The United States in the Middle East

The United States in the Middle East

A HISTORICAL DICTIONARY

DAVID SHAVIT

Greenwood Press
NEW YORK · WESTPORT, CONNECTICUT · LONDON

For Penny

Library of Congress Cataloging-in-Publication Data

Shavit, David.
  The United States in the Middle East : a historical dictionary /
David Shavit.
    p.   cm.
  Bibliography: p.
  Includes index.
  ISBN 0–313–25341–2 (lib. bdg. : alk. paper)
  1. Middle East—Relations—United States—Dictionaries. 2. United
States—Relations—Middle East—Dictionaries. 3. United States—
Biography—Dictionaries. 4. Middle East—History—1517– —
Dictionaries. I. Title.
DS63.2.U5S384   1988
303.4′8273′056—dc19   87–24965

British Library Cataloguing in Publication Data is available.

Library of Congress Catalog Card Number: 87–24965
ISBN: 0–313–25341–2

First published in 1988

Greenwood Press, Inc.
88 Post Road West, Westport, Connecticut 06881

Printed in the United States of America

The paper used in this book complies with the
Permanent Paper Standard issued by the National
Information Standards Organization (Z39.48–1984).

10 9 8 7 6 5 4 3 2 1

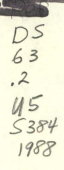
Contents

Preface

Contacts between the United States and the Middle East began in the eighteenth century when New England merchants arrived on the eastern shores of the Mediterranean Sea. They were followed by ships and officers of the U.S. Navy, missionaries, diplomats, archaeologists, travelers and tourists, army officers, educators, authors and artists, scientists, engineers, petroleum geologists, and other Americans and American institutions, organizations, and business firms which established a whole gamut of relationships between the United States and the Middle East.

This dictionary provides in alphabet format information about the persons, institutions, and events that affected the relationships between the United States and the Middle East; persons who actually have been in the Middle East, and particularly those who have left written or visual records of their stay; organizations and institutions that functioned in the Middle East itself; and events that occurred in that area.

The term *Middle East* includes all the countries from Morocco in the west, Afghanistan in the east, Turkey in the north, to the Sudan and Yemen in the south. Geographical names have been modernized, but the names used in a specific entry are the ones relevant to the period covered.

The dictionary attempts to be comprehensive, including all persons, institutions, and events that brought the United States into contact with the Middle East. The choice of entries in a historical dictionary is always difficult. For example, of 256 chiefs of diplomatic missions who served in the Middle East between 1831 and 1976, only 73 appear as entries in the book. Only those who contributed to U.S.-Middle Eastern relations in some significant way are included, even if this contribution consisted of only a book of memoirs of their service in the area. A complete list of all chiefs of American diplomatic missions in the Middle East is included in this book.[1]

Specifically excluded are U.S. military personnel who served in North Africa during World War II. Only a limited number of travelers, government agencies, and business firms are included.

With regard to travelers, only those whose travel reports are of particular interest and influence are covered.[2] Although many governmental agencies, in addition to the Department of State, were involved with the Middle East, only a few had establishments in the area.[3] Finally, as regards business, only a few business firms, particularly oil companies, are covered in this dictionary. For those who are interested, lists of firms that sold their products in the Middle East are available in several sources.[4]

The references at the end of each entry note whether the subject is listed in the general biographical dictionaries, such as the *Dictionary of American Biography*, *National Cyclopaedia of American Biography*, *Appleton Cyclopaedia of American Biography*, *Notable American Women*, *Who's Who in America*, *Who Was Who in America*, and *Contemporary Authors*. The references also attempt to list every book and article written about the subject, but references that appear in the *Dictionary of American Biography* and *Notable American Women* have not been duplicated. Volume and page numbers are provided only for the *National Cyclopaedia of American Biography*, because it is not arranged in alphabetical order. Asterisked entries indicate that the subject is covered separately in this volume.

Efforts have been made to include complete and accurate information, but this was not always possible because some information is no longer available and other information could not be located. Unfortunately, mistakes are inevitable in a work of this scope. The author would appreciate receiving corrections and emendations.

Many individuals provided valuable assistance, especially librarians, archivists, and officials of missionary societies. The dictionary would have been far less complete without their help. Special thanks are also due to Loretta Rielly, my research assistant, and to the staff of the Interlibrary Loan Office of Northern Illinois University, DeKalb, Illinois.

NOTES

1. A complete list is available in U.S. Department of State, *United States Chiefs of Mission 1778–1986* (Washington, D.C., 1987). A complete list of consuls who served in the Middle East is available only through 1865 in Walter B. Smith II, *America's Diplomats and Consuls of 1776–1865: A Geographic and Biographic Directory of the Foreign Service from the Declaration of Independence to the End of the Civil War* (Washington, D.C., 1986).

2. Several lists provide an almost complete bibliography of travel accounts of the nineteenth century. There are no such lists for the twentieth century. Davis F. Finnie, *Pioneers East: The Early American Experience in the Middle East* (Cambridge, Mass., 1967), pp. 287–294, lists publications by Americans that relate to American activities in the Middle East before 1850. Other lists include Yohai Goell and Martha B. Katz-Hyman, "Americans in the Holy Land, 1850–1900: A Select Bibliography." in *With Eyes Toward Zion*, ed. Moshe Davis (New York, 1977), pp. 100–125; Morroe Berger, *Cairo to the American Traveler of the Nineteenth Century* (Princeton, N.J., 1974); Harold F. Smith,

American Travels Abroad: A Bibliography of Accounts Published Before 1900 (Carbon-dale, Ill., 1969); and Richard W. Bevis, *Bibliotheca Cisorientalia: An Annotated Checklist of Early English Travel Books on the Near and Middle East* (Boston, 1973).

3. A comprehensive list of current governmental agencies involved with the Middle East is available in Steven R. Dorr, *Scholars' Guide for Washington, D.C., for Middle Eastern Studies* (Washington, D.C., 1981), pp. 256–375.

4. *A Survey of American Interests in the Middle East Covering Business, Philanthropic, Welfare, Educational and Cultural, Governmental and International Organizations with Major Interests in the Middle East*, ed. by Frances C. Mattison (Washington, D.C., 1953) which lists 512 business firms; *African Programs of U.S. Organizations: A Selective Directory*, comp. by Jacqueline S. Mithun (Washington, D.C., 1965) for Middle Eastern countries in Africa; and *Directory of American Firms Operating in Foreign Countries* (New York, 1955/56–   ).

Abbreviations

ACAB	*Appleton's Cyclopaedia of American Biography* (New York, 1888–1901)
ACWW	*American Catholic Who's Who*
AJA	*American Journal of Archaeology*
Amherst	*Amherst College Biographical Record, 1973; Biographical Record of the Graduates and Non-Graduates of the Classes of 1822–1971 Inclusive* (Amherst, 1973)
AMWS	*American Men and Women of Science*
AndoverTS	*General Catalogue of Andover Theological Seminary* (Boston, 1908)
AuburnTS	*General Biographical Catalogue of Auburn Theological Seminary 1818–1918* (Auburn, N.Y., 1918)
AWM	*Aramco World Monthly*
BA	*Biblical Archaeologist*
BAAPG	*Bulletin of the American Association of Petroleum Geologists*
BangorTS	*Historical Catalogue of Bangor Theological Seminary* (Bangor, Me., 1928)
BASOR	*Bulletin of the American Schools of Oriental Research*
BDAC	*Biographical Directory of the American Congress 1774–1971* (Washington, D.C., 1971)
BDABL	John H. Ingham, *Biographical Dictionary of American Business Leaders* (Westport, Conn., 1983)
BDAE	John F. Ohles, ed., *Biographical Dictionary of American Educators* (Westport, Conn., 1978)
BDAS	Clark A. Elliott, *Biographical Dictionary of American Science: The Seventeenth Through the Nineteenth Centuries* (Westport, Conn., 1979)

BDC	Jon L. Wakelyn, *Biographical Dictionary of the Confederacy* (Westport, Conn., 1977)
BDI	Warren F. Kuehl, ed., *Biographical Dictionary of Internationalists* (Westport, Conn., 1983)
BMNAS	*Biographical Memoirs of the National Academy of Science*
Boardman	Francis Boardman, *Institutions of Higher Learning in the Middle East*, 2nd ed. (Washington, D.C., 1977)
BRDS	*Biographical Register of the Department of State*
CA	*Contemporary Authors* (Detroit, 1967–)
Corners	Robert McAdams and Corinne S. Schelling, eds., *Corners of a Foreign Field: Discussions About American Overseas Research Centers in the Humanities and the Social Sciences* (New York, 1979)
CWD	Mark M. Boatner, *The Civil War Dictionary* (New York, 1959)
DAA	Oscar Fay Adams, *Dictionary of American Authors*. 5th rev. and enlarged ed. (New York, 1904)
DAB	*Dictionary of American Biography* (New York, 1928–)
DACB	John H. Delaney, *Dictionary of American Catholic Biography* (Garden City, N.Y., 1984)
DADH	John E. Findling, *Dictionary of American Diplomatic History* (Westport, Conn., 1980)
DAMB	Howard A. Kelly, *Dictionary of Medical Biography* (Boston, 1928)
DAMIB	Roger J. Spiller, ed., *Dictionary of American Military Biography* (Westport, Conn., 1984)
DANFS	*Dictionary of American Naval Fighting Ships* (Washington, D.C., 1959–1981)
DARB	Henry W. Bowden, *Dictionary of American Religious Biography* (Westport, Conn., 1977)
DAS	*Dictionary of American Scholars*
DFAF	*Directory, Foreign-Area Fellows, 1952–72* (New York, 1973)
DLB	*Dictionary of Literary Biography* (Detroit, 1978–)
DNB	*Dictionary of National Biography* (Oxford, 1885–)
DSB	*Dictionary of Scientific Biography* (New York, 1970–1976)
EAJ	Donald Paneth, *Encyclopedia of American Journalism* (New York, 1983)
EJ	*Encyclopaedia Judaica* (Jerusalem, 1972–)
EM	*Encyclopaedia of Missions* (New York, 1891–1904)
EMCM	Burton L. Goddard, ed., *The Encyclopedia of Modern Christian Missions: The Agencies* (Camden, N.J., 1967)

ESBS	*Encyclopedia of Southern Baptists* (Nashville, Tenn., 1958–1982)
FRWW	*Federal Records of World War II* (Washington, D.C., 1951)
GSAB	*Geological Society of America Bulletin*
HDRCA	Peter N. VandenBerge, *Historical Directory of the Reformed Church in America 1628–1978* (Grand Rapids, Mich., 1978)
Hesseltine	William B. Hesseltine and Hazel C. Wolfe, *The Blue and the Gray on the Nile* (Chicago, 1961)
Hewitt	John M. Hewitt, *Williams College and Foreign Missions* (Boston, 1914)
Hill	Richard Leslie Hill, *A Biographical Dictionary of the Anglo-Egyptian Sudan*, 2nd ed. (London, 1967)
IAB	R. E. Banta and Donald R. Thompson, *Indiana Authors and Their Books* (Bloomington, Ind., 1949–1974)
IHU	*International Handbook of Universities and Other Institutions of Higher Education*
IPE	*International Petroleum Encyclopedia*
JAOS	*Journal of the American Oriental Society*
LE	Leaders in Education
MBEP	Turner Browne and Elaine Partnow, *Macmillan Encyclopedia of Photography* (New York, 1983)
MEA	*Macmillan Encyclopedia of Architects* (New York, 1982)
MEJ	*Middle East Journal*
MENA	*Middle East and North Africa: A Survey and Directory of the Countries of the Middle East* (London, 1948–)
Mount Holyoke	*General Catalogue of Mount Holyoke College, 1837–1924* (South Hadley, Mass., 1924)
MW	*Muslim World*
NAW	*Notable American Women* (Cambridge, Mass., 1971–1980)
NCAB	*National Cyclopaedia of American Biography* (New York, 1898–)
NYHSD	George C. Groce and Davis H. Wallace, *The New-York Historical Society's Dictionary of Artists in America* (New York, 1957)
NYT	*New York Times*
OAB	William Coyle, ed., *Ohio Authors and Their Books* (Cleveland, 1962)
PGSA	*Proceedings of the American Geological Society*
PolProf	*Political Profiles*, Nelson Lichtenstein, ed. (New York, 1976–1978)

PrincetonTS	*Biographical Catalogue of the Princeton Theological Seminary, 1815–1932* (Princeton, N.J., 1933)
Qubain	Fahim I. Qubain, *Education and Science in the Arab World* (Baltimore, 1966)
RAGMA	*Annual Report of the Association of Graduates of the U.S. Military Academy*
S	Supplement
Schools	*Schools Abroad of Interest to Americans*, 5th ed. (Boston, 1982–1983)
Stone	Frank Andrew Stone, *Academies for Anatolia* (Lanham, Md., 1984)
Touval	Saadia Touval, *The Peace Mediators in the Arab-Israeli Conflict, 1948–1979* (Princeton, N.J., 1982)
UnionTS	*Alumni Catalogue of the Union Theological Seminary in the City of New York, 1839* (New York, 1937)
WAMB	*Webster American Military Biographies* (Springfield, Mass., 1978)
WWA	*Who's Who in America*
WWE	*Who's Who in the East*
WWS	*Who's Who in the South and Southwest*
WWW	*Who's Who in the West*
WWWA	*Who Was Who in America*
WWWE	Warren R. Dawson and Eric P. Uphill, *Who Was Who in Egyptology*, 2nd rev. ed. (London: 1972)
WWWJ	*Who's Who in World Jewry*

*A separate entry included in the *Dictionary*

Place Names

Since geographical names in the Middle East appear in several versions, the following names have been used in the dictionary. In those cases where names have changed, the dictionary has followed the usage of the times.

Current Name	Former Name
Adana	
Amara [Amarah]	
Assiut [Asyut, Assoiut]	
Basra [Basrah]	
Bitlis	
Bursa	Brusa [Brousa]
Dhahran	
Diyarbakir [Diarbekr]	
Erzurum [Erzerum]	
Gaziantep	Aintab
Goksun	Hadjin
Harput [Harpoot]	
Istanbul	Constantinople
Izmid [Izmit]	Nicomedia
Izmir	Smyrna
Kayseri	[Caesarea]
Leninakan	Alexandropol
Maras	Marash
Massawa	
Merzifon	Marsovan
Rezaiych	Urmia [Urumia]

Riyadh
Sivas
Tarsus
Trabzon   Trebizond
Urfa
Üsküdar   Scutari

Chronology

1787–1792	Ottoman-Russian War
1794	Founding of the Qajar dynasty in Persia
1798	Napoleon Bonaparte's Egyptian expedition; Battle of the Pyramids; Battle of Abu Qir
1799	Napoleon invades Palestine
1801	French evacuate Egypt
1801–1805	Barbary Wars
1804–1812	Russo-Persian War
1805–1848	Muhammad Ali, Viceroy of Egypt
1806–1812	Ottoman-Russian War
1807–1808	Revolt of the Jannissaries, murder of Sultan Selim III
1808–1839	Mahmud II, Ottoman Sultan
1811	Muhammad Ali massacres the Egyptian Mamelukes; first American commercial house founded in Smyrna, Turkey
1811–1818	Muhammad Ali's campaigns against the Wahhabis in Arabia
1815	War with Algiers
1819	First American missionaries arrive in the Middle East
1820–1822	Muhammed Ali conquers the Sudan
1821–1823	Ottoman-Persian War
1821–1830	Greek War of Independence
1825–1828	Russo-Persian War
1826	Mahmud II massacres the Janissaries in Istanbul and reorganizes the Ottoman army
1827	Battle of Navarino
1828–1829	Ottoman-Russian War
1830	France invades Algiers

1832–1841	Ottoman-Egyptian War
1834	American Press established in Beirut; Nestorian mission established in Urmia, Persia
1839–1842	First Afghan War
1839	Hatt-i Sherif of Gulhane—reforms guaranteeing liberties of Ottoman subjects promulgated; British occupy Aden
1839–1840	Ottoman-Egyptian War
1844	Beginning of the Baha'i movement in Persia
1853	Koszta Affair
1854	American mission established in Egypt
1854–1856	Crimean War
1856	Hatt-I Humayun promulgated extending the rights granted by Hatt-i Sherif; Anglo-Persian War
1857	Alexandria-Cairo railroad opened
1860	Founding of Robert College in Istanbul
1860–1861	Civil war in Lebanon
1863–1879	Ismail, Viceroy and then Khedive of Egypt
1866	American colony established in Jaffa, Palestine
1866	Syrian Protestant College (later American University of Beirut) founded in Beirut; Anatolia College founded in Marsovan, Turkey
1869	Opening of the Suez Canal
1874–1879	General Charles Gordon, Governor of the Sudan
1875–1879	Egyptian-Abyssinian War
1875	Establishment of the Mixed Courts in Egypt
1876	Proclamation of Ottoman Constitution; Central Turkey College founded in Aintab, Turkey
1876–1909	Abdulhamid II, Sultan of Turkey
1877	Opening of the Ottoman Parliament
1877–1878	Russo-Ottoman War
1878	Ottoman Constitution suspended; Congress of Berlin; Armenia College (later Euphrates College) founded in Harput, Turkey
1878–1879	Second Afghan War
1881	French occupy Tunisia; American colony established in Jerusalem
1881–1882	Urabi revolt in Egypt
1882	British bombard Alexandria; Battle of Teal al-Kabir; British occupy Egypt
1883–1907	Lord Kromer, British resident and consul general in Egypt
1883–1885	Mahdist revolt in the Sudan

1885	Fall of Khartoum; death of General Gordon
1889	Arabian mission established
1890–1897	Armenian revolts in Ottoman Empire
1892–1914	Abbas Hilmi II, Khedive of Egypt
1896–1898	Anglo-Egyptian reconquest of the Sudan
1898	Battle of Omdurman in the Sudan; Fashoda Incident
1899	Anglo-Egyptian Condominion established in the Sudan
1900	American School of Oriental Research founded in Jerusalem
1901	The Wahhabis capture Riyadh
1900–1908	Hijaz railroad built
1905	Perdicaris Affair
1905–1909	Constitutional revolution in Persia
1906	Algeciras Conference
1908–1909	Young Turk revolt restores constitution in Turkey
1909	Sultan Abdul Hamid deposed; formation of the Anglo-Persian Oil Co.
1911–1912	Ottoman-Italian War over Libya
1911	Shuster Mission to Persia
1912–1913	Balkan Wars
1912	Morocco became a French protectorate
1914	Turkey enters World War I on the side of the Central Powers; Egypt became British protectorate; Britain annexes Cyprus
1915–1916	Gallipoli campaign
1915–1916	Siege of Kut-el-Amara in Mesopotamia
1915–1930	Near East Relief
1916–1917	Arab revolt against Turkey
1917	Balfour Declaration; British conquest of Palestine
1917–1936	Ahmad Fuad, King of Egypt
1918	British conquer Syria; Mudros Armistice
1919	Harbord Mission; King-Crane Commission; American University in Cairo founded
1919–1922	Turkish war of liberation against Greece and the Allied forces
1919–1929	Amanullah, amir of Afghanistan
1920	League of Nations assigned mandates over Iraq, Palestine and Transjordan to British, and over Lebanon and Syria to France; French occupy Syria
1920–1921	Greco-Turkish War
1921	Arab riots in Palestine
1921–1933	Faisal, king of Iraq

1921–1951	Abdallah, emir and later king of Transjordan
1922	Egypt declared independent; Sultanate is abolished
1922–1927	First Millspaugh mission to Persia
1923	Treaty of Lausanne between Turkey and the Allied Powers; sultan deposed and Turkey proclaimed a republic; Transjordan recognized as autonomous state
1923–1938	Mustafa Kemal Attaturk, President of Turkey
1925	Druse insurrection in Syria; Hebrew University founded in Jerusalem
1925–1926	Riffian War in Morocco
1925–1941	Reza Shah Pahlvai, Shah of Persia
1926–1953	Abd al-Aziz Ibn Saud, King of the Hejaz and later King of Saudi Arabia
1929	Wailing Wall incident and Arab riots in Palestine
1932	Iraq is granted independence
1935	Iran becomes the official name for Persia
1936	Anglo-Egyptian Treaty
1936–1938	Arab rebellion in Palestine
1936–1952	Faruq, king of Egypt
1937	Montreux Conference abolishes the capitulations in Egypt
1938–1950	Ismet Inonu, president of Turkey
1939	British White Paper on Palestine
1941	Anglo-Soviet troops occupy Iran; Riza Shah deposed and replaced by his son
1941–1979	Mohammed Reza Pahlabi, Shah of Iran
1941	Rashid Ali revolt in Iraq
1942	Allied invasion of North Africa
1942–1945	Persian Gulf Command
1943–1945	Second Millspaugh mission to Iran
1944	Culbertson Mission
1945	Formation of the Arab League; Anglo-American Committee of Inquiry to investigate the future of Palestine
1945–1946	Azerbaijan crisis
1946	French troops evacuate Lebanon and Syria; Transjordan becomes independent
1947	Truman Doctrine announced
1948	State of Israel established
1948–1949	Arab-Israel War
1949	Military revolts in Syria

1951	Libya becomes independent; King Abdullah of Jordan assassinated
1951–1953	Muhammad Musaddeq, Prime Minister of Iran
1952	Military revolution in Egypt overthrows the monarchy and established a republic
1952–	Hussain, king of Jordan
1953–1964	Saud ibn Abdul Aziz, King of Saudi Arabia
1954–1956	Revolt in Algeria
1954	Anglo-Egyptian Treaty; British troops evacuated Egypt
1955	Start of the Baghdad Pact
1956	Sudan gains independence; Morocco and Tunis gain independence; Egypt nationalized the Suez canal; Suez crisis; Anglo-French invasion of Egypt; Second Israel-Arab War (Sinai War)
1956–1970	Gamal Abdel Nasser, President of Egypt
1957	Eisenhower Doctrine announced
1958	Military revolt in Iraq overthrew monarchy and established a republic; U.S. marines in Lebanon
1958–1962	United Arab Republic
1960	Military coup in Turkey; Cyprus becomes independent
1961	Kuwait gains independence
1962	Civil war in Yemen overthrows the monarchy; Algeria gains independence
1964	Palestine Liberation Organization founded
1964–1975	Faisal, King of Saudi Arabia
1967	Third Arab-Israeli War (Six-Day War); Israeli attack on the U.S.S. *Liberty*; Israel occupies the West Bank and Jerusalem
1968	Southern Yemen becomes independent
1969	Military *coup* overthrows Monarchy in Libya and establishes the Libyan Arab Republic; Rogers Plan
1969–1970	Fourth Israel-Arab War ("War of Attrition")
1970	Civil war in Jordan
1971	Aswan High Dam inaugurated in Egypt; Oman becomes independent; Britain leaves the Gulf states
1973	Fifth Arab-Israeli War (Yom Kippur War)
1974	Turkey invades Cyprus
1975–1976	Lebanon Civil War
1975	King Faisal of Saudi Arabia assassinated; Suez Canal reopened
1977	President Sadat's peace mission to Israel
1978	Camp David Accords

1979   Peace treaty signed between Israel and Egypt; Shah Mohammed
                Reza Pahlavi leaves Iran, and Islamic republic established in
                Iran

1979–1981   American hostages in Teheran

1979   Soviets invaded Afghanistan

1980–   Iraq-Iran War

1981   Anwar al-Sadat assassinated

1982   Israel invades Lebanon

1982–84   U.S. Marines in Lebanon

1986   U.S. raid on Libya

Introduction

American trade with the Middle East began before the Revolutionary War, although the first trader whose name is known to us was one Perkins, a loyalist from Boston, who settled in Smyrna during the Revolution. As American trade, and the number of ships carrying this trade, increased, American merchant ships were attacked by Barbary pirates. The first American hostages were taken in 1784, and the U.S. government tried through both diplomatic (including the payment of tribute) and military means to release them and the other hostages who followed. These efforts eventually led to a series of wars with the Barbary States conducted intermittently between 1801 and 1815, in which the U.S. Navy succeeded in releasing all the hostages and eliminating the tribute and the disruption of American trade in the Mediterranean. By that time, American commercial houses were already established in Smyrna.

Missionaries representing several missionary societies arrived in the Middle East in 1819. The more important of them were the American Board of Commissioners for Foreign Missions and the boards of missions of the Presbyterian Church, the United Presbyterian Church, and the Reformed Church of America. They established missionary stations in most countries of the Middle East. They explored various areas of the Middle East, established schools and colleges, hospitals and clinics, and published books and newspapers in the vernacular languages. The most important educational institutions established by Americans were Robert College in Constantinople, the Syrian Protestant College (later the American University of Beirut), and the American University in Cairo. But the missionaries' role went beyond educational and medical work; they also instigated social, cultural, and economic change in the Middle East.

American diplomats soon followed. Consular offices were established in Tangier, Tunis, Algiers, and Tripoli in the late eighteenth century, and the first diplomatic mission in the Middle East was established in Constantinople in 1831. One of the most important tasks assigned to diplomats through much of the nineteenth century until the end of World War I was the protection of missionaries. Another important task was the fostering of American trade with the Middle

East. Treaties of friendship and commerce were signed with the Ottoman Empire in 1831, with Muscat in 1838, and with Persia in 1857.

American missionaries and diplomats provided humanitarian and philanthropic aid to Armenians, Jews, and other minorities in the Middle East, particularly in the Ottoman Empire. This role was later assumed by other philanthropic organizations, particularly Near East Relief and the Near East Foundation, as well as agencies of the U.S. government. Other advisers also came from the United States, including naval constructors, cotton-growing specialists, mining engineers, and army and naval officers who served in the Turkish and Egyptian navies and armies. Before World War II Middle Eastern governments invited various economic missions, including the Shuster and Millspaugh missions to Persia. Their number increased many fold after the war, as the U.S. government increased its role in technical and economic aid.

Travelers came to the Middle East at an early date. The lure of the Holy Land and Egypt was strong, and an increasing number of American tourists, among whom were many authors and artists, began to arrive. Many of them recorded their impressions on paper and on canvas. Those interested in the ancient history and antiquities of the area soon followed. Mendes Cohen brought the first large collection of Egyptian antiquities back to the United States. The first important researcher of ancient Palestine was Edward Robinson, who was followed by other biblical scholars. After the end of the nineteenth century, a growing number of archaeologists and anthropologists excavated many locations in the area, and studied its people and culture, both ancient and modern. A great number of archaeological expeditions in the area were sponsored by American museums and universities. Other scholars studied the geology, climatology, and flora and fauna of the Middle East. While commerce was not extensive until after World War II, certain American products, such as sewing machines, kerosene lamps, wagons, and agricultural implements, began to play a significant role in the Middle East in the second half of the nineteenth century. The most important American commercial relationship to develop after World War I was the involvement of American companies in the development of petroleum.

Since World War II, the role of the United States in the Middle East has changed drastically. Political and strategic conditions have dictated a policy in which the United States has become directly involved in the area. The United States was a major participant in the creation of the state of Israel, in the Arab-Israeli dispute, the wars in Cyprus, Lebanon, and the Yemen War, and the Iranian revolution. American ships are stationed in the eastern Mediterranean and the Persian Gulf, protecting American strategic, political, and commercial interests, particularly the free flow of petroleum. The United States has tried to stabilize the Middle East and to bring peace to the area through various negotiators and intermediaries, some of whose efforts have been successful.

The United States
in the
Middle East

A

ABCFM. *See* American Board of Commissioners for Foreign Missions.

ADAMS, CHARLES CLARENCE (1883–1948). Missionary and Orientalist, born January 15, 1883, in West Sunbury, Pennsylvania. Adams graduated from Westminster College (New Wilmington, Pa.), Pittsburgh (later Pittsburgh-Xenia) Theological Seminary, and the University of Chicago, studied at the Kennedy School of Missions, and was ordained in 1908. He served as a missionary under the United Presbyterian Church of North America Board of Foreign Missions in Egypt from 1908 to 1939, was chairman of the faculty of the Evangelical Theological Seminary in Cairo from 1919 to 1938, and dean of the school of Oriental Studies at the American University in Cairo* from 1939 until his death. He wrote *Islam and Modernism in Egypt* (London, 1933). Died March 9, 1948, in Cairo. *References*: *NYT*, March 10, 1948; *WWWA*.

ADAMS, GEORGE WASHINGTON (1811–1880). Religious zealot, born in Oxford, New Jersey. Adams became a lay Methodist preacher, but in 1840 joined the Church of the Latter-Day Saints and was ordained a Mormon elder. He was also an actor and a manager of a touring theatrical troupe. In the 1850s he became a Campbellite preacher in Vermont, established the Church of the Messiah, and in 1862 began publishing *The Sword of Truth and Harbinger of Peace*. In 1864 he moved to Indian River, Maine, and in 1865 he established the Palestine Emigration Association and was its president. In the same year, he went with his partner Abraham McKenzie, a storekeeper from Indian River, Maine, on an exploratory tour to Palestine. In 1866 he took a group of American Colonists to Palestine and established the American Colony* in Jaffa. The colony failed in 1867, and he returned to the United States in 1868. Died May 11, 1880, in Philadelphia. *References*: Peter Amann, ''Prophet in Zion: The Saga of George J. Adams,'' *New England Quarterly* 37 (1964): 477–500; Reed M. Holmes, *The Forerunners* (Independence, Mo., 1981).

ADAMS, JAMES MCKEE (1886–1945). Biblical scholar, born October 17, 1886, in Raleigh, North Carolina. Adams graduated from Wake Forest College (N.C.), and Crozer and Southern Baptist theological seminaries. He was a pastor from 1912 to 1916 and became a member of the faculty of Southern Baptist Theological Seminary in 1921. He made eleven trips to the Middle East in connection with his research work on the geography of the Bible, and wrote *The Heart of the Levant, Palestine-Syria; a survey of Ancient Countries in the Interest of Modern Missions* (Richmond, 1937). Died September 17, 1945, in Louisville, Kentucky. *References*: *ESB*; *WWWA*.

ADAMS, KATHRYN NEWELL (1876–1966). Educator, born March 2, 1876, in Prague, Bohemia, and brought to the United States in that same year. Adams graduated from Beloit and Radcliffe colleges and Columbia University. She taught at Fargo College, was dean of women at Huron (S.D.), Beloit, Drury (Springfield, Mo.) and Yankton (S.D.) colleges, and served as principal of Kawalao Seminary in Honolulu. She was president of Istanbul College for Women from 1924 to 1931 but following a series of disagreements with the Turkish authorities, who complained that the college did not provide practical education for Turkish women, left Turkey. She later resided in Walpole, Massachusetts. Died January 24, 1966, in Norwood, Massachusetts. *References*: *Walpole Times*, January 27, 1966; *WWAW*.

ADAMS, ROBERT MCCORMICK (1926–   ). Anthropologist and archaeologist, born July 23, 1926, in Chicago. Adams served in the navy in World War II and later graduated from the University of Chicago. He conducted archaeological fieldwork in Jarmo, Iraq, in 1950–1951 and in Yucatan in 1953. He became a member of the faculty of the University of Chicago in 1954 and professor of anthropology in 1963, as well as professor at the Oriental Institute in 1962, director of the Oriental Institute from 1962 to 1968 and from 1981 to 1983, and provost of the University of Chicago from 1982 to 1984. Adams conducted field studies of irrigation and settlement patterns in central and southern Iraq in 1956–1958, 1960, 1967, and 1968–1969, in Saudi Arabia from 1956, and in Iran during 1960–1961; supervised the Iraq surface survey between the Tigris and the Euphrates; and conducted excavations in Iran in 1963 and in Syria in 1970. He wrote *Land Behind Baghdad: A History of Settlement on the Diyala Plains* (Chicago, 1965), and *Heartland of Cities* (Chicago, 1981), and was co-author of *Uruk Countryside: The Natural Setting of Urban Societies* (Chicago, 1972). He became director of the Smithsonian Institution in 1984. *References*: *AMWS*; *CA*; *MENA*; "The Secretary," *New Yorker* 60 (January 21, 1985): 24–25; and *WWA*.

ADAMS, WILLIAM YEWDALE (1927–   ). Archaeologist, born August 6, 1927, in Los Angeles. Adams served in the navy and graduated from the University of California at Berkeley and the University of Arizona. He was senior archaeologist at the Glen Canyon archeological salvage project in northern Arizona from 1957 to 1959, program specialist in archaeology for UNESCO in liaison with the Sudan Antiquities Service and director of the archaeological salvage program in Nubia from 1959 to 1966. He became associate professor of anthropology at the University of Kentucky in 1966 and professor in 1971. He wrote *Nubia, Corridor to Africa* (Princeton, N.J., 1977), and *Ceramic Industries of Medieval Nubia* (Lexington, Ky., 1986). *References*: *AMWS*; *CA*; and *WWS*.

AGRANAT, SHIMON (1906–   ). Jurist, born September 5, 1906, in Louisville, Kentucky. Agranat graduated from the University of Chicago. Attracted to Zionism, he settled in Palestine in 1930, and practiced law in Haifa. He was appointed a magistrate in 1940 and president of the Haifa District Court in 1948. In 1950 he was appointed justice of the Supreme Court of Israel, becoming deputy president of the court in 1960 and its president from 1965 until his retirement in 1976. In 1974 he served as chair of the Commission (known as the Agranat Commission) to investigate and report on the civil and military aspects of the Yom Kippur War. *References*: *EJ*; *WWAJ*.

AGRON (AGRONSKY), GERSHON (1893–1959). Journalist, born in Mina, Ukraine, and brought to the United States in 1906. Agron enlisted in the Jewish Legion in 1918 and remained in Palestine after demobilization. He was editor of the Jewish Telegraphic Agency from 1921 to 1924 and correspondent for international press agencies and several English newspapers. In 1932 he founded and edited the English-language newspaper *Palestine Post* (later the *Jerusalem Post*). He was director of the Israel Government Information Services from 1949 to 1951, and mayor of Jerusalem from 1955 until his death. Died November 1, 1959, in Jerusalem. *References*: *EJ*; *NYT*, November 2, 1959; and H. M. Sachar, *Aliyah: The People of Israel* (Cleveland, 1961), pp. 39–70.

AJAX, OPERATION. Code name for the Central Intelligence Agency's successful covert operation in 1953 to oust Iran's Premier Muhammed Mossadegh and reinstate Shah Mohammad Reza Pahlavi. *References*: Stephen Ambrose, *Ike's Spies: Eisenhower and the Espionage Establishment* (Garden City, N.Y., 1981), chs. 14–15; Donald N. Wilber, *Adventures in the Middle East: Excursions and Incursions* (Princeton, N.J., 1986), ch. 14.

AKINS, JAMES ELMER (1926–   ). Diplomat, born October 15, 1926, in Akron, Ohio. Akins graduated from the University of Akron and joined the navy. He did relief work with a nonprofit organization from 1948 to 1950, taught in Lebanon in 1951–1952, and was assistant editor of a research organization in 1953–1954. He entered the foreign service in 1954 and successively served in Naples, Paris, Strasbourg, Damascus, Beirut, Kuwait, and Baghdad. He was director of the Office of Fuels and Energy from 1967 to 1972, served in the

White House detail in 1972 and 1973, and was ambassador to Saudi Arabia from 1973 to 1975 when he was dismissed because of disagreements with the secretary of state. In 1976 he became a consultant on foreign policy and energy in Washington, D.C. *Reference*: *WWE*.

ALBORZ COLLEGE, TEHERAN. Founded in 1925 as the American College in Teheran, a junior college, by Presbyterian missionaries, and given a charter from the Board of Regents of the State of New York. The name was changed to Alborz College (named after the Alborz Mountains Range in Iran) in 1935. The Iranian government closed it in 1940, when all missionary schools were taken over by the Ministry of Education and operated as public state schools. *Reference*: Arthur C. Boyce, "Alborz College of Teheran and Dr. Samuel Martin Jordan, Founder and President," in Ali Pasha Saleh, *Cultural Ties Between Iran and the United States* (Teheran, 1976), pp. 155–234.

ALBRIGHT, WILLIAM FOXWELL (1891–1971). Orientalist and archaeologist, born May 24, 1891, in Coquimbo, Chile, to American parents. Albright graduated from Upper Iowa and Johns Hopkins universities, and served in World War I. He was acting director of the American Schools of Oriental Research (ASOR),* Jerusalem, in 1920–21 and director from 1921 to 1929 and again from 1933 to 1936. He was professor of Semitic languages at Johns Hopkins University from 1929 to 1958 and research professor at the Jewish Theological Seminary from 1957 to 1959. Albright was director of excavations at Gibea of Saul, Tell Beit Mirsim, and Bethel in Palestine. He wrote *Excavations and Results at Tell el Ful (Gibea of Saul)* (New Haven, Conn., 1924), *The Excavation of Tell Beit Mirsim* (New Haven, Conn., 1932–1943), *Recent Discoveries in Bible Lands* (New York, 1936), and was co-author of *The Spoken Arabic of Palestine* (Jerusalem, 1937), and *The Excavation of Bethel (1934–1960)* (Cambridge, Mass., 1968). He was chief archaeologist for the University of California expedition in Sinai in 1947–1948 and for the American Foundation for the Study of Man expedition in South Arabia in 1950–1951. Died September 19, 1971, in Baltimore. His autobiography appeared in *American Spiritual Autobiographies*, ed. by Louis Finkelstein (New York, 1948), pp. 156–81. *References*: *BASOR* 205 (1972): 3–13; E. F. Campbell, Jr., and J. M. Miller, "W. F. Albright and Historical Reconstruction," *BA* 42 (Winter 1979): 37–47; *CB* 1955; *NCAB* 56:222; *NYT*, September 20, 1971; Leona G. Running and Davis N. Freedman, *William Foxwell Albright: A Twentieth Century Genius* (New York, 1975); and *WWWA*.

ALEPPO COLLEGE. Founded in 1876 in Aintab, Turkey, by Tillman Conklin Trowbridge,* as Central Turkey College,* which was closed as a result of World War I. Aleppo College was reopened in Aleppo, Syria, in 1924 under the name Boys High School. In 1937 it combined with North Syria School for Boys, which had been established there in 1927, to form Aleppo College, a junior college.

The institution was managed by the American Board of Commissioners for Foreign Missions (ABCFM)* and the Board of Foreign Missions of the Presbyterian Church in the U.S.A.* It became a secondary school in 1952, and formal connections with American missionary societies were severed in 1967. *References*: George Miller, ''Aleppo College: Failure or Fulfillment,'' *MW* 57 (1967): 42–45; *Qubain*, pp. 435–437; and *Survey*.

ALEXANDER, JOHN ROMICH (1849–1940). Missionary, born May 23, 1849, in Wooster, Ohio. Alexander graduated from Ohio Central College and Xenia Theological Seminary, and was ordained in 1875. He became a missionary under the United Presbyterian Church of North America Board of Foreign Missions* in Egypt in 1875. He was general superintendent of Assiut College* from 1875 to 1887, its president from 1887 to 1910, college pastor and the librarian at the Mission Theological Seminary in Cairo from 1910 to 1913, and professor of church history and church government from 1913 to 1925. He was director of Protestant educational work in Egypt from 1880 to 1903 and the moderator of the Synod of the Nile in 1911–1912. Alexander wrote *The Truth About Egypt* (London, 1911), *A Sketch of the Story of the Evangelical Church of Egypt, Founded by the American Mission, 1854–1930* (Alexandria, 1930), and ''Knowest Thou Yesterday,'' a manuscript history of the mission in Egypt from 1854 to 1934. Died April 16, 1940. *Reference*: WWWA.

ALGIERS, WAR WITH (1815). When American naval vessels withdrew from the Mediterranean during the War of 1812, the Dey of Algiers declared war on the United States and began to seize American vessels. In 1815 an American naval force commanded by Stephen Decatur, Jr.,* destroyed the Algerian naval forces, entered Algiers Harbor, and forced the country to accept a treaty on American terms, releasing all American prisoners, canceling the tribute, and ceasing all piratical activity against American shipping.

AL-HIKMA UNIVERSITY OF BAGHDAD. A Catholic university, founded in 1956 in Baghdad, Iraq, by the Society of Jesus of the United States, organized and administered by Jesuit priests from the United States. In 1968 it became part of the Iraqi state university system and was later dissolved into Baghdad University. *Reference*: *Qubain*, pp. 232–235.

ALLEN, GEORGE VENABLE (1903–1970). Diplomat, born November 3, 1903, in Durham, North Carolina. Allen graduated from Duke and Harvard universities. He was teacher and principal in public schools from 1924 to 1928, and a reporter for local newspapers until 1929. He entered the foreign service in 1930, serving in Kingston, Jamaica; Shanghai; Patras, Greece; and Cairo. From 1938 to 1945 he served with the Near Eastern Division. He was ambassador to Iran from 1946 to 1948, and played a crucial role in resolving the Iranian crisis of 1946, when the Soviet government tried to create an autonomous republic in Azerbaijan, in northern Iran. He was assistant secretary of state from 1948 to 1950, ambassador to Yugoslavia from 1950 to 1953, ambassador to India and Nepal in 1953–1954, assistant secretary of state in the Bureau of Near Eastern, South Asian, and African Affairs in 1955–1956, and ambassador to Greece in 1956–1957. He was director of the U.S. Information Agency from 1957 to 1960 and director of the Foreign Service Institute from 1966 until his retirement in 1968. Allen was president of the Tobacco Institute from 1960 to 1966, and became ambassador-in-residence at George Washington University in 1968. Died July 11, 1970, in Bahama, near Durham, North Carolina. His wife, **KATH-ERINE M(ARTIN) ALLEN**, wrote *Foreign Service Diary* (Washington, D.C., 1967). *References*: Papers, Allen-Angier Family Papers, Duke University Library; "Mission to Iran," Ms. Harry S. Truman Library, Independence, Missouri; *NCAB* I:156; *NYT*, July 13, 1970; Richard Pfau, "Containment in Iran, 1946: The Shift to an Active Policy," *Diplomatic History* 1 (1977): 359–372; *PolProf: Eisenhower*; *PolProf: Truman*; and *WWWA*.

ALLEN, HAROLD B(OUGHTON) (1891–1970). Association executive, born August 4, 1891, in Carlton, New York. Allen graduated from Rutgers University. He was an assistant in agricultural education at Rudgers University from 1922 to 1926, and educational director for the Caucasus area for Near East Relief* from 1926 to 1928. He was director of education for Near East Relief and the Near East Foundation from 1928 to 1939 and conducted an experiment in rural education in Macedonia, Greece. Between 1930 and 1939 he also organized and supervised rural education programs in Syria, Palestine, Turkey, and Cyprus, made a study of agricultural problems in Cyprus for the British government in 1935, and a survey of rural and elementary education for the Syrian government in 1937. He was president of the National Farm school in Bucks County, Pennsylvania, from 1939 to 1943. He returned to his position of director of education for the Near East Foundation* in 1943 and served until 1957. Allen prepared a report for the Middle East Supply Center on *Rural Education and Welfare in the Middle East* (London, 1946). He was head of the UNESCO mission in fundamental education to the Arab States in 1950, and wrote *Rural Reconstruction in Action: Experience in the Near and Middle East* (Ithaca, N.Y., 1953). Died July 10, 1970, after being struck by a car, in Red Bank, New Jersey. *Reference*: *NYT*, July 11, 1970.

ALLEN, ORSON PARDA (1827–1918). Missionary, born November 6, 1827, in Smyrna, New York. Allen graduated from Amherst College and Andover Theological Seminary, and was ordained in 1855. He was a missionary under the American Board of Commissioners for Foreign Missions (ABCFM) in Smyrna and Trebizond, Turkey, in 1856–1857, and in Harput from 1857 to 1896. He taught at Harput Theological Seminary and was its president for some time. He returned to the United States in 1896, but went back to Turkey in 1912 and served in Brusa and Constantinople. Died June 21, 1918, in Constantinople. *References*: *Amherst*; *AndoverTS*.

AMERICAN BIBLE SOCIETY. A nondenominational specialized agency, founded in New York in 1816 to translate, produce, publish, and distribute the Bible, and to prepare literacy materials for both religious and secular use. The first overseas office was established in Smyrna in 1836, and the Middle East was the largest and most important foreign agency of the society throughout the nineteenth century. *References*: Archives, American Bible Society Library, New York City; Henry O. Dwight, *The Centennial History of the American Bible Society* (New York, 1916); *EMCM*; John M. Gibson, *Soldiers of the Word: The Story of the American Bible Society* (New York, 1958); and Creighton Lacy, *The Word-Carrying Giant: The Growth of the American Bible Society (1816–1966)* (South Pasadena, Calif., 1977).

AMERICAN BOARD OF COMMISSIONERS FOR FOREIGN MISSIONS (ABCFM). Founded in 1810 by Congregational churches. The ABCFM began work in the Middle East in 1819. It established missions in Palestine in 1819 (merged in 1826 with the Syria mission),* in Turkey in 1820, in Syria in 1823, and in Persia in 1838. It conducted educational, medical, and religious activities. It transferred the Persia and Syria missions to the Presbyterian Church in the U.S.A. Board of Foreign Missions* in 1870. In 1961 it merged into the United Church Board for World Ministries. *References*: Archives, Houghton Library, Harvard University; *Papers of the American Board of Commissioners for Foreign Missions. Unit 5: The Near East, 1817–1919* [Microfilm edition]; Clifton J. Phillips, *Protestant America and the Pagan World: The First Half Century of the American Board of Commissioners for Foreign Missions, 1810–1860* (Cambridge, Mass., 1969); Fred F. Goodsell, *You Shall Be My Witness* (Boston, 1959); and William E. Strong, *The Story of the American Board: An Account of the First Hundred Years of the American Board of Commissioners for Foreign Missions* (Boston, 1910).

AMERICAN COLLEGE, TEHERAN. *See* Alborz College, Teheran.

AMERICAN COLLEGE FOR GIRLS, CAIRO. Founded in 1861 by the United Presbyterian Church of North America's mission as a primary school and the first American School in Egypt, the College was expanded in 1910, covering all grades from kindergarten through junior college. *Reference*: *Survey*.

AMERICAN COLLEGE FOR GIRLS, CONSTANTINOPLE. Founded in 1871 as the Home School for Girls by the Women's Board of Missions in Boston. Renamed the American College for Girls in 1890, it became independent in 1904. It was later known as the Constantinople Woman's College and the Istanbul Woman's College. It merged in 1971 with Robert College.* *References*: Mary

M. Patrick, *A Bosporus Adventure: Istanbul (Constantinople) Woman's College, 1871–1924* (London, 1934); *Survey*.

AMERICAN COLLEGIATE INSTITUTE FOR GIRLS, SMYRNA. Founded in 1877 in Smyrna by the American Board of Commissioners for Foreign Missions (ABCFM) as the American Collegiate Institution, it became a high school and a college preparatory school. It was later renamed Izmir Amerikan Kiz Lisesi. *References*: *Schools*; *Survey*.

AMERICAN COLONY, JAFFA. Established in 1866 when a group of forty-three families (157 persons) led by George Washington Adams* arrived in Jaffa, Palestine. The group brought the first agricultural machines to Palestine and settled in Jaffa. The colony existed only a year. The people were dependent on Adams for food and shelter; the land chosen was poor and the crop failed. The colony was dismantled in 1867 when most of its members returned to the United States. Adams left Palestine in 1868. Only twenty-two persons remained in Palestine. *References*: Peter Amann, "U.S. Colonists in the Holy Land," *American History Illustrated* 5 (January 1971): 28–33; George W. Chamberlain, "A New England Crusade," *New England Magazine* 34 (1907): 195–207; Harold Davis, "The Jaffa Colonists from Downeast," *American Quarterly* 3 (1951): 344–356; Shlomo Eidelberg, "The Adams Colony in Jaffa (1866–1868)," *Midstream* 3 (Summer 1957): 52–61; and Reed M. Holmes, *The Forerunners* (Independence, Mo., 1981).

AMERICAN COLONY, JERUSALEM. Established by Horatio Gates Spafford,* who came to Jerusalem with a group of nineteen persons in 1881 for religious reasons. It later established a hotel (now the American Colony Hotel), the Anna Spafford Child Care Center in the Old City of Jerusalem, and a photographic studio which produced a guidebook to Jerusalem and other publications. *References*: Alexander Hume Ford, "Our American Colony at Jerusalem," *Appleton's Magazine* 7 (December 1906): 643–655; Helga Dudman, *Street People* (Jerusalem, 1982), ch. 7; Paul Elman. "The American-Swedish Kibbutz," *Swedish Pioneer Historical Quarterly* 32 (July 1981): 205–218; G. S. Hobart, " 'The Matson Collection': A Half Century of Photography in the Middle East," *The Quarterly Journal of the Library of Congress* 30 (January 1973): 19–43; and Bertha Spafford Vester, *Our Jerusalem: An American Family in the Holy City, 1881–1949* (Garden City, N.Y., 1950).

AMERICAN INDEPENDENT OIL COMPANY (AMINOIL). Founded in 1947 in Delaware by several companies pooling their resources. In 1948 it received an oil concession from Kuwait for the Neutral Zone—the desert land between Kuwait and Saudi Arabia. It struck oil in 1953 and later shared oil production equally with the Getty Oil Company.* The company's interests were nationalized by the Kuwaiti government in 1977. *Reference*: *IPE*.

AMERICAN MILITARY MISSION TO ARMENIA. *See* Harbord Mission.

AMERICAN MISSION, EGYPT. Begun in 1854 by the Associate Reformed Church of the West, one of the bodies that later joined to constitute the United Presbyterian Church of North America Board of Foreign Missions.* It conducted evangelical, educational, medical, and literary programs in Egypt and was responsible for the emergence of Protestant churches in Egypt, particularly the Coptic Evangelical Church. *References*: Records, 1850–1958. Presbyterian Historical Society Collections, Philadelphia; Earl E. Elder, *Vindicating a Vision: The Story of the American Mission in Egypt 1854–1954* (Philadelphia, 1958); *EMCM*; Stanley H. Skreslet II, "The American Presbyterian Mission in Egypt: Significant Factors in Its Establishment," *American Presbyterians* 64 (Summer 1986): 83–95; and Andrew Watson, *The American Mission in Egypt, 1854–1896* (Pittsburgh, 1904).

AMERICAN MISSION, SUDAN. Began in 1900 in Khartoum. The mission was an extension of the work in Egypt by the United Presbyterian Church of North America, Board of Foreign Missions.* The missionaries were expelled from the south of Sudan in 1964 by the Sudanese government because they were suspected of sympathizing with the tribal revolution in southern Sudan. *References*: *EMCM*; Reid F. Shields, *Behind the Garden of Allah* (Philadelphia, 1937).

AMERICAN NATIONAL RED CROSS. Established in 1881 in Washington, D.C., as the American Association of the Red Cross; became the American National Red Cross in 1893 and received a federal charter in 1900. The Red Cross was involved in various activities in the Middle East, including a relief expedition to aid Armenian victims of Turkish massacres in 1896, relief work in Palestine in 1918–1919, evacuation of Greek refugees from Smyrna in 1922, and many activities during and after World War II. *References*: Archives, National Archives and Records Center and American Red Cross Archives, Washington, D.C.; Clara Barton, *The Red Cross: A History of This Remarkable Movement in the Interest of Humanity* (Washington, D.C., 1898); Foster R. Dulles, *The American Red Cross: A History* (New York, 1950); and "The History of the American National Red Cross," Ms., American Red Cross National Headquarters Library, Washington, D.C.

AMERICAN NAVAL DETACHMENT IN TURKISH WATERS. 1919–1924. *See* U.S. Naval Detachment in Turkish Waters.

AMERICAN PALESTINE EXPLORATION SOCIETY. Founded in 1870 to cooperate with the British Palestine Exploration Fund in the exploration of Palestine. The chief task of the society was to explore the area east of the Jordan River. The first expedition, led by Lieutenant Edgar Zell Steever,* explored and surveyed Moab (southwest Jordan) in 1873, and a second expedition, led by

James Crandall Lane,* surveyed the area east of the River Jordan in 1875. Selah Merrill* explored that area for the society in 1876–1877. The society was disbanded in 1884. *Reference*: Warren J. Moulton, ''The American Palestine Exploration Society,'' *Annals of the American Schools of Oriental Research* 8 (1926–27): 55–78.

AMERICAN PRESS. Established by the American Board of Commissioners for Foreign Missions (ABCFM)* in Malta in 1822. The Arabic-language work was moved to Beirut in 1834 (the rest being moved to Smyrna and becoming later the Redhouse Press*) and was initially directed by Eli Smith.* It has printed a large amount of material in Arabic and in 1900 it was the largest Arabic printing establishment in the world. It also produced matrices in Arabic for print shops all over the Middle East. *Reference*: *Centennial of the American Press of the Board of Foreign Missions of the Presbyterian Church in the USA, Beirut, Syria, 1822–1922* (Beirut, 1923).

AMERICAN PROTESTANT EPISCOPAL CHURCH. *See* Protestant Episcopal Church in the United States of America: Board of Missions.

AMERICAN RESEARCH CENTER IN EGYPT, INC. (ARCE). Independent private, nonprofit research institution founded in 1948 by a consortium of twenty-six universities and museums, which has established a center in Cairo, which has become the major American base for research in Egypt. The center's task is to promote and fund scholarly research on Egypt and the Middle East in the fields of archaeology, history, culture, and the social sciences; to train specialists in Middle Eastern studies and in academic disciplines which require familiarity with Egypt; to disseminate knowledge about Egypt; and to promote United States-Egyptian cultural relations. ARCE supports archaeological, historical, and literary projects, and assists in archaeological and scientific expeditions in Egypt. *References*: *Corners*, pp. 133–135.

AMERICAN SCHOOLS OF ORIENTAL RESEARCH (ASOR). Founded in 1900 in Jerusalem to support the activities of independent archaeological institutions in the United States and Canada. Biblical archaeology has been the major focus of its activity in the past. The Baghdad School was founded in 1923. ASOR conducted many excavations under its auspices, including some of the most significant excavations in the Middle East, and shared in the discovery, decipherment, and publication of the Dead Sea Scrolls. It overseas a large number of projects in various Middle Eastern countries, and has an active publications program. The center in Jerusalem was renamed the W. F. Albright Institute of Archaeological Research (AIAR). Other components of ASOR are the American Center of Oriental Research (ACOR) in Amman, and the Cyprus American Archaeological Research Institute (CAARI) in Nicosia, which have been centers for scholarly research in these countries. *References*: *Corners*, pp. 143–145;

Philip J. King, *American Archaeology in the Mideast: A History of the American Schools of Oriental Research* (Philadelphia, 1983).

AMERICAN UNIVERSITY IN CAIRO. Nondenominational, American-type, independent liberal arts college, founded by private interests in 1919 and incorporated under the laws of Washington, D.C. It is governed by a self-perpetuating American Board of Trustees. The university began operations in 1920 and added the School of Oriental Studies in 1921. It established a division of public service, providing adult education programs, in 1924; a Social Research Center in 1953; and a graduate faculty in 1956. *References: Boardman*; Edward F. Gossett, "The American Protestant Missionary Endeavour in North Africa from Its Origins to 1939," Ph.D. diss., University of California, Los Angeles, 1960, ch. vii; *IHU*; *Qubain*, pp. 68–70; and William Tuohy, "Egyptian Education American Style," *AWM* 23 (March–April 1972): 28–34.

AMERICAN UNIVERSITY OF BEIRUT. Private, nondenominational university, founded in 1866 by missionaries as the Syrian Protestant College under charter from the Board of Regents of the State of New York. The School of Medicine was added in 1867 and the School of Pharmacy in 1871. It was rechartered in 1920 when the present name was adopted. Schools of engineering and architecture, agriculture and public health were added later. The university played an important role in the educational and political development of the Arab Middle East. The civil war in Lebanon in 1975–76 and after 1978 disturbed the activities of the university. President Malcolm H. Kerr* was assassinated and several of its American deans and faculty members were kidnapped by terrorist groups and held as hostages. *References: Boardman*; Bayard Dodge, *The American University of Beirut* (Beirut, 1958); Faith Hanna, *An American Mission: The Role of the American University of Beirut* (Boston, 1979); *IHU*; John M. Munro, *A Mutual Concern: The Story of the American University of Beirut* (Delmar, N.Y., 1977); Stephen B. L. Penrose, Jr., *That They May Have Life: The Story of the American University of Beirut 1866–1941* (Princeton, 1941); *Qubain*, 346–91; A. L. Tibawi, "The Genesis and Early History of the Syrian Protestant College," *MEJ* 21 (1967): 1–15.

AMERICAN WOMEN'S HOSPITALS (AWH). Founded in 1917 by the American Medical Women's Association as an international philanthropic medical relief service. It has supported medical and hospital service carried by American physicians and nurses. The first hospital was established in France in 1918. It provided medical service in the Armenian Republic of Erivan in 1919–1920, and was active in Turkey and Greece in 1922–1923, work described by Esther P. Lovejoy* in *Certain Samaritans* (New York, 1927; 2nd ed. 1933). It was renamed the American Women's Hospitals Service (AWHS) in 1959. *Reference*: Esther P. Lovejoy, *Women Doctors of the World* (New York, 1957), chs. 21–24.

AMERICAN ZIONIST MEDICAL UNIT (AZMU). Organized by Hadassah, the Women's Zionist Organization of America,* at the request of the World Zionist Organization. AZMU went to Palestine in 1918, headed by Isaac Max Rubinow.* It dealt with the health problems that arose during World War I, and it established regular health services in Palestine. It was renamed the Hadassah* Medical Organization in 1922. *Reference*: *EJ*.

AMINOIL *See* American Independent Oil Company (AMINOIL).

ANATOLIA COLLEGE. Founded in 1886 by Charles Chapin Tracy* in Marsovan, Turkey. Antolia was incorporated as a college in 1894 and received imperial recognition from the Ottoman government in 1899, although several teachers and students were implicated in Armenian revolutionary activities in 1893. It was closed in 1916, reopened in 1919, but, because of Turkish government interference, it was relocated to Saloniki, Greece, in 1925. *References*: *Stone*, ch. 9; George E. White, *Adventuring with Anatolia College* (Grinnell, Iowa, 1940).

ANDERSON, HENRY JAMES (1799–1875). Physician and scientist, born February 6, 1799, in New York City. Anderson graduated from Columbia College and the College of Physicians and Surgeons, and was professor of mathematics and astronomy at Columbia College from 1825 to 1850. He traveled in Egypt, Nubia, and Abyssinia in 1843, and in 1848 he served as geologist and physician on the Expedition to the River Jordan and the Dead Sea,* later publishing several reports on his geological findings. He also collected antiquities which he gave to the New York Historical Society (later transferred to the Brooklyn Museum). In 1875 he joined the scientific expedition to observe the transit of Venus in Australia, visiting India on the way. He became sick while exploring the Himalayas. Died October 19, 1875, in Lahore, India. *References*: *ACAB*; *DACB*; *NCAB* 6:389; and *WWWA*.

ANDERSON, ROBERT VAN VLECK (1884–1949). Geologist, born April 18, 1884, in Galesburg, Illinois. Anderson graduated from Stanford University. He conducted geological and zoological work in Japan in 1905; was geological aide, assistant geologist, and geologist for the U.S. Geological Survey from 1906 to 1913; geologist for S. Pearson and Son, Ltd. of London, from 1913 to 1918; representative of the U.S. War Trade Board in Sweden; and a delegate on the Inter-Allied Trade Commission in Stockholm in 1918–1919. He was employed by Whitehall Petroleum Corporation of London from 1918 to 1923, was their chief geologist from 1923 to 1925, and was engaged in independent scientific work from 1927 to 1934. He was a collaborator in the Service de la Carte Geologique de l'Algerie from 1930 to 1932, conducted research in Algeria in 1933, and wrote *Geology in the Coastal Atlas of Western Algeria* (New York, 1936). He was with Socony Vacuum Oil Company from 1934 to 1944 and served as research associate at Stanford University after 1945. Died June 6, 1949, in Palo Alto, California. *References*: *GSAP*, 1933–1957, pp. 81–84; *WWWA*.

ANDERSON, RUFUS (1796–1880). Clergyman, born August 17, 1796, in North Yarmouth, Maine. Anderson graduated from Bowdoin College and Andover Theological Seminary. He was editor-in-chief of *Millionary Herald*, assistant to the secretary of the American Board of Commissioners for Foreign Missions (ABCFM)* from 1822 to 1824, assistant secretary from 1824 to 1832, and corresponding secretary from 1832 to 1866. He toured the Middle East in 1828–1829 and again in 1843–1844. Each visit was followed by changes in the organization of local mission work. He wrote *Memorial Volume of the First Fifty Years of the American Board of Commissioners for Foreign Missions* (Boston, 1861), and *History of the Missions of the American Board of Commissioners for Foreign Missions to the Oriental Churches* (Boston, 1872). Died May 30, 1880, in Boston. *References*: R. P. Beaver, ed., *To Advance the Gospel: Selections from the Writings of Rufus Anderson* (Grand Rapids, Mich., 1967); *ACAB*; *AndoverTS*; *NCAB* 24:153; Robert A. Schneider, "The Senior Secretary: Rufus Anderson and the American Board of Commissioners for Foreign Missions, 1810–1880," Ph.D. diss., Harvard University, 1980; and *WWWA*.

ANDERSON MISSION, 1955–1956. Robert Bernerd Anderson (1910–   ), secretary of the navy in 1953–1954, and deputy secretary of defense in 1954–1955, was President Dwight D. Eisenhower's special envoy to the Middle East from December 1955 to March 1956 in an unsuccessful effort to initiate direct talks between Israel and Egypt and to bring about an Egyptian-Israeli agreement. *References*: *NCAB* I:15; Donald Neff, *Warriors at Suez: Eisenhower Takes America Into the Middle East* (New York, 1981), ch. 6; *PolProf: Eisenhower*; and *Touval*, ch. 5.

ANDREWS, FANNIE FERN PHILLIPS (1867–1950). Publicist and author, born September 25, 1867, in Margaretville, Nova Scotia. Andrews graduated from Radcliffe College. She was a school teacher at Lynn, Massachusetts, from 1884 to 1890, and the founder, secretary, and later president of the Boston Home and School Association from 1907 to 1918. In 1925 she traveled through the Middle East to study the mandatory system. She wrote *The Holy Land under Mandate* (Boston, 1931), and later her memoirs, *Memory Pages of My Life* (Boston, 1948). Died January 23, 1950, in Somerville, Massachusetts. *References*: Papers, Schlesinger Library, Radcliffe College; *BDI*; *NAW*; *NCAB* A:356; and *WWWA*.

ANDRUS, ALPHEUS NEWELL (1843–1919). Missionary, born July 17, 1843, in New York City. Andrus graduated from Williams College and Union Theological Seminary, and was ordained in 1858. He became a missionary under the American Board of Commissioners for Foreign Missions (ABCFM)* in

Turkey in 1859 and was stationed in Mardin. He opened a school and a theological seminary in Mardin, was involved in relief work following the massacre of 1895, and later devoted special attention to the Yezidees and the Kurds. He transliterated the New Testament in Arabo-Kurdish and prepared a Kurdish grammar. Died January 11, 1919, in Poughkeepsie, New York. *References*: *NCAB* 18:24; *UnionTS*.

ANGLO-AMERICAN COMMITTEE OF INQUIRY. A joint committee appointed in 1945 to inquire about the problems of Jewish displaced persons in Europe and the capacity of Palestine to absorb them. The six American members, appointed by President Harry S. Truman, were Joseph Chapelle Hutcheson, Jr. (1879–1973), chief judge of the Southern District of Texas, who was co-chairman of the committee; Frank Aydelotte (1880–1956), former president of Swarthmore College; Frank W. Buxton (1877–1974), editor of the Boston *Herald*; Bartley Cavanaugh Crum (1900–1959), a San Francisco attorney; James Grover McDonald* (1886–1964), former League of Nations High Commissioner for Refugees; and William Phillips (1878–1968), former undersecretary of state and ambassador to Belgium and Italy. The committee went to the Middle East in 1946, and conducted hearings in Cairo and Jerusalem. The recommendation adopted by President Truman was the immediate admission of 100,000 Jews in Palestine, but the British government never implemented any of the recommendations. *References*: Leonard Dinnerstein, "America, Britain, and Palestine: The Anglo-American Committee of Inquiry and the Displaced Persons, 1945–46," *Diplomatic History* 4 (1980): 283–301; *America and the Survivors of the Holocaust* (New York, 1982), ch. 3.

ANTES, JOHN [JOHANN] (1740–1811). Musician and missionary, born March 24, 1740, in Frederick, near Bethlehem, Pennsylvania. In 1764 Antes went to Saxony for training and was ordained in 1769. In 1770 he was sent as the first American missionary to Egypt. In 1779 henchmen of Osman Bey, intent on extorting money from him, captured, tortured and imprisoned him. He was released through the intervention of a friend. While recovering in Cairo, he composed three string trios, the earliest known chamber music by a native American composer. He left Egypt in 1781 and later lived in England. He wrote *Observations on the Manners and Customs of the Egyptians; the Overflowing of the Nile, and Its Effects; with Remarks on the Plague, and Other Subjects Written During a Residence of Twelve Years in Cairo and Its Vicinity* (London, 1800). Died December 17, 1811, in Bristol, England. *References*: J. Taylor Hamilton, "Experiences of the First American Missionary in Egypt," *Transactions of the Moravian Historical Society* 12, Part 1 (1938): 26–39; Donald M. McCorkle, "John Antes, 'American Dilettante'," *Musical Quarterly* 42 (October 1956): 486–499; *The New Grove Dictionary of Music and Musicians* (London, 1980); and *WWWA*.

ANTOUN, RICHARD T(AFT) (1932–   ). Anthropologist, born March 31, 1932, in Massachusetts. Antoun graduated from Williams College, Johns Hopkins, and Harvard universities. He was assistant professor, and associate professor of anthropology at Indiana University from 1963 until 1967, and professor at the State University of New York in Binghamton after 1970. He conducted anthropological research in Jordan, and wrote *Arab Village: A Social Structure Study of a Transjordanian Peasant Community* (Bloomington, Ind., 1972) and *Low-key Politics: Local-level Leadership Change in the Middle East* (Albany, N.Y., 1979). *Reference: CA.*

APPLETON, THOMAS GOLD (1812–1884). Author, born March 31, 1812, in Boston. Appleton attended Harvard College, but had no fixed occupation and traveled widely. He toured Egypt and Syria in 1874–1885, and wrote *A Nile Journey* (Boston, 1876) and *Syrian Sunshine* (Boston, 1877). Died April 17, 1884, in Boston. *References: ACAB; DAB;* Susan Hale, *Life and Letters of Thomas Gold Appleton* (New York, 1885); *NCAB* 8:391; *NYHSD;* Louise H. Thorpe, *The Appletons of Beacon Hill* (Boston, 1973); and *WWWA.*

ARABIAN AMERICAN OIL COMPANY (ARAMCO). In 1933 Standard Oil Company of California obtained an oil concession for an area of eastern Saudi Arabia and established the California Arabian Oil Company (CASOC).* In 1936 it combined its operations with Texas Company. The company's name was changed to the Arabian American Oil Company (ARAMCO) in 1944. Standard Oil Company (New Jersey) and Socony Vacuum became part owners. The government of Saudi Arabia acquired 25 percent of the company's production assets in 1972, increasing it to 60 percent in 1974 and to 100 percent in 1980, but the company continues to operate the oil fields. *References:* Irvine H. Anderson, *Aramco, the United States, and Saudi Arabia: A Study in the Dynamics of Foreign Oil Policy, 1930–1950* (Princeton, N.J., 1981); "Aramco: A Celebration," *AWM* 35 (May-June 1984), entire issue; *Aramco and Its World: Arabia and the Middle East,* ed. Ismail I. Nawwab et al. (Dharan, Saudi Arabia, 1986); Philip C. McConnel, *The Hundred Men* (Peterborough, N.H., 1965); and Wallace Stegner, *Discovery* (Beirut, 1971).

ARABIAN MISSION. Founded in 1889 as an independent mission by James Cantine* and Samuel Marinus Zwemer,* who opened the first station in August 1891 in Basra, Iraq. It was transferred to the Reformed Church of America in 1894. Mission stations were eventually established in Muscat, Bahrain, Kuwait, and Iraq. Activities concentrated on medical care and education. *References:* Alfred D. Mason and Fredrick J. Barny, *History of the Arabian Mission* (New York, 1926); Dorothy Van Ess, *History of the Arabian Mission 1926–1957* (n.p., 195–).

ARAMCO. *See* Arabian American Oil Company (ARAMCO).

ASCHAM, JOHN BAYNE (1873–1950). Clergyman, born February 12, 1873, in Vanlue, Ohio. Ascham graduated from Ohio Wesleyan, Harvard, and Boston universities, and was ordained in 1897. He served in various communities in Ohio from 1897 to 1923, was a student at the American Schools of Oriental Research (ASOR)* in 1913, made an extensive tour of Palestine, and wrote *A Syrian Pilgrimage* (New York, 1914). He was a chaplain in World War I, social service representative of the A. Nash Company, and educational adviser of Turk Ojaq of Turkey from 1925 to 1928. He was executive vice president of the Children's Home in Cincinnati from 1928 until his retirement in 1943. Died November 14, 1950, in Cincinnati. *References*: *OAB*; *WWWA*.

ASOR. *See* American Schools of Oriental Research.

ASSEMBLIES OF GOD. Began missionary activities in 1908 in Assiut, Egypt, and in Es Salt, Palestine, and in 1924 in Minia, Egypt. Its most publicized activity has been the sponsorship of the Assiut Orphanage founded by Lillian Hunt Trasher* in 1911 in Assiut. *References*: *EMCM*; Irwin Winehouse, *The Assemblies of God* (New York, 1959).

ASSIUT COLLEGE, ASSIUT. Founded in 1865 by the American Mission, Egypt.* It served as the center of the mission's cultural activity in Upper Egypt. Postsecondary work was offered at one time, but the college later reverted to a secondary school. It included an agricultural department and a dairy farm which experimented in breeding Egyptian cattle and Jerseys. In 1958 it came under the control of the Egyptian Ministry of Education.

ATHERTON, ALFRED LEROY, JR. (1921–   ). Diplomat, born November 22, 1921, in Pittsburgh, and grew up in Springfield, Massachusetts. Atherton graduated from Harvard University, and served in the army during World War II. He entered the foreign service in 1947, and served in Stuttgart, and Bonn, Germany. He was 2nd secretary in Damascus from 1953 to 1956, and consul in Aleppo, Syria, in 1957–1958, international relations officer in the Bureau of Near Eastern and South Asian Affairs from 1959 to 1961, consul in Calcutta from 1962 to 1965, deputy director of the Office of Near Eastern Affairs in 1965–1966, country director, Arab States North, in 1966–1967, and Israel and Arab-Israel Affairs from 1967 to 1969. He was deputy assistant secretary of state in the Bureau of Near Eastern and South Asian Affairs from 1970 to 1974, and assistant secretary from 1974 to 1978. He was ambassador at large in 1978–1979, with special responsibility for Middle East peace negotiations, and ambassador to Egypt from 1979 to 1983. He was director general of the Foreign Service from 1983 until his retirement in 1984. *References*: *MENA*; *NYT*, December 2, 1977; and *WWA*.

ATKINS, PAUL MOODY (1892–1977). Economist, financial and management consultant, born April 3, 1892, in Boston. Atkins graduated from Yale University and the universities of Chicago and Paris, and served in the army in World War I. He worked for various corporations until 1932 and was special liquidator of securities for the U.S. Comptroller of Currency from 1932 to 1937. In 1938 he became financial and management consultant and served as a consultant on financial missions to Peru and Japan. In 1943–1944 he was an economic advisor to the Ministry of Finance of Iran, a member of Arthur Chester Millspaugh's* second mission to Iran, and director of the opium and tobacco monopolies. In 1944 he prepared a report on the economic conditions of the Middle East countries. Died January 31, 1977, in Glen Ridge, New Jersey. *References*: Papers, Sterling Memorial Library, Yale University; *CA*; *NYT*, February 2, 1977; and *WWWA*.

AVERY, BENNETT F(RANKLIN) (1901–   ). Physician, born September 21, 1901, in Vassar, Michigan. Avery graduated from the University of Michigan and served in World War I in France with the Red Cross Ambulance Corps. He was adjunct professor of anatomy at the American University of Beirut* from 1926 until 1929, associate professor from 1930 to 1939, professor from 1939 to 1941, and professor of anatomy and dean of the School of Medicine at Boston University from 1940 to 1944. From 1944 to 1949 he served as director general of public health in Iran and as an adviser to the Imperial Iranian Ministry of Health. He was medical officer in the Norfolk, Virginia, naval base from 1950 to 1952, director of publications in the Bureau of Medicine and Surgery in the Department of the Navy from 1952 to 1958, editor of the *U.S. Armed Forces Medical Journal* from 1955 to 1958, and national coordinator of medical education for national defense programs from 1958 until his retirement in 1963, with the rank of captain. *References*: *AMWS*; *NCAB* J:115.

B

BACON, FRANCIS H(ENRY) (1856–1940). Architectural archaeologist and designer, born July 3, 1856, in Chicago. Bacon graduated from the Massachusetts Institute of Technology and was engaged in architectural work in New York City. He traveled in Europe in 1878–1879, toured the Aegean Sea in a small craft, and visited Assos in Asia Minor. He took part in the first American archaeological expedition to Asia Minor as an engineer and architect in the excavation of Assos from 1881 to 1883, and completed the report of the excavations which was published as *Investigations at Assos* (Cambridge, Mass., 1902–1921). He wrote of his experiences in Assos in the September 1886 issue of *Century Magazine*. Bacon was later draughtsman with the architect H. H. Richardson, a furniture designer and decorator in Boston, and in 1908 he became a manufacturer of furniture and an interior decorator. Died February 5, 1940, at Chanakkale on the Dardanelles, Turkey. *References*: "The Log of the Dorian" and "Assos Days," Mss., Archaeological Institute of America; Letters in William Berry Mckoy Papers, Duke University Library; drawings done in Turkey in 1881 in Museum of Fine Arts, Boston; "Assos Journals of Francis H. Bacon," ed. Lenore K. Congdon, *Archeology* 27 (April 1974): 83–95; and *AJA* 44 (1940): 117.

BACON, HENRY (1839–1912). Painter and illustrator, born September 10, 1839, in Haverhill, Massachusetts. Bacon enlisted in the army in 1857 and served in the Civil War as a field artist for *Leslie's Weekly*. In 1864 he went to Europe; he studied art in Paris, where he spent most of his professional life. After visiting Egypt, he specialized in Egyptian subjects and became noted for his watercolor paintings of life in Egypt. Died March 13, 1912, in Cairo. *References*: *ACAB*; Sara C. Junkin, "The Europeanization of Henry Bacon (1839–1912): American Expatriate Painter," Ph.D. diss., Boston University, 1986; and *NYHSD*.

BADÈ, WILLIAM FREDERIC (1871–1936). Educator and archaeologist, born January 22, 1871, in Carver, Minnesota. Badè graduated from Moravian College and Theological Seminary (Bethlehem, Pa.), and studied at Yale and Leigh universities and at the universities of Berlin and Paris. From 1896 to 1898 he was on the faculty of Moravian College, and from 1898 to 1902, on the faculty of Moravian Theological Seminary. In 1902 he moved to the Pacific Theological Seminary (later Pacific School of Religion), which he served as professor of Semitic languages and Old Testament literature until his death. He was also dean of faculty from 1922 to 1928, and acting president from 1920 to 1922. In 1928 he established the Palestine Institute of the Pacific School of Religion and was its director. In 1926 he and William Charles Gotshall* undertook the excavation of Tell en-Nasbeh, north of Jerusalem, and continued to excavate it for four more seasons. He wrote two progress reports and *A Manual of Excavation in the Near East: Methods of Digging and Recording of the Tell en-Nasbeh Expedition in Palestine* (Berkeley, Calif., 1934). The final publication of the results appeared after his death. Died March 4, 1936, in Berkeley, California. *References*: Papers, Pacific School of Religion Library; *DAB S2*; *NCAB* 27:180; and *WWWA*.

BADEAU, JOHN STOTHOFF (1903–   ). Educator and diplomat, born February 24, 1903, in Pittsburgh, Pennsylvania. Badeau graduated from Union College and the New Brunswick Theological Seminary, and was ordained in 1928. From 1928 to 1935 he served as a missionary of the United Mission in Mesopotamia, stationed at Mosul from 1928 to 1930, and at Baghdad from 1930 to 1935. He was associate professor of religion and philosophy at the American University in Cairo* from 1936 to 1938, dean of the Faculty of Arts and Sciences from 1938 to 1944, and president from 1945 to 1953. From 1943 to 1945 he served as a religion specialist in the Office of War Information in Washington, D.C. He was president of the Near East Foundation* from 1953 to 1961 and ambassador to Egypt from 1961 to 1964. From 1964 to 1971 he was professor of Middle Eastern studies at Columbia University. He wrote *East and West of Suez: The Story of the Modern Near East* (New York, 1943), *The Emergence of Modern Egypt* (New York, 1953), *The Lands Between* (New York, 1958), *The American Approach to the Arab World* (New York, 1968), and his autobiography, *The Middle East Remembered* (Washington, D.C., 1983). *References*: *DAS*; *MENA*; *PolProf: Kennedy*; and *WWA*.

BAHRAIN PETROLEUM COMPANY (BAPCO). Originally incorporated in Canada in 1929 as a wholly owned subsidiary of Standard Oil Company of California. BAPCO struck oil in Bahrain in 1932 and began production in the mid–1930s. Texas Company (later Texaco) acquired a 50 percent interest in the company in 1936. It constructed a refinery in 1936 which was expanded to become one of the region's largest. The Bahraini government acquired 60 percent interest in the company in 1974 and increased its ownership to 100 percent in 1980. *References*: *IPE*; *Survey*.

BAIN, ROBERT E(DWARD) M(ATHER) (1858–1932). Photographer, born August 9, 1858, in Chicago. Bain graduated from Washington University and was a member of the Missouri House of Representatives from 1884 to 1886. A well-known amateur photographer, he traveled, with James Wideman Lee,* in 1894 in Lower Egypt, Palestine, and Turkey, producing photographs to illustrate the book *Early Footsteps of the Man of Galilee: Being Five Hundred Original Photographic Views and Descriptions of the Places Connected with the Earthly Life of Our-Lord and His Apostles, Traced with Note Book and Camera*, written by Lee and John Heyl Vincent* (New York, 1894), as well as the photographs for *The Self-Interpreting Bible* (St. Louis, 1895–1898). He was later president of the American Outdoor Photographers' Association, and the International Mercantile Marine Company's general passenger manager for the Southwest from 1903 to 1925. Died May 22, 1932, in St. Louis, Missouri. *References*: Photograph Collection, Prints and Photographs Division, Library of Congress; *WWWA*.

BAINBRIDGE, WILLIAM (1774–1833). Naval officer, born May 7, 1774, in Princeton, New Jersey. Bainbridge went to sea at fifteen and until 1798 commanded vessels in the European trade. In 1798 he was commissioned a lieutenant commander in the navy, received the command of *Retaliation*, and served in the quasi-war with France. In 1800 he commanded the frigate *George Washington* and delivered the American tribute to the Dey of Algiers. Bainbridge was forced to sail, under Ottoman flag, to Constantinople to carry presents from the Dey to the Sultan. He commanded the frigate *Philadelphia** in 1803, when the ship ran aground in the Tripoli Harbor and Bainbridge was obliged to surrender, and was held prisoner in Tripoli until 1805. After his return to the United States, Bainbridge served again as captain and part owner of a merchant ship. He served in the navy during the War of 1812 and commanded the *Independence* in the War with Algiers. He returned to the Mediterranean a fifth time in 1820. Died July 27, 1833, in Philadelphia. *References*: Papers, Library of Congress; *ACAB*; *DAB*; *DAMIB*; David F. Long, *Ready to Hazard: A Biography of Commodore William Bainbridge, 1774–1833* (Boston, 1981); *NCAB* 8:93; *WAMB*; and *WWWA*.

BALDWIN, E. F. (fl. 1884–1890). Missionary. Baldwin served as a Baptist minister in North Carolina, and in 1884 he conducted an exploratory investigation of Algeria for the Foreign Missions Board of the Southern Baptist Convention.* When the convention decided not to enter this mission field, he became a missionary in the English Kabyle Mission in 1884 and was the first superintendent of the Southern Morocco Mission. He severed his relations with the Kabyle Mission in 1888 and launched into independent missionary work in Morocco until 1890 when he moved to Syria.

BALDWIN, MARY BRISCOE (1811–1877). Missionary, born May 20, 1811, in the Shenandoah Valley of Virginia. Baldwin taught in a seminary for women in Staunton, Virginia, and in 1832 went to Athens as a missionary under the Domestic and Foreign Missionary Society of the Protestant Episcopal Church.* She established a girls' boarding school in Athens and taught there from 1835 to 1869. She played an important role in the American relief operations for the Cretans in the 1860s. In 1869 she moved to Palestine. She was a teacher in the Tabitha mission girls' school and in a boys' school established by the Englishwoman Walker Arnot in Jaffa, Palestine, until her death. Died June 21, 1877, in Jaffa. *Reference*: Emma R. Pitman, *Mission Life in Greece and Palestine; Memorial of Mary Briscoe Baldwin, Missionary to Athens and Joppa* (London, 1881).

BALLANTINE, DUNCAN SMITH (1912–   ). Educational administrator, born November 5, 1912, in Garden City, New York. Ballantine graduated from Amherst College and Harvard University, and served in the navy during World War II. He was assistant professor and associate professor of history at the Massachusetts Institute of Technology from 1947 to 1952, and president of Reed College (Portland, Ore.) from 1952 to 1955. From 1955 until 1961 he was president of Robert College* and the American College for Girls* in Istanbul. He turned Robert College* into a coeducational institution, instituted a graduate program, and established a school of business administration and economics. After his return to the United States, he became director of the Education Department of the International Bank for Reconstruction and Development (the World Bank) from 1962 until 1977, and consultant to the bank afterwards. *References*: *Amherst*; *AMWS*; *LE*; and *WWS*.

BALLANTINE, HENRY (1846–1914). Consul, born November 18, 1846, in Ahmednagar, India, to American parents. Ballantine graduated from Amherst College. He was a merchant in Bombay, India, from 1870 until 1872, and in New York City from 1872 until 1891. In 1875 he traveled in the Persian Gulf, visiting Muscat and Bahrain, and then from Bushire, through the interior of Persia to the Caspian Sea. He described his travels in *Midnight Marches Through Persia* (Boston, 1879). He was consul in Bombay from 1891 to 1896, and later a claims adjuster for an insurance company. In private business he maintained offices in Bombay, Calcutta, and other cities in India, until his death. Died October 30, 1914, in Seattle, Washington. *Reference*: *Amherst*.

BALLANTINE, WILLIAM GAY (1848–1937). Educator, born December 7, 1848, in Washington, D.C. Ballantine graduated from Mariette (Ohio) College and studied at Union Theological Seminary and the University of Leipzig. He was assistant engineer in the American Palestine Exploration Society's* first expedition in the area east of the Jordan River in 1873. He was professor of chemistry and geology at Ripon College from 1873 to 1876, professor of Greek at Indiana University from 1876 to 1878, professor of Hebrew and Greek at

Oberlin Theological Seminary from 1878 to 1891, president of Oberlin College from 1891 to 1896, and professor of Bible at the Young Men's Christian Association (YMCA)* College in Springfield, Massachusetts, from 1897 until his retirement in 1920. Died January 10, 1937, in Springfield. *References*: *NCAB* 27:288; *OAB*; *UnionTS*; and *WWWA*.

BALLOU, HENRY ARTHUR (1872–1937). Entomologist, born in Swanzey, New Hampshire. Ballou graduated from the Massachusetts Agricultural College (Fitchburg, Mass.). He went to Barbados in 1903 as representative of the Imperial Department of Agriculture, and later was professor of entomology at the Imperial College in Trinidad. In 1916–1917 he was in Egypt, studying the pink bollworm of the cotton in Egypt and published a report *The Pink Boll-worm in Egypt in 1916–1917* (Cairo, 1920). He was commissioner of agriculture of the British West Indies until his retirement in 1934. Died November 3, 1937, in Bridgetown, Barbados. *Reference*: *NYT*, November 4, 1937.

BANGOR. River paddle steamer, owned by Boston and Bangor Steamsboat Co. from 1834 to 1842 served from Boston to Bangor, Maine. She was sold in 1842 to the Ottoman government, renamed *Sudaver* and was placed on passenger service between Princes' Island in the Sea of Marmara and Constantinople. She was later transferred to a private Turkish company which continued to run her in the same route until the 1880s when she was laid up in the Imperial Ottoman Dockyard. She was scrapped about 1888. *References*: Erik Heyl, *Early American Steamer* (Buffalo, N.Y., 1956), 2:13; H. Parker and Frank C. Bowen, *Mail and Passenger Steamships of the Nineteenth Century* (London, 1928), pp. 28–29.

BANKS, EDGAR JAMES (1866–1945). Archaeologist, born May 23, 1866, in Sunderland, Massachusetts. Banks graduated from Amherst College and Harvard University, and studied at the University of Breslau. He was consul in Baghdad from 1897 to 1898, taught at Robert College* in 1902–1903, and was private secretary to the U.S. minister to Turkey in 1903. In 1899 he organized an expedition to excavate Ur, but was refused permission by the Turkish government. He was field director of the Babylonian expedition, an instructor at the University of Chicago from 1903 to 1906, and excavated Bismya in Mesopotamia in 1903–1904. He wrote *Bismya, or the Lost City of Adab: A Story of Adventure, of Exploration, and of Excavation Among the Ruins of the Oldest of the Buried Cities of Babylonia* (New York, 1912), *The Bible and the Spade* (New York, 1913), and *Armenian Princess: A Tale of Anatolian Peasant Life* (Boston, 1914), a book of fiction. He was the first American to climb to the summit of Mount Ararat on August 20, 1912. Banks was later professor of Oriental languages and archaeology at Toledo University, lecturer for the extensioin division of the University of Pennsylvania, and, after 1906, a freelance lecturer. He established Sacred Films, Inc., and was later president of Seminole Films, Inc. Died May 4, 1945, in Eustis, Florida. *References*: *ACAB*; *NYT*, May 9, 1945; and *WWWA*.

BANVARD, JOHN (1815–1891). Panorama painter, born November 15, 1815, in New York City. Banvard went to Louisville, Kentucky, at fifteen, and became an itinerant portraitist in the 1830s, working along the Ohio River. In 1840 he began to travel along the Mississippi River, drawing the life on the river. The sketches he made on the spot were later transformed into a panorama of the Mississippi River, which was completed in 1846 and exhibited throughout the United States and in London. In 1850 or 1851 he traveled in the Middle East, particularly Palestine and Egypt, where he painted scenes that were transformed into several panoramas. The panorama of Jerusalem and the Holy Land, which was exhibited in New York and other cities beginning in 1852, represented the first "moving pictures" of the Holy Land. Banvard provided guides to the panoramas in pamphlets, including *Description of Banvard's Pictures of Jerusalem and the Holy Land* (New York, 1852) and *Banvard's Historical Landscape of the Sea of Galilee* (New York, 1863). Died May 17, 1891, in Watertown, North Dakota. *References*: Papers, Archives and Manuscripts Division, Minnesota Historical Society, St. Paul, Minnesota; Nan H. Agle and Frances A. Bacon, *The Ingenious John Banvard* (New York, 1966); *ACAB*; *DAB*; *NCAB* 5:326; *NYHSD*; Doane Robinson, "John Banvard," *South Dakota Historical Collections* 21 (1942): 567–594; *WWWA*.

BAPCO. *See* Bahrein Petroleum Company (BAPCO).

BARBARY WARS (1801–1805). In order to avoid attacks by the Barbary States (Algeria, Morocco, Tripoli, and Tunis) on American shipping in the Mediterranean, the United States paid annual tributes to these states. In 1801 the Pasha of Tripoli declared war on the United States. The U.S. Navy conducted several naval engagements against the ships and ports of Morocco and Tripoli, as well as a land expedition against Darna in Tripoli led by William Eaton.* In 1805, the Pasha of Tripoli signed a peace treaty with the United States and the Bey of Tunis was forced to make peace. Only Algiers continued to receive tribute until 1815. *References*: *Naval Documents Related to the United States' Wars with the Barbary Powers* (7 vols., Washington, D.C., 1939–1945); Syed Z. Abedin, "In Defense of Freedom: America's First War: A New Look at U.S.-Barbary Relations, 1776–1816," Ph.D. diss., University of Pennsylvania, 1974; Gardner W. Allen, *Our Navy and the Barbary Corsairs* (Cambridge, Mass., 1905); Glenn Tucker, *Dawn Like Thunder: The Barbary Wars and the Birth of the U.S. Navy* (Indianapolis, 1963); and L. B. Wright and J. H. MacLeod, *The First Americans in North Africa: William Eaton's Struggle for a Vigorous Policy Against the Barbary Pirates, 1799–1805* (Princeton, N.J., 1945).

BARBER & COMPANY. Formed in New York in 1883 by James Wells and Herbert Barber and incorporated in 1901. It inaugurated a direct steamship line between New York and the principal Turkish ports in February 1899, but after a rate war with British shipping companies, it discontinued service in January 1902. *References*: *NCAB* 31:38, 35:32.

BARBOUR, WALWORTH (1908–1982). Diplomat, born June 4, 1908, in Cambridge, Massachusetts. Barbour graduated from Harvard University, entered the foreign service in 1931, and served in Naples, Athens, Baghdad, and Sofia. He was second secretary in Athens in 1944, assistant chief, and later chief of the Division of Southern (and later Southeast) European Affairs from 1945 to 1948, and counselor with the rank of minister in Moscow from 1949 to 1951. He served in the Office of East European Affairs and was deputy assistant secretary of state for European affairs from 1951 to 1955, and minister in London from 1956 to 1961. He was ambassador to Israel from 1961 until his retirement in 1973. Barbour cultivated close relations with political leaders in Israel and was credited with heading off several crises in U.S.-Israeli relations. Died July 21, 1982, in Gloucester, Massachusetts. *References*: *BRDS*; *DADH*; *NYT*, July 26, 1982; *WWWA*; and *WWAP*.

BARCLAY, HAROLD B(ARTON) (1924–   ). Anthropologist, born January 3, 1924, in Newton, Massachusetts. Barclay graduated from Boston and Cornell universities. He taught at the American University in Cairo* from 1956 to 1959, and in 1959–1960 he conducted anthropological research in the Sudan, and wrote *Buuri al Lamaab: A Suburban Village in the Sudan* (Ithaca, N.Y., 1964). He was a member of the faculty of Knox College and the University of Oregon, and in 1966 he became associate professor and later professor of anthropology at the University of Alberta (Edmonton). *References*: *AMWS*; and *CA*.

BARCLAY, JAMES TURNER (1807–1874). Missionary, born in Hanover, Virginia. Barclay was the first missionary of the American Christian Missionary Society of the Disciples of Christ, and served in Jerusalem from 1851 to 1854 and from 1858 to 1861. He discovered Barclay Gate in Jerusalem and was possibly the first American photographer in Jerusalem; he photographed the city in the 1850s. He wrote *The City of the Great King; or Jerusalem As it Was, As It Is, As It Is to Be* (Philadelphia, 1858) and prepared a map of Jerusalem, *Jerusalem and Environs, From Actual and Minute Survey, Completed on the Spot* (Philadelphia, 1856). He resigned his mission for lack of support and returned to the United States. Papers of his wife, **JULIA ANN BARCLAY (1813–1908)**, are in the Disciples of Christ Historical Collections, Nashville, Tennessee.

BARCLAY, THOMAS (1728–1793). Merchant of Philadelphia. Barclay was involved in commercial activities in France from 1781, resided at Bordeaux, where he served as vice consul, and was employed by the U.S. government as special commissioner to settle U.S. debts in Europe. In 1785 he was appointed an agent to conclude a treaty with Morocco, went to Morocco in 1786 where he conducted negotiations, and concluded a treaty of peace and friendship in

1787. In 1791 he was appointed a member of a commission to Algiers to ransom American hostages there (see Hostages in Barbary States). Died January 19, 1793, in Lisbon. *References*: *Papers of Thomas Jefferson*, ed. Julian P. Boyd (Princeton, N.J., 1955), 11: 493–500. *Treaties and Other International Acts of the United States of America*, ed. Hunter Miller (Washington, D.C., 1931), 2:185–227.

BARGER, THOMAS CHARLES (1909–1986). Geologist and oil executive, born August 30, 1909, in Minneapolis, Minnesota. Barger graduated from the University of North Dakota, worked as a mining engineer in Ontario and the North West Territory from 1931 to 1935, and was associate professor of mining at the University of North Dakota from 1935 to 1937. He joined California Arabian Standard Oil Company (CASOC)* as a geologist in 1937, was a geologist in Dhahran from 1938 to 1941, and made the initial geological survey in al-Kharj, Saudi Arabia, in 1941. He spent World War II exploring and mapping the Empty Quarter in Saudi Arabia. He was later local government relations manager and Arabian American Oil Company (ARAMCO)* representative to the Saudi Arabian government. He became vice president of ARAMCO in 1958, president in 1959, chief executive officer from 1961 to 1968, and chairman of the board from 1968 until his retirement in 1969, when he was petroleum consultant to private corporations and to the Board of National Estimates. He wrote *Energy Policies of the Arab States of the Persian Gulf* (Newark, Del., 1975). His reminiscences appeared in the May–June 1984 issue of *AWM*. Died June 30, 1986, in San Diego. *References*: Paul F. Hoye, "Tom Barger: Myth or Man?" *AWM* 20 (September-October 1969): 4–13; *NYT*, July 12, 1986; and *WWA*.

BARLOW, CLAUDE HEMAN (1876–1969). Medical researcher, born October 13, 1876, in Lyon, Michigan. Barlow graduated from Northwestern University and the London School of Tropical Medicine. He served as a medical missionary in China from 1908 to 1928, and as a port physician for the Chinese Maritime Customs in Ningpo from 1925 to 1928. In 1929 he became head of schistosomiasis studies for the International Health Division of the Rockefeller Foundation in Egypt. He was also the director of the Bilharzia Snail Destruction Section in the Egyptian Ministry of Public Health in Cairo, where he conducted research on hookworm and schistosomes, and wrote articles on the control of schistosomiasis in Egypt. He later worked on control of the Bilharzia snail hosts in South Africa. Died October 9, 1969, in Trumansburg, New York. *References*: Papers, Rockefeller Foundation Archives, New York; Lawrence K. Altman, *Who Goes First? The Story of Self-experimentation in Medicine* (New York, 1987), pp. 171–177; *NYT*, October 11, 1969; and *WWWA*.

BARLOW, JOEL (1754–1812). Poet and diplomat, born March 24, 1754, in Redding, Connecticut. Barlow graduated from Yale College and served in the American Revolution as a chaplain. He was one of the "Hartford Wits" and began publishing his writings in 1787. He was admitted to the bar in 1786, became associated with a land speculation company, and went to France in 1787 as its agent. He lived in London from 1790 to 1792, when he went back to France and speculated in French bonds. In 1795 he was appointed consul in Algiers. He obtained treaties with Algiers and worked to secure the release of American hostages in the Barbary States (see Hostages in the Barbary States). He returned to the United States in 1805, settled near Washington, D.C., and continued to write. In 1811 he became minister to France. Died December 26, 1812, in Zarnowiec, Poland, while returning from a journey to meet Napoleon. *References*: "A Connecticut Yankee in a Barbary Court: Joel Barlow's Algerian Letters to His Wife," ed. Milton Cantor, *William and Mary Quarterly* 19 (1962): 86–109; Papers, Houghton Library, Harvard University; *ACAB*; Milton Cantor, "The Life of Joel Barlow," Ph.D. diss., Columbia University, 1954; Milton Cantor, "Barlow's Mission to Algiers," *Historian* 25 (1963):179–194; *DADH*; *DAB*; *DLB*; *NCAB* 3:186; James Woodress, *A Yankee's Odyssey: The Life of Joel Barlow* (Philadelphia, 1958); and *WWWA*.

BARNARD, CHARLES INMAN (1850–1942). Correspondent, born March 15, 1850, in Boston, Massachusetts. Barnard graduated from Massachusetts Institute of Technology and Harvard Law School. He served as military secretary to General Charles Pomeroy Stone* in Egypt from 1875 to 1879, and was also employed by the Egyptian government on various missions to Constantinople, Khartoum, and Massawa, and on a mission to Abyssinia in 1876. In 1877–1878 he was chief of the Sudan bureau of General Charles Gordon, governor general of the Sudan, and then tutor to Prince Mahmud Hilmy, son of the Khedive Ismail. He was a member of Egypt's Superior Council on Public Instruction in 1881–1882. In 1882–1883 he served as war correspondent for the *New York Herald* in Egypt and, after 1897, as Paris correspondent of the *New York Tribune*. He wrote *Paris War Days: Diary of an American* (Boston, 1914). Barnard was later associated with an American international law firm in Paris. Died May 11, 1942, in Paris. *Reference*: *WWWA*.

BARNETT, JAMES (1817–1884). Missionary, born June 16, 1817, in Hanover, Dauphin County, Pennsylvania. Barnett graduated from Miami University and the Associate Reformed Seminary (Oxford, Ohio), and was ordained in 1844. He went to Syria in 1845 as a missionary under the Associate Reformed Church, and served in Damascus. In 1854 he went with Thomas McCague* to Egypt where they founded the American Mission* in Cairo. He made several tours through Palestine, and visited Palmyra in Syria and Sinai. He remained in Cairo until 1875, when he returned to the United States. Died October 2, 1884, in Emporia, Kansas. *Reference*: Andrew Watson, *The American Mission in Egypt, 1854–1896*, 2nd ed. (Pittsburgh, 1904).

BARNUM, HENRY SAMUEL (1837–1915). Missionary, born August 13, 1837, in Stratford, Connecticut. Barnum graduated from Yale College and Auburn Theological Seminary, and was ordained in 1867. He served as a missionary under the American Board of Commissioners for Foreign Missions (ABCFM)* in Harput, Turkey, from 1867 to 1872, and in Van, Turkey, from 1872 to 1883. After 1883, he was stationed in Constantinople, editing a weekly paper in Armenian and Turkish from 1884 until 1907 and in 1911–1912. Died December 10, 1915, in Constantinople. *References*: *Auburn*; *WWWA*.

BARNUM, HERMAN NORTON (1826–1910). Missionary, born December 5, 1826, in Auburn, New York. Barnum graduated from Amherst College and Andover Theological Seminary, and was ordained in 1855. He served as a home missionary-at-large in Vermont in 1855–1856, and was a missionary under the American Board of Commissioners for Foreign Missions (ABCFM)* in Turkey from 1858 to 1910. He taught at Harput Theological Seminary and at Euphrates College, and was engaged in general missionary work. He was also an adviser to Turkish officials in Armenia. Died May 19, 1910, in Harput, Turkey. *References*: *Amherst*; *AndoverTS*; and *WWWA*.

BARRINGER, VICTOR CLAY (1827–1896). Jurist, born March 29, 1827, near Concord, North Carolina. Barringer graduated from the University of North Carolina. After serving as private secretary to the minister to Spain, he practiced law in North Carolina, and in 1860 he was elected to the state legislature. He was later appointed one of the commissioners to compile the revised statutes of the United States. In 1874 he was appointed to the Court of Appeals of the Mixed Courts of Egypt* and served until 1894. Died May 27, 1896, in Washington, D.C. *References*: Papers, University of Virginia Library; *NCAB* 13:351.

BARRON, SAMUEL (1763–1810). Naval officer, born September 25, 1765, in Hampton, Virginia. In 1798 Barron commanded the brig *Augusta* in the quasi-war with France. In 1805 he commanded the fleet sent to the Mediterranean to cooperate with William Eaton* against Tripoli. Because of ill health, he transferred his command to John Rodgers* and returned to the United States. Died October 29, 1810, in Hampton, Virginia. *References*: *ACAB*; *NCAB* 4:417.

BARROWS, JOHN OTIS (1833–1918). Missionary, born August 4, 1833, in Mansfield, Connecticut. Barrows graduated from Amherst College, studied at the Theological Institute of Connecticut (Hartford), graduated from Andover Theological Seminary, and was ordained in 1864. He served as a pastor in North Hampton and Exeter, New Hampshire, from 1863 to 1869, and was a missionary under the American Board of Commissioners for Foreign Missions (ABCFM)* in Turkey from 1869 to 1880. He was stationed in Kayseri from 1869 to 1875, in Manisa from 1875 to 1877, and in Constantinople from 1877 to 1880. He wrote *On Horseback in Cappadocia; or, a Missionary Tour* (Boston, 1884).

After his return to the United States, Barrows again served as a pastor in Atkinson, New Hampshire, and Newington, and Stonington, Connecticut, until his retirement in 1908. Died January 26, 1918, in Norwichtown, Connecticut. *References*: *Amherst*; *AndoverTS*; and *WWWA*.

BARTLETT, CORNELIA STORRS (1859–1940). Missionary educator, born June 22, 1859, in Columbus, New York. Bartlett went to Turkey in 1867 with her missionary parents, returned to the United States in 1875, graduated from Mount Holyoke and Wellesley colleges, and was trained as a kindergarten teacher in Minneapolis. She returned to Turkey in 1884 as a missionary under the American Board of Commissioners for Foreign Missions (ABCFM),* and established the first kindergarten in Turkey in 1885 in Smyrna and a normal school that later became a training school for kindergarten teachers. These two schools were ultimately incorporated into the Collegiate Institute for Girls. Bartlett returned to the United States in 1902. Died March 21, 1940, in Pasadena, California. *References*: Lyman Bartlett, "Kindergarten Work of Cornelia S. Bartlett," Ms., Mount Holyoke College Archives,* Mount Holyoke; and Frank A. Stone, "Mt. Holyoke's Impact on the Land of Ararat," *MW* 66 (1976): 44–57.

BARTLETT, SAMUEL COLCORD (1817–1898). Clergyman, born November 25, 1817, in Salisbury, New Hampshire. Bartlett graduated from Dartmouth College and Andover Theological Seminary, and was ordained in 1843. He was a pastor at Monson, Massachusetts, from 1843 to 1846, professor of intellectual philosophy and rhetoric at Western Reserve College (Hudson, Ohio) from 1846 to 1852, and pastor in Manchester, New Hampshire, from 1852 to 1857, and in Chicago from 1857 to 1859. He was professor of biblical literature and sacred theology at the Chicago Theological Seminary from 1858 to 1877, and president of Dartmouth College from 1877 until 1892. He traveled in the Middle East in 1873–1874, and wrote *From Egypt to Palestine Through Sinai, the Wilderness and the South Country* (New York, 1879). Died November 16, 1898, in Hanover, New Hampshire. *References*: *ACAB*; *DAB*; *NCAB* 9:89; *UnionTS*; and *WWWA*.

BARTON, GEORGE AARON (1859–1942). Educator and Orientalist, born November 12, 1859, in Farnham, Province of Quebec, Canada. Barton graduated from Haverford College and Harvard University. He was a teacher in Providence, Rhode Island, from 1884 to 1889; lecturer at Haverford College from 1891 to 1895; professor of biblical literature and Semitic languages at Bryn Mawr College from 1891 to 1922; and professor of Semitic languages and history of religion at the University of Pennsylvania from 1922 until his retirement in 1932. He was also professor of New Testament literature and language at the Divinity School of the Protestant Episcopal Church in Philadelphia from 1921 to 1937. From 1879 to 1918, he was minister of the orthodox branch of the Society of Friends but joined the Episcopal Church in 1919. Barton was resident director

of the American Schools of Oriental Research (ASOR)* in Jerusalem in 1902–
1903, and wrote *A Year's Wandering in Bible Lands* (Philadelphia, 1904). His
book *Archaeology and the Bible* (Philadelphia, 1916) went into seven editions.
Died June 28, 1942, in Weston, Massachusetts. *References*: *DAB S3*; *NCAB*
D:441; *NYT* June 29, 1942; and *WWA*.

BARTON, JAMES LEVI (1855–1936). Missionary and organizer of the Near
East Relief,* born September 23, 1855, in Charlotte, Vermont. Barton graduated
from Middlebury College and Hartford Theological Seminary, and was ordained
in 1885. He was a missionary under the American Board of Commissioners for
Foreign Missions (ABCFM)* in Harput, Turkey, from 1885 until 1892, responsible for the supervision of the mission schools. He became president of
Euphrates College in 1893, but returned to the United States in 1894 because
of his wife's ill health, and later wrote *Daybreak in Turkey* (Boston, 1908). He
served as foreign secretary of the ABCFM from 1894 to 1927 and was a member
of various committees and commissions for Middle East missions and philanthropies. In 1919 he was head of the American Committee for Armenian and
Syrian Relief (ACASR) commission to the Middle East, and represented the
Foreign Missions Conference of North America at the London and Lausanne
conferences in which a peace treaty was negotiated between the Allies and
Turkey. He organized Near East Relief* and wrote *Story of Near East Relief
(1915–1930): An Interpretation* (Boston, 1930). Died July 21, 1936, in Brookline, Massachusetts. His "Reminiscences" appeared in the *Missionary Herald*
from January through December 1927. *References*: "Memoirs," Ms., ABCFM
Archives; *DAB S2*; Fred F. Goodsell, *James Levi Barton* (Boston, 1964); *NCAB*
27:130; *NYT*, July 22, 24, 1936; and *WWWA*.

BARTON, WILLIAM ELEAZER (1861–1930). Clergyman and author, born
June 28, 1861, in Sublette, Illinois. Barton graduated from Berea College and
Oberlin Theological Seminary, and was ordained in 1885. He served as a pastor
in Robbins, Tennessee, Litchfield and Wellington, Ohio, Boston, and Oak Park,
Illinois, from 1885 to 1924, and was a lecturer at the Chicago Theological
Seminary from 1905 to 1909 and from 1911 until his retirement in 1924. He
visited Palestine in 1902, became interested in the Samaritans, and wrote about
them in *The Old World in the New Century; Being a Narrative of a Tour of the
Mediterranean, Egypt and the Holy Land* (Boston, 1902), with illustrations made
from photographs. He was the founder and principal agent of the American
Samaritan Committee, visited Palestine again in 1926, and distributed the assets
of the committee. Died December 7, 1930, in Brooklyn, New York. *The Autobiography of William E. Barton* (Indianapolis, 1932) was published after his
death. *References*: *ACAB*; *DAB S1*; *NCAB* 42:304; *OAB*; James D. Purvis, "Studies on Samaritan Materials in the W. E. Barton Collection in the Boston University Library," in *Proceedings of the Fifth World Congress of Jewish Studies*
(Jerusalem, 1972), pp. 134–143.

BASKERVILLE, HOWARD C. (1885–1909). Teacher, born April 10, 1885, in Nebraska. Baskerville graduated from Princeton University and Princeton Theological Seminary. He came to Persia in 1907 to teach in the mission school in Tabriz. He became involved in the Persian Revolution, aided and joined the Constitutionalists, and was killed on April 19, 1909, in Tabriz. *Reference*: S. R. Shafaq, "Howard Baskerville," in Ali Pasha Saleh, *Cultural Ties Between Iran and the United States* (Teheran, 1976), pp. 311–328.

BASS, GEORGE F(LETCHER) (1932–   ). Archaeologist, born December 9, 1932. Bass graduated from Johns Hopkins University and the University of Pennsylvania. He was research associate at the University Museum in 1963–1964, assistant professor at the University of Pennsylvania from 1964 to 1968, and became associate professor of classical archaeology in 1968. He excavated in Greece and in 1960 began the underwater excavation of a shipwreck at Cape Gelidonya, Turkey. He directed underwater excavations at Yassi Ada, an island off the coast of Turkey, from 1961 to 1974. He wrote *Archaeology Beneath the Sea* (New York, 1975), an account of his work in scientific underwater archaeology, *Cape Gelidonya: A Bronze Age Shipwreck* (Philadelphia, 1967), and was co-author of *Yassi Ada* (College Station, Tex., 1982). He became president of the Institute of Nautical Archaeology in 1973 and professor of anthropology at Texas A & M University in 1980. *Reference: DAS.*

BASSETT, JAMES (1834–1906). Missionary, born January 31, 1834, at Mundos, near Hamilton, Ontario, Canada. Bassett graduated from Wabash College and Lane Theological Seminary, and served as a pastor before and after the Civil War in which he served as a chaplain in the Union Army. In 1871 he was appointed a missionary to Persia under the Presbyterian Church in the U.S.A. Board of Foreign Missions*. He went to Urmia in 1871 and opened the mission station in Teheran in 1872. He was the first American missionary in Teheran. He opened schools, obtained his own printing press in 1878, was in charge of all boys' schools after 1881, and became head of the Eastern part of the Persian Mission in 1882. He also collaborated on the translation of the Bible into Persian. He resigned in 1884, returned to the United States and wrote *Persia: The Land of the Imams. A Narrative of Travels and Residence, 1871–1885* (New York, 1886), and *Persia: Eastern Mission: A Narrative of the Founding and Fortunes of the Eastern Persia Mission* (Philadelphia, 1890). Died March 10, 1906, in Los Angeles. *References: ACAB; DAB.*

BATCHELLER, GEORGE SHERMAN (1837–1908). Lawyer, born July 25, 1837, in Batchellerville, Saratoga County, New York. Batcheller graduated from Harvard College and Harvard Law School, and was admitted to the bar in 1858. He served in the Civil War, and later became inspector general of the New York militia, practiced law in New York City, and was a member of the New York Assembly. Because of his prominence as a lawyer and a politician, he was appointed judge of the Mixed Courts of Egypt* in 1876 and served until 1885. He was reappointed in 1898 at the request of the Egyptian government, was promoted in 1902 to the Court of Appeals and served until 1908. He became president of the Court of Appeals in 1902. In 1889 he was assistant secretary of war and from 1890 to 1893 minister to Portugal. From 1893 to 1897, Batcheller worked in Europe as manager of the European interests of American companies, and in 1897 he presided over the Universal Postal Congress. Died July 2, 1908 in Paris. *References*: *DAB*; *DADH*, *NCAB* 4:464; *NYT*, July 3, 1908; and *WWWA*.

BATES, ORIC (1883–1918). Archaeologist, born December 8, 1883, in Boston. Bates graduated from Harvard and Berlin universities. In 1906 he joined the staff of the Egyptian Department of the Boston Museum of Fine Arts. He took part in the archaeological survey of Nubia and excavated in the Sudan in 1911–1912 and 1915. He conducted an expedition to Tripoli in 1909, made archaeological explorations in the Libyan Desert in 1910–1911, and wrote *The Eastern Libyans* (London, 1913). In 1914 Bates became curator of African archaeology and ethnology at the Peabody Museum of Harvard University. Died October 8, 1918, in Louisville, Kentucky, while training for military service. *References*: *Hill*; *WWWA*; and *WWWE*.

BAUSMAN, BENJAMIN (1824–1909). Clergyman and author, born January 28, 1824, near Lancaster, Pennsylvania. Bausman graduated from Marshal College, studied at the Theological Seminary at Mercerburg, Pennsylvania, and was ordained in 1853. He served as a pastor in Reading, Pennsylvania, from 1863 to 1909 and was also the editor of several religious magazines. In 1856–1857 he traveled in Palestine, and he recorded his observations and impressions in *Sinai and Zion; or, A Pilgrimage Through the Wilderness to the Land of Promise* (Reading, Pa., 1861), which ran through eleven editions. Died May 8, 1909, in Reading, Pennsylvania. *References*: *DAB*; and *WWWA*.

BAYLEY, JAMES ROOSEVELT (1814–1877). Clergyman, born August 23, 1814, in Rye, New York. Bayley graduated from Trinity College (Hartford) and the Seminary of St. Sulpice in Paris. He converted to Roman Catholicism and was ordained to the priesthood in 1844. He was a priest in New York City from 1848 to 1853, secretary to Archbishop John Joseph Hughes of New York, first bishop of Newark, New Jersey, from 1853 to 1872, and archbishop of Baltimore from 1872 to 1877. He traveled to Palestine in 1867 and was the first American prelate to visit the Holy Land. Died October 3, 1877, in Newark. *References*: Diary and papers, Archives of the Catholic Archdiocese of Baltimore; Seton Hall University Library, Orange, N.J.; *ACAB*; *DAB*; *DACB*; *DARB*; *NCAB* 1:487; and *WWWA*.

BEALE, TRUXTON (1856–1936). Diplomat, born March 6, 1856, in San Francisco. Beale graduated from the Pennsylvania Military College (Chester, Pa.) and Columbia University Law School. He was admitted to the bar in 1878, but instead of entering his field managed his father's ranch in Kern County, California, from 1878 to 1891. He married the daughter of Secretary of State James G. Blaine, and was appointed minister to Persia, serving from 1891 to 1892. Beale obtained permission for American missionaries to hold land; he sent animals, plants, and seeds to the Department of Agriculture; and he secured the first two molds of cuneiform inscriptions from Persepolis for the National Museum. He was minister to Greece, Rumania, and Serbia from 1892 to 1894. Between 1894 and 1896 he traveled in Siberia, Central Asia, and Chinese Turkestan. He later lived in California. Died June 2, 1936, near Annapolis, Maryland. *References*: *DADH*; *NCAB* 27:407; *NYT*, June 3, 1936; and *WWWA*.

BEAM WILLIAM (1866–1919). Research chemist. Beame became head of the Chemical Section at the Wellcome Tropical Research Laboratories at Gordon College in Khartoum, the Sudan, in 1904. He did research on gum production and made valuable contributions to soil chemistry. Died April 15, 1919, in Khartoum. *References*: *Hill*; *Sudan Notes and Records* 3 (1920): 83.

BECHTEL CORPORATION. Construction and engineering company, founded in 1898 and incorporated in 1925. In 1931 Bechtel organized the consortium that built Hoover Dam. It began its first work in the Middle East in 1943 and continued to work under various subsidiaries. It was responsible for the engineering and construction of facilities for gathering, transporting, and refining oil, a variety of public works, marine terminals, refineries, international airports at Jidda and Riyadh, a railroad from the Persian Gulf to Riyadh, the Trans-Arabian pipeline (Tapline) system, and the Kirkuk to Banias pipeline. *References*: Richard Finnie, *Bechtel in Arab Lands: A Fifteenth-year Review of Engineering and Construction Projects* (San Francisco, 1958); Milton Moskowitz et al., *Everybody's Business: An Almanac* (New York, 1980), pp. 857–861.

BEIRUT UNIVERSITY COLLEGE. Founded in 1835 by the American Board of Commissioners for Foreign Missions (ABCFM)* missionaries as the American School for Girls, the first in the Ottoman Empire. The college was reorganized in 1926 as the American Junior College for Women. It expanded in 1950 to a four-year program and changed its name to the Beirut College for Women. In 1955 it received a charter from the New York State Board of Regents, and in 1973 it was renamed Beirut University College. It is now an independent, nonprofit corporation. *References*: *Boardman*; *IHU*; *Qubain*, pp. 357–358; Marie A. Sabri, *Pioneering Profiles: Beirut College for Women* (Beirut, 1967); and *Survey*.

BELL, ARCHIBALD ("ARCHIE") (1877–1943). Reporter, born March 17, 1877, in Geneva, Ohio. Bell became a correspondent and music and drama critic for Cleveland newspapers in 1905, and was associated for more than twenty years with the Cleveland *News*. He was a world traveler and the author of several books about his travels in the Middle East, including *The Spell of the Holy Land* (Boston, 1915) and *The Spell of Egypt* (Boston, 1916). Died January 23, 1943, in Cleveland. *References*: "Diary and Notes on a Trip to the Holy Land and Egypt, 1914," Ms., Cleveland Public Library; *NYT*, January 27, 1943; *OAB*; and *WWWA*.

BELLOWS, HENRY WHITNEY (1814–1882). Clergyman, born June 11, 1814, in Boston. Bellows graduated from Harvard College and Harvard Divinity School. He was a preacher in Mobile, Alabama, and in New York City, and the originator, founder, and president of the U.S. Sanitary Commission during the Civil War. He traveled in the Middle East, and his travel book *The Old World in Its New Face* (New York, 1868) went through five printings. He was editor of the *Christian Examiner* from 1866 to 1877 and became involved in civil service reform. Died January 30, 1882, in New York City. *References*: *ACAB*; *DAB*; *NCAB* 3:261; *NYT*, January 27, 1882; and *WWWA*.

BENDINER, ALFRED (1899–1964). Architect and illustrator, born July 23, 1899, in Pittsburgh, and grew up in Philadelphia. Bendiner graduated from the University of Pennsylvania and worked as a draughtsman until 1929 when he opened his own architectural office. He was artist-architect with the archaeological expedition of the University Museum of the University of Pennsylvania in Tepe Gawra and Khafajeh in Iraq in 1936–1937, and with an expedition to Tikal, Guatemala, in 1960. He published many illustrated articles in newspapers and magazines and executed several murals. Died March 19, 1964, in Philadelphia. *Translated from the Hungarian: Notes Toward an Autobiography* (New York, 1967), was published after his death. *References*: Davis Crownover, "Alfred Bendiner and Iraq," *Expedition* 12 (Spring 1970): 14–16; *Expedition* 6 (Summer 1964): 20–27; *NYT*, March 20, 1964; and *WWWA*.

BENJAMIN, NATHAN (1811–1855). Missionary, born December 14, 1811, in Catskill, New York. Benjamin graduated from Williams College, studied at Auburn Theological Seminary, and graduated from Andover Theological Seminary. He became a missionary under the American Board of Commissioners of Foreign Missions (ABCFM)* in 1834, studied medicine in New Haven and New York in 1834–1835, and was ordained in 1836. He served in Argos and Athens, Greece, from 1836 until 1845, when he moved to the Armenian Mission in Trebizond, Turkey. He returned to the United States in 1846 because of his wife's health, but was back in Smyrna in 1847 and moved to Constantinople in 1852. An editor and translator, he founded the *Morning Star*, the first Armenian newspaper. Died January 27, 1855, in Constantinople. *References*: *ACAB*; *AuburnTS*; *DAB*; *EM*; *Hewitt*; and *WWWA*.

BENJAMIN, SAMUEL GREENE WHEELER (1837–1914). Author and diplomat, born February 13, 1837, in Argos, Greece, son of Nathan Benjamin.* Benjamin grew up in Greece and Asia Minor, came to the United States in 1855, and graduated from Williams College. He was an assistant in the New York State Library in Albany from 1861 to 1864, established himself in the 1870s in Boston as a marine painter, and began to publish. His first book was *Constantinople, the Isle of Pearls, and Other Poems* (Boston, 1860). He also wrote *The Turk and the Greek: or, Creeds, Races, Society, and Scenery in Turkey, Greece, and the Isles of Greece* (New York, 1867). He traveled extensively and made forty-five Atlantic crossings. He was the first minister to Persia from 1883 to 1885, and drafted the diplomatic code used by the American legation in Persia. After his return to the United States, he wrote *Persia and the Persians* (Boston, 1886), and an autobiography, *The Life and Adventures of a Free Lance*, ed. Fannie N. Benjamin (Burlington, Vt., 1914). Died July 19, 1914, in Burlington, Vermont. *References*: *ACAB*; *DAB*; *DADH*; James F. Goode, "A Good Start: The First American Mission to Iran, 1883–1885," *MW* 74 (April 1984): 100–118; *NCAB* 7:26; *NYHSD*; *NYT*, July 20, 1914; and *WWWA*.

BENNETT, ARTHUR KING (1881–1966). Medical missionary, born March 27, 1881, in Watkins Glen, New York. Bennett graduated from the University of Michigan, and studied at the University of Liverpool and the Sorbonne. He served in the Arabian Mission* from 1904 until 1916. He was stationed in Basra, Iraq, supervised the construction of the Lansing Memorial Hospital there, and served as its chief of staff. He was transferred to Matrah, Oman, in 1910, to take charge of a hospital and dispensary. From 1914 to 1916, he served with the British Red Cross. He returned to the United States in 1916 and practiced in Marquette, Michigan, until his retirement in 1951. Died September 13, 1966, in Marquette. His wife, **CHRISTINE IVERSON BENNETT (1881–1916)**, medical missionary, was born in Denmark, and came to the United States in 1893. She graduated from Yankton College and the University of Michigan Medical School, was a physician in the Michigan Asylum, and served in the Arabian Mission in Basra. Died March 21, 1916, in Basra. *References*: James H. Franklin, *Ministers of Mercy* (New York, 1919), pp. 31–50; *HDRCA*; and *NCAB* 53:520.

BERKSON, ISAAC BAER (1891–1975). Educator, born in New York City. Berkson graduated from City College of New York and Columbia University, began teaching at the Central Jewish Institute in New York, and became its director in 1917. From 1918 to 1927 he supervised the schools and the extension program of the Bureau of Jewish Education in New York, and in 1927, he was also teaching at the Jewish Institute of Religion. He surveyed the Jewish schools in Palestine in 1927 and was superintendent of the Jewish school system in Palestine from 1927 to 1935. He joined the faculty of the City College of New York in 1938 and was professor of the philosophy of education from 1955 until his death. Died March 10, 1975, in New York City. *References*: Papers, Central Zionist Archives, Jerusalem; *EJ*; *NYT*, March 13, 1975; and Henry F. Skirball, "Isaac Baer Berkson and Jewish Education," Ph.D. diss., Columbia University Teachers College, 1976.

BERMAN, SIMEON (or SIMON) (1818–1884). Colonizer, born in Cracow, Poland, immigrated to the United States in 1852, and settled in New York City. Berman made several unsuccessful attempts to found societies for agricultural settlement. He went to Palestine in 1870, received permission from the Ottoman government to buy land, and founded the Holy Land Settlement Society, a cooperative agricultural settlement. He went abroad to publicize the scheme but returned to Palestine. He wrote a book in Yiddish about his travels. Died in Tiberias, Palestine. *References*: *EJ*.

BERRY, BURTON YOST (1901–   ). Diplomat, born August 31, 1901, in Fowler, Indiana. Berry graduated from Indiana University and the University of Paris, entered the foreign service in 1928, served in Istanbul, Athens, Naples, and Cairo, and was staff adviser to the Mediterranean Command during World War II. He was representative to Rumania from 1944 to 1947, and special assistant to the chief of the aid mission to Greece in 1947. He was ambassador to Iraq from 1949 to 1952, administering the Point Four program. He retired in 1956, built a house near Rumeli Hisar above the Bosporus in Turkey, and became an expert on Islamic antiquities. He wrote *Out of the Past: The Istanbul Great Bazaar* (New York, 1977). *References*: Papers, Lilly Library, Indiana University; *CA*; *DADH*; and *WWA*.

BIBLE HOUSE, CONSTANTINOPLE. Completed in 1872 with money raised by Isaac Grout Bliss,* agent of the American Bible Society.* Bible House became known as the "American Khan," and served as the offices and storerooms for the American Bible Society and the American Board Mission, and as residence for missionaries. *Reference*: *EM*.

BIDDLE, JAMES (1783–1848). Naval officer, born February 18, 1783, in Philadelphia. Biddle studied at the University of Pennsylvania and was appointed a midshipman in the navy in 1800. In 1802 he served on the *Constellation* in the Mediterranean, and in 1803 he was transferred to the *Philadelphia.* When the *Philadelphia* was grounded near Tripoli Harbor and its crew surrendered, he was held prisoner in Tripoli for nineteen months. After the conclusion of peace he returned to the United States, served in the War of 1812, and commanded the ship that sailed to the Columbia River to take possession of the Oregon territory in 1817. He commanded the Mediterranean Squadron from

1829 to 1832 and was a member of the commission that negotiated the first treaty between the United States and Turkey. From 1845 to 1848 he commanded the East Indian Squadron and in 1846 exchanged the ratifications of the Treaty of Wanghia between the United States and China. He commanded the Pacific Coast Squadron during the Mexican War. Died October 1, 1848, in Philadelphia. *References*: *ACAB*; *DAB*; *DAMIB*; David F. Long, *Sailor-Diplomat: A Biography of Commodore James Biddle, 1783–1848* (Boston, 1983); *NCAB* 6:55; Nicholas Wainwright, *Commodore James Biddle and His Sketch Book* (Philadelphia, 1966); *WAMB*; and *WWWA*.

BILKERT, HENRY ARJEN (1892–1929). Missionary, born January 24, 1892, in Kalamazoo, Michigan. Bilkert graduated from Hope College and New Brunswick Theological Seminary, and was ordained in 1917. He served as a missionary in the Arabian Mission* from 1917 to 1929. Killed January 21, 1929, by a raiding party of Ikhwan, members of a religious and military movement in Saudi Arabia, on the road between Kuwait and Basra, Iraq. *References*: *HDRCA*; *NYT*, January 22, 1929.

BIRD, ISAAC (1793–1876). Missionary, born June 19, 1793, in Salisbury, Connecticut. Bird graduated from Yale College and Andover Theological Seminary, and was ordained in 1821. He became a missionary under the American Board of Commissioners for Foreign Missions (ABCFM)* in 1822, and served in Malta, Beirut, and Smyrna. Although called a missionary to Palestine, he was stationed in Beirut. In 1824 he conducted a tour of Palestine, and his account of his swim in the Dead Sea is reputed to be the earliest such mention by an American. In 1829 he made a missionary tour to Tripoli and Tunis, and wrote an account of his journey in the *Missionary Herald*. He returned to the United States in 1836, was professor of sacred literature in the Gilmanton (N.H.) Seminary from 1838 to 1845, and then established a school in Hartford, Connecticut. He wrote *The Martyr of Lebanon* (Boston, 1864), and *Bible Work in Bible Lands; or, Events in the History of the Syria Mission* (Philadelphia, 1872). Died June 12, 1876, in Hartford. His son, **WILLIAM BIRD (1823–1902)**, a missionary, was born August 17, 1823, in Valetta, Malta, graduated from Dartmouth College and Andover Theological Seminary, and was ordained in 1852. He was a missionary under the ABCFM in Syria from 1853 until his death. Died August 30, 1902, in Beirut, Syria. *References*: Isaac Bird's ''Journal,'' Ms., Sterling Memorial Library, Yale University; *AndoverTS*; and *EM*.

BIRD, WILLIAM (1888–1963). Journalist, born January 2, 1888, in Buffalo, New York. Bird graduated from Trinity College (Hartford). In 1920 he started a wire service, Consolidated Press Service, handling its Paris office. He also established a private press in Paris. After dissolving the Consolidated Press in 1933, he became chief foreign correspondent for the New York *Sun* and also served as correspondent for the New York *Post*. He served as war correspondent during World War II, moved to Tangier after the war, and was editor of the *Tangier Gazette*, an English-language weekly newspaper. In 1948 he was appointed American representative to the Legislative Assembly of the Tangier International Zone. In 1960 the Moroccan government closed the newspaper, and he returned to France. Died August 2, 1963, in Paris. *References*: Papers, Lilly Library, Indiana University; *DLB*; and *NYT*, August 6, 1963.

BIRGE, JOHN KINGSLEY (1888–1952). Missionary educator and Turcologist, born March 4, 1888, in Bristol, Connecticut. Birge graduated from Yale University and Hartford Theological Seminary, and was ordained in 1914. From 1914 to 1923 he was a professor at the International College in Smyrna. He helped in relief work during the Greco-Turkish war and served on the commission to exchange prisoners. In 1921 he prepared a survey of social conditions in Izmir. He returned to the United States in 1923 and was president of his family's textile manufacturing company, but was back in Istanbul in 1927 as head of the American Board of Commissioners for Foreign Missions (ABCFM)* publications department. He became an authority on Turkish history and languages, wrote *The Bektashi Order of Dervishes* (London, 1937), and prepared *A Guide to Turkish Area Study* (Washington, D.C., 1949). In 1950 he published, after twelve years of work, a revision of the *Redhouse English-Turkish Dictionary*. Died August 14, 1952, in Istanbul. *Reference*: *NYT*, August 17, 1952.

BLACK, FLOYD H(ENSON) (1888–1983). Educator, born February 2, 1888, in Bridgeport, Illinois. Black graduated from Carson-Newman College (Jefferson City, Tenn.), Southern Baptist and Andover theological seminaries, and Chicago and Harvard Divinity schools. He was instructor in English and Latin at Robert College* from 1911 to 1914, professor of Latin from 1919 to 1926, president of the American College of Sofia, Bulgaria, from 1926 to 1942, and president of Robert College and the American College for Girls* in Istanbul from 1944 to 1955. During World War II he was special assistant to the consul general in Istanbul. He wrote *The American College in Sofia: A Chapter in American-Bulgarian Relations* (Boston, 1958). Died December 28, 1983, in Princeton. *References*: *AndoverTS*; *LE*; *MENA*; *NYT*, December 31, 1983; and *WWWA*.

BLAKE, MAXWELL (1877–1959). Diplomat, born November 15, 1877, in Kansas City, Missouri. Blake graduated from Scaritt College and the University of Missouri, entered the foreign service in 1906, and served in Funchal, Madeira Islands, Dunfermline, Scotland, and Bogotá. He was consul general in Tangier from 1910 to 1912, secretary of legation in Morocco in 1912, and chargé d'affaires ad interim from 1912 to 1917. He served on the staff of the American delegation to the Paris Peace Conference in 1919 and was consul general in Australia from 1923 to 1925. From 1925 to 1940 he was diplomatic agent and consul general in Morocco, and member of several international commissions and committees there. He retired in 1941. Died January 1959. *References*: *DADH*; *WWWA*.

BLAKE, ROBERT P(IERPONT) (1886–1950). Educator, born November 1, 1886, in San Francisco. Blake graduated from the University of California, Harvard University, and the University of Petrograd. He taught briefly in Tiflis in the Georgian Republic, after which he became a member of the faculty of Harvard University in 1920. He was director of the university library from 1928 to 1937, became professor of history in 1930, and president of the Byzantine Institute in 1948. With Kirsopp Lake* he explored the Sinai Peninsula in 1927. While in Jerusalem he catalogued the Georgian manuscripts in the Greek Patriarchal library. Died May 9, 1950, in Boston. *References*: *NYT*, May 10, 1950; *WWWA*.

BLAKELY, ELLEN M. (1859–1937). Missionary educator, born October 7, 1859, in Rodmen, New York. Blakely graduated from Mount Holyoke Seminary, and taught in Gilmanton, New Hampshire, and Oxford, Ohio. She taught at the Central Turkey Girls' College in Marash from 1885 to 1923, was its principal from 1892 to 1922, and wrote *The Central Turkey Girls' School, Marash* (Chicago, 1911). She was then a missionary from 1923 to 1929. Died February 21, 1937, in Pasadena, California. *Reference*: *Mount Holyoke*.

BLASHFIELD, EDWIN HOWLAND (1848–1936). Painter, born December 15, 1848, in Brooklyn, New York. Blashfield graduated from Massachusetts Institute of Technology. In 1867 he went to Europe, studying in Paris until 1870, and again from 1874 to 1880. He had a studio in New York City from 1871 to 1874, and from 1881 until 1933. He traveled in Egypt in 1886–1887 and in 1890, and illustrated several articles written by his wife, **EVANGELINE WILBOUR BLASHFIELD (1858–1918)**, about their Egyptian experiences and published in *Scribner's Magazine* in 1891–1892. He later executed many murals on large public buildings. Died October 12, 1936, in South Dennis, Cape Cod, Massachusetts. *References*: Letter-diaries, New York Historical Society; *ACAB*; Leonard N. Amico, *The Mural Decorations of Edwin Howland Blashfield* (Williamstown, Mass., 1978); *DAB S2*; *NCAB* 27:181; *NYT*, October 13, 1936; and *WWWA*.

BLATCHFORD, EDWARD WILLIAMS (1868–1956). Association executive and consul, born July 13, 1868, in Chicago. Blatchford graduated from Amherst College and Chicago Theological Seminary. He was in business in Colorado Springs, Colorado, from 1893 to 1897, in Chicago from 1897 to 1899, in London from 1899 to 1901, and was assistant manager of E. W. Blatchford and Company in Chicago from 1902 to 1918. From 1918 to 1922 he worked under the Young Men's Christian Association (YMCA)* in London, Copenhagen, and Istanbul, and was in charge of Near East Relief* work in Palestine from 1922 to 1929.

He was vice consul in Jerusalem from 1930 until his retirement in 1948. Died May 18, 1956, in Chicago. *References*: *Amherst*; *BRDS*.

BLATTER, DOROTHY (GERTRUDE) (1901–1977). Missionary educator, born July 15, 1901, in Albion, Nebraska. Blatter graduated from Doane College, the University of Colorado, and Columbia University. She was a teacher in New Mexico from 1925 to 1931, and in 1931 she became a teacher under the American Board of Commissioners of Foreign Missions (ABCFM)* in Turkey. She taught art and English at Merzifon from 1931 to 1937 and at Uskudar Academy for Girls from 1939 to 1945. From 1945 to 1961 she worked in the publications department of the mission in Istanbul, and from 1961 until her retirement in 1967, she was children's editor and inaugurated a program of books for children, including her books, *Uncle Ali's Secret: A Story of New Turkey* (Chicago, 1939), *The Thirsty Village* (New York, 1950), and *Cap and Candle* (New York, 1961), some of which were also published in Turkish. Died October 28, 1977, in Kansas City, Missouri. *Reference*: *CA*.

BLEGEN, CARL W(ILLIAM) (1887–1971). Archaeologist, born January 27, 1887, in Minneapolis, Minnesota. Blegen graduated from Augsburg College, the University of Minnesota, and Yale University, and studied at the American School of Classical Studies in Athens. In 1918–1919 he served with the American Red Cross* in Greece. He was secretary, assistant director, and acting director of the American School of Classical Studies from 1913 to 1927, and in 1927 he became professor of classical archaeology at the University of Cincinnati. He was field director of the university's archaeological expedition to Turkey and Greece, and director of the expedition to Troy from 1932 to 1938. In 1939 he found the Palace of Nestor. He served with the Office of Strategic Services in World War II in Washington, and was cultural relations attaché in the embassy in Athens in 1945–1946. He wrote *Troy: Excavations Conducted by the University of Cincinnati, 1932–1938* (Princeton, N.J., 1950–58), and *Troy and the Trojans* (New York, 1963). Died August 24, 1971, in Athens. *References*: *CA*; *NYT*, August 26, 1971; and *WWWA*.

BLISS, DANIEL (1823–1916). Missionary educator, born August 17, 1823, in Georgia, Vermont. Bliss graduated from Amherst College and Andover Theological Seminary, and was ordained in 1855. He became a missionary under the American Board of Commissioners for Foreign Missions (ABCFM)* in 1856 in Syria and worked in the Abeih mission station until 1858. He was in charge of a girls' boarding school in Suq el Gharb until 1862. In 1862 he was assigned the task of organizing and presiding over the Syrian Protestant College in Beirut which was opened in 1866. He was its president and also served as professor of Bible and ethics and treasurer. He resigned in 1902. Died July 27, 1916, in Beirut, Syria. *The Reminiscences of Daniel Bliss*, ed. and supplemented by

Frederic J. Bliss (New York, 1920), appeared after his death. *References*: *ACAB*; *Amherst*; *AndoverTS*; *DAB*; *NCAB* 19:176; *NYT*, August 8, 1916; and *WWWA*.

BLISS, EDWIN ELISHA (1817–1892). Missionary, born April 12, 1817, in Putney, Vermont. Bliss graduated from Amherst College and Andover Theological Seminary, and was ordained in 1843. He went to Turkey in 1843 and served as a missionary under the American Board of Commissioners for Foreign Missions (ABCFM)* to the Armenians in Trebizond from 1843 to 1851. He opened a station in Marsovan in 1851, stayed there until 1856 when he was transferred to Constantinople, and worked in the publications department until 1892. He was editor of a newspaper in Armenian and Turkish, and wrote *Condensed Sketch of the Missions of the American Board in Asiatic Turkey* (Boston, 1877). Died December 20, 1892, in Constantinople. *References*: *Amherst*; *AndoverTS*; *DAB*; and *WWWA*.

BLISS, EDWIN MUNSELL (1848–1919). Missionary and editor, son of Isaac Grout Bliss,* born September 12, 1848, at Erzerum, Turkey. Bliss grew up in Constantinople. He attended Robert College,* and graduated from Amherst College and Yale Divinity School. He went to Constantinople in 1872 and spent three years as assistant agent of the American Bible Society,* traveling extensively in Turkey, Egypt, Persia, and Palestine. He returned to Yale University in 1875 and was ordained in 1877. He went back to the Middle East as assistant agent of the American Bible Society and from 1885 to 1887 was stationed in Constantinople. He resigned in 1888, returned to the United States, and served as editor of the two editions of the *Encyclopaedia of Missions* in 1889–1891 and 1904. He wrote *Turkey and the Armenian Atrocities* (Boston, 1896), which appeared in several editions. Died August 6, 1919, in Washington, D.C. *References*: *Amherst*; *DAB*; *NYT*, August 8, 1919; and *WWWA*.

BLISS, FREDERIC JONES (1859–1937). Archaeologist, son of Daniel Bliss,* born January 22, 1859, in Suq al Gharb near Beirut, Syria. Bliss graduated from Amherst College and Union Theological Seminary. He was principal of the preparatory department of the Syrian Protestant College from 1880 to 1883, and spent two years conducting research on the customs and religion of Syria. He was invited by the Palestine Exploration Fund to continue the excavation of Tell el-Hesi in southern Palestine, begun in 1890 by Flinders Petrie. He excavated the site from 1891 to 1893, and wrote *A Mound of Many Cities; or, Tell el Hesy Excavated* (New York, 1894). He excavated in Jerusalem on behalf of the fund from 1894 to 1897, and was co-author of *Excavations at Jerusalem 1894–97* (London, 1898). He made soundings in a series of mounds in Judah and reported the results in *Excavations of Palestine During the Years 1898–1900* (London, 1902). He was dean of men at the University of Rochester from 1 11 to 1914. He wrote *The Development of Palestine Exploration* (New York, 1906), and *The Religions of Modern Syria and Palestine* (New York, 1912). Died June 3,

1937, in White Plains, New York. *References*: Papers, Palestine Exploration Fund, London; *Amherst*; *DAB S2*; *NYT*, June 5, 1937; Olga Tufnell, "'Excavator's Progress: Letters of F. J. Bliss, 1889–1900,'" *Palestine Exploration Quarterly* 97 (1965): 112–127; *UnionTS*; and *WWWA*.

BLISS, HOWARD SWEESTER (1860–1920). Missionary educator, son of Daniel Bliss,* born December 6, 1860, in Suq al Gharb, Syria. Bliss grew up in Beirut, graduated from Amherst College and Union Theological Seminary, studied at Mansfield College, Oxford, and Berlin and Gottingen universities, and was ordained in 1890. He served as a pastor in Brooklyn and Upper Montclair, New Jersey. In 1902 he was selected to succeed his father as president of the Syrian Protestant College, and served from 1903 until his death. He broadened the role of the college, established schools of nursing and dentistry, and strengthened the medical school. Died May 2, 1920, in Saranac Lake, New York. *References*: *Amherst*; *DAB*; *NCAB* 19:177; *UnionTS*; and *WWWA*.

BLISS, ISAAC GROUT (1822–1889). Missionary, born July 5, 1822, in Springfield, Massachusetts. Bliss graduated from Amherst College and Andover and Yale theological seminaries, and was ordained in 1847. He was a missionary under the American Board of Commissioners for Foreign Missions (ABCFM)* and was stationed in Erzurum, Turkey, until 1852. At that time he returned to the United States, resigned from ABCFM, and was a pastor in Southbridge and Boylston, Massachusetts. He returned to the Middle East in 1857 as an agent of the American Bible Society.* He was stationed in Constantinople, reorganized the distribution of the Bible, and obtained the funds to build the Bible House* in Constantinople which was completed in 1872. Died February 16, 1889, in Assiut, Egypt. He wrote *Twenty-five Years in the Levant* in the *67th Report of the American Bible Society* (1883). *References*: *Amherst*; *AndoverTS*; and *EM*.

BLOWERS, GEORGE (ALBERT) (1906–1969). Banker and financial consultant, born March 5, 1906, in Pineville, Kentucky. Blowers graduated from Harvard University, worked at the National City Bank from 1928 to 1937, and at the Bank of Monrovia in Liberia from 1937 to 1943, and was later governor of the State Bank of Ethiopia. In 1950 he headed the United Nations mission on currency and banking problems to Libya, which planned the banking system and the currency for that country. From 1952 to 1954, he was the first governor of the Saudi Arabian Monetary Agency and organized the central bank of Saudi Arabia. He was director of the Export-Import Bank from 1954 to 1961. Died October 19, 1969, in New York City. *Reference*: *NYT*, October 20, 1969.

BLUEBOLT, **OPERATION** *See* Lebanon, Marines in (1958).

BOKER, GEORGE HENRY (1823–1890). Poet, playwright, and diplomat, born October 6, 1823, in Philadelphia. Boker graduated from Princeton University. His first book of poems was published in 1848, and his first play was produced in London in 1849. He served as the president of the Union League of Philadelphia and the Fairmount Park Commission. He was minister to Turkey from 1872 to 1875, and negotiated a treaty recognizing the status of neutralized American citizens. He recommended the purchase of Bab el Mandeb at the entrance to the Red Sea by the United States. He was minister to Russia from 1875 to 1878, and after his return to the United States continued to write. Died January 2, 1890, in Philadelphia. *References*: *ACAB*; *DAB*; *DADH*; Oliver H. Evans, *George Henry Boker* (Boston, 1984); *NCAB* 6:73; *NYT*, January 3, 1890; and *WWWA*.

BORDEN, MARY (SPEARS) (1886–1968). Author, born May 15, 1886, in Chicago. Borden graduated from Vassar College, and organized and directed a field hospital in France during World War I. She married Sir Edward (Louis) Spears (1886–1974) in 1918, when he was head of the British Military Mission in Paris, and later lived in England. In World War II she ran a field hospital in France, later equipped and staffed a field hospital in the Middle East, and then was official hostess in the British legations in Beirut and Damascus when her husband was the British minister to Syria and Lebanon from 1942 to 1944. *Journey Down a Blind Alley* (London, 1946) is her account of her wartime experiences. Died December 2, 1968, in Bracknel, Berkshire, England. *References*: *CA*; *NYT*, December 3, 1968; and *WWWA*.

BOWEN, HERBERT WOLCOTT (1856–1927). Diplomat, born February 29, 1856, in Brooklyn. Bowen graduated from Yale College and Columbia Law School. From 1890 to 1899 he was consul and later consul general in Barcelona. He was minister to Persia from 1899 to 1901, and minister to Venezuela from 1901 until his retirement in 1905. He wrote his memoirs, *Recollections Diplomatic and Undiplomatic* (New York, 1927). Died May 29, 1927, in Woodstock, Connecticut. *References*: *ACAB*; *DAB*; *DADH*; *NCAB* 20:46; *NYT*, May 30, 1927; and *WWWA*.

BOWEN, MARCELLUS (1846–1916). Clergyman, born April 6, 1846, in Marion, Ohio. Bowen graduated from Yale University and Union Theological Seminary, and was ordained in 1872. He was a pastor in Springfield, New Jersey, from 1872 to 1874, a missionary under the American Board of Commissioners for Foreign Missions (ABCFM)* at Smyrna from 1874 to 1884, and principal of a private school for boys in Hartford, Connecticut, from 1885 until 1888. He was an agent of the American Bible Society* in Constantinople from

1888 until his death. Died October 3, 1916, in Geneva, Switzerland. *References*: *NYT*, October 6, 1916; *UnionTS*; and *WWWA*.

BOWEN, RICHARD LE BARON, JR. (1919–   ). Chemical engineer and archaeologist, born April 2, 1919, in Providence, Rhode island. Bowen graduated from Princeton University and the Massachusetts Institute of Technology. From 1949 to 1977 he was vice president and president of Coated Textile Mills, and president and treasurer of Tensco, Inc. after 1977. He was interested in nautical archaeology and in Arabian archaeology and ethnology, conducted archaeological excavations in Arabia, and was co-author of *Archaeological Discoveries in South Arabia* (Baltimore, 1958), and *The Early Arabian Necropolis of Ain Jawan: Pre-Islamic and Early Islamic Site on the Persian Gulf* (New Haven, Conn., 1950). He also studied the traditional Arab dhow boats and dhow sailors of the Persian Gulf, wrote several articles in the *American Neptune* between 1949 and 1955, and *Arab Dhows of Eastern Arabia* (Rehoboth, Mass., 1949). *Reference*: *AMWS*.

BOWLES, PAUL FREDERIC (1910–   ). Author and composer, born December 30, 1910, in New York City. Bowles graduated from the University of Virginia, and from 1942 to 1946, he was music critic of the *New York Herald Tribune*. After 1947 he lived in Tangier or on an island near Sri Lanka. His novel *The Sheltering Sky* (New York, 1949) is set in Algeria, and the novel *Let It Come Down* (New York, 1952) is set in Tangier. He also wrote two travel books about North Africa, *Yallah* (New York, 1957) and *Their Heads Are Green and Their Hands Are Black* (New York, 1963). He also wrote *Without Stopping: An Autobiography* (New York, 1972). In 1959 Bowles collected Moroccan music for the Archive of Folk Song of the Library of Congress. His wife, **JANE (SYDNEY) BOWLES (1917–1973)**, author and dramatist, was born February 22, 1917, in New York City. She came to Morocco after World War II and settled in Tangier in 1952. Died May 3, 1973, in Malaga, Spain. *References*: Papers, Humanities Research Center, University of Texas; *CA*; Millicent Dillon, *A Little Original Sin: The Life and Work of Jane Bowles* (New York, 1981); *DLB*; Lawrence D. Stewart, *Paul Bowles; The Illumination of North Africa* (Carbondale, Ill., 1974); and *NYT*, May 31, 1973.

BOYCE, ARTHUR C(LIFTON) (1884–1959). Missionary educator, born September 24, 1884, in Tuscola, Illinois. Boyce graduated from Lafayette College and the universities of Illinois and Chicago. He was a teacher in Persia in 1906–1907 and in the American High School in Teheran from 1907 to 1910. He served as a missionary in Iran under the Presbyterian Church in the U.S.A. Board of Foreign Missions* from 1915 to 1949, was associate and acting principal of the American boys' school in Teheran from 1915 to 1923, and later vice president of Alborz College* in Teheran. He retired in 1949. He wrote *Alborz College of Teheran and Dr. Samuel Martin Jordan, Founder and President* (Duarte, Calif.,

1954). Died August 30, 1959, in Duarte, California. *Reference*: *NYT*, September 1, 1959.

BRADISH, LUTHER (1783–1863). Lawyer and diplomat, born September 15, 1783, in Cummington, Massachusetts. Bradish graduated from Williams College, was admitted to the bar in 1804, practiced law, and served in the War of 1812. In 1820 he was sent on a secret, but unsuccessful, special mission to Constantinople to negotiate with the Turkish government concerning American trade. After negotiations broke off, he left Constantinople and traveled in Egypt, Palestine, Syria, and Europe until 1826. He served in the New York Assembly from 1827 to 1830 and from 1835 to 1838, was lieutenant governor of New York State in 1838, and assistant U.S. treasurer. Died August 30, 1863, in Newport, Rhode Island. *References*: Papers, New York Historical Society; *ACAB*; *DAB*; Louis B. Gimelli, "Luther Bradish, 1783–1863," Ph.D. diss., New York University, 1964; *NCAB* 3:463; *WWWA*; and *WWWE*.

BRAIDWOOD, ROBERT J(OHN) (1907–   ). Prehistorian, born July 29, 1907, in Detroit. Braidwood graduated from the universities of Michigan and Chicago. He was field assistant in archaeology for the University of Michigan in Iraq in 1930–1931 and for the University of Chicago in Syria from 1933 to 1938. He was instructor, assistant professor, and professor of prehistoric archaeology at the Oriental Institute. He also became professor in the Department of Anthropology of the University of Chicago in 1947. He conducted prehistoric studies in Iraq, Iran, and Turkey, especially the Iraq-Jarmo prehistoric project in northern Iraq, from 1950 to 1955, and excavated Qalal Jarmo. He was co-author of *Excavations in the Plain of Antioch* (Chicago, 1960), and *Prehistoric Investigation in Iraqi Kurdistan* (1960). His wife, **LINDA S(CHREIBER) BRAIDWOOD**, archaeologist and associate at the Oriental Institute, wrote *Digging Beyond the Tigris: An American Woman Archaeologist's Story of Life in a "Dig" in the Kurdish Hills of Iraq* (New York, 1953), and co-edited *Prehistoric Archaeology Along the Zagros Flanks* (Chicago, 1983). *References*: *The Hilly Flanks and Beyond: Essays on the Prehistory of Southwestern Asia, Presented to Robert J. Braidwood*, ed. by T. Cuyler Young et al. (Chicago, 1983); *AMWS*; *DAS*; and *WWA*.

BRAMKAMP, RICHARD A(LLEN) (1910–1958). Petroleum geologist, born February 3, 1910, in Richmond, Indiana. Bramkamp graduated from Pomona College and the University of California at Berkeley, and was curator of the Museum of Paleontology of the University of California. In 1936 he joined Standard Oil Company of California, was transferred to California Arabian Standard Oil Company (CASOC)* and went to Saudi Arabia. He became senior palentologist in 1944, chief field geologist in 1947, and chief geologist of Arabian American Oil Company (ARAMCO)* in the same year. He played a major part in Aramco's discovery of oil reserves in Saudi Arabia. He became sick in Saudi

Arabia and died September 1, 1958, in New York City. *References*: *NYT*, September 3, 1958; *PAAPG* 43 (February 1959): 261–263.

BREASTED, JAMES HENRY (1865–1935). Egyptologist, archaeologist, and historian, born August 27, 1865, in Rockford, Illinois. Breasted attended North-Western (now North Central) College (Naperville, Ill.), graduated from the Chicago College of Pharmacy, and studied at the Congregational Institute (now Chicago Theological Seminary), Yale University, and the University of Berlin. He was assistant in Egyptology and assistant director of Haskell Oriental Museum at the University of Chicago from 1895 to 1901, and director of the Haskell Museum from 1901 to 1935. Breasted became instructor in Egyptology and Semitic languages in 1896; professor of Egyptology and Oriental history from 1905 to 1933; holder of the first chair of Egyptology in America; and founder of the Oriental Institute at the University of Chicago. He gathered inscriptions in Egypt from 1899 to 1904, was director of the University of Chicago expedition to Nubia from 1905 to 1907, and wrote *Egypt Through the Stereoscope: A Journey Through the Land of the Pharaohs* (New York, 1905), *The Temples of Lower Nubia, Report of the Work of the Egyptian Expedition, Season of 1905–1906* (Chicago, 1906), and *The Monuments of Sudanese Nubia, Report of the Work of the Egyptian Expedition, Season of 1906–07* (Chicago, 1908). He led the American Scientific Mission to the Middle East in 1919–1920 and made an exploratory expedition to Dura Europos in Syria which he described in *Oriental Forerunners of Byzantine Painting* (Chicago, 1924). He made his last trip to the Middle East in 1935. Died December 2, 1935, in New York City. *References*: *BASOR* 61 (1936): 1–4; Charles Breasted, *Pioneer to the Past: The Story of James Henry Breasted, Archaeologist* (New York, 1945); *DAB*; *NCAB* 29:257; John A. Wilson, "James Henry Breasted—The Idea of an Oriental Institute," in *Near Eastern Archaeology in the Twentieth Century*, ed. by James A. Sandeers (Garden City, N.Y., 1970), pp. 41–56; *WWWA*; and *WWWE*.

BREATH, EDWIN (1808–1861). Missionary printer, born January 22, 1808, in New York City. A trained printer, Breath was sent by the American Board of Commissioners for Foreign Missions (ABCFM)* to the mission in Urmia, Persia. In 1837 he tried, unsuccessfully, to get a printing press to Urmia, but he returned in 1840 with a special press which he designed and built and which could be dissembled. He cut the first fonts of Syriac type and printed some 80,000 volumes on his press. Died November 18, 1861, in Urmia. *Reference*: *EM*.

BREWER, JOSIAH (1796–1872). Missionary, born June 1, 1796, in Monterey, Berkshire County, Massachusetts. Brewer graduated from Yale College and Andover Theological Seminary, and was ordained in 1826. He was one of the first volunteers as missionaries to Turkey under the American Board of Commissioners for Foreign Missions (ABCFM).* He served first in Greece and, from

1830 until 1838, in Constantinople, and wrote *A Residence at Constantinople, in the Year 1827* (New Haven, Conn., 1830). He traveled in Asia Minor and wrote *Patmos, and the Seven Churches of Asia*, compiled from the Ms. Journals of Reverend Josiah Brewer by John W. Barber (Bridgeport, Conn., 1851). He was later chaplain of the Connecticut State Prison, principal of girls' seminaries in New Haven and Middletown, Connecticut, and a pastor in Housatonic, Massachusetts. Died November 19, 1872, in Stockbridge, Massachusetts. *References*: Brewer family papers, Yale University Library; *AndoverTS*; and *NCAB* 2:228.

BRIDGEMAN, CHARLES THORLEY (1893–1967). Clergyman, born February 21, 1893, in New York City. Bridgeman graduated from Bard College and General Theological Seminary, and was ordained in 1917. He served in Brooklyn and in Newton, Pennsylvania. He went to Jerusalem in 1924 as the representative of the National Council of the Episcopal Church in the United States in Palestine, and as liaison officer for relations with the eastern churches. He was the representative of the American Church on the staff of the Anglican Bishop in Jerusalem, the residentiary canon of St. George's Collegiate Church in Jerusalem, professor of theology in the Armenian Seminary from 1929 until 1944, and special correspondent for the *Times* of London and other newspapers. In 1943–1944 he was archdeacon of Syria and Lebanon. He returned to the United States in 1944 and served as curate of Trinity Episcopal Church in New York from 1945 to 1964. He wrote *Jerusalem at Worship* (Jerusalem, 1932), *Religious Communities of the Christian East* (n.p., 1932), and *The Episcopal Church and the Middle East* (New York, 1958). Died May 6, 1967, in Orange, New Jersey. *Reference*: *NYT*, May 7, 1967.

BRIDGMAN, FREDERICK ARTHUR (1847–1927). Painter, born November 10, 1847, in Tuskegee, Alabama. Bridgman moved north with his family at an early age. In 1863 he was apprenticed to the American Bank-Note Company, worked as a bank note engraver, and also studied drawing and painting at the Brooklyn Art Academy. In 1866 he went to France, studied in Paris until 1871, and spent summers in the Pont-Aven artists' colony and in the Pyrenees. He spent the winter of 1872–1873 in Algeria and the winter of 1873–1874 in Egypt, Nubia, and the Nile, making a voyage up the Nile as far as the second cataract. He returned to Paris in 1874 with 300 sketches and studies and quantities of costumes and curiosities that were utilized in the scenes of contemporary life in the Near East to which he devoted most of his attention. He wrote *Winters in Algeria* (New York, 1890). Bridgman remained in France for the rest of his life. Died January 13, 1927, in Rouen, France. *References*: *ACAB*; *DAB*; *NCAB* 2:110; and *WWWA*.

BRINTON, JASPER YEATES (1878–1973). Jurist, born October 5, 1878, in Philadelphia. Brinton graduated from the University of Pennsylvania and its law school, and was admitted to the bar in 1901. He practiced admiralty law in Philadelphia from 1901 until 1921, was assistant U.S. attorney for the Eastern District of Pennsylvania from 1904 to 1912, and served in the Judge Advocate General's Department in World War I. In 1919 he was a member of the American military mission to Armenia, and in 1921 he was solicitor of the U.S. Shipping Board. In 1921 he became judge on the Court of Appeals of the Mixed Courts of Egypt,* and from 1943 to 1948 he was president of the Mixed Courts. From 1948 to 1953 he was legal adviser to the embassy in Cairo. He wrote *Mixed Courts of Egypt* (New Haven, Conn., 1930; rev. ed., New Haven, Conn., 1968), and *The American Effort in Egypt: A Chapter in Diplomatic History in the Nineteenth Century* (Alexandria, Egypt, 1972). Died August 1973 in Alexandria. *References*: *NYT*, August 13, 1973; William Tracy, "Jasper Yeates Brinton: An American Judge in Egypt," *AWM* 21 (September-October 1970): 18–21; and *WWWA*.

BRISTOL, MARK LAMBERT (1868–1939). Naval officer and diplomat, born April 17, 1868, in Glassboro, New Jersey. Bristol graduated from the U.S. Naval Academy in 1887. He served in the Spanish-American War, and in 1913 he became director of naval aeronautics. During World War I he commanded the armored cruiser *North Carolina** and the battleship *Oklahoma*. In 1919 he was ordered to Constantinople to command a naval detachment to protect American interests in the Middle East, became high commissioner to Turkey, and served until 1927. He organized the U.S. Naval Detachment in Turkish Waters,* and assisted in the distribution of relief supplies and the evacuation of Americans and refugees. He was one of the observers to the Lausanne Conference, which negotiated the peace treaty between the Allies and Turkey in 1922, and was later commander-in-chief of the Asiatic Fleet. He retired with the rank of admiral. Died May 13, 1939, in Washington, D.C. *References*: Papers, Manuscript Division, Library of Congress; Thomas A. Bryson, "Admiral Mark Lambert Bristol: An Open Door Diplomat in Turkey," *International Journal of Near Eastern Studies* 5 (1974): 450–467; Peter M. Buzanski, "Admiral Mark L. Bristol and Turkish-American Relations, 1919–1922," Ph.D. diss., University of California at Berkeley, 1960; *DAB S2*; *DADH*; *NCAB* 34:256; *NYT*, May 14, 1939; *WAMB*; and *WWWA*.

BROOKS, NOAH (1830–1903). Journalist, born October 24, 1830, in Castine, Maine. Brooks began his newspaper career in Boston but went to California in 1859, and established the *Marysville Appeal*. He was a war correspondent in the Civil War, naval officer of the port of San Francisco, Washington correspondent for the *Sacramento Union*, and managing editor of *Alta California* in San Francisco. He was on the staff of the *New York Tribune* from 1871 to 1874, the *New York Times* from 1875 to 1884, and the Newark (N.J.) *Advertiser* from

1884 to 1894. In 1894–1895 he toured Egypt, Turkey, and Palestine, and wrote *The Mediterranean Trip: A Short Guide to the Principal Points on the Shores of the Western Mediterranean and the Levant* (New York, 1895). Died August 16, 1903, in Castine, Maine. *References*: *ACAB*; *DAB*; *NCAB* 7:57; and *WWWA*.

BROWN, DEMETRA (VAKA) (1877–1946). Author, born near Constantinople, and came to the United States in 1894. Brown was on the editorial staff of a Greek newspaper in New York City and a teacher of French at Comstock school. She traveled through the Balkans and Asia Minor, was in Greece during World War I, and traveled to Constantinople and Asia Minor in 1921 to write for *Asia Magazine*. Under the pen name Demetra Vaka, she wrote *Haremlik: Some Pages from the Life of Turkish Women* (Boston, 1909), and *The Unveiled Ladies of Stamboul* (Boston, 1923). Died December 17, 1946, in Chicago. *References*: *NYT* December 19, 1944; Grant Overton, *The Women Who Make Our Novels*, rev. ed. (New York, 1928), 315–317; and *WWWA*.

BROWN, GLEN FRANCIS (1911–   ). Geologist born December 14, 1911, in Graysville, Indiana. Brown graduated from the New Mexico School of Mines and Northwestern University. He was a geologist with the Philippine Bureau of Mines from 1936 to 1938, and a junior geologist with the U.S. Geological Survey from 1938 to 1941. He served with the Foreign Economic Administration as assistant geologist and senior geologist from 1941 to 1946 and returned to the U.S. Geological Service in 1946. He was acting chief of mission to Thailand in 1949, chief of the field party in Saudi Arabia from 1950 to 1954, chief of the Saudi Arabian project in Washington from 1955 to 1957, and geological adviser to the Kingdom of Saudi Arabia from 1957 to 1958. He was a member of the World Bank Mission to Saudi Arabia in 1960 and to Kuwait in 1962, and chief of the field party from 1963 to 1969. In 1969 he became senior chief geologist for Mideastern Affairs in the U.S. Geological Survey. He wrote *The Geology and Ground Water of Al Kharj District, Nejd, Saudi Arabia* (Evanston, Ill., 1948). *References*: *AMWS*; *IAB*.

BROWN, JOHN PORTER (1814–1872). Diplomat and Orientalist, born August 17, 1814, in Chillicote, Ohio. Brown joined his uncle, Davis Porter,* in Turkey in 1832, studied Arabic and Turkish, and held various positions in the legation in Turkey until his death. He became consul in 1835, dragoman in 1836, and consul general in 1857. In 1850 he helped secure the first Turkish military mission to the United States, and in 1853 he was involved in the Koszta affair* and supported Duncan Nathaniel Ingraham's* ultimatum to the Austrians in Smyrna to surrender Martin Koszta. From 1858 to 1872 he was secretary of legation and served nine times as chargé d'affaires. He translated *Turkish Evening Entertainments. The Wonders of Remarkable Incidents and the Rarities of Anecdotes* (New York, 1850), a collection of fairy tales, and wrote *The Dervishes, or Oriental Spiritualism* (London, 1868; rev. ed. by H. A. Rose, London, 1927).

Died April 28, 1872, in Constantinople. *References*: *ACAB*; Gary C. Conn, "John Porter Brown, Father of Turkish-American Relations; An Ohioan at the Sublime Porte, 1832–1872," Ph.D. diss., Ohio State University, 1973; *DAB*; *DADH*; *OAB*; and *WWWA*.

BROWN, JULIUS ARTHUR (1880–1970). Physicist and educator, born May 8, 1880, in New York City. Brown graduated from Dartmouth College and was New Hampshire's first Rhodes scholar at Oxford University. He was assistant professor of physics at Dartmouth College from 1907 to 1909, professor of physics at the Syrian Protestant College from 1909 to 1919, deputy commissioner of the American Red Cross* for Palestine and Egypt in 1919, and professor of astronomy and director of the observatory at the American University of Beirut* from 1919 until his retirement in 1945. Died May 2, 1970, in Laconia, New Hampshire. *Reference*: *NYT*, May 5, 1970.

BROWN, PHILIP MARSHALL (1875–1966). Educator, born July 31, 1875, in Hampden, Maine. Brown graduated from Williams College and Harvard University. He entered the foreign service in 1900; was secretary to the minister in Constantinople and second secretary of legation in Constantinople from 1900 to 1903; secretary of legation in Honduras and Guatemala from 1903 to 1907; secretary and chargé d'affaires in Constantinople in 1907–1908; and minister to Honduras from 1908 to 1910. He wrote *Foreigners in Turkey* (Princeton, N.J., 1914). Brown was an attaché on the staff of General Edmund Allenby in Egypt and Palestine, and an observer on the staff of the American Commission at the Paris Peace Conference in 1919. He was assistant professor, and professor of international law at Princeton University from 1913 until his retirement in 1935. Died May 10, 1966, in Williamstown, Massachusetts. *References*: *American Journal of International Law* 60 (1966): 515–516; *NYT*, May 12, 1966; and *WWWA*.

BROWNE, JOHN ROSS (1821–1875). Traveler and author, born February 11, 1821, in Dublin, Ireland. Browne came to the United States with his parents in 1833 and grew up in Louisville, Kentucky. He was a porter in the U.S. Senate in 1841–1842, shipped as a sailor on a whaler from New Bedford, Massachusetts, in 1842, traveled extensively for the next twenty years, and was official reporter to the first constitutional convention of California in 1849. In 1851 he traveled in the Middle East and wrote *Yusef; or, the Journey of the Franji; a Crusade in the East* (New York, 1853). He was later a confidential agent for the Treasury Department in the west and minister to China in 1870–1871. He settled in Oakland, California. Died December 8, 1875, in Oakland. *References*: *J. Ross Browne: His Letters, Journals and Writings*, ed. Lina F. Browne (Albuquerque, N.M., 1969); *ACAB*; *DAB*; Franklin Walker, *Irreverent Pilgrims: Melville, Browne, and Mark Twain in the Holy Land* (Seattle, Wash., 1974), chs. 2–4; *NCAB* 8:117; and *WWWA*.

BROWNELL, CLARENCE MELVILLE (1828–1862). Physician and explorer, born in East Hartford, Connecticut. Brownell studied in medical schools in Pittsfield, Woodstock, and New York, and practiced medicine in Wauwatosa, Wisconsin, and at East Hartford, Connecticut. He began traveling in 1859 and went to Canada and the Amazon River. In 1861 he went to Egypt, traveled through the Nubian Desert to Khartoum where he joined the Welsh explorer and trader John Petherick and his wife, and went on a trading expedition to the Upper White Nile. He contracted fever on the voyage. Died May 20, 1862, near Aliyab, on the east bank of the White Nile. *References*: Diary and papers in private hands; *Hill*.

BRYANT, WILLIAM CULLEN (1794–1878). Poet and journalist, born November 3, 1794, in Cummington, Massachusetts. Bryant graduated from Williams College. In 1825 he became co-editor of the *New York Review and Athenaeum* and then of the New York *Evening Post*, and in 1829 he became the editor of that newspaper. He traveled to Egypt and Palestine in 1852–1853, and sent letters to the *Evening Post* which were later printed in *Letters from the East* (New York, 1869). Died June 12, 1878, in New York City. *References*: Diary and papers in private hands (microfilm in the New York Public Library); *ACAB*; Charles H. Brown, *William Cullen Bryant* (New York, 1971); *DAB*; *DLB*; *NCAB* 4:79; and *WWWA*.

BUCKLER, WILLIAM HEPBURN (1867–1952). Archaeologist and diplomat, born February 1, 1867, in Paris, to American parents. Buckler studied at Trinity College, Cambridge University, the Law Department of the University of Maryland, and practiced law in Baltimore from 1894 to 1902. He was secretary of legation in Madrid from 1907 to 1909, member of the archaeological expedition to Sardis, Asia Minor, from 1910 to 1914, and special agent in the embassy in London from 1914 to 1918. He made additional journeys in Asia Minor in 1924, 1926, 1930, and 1933, was co-editor of *Monuments and Documents from Eastern Asia and Western Galatia* (Manchester, 1933), and of *Monuments and Documents from Phryggia and Caria* (Manchester, 1939). Died March 2, 1952, in Oxford, England. *Reference*: *WWWA*.

BUCKNAM, RANSFORD D. (1869–1915). Shipbuilder and naval adviser, born in Hansport, Nova Scotia, and moved to Maine as an infant. Bucknam went to sea at the age of fourteen, served on merchant ships in the Atlantic and Pacific oceans and in the Great Lakes, and was superintendent of the American Steel Barge Company of New York, the Pacific Mail Steamship Company of Panama, and Cramp Company's shipyards in Philadelphia. He was trial commander of the U.S.S. *Maine*, and of the Imperial Ottoman warship *Medjidia* which was built by Cramp and which he brought to Turkey early in 1904. He was retained by Sultan Abdul Hamid as naval adviser and personal aide-de-camp, continuing in that capacity until his death. Died May 27, 1915, in Constantinople. *Reference*: *WWWA*.

BULL, LUDLOW SEGUINE (1886–1954). Egyptologist, born January 10, 1886, in New York City. Bull graduated from Yale University and Harvard Law School, was admitted to the bar in 1911, and practiced law in New York City from 1910 to 1915. He served in the army in World War I. He changed his field of interest from law to Egyptology, and studied at the University of Chicago. He was assistant curator in the Egyptian Department of the Metropolitan Museum of Art from 1922 to 1928, and associate curator from 1928 until his death. He was a member of the Oriental Institute expeditions to Egypt, Iraq, and Syria in 1919–1920 and to Egypt in 1922–1923. From 1925 until his death he was also associate curator of the Egyptian Collection at Yale University, lecturer of Egyptology from 1925 to 1936, and research associate with rank of professor after 1936. Died July 1, 1954, in Litchfield, Connecticut. *References*: *BASOR* 135 (1954): 2–3; *NCAB* 42:690; *NYT*, July 2, 1954; and *WWWE*.

BULL, ROBERT J(EHU) (1920–   ). Archaeologist, born October 21, 1920, in Harrington, Delaware. Bull graduated from Randolph-Macon College and Duke and Yale universities. He was instructor, assistant and associate professor at Drew University from 1955 to 1970, and professor of church history in 1970. He became director of the Institute for Archaeological Research in 1968. He was field supervisor of the Drew University-McCormick archaeological expeditions to Shechem from 1956 to 1958, to Tell Balatah in 1960, 1962, and 1964, and to Tell (Ai) in 1964, field supervisor of the Wooster expedition to Pella in 1966, and director of Tell er Ras expedition in 1966, 1968, and 1971. He was director of the American Schools of Oriental Research (ASOR)* in Jerusalem in 1970–1971, and field director of the joint expedition to Khirbet Shema from 1970 to 1972, and to Caesarea in 1971 to 1974, 1976, and 1978–1979. He was co-editor of *The Joint Expedition to Caesarea Maritima* (Missoula, Mont., 1975), and wrote *Come See the Place: The Holy Land Jesus Knew* (Englewood Cliffs, N.J., 1978). *Reference*: *CA*.

BULLARD, ARTHUR ("ARTHUR EDWARDS") (1879–1929). Author, born December 8, 1879, in St. Joseph, Missouri. Bullard graduated from Hamilton College (Clinton, N.Y.). He was probation officer for the Prison Association of New York from 1903 to 1905 and was also connected with university settlement. He became a foreign correspondent in 1905, went to North Africa several times, spending a year or more each time, and wrote *The Barbary Coast; Sketches of French North Africa* (New York, 1913), and *The Stranger* (New York, 1920), a novel about North Africa. He was correspondent for *The Outlook* in the Balkan War of 1912–1913 and war correspondent for a group of American magazines from 1914 to 1917. From 1917 to 1919 he was a member of the Committee on Public Information, and director of the Russian division in the Department of

State. Bullard continued to serve in the State Department until 1921, was associated for many years with the League of Nations as the representative of the American League of Nations Association, and was a member of the secretariat of the League of Nations in 1926–1927. Died September 10, 1929, in Geneva, Switzerland. *References*: *NCAB* 21:392; *NYT*, September 11, 1929; and *WWWA*.

BUNCHE, RALPH JOHNSON (1904–1971). Diplomat, born August 7, 1904, in Detroit. Bunche graduated from the University of California at Los Angeles and Harvard University. He was instructor, assistant professor, assistant to the president, associate professor, and professor of political science at Howard University from 1928 to 1941. During World War II he was analyst in charge of research on Africa and other colonial areas in the Office of Strategic Services, and in 1944 he became an adviser to the State Department. In 1946 he was appointed director of the Division of Trusteeship in the United Nations. He was acting mediator on Palestine in 1948–1949 and succeeded in reaching cease-fire agreements in the Arab-Israeli War, for which he received the Nobel Peace Prize in 1950. In 1955 Bunche was appointed undersecretary of the United Nations (U.N.), was U.N. special representative in the Congo in 1960, head of the U.N. mission to Yemen in 1962, and took charge of the peace-keeping forces in Cyprus in 1964. In 1968 he became undersecretary general of the United Nations. Died December 9, 1971, in New York City. *References*: Papers, University of California at Los Angeles Library; *CB* 1948; *DADH*; Peggy Mann, *Ralph Bunche: UN Peaceman* (New York, 1975); *NCAB* 57:304; *NYT*, December 10, 1971; *PolProf: Eisenhower*; *PolProf: Truman*; and *Touval*, ch. 3.

BUNGER, MILLS EMERSON (1886–   ). Consulting engineer, born July 16, 1886, in Fort Morgan, Colorado. Bunger graduated from the Colorado School of Mines and was involved in various surveying and engineering jobs in Golden, Denver, and Pueblo, Colorado, and in San Francisco. He was engineering manager of the Model Lands and Irrigation Company in Trinidad, Colorado, from 1917 to 1945, with the U.S. Bureau of Reclamation from 1946 to 1948, and consulting engineer with Ford, Bacon, Davis in New York City from 1949 to 1951. He was chief of water resources development for the Hashemite Kingdom of Jordan from 1952 to 1954, and in 1953 he prepared a plan for the development of the Jordan River Valley. In 1955 he became a consulting engineer on water problems in Denver. *Reference*: *WWW*.

BUNKER MISSION, 1963. A military coup d'etat in Yemen in 1962 led to a civil war in Yemen and the military conflict between Egypt, which supported the revolutionaries, and Saudi Arabia, which supported the royalists. Ambassador Ellsworth Bunker (1894–1984) was sent by President John F. Kennedy as presidential emissary to Saudi Arabia in 1963 in an effort to reduce the tensions between Saudi Arabia and Egypt. He conducted a series of "shuttle diplomacy" flights between Riyadh and Cairo, and secured a disengagement agreement between the two countries. The United Nations took over the implementation of the agreement. *References*: *DADH*; Christopher J. McMullen, *Resolution of the Yemen Crisis, 1963: A Case Study in Mediation* (Washington, D.C., 1980); and *PolProf: Johnson*.

BURNS, NORMAN (1905–   ). Economist and educator, born November 14, 1905, in Versailles, Ohio. Burns graduated from Wittenberg and Yale universities and studied at the University of Montpellier, France. He was assistant professor of economics at the American University of Beirut* from 1929 to 1932, and wrote *The Tariff of Syria, 1919–1932* (Beirut, 1933). He was a foreign trade economist in the U.S. Tariff Commission from 1934 to 1944, adviser on international trade policy in the State Department from 1944 to 1949, and director of the Foreign Service Institute and deputy regional director for Near East, South Asia, and Africa Affairs in the International Co-operation Administration from 1956 to 1959. He was chief economic adviser to the United Nations Relief and Works Agency (UNRWA) for Palestine Refugees in the Near East in Beirut from 1953 to 1956, and director of the U.S. Operations Mission to Jordan from 1959 to 1961. From 1961 until 1965 he served as president of the American University of Beirut. *References*: *MENA*; and *WWA*.

BURROWS, MILLAR (1889–1980). Biblical scholar, born October 26, 1889, in Wyoming, Ohio, and grew up in Buffalo, New York. Burrows graduated from Cornell University, Union Theological Seminary, and Yale University, and was ordained in 1915. He was a pastor in Wallace, Texas, from 1915 to 1919; pastor and professor of biblical history and literature at Tusculum College (Greenville, Tenn.) from 1920 to 1923; and associate professor and professor of biblical literature and history of religion at Brown University from 1925 to 1934. He was professor of biblical theology at Yale Divinity School from 1934 until his retirement in 1958. Burrows was director of the American Schools of Oriental Research (ASOR)* in Jerusalem in 1931–1932 and 1947–1948, and president of the ASOR from 1934 to 1948. While he was director of ASOR, the Dead Sea Scrolls were discovered and he wrote two best-selling books on the subject. He wrote *What Mean These Stones? The Significance of Archaeology to Biblical Studies* (New Haven, Conn., 1941), and *Palestine Is Our Business* (Philadelphia, 1949). He was president of Middle East Relief from 1954 to 1957. Died April 1980 in Ann Arbor, Michigan. *References*: *BA* 44 (Spring 1981): 116–121; *CA*; *CB*, 1956; *NYT*, May 3, 1980; *OAB*; *UnionTS*; and *WWWA*.

BURT, NATHANIEL CLARK (1825–1874). Clergyman, born April 23, 1825, in Fairton, New Jersey. Burt graduated from Princeton University and Princeton Theological Seminary, and was ordained in 1850. He served as pastor in Springfield, Ohio, Baltimore, and Cincinnati. He traveled in the Middle East in 1866–1867, and wrote *The Far East; or, Letters from Egypt, Palestine and Other Lands of the Orient* (Cincinnati, 1868), and *The Land and Its Story: or the Sacred*

Geography of Palestine (New York, 1869). He was president of Ohio Female College from 1868 to 1870, and spent the rest of his life in southern Europe because of his poor health. Died March 4, 1874, in Rome. *References*: *ACAB*; and *OAB*.

BURTON, HARRY (1879–1940). Archaeologist and photographer. Burton took part in the excavations of Theodore Monroe Davis* in the Valley of the Kings and Thebes in Egypt. In 1914 he joined the staff of the Egyptian Expedition of the Metropolitan Museum of Art as a photographer and made photographic records of the excavations and of many tombs in Thebes. He lent his services to Lord Carnarvon and Howard Carter in 1922, and he took all the pictures of the tomb of Tutankhamen and its contents. He became sick in April 1940 while working in Luxor and died June 27, 1940, in Assiut. *References*: *Bulletin of the Metropolitan Museum of Art* 35 (1940): 165; and *WWWE*.

BUTLER, HOWARD CROSBY (1872–1922). Archaeologist, born March 7, 1872, at Croton Falls, New York. Butler graduated from Princeton College and Columbia University School of Architecture, and studied at the American School of Classical Studies in Rome and Athens. He was lecturer on architecture at Princeton University from 1895 to 1897, and professor of art and archaeology from 1901 to 1922. He organized and conducted the first archaeological expedition to the deserts of northcentral Syria in 1899–1900, 1904–1905, and 1909, and directed the excavation of Sardis from 1910 to 1922. He was co-author of *Sardis* (Leyden, 1922), wrote *Early Churches in Syria, Fourth to Seventh Centuries* (Princeton, N.J., 1929), and many reports on the Syrian archaeological expeditions. Died August 13, 1922, in Neuilly, France, on his return from Sardis. *References*: *BDAE*; *DAB*; *NCAB* 20:56; *NYT*, August 16, 1922; and *WWWA*.

BUTLER, MILLARD ANGLE (1879–1943). Engineer, born October 17, 1879, in Minneapolis. Butler graduated from the University of Minnesota. He was assistant to the division engineer of the Great Northern Railway in St. Paul, from 1902 to 1916, chief engineer with the Twin City Belt Line Railway in St. Paul, in 1916–1917, and served with the U.S. Army from 1917 to 1920. He was in private practice in Norfolk, Virginia, from 1920 to 1927, and engineer of the southern lines of the Persian National Railways as representative of Ulen and Company* from 1927 to 1930. He was in Honduras for the same company in 1930–1931, and returned to private practice in Norfolk, Virginia. He was again with the U.S. Army from 1940 until his death. Died June 3, 1943, in Charleston, West Virginia. *Reference*: *NCAB* 34:23.

C

CADET. Brig of Salem, Massachusetts. Commanded by Captain Charles Derby, the *Cadet* made a trip to Muscat in 1795, the first American ship to visit Muscat and to open trade with it. *Reference*: James D. Phillips, *Salem and the Indies* (Boston, 1947).

CAFFERY, JEFFERSON (1886–1974). Diplomat, born December 1, 1886, in Lafayette, Louisiana. Caffery graduated from Tulane University and was admitted to the bar in 1909. He entered the foreign service in 1911 and served in Caracas, Venezuela, Stockholm, Teheran, Madrid, and Athens; was counselor in Tokyo from 1923 to 1925 and in Berlin in 1925–1926; minister to El Salvador from 1926 to 1928; ambassador to Cuba from 1934 to 1937; ambassador to Brazil from 1937 to 1944; and ambassador to France from 1944 to 1949. He was ambassador to Egypt from 1949 until his retirement in 1955. Following the Egyptian Revolution of 1952, he served as an intermediary in the negotiations between the Egyptian and the British governments leading to the withdrawal of British forces from the Suez Canal Zone. Died April 12, 1974, in Lafayette, Louisiana. *References*: Papers, Southwestern Archives and Manuscripts Collection, University of Southwestern Louisiana, Lafayette; *CB* 1943; *DADH*; Philip F. Dur, "Jefferson Caffery of Louisiana: Highlights of His Career," *Louisiana History* 15 (1974): 9–34, 367–402; *NYT*, April 15, 1974; and *WWWA*.

CALHOUN, SIMEON HOWARD (1804–1875). Missionary, born August 15, 1804, in Boston. Calhoun graduated from Williams College and was ordained in 1836. He went to the Middle East in 1837 as agent of the American Bible Society,* and became a missionary under the American Board of Commissioners for Foreign Missions (ABCFM)* in 1843. He served in the Syria mission, was in charge of the seminary at Abeih, and was pastor of a church on Mount Lebanon until 1875. He assisted William Goodell* in translating the Bible into Turkish. Died December 14, 1875, in Buffalo, New York, during a visit to the United States. *References*: *ACAB*; *EM*; and *Hewitt*.

CALIFORNIA ARABIAN STANDARD OIL COMPANY (CASOC). Company incorporated in 1933 by the Standard Oil Company of California to conduct operations in Saudi Arabia and to develop, explore, refine, and ship petroleum. Texas Company acquired half-interest in 1936. The name was changed to the Arabian American Oil Company (ARAMCO)* in 1944.

CALLAWAY, JOSEPH A(TLEE) (1920–   ). Archaeologist, born March 31, 1920, in Warren, Arkansas. Callaway graduated from Ouachita Baptist College and Southern Baptist Theological Seminary (Lexington, Ky.). He was instructor of Hebrew in the Southern Baptist Theological Seminary in 1956–1957, associate professor of Old Testament in 1958–1959, and professor of Biblical archaeology after 1967. He was supervisor of archaeological expeditions in Israel from 1960 to 1964 and director of the joint archaeological expedition to Ai (et-Tell) from 1964 to 1974. He wrote *Pottery from the Tombs at Ai (et-Tell)* (London, 1964), *The Early Bronze Age Sanctuary at Ai (et-Tell)* (London, 1972), and *The Early Bronze Age Citadel and Lower City at 'Ai (et-Tell)* (Cambridge, Mass., 1980). *References*: *CA*; *DAS*.

CALUMET. Ship owned by Samuel D., John, and Jonathan Harris of Boston, with E. T. Holmes, master. The *Calumet* was probably the first American ship to penetrate the Dardanelles and to enter the Black Sea in 1810. *Reference*: Samuel E. Morison, "Forcing the Dardanelles in 1810, with Some Account of the Early Levant Trade of Massachusetts," *New England Quarterly* 1 (1928): 208–225.

CALVERLEY, EDWIN E(LLIOTT) (1882–1971). Missionary and Orientalist, born October 26, 1882, in Philadelphia. Calverley graduated from Princeton University and Princeton Theological Seminary, and was ordained in 1908. He served in the Arabian Mission* from 1909 to 1930, and was stationed in Bahrain, in Basra and Amara in Iraq, and in Kuwait. He was professor of Arabic and Islamics in the Kennedy School of Missions of the Hartford Seminary Foundation from 1930 to 1952, acting dean of the School of Oriental Studies of the American University in Cairo* in 1944–1945, and consulting Arabist to the Arabian American Oil Company (ARAMCO)* in Dhahran, Saudi Arabia, from 1952 to 1957. Died April 22, 1971, in Hartford, Connecticut. His wife, **ELEANOR JANE (TAYLOR) CALVERLEY (1886–1968)**, was a medical missionary, born March 24, 1886, in Woodstown, New Jersey, and graduated from the Woman's Medical College in Philadelphia. She served in the Arabian Mission from 1909 to 1931 and became a lecturer on hygiene to missionaries at the Kennedy School of Missions in 1931. She wrote an autobiography, *My Arabian Days and Nights* (New York, 1958). Died December 22, 1968, in Hartford, Connecticut. *References*: Papers, Case Memorial Library, Hartford Seminary Foundation; *MW* 61 (1971): 155–160; *NCAB* 56:561, 56:562; *NYT*, April 23, 1971; and *WWWA*.

CAMERON, GEORGE GLENN (1905–1979). Archaeologist, born July 30, 1905, in Washington, Pennsylvania. Cameron graduated from Washington and Jefferson and Muskingum (New Concord, Ohio) colleges and the University of Chicago. He was assistant professor of Oriental languages at the Oriental Institute of the University of Chicago from 1933 to 1948, associate professor of Near Eastern cultures at the University of Michigan from 1945 to 1948, and professor from 1948 until his retirement in 1975. He was annual professor at the American Schools of Oriental Research (ASOR)* in Baghdad in 1948–49. He was a member of the Persepolis expedition of the Oriental Institute in 1939 and director of the expedition to the Bisitun (Behistun) monument in Iran, in 1947–1948. Cameron climbed the Bisitun Rock to take new photographs of portions of the text that had not been accessible before. He returned to Bisitun in 1957. In 1951 he directed the University of Michigan expedition to Iraqi Kurdistan. He wrote *History of Early Iran* (Chicago, 1936). Died September 15, 1979, in Ann Arbor, Michigan. *References*: *Michigan Oriental Studies in Honor of George G. Cameron*, ed. Louis L. Orlin (Ann Arbor, Mich., 1976); *CA*; *DAS*; *NYT*, September 17, 1979; Matthew W. Stolper, "George W. Cameron 1905–1979," *BA* 43 (1980): 183–189; and *WWWA*.

CAMINOS, RICARDO AUGUSTO (1915–   ). Egyptologist, born July 11, 1915, in Buenos Aires, Argentina. Caminos graduated from the universities of Buenos Aires and Chicago and Oxford University, and studied at the Oriental Institute. He was epigraphist of the expedition at Luxor, Upper Egypt, from 1947 to 1950. He became a member of the faculty of Brown University in 1952, serving as professor from 1964 until his retirement in 1980. He was field director of the Egypt Exploration Society and Brown University expedition to Gebel es-Silsilah, Upper Egypt, from 1955 to 1982, Bulen, Sudan, in 1960–1961, Kasr Ibrim, Egyptian Nubia, in 1961–1962, Semna, Sudanese Nubia, in 1962–1963, Kumma, Sudanese Nubia, from 1963 to 1965, and the Egypt Exploration Society expedition to Wadi el-Shatt el-Rigal in Upper Egypt in 1982–1983, copying and recording inscriptions. He wrote *The Shrines and Rock-inscriptions of Ibrim* (London, 1968) and *The New Kingdom Temples of Buhen* (London, 1974). *References*: *DAS*; *WWA*.

CAMP DAVID ACCORDS. Following secret negotiations and the visit of Anwar Sadat, president of Egypt, to Jerusalem on November 19–20, 1977, Sadat, Menachem Begin, Prime Minister of Israel, and President Jimmy Carter met at Camp David from September 5 to 17, 1978. On September 17 Sadat and Begin signed the Camp David Accords at the White House (witnessed by Carter), setting forth the outline for dealing with the West Bank and Gaza, and detailing the formula for reaching an Egyptian-Israeli peace treaty. Following additional negotiations, Begin and Sadat signed the Egyptian-Israel peace treaty in Washington on March 26, 1979. *Reference*: William R. Quandt, *Camp David: Peacemaking and Politics* (Washington, D.C., 1986).

CAMPBELL, EDWARD F(AY), JR. (1932–   ). Archaeologist, born January 5, 1932, in New Haven, Connecticut. Campbell graduated from Yale University, McCormick Theological Seminary, and Johns Hopkins University, and was ordained in 1956. He was an assistant pastor in Baltimore from 1956 to 1958, became a member of the faculty of McCormick Theological Seminary in 1958, and professor of Old Testament in 1966. He was acting director and annual professor of the Albright Institute in 1964–1965, vice president from 1967 to 1970, and president in 1970–1971. He was a staff member of the Drew-McCormick Joint Expedition to Shechem in 1957, 1960, 1962, and 1964, assistant director from 1960 to 1962, associate director in 1964, and archaeological director of the expedition in 1966 and 1968. *References*: *CA*; *DAS*; and *WWA*.

CAMPBELL, THOMAS DONALD (1881–1966). Agriculturist, mechanical and agricultural engineer, born February 19, 1881, in Grand Rapids, North Dakota. Campbell graduated from the University of North Dakota and Cornell University, and began farming in 1898. In 1922 he became president and chief engineer of the Campbell Farming Corporation which operated a wheat farm in Montana and a cattle ranch in New Mexico. He was a special adviser for the Russian government in 1929 and a special adviser to the British government in 1941. He served in North Africa in World War II and made a survey of its possible wheat production. He returned to North Africa in 1947–1948 at the request of the French government to advise farmers on problems of soil and moisture conservation and increased wheat production. He retired in 1961. Died March 18, 1966, in Pasadena, California. *References*: *NCAB* 54:86; *NYT*, March 19, 1966; and *WWWA*.

CAMPBELL, WILLIAM P.A. (–1874). Naval officer, born in Tennessee. Campbell graduated from the U.S. Naval Academy in 1853 and served in the Confederate Navy during the Civil War. He entered the Egyptian service in 1870 and, together with Alexander McComb Mason,* was in charge of the Egyptian government steamers between Alexandria and Constantinople. In 1874 he was appointed to the staff of General Charles Gordon on the Upper White Nile and was in charge of military stores at Gondokoro. Died October 10, 1874, in Khartoum, the Sudan. *References*: *Hesseltine*; *Hill*.

CANTINE, JAMES (1861–1940). Missionary, born March 3, 1861, in Stone Ridge, Ulster County, New York. Cantine graduated from Union College and New Brunswick Theological Seminary, and was ordained in 1889. One of the founders of the Arabian Mission,* he served as a missionary from 1889 to 1929. He toured parts of Iraq, Arabia, and Oman. He was later acting corresponding secretary of the Board of Foreign Missions of the Reformed Church of America,* and served a few years in the United Mission in Mesopotamia. He was co-author of *The Golden Milestone* (New York, 1938). Died July 1, 1940, in Kingston, New York. *References*: *MW* 30 (1940):331; *NYT*, July 2, 1940.

CARLETON, ALFORD (1903–1983). Missionary, born March 26, 1903, in Albany, New York. Carleton graduated from Oberlin College and Hartford Theological Seminary, was a tutor at St. Paul's College at Tarsus from 1924 to 1927, and was ordained in 1929. He became a missionary under the American Board of Commissions for Foreign Missions (ABCFM)* in the Middle East in 1930; was principal of a boy's high school in Aleppo, Syria, in 1931; acting principal of the American school for boys in Talas, Turkey, in 1934–1935; teacher at Tarsus College from 1935 to 1937; and president of Aleppo College* from 1937 to 1953. During World War II he served as regional director of the American Red Cross* in North Syria. He was elected executive vice president of ABCFM in 1954 and was leader of the United Church of Christ's Board for World Ministries from 1957 until his retirement in 1970. Died August 22, 1983, in Columbus, Ohio. Carleton published his memoirs, *Vagaries of a Missionary Career: Recollections and Reflections*, ed. J. Martin Bailey (New York, 1983). *Reference*: *NYT*, August 23, 1983.

CARPENTER, FRANK GEORGE (1855–1924). Journalist and traveler, born May 8, 1855, in Mansfield, Ohio. Carpenter graduated from the University of Wooster. He became legislative correspondent for the *Cleveland Leader* in 1879 and its Washington correspondent in 1882. He traveled to Europe and Egypt in 1881, and in 1888 he began traveling around the world, publishing a weekly foreign travel letter for a newspaper syndicate. He traveled in Africa in 1906–1907, going from Morocco to Egypt and from Cairo to the Cape, and traveled in Turkey, Palestine, and Egypt in 1909. He wrote *The Holy Land and Syria* (Garden City, N.Y., 1922), *Cairo to Kismu; Egypt-the Sudan-Kenya Colony* (Garden City, N.Y., 1923), and *Travels in Egypt and the Sudan; From Tangier to Tripoli: Morocco, Algeria, Tunisia, Tripoli, and the Sahara* (Garden City, N.Y., 1923). All his books included original photographs. Died June 18, 1924, in Nanking, China. *References*: Photographs collection, Prints and Photographs Division, Library of Congress; *DAB*; Milton Kaplan, "Africa Through the Eye of a Camera," *Quarterly Journal of the Library of Congress* 27 (1970): 222–237; *NYT*, June 18, 1924; and *WWWA*.

CARREL, MORTON D(REW) (1877–1955). Government official and businessman, born February 1, 1877, in Reading, Michigan. Carrel was a member of President Roosevelt's financial commission to the Dominican Republic in 1901–1902 and private secretary to the governor of Cuba. He became secretary of state for Puerto Rico in 1909 and was acting governor from 1912 to 1914. He later organized the Buenos Aires branch of the National City Bank of New York and was adviser on Latin American Affairs in the State Department in 1921–1922. From 1922–1932 he was vice president of Ulen and Company of New York in charge of business development in foreign countries. He went to Persia in 1928 and received the concession to construct the southern part of the

Trans-Persian Railway line. Died April 4, 1955, in Orlando, Florida. *References*: *NYT*, April 6, 1955.

CARROLL, CHARLES JOSEPH (1877–1941). Civil engineer, born September 18, 1877, in Barclay, near Towanda, Pennsylvania. Carroll graduated from the Sheffield Scientific School of Yale University, served on the construction staff of railway companies in Mexico from 1899 to 1911, had a consulting practice in Mexico and Texas, and worked in China from 1915 until 1927 as engineer-in-chief of the Hu-Kuand Railways in Central China. He went to Persia in 1927 as chief engineer of surveys for the railway administration of Persia, and was later director general and engineer-in-chief of the Southern Persian State Railway. He resigned in 1933. He was vice chairman of the American Economic Mission to China and Japan in 1935, and retired in 1936. Died July 9, 1941, in Jacksonville, Florida. *References*: *NCAB* 31:58; *NYT*, July 10, 1941.

CARTER, THERESA HOWARD (1929–   ). Archaeologist, born May 15, 1929, in Millbrook, New York. Carter graduated from Syracuse University, the University of Pennsylvania, and Bryn Mawr College. She was research assistant and research associate at the University Museum of the University of Pennsylvania from 1960 to 1964, annual professor at the American Schools of Oriental Research in Baghdad in 1965–1966, and research associate in the Near Eastern section of the University Museum after 1966. She directed the University of Pennsylvania excavations at Leptis Magna, Libya, in 1960–1961; was director of the coastal survey of Cyrenaica, Libya, in 1962; co-director of the Tell al-Rimah expedition to Northern Iraq from 1964 to 1966; and director of the Johns Hopkins University expeditions to the Syrian Euphrates Valley and to the Persian Gulf from 1972 to 1974. *References*: *DAS*; *WWAW*; and *WWA*.

CARTER DOCTRINE. Following the Soviet invasion of Afghanistan in December 1979, President Jimmy Carter announced the Carter Doctrine in January 1980. The doctrine acknowledged United States interests in the Persian Gulf Region. It declared that any attempt by any outside power to gain control of the Persian Gulf Region will be regarded as a threat to the vital interests of the United States which will respond to it by any means necessary, including military force. *Reference*: Cecil V. Crabb, Jr., *The Doctrines of American Foreign Policy: Their Meaning, Role, and Future* (Baton Rouge, La., 1982), ch. 8.

CARY, MAUDE (1878–1967). Missionary, born in Little Falls, Minnesota. Cary graduated from the Bible Institute in Kansas City. She was a missionary in Leavenworth, Kansas, and was the first woman missionary under the Gospel Missionary Union* in Morocco from 1901 until 1951. Died July 15, 1967, in Kansas City, Missouri. *Reference*: Evelyn Stenbock, *"Miss Terri": The Story of Maude Cary, Pioneer Gospel Union Missionary in Morocco* (Lincoln, Neb., 1970).

CASOC. *See* California Arabian Standard Oil Company.

CATHCART, JAMES LEANDER (1767–1843). Consul, born June 1, 1767, in Mount Murragh, County Westmeath, Ireland, and brought to the United States as a child. In 1779 Cathcart became a midshipman in the Continental Navy. In 1782 he entered the merchant service, and in 1785 his ship was captured by Algerian pirates and he was sold into slavery in Algiers. He became clerk of the Algerian Marine, clerk of the prison of the galley slaves and keeper of the prison tavern, and clerk to the prime minister. In 1792 he became chief Christian secretary to the Dey and Regency of Algiers. He was released in 1796 as a result of the negotiations conducted by Joseph Donaldson, Jr.* He was appointed consul in Tripoli in 1797 but did not proceed there. In 1798 he went as a special diplomatic agent to Tunis, proceeded to Tripoli in 1799 and obtained a settlement with the Pasha, but left Tripoli in 1801. He was appointed consul general to Algiers in 1802 and consul to Tunis in 1803, but was refused. He was later consul in Madeira from 1807 to 1815, and in Cadiz from 1815 to 1817, naval agent in Florida from 1818 to 1820, and was employed by the Treasury from 1820 until his death. He published a journal of his Algerian captivity. Died October 6, 1843, in Washington, D.C. *References*: *The Captives: Eleven Years a Prisoner in Algiers*, ed. Jane B. Newkirk (LaPorte, Ind., 1899) and *Tripoli . . . Letter-Book by James Leander Cathcart*, ed. Jane B. Newkirk (LaPorte, Ind., 1901); Papers, Manuscript Division, Library of Congress; New York Public Library. "The Diplomatic Journal and Letter Book of James Leander Cathcart, 1788–1796," *Proceedings of the American Antiquarian Society* 64, pt. 2 (1955): 303–436; *DAB*; and *WWWA*.

CENTRAL TURKEY COLLEGE, AINTAB. College for men, founded in 1874 in Aintab by Tillman Conklin Trowbridge.* Disrupted by World War I, it was transferred to Aleppo, reopened as a high school in 1924, and became Aleppo College* in 1927. *Reference*: *Stone*, ch. 7.

CESNOLA, LUIGI PALMA DI (1832–1904). Archaeologist, born June 29, 1832, in Rivarolo, near Turin, Italy. Cesnola graduated from the Royal Military Academy in Turin and served in the Sardinian Army. He came to the United States in 1860, served in the Civil War, and became a citizen in 1865. He was consul in Cyprus from 1865 to 1876, and at his own expense, pioneered in the excavation of archaeological sites on the island. Many of the objects he found were later bought by the Metropolitan Museum of Art and were described in *Handbook of the Cesnola Collection of Antiquities from Cyprus* by John L. Myers (New York, 1914). Cesnola was secretary of the Metropolitan Museum of Art in New York City from 1877 to 1879 and director of the museum from 1879 until his death. He wrote *Cyprus: Its Ancient Cities, Tombs, and Temples* (New York, 1878). Died November 20, 1904, in New York City. *References*: *ACAB*; *DAB*; Elizabeth McFadden, *The Glitter and the Gold: A Spirited Account* *of the Metropolitan Museum of Art's First Director, the Audacious and High-Handed Luigi Palma de Cesnola* (New York, 1971); *NCAB* I:422; *NYT*, November 22, 1904; and *WWWA*.

CHAILLÉ-LONG, CHARLES (1842–1917). Army officer and explorer, born July 2, 1842, in Princess Anne, Somerset County, Maryland. Chaillé-Long served in the Confederate Army in the Civil War. He joined the Egyptian Army in 1869, and in 1874 he was chief of staff to General Charles Gordon, governor of Equatoria Province in southern Sudan, who was suppressing the slave traffic in the region of the White Nile. The Khedive sent Chaillé-Long on a secret mission to King Mutesa of Uganda, and recorded his journey in *Central Africa: Naked Truths of Naked People; an Account of Expeditions to the Lake Victoria Nyanza and the Makrak Niam-Niam, West of the Bahr-el-Abiad (White Nile)* (London, 1876). On this journey he explored the Upper Nile basin. In 1875 he made another trip from Gondokoro, along the Congo-Nile divide region. He returned to the United States in 1877 because of ill health, studied law at Columbia University, and in 1882 went back to Alexandria, Egypt, where he practiced international law and acted as consul general in the absence of U.S. consular officials. He moved to Paris in 1882 and was engaged in international law. He wrote *The Three Prophets: Chinese Gordon, Mohammed-Ahmed (el Mahdi), Arabi Pasha. Events Before and After the Bombardment of Alexandria* (New York, 1884). From 1887 to 1889 he was consul general and secretary of legation in Korea. He wrote an autobiography, *My Life in Four Continents* (London, 1912). Died March 24, 1917, at Virginia Beach, Norfolk, Virginia. *References*: David Icenogle, "The Expeditions of Chaillé-Long," *AWM* 29 (November-December 1978): 2–7; *DAB*; *Hesseltine*; *NCAB* 10:28; *NYT*, March 26, 1917; *WAMB*; and *WWWA*.

CHAUNCEY, ISAAC (1772–1840). Naval officer, born February 20, 1772, in Black Rock, Fairfield County, Connecticut. Chauncey served in the merchant marine and was appointed a lieutenant in the navy in 1798. He commanded the frigate *Chesapeake* in Tripoli in 1802. He was commander of the New York Navy Yard and served in the War of 1812. From 1816 to 1818 he was commander of the Mediterranean Squadron and acting commissioner to conclude a treaty with Algiers. He was navy commissioner from 1820 to 1824, again commander of the New York Navy Yard from 1824 to 1833, and served on the Board of Navy Commissioners until his death. Died January 27, 1840, in Washington, D.C. *References*: *ACAB*; *DAB*; *DAMIB*; *NCAB* 8:95; *WAMB*; and *WWA*.

CHESTER, COLBY MITCHELL (1844–1932). Naval officer, born February 27, 1844, in New London, Connecticut. Chester graduated from the U.S. Naval Academy in 1863, served in the Pacific Squadron from 1869 to 1873, and was on duty in the Naval Academy from 1874 to 1877 and again from 1891 to 1894. He served in the Coast Survey and Hydrographic Office, and commanded the

Galena from 1885 to 1888 and the cruiser *Cincinnati* during the Spanish-American War. In 1900 he went to Constantinople in command of the cruiser *Kentucky* to support American damage claims. He was superintendent of the Naval Observatory from 1902 until his retirement in 1906. In 1908 Chester returned to Turkey and obtained concessions for a railway in eastern Anatolia and for petroleum and mineral rights. Died May 4, 1932, in Rye, New York. *References*: *ACAB*; *DAB S1*; *NCAB* 33:185; *NYT*, May 5, 1932; and *WWWA*.

CHESTER PROJECT. A program for railroad building and mineral development in Asiatic Turkey. Admiral Colby Mitchell Chester* visited Turkey in 1908 and applied for a contract to install a telephone system in Constantinople. In 1909 he organized the Ottoman-American Development Company. The project to build a railroad was defeated by German pressure. He revived the scheme in 1920 but without success. *Reference*: John A. DeNovo, ''A Railroad for Turkey: The Chester Project, 1908–1913,'' *Business History Review* 33 (1959): 300–329.

CHIERA, EDWARD (1885–1933). Orientalist, born August 5, 1885, in Rome, and came to the United States in 1907. Chiera graduated from Crozer Theological Seminary (Chester, Pa.) and the University of Pennsylvania. He was instructor, assistant professor, and professor of Assyriology at the University of Pennsylvania from 1913 to 1927, after which he became professor of Assyriology at the University of Chicago. He was research fellow at the Ottoman Museum in 1923 and annual professor at the American Schools of Oriental Research (ASOR)* in Baghdad in 1932–1933. In 1924–1925 and 1927–1928 he conducted excavations at Nuzi, Iraq, and in 1928–1929 he was director of the excavations at Khorsabad, Persia, for the Oriental Institute. Died June 20, 1933, in Chicago. His book *They Wrote on Clay: The Balylonian Tables Speak Today*, edited by G. G. Cameron, was published posthumously (Chicago, 1938). *References*: *DAB S1*; *NCAB* 24:152; and *WWWA*.

CHILDS, JAMES RIVES (1893–   ). Diplomat, born February 6, 1893, in Lynchburg, Virginia. Childs graduated from Randolph-Macon College and Harvard University, served in World War I and later on the military staff of the U.S. Commission to Negotiate Peace. He was correspondent for the Associated Press from 1919 to 1921, and assistant and then supervisor of the Kazan District for the American Relief Administration in Russia from 1921 to 1923. He entered the diplomatic service in 1923, was consul in Jerusalem and Bucharest, second secretary in Cairo, Teheran, and again in Cairo, and served in the Division of Near Eastern Affairs from 1937 to 1941. He was chargé d'affaires in Tunis and chargé d'affaires ad interim in Morocco from 1941 until 1945; minister to Saudi Arabia and Yemen from 1946 until 1949; first ambassador to Saudi Arabia in 1949–1950; and ambassador to Ethiopia from 1951 until his retirement in 1953. Under the pseudonym Henry Filmer, he wrote *The Pageant of Persia: A Record of Travel by Motor in Persia With an Account of Its Ancient and Modern Days*

(Indianapolis, 1936), and *Escape to Cairo* (Indianapolis, 1938), a novel. He wrote an autobiography, *Foreign Service Farewell: My Years in the Near East* (Charlottesville, Va., 1969), and *Vignettes, or Autobiographical Fragments* (New York, 1977). In 1966 he became scholar in residence at Randolph-Macon College. *References*: Papers, University of Virginia Library; *WWA*.

CHRISTIAN AND MISSIONARY ALLIANCE: FOREIGN DEPART-MENT. Formed in 1897 by the union of the Christian Alliance and the International Missionary Alliance, both of which were established in 1887. The International Missionary Alliance established the Jerusalem Faith Mission in Jerusalem in 1890. It also established stations in Hebron, Jaffa, and Safed. The Alliance constructed the first American church in Jerusalem. *References*: Robert B. Ekvall et al., *After Fifty Years: A Record of God's Working Through the Christian and Missionary Alliance* (Harrisburg, Pa., 1939), ch. xi; James H. Hunter, *Beside All Waters: The Story of Seventy-five Years of World-wide Ministry of the Christian and Missionary Alliance* (Harrisburg, Pa., 1964).

CHRISTIE, THOMAS DAVIDSON (1843–1921). Missionary educator born January 21, 1843, in Sion Mills, County Tyrone, Ireland, and brought to the United Sates as an infant. Christie served in the Civil War, graduated from the University of Wisconsin, Beloit College, and Andover Theological Seminary, and was ordained in 1877. He was a missionary under the American Board of Commissioners for Foreign Missions (ABCFM)* in Turkey, professor of church history and New Testament Greek at Marash Theological Seminary from 1877 and 1893, and president of St. Paul's College,* Tarsus, from 1893 until 1915. He traveled in the Taurus Mountains and carried relief work among the Armenians following the 1909 massacre. Christie was compelled to leave Turkey in July 1915. He served as a pastor in southern California until he returned to Tarsus in 1919. Died May 25, 1921, in Pasadena, California. *References*: Christie family Papers, Minnesota Historical Society Collections; *AndoverTS*; *NCAB* 19:217; *NYT*, May 27, 1921; and *WWWA*.

CHURCH, FREDERIC EDWIN (1826–1900). Painter, born May 4, 1826, in Hartford, Connecticut. Church studied art with Thomas Cole from 1844 to 1848. In 1853 and again in 1857 he visited Ecuador and Colombia, in 1855 Panama and Jamaica, and in 1859 Newfoundland and Labrador. From 1867 until 1869 he traveled in Europe, and in 1868 he traveled and painted in the Middle East. He was the first American painter to paint Petra. He later lived in Olana in the Hudson Valley. Died April 7, 1900, in New York City. *References*: "Diary," Ms. in private hands; *ACAB*; *DAB*; Elaine E. Dee, *To Embrace the Universe: Drawings by Frederic Edwin Church* (Yonkers, N.Y., 1984); David C. Huntington, *The Landscapes of Frederic Edwin Church: Vision of an American Era* (New York, 1966); *NCAB* 20:291; and *NYHSD*.

CHURCH OF GOD, MISSIONARY BOARD (ANDERSON, INDIANA). Founded in 1881. The Church of God began its missionary work in the Middle East in 1908 when its first missionary went to Egypt. It began missionary activities in Syria in 1912. *References*: Lester A. Crose, *Passport for a Reformation: A History of the Church of God Movement's Missionary Endeavors Outside North America* (Anderson, Ind., 1981); Albert F. Gray, *Church of God Missions Abroad* (Anderson, Ind., 1929).

CLAGUE, RICHARD (1821–1873). Painter, probably born in Paris while his parents were visiting there, and grew up in New Orleans. In 1832 Clague moved back to Paris and then studied art in Switzerland. From 1844 until 1857 he lived, studied, and exhibited in Paris. In 1856 he joined Ferdinand de Lesseps on a French expedition to Egypt to plan the digging of the Suez Canal, serving as the expedition's draftsman. In 1857 he returned to New Orleans and served in the Confederate Army during the Civil War. Died in New Orleans. *References*: *NYHSD*; Roulhac Toledano, *Richard Clague, 1821–1873* (New Orleans, 1974).

CLAPP, FREDERICK GARDNER (1879–1944). Consulting geologist, born July 20, 1879, in Boston. Clapp graduated from Massachusetts Institute of Technology. He was a geologist with the U.S. Geological Survey from 1902 to 1908, and in 1908 he became a consulting geologist and petroleum geologist specializing in reports on oil and gas properties. He was managing geologist of the Associated Geological Engineers from 1912 to 1918, and later its chief geologist. He was petroleum and natural gas expert for the Canadian Department of Mines from 1911 to 1915, in charge of geological explorations in China from 1913 to 1915, and in Australia and New Zealnd from 1923 to 1925. He was petroleum adviser to the Persian government in 1927, 1928, and 1933; conducted oil explorations in Iran and Afghanistan from 1935 to 1938 for the Amiranian Oil Company and the Inland Exploration Company; and supervised a reconnaissance of Afghanistan for Seabord Oil Company in 1937–1938. He published several articles describing his surveys in the Middle East and wrote on the geology of Eastern Iran. He supervised oil operations in Oklahoma from 1939 to 1943. Died February 18, 1944, in Chickasha, Oklahoma. *References*: *BAAPG* 29 (1945): 402–409; *Economic Geology* 39 (1944): 248–249; *NCAB* 32:355; and *WWWA*.

CLAPP, GORDON RUFUS (1905–1963). Government official, born October 28, 1905, in Ellsworth, Wisconsin. Clapp graduated from Lawrence College and the University of Chicago. He joined the Tennessee Valley Authority in 1933 as assistant director of personnel, becoming director of personnel in 1936, general manager in 1939, and chairman of the board in 1946. In 1954–1955 he was deputy city administrator of New York City. In 1955 he became president of Development and Resources Corporation, a private consulting engineering firm, which he headed until his death. In 1949 he headed the United Nations

Economic Survey Mission for the Middle East (Clapp Mission) to study its economic problems. The final report was published in 1949, and he summarized it in the April 1950 issue of *International Conciliation*. Died April 28, 1963, in New York City. *References*: *CB* 1947; *NCAB* 49:296; *NYT*, April 29, 1963; and *WWWA*.

CLARK, EUGENIE (1922–   ). Ichthyologist, born May 4, 1922, in New York City. Clark graduated from Hunter College and New York University. She was assistant ichthyologist at the Scripps Institute of Oceanography in 1946–1947 and the New York Zoological Society in 1947–1948; assistant in animal behavior at the American Museum of Natural History in 1947–1948; and research associate from 1950 to 1966. In 1951 she conducted research at the Marine Biological Station at Ghardaqa on the Red Sea, published papers in the journal of Egypt's Marine biological Station, articles on the Red Sea in the *National Geographic Magazine*, and wrote a memoir, *Lady with a Spear* (New York, 1953). Clark made seventeen trips to the Red Sea for scientific study. She was director of marine biology at the Cape Haze Marine Laboratory from 1955 to 1966, associate professor at the University of Maryland from 1969 to 1973, and professor of zoology in 1973. *References*: *AMWS*; *CA*; *CB* 1953; Anne LaBastille, *Women and Wilderness* (San Francisco, 1980), pp. 159–172; *WWA*; and *WWAW*.

CLARK, HARLAN B(ENDELL) (1913–   ). Diplomat, born January 5, 1913, in Brookfield, Ohio. Clark graduated from Michigan State College and Fletcher School of Law and Diplomacy, entered the foreign service in 1937, and served in Zurich, Birmingham, Bangkok, Capetown, and Pretoria. He was principal officer in Aden from 1944 to 1946. In 1945 he was member and administrative officer of the special diplomatic mission to Yemen, and reported on this trip in the November 1947 issue of *National Geographic Magazine*. He was deputy chief of mission in Jiddah in 1946–1947 and second secretary and consul in San'a; deputy chief of mission in Syria from 1951 to 1954; political officer and consul general in Japan from 1957 to 1959; consul general in Alexandria from 1960 to 1964; counselor, consul general, and chargé d'affaires with the rank of minister in Yemen from 1964 to 1966; and diplomatic adviser to the commandant of the Army War College from 1967 until his retirement in 1970. *Reference*: *BRDS*.

CLARK, HERBERT EDGAR (1856?–1921). Tourist guide. Clark went to Palestine in 1866 with his family who were members of the American Colony* in Jaffa. His father died soon after, but his mother remained in Palestine. He moved to Jerusalem, became involved in tourism, was agent for Thomas Cook & Son, and was named vice-consul in Jerusalem. He collected antiquities which are now exhibited in the Young Men's Christian Association (YMCA)* in Jerusalem.

CLARK, KENNETH WILLIS (1898–1979). New Testament scholar, born January 11, 1898, in New York City. Clark graduated from Yale University and Colgate-Rochester Divinity School, and was ordained in 1926. He was a pastor in 1926–1927, and instructor, assistant professor, associate professor, and from 1945 until 1979, a professor of New Testament at the Divinity School of Duke University. He was annual professor in the American Schools of Oriental Research (ASOR)* in Jerusalem in 1949–1950; director of the microfilm expedition to the Greek Patriarchal Library in Jerusalem in 1949–1950; and general editor of the expedition to St. Catherine's Monastery on Mount Sinai in 1950. He conducted the microfilm project of New Testament manuscripts in Sinai and Jerusalem and was general editor of the microfilm project. Died July 27, 1979, in Durham, North Carolina. *References*: *DAS*; *WWWA*.

CLARK, LEWIS (1895–1978). Diplomat, born November 16, 1895, in Montgomery, Alabama. Clark graduated from the University of Virginia and served in the navy during World War I. He was clerk and manager of a cotton firm from 1919 to 1922; entered the foreign service in 1925, serving in Peking, Hankow, Peiping, and Paris; was second secretary and consul, first secretary, consul general, and counselor in Ottawa from 1941 to 1945; and counselor in London in 1946 and in Nanking in 1947. In 1951–1952 he was American commissioner to Libya and the American representative, with the personal rank of ambassador, on the Council for Libya, which helped the people of Libya to formulate a constitution and establish an independent government. Clark was consul general in Algiers from 1953 until his retirement in 1957. Died October 28, 1978. *References*: *BRDS*; Adrian Pelt, *Libyan Independence and the United Nations: A Case of Planned Decolonization* (New Haven, Conn., 1970).

CLARK, STANLEY PENRHYN (1883– ?). Agriculturist, born May 14, 1883, in Wakefield, Kansas. Clark graduated from Kansas State Agricultural College. He was superintendent of the Branch Experimental Farm in Colby, Kansas, from 1914 to 1918, and assistant agronomist at the University of Arizona Agricultural Experimental Station, Tucson, from 1919 until 1931. He was employed by the Turkish government from 1931 to 1940, and worked in the Seed Improvement Station at Adana to improve cotton production and quality. He wrote *Crop Experiments, 1934 to 1940: Seed Improvement Station, Adana, Turkey* (Beirut, 1941).

CLARK, WALLACE (1880–1948). Consulting engineer, born July 27, 1880, in Cincinnati, Ohio. Clark was employed by the Remington Typewriter Company from 1907 to 1917, was staff engineer with the H. L. Gantt Company in 1919–1920, served as head of the scheduling division of the U.S. Shipping Board in 1918, and became head of Wallace Clark and Company, industrial and engineering consultants, in 1920. He was a member of the Kammerer Finance Commission to Poland in 1920, made a survey of the Turkish tobacco, alcohol, and salt monopolies in 1933 and, when the study was completed, was engaged by the Turkish government to implement his recommendations in 1933–1934. Died July 4, 1948, in New York City. *References*: *NCAB* 36:80; *NYT*, July 5, 1948; and *WWWA*.

CLARY, (CORA A.) PHOEBE (1894–   ). Association official, born October 25, 1894, in Syracuse, New York. Clary graduated from Syracuse University, was a teacher in Roxbury, South Byron, and South Syracuse, New York, from 1916 to 1923, and served at the Young Women's Christian Association (YWCA) in Johnstown, Pennsylvania, from 1923 to 1927. She went to Turkey in 1927 as a field worker for the YWCA and was executive director of the Istanbul Service Center for Girls of the YWCA from 1932 until 1945. She wrote a memoir, *When Latticed Windows Opened: Experiences of an American in Turkey* (as told to Marion O. Robinson) (New York, 1969). In 1955 she conducted a survey of the needs of girls and women in Ethiopia and was later executive director of the YWCA in White Plains, New York. *Reference*: *WWAW*.

CLAY, ALBERT TOBIAS (1866–1925). Orientalist, born December 4, 1866, in Hanover, Pennsylvania. Clay graduated from Franklin and Marshall College, Mount Airy Theological Seminary, and the University of Pennsylvania, and was ordained in 1893. He taught Assyriology and Hebrew at the University of Pennsylvania from 1892 to 1895, Old Testament theology at the Chicago Lutheran Seminary from 1895 to 1899, and Hebrew at Mount Airy Theological Seminary from 1905 to 1910. He was lecturer in Hebrew, Assyrian, and Semitic archaeology from 1899 to 1903; assistant professor from 1903 to 1909; professor of Semitic philology and archaeology at the University of Pennsylvania in 1909–1910; and assistant curator of Babylonian and Semitic antiquities from 1899 to 1910. He was professor of Assyriology and Babylonian literature at Yale University from 1910 until his death and curator of the Yale Babylonian collection. He was annual professor of the American Schools of Oriental Research (ASOR)* in Jerusalem in 1919–1920, was instrumental in establishing the Oriental Society of Palestine in Jerusalem, and was sent to Iraq by the Mesopotamian Committee of the Archaeological Institute of America to ascertain the practicability of establishing an American School of Oriental Research in Iraq. He was the first annual professor in Baghdad in 1923–1924. Died September 14, 1925, in New Haven, Connecticut. *References*: *DAB*; Albrecht Goetze, "Professor Clay and the Amurrite Problem," *Yale University Library Gazette* 36 (1962): 133–137; *NCAB* 22:130; *NYT*, September 15, 1925; and *WWWA*.

CLELAND, (WILLIAM) WENDELL (1888–1972). Educator, born December 14, 1888, in Aledo, Illinois. Cleland graduated from Westminster College (New Wilmington, Pa.), Princeton and Columbia universities, and the New York School of Social Work. He was educational secretary to the United Presbyterian Church of North America Board of Foreign Missions* in Philadelphia from 1911 to 1913, and secretary to the comptroller of the state of New York in Albany from 1915 to 1917. In 1917 Cleland went to Cairo to help organize the American University in Cairo,* and became a member of its faculty. In World War I he aided in the distribution of the Syrian-Palestinian Relief funds, was later captain in the American Red Cross,* and served in Jerusalem and Syria. From 1920 to 1925 he was the bursar of the university, and in 1924 he established its Division of Public Service and was its director until 1947. He was also involved in the activities of the Division of Extension. He taught sociology and helped found the Cairo School of Social Work. Cleland studied poverty in Egypt and wrote *The Population Problem of Egypt: A Study of Population Trends and Conditions in Modern Egypt* (Lancaster, Pa., 1936). During World War II he served in the Office of War Information, and from 1947 to 1958 in the State Department. In 1954 he was acting president of the American University in Cairo. He was professor of Middle East Studies in the School of International Service in the American University (Washington, D.C.) from 1954 to 1958. Died December 2, 1972, in Highland Park, Illinois. *References*: *CA*; *NCAB* 57:593; and *NYT*, December 4, 1972.

CLEMENT, CLARA ERSKINE. *See* Waters, Clara Erskine Clement.

CLERGUE, FRANCIS HECTOR (1856–1939). Businessman, born May 28, 1856, in Bangor, Maine. Clergue graduated from the University of Maine and was admitted to the bar in 1877. In 1880 he became involved in manufacturing and hydraulic engineering, and in 1881 he organized the first electric railway in Maine. He went to Teheran, Persia, in 1888 as representative of the Persia Company seeking concessions to build railroads and establish industrial enterprises. In 1889 he received a sixty-year general electric concession for all of Persia which was never implemented. He was later involved in banking in Mobile, Alabama, became president of Lake Superior Power Company, Algoma Steel Company, and Algoma Central Railway in 1904, and began the development of the hydraulic power of the Falls of St. Mary at Sault Ste. Marie, Michigan, and Ontario. Died January 19, 1939, in Montreal, Canada. *References*: *NYT*, January 20, 1939; *WWWA*.

CLEVELAND, RAY L(EROY) (1929–   ). Archaeologist, born April 29, 1929, in Scotbluff, Nebraska. Cleveland graduated from Westmont College and Johns Hopkins University. He was research associate in Arabian archaeology at Johns Hopkins University from 1956 to 1964 and a research fellow in Jordan from 1964 to 1966. In 1958 he conducted excavations in Sohar in Oman, and in 1960 he led an archaeological expedition to Dhofar in Oman. He wrote *The Excavation of the Conway High Place (Petra) and Soundings at Khirbet Ader* (New Haven, Conn., 1960), and *An Ancient South Arabian Necropolis* (Baltimore, 1965). In 1967 he became associate professor of history at the University of Saskatchewan (Regina), was professor from 1971 to 1974, and professor of history at the University of Regina after 1974. *References*: *CA*; *DAS*.

COAN, GEORGE WHITEFIELD (1817–1879). Missionary, born December 30, 1817, in Bergen, Genesee County, New York. Coan graduated from Williams College and Union Theological Seminary, and was ordained in 1849. He served as a missionary under the American Board of Commissioners for Foreign Missions (ABCFM)* in Persia from 1849 until 1874. Died December 21, 1879, in Wooster, Ohio. His son, **FREDERICK GAYLORD COAN (1859–1943)**, a missionary, was born May 23, 1859, in Urmia, Persia. He graduated from Wooster University and Western and Princeton theological seminaries, and was ordained in 1885. He served as a missionary in Persia from 1885 until 1904. He was stationed at Salmas in 1885–1886, at Urmia from 1886 to 1916, and at Hamadan from 1920 to 1923. He was in charge of Urmia College and was superintendent of village schools from 1904 to 1912. He traveled in Persia, Turkey, and parts of Arabia. He retired in 1932 and published his memoirs, *Yesterdays in Persia and Kurdistan* (Claremont, Calif., 1939). Died March 23, 1943, in Shreve, Ohio. *References*: *EM*; *Hewitt*; *NYT*, March 24, 1943; and *WWWA*.

COBB, STANWOOD (1881–1982). Educator, born November 6, 1881, in Newton Highlands, Massachusetts. Cobb graduated from Dartmouth College and Harvard Divinity School, and joined the Baha'i faith in 1906. He was an instructor in English and Latin at Robert College* from 1907 to 1910. He wrote *The Real Turk* (Boston, 1914), a study of social life and customs, and *Ayesha of the Bosphorus: A Romance of Constantinople* (Boston, 1914), a novel. He taught in Annapolis, Maryland, and Asheville, North Carolina, from 1911 to 1913, and at the U.S. Naval Academy from 1914 to 1919. He founded the Chevy Chase Country Day School in 1919 and was its principal until his retirement in 1961. He wrote *A Saga of Two Centuries: Autobiography* (Washington, D.C., 1979). Died December 28, 1982, in Chevy Case, Maryland. *References*: *DAEB*; *Washington Post*, January 1, 1983; and *WWWA*.

COCHRAN, JOHN WEBSTER (1814–   ?   ). Inventor, born May 16, 1814, in Enfield, New Hampshire. In 1832 Cochran moved to Boston and patented a steam-heating apparatus, and in 1834 he invented a revolving, breech-loading rifled cannon. He visited France in 1835 and showed his invention to the Turkish ambassador in Paris. He was invited by Sultan Mahmud to Constantinople, and he remained in Turkey several years. He lived in France from 1839 to 1847, and later in England. After his return to the United States, Cochran was engaged in the manufacture of firearms and projectiles. *References*: *ACAB*; *NCAB* 11:269.

COCHRAN, JOSEPH GALLUP (1817–1871). Missionary, born February 5, 1817, in Springville, New York. Cochran graduated from Amherst College and Union Theological Seminary, and was ordained in 1847. He was a missionary under the American Board of Commissioners for Foreign Missions (ABCFM)* to the Nestorians from 1847 to 1871. He was stationed in Erzurum from 1847 to 1848, taught at the male seminary at Mount Seir from 1851 to 1857, and was its principal from 1857 until 1865. He was a voluminous author and translator in the Syriac and prepared textbooks in that language. He wrote *The Persian Flower: A Memoir of Judith Perkins of Oroomiah, Persia* (Boston, 1853). Died November 21, 1871, near Urmia, Persia. *References*: *Amherst*; *AndoverTS*; and *EM*.

COCHRAN, JOSEPH PLUMB (1855–1905). Medical missionary, son of Joseph Gallup Cochran,* born in Persia. Cochran graduated from Yale College, Buffalo Medical College, and Bellevue Medical College (New York City). He served as a missionary under the Presbyterian Church in the U.S.A. Board of Foreign Missions* in Persia from 1878 until 1905. He built Westminster Hospital, the first American hospital in Persia, in 1890, and trained several Persian assistants as doctors. Died August 18, 1905, in Urmia, Persia. *References*: *EM*; Robert E. Speer, *"The Hakim Sahib," The Foreign Doctor: A Biography of Joseph Plumb Cochran, M.D. of Persia* (New York, 1911).

COCHRANE, HENRY CLAY (1842–1913). Marine corps officer, born November 7, 1842, in Chester, Pennsylvania. Cochrane was appointed second lieutenant in 1861 and served as marine officer in the Civil War. He commanded the arsenal in Washington, D.C., in 1881, and was fleet marine officer of the European squadron from 1881 to 1884. In 1882 he was present at the British bombardment of Alexandria and assisted in the reestablishment of the U.S. consulate. He served in the Spanish-American War and in the Boxer Rebellion. He retired in 1905 with the rank of brigadier general. Died April 28, 1913, in New York City. *References*: Papers and diary, Marine Corps History and Museums Division, Washington, D.C.; *DAB*; *NCAB* 17:133; *NYT*, April 28, 1913; and *WWWA*.

COHEN, MENDES ISRAEL (1796–1879). Banker, traveler, and collector, born in Baltimore. Cohen served in the War of 1812 and retired from his family's banaking business in 1829. In 1832 he made a tour of the Middle East, visiting Egypt, sailing up the Nile, and reaching the second Cataract at Wadi Halfa, the first American to enter the Nile Valley and to explore it. He constructed an American flag, believed to be the first ever flown upon the Nile. He purchased antiquities, brought nearly 700 objects back to the United States, and founded the first American collection of Egyptian antiquities. He placed his collection at the disposal of George Robins Gliddon* in 1845. After Cohen's death the collection passed to his nephews who presented it to Johns Hopkins University in

1884. *References*: Dairy and papers, Maryland Historical Society; Lynn Poole, "Cohen's First Out of Egypt," *Art News* 47 (1949): 38–39; and *WWWE*.

COLMAN, SAMUEL, JR. (1832–1920). Painter, born March 4, 1832, in Portland, Maine. Colman studied art in New York City, opened a studio there, and then studied in Paris and Spain. Between 1871 and 1875 he toured Algeria, Morocco, and Egypt. In his later years he lived in Newport, Rhode Island. Died March 20, 1920, in New York City. *References*: Wayne Craven, "Samuel Colman (1832–1920): Rediscovered Painter of Far-away Places," *American Art Journal* 8 (May 1976): 16–37; *DAB*; *NCAB* 7:546; *NYHSD*; and *WWWA*.

COLSTON, RALEIGH EDWARD (1825–1896). Soldier, born October 31, 1825 in Paris to American parents, and came to America in 1842. Colston graduated from the Virginia Military Institute in 1846 and remained there as an assistant professor, becoming a professor in 1854. He served in the Confederate Army in the Civil War, and later conducted a private military school. In 1874 he was appointed to the Egyptian General Staff and served in Egypt and the Sudan until 1878. He conducted exploring an expedition to the Nubian Desert and to Kordofan. Colston was seriously injured by a fall from a camel and handed over the command of the expedition to Henry Goslee Prout.* The results were reported in the publications of the Egyptian General Staff. He returned to the United States in 1878, and was clerk in the War Department until 1894. Died July 29, 1896, in Richmond, Virginia. *References*: Papers and diary, Southern Historical Collection, University of North Carolina; *ACAB*; *BDC*; *DAB*; *Hesseltine*; *Hill*; *NCAB* 12:122; and *WWWA*.

COLT, HARRIS DUNSCOMB (1901–1973). Archaeologist, born January 29, 1901, in New York City. Colt traveled widely. In 1921 he excavated at Richborough, Kent, England, and later in Malta. He participated in Flinders Petrie's excavations in the Negev in Palestine from 1919 to 1932, and provided the financial backing for James L. Starkey's expedition to Tell ed Duweir (Lachish) in 1932–1933. He was director of the Colt Archaeological Expedition to investigate the ruins of Byzantine cities in the Negev from 1935 to 1937, and excavated at Nessana. He established the Colt Archaeological Institute, and he wrote *Colt Archaeological Expedition, 1936–1937* (London, 1950) and *Excavations in Nessana* (Princeton, N.J., 1950; Jerusalem, 1962). He was also a student of the engraving art. Died November 8, 1973. *Reference*: *Proceedings of the American Antiquarian Society* 84, pt. 1 (1974): 21–24.

COLT, JAMES W(OOD) (1858?–1941). Railroad construction engineer, born in Geneseo, New York. Colt entered the railroad business in St. Paul, Minnesota, became a partner in the contracting firm of Shepard, Selmes and Company, and participated in the construction of various railroads. In 1909 he went to Turkey as field representative of the Ottoman-American Development Company, promoting a proposed railway to run from central Asia Minor to the Persian border, and a survey of the territory through which the proposed railway would pass. He later moved to Santa Barbara, California. Died February 17, 1941, in Geneseo, New York. *Reference*: *NYT*, February 18, 1941.

COLTON, WALTER (1797–1851). Naval chaplain and journalist, born May 9, 1797, in Rutland County, Vermont. Colton graduated from Yale College and Andover Theological Seminary, and was ordained in 1825. From 1828 to 1830 he was editor of *The American Spectator and Washington City Chronicle*, and in 1831 he became a naval chaplain. He traveled in the Middle East from 1832 to 1835, and wrote *Ship and Shore: or, Leaves from the Journal of a Cruise to the Levant* (New York, 1835), and *A Visit to Constantinople and Athens* (New York, 1836). He traveled to the Pacific in 1845, became chief judge of Monterey, California, and established *The Californian* in 1846. Died January 22, 1851, in Philadelphia. *References*: *ACAB*; *AndoverTS*; *DAB*; *NYHSD*; and *WWWA*.

CONNOLLY, DONALD H(ILARY) (1880–1969). Army officer, born February 11, 1880, in Fort Mojave, Arizona. Connolly graduated from the U.S. Military Academy in 1910, after which he served as district engineer on several rivers and harbors projects. He was administrator of the Los Angeles Civil Works Administration in 1934 and of the Works Progress Administration in Los Angeles from 1935 to 1939, corps engineer of the Ninth Army Corps in 1939–1940, and administrator of civil aeronautics in the Department of Commerce from 1940 to 1942. He was commanding general of the Persian Gulf Command* from 1942 to 1944. He retired in 1948 with the rank of major general and was director of the Baltimore Department of Aviation from 1948 to 1956. Died June 18, 1969, in Fort Meade, Maryland. *Reference*: *WWWA*.

CONSTANTINOPLE WOMAN'S COLLEGE. *See* American College for Girls, Constantinople.

COOLEY, JOHN K(ENT) (1927–   ). Journalist, born November 25, 1927, in New York City. Cooley studied at the universities of Zurich and Vienna, Dartmouth College, and the New School of Social Research, and served in the Signal Corps in 1947–1948. He was a freelance reporter from 1949 to 1957, editor of a weekly newspaper for construction workers on the U.S. air base in Ben Guerir, Morocco, in 1953, and served with the Army Engineers in Nouassaeur, Morocco, from 1955 to 1957. He was a special correspondent for the *Christian Science Monitor* in North Africa from 1958 to 1964 and became its Middle East correspondent in 1965, based in Beirut. He wrote *Baal, Christ, and Mohammed: Religion and Revolution in North Africa* (New York, 1965), *Green March, Black September: The Story of the Palestinian Arabs* (London, 1973), and *Libyan Sandstorm* (New York, 1982). *References*: *CA*; *WWA*.

COON, CARLETON (STEVENS) (1904–1981). Anthropologist, born June 23, 1904, in Wakefield, Massachusetts. Coon graduated from Harvard University. He taught at Harvard University from 1934 to 1948, was later curator of ethnology at the University Museum, Philadelphia, and professor of anthropology at the University of Pennsylvania until his retirement in 1963. From 1924 to 1928 he conducted fieldwork among the Riffian tribes of Morocco, and wrote *Tribes of the Rif* (Cambridge, Mass., 1932), and two works of fiction, *Flesh of the Wild Ox* (New York, 1932) and *The Riffian* (Boston, 1933). In 1933–1934 he conducted anthropological measurements in Aden, Yeman, and Hadramaut, described in *Measuring Ethiopia and a Flight into Arabia* (Boston, 1935). During World War II Coon served with the Office of Strategic Services in North Africa, and recounted his experiences in *A North African Story: The Anthropologist as OSS Agent 1941–1943* (Ipswich, Mass., 1980). He later conducted several expeditions and excavated caves in Iraq, Iran, Afghanistan, the Syrian Desert, and Saudi Arabia, and wrote *The Seven Caves: Archeological Explorations in the Middle East* (New York, 1957). He also wrote *Caravan* (New York, 1951). Died June 4, 1981, in Gloucester, Massachusetts. His autobiography, *Adventures and Discoveries* (Englewood Cliffs, N.J., 1981), appeared after his death. *References*: AJPA 58 (1982): 239–241; AMWS; CA; CB 1955; McGraw-Hill Modern Scientists and Engineers (New York, 1980); NCAB I:108; NYT; June 6, 1981.

COOPER, CLAYTON SEDGWICK (1869–1936). Author and lecturer, born May 24, 1869, in Henderson, New York. Cooper graduated from Brown University and Union and Rochester theological seminaries, and was ordained in 1898. He was a pastor in Lynn, Massachusetts, until 1902, and college secretary for Bible study for the United States and Canada for the International Committee of Young Men's Christian Association (YMCA) from 1902 to 1909. He traveled in Egypt in 1912–1913, investigating educational and industrial conditions, lived among the bedouins in the Libyan Desert, and wrote *The Man of Egypt* (New York, 1913). From 1918 to 1922 he was editorial director of publications for W. R. Grace and Company. In 1927 he made another industrial survey of North Africa and the Middle East. He later lived in Miami Beach, Florida. Died October 13, 1936, in Rochester, Minnesota. His wife, **ELIZABETH (GOODNOW) COOPER (1877–1945)**, an author, born May 10, 1877, in Homer, Iowa. She worked in the Greenwich Settlement in New York City and with the Immigration Commission in 1908–1909. She lived for ten years in Shanghai, made extensive trips in the Far East, and completed two trips around the world, studying the status of women in Oriental lands. She wrote *The Women of Egypt* (New York, 1914) and *The Harim and the Purdah: Studies of Oriental Women* (New York, 1915). Died in Sarasota, Florida. *References*: NCAB 27:209; WWWA.

COOPER, HUGH LINCOLN (1865–1937). Hydrological engineer, born April 28, 1865, in Seldon, Minnesota. In 1883 Cooper became involved with several bridge engineering projects, but in 1895 he began his association with hydroelectric power development, and in 1905 established his own firm, Hugh L. Cooper and Company. He designed and supervised hydroelectric projects in Mexico, Brazil, Chile, Canada, and the United States. He was involved in the beginnings of the Tennessee Valley Authority and served as a consultant to the Soviet government. In 1914 he was a consultant to the Egyptian government on the practicability of using the Nile water at the Aswan Dam for power, and in 1928 he was a member of a committee of experts which advised the Egyptian government on the projected heightening of the Aswan Dam and formulated the plans for this project. Died June 24, 1937, in Stamford, Connecticut. *References*: *DAB S2*; *NCAB* 33:172; and *WWWA*.

COOPER, MERIAN C. (1894–1973). Motion picture director, producer, and author, born October 24, 1894, in Jacksonville, Florida. Cooper attended the U.S. Naval Academy, and served as a pilot in World War I and in the Kosciusko Squadron in Poland in 1920. He traveled as a newspaper and magazine correspondent, making motion pictures. In 1924–1925 he traveled to Persia to record the annual tribal migration of the Bakhtiary tribe. He spent six months with the tribe, producing the documentary film *Grass* which was released in 1925. He also wrote *Grass* (New York, 1925). Cooper was later vice president in charge of production for MGM and for Columbia Pictures. He was the creator of *King Kong* and produced other movies for RKO. Died April 21, 1973, in San Diego, California. *References*: Davis Thompson, *Biographical Dictionary of Film*, 2nd ed. (New York, 1981); *Cinema, a Critical Dictionary: The Major Film Makers*, ed. Richard Roud (New York, 1980) 2:910–917; *NYT*, April 22, 1973; and *WWWA*.

COPELAND, MILES (1916–   ). Intelligence agent, born July 16, 1916, in Birmingham, Alabama. Copeland was a jazz arranger for several bands during the 1930s. He served in the army and in the Office of Strategic Services during World War II, worked for the Department of Defense as a specialist in intelligence matters from 1945 to 1947 and from 1950 to 1953, and was political attaché in Beirut from 1947 to 1950. He was management consultant with Booz-Allen and Hamilton and Central Intelligence Agency officer in Cairo from 1953 to 1955; consultant to the Department of State from 1955 to 1957; and senior partner with Kermit Roosevelt Associates in 1957. He was later chairman of the board of Interser, New York, and president of SCOPE Ltd., Geneva, Switzerland. He wrote *The Game of Nations: The Amorality of Power Politics* (New York, 1969), and *Without Cloak or Dagger: The Truth about the New Espionage* (New York, 1974). *Reference*: *CA*.

COWDERY, JONATHAN (1767–1852). Naval surgeon, born April 22, 1767, in Sandisfield, Massachusetts. Cowdery was appointed an assistant surgeon in the navy in 1800 and surgeon in 1804. He served on the frigate *Philadelphia***** which was lost in Tripoli in 1804 and was prisoner in Tripoli for nearly two years. On his return he published the journal of his captivity, *American Captives in Tripoli* (Boston, 1806).

COX, SAMUEL SULLIVAN ("SUNSET") (1824–1889). Politician and diplomat, born September 30, 1824, in Zanesville, Ohio. Cox graduated from Ohio and Brown universities and practiced law in Cincinnati. He went to the Middle East in 1851 and described his trip in *A Buckeye Abroad; or, Wanderings in Europe and the Orient* (New York, 1852). He was a congressman from 1857 to 1865, from 1869 to 1885, and from 1886 to 1889. He went to Algiers in 1869, traveled again in the Middle East in 1881, and wrote *Oriental Sunbeams or from the Porte to the Pyramids, by Way of Palestine* (New York, 1882). He was minister to Turkey in 1885–1886 and wrote *Diversions of a Diplomat in Turkey* (New York, 1887). He spent 1886 on the Isles of Princes, or Prinkipo, in the Sea of Marmara, and wrote *The Isle of the Princes; or the Pleasures of Prinkipo* (New York, 1888). Died September 10, 1889, in New York City. *References*: *ACAB*; *DAB*; *DADH*; David Lindsey, *"Sunset" Cox, Irrepressible Democrat* (Detroit, 1959); *NCAB* 6:369; and *WWWA*.

CRABITES, PIERRE (1877–1943). Judge and author, born February 17, 1877, in New Orleans. Crabites graduated from the College of Immaculate Conception (New Orleans), Tulane University, and the University of Paris, and was admitted to the bar in 1900. He practiced in New Orleans until 1911. He was a judge on the Mixed Courts of Egypt* in Cairo from 1911 to 1936. He was a special lecturer at the Louisiana State University Law School from 1936 to 1941, special assistant to the minister in Cairo from 1942 to 1943, and legal assistant to the minister in Baghdad in 1943. He wrote several historical studies about Egypt, including biographies of the khedives Ibrahim Pasha and Isam'il and *Americans in the Egyptian Army* (London, 1938). Died October 9, 1943, in Baghdad. *References*: *NYT*, October 11, 1943; *WWWA*.

CRANE, CHARLES RICHARD (1858–1939). Businessman and philanthropist, born August 7, 1858, in Chicago. Crane began to work in his father's foundry at age of fourteen. In 1877 he traveled in the Middle East and met Richard Burton in Damascus. He was vice president of Crane Company from 1894 to 1912 and its president from 1912 to 1914. In 1909 he was appointed minister to China but did not serve. In 1917 he was a member of the special diplomatic mission to Russia, and in 1919 he was a member of the Inter-Allied Commission on Mandates in Turkey (the King-Crane Commission*). He was minister to China in 1920–1921. Crane visited Yemen and reported on his visit to the Red Sea Littoral and to Yemen in the *Journal of the Royal Central Asian Society* in 1928. He sent American engineers to Yemen to build roads and irrigation systems at his own expense. In 1930 he visited Saudi Arabia at the invitation of King 'Abd al-'Aziz, and later sent Karl Saben Twitchell* to examine water and mineral resources in Saudi Arabia. In 1925 he established and endowed the Institute of Current World Affairs. Died February 15, 1939, in Palm Springs, California. *References*: Papers, Institute of Current World Affairs; Leo J. Bocage, "The Public Career of Charles R. Crane," Ph.D. diss., Fordham University, 1962; *DAB S2*; *DADH*; *NCAB* 30:221; *NYT*, February 16, 1939; and *WWWA*.

CRANE, WILLIAM MONTGOMERY (1784–1846). Naval officer, born February 1, 1784, in Elizabeth, New Jersey. Crane was commissioned a midshipman in the navy in 1799. He participated in the attack on Tripoli in 1804, commanding gunboat No. 7. Later, he served in the War of 1812. He commanded the *Erie* during the naval demonstration against Algiers in 1815. He was commander of the Mediterranean squadron from 1827 to 1829. With Davis Offley,* he was joint commissioner to negotiate a commercial treaty with Turkey in 1828–1829. He was commandant of the Portsmouth, New Hampshire, Navy Yard from 1832 to 1840, member of the Board of Navy Commissioners in 1841–1842, and chief of the Bureau of Ordnance and Hydrography from 1842 to 1846. Died March 18, 1846, in Washington, D.C. *References*: *DAB*; *NCAB* 12:422; and *WWWA*.

CRAWFORD, F(RANCIS) MARION (1854–1909). Author, born August 2, 1854, in Bagni di Lucca, Tuscany, to American parents, and came to the United States in 1866. Crawford graduated from Trinity College, Cambridge, and studied at Karlsruhe and Heidelberg universities. In 1879 he went to India and edited a newspaper in Allahabad from 1879 to 1880. He returned to Rome because of illness and lived there for the rest of his life. His first novel was published in 1882. He was in Constantinople in 1884, traveled to Arabia and Baghdad in 1891, and wrote two novels with Middle Eastern backgrounds, *Paul Patoff* (New York, 1887) and *Khaled: A Tale of Arabia* (New York, 1891). He also wrote *Constantinople* (New York, 1895). Died April 9, 1909, in Sorrento, Italy. *References*: *ACAB*; *DAB*; John C. Moran, *An F. Marion Crawford Companion* (Westport, Conn., 1981); *NCAB* 2:502; John Pilkington, Jr., *Francis Marion Crawford* (New York, 1964); and *WWWA*.

CRAWFORD, VAUGHN EMERSON (1917–1981). Sumerologist, born in Princeton, Indiana. Crawford graduated from Bethel College (McKenzie, Tenn.), Yale Divinity School, and Yale University. In 1957 he joined the staff of the Metropolitan Museum of Art as assistant curator. He was research associate in the Department of Near Eastern Art, associate curator in the Department of Ancient Near Eastern Art from 1963 to 1973, and curator from 1973 until his death. He took part in the excavations of Tell Leilan in Syria and Hasanlu in Iran; and represented the Metropolitan Museum of Art at the excavations at Nimrud and the excavations and regional surveys at Nippur and at Tell Abu Salibikh in southern Iraq. In 1969 he was project director for the Metropolitan Museum of Art excavation at Tell al Hiba in southern Iraq. He was director of the American Schools of Oriental Research (ASOR)* in Baghdad in 1956–1957.

Died September 25, 1981, in Port Chester, New York. *References*: *NYT*, September 27, 1981.

CRESSON, WARDER (1798–1860). Religious zealot, born July 1, 1798, in Philadelphia. A Quaker, Cresson farmed near the city. He became involved in various religious sects and mysticism. He was appointed first counsul in Jerusalem in 1844. Although the commission was revoked, he went to Palestine, remaining in Jerusalem until 1848 when he was converted to Judaism. That same year he returned to Philadelphia where he became involved in a legal battle with his family which he won. He returned to Jerusalem in 1852, adopted the name Michael Boaz Israel, and propagandized for the agricultural colonization of Jews in Palestine. Died October 27, 1860, in Jerusalem. *References*: *EJ*; Frank Fox, "Quaker, Shaker, Rabbi: Warder Cresson, the Story of a Philadelphia Mystic," *Pennsylvania Magazine of History and Biography* 95 (1971): 147–194; and Abraham J. Karp, "The Zionism of Warder Cresson," in *Early History of Zionism in America*, ed. Isidore S. Meyer (New York, 1958), pp. 1–20.

CROSBY, HOWARD (1826–1891). Clergyman and educator, born February 27, 1826, in New York City. Crosby graduated from the University of the City of New York. He traveled in the Middle East in 1849 and wrote *Lands of the Moslem. A Narrative of Oriental Travel. By El-Mukattem* (New York, 1851). He was professor of Greek at the University of the City of New York from 1851 to 1859, was ordained in 1861, served as a pastor in New York City from 1861 until 1891, and was chancellor of the University of the City of New York from 1870 to 1881. Died March 29, 1891, in New York City. *References*: *ACAB*; *DAB*; *NCAB* 4:193; *NYT*, March 30, 1891; and *WWWA*.

CROSS, FRANK MOORE, JR. (1921–   ). Biblical scholar, born July 13, 1921, in Ross, California. Cross graduated from Merryville (Tenn.) College, McCormick Theological Seminary, and Johns Hopkins University. He was an instructor, assistant professor, and associate professor of Old Testament at McCormick Theological Seminary from 1951 until 1957, and became professor of Hebrew and other Oriental languages at Harvard University in 1957. He was a curator of the Semitic Museum and became its director in 1975. He was annual professor of the American Schools of Oriental Research (ASOR)* in Jerusalem in 1953–1954, co-director of the archaeological expedition to Judean Buqei'ah in 1955, archaeological director of the Hebrew Union College in Jerusalem in 1963–1964, and principal investigator of the expedition to Carthage in 1975–1976. He was a member of the international staff that edited the Dead Sea Scrolls. He wrote *Ancient Library of Qumran and Modern Biblical Studies* (Garden City, N.Y., 1958). *References*: *CA*; *DAS*; and *WWA*.

CULBERTSON, WILLIAM SMITH (1884–1966). Lawyer, born August 5, 1884, in Greensburg, Pennsylvania. Culbertson graduated from the College of Emporia (Kansas) and Yale University, studied at the universities of Leipzig and Berlin, and was admitted to the bar in 1912. He practiced law in Washington, D.C., from 1912 to 1915, and was with the U.S. Tariff Commission from 1916 to 1925, first as a special counsel and a member of its board of review, and then as a member and chairman of the commission. He was minister to Rumania from 1925 to 1928 and minister to Chile from 1928 to 1933. In 1933 he returned to the practice of law in Washington, specializing in international law. He served in the army during World War II, and in 1944 he was the chairman, with the rank of ambassador, of a special mission to French North Africa and the Middle East and later also to Italy and France. Died August 12, 1966, in Washington, D.C. *References*: "Ventures in Time and Space," Ms., memoirs and papers, Manuscript Division, Library of Congress; *NCAB* 54:101; *NYT*, August 14, 1966; John R. Snyder, *William S. Culbertson: In Search of a Rendezvous* (Washington, D.C., 1980); and *WWWA*.

CULBERTSON MISSION. Special economic mission, headed by William Smith Culbertson,* sent in 1944 to North Africa and the Middle East to study American trade relations and to survey postwar prospects for American business. Culbertson traveled in North Africa and the Middle East. *Reference*: John DeNovo, "The Culbertson Economic Mission and Anglo-American Tensions in the Middle East, 1944–1945," *Journal of American History* 63 (1977): 913–936.

CURTIS, GEORGE WILLIAM (1824–1892). Journalist and author, born February 24, 1824, in Providence, Rhode Island. Curtis was a member of Brook Farm Community in 1842–1843. He traveled abroad from 1846 to 1850, was in the Middle East in 1850, and wrote *Nile Notes of a Howadji* (New York, 1851) and *The Howadji in Syria* (New York, 1856), based on letters he sent to the *New York Tribune*. He was associate editor of the *New York Tribune* from 1852 to 1857, and editor of *Harper's Weekly* in 1863. Died August 31, 1892, in Staten Island, New York. *References*: *ACAB*; *DAB*; *NCAB* 3:96; *WWWA*; and *WWWE*.

CURTIS, WILLIAM ELEROY (1850–1911). Journalist, born November 5, 1850, in Akron, Ohio. Curtis graduated from Western Reserve College. He was a staff member of the *Chicago Inter Ocean* from 1873 to 1887, as well as Washington correspondent of the *Chicago Record* and later the *Chicago Record-Herald*. He was special commissioner to the republics of Central and South America, and the first director of the Bureau of the American Republics from 1889 to 1893. He traveled in the Middle East for the *Chicago Herald*, and wrote *To-day in Syria and Palestine* (Chicago, 1904), and *Egypt, Burma, and British Malaysia* (Chicago, 1905). Died October 5, 1911, in Washington, D.C. *References*: *ACAB*; *DAB*; *NCAB* 5:43; and *WWWA*.

CURTISS, SAMUEL IVES (1844–1904). Theologian, born February 5, 1844, in Union, Connecticut. Curtiss graduated from Amherst College, Union Theological Seminary, and the University of Leipzig. He was engaged in missionary work in New York City and was ordained in 1874. He was a pastor in Leipzig from 1874 to 1878, and became professor of biblical literature at Chicago Theological Seminary in 1878. He was president of the Chicago City Missionary Society from 1888 to 1898 and from 1899 to 1903. His book *Primitive Semitic Religion Today* (Chicago, 1902) was based on his observations in Syria, Palestine, and Sinai from 1898 to 1901. Died September 22, 1904, in Chicago. *References*: *ACAB*; *DAB*; *NCAB* 13:395; and *WWWA*.

CUSHMAN, EMMA DARLING (1863–1930). Missionary nurse, born July 20, 1863, in Burlington, New York. Cushman graduated from Manhattan (Kans.) State College. She served under the American Board of Commissioners for Foreign Missions (ABCFM)* in the mission hospital in Kayseri, Turkey, from 1900 until 1907, and then in an independent mission hospital in Konya. In 1919 she served Near East Relief* and helped refugee children in Asia Minor. She moved to Corinth, Greece, in 1923. Died in Corinth. *Reference*: Lucius E. Thayer, "Miss Valiant," *Andover Newton Quarterly* 7 (1967): 158–167.

CYPRUS MINES CORPORATION. American corporation founded in 1916 to produce cooper from ancient copper mines in Cyprus rediscovered by Charles Godfrey Gunther.* Operations in Cyprus ceased in 1974. *Reference*: David Lavender, *Story of the Cyprus Mines Corporation* (San Marino, Calif., 1962).

D

DALE, RICHARD (1756–1826). Naval officer, born November 6, 1756, in Norfolk County, Virginia. Dale served in the Virginia and the Continental navies during the Revolution, and was first lieutenant on the *Bon Homme Richard* under John Paul Jones in 1779. He served in the merchant marine from 1783 to 1794, was active in the China trade, and was commissioned a captain in the U.S. Navy in 1794. He commanded a squadron in the Mediterranean during the war with Tripoli, and in the frigate *Essex*, maintained a successful blockade of Tripoli. After the war he returned to private life. Died February 26, 1826, in Philadelphia. *References*: *DAB*; *NCAB* 2:17; *WAMB*; and *WWWA*.

DALENBERG, CORNELIA (1893–   ). Missionary nurse, born October 4, 1893, in South Holland, Illinois. Dalenberg graduated from the West Side School of Nurses in Chicago. She served in the Arabian Mission from 1921 to 1962, first in a hospital in Bahrain and, from 1930 to 1941, in Amara, Iraq. She prepared handbooks on nursing in Arabic. She retired to North Holland, Illinois, and wrote her memoirs (with David de Groot), *Sharifa* (Grand Rapids, Mich., 1983).

DALES, GEORGE FRANKLIN (1927–   ). Archaeologist, born August 13, 1927, in Akron, Ohio. Dales graduated from the University of Pennsylvania, was assistant curator of Near East archaeology at the Royal Ontario Museum from 1960 to 1963, assistant professor at the University of Pennsylvania from 1963 to 1966, and associate professor and associate curator at the University Museum from 1966 to 1972. He became professor of Near East and South Asian archaeology at the University of California at Berkeley in 1972. He was the principal investigator on Afghanistan archaeology for the National Science Foundation from 1969 to 1972, conducted a survey of Seistan in 1970, and became director of archaeological excavations at Balakot, Pakistan, in 1973. He wrote *New Excavations at Nad-i-Ali (Sarkh Dagh), Afghanistan* (Berkeley, Calif., 1977). *Reference*: *DAS*.

DALES, SARAH B. (1820–1889). Missionary, born July 30, 1820, in Moscow, New York. Dales went to Syria in 1854 as a missionary under the Associate Reformed Church. In 1857 she fell from a horse and sustained serious injuries which forced her to suspend her work. She moved to Alexandria, Egypt, in 1859, taking charge of a girls' school. She was transferred to Cairo in 1860, and also took charge of a girls' school. She married Gulian Lansing.* Died November 26, 1889, in Cairo. *Reference*: *In the King's Service* (Philadelphia, 1905), pp. 81–105.

DAME, LOUIS PAUL (1886–1953). Medical missionary, born December 16, 1886, in Groningen, the Netherlands. Dame graduated from Lewis Institute (Chicago) and the University of Illinois Medical College, and served in the medical corps in World War I. He served under the Arabian Mission* in Bahrain from 1919 to 1936. From 1921 to 1933 he made a series of trips through Arabia, visited Hasa in 1929, went to Taif in 1932 and to Riadh in 1933, and toured Qatar in 1934 and the northern part of Najd in 1935. He was later medical adviser to the Arabian American Oil Company (ARAMCO)* in Saudi Arabia. He returned to the United States in 1941 and practiced in Rockford, Illinois, from 1942 until his death. Died July 2, 1953, in Rockford. *References*: *HDRCA*; *Rockford Morning Star*, July 3, 1953.

DANA, CHARLES A(NDERSON) (1819–1897). Editor, born August 8, 1819, in Hinsdale, New Hampshire. Dana graduated from Harvard University, was managing trustee of Brook Farm from 1841 to 1846, assistant editor of *Boston Daily Chronologue* in 1846–1847, city and managing editor of the *New York Tribune* from 1847 to 1862, assistant secretary of war in 1863–1864, editor of *Chicago Republican* in 1865, and owner and editor of the *New York Sun* from 1868 to 1897. He visited the Middle East, and his book *Eastern Journeys: Some Notes of Travel in Russia, in the Eastern Caucasus and to Jerusalem* (New York, 1898) was intended to encourage Americans to travel in Eastern Europe and the Middle East. Died October 17, 1897, in West Island, Long Island, New York. *References*: *DAB*; *DLB*; *NCAB* 1:307; and *WWWA*.

DANIEL, JOHN FRANKLIN, III (1910–1948). Archaeologist, born June 8, 1910, in Ann Arbor, Michigan. Daniel graduated from the University of California, and studied at the universities of Freiburg, Munich, and Pennsylvania. He excavated at Kourion for the Cyprus expedition of the University Museum from 1934 to 1939, and at Tarsus, Turkey, with the Bryn Mawr expedition to Cilicia in 1939. He became assistant curator of the Mediterranean section in the University Museum in 1940, served with the Office of Strategic Services in Washington in 1942, and was commanding officer of the U.S. Army in Cyprus from 1943 to 1945. In 1946 he became curator of the Mediterranean section of the University Museum, and in 1948 professor of practical archaeology at the University of Pennsylvania. In 1948 he conducted excavations in Cyprus for the

University Museum and made a reconnaissance trip in Turkey. Died December 17, 1948, in Ankara, Turkey. *References*: *AJA* 52 (1948): 485; *NYT*, December 19, 1948.

DAVENPORT, HOMER CALVIN (1867–1912). Cartoonist, born March 8, 1867, in Silverton, Marion County, Ohio. Davenport was a jockey, railroad foreman, clown in a circus, cartoonist on the Portland *Oregonian* and on the *San Francisco Examiner*, and in 1895 cartoonist on the *New York Evening Journal*. In 1906 the Sultan Abdulhamid II granted him permission to export Arabian horses, traveled to Aleppo, Syria, purchased horses from the 'Anazah tribe, and wrote of his experiences in *My Quest of the Arab Horse* (New York, 1909). Died May 2, 1912, in Morristown, New Jersey. *References*: Anthony Amaral, "Quest for Arabian Horses Becomes a Desert Odyssey," *Smithsonian* 6 (September 1975): 42–49; *DAB*; Leland Huot and Alfred Powers, *Homer Davenport of Silverton; Life of a Great Cartoonist* (Binger, Wash., 1973); *NCAB* 11:25; and *WWWA*.

DAVIES, FRED A(LEXANDER) (1894–). Mining engineer and oil executive, born April 17, 1894, in Aberdeen, South Dakota. Davies graduated from the University of Minnesota and served in World War I. He worked for the Greenwood Company in Kansas and the Anaconda Copper Mining Company, was an oil geologist for the Standard Oil Company of California from 1919 to 1930, and assistant manager from 1931 to 1934. He conducted a geological survey of Bahrain in 1930, was field manager in Bahrain for the Bahrain Petroleum Company (BAPCO)* and the California Arabian Standard Oil Company (CASOC)* from 1934 to 1937 and for BAPCO and the foreign division of Standard Oil Company of California from 1937 to 1940. He was president of CASOC from 1940 until 1947, vice president and executive vice president of the Arabian American Oil Company (ARAMCO)* in charge of production and exploration from 1947 to 1952, and later chairman of the board and chief executive officer of ARAMCO. *Reference*: *Business World*, April 5, 1947.

DAVIS, DARIUS A(LTON) (1883–1970). YMCA official, born May 6, 1883, at Skerry, New York. Davis graduated from Syracuse University and was director of religious work of the Young Men's Christian Association (YMCA)* in Washington, D.C., from 1907 to 1910. From 1910 to 1915, he headed the YMCA in Constantinople, the first representative under salary to be appointed in the Middle East, and worked on behalf of Turkish soldiers during the first Balkan War. He directed YMCA aid to prisoners of war in World War I, later worked with displaced persons, and was associate director general for the World Alliance of YMCA in Geneva. In World War II, he resumed work for prisoners of war. He retired in 1950. Died May 20, 1970, in Westwood, New Jersey. *Reference*: *NYT*, May 22, 1970.

DAVIS, JAMES BOLTON (1809–1855). Physician and planter, born December 31, 1809, at Monticello, Fairfield County, South Carolina. Davis graduated from South Carolina College, the Medical College of Charleston, and the Medical College of Pennsylvania, and became involved in agriculture and stock raising. In 1846 he went to Turkey and brought with him six slaves to teach the Turks how to grow cotton. He introduced cotton culture into Turkey and set up a cotton-growing experiment in a farm at San Stefano (today Yesilkoy), on the Sea of Marmara. The efforts to grow cotton were unsuccessful, however, and his contract was not renewed. He sent to Persia for Angora or Cashmere goats which he brought back to the United States, together with blackwater buffalos whijch he purchased in Turkey. He returned to the United States in 1848 and continued farming. Died May 6, 1855, in Monticello, South Carolina. *Reference*: *History of the State Agricultural Society of South Carolina from 1839 to 1845* (Columbia, S.C., 1916), pp. 223–229.

DAVIS, JOHN HERBERT (1904–   ). Agriculturist and economist, born October 9, 1904, in Wellsville, Missouri. Davis graduated from Iowa State University of Science and Technology and the University of Minnesota. He was economist at the Department of Agriculture in 1935–1936 and 1941–1942; chief of the Wheat Section in the Commodity Credit Corporation from 1942 to 1944; executive vice president of the National Council of Farmer Co-operatives from 1942 to 1952; general manager of the National Wool Marketing Corporation in 1952–1953; assistant secretary of agriculture; president of the Commodity Credit Corporation; president of the Federal Crop Insurance Corporation in 1953–1954; and director of the Program in Agriculture and Business at the Graduate School of Business Administration of Harvard University from 1954 to 1959. He was commissioner-general of the United Nations Relief and Works Agency in Beirut from 1959 to 1964, and president of the American Middle East Refugee Aid, Inc. from 1968 to 1976. He wrote *The Evasive Peace: A Study of the Zionist-Arab Problem* (London, 1968). *Reference*: *CA*.

DAVIS, MOSHE (1916–   ). Educator, born June 12, 1916, in Brooklyn, New York. Davis graduated from Columbia University Teachers College and the Jewish Theological Seminary Teachers Institute, studied at the Hebrew University in Jerusalem in 1937, and was the first American to receive a doctoral degree from that institution. He was ordained in 1942. Davis was dean of the Jewish Theological Seminary Teachers Institute and the College of Jewish Studies and provost of the seminary. He went to Israel in 1959, founded the Institute of Contemporary Jewry at the Hebrew University, and was professor of American Jewish history and institutions. He was project director and general editor of the American-Holy Land Studies. *Contemporary Jewry: Studies in Honor of Moshe Davis*, ed. Geoffrey Wigodor (Jerusalem, 1984). *References*: *CA*; *DAS*; *WWA*; and *WWAJ*.

DAVIS, RICHARD HARDING (1864–1916). Journalist, born April 18, 1864, in Philadelphia. Davis graduated from Lehigh and Johns Hopkins universities, was a reporter for the *Philadelphia Record* and then the *Philadelphia Press* from 1886 to 1889, the New York *Evening Sun* from 1889 to 1891, and managing editor of the *Harper's Weekly* from 1891 to 1893. In 1893 he traveled in the Middle East and wrote *The Rulers of the Mediterranean* (New York, 1894). In 1897 he covered the Turkish-Greek War for the *New York Herald* and the London *Times*. Davis became famous as war correspondent and novelist of adventure-style fiction. Died April 12, 1916, in Mount Kisco, New York. *References*: *DAB*; *DADH*; *DLB*; Fairfax Downey, *Richard Harding Davis: His Day* (New York, 1948); *EAJ*; Gerald Langford, *The Richard Harding Davis Years* (New York, 1961); *NYT*, April 13, 1916; Scott C. Osborn and Robert L. Phillipts, Jr., *Richard Harding Davis* (Boston, 1978); and *WWWA*.

DAVIS, THEODORE MONROE (1837–1915). Businessman and philanthropist, who lived and worked in New York City and Newport, Rhode Island. Davis first visited Egypt in 1899, became interested in Egyptology, financed excavations in Egypt, and from 1903 to 1912 had a permit to explore the Valley of the Kings. Most of the objects discovered went to the Cairo Museum and were exhibited in a special gallery known as the Salle Theodore Davis. His private colalection went to the Metropolitan Museum of Art, New York. Died February 23, 1915, in Florida. *References*: Emma B. Andrews, ''Diary Kept on the Dahabiya of Theodore M. Davis during 17 Trips to Egypt, 1889–1912.'' Ms., Metropolitan Museum of Art; *NYT*, February 24, 1915; and *WWWE*.

DECATUR, STEPHEN, JR. (1779–1820). Naval officer, born January 5, 1779, in Sinepuxent, Maryland. Decatur was commissioned midshipman in the navy in 1798, served in the Mediterranean in 1801, 1802–1803, and in the War with Tripoli in 1804–1805, and led the raid into Tripoli Harbor to destroy the U.S.S. *Philadelphia*.* He served in the War of 1812 and returned to the Mediterranean in 1815, in command of the squadron that ended the Algiers War and the payment of tribute, and secured reparations to American shipping. From 1815 until his death, he was a member of the Board of Naval Commissioners. Killed March 22, 1820, in a duel, near Bladensburg, Maryland. *References*: *DAB*; *DAMIB*; Charles L. Lewis, *The Romantic Decatur* (Philadelphia, 1937); *NCAB* 4:56; John H. Schroeder, ''Stephen Decatur: Heroic Ideal of the Young Navy,'' in *Command Under Sail: Makers of the American Naval Tradition 1775–1850*, ed. James C. Bradford (Annapolis, Md., 1985), pp. 199–219: *WAMB*; and *WWWA*.

DE COU, HERBERT FLETCHER (1868–1911). Epigrapher, born June 10, 1868, in Good Harbor, Michigan. De Cou graduated from the University of Michigan, was an instructor of Greek and Sanskrit at the University of Michigan from 1892 to 1895 and of Greek in 1899–1900, and secretary and lecturer at the American Schools of Classical Studies in Athens and Rome. He participated in the archaeological expedition to Cyrene, Libya, in 1910–1911. Murdered March 11, 1911, in Cyrene. *References*: Richard G. Goodrich, "A Hole in the Heaven," in *Lybian Studies*, ed. Joyce Reynolds (London, 1970), pp. 290–297, and "Death of an Epigrapher: The Killing of Herbert De Cou," *Michigan Quarterly Review* 8 (1969): 149–154.

DE FOREST, HENRY ALBERT (1814–1858). Medical missionary, born May 15, 1814. De Forest served as a missionary under the American Board of Commissioners for Foreign Missions (ABCFM)* in Syria from 1842 to 1854. He toured Mount Lebanon, Lake Huleh, and the Bekaa Valley, made an extended series of meteorological observations, studied the climatology of Palestine, and wrote descriptions of the antiquities of North Syria. Died November 24, 1858. His brother was **JOHN WILLIAM DE FOREST (1826–1906)**, author, born May 31, 1826, in Humphreysville (later Seymour), Connecticut. In 1846–1847 he traveled in the Middle East to visit his brother, and wrote *Oriental Acquaintances; or, Letters from Syria* (New York, 1856), and the novel *Irene the Missionary* (Boston, 1879), based on his recollections of Syria. Died July 17, 1906, in New Haven, Connecticut. *References*: Papers, Yale University Library; *DAB*; *DLB*; and James F. Light, *John William DeForest* (New Haven, Conn., 1965).

DEGOLYER, E(VERETTE) L(EE) (1886–1956). Petroleum geologist and geophysicist, born October 9, 1886, in Greensburg, Kansas. DeGolyer graduated from the University of Oklahoma. He was employed by the U.S. Geological Service from 1906 to 1909, and served with the Mexican Eagle Oil Company from 1909 to 1914. He was a consultant from 1914 to 1919, vice president and general manager and later chairman of the board of Amerada Corporation from 1926 to 1932, became vice president and general manager of Geophysical Research Corporation in 1932, and senior member of DeGolyer and McNaughton in 1936. He was assistant deputy of the Petroleum Administration for War from 1941 to 1943, and in 1943 he was head of a technical mission to the Middle East for the Department of the Interior to evaluate oil resources for the Petroleum Reserves Corporation, and published a report on the mission. He became a member of the National Petroleum Council in 1946, and served in several advisory commissions dealing with natural resources. Died December 14, 1956, in Dallas, Texas. *References*: *BAAPG* 41 (1957): 969–974; *BMNAS* 33 (1959): 65–86; *NCAB* 43:12; *PGSA* for 1957 (1958): 95–103; Lon Tinkle, *Mr. De: A Biography of Everette Lee DeGolyer* (Boston, 1970); and *WWWA*.

DE HASS, FRANK S. (fl. 1873–1884). Clergyman. De Hass served as consul in Jerusalem from 1873 to 1877, and wrote *Recent Travels and Exploration in Bible Lands Consisting of Sketches Written from Personal Observation* (Pittsburgh, 1880), and *Buried Cities Recovered or, Exploration in Bible Lands* (Richmond, Va., 1884).

DEKAY, GEORGE COLMAN (1802–1849). Naval officer, brother of James Ellsworth DeKay,* born March 5, 1802, in New York City. DeKay served in the Argentine Navy from 1826 until 1830. In 1831 he sailed a corvette built by Henry Eckford* for the Sultan of Turkey to Constantinople. He was offered the command of a division in the Ottoman fleet, but turned it down. He was the first American to swim the Hellespont. He returned to the United States in 1832. He later led the relief efforts during the Irish famine of 1847 and sailed on the *Macedonian* with supplies to Ireland. Died January 31, 1849, in Washington, D.C. *References*: *DAB*; *NCAB* 9:205; and *WWWA*.

DEKAY, JAMES ELLSWORTH (1792–1851). Naturalist and physician, born October 12, 1792, in Lisbon, Portugal, brother of George Colman DeKay,* and brought to the United States in 1794. DeKay studied medicine at the University of Edinburgh, practiced medicine in New York City, and was involved with the Lyceum of Natural History. He sailed with Henry Eckford* and his brother to Turkey in 1831, remained there until 1832, and published his impressions in *Sketches of Turkey in 1831 and 1832* (New York, 1833). He later prepared the zoological section of the natural history survey of New York State. Died November 21, 1851, in Oyster Bay, Long Island, New York. *References*: *BDAS*; *DAB*; *DAMB*; *NCAB* 9:204; and *WWWA*.

DELANO, FREDERIC ADRIAN (1863–1953). Engineer and railroad executive, born September 10, 1863, in Hong Kong, to American parents. Delano graduated from Harvard University and in 1885 began a railway career as a machinist, rising to be general manager and director of several railroads. In 1914 he became a member of the Federal Reserve Board, resigning in 1918 to join the army. In 1925 he became chairman of the League of Nations Commission of Inquiry into the production of opium in Persia and the possible substitution of other crops or industries, and went to Persia to study its opium problem in its local setting. Delano was later involved in various government and civic organizations. Died March 28, 1953, in Washington, D.C. *References*: David C. Coyle, "Frederick A. Delano: Catalyst," *Survey Graphic* 35 (1946): 252–254; *NCAB* 40:5564; *NYT*, March 29, 1953; and *WWWA*.

DE LEON, EDWIN (1818–1891). Diplomat, born May 4, 1818, in Columbia, South Carolina. De Leon graduated from South Carolina College, was admitted to the bar, and was editor of newspapers in Savannah, Georgia, and Washington, D.C. He was agent and consul general in Egypt from 1853 to 1861. He served the Confederacy as a publicity agent in Europe from 1861 to 1864 and visited Turkey in 1864. He remained in Europe and Egypt for the rest of his life. He wrote *Askaros Kassis, the Copt. A Romance of Modern Egypt* (Philadelphia, 1870), *The Khedive's Egypt or, the Old House of Bondage Under New Masters* (London, 1877), *Under the Stars and Under the Crescent. A Romance of East and West* (London, 1877), and an autobiography, *Thirty Years of My Life on*

Three Continents (London, 1890). Died December 1, 1891, in New York City. *References*: Papers, South Caroliniana Library, University of South Carolina; *BDC*; *DADH*; *NCAB* 4:94; and *WWWA*.

DELOUGAZ, PINHAS PIERRE (1901–1975). Archaeologist, born July 16, 1901, in Russia, went as a child with his parents to Palestine, came to the United States in 1938, and was naturalized in 1944. Delougaz graduated from the universities of Paris and Chicago. He was on the faculty of the University of Chicago from 1949 to 1967, professor of archaeology from 1960 to 1967, curator of the Oriental Institute Museum from 1944 to 1967, and professor of archaeology at the University of California in Los Angeles from 1969 to 1975. He was architectural assistant to the Harvard-American Schools of Oriental Research (ASOR)* Expedition to Nuzi, Iraq, in 1928–1929; field assistant in the Oriental Institute's Iraq expedition of 1929–1931; field director of the University Museum of the University of Pennsylvania and ASOR joint expedition to Khafaje, Iraq, from 1931 to 1937; field director of the Iraq expeditions from 1948 to 1975; and director of the Israel expedition from 1952 to 1975, and the Iran expedition from 1961 to 1975. He wrote *The Temple Oval at Khafajah* (Chicago, 1940), *Pottery from the Diyala Region* (Chicago, 1952), and was co-author of *Pre-Sargonid Temples in the Diayala Region* (Chicago, 1942), *A Byzantine Church at Khirbet al-Karak* (Chicago, 1960), and *Private Houses and Graves in the Diyala Region* (Chicago, 1967). Died March 29, 1975, in Los Angeles. *References*: *EJ*; *NYT*, April 2, 1975; and *WWWA*.

DENNIS, JAMES SHEPARD (1842–1914). Missionary, born December 15, 1842, in Newark, New Jersey. Dennis graduated from Princeton University and Princeton Theological Seminary, and was ordained in 1868. He served as a missionary under the Presbyterian Church in the USA Board of Foreign Missions* in Syria from 1868 to 1891. He was stationed in Sidon and Zahleh, was principal and professor at the theological seminary in Beirut from 1873 to 1891, and wrote *A Sketch of the Syrian Mission* (New York, 1872). He resigned in 1892, and was later historian and statistician of missions for the Presbyterian Board of Foreign Missions. Died March 21, 1914, in Montclair, New Jersey. *References*: William H. Berger, "James Shepard Dennis: Syrian Missionary and Apologist," *American Presbyterians* 64 (Summer 1986): 97–111; *DAB*; *NCAB* 22:320; and *WWWA*.

DENNIS, JAMES TEACKLE (1865–1918). Attorney and Egyptologist, born October 6, 1865, in Baltimore. Dennis graduated from Lafayette College, studied at Johns Hopkins University, and was admitted to the bar in 1889. He served as state's attorney for Somerset County, Maryland, from 1890 to 1893. He traveled in Egypt in 1895 and in 1903–1904, assisted in the excavations at Deir el-Bahri from 1903 to 1907, discovered the Hathor Shrine in 1906, and continued to work there in 1909–1910. He traveled in the Sudan, took a journey down the

Nile into Uganda, and wrote about his experiences in *From Cataract to Equator* (Boston, 1910). Died March 31, 1918, in Baltimore. *References*: Bill Needle, *The Dennis Collection of Egyptian Antiquities* (Normal, Ill., 1978); *NYT*, April 2, 1918; *WWWA*; and *WWWE*.

DENNISON, JAMES ALFRED (1846–1900). Soldier, born in Indiana. Dennison served in the Union Army during the Civil War, attended Mount Vernon College (Ia.), graduated from the U.S. Military Academy in 1870, and was commissioned second lieutenant in the cavalry. He resigned from the army in 1872, studied at the Albany Law school, was admitted to the bar in 1873, and practiced in Little Falls and Johnstons, New York, and New York City. He joined the Egyptian General Staff in 1874 as major of engineers and served as staff officer in the Egyptian-Abyssinian War of 1875. He was stationed with a small Egyptian detachment a few miles away from the battle of Gundet, and later succeeded in regaining Massawa. He contributed to the great map of Africa completed by the Egyptian General Staff in 1877. He returned to the United States in 1876, was assistant attorney general of the state of New York, and practiced law in New York City. Died July 12, 1900, in New York City. *References*: *Hesseltine*; *RAGMA*, 1901.

DERRICK, HENRY CLAY (1832–1915). Civil engineer, born January 13, 1832. Derrick served in the Confederate Army during the Civil War. He joined the Egyptian General Staff in 1875, was chief engineer to the commander-in-chief of the Egyptian Army invading Abyssinia in 1876, and fought in the battle of Gura. With Samuel Henry Lockett,* he explored and mapped the region southwest of Massawa, explored and mapped districts of Berber and Harrar, and assisted in the compilation of the map of Africa which the general staff prepared in 1877. He was discharged in 1878, returned to the United States, and lived near Halifax, Virginia. Died May 9, 1915, in Fairfax County, Virginia. *References*: "Diary," Manuscript Division, Library of Congress; *Hesseltine*.

DES MOINES, U.S.S. Protected cruiser. From May 1915 to April 1917 the *Des Moines* protected American citizens and interests threatened in the Middle Eastern theater of war. The cruiser carried missionaries and refugees out of Turkey and Syria, carried U.S. officials, and delivered relief funds. *Reference*: *DANES*.

DETWEILER, A(LBERT) HENRY (1906–1970). Archaeologist, born October 4, 1906, in Perkasie, Pennsylvania. Detweiler graduated from the University of Pennsylvania. He participated in the University of Pennsylvania expedition to Tell Billa and Tepe Gawra in Iraq from 1930 to 1933, in the excavations at Tell Beit Mirsim, Gerasa, Bostra, and Samaria, in Palestine, from 1932 to 1935; was a member of the Yale University expedition to Dura Europos, Syria, from 1935 to 1937; assisted in a survey of Mosque d'Jumma in Isfahan,

Iran; and worked with the University of Michigan expedition to Seleucia-on-the-Tigris, Syria, in 1936. In 1939 he became a member of the faculty of Cornell University, was professor of architecture from 1948 until 1956, and associate dean of the College of Architecture from 1956 until 1970. Detweiler was acting director of the American Schools of Oriental Research (ASOR)* in Jerusalem in 1949, director in 1953–1954, and president from 1955 to 1966. He conducted a survey of Medaba in Jordan in 1949, was a consultant on Roman architectural problems at the Jericho excavation in 1951, and from 1958 until his death he was associate director of the Cornell-Harvard excavations in Sardis. During the 1960s he served as adviser to the U.S. and Egyptian governments regarding the salvage of Abu Simbel and the preservation and restoration of antiquities and monuments in Jordan and Cairo. He wrote *Manual of Archaeological Surveying* (New Haven, Conn., 1948). Died January 30, 1970, in New York City. *References*: NCAB 55:152; *NYT*, February 1, 1970; and *WWWA*.

DEVER, WILLIAM GWINN (1933–   ). Archaeologist, born November 27, 1933, in Louisville, Kentucky. Dever graduated from Milligan College, Christian Theological Seminary (Ind.), and Butler and Harvard universities. He was senior archaeological fellow in the Biblical and Archaeological School of the Hebrew Union College in Jerusalem in 1966–1967, assistant professor and professor of ancient Near East history and archaeology from 1967 to 1975, resident director from 1968 to 1971, and professor of Near Eastern archaeology at the University of Arizona in 1975. He was director of the Hebrew Union College-Harvard Semitic Museum excavation at Gezer, Israel, from 1966 to 1971, and director of the Hebrew Union College excavations at Khalit el-Ful, Hebron, in 1967–1968 and 1971. From 1971 to 1975 he was director of the W. F. Albright Institute for Archaeological Research in Jerusalem, and director of the institute's excavations at Shechem in 1972–1973. He was co-author of *Gezer* (Jerusalem, 1970–1974), wrote *Biblical Archaeology* (New York, 1973), and also co-authored *A Manual of Field Excavation: Handbook for Field Archaeologists* (Cincinnati, 1978). *References*: CA; *DAS*.

DEWEY, JOHN (1859–1952). Philosopher and educator, born October 20, 1859, in Burlington, Vermont. Dewey graduated from the University of Vermont and Johns Hopkins University. He taught philosophy at the universities of Minnesota and Michigan and was head of the Department of Philosophy, Psychology and Pedagogy at the University of Chicago from 1894 to 1904, established the Laboratory School in 1896, and was its director until 1904. He was professor of philosophy at Columbia University from 1904 until his retirement in 1930. In 1924 at the invitation of the Turkish government, he visited Turkey to survey that country's educational system and to recommend ways for its improvement. He traveled through Turkey's provinces and prepared a "Report and Recommendation upon Turkish Education." The Report was responsible for the growth of many progressive steps in Turkish education. He also wrote a series of articles about Turkey for the *New Republic* in 1924 and 1925 which were republished as *Impressions of Soviet Russia and the Revolutionary World: Mexico China Turkey* (New York, 1929). Died June 1, 1952, in New York City. *References*: *DAB S5*; George Dykhuizen, *The Life and Mind of John Dewey* (Carbondale, Ill., 1973); *NCAB* 40:1; *NYT*, June 2, 1952; and *WWWA*.

DHAHRAN AIRFIELD. Following an agreement with the Saudi Arabian government, construction of the airfield in Dhahran, in eastern Saudi Arabia, began in 1945 and was completed in 1946. The U.S. government leased facilities until 1962, when the agreement expired and the airbase was evacuated and turned over to the Saudi government. *References*: James L. Gormly, "Keeping the Door Open in Saudi Arabia: The United States and the Dhahran Airfield, 1945–46," *Diplomatic History* 4 (1980): 189–205.

DICKINSON, CHARLES MONROE (1842–1924). Lawyer, journalist, and diplomat, born November 15, 1842, near Lowville, Lewis County, New York. Dickinson studied law and was admitted to the bar in 1865. He practiced law in Binghamton, New York, and New York City until 1877, and was editor and proprietor of the *Binghamton Republican* from 1878 until 1911. From 1897 to 1906 he was consul general to Turkey, and from 1901 to 1903 he was also diplomatic agent to Bulgaria. Dickinson was involved with the settlement and release of Ellen M. Stone, a missionary kidnapped by Bulgarian robbers. From 1906 to 1908 he was consul general at-large. Died July 3, 1924, in Binghampton, New York. *References*: Papers, Manuscript Division, Library of Congress; *DAB*; *NCAB* 11:91; and *WWWA*.

DICKSON, WALTER (1799–1860). Missionary, born in Groton, Massachusetts. Dickson went to Palestine in 1854 as an agricultural missionary, independent of church sponsorship, to train the Jews in modern agricultural practices. He joined Mount Hope Colony,* Jaffa, and remained in Jaffa after the death of Clorinda S. Minor,* an American religious zealout who established the colony. When his son-in-law was killed, he himself was wounded, and his wife and daughter were raped in an attack on his home by Arab burglers on January 11, 1858, he returned with his family to the United States. The attack caused diplomatic repercussions between the United States and the Ottoman governments. The case of Walter Dickson was settled in 1860, when the Ottoman government agreed to punish the offenders and to pay him indemnity. *References*: S. A. Green, "Walter Dickson's Family," *Groton Historical Series* II, no. 8 (Cambridge, 1888): 238–240; *Treaties and Other International Acts of the United States of America*, ed. Hunter Miller (Washington, 1948), 8:519–532.

DILLER, JOSEPH SILAS (1850–1928). Geologist, born August 27, 1850, near Plainfield, Pennsylvania. Diller graduated from Lawrence Scientific School of Harvard University, studied at Harvard and Heidelberg universities, and taught at the State Normal School (Westfield, Mass.) from 1873 to 1877. He was a geologist at the archaeological expedition to Assos, Mount Ida, and the Troad in Turkey from 1881 to 1883, and published some of the results in papers on the geology of Assos and the Troad. He was a geologist with the U.S. Geological Survey from 1883 until his death. Died November 13, 1928, in Washington, D.C. *References*: *DAB S1*; *NCAB* 3:514; and *WWWA*.

DODD, EDWARD MILLS (1824–1865). Missionary, born June 22, 1824, in Bloomfield, New Jersey. Dodd graduated from Princeton College and Union Theological Seminary, and was ordained in 1848. He went to Turkey in 1849 as a missionary under the American Board of Commissioners for Foreign Missions (ABCFM)* on a mission to the Jews in Salonika. He returned to the United States in 1852 because of health reasons. Upon recovery in 1855, he went to Smyrna, working among the Armenians until 1863. At that time he was transferred to Marsovan and opened a girls' school in 1865. Died August 19, 1865, in Marsovan, Turkey. *References*: *EM*; *NYT*, September 23, 1865; and *UnionTS*.

DODD, EDWARD MILLS (1887–1967). Medical missionary, son of William Schauffler Dodd,* born in Kayseri, Turkey. Dodd graduated from Princeton University and Cornell University Medical School. He served as a medical missionary under the United Presbyterian Board of Missions in Persia from 1916 to 1925, and was later medical secretary to the Board of Foreign Missions of the United Presbyterian Church of North America*. He was co-author of *Mecca and Beyond* (Boston, 1937). Died June 28, 1967, in Upper Monclair, New Jersey. *References*: "Near East Vortex," Ms., Presbyterian Historical Society, Philadelphia; *NYT*, July 3, 1967.

DODD, STUART C(ARTER) (1900–1975). Sociologist, son of William Schauffler Dodd,* born October 3, 1900, in Talas, Turkey. Dodd graduated from Princeton University. He was adjunct professor at the American University of Beirut* from 1927 to 1930, associate professor from 1930 to 1936, professor of sociology from 1936 to 1947, and director of the social science research section from 1929 to 1947. He served in the army in 1943–1944, was research professor in sociology at the University of Washington from 1947 to 1971, and director of the Washington Public Opinion Laboratory from 1947 to 1961. He wrote *Social Relations in the Near East* (Beirut, 1931; rev. and enlarged ed., Beirut, 1940), *A Controlled Experiment on Rural Hygiene in Syria* (Beirut, 1934), and *A Pioneer Radio Poll in Lebanon, Syria, and Palestine* (Jerusalem, 1943). Died December 26, 1975. *References*: *AMWS*; *CA*; *International Encyclopedia of the Social Sciences* (New York, 1979), 18:147–150; and *Public Opinion Quarterly* 40 (1976): 411–412.

DODD, WILLIAM SCHAUFFLER (1860–1928). Medical missionary, born December 27, 1860, in Smyrna, Turkey, father of Edward Mills Dodd* (1887–1967), and grew up in Mendham, New Jersey. Dodd graduated from Princeton University and the College of Physicians and Surgeons, returned to Turkey in 1886, and served in the hospital in Kayseri. In 1887 he moved to a hospital in Talas, and in 1912 he moved his hospital to Koniya. He left Turkey in 1916 and was a member of the Palestine Red Cross expedition in 1919. He returned to Turkey in 1919, and was stationed in Adana and later in Konya. Died January 24, 1928, in Bloomfield, New Jersey. *Reference*: Edward M. Dodd, *The Beloved Physician: An Intimate Life of William Schauffler Dodd* (n.p., 1931).

DODGE, ASA (1802–1835). Medical missionary, born November 15, 1802, in Newcastle, Maine. Dodge graduated from Bowdoin College. He was the first physician sent by the American Board of Commissioners for Foreign Missions (ABCFM)* to the Middle East. In 1833 he went to Beirut, and in 1834 he was transferred to Jerusalem, where he performed many cataract operations. Died January 28, 1835, in Jerusalem.

DODGE, BAYARD (1888–1972). Educator, born February 5, 1888, in New York City. Dodge graduated from Princeton University, Princeton Theological Seminary, and Columbia University, and became a member of the faculty at the American University of Beirut* in 1913. During World War I he aided relief efforts in Lebanon, and was director of Near East Relief* for Syria and Lebanon in 1920–1921. He was associate principal of the preparatory school in 1920–1921 and president of the American University of Beirut from 1923 to 1948. Dodge made the university coeducational in 1924, strengthened the schools of medicine and dentistry, and increased the student body. He was the regional cultural officer in the U.S. Information Service in Cairo in 1955–1956. He wrote *The American University of Beirut: A Brief History of the University and the Lands Which It Serves* (Beirut, 1958), and *Al Azhar: A Millennium of Muslim Learning* (Washington, D.C., 1961). Died May 30, 1972, in Princeton, New Jersey. *References*: Jerome Beatty, *Americans All Over* (New York, 1940), 76–85; *CA*; *CB* 1948; *NCAB* 57:635; *NYT*, June 1, 1972; and *WWWA*.

DODGE, WENDELL PHILLIPS (1883–1976). Explorer, theater producer, and author, born August 12, 1883, in Manchester, New Hampshire. Dodge studied at the Chicago Art Institute, the National Academy of Design, the Art Students' League of New York, and New York University, and had various engineering, industrial, commercial, and reportorial assignments from 1905 to 1913. He explored the Dead Sea, the Jordan Valley, and the Syrian Desert, and he excavated the mounds of Balawat, east of Mosul, Iraq, and at the tomb of Cyrus in Pasargadae, Persia, in 1900–1901. He was the founder and proprietor of the World Wide News Service in 1913, becoming its general manager and managing editor; founded the American Theater in Paris in 1929, serving as its director; and was the editor of *The Maine News* from 1943 to 1950 and of *The Explorer's Journal* until his retirement in 1954. Died May 26, 1976, in Jackson Heights, Queens, New York. *References*: *CA*; *NYT*, May 28, 1976; and *WWWA*.

DONALDSON, BESS ALLEN (1879–1984). Missionary, born December 5, 1879, in Galesburg, Illinois. Donaldson graduated from Knox College, taught several years in Illinois, and in 1910 went to Persia as a missionary under the Prebyterian Church in the U.S.A. Board of Foreign Missions*. She was stationed in Teheran from 1910 until 1918 and in Meshed from 1927 to 1937. She served in India from 1937 until her retirement in 1951. Donaldson wrote *The Wild Rue: A Study of Muhammedan Magic and Folklore in Iran* (London, 1938), and her memoirs, *Prairie Girl in Iran and India* (Galesburg, Ill., 1972). Died December 20, 1984, in Lakeland, Florida. *References*: Papers, Knox College Library; *Galesburg Register Mail*, January 16, 1975.

DONALDSON, JOSEPH, JR. (fl. 1795–1796). Diplomat from Philadelphia. In 1795 Donaldson was sent as an agent to Algiers to negotiate for peace and for the release of American hostages in the Barbary States (see Hostages in Barbary States). He reached a financial settlement and a treaty with Algiers, and left Algiers in 1796. *References*: Frank E. Ross, "The Mission of Joseph Donaldson, Jr. to Algiers: 1795–97," *Journal of Modern History* 7 (1935): 422–433.

DOOLITTLE, HOOKER AUSTIN (1889–1966). Diplomat, born January 27, 1889, in Mohawk, New York. Doolittle graduated from Cornell University, was involved in commerce in Rahway, New Jersey, Atlanta, and New Orleans from 1911 to 1916, and was commercial agent for the Bureau of Foreign and Domestic Commerce in 1916. He was vice consul in Tiflis, the Georgian Republic, Madras, India, and Marseille; consul in Bilbao, Spain, and Sarnia, Ontario, Canada; and secretary of legation in Tangier. He conducted prehistoric excavations in the Mughâret el 'Aliya at Cape Ashakar in Tangier from 1936 to 1940. He was consul general in Rabat, first secretary in Cairo in 1943, and consul general in Tunis and in Alexandria in 1944; established the first American consulate in Lahore, Pakistan, in 1947; and was representative to the U.N. commission for Indonesia in 1950. He lived in Tangier after his retirement in 1950, was director of the *Tangier Gazette*, president of the American School of Tangier, and a member of the Legislative Assembly for the International Zone of Tangier until it was dissolved in 1956. Died November 30, 1966, in Tangier. *References*: *NYT*, December 1, 1966; *WWWA*.

DORR, BENJAMIN (1796–1869). Clergyman, born March 22, 1796, in Salisbury, Massachusetts. Dorr graduated from Dartmouth College and the General Theological Seminary, and was ordained in 1823. He was a rector of churches in Lansingburg, Waterford, and Utica, New York, and Philadelphia. In 1853 he traveled in the Middle East and wrote *Notes on Travel in Egypt, the Holy Land, Turkey and Greece* (Philadelphia, 1856). Died September 18, 1869, in Philadelphia. *Reference*: *NCAB* 11:221.

DORR, GOLDTHWAITE HIGGINSON (1876–1977). Lawyer, born October 21, 1876, in Newark. Dorr graduated from Harvard University and Columbia University Law School, and was admitted to the bar in 1904. He practiced law in New York City, was assistant U.S. attorney in New York, Special assistant to the U.S. attorney general at various times between 1906 and 1921, and assistant director of munitions in World War I. He was chief assistant to Walker Downer Hines,* and after his death, head of the economic survey of Turkey in 1934 to prepare a plan for its future economic development. He was assistant to Secretary of War Henry Stimson during World War II and member of President Harry S. Truman's cabinet commission on Palestine in 1946. He continued to practice law with Mudge, Rose, Guthrie and Alexander in New York City, until his retirement in 1974. Died December 7, 1977, in Carmel, New York. *References*: *NCAB* E:347; *NYT*, December 13, 1977; and *WWWA*.

DOS PASSOS, JOHN (RODERIGO) (1896–1970). Author, born January 14, 1896, in Chicago. Dos Passos graduated from Harvard University, and served in the volunteer ambulance corps and later in the U.S. Army in World War I. In 1921–1922 he traveled to the Middle East. He wrote articles about his trip which were collected in his book *Orient Express* (New York, 1927). In 1926–1927 he traveled to Morocco and Tangier. His major work was the trilogy *U.S.A.* which appeared between 1930 and 1936. He wrote other novels as well as historical studies and biographies. Died September 28, 1970, in Baltimore. *References*: *The Fourteenth Chronicle; Letters and Diaries of John Dos Passos*, ed. and with a biographical narrative by Townsend Ludington (Boston, 1973); *CA*; Virginia S. Carr, *Dos Passos: A Life* (Garden City, N.Y., 1984); *DLB*; Townsend Ludington, *John Dos Passos: A Twentieth Century Odyssey* (New York, 1980); *NYT*, September 29, 1970; and *WWWA*.

DOTY, WILLIAM FURMAN (1870–1963). Consul, born December 1, 1870, in Brooklyn, New York. Doty graduated from Princeton University and Princeton Theological Seminary. He was a government teacher and agent for the Eskimo in St. Lawrence Island, Bering Strait, from 1897 to 1898 and in 1900, and was ordained in 1902. He was a clerk and consul in Tahiti from 1900 to 1906, and consul in Tabriz, Persia, from 1906 to 1910. Doty was involved in the diplomatic imbroglio between the United States and Persia, resulting from the murder of the American missionary Benjamin Woods Labaree,* in 1904 and of Howard C. Baskerville during the Persian Revolution. He was later consul in Riga, Russia; Nassau, Bahama Islands; and Cardiff, Wales. Died April 9, 1963. *Reference*: *WWWA*.

DOUGHERTY, RAYMOND PHILIP (1877–1933). Assyriologist, born August 5, 1877, in Lebanon, Pennsylvania. Dougherty graduated from the Lebanon Valley (Pa.) College, Bonebrake Theological Seminary, and Yale University, and was ordained in 1904. He was principal of the Albert Academy in Freetown, Sierra Leone, from 1904 to 1914; vice consul in Freetown in 1905–1906 and in 1912–13; professor of biblical literature at Goucher College from 1918 to 1926; and professor of Assyriology and Babylonian Literature and curator of the Babylonian Collection at Yale University from 1926 until his death seven years later. He was annual professor of the American Schools of Oriental Research (ASOR)* in Baghdad in 1925–26, conducted an archaeological survey of southern Babylonia in 1926, and wrote *Searching for Ancient Remains in Lower Iraq: Report of an Archaeological Survey Made in Southern Babylonia* (New Haven, Conn., 1927). He also wrote *The Sealand of Ancient Arabia* (New Haven, Conn., 1932). Died July 13, 1933, in New Haven. *References*: *AJA* 36 (1933): 467; *DAB S1*; and *WWWA*.

DOWNEY, GLANVILLE (1908–   ). Archaeologist, born June 14, 1908, in Baltimore. Downey graduated from Princeton University. He conducted an archaeological expedition for the excavation of Antioch in Syria from 1932 until 1939. He served in the army during World War II, became a member of the faculty of Dumbarton Oaks Research Library and Collection in 1945, and was a member of the faculty of Indiana University from 1964 to 1978. He wrote *Ancient Antioch* (Princeton, N.J., 1963). *References*: *CA*; *DAS*; and *WWA*.

DUELL, PRENTICE (1894–1960). Archaeologist, born August 17, 1894, in New Albany, Indiana. Duell graduated from the universities of California and Arizona and Harvard University, and studied in Paris and at the American School of Classical Studies in Athens. He served as balloon-pilot observer in World War I. He was an instructor in the history of architecture at the University of Illinois, assistant professor and professor at the University of Cincinnati, lecturer and associate professor in classical archaeology at Bryn Mawr College, and architect in the restoration of Williamsburg, Virginia, from 1929 to 1931. He was field director of the Sakkarah, Egypt, expedition for the Oriental Institute from 1930 to 1936, and was co-author of *The Mastaba of Mereruka, by the Sakkarah Expedition* (Chicago, 1938). He conducted research in London and Vienna from 1936 to 1938, and became research fellow in Etruscan art at the Fogg Museum of Art of Harvard University in 1939. Died April 16, 1960, in Cambridge, Massachusetts. *References*: *IAB*; *NCAB* 44:226; *NYT*, April 20, 1960; and *WWWA*.

DULLES, JOHN WELSH (1823–1887). Missionary and editor, born November 4, 1823, in Philadelphia. Dulles graduated from Yale College and Union Theological Seminary, and studied medicine. He was a missionary in Southern India from 1849 until 1853. In 1856 he became the secretary of the publications committee for the Presbyterian General Assembly, and later editorial secretary for the United Presbyterian Church. In 1879–1880 he traveled in Egypt, Syria, and Asia Minor, and wrote *The Ride Through Palestine in 1879, Made by Seven Presbyterian Clergymen on Horseback* (Philadelphia, 1881). In 1884 he journeyed through Algeria. Died April 13, 1887, in Philadelphia. *References*: *EM*; *NCAB* 6:258; and *UnionTS*.

DUNAWAY, JOHN ALLDER (1886–1969). Economist, born October 10, 1886, in Stockton, Missouri. Dunaway graduated from Park College (Parkville, Mo.) and the Wharton School of the University of Pennsylvania, and was a Chautauqua lecturer. He was treasurer of the Near East Relief* in the Aleppo district in 1919; assistant chief and chief of the research division of the Bureau of Foreign and Domestic Commerce in 1921–1922; and statistician and provincial director of finances for the American Finance Commission to Persia from 1922 to 1928. He was economist, and later senior marketing specialist, in the dairy section of the Agricultural Adjustment Administration from 1933 to 1935; supervisor of revenues for the Republic of Liberia from 1935 to 1938; and financial adviser in 1938. Dunaway was acting director of the Technical Cooperation Administration in Saudi Arabia and chief of the Public Administration Division and senior expert in Arthur Nichols Young's* mission to Saudi Arabia, dealing with customs administration. He retired in 1953. Died June 20, 1969, in Phoenix, Arizona. *Reference*: *WWWA*.

DUNHAM, DOWS (1890–1984). Egyptologist, born June 1, 1890, at Irvington-on-Hudson, New York. Dunham graduated from Harvard University. He served as ambulance driver in France and in the army in World War I. He became a staff member of the Boston Museum of Fine Arts in 1915, was a member of the Harvard University-Boston Museum of Fine Art expeditions in Egypt from 1915 to 1927, and director of the expedition in 1946–1947. He conducted excavations at Giza Naga-ed-Der and Coptos, Gammai, Gebel Berkal, Nuri, and Meroe. He became assistant curator of the Egyptian Department of the Boston Museum of Fine Arts in 1928, later associate curator, and curator from 1942 until his retirement in 1956. He was co-author of *Second Cataract Forts* (Boston, 1960), *The Predynastic Cemetery N7000 Naga-ed-Der* (Berkeley, Calif., 1965), *The Royal Cemetries of Kush* (Cambridge, Mass., 1950–1967), and *The Berkal Temples* (Boston, 1970), and wrote *The Egyptian Department and Its Excavations* (Boston, 1958), and a memoir, *Recollections of an Egyptologist* (Boston, 1972). Died January 10, 1984, in Boston. *References*: *Studies in Ancient Egypt, the Aegean, and the Sudan; Essays in Honor of Dows Dunham in the Occasion of His 90th Birthday, June 1, 1980*, ed. William K. Simpson and Whitney M. Davis (Boston, 1981); *AJA* 84 (1980): 190; and *Boston Globe*, January 11, 1984.

DUNMORE, GEORGE W(ASHINGTON) (1820–1862). Missionary, born October 5, 1820, in Rush, Pennsylvania. Dunmore graduated from the University of the City of New York and the Bangor Theological Seminary, and was ordained in 1850. He was a missionary under the American Board of Commissioners for Foreign Missions (ABCFM)* in Turkey from 1850 to 1861, and was stationed in Aintab, Diyarbekir, Harput, and Erzurum. He came to Constantinople in 1860 and resigned in 1861. He traveled extensively in Turkey, Persia, and Russia. He served as chaplain in the Civil War and was killed in battle on August 3, 1862, at L'Arguille Ferry, Arkansas. *Reference*: *BangorTS*.

DUNNING, HARRY WESTBROOK (1871–1960). Author and tourism expert, born December 7, 1871, in Roxbury, Massachusetts. Dunning graduated from Yale University and was an instructor in Semitic languages at Yale University from 1896 to 1899. In 1899 he established H. W. Dunning and Company, a travel agency in Boston, of which he was president, and Temple Tours. He organized and managed tours to the Middle East and later to other parts of the world. An experienced guide, he visited Palestine ten times between 1890 and 1905 and made six visits to Egypt. He wrote *To-Day on the Nile* (New York, 1905) and *To-Day in Palestine* (New York, 1907). Died June 27, 1960, in Waban, Massachusetts. *References*: *NCAB* 55:386; *WWWA*.

DUPREE, LOUIS (BENJAMIN) (1925–   ). Anthropologist, born August 23, 1925, in Greenville, North Carolina. Dupree graduated from Harvard University, and was merchant seaman and paratrooper in World War II. He was a member of the American Museum of Natural History expeditions in Afghanistan in 1949 and 1950–1951 and the University of Michigan Museum expedition to Iran in 1951, excavated at Deh Morasi Ghundi in 1950, and conducted surveys and excavations of prehistoric and other sites in 1959. He was assistant professor and associate professor of Middle Eastern studies at the Air University from 1954 to 1957, and associate professor of anthropology at Pennsylvania State University from 1957 to 1966. He became associate in Afghan studies for the American Universities Field Staff in 1959. Dupree wrote *Shamshir Ghar: Historic Cave Site in Kandahar Province, Afghanistan* (New York, 1958), and *Deh Morasi Ghundai A Chalcolitic Site in South-Central Afghanistan* (New York, 1963). His wife, **NANCY HATCH DUPREE**, assisted the Afghan Tourist Organization. She wrote *The Road to Balkh* (Kabul, 1967), *The Valley of Bamiya* (Kabul, 1963), *An Historical Guide to Afghanistan* (Kabul, 1965), and co-authored *An Historical Guide to Kabul* (Kabul, 1965). *References*: *AMWS*; *CA*; and *WWA*.

DURBIN, JOHN PRICE (1800–1876). Clergyman, born October 10, 1800, in Bourbon County, near Paris, Kentucky. Durbin graduated from Miami University and was ordained in 1842. He was professor of languages at Augusta (Ky.) College from 1825 to 1831, professor of natural sciences at Wesleyan University from 1831 to 1834, and at Dickinson College in 1834–1835. He traveled to the Middle East in 1842 and wrote *Observations in the East: Chiefly in Egypt, Palestine, Syria and Asia Minor* (New York, 1845) which appeared in ten editions before 1854. He was a pastor in Philadelphia from 1845 to 1850, secretary of the Missionary Society of the Methodist Church from 1850 to 1872, and vice president of the American Society for Ameliorating the Conditions of the Jews. Died October 19, 1876, in New York City. *References*: *DAB*, *NCAB* 6:463; and *WWWA*.

DUSHKIN, ALEXANDER MORDECAI (1890–1976). Educator, born August 21, 1890, in Suwalki, Russia, and came to the United States in 1902. Dushkin graduated from City College of New York and Teachers College, Columbia University. He went to Palestine in 1919, was instructor in English and school administration in Teachers' Seminary, Jerusalem, from 1919 to 1921; secretary of the pedagogic committee of the Board of Education of the Yishuv in Palestine; first government inspector of Jewish schools; and leader of the scout movement in Palestine. In 1921 Dushkin prepared a survey of Jewish education in Palestine for the Palestine government. He was director of the Chicago Board of Jewish Education from 1921 to 1934; principal of the Hebrew University secondary school in Jerusalem and director of the Department of Teacher Training from 1934 to 1939; and executive director of the Jewish Education Committee of New York from 1939 to 1949. From 1949 until his death, he was executive dean for undergraduate studies at the Hebrew University. He wrote *Living Bridges: Memoirs of an Educator* (Jerusalem, 1975). Died June 2, 1976, in Jerusalem. *References*: *CA*; *Jewish Education* 41 (Summer-Fall 1971), entire issue; and *NYT*, June 4, 1976.

DWIGHT, HARRISON GRAY OTIS (1803–1862). Missionary, born November 22, 1803, in Conway, Franklin County, Massachusetts. Dwight graduated from Hamilton College and Andover Theological Seminary, and was ordained in 1830. In 1830 he became a missionary under the American Board of Commissioners for Foreign Missions (ABCFM)*, and in 1830–1831 went with Eli Smith* on a tour of exploration of Armenia. He and Smith co-authored *Missionary Researchers in Armenia: Including a Journey Through Asia Minor, and into Georgia and Persia, with a Visit to the Nestorians and Chaldean Christians at Oormiah and Salmas* (Boston, 1833). He became a missionary to the Armenians in Constantinople in 1831, and in 1859–1860 he made an extensive trip on horseback through the whole area. He wrote *Christianity Revived in the East; or, A Narrative of the Work of God Among the Armenians of Turkey* (New York, 1850). Died January 25, 1862, in a railroad accident at Salisbury, Vermont. *References*: *AndoverTS*; *DAB*; *EM*; and *NCAB* 10:490.

DWIGHT, HARRISON GRISWOLD (1875–1959). Author, son of Henry Otis Dwight,* born August 6, 1875, in Constantinople. Dwight graduated from Amherst College, was correspondent for the *Chicago Record-Herald* from 1898 to 1902, served as curator of the Authors Club in New York from 1903 to 1906, and worked for magazines in Europe and the Middle East from 1906 to 1914. He served with the Supreme War Council in Versailles and with the Peace Commission in Paris in 1918–1919; was a special assistant in the Department of State from 1920 to 1925 and from 1930 to 1933; and assistant director of the Frick Collection in New York City from 1936 to 1946. Dwight wrote *Constantinople, Old and New* (New York, 1915), *Stamboul Nights* (Garden City, N.Y., 1916), *Persian Miniatures* (Garden City, N.Y., 1917), and *Emperor of Elam and Other Stories* (Garden City, N.Y. 1920). Died March 24, 1959, in New York City. *References*: *Amherst*; *NYT*, March 26, 1959; and *WWWA*.

DWIGHT, HENRY OTIS (1843–1917). Missionary and author, son of Harrison Gray Otis Dwight,* born June 3, 1843, in Constantinople. Dwight graduated from Ohio Wesleyan University and served in the Civil War. He was the business agent of the American Board of Commissioners for Foreign Missions (ABCFM)* mission in Constantinople from 1867 to 1872, and editor of its Turkish publications from 1872 to 1899. He revised and edited the second edition of James William Redhouse's lexicon of the Turkish language which was published in Constantinople in 1877. From 1875 until 1892 he was also the Constantinople correspondent for *The New York Tribune*. Dwight was ordained in 1880, resigned in 1901, and was involved in literary and editorial work from 1901 to 1904. He was editor-in-chief of the *Encyclopedia of Missions* and became recording secretary of the American Bible Society* in 1907. He wrote the history of the American Bible Society; *Turkish Life in Wartime* (New York, 1881), *Treaty Rights of American Missionaries in Turkey* (New York, 1893), *Constantinople and Its Problems: Its Peoples, Customs, Religions and Progress* (New York, 1901), and *A Muslim Sir Galahad: A Present Day Story of-Islam in Turkey* (New York, 1913). *References*: *DAB*; *NCAB* 10:490; and *WWWA*.

DYE, WILLIAM MCENTYRE (1831–1899). Soldier, born February 1831 in Pennsylvania. Dye graduated from the U.S. Military Academy in 1853 and served in the Union Army during the Civil War. He resigned from the army in 1870 and went into farming. Looking for adventure, he joined in 1873 the Egyptian General Staff as an assistant to General Charles Pomeroy Stone.* He participated in the battle of Gura in the Egyptian-Abyssinian War of 1875–1876 and was wounded. He returned to the United States in 1878, and he wrote an account of the war in *Moslem Egypt and Christian Abyssinia, or Military Service Under the Khedive, in his Provinces and beyond their Borders* (New York, 1880). Later he served as chief of police in Washington, D.C. He was chief military adviser to the Korean government from 1888 until 1899. Died November 13, 1899, in Muskegon, Michigan. *References*: *CWD*; *DAB*; Herman M. Katz, *Brig-*

adier General William McEntire Dye: A Pioneer of U.S. Military Contributions to Korea (n.p., 1982); and *WAMB*.

DYKSTRA, DIRK (1879–1956). Missionary, born in Welsryp, the Netherlands. Dykstra graduated from Hope College and Western Theological Seminary, and was ordained in 1914. He served in the Arabian Mission* from 1906 to 1952 and established a hospital in Muscat. Died November 1, 1956, in Holland, Michigan. *References*: *HDRCA*; *The Holland* [Michigan] *Evening Sentinel*, November 2, 1956.

DYSON, ROBERT H(ARRIS), JR. (1927–   ). Archaeologist and museum director, born August 2, 1927, in York, Pennsylvania. Dyson graduated from Harvard University. He was assistant curator at the University Museum of the University of Pennsylvania from 1955 to 1962, associate curator from 1962 to 1967, curator in 1967, and director of the museum in 1982. Dyson was field director of the University Museum and the Iranian Archaeological Service archaeological expedition to Tepe Hasanlu, Iran, from 1956 until 1977. *References*: *AMWS*; *WWA*.

E

EATON, WILLIAM (1764–1811). Army officer and diplomat, born February 23, 1764, in Woodstock, Connecticut. Eaton graduated from Dartmouth College and was commissioned captain in the U.S. Army in 1792. He served in the Army of the West and later in Georgia from 1792 to 1795 and in Philadelphia from 1795 to 1797; was consul to Tunis from 1798 to 1804; and was navy agent to the Barbary States. In 1804–1805 he led a unit of marines and mercenaries in a 600-mile march across the Libyan Desert from Alexandria, Egypt, to Derna, Tripoli, to try to restore the exiled ruler of Tripoli to his throne. He captured Derna, but was then recalled when Tobias Lear,* consul general in Algiers, signed a treaty with the illegal ruler of Tripoli. Eaton was later a member of the Massachusetts legislature. Died June 1, 1811, in Brimfield, Massachusetts. *References*: Correspondence, New York Historical Society; *ACAB*; *DAB*; Samuel Edwards, *Barbary General: The Life of William Eaton* (Englewood Cliffs, N.J., 1968); *NCAB* 11:505; John H. Sedgwick, "William Eaton: A Sanguine Man," *New England Quarterly* 1 (1928): 107–123; *WAMB*; and *WWWA*.

ECKFORD, HENRY (1775–1832). Marine architect and shipbuilder, born March 12, 1775, in Kilwinning, near Irvine, Scotland, and came to the United States in 1796. Eckford was superintendent of shipbuilding in Lake Ontario during the War of 1812 and naval contractor in the Brooklyn Navy Yard from 1817 to 1820. He established his own yard in 1821 and built the steamer *Robert Fulton*, which made the first successful steam voyage from New York City to New Orleans and Havana, Cuba, in 1822. The last ship he built was a corvette for the Sultan of Turkey. Eckford sailed to Turkey on board this ship and was placed in charge of naval construction in Turkey. Died while reorganizing the Turkish navy yard on November 12, 1832, in Constantinople. *References*: *ACAB*; *DAB*; *NCAB* 1:350; Phyllis D. Wheelock, "Henry Eckford (1775–1832), an American Shipbuilder," *American Neptune* 7 (1947): 186–195; and *WWWA*.

EDDY, DANIEL CLARKE (1823–1896). Clergyman and author, born May 21, 1823, in Salem, Massachusetts. Eddy graduated from New Hampshire Theological Institution and held pastorates in Lowell, Massachusetts, Boston, Brooklyn, Philadelphia, Fall River, Massachusetts, and Hyde Park, New York. In 1861 he traveled in the Middle East and wrote the first American children's books about that area of the world, *Walter's Tour in the East* series (New York, 1862–1864). This series was composed of five volumes: *Walter in Egypt*, *Walter in Jerusalem*, *Walter in Damascus*, *Walter in Samaria*, and *Walter in Constantinople*. Died July 26, 1896, in Cottage City on Martha's Vineyard, Massachusetts. *References*: *DAB*; *NCAB* 9:501; and *WWWA*.

EDDY, WILLIAM ALFRED (1896–1962). Educator and diplomat, born on March 9, 1896, in Sidon, Syria, to American parents. Eddy graduated from Princeton University and served in the marines in World War I. From 1923 to 1928 he was chairman of the English Department at the American University in Cairo,* and while there is credited with having introduced basketball to Egypt. He was assistant professor of English at Dartmouth College from 1928 to 1936, and president of Hobart and William Smith colleges in Geneva, New York, from 1936 to 1942. He served in the Office of Strategic Services during World War II; was naval attaché in Cairo in 1941 and in Tangier in 1942; served on the staff of Allied Forces Headquarters in Algiers in 1943; and was ambassador to Saudi Arabia from 1944 to 1946. Eddy served as interpreter at President Franklin D. Roosevelt's meeting with King Ibn Saud in 1945 and wrote *FDR Meets Ibn Saud* (Washington, D.C., 1954). He was also chief of a special diplomatic mission to the Kingdom of Yemen, special assistant to the secretary of state in charge of research and intelligence in 1946–1947, and Middle East consultant to the Arabian American Oil Company (ARAMCO)* and Tapline from 1947 to 1962. Died May 3, 1962, in Beirut. *References*: *NCAB* 49:177; *NYT*, May 5, 1962; and *WWWA*.

EDDY, WILLIAM WOODBRIDGE (1825–1900). Missionary, born December 18, 1825, in Penn Yan, New York. Eddy graduated from Williams College and Union Theological Seminary, and was ordained in 1851. In 1851 he went to Syria as a missionary under the American Board of Commissioners for Foreign Missions (ABCFM)*, was stationed in Aleppo from 1851 to 1854, in Sidon, where he established a girls' seminary, from 1854 to 1874, and in Beirut from 1875 to 1900. In 1878 he became instructor at the theological seminary in Beirut, performing pastoral and editorial work. Died January 26, 1900, in Beirut. His daughter, **MARY PIERSON EDDY (1864–1923)**, was born September 21, 1864, in Sidon, Syria, and graduated from Elmira College and the Woman's Medical College of the New York Infirmary, and was a medical missionary in Syria under the Presbyterian Church in the USA Board of Foreign Missions* from 1893 to 1914. She was the first woman granted a license to practice medicine in the Ottoman Empire, and in 1908 established near Beirut the first tuberculosis sanitarium in that country. Died September 11, 1923, in Beirut, Syria. *References*: *Hewitt*; *UnionTS*.

EDDY-MIKESELL MISSION. Economic mission composed of George Eddy, gold expert in the Office of International Finance of the Treasury Department, and Raymond French Mikesell,* representative of the Department of the Treasury in the Middle East, which went to Saudi Arabia in 1948 to look at its monetary system and to give informal technical advice on monetary problems.

EDGERTON, WILLIAM FRANKLIN (1893–1970). Egyptologist, born September 30, 1893, in Binghamton, New York. Edgerton graduated from Cornell University and the universities of Pennsylvania and Chicago, and served in World War I and World War II. He was assistant professor of ancient history at the University of Louisville in 1924–1925, professor of history at Vassar College in 1925–1926, associate professor of Egyptology at the University of Chicago from 1929 to 1937, and professor from 1937 until his retirement in 1959. He participated in an archaeological survey in Iraq and Syria for the Oriental Institute in 1920; was epigrapher in the epigraphic and architectural survey conducted by the Oriental Institute in Luxor, Egypt, from 1926 to 1929; and collected graffiti at Medinet Habu, near Luxor, for the Oriental Institute, from 1931 to 1933. Died March 1970 in Chicago. *Reference*: *WWWA*.

EILTS, HERMANN FREDERICK (1922–   ). Diplomat, born March 23, 1922, in Weissenfels Saale, Germany, came to the United States in 1926, and was naturalized in 1930. Eilts graduated from Ursinus College, Johns Hopkins University's School of Advanced International Studies, and the University of Pennsylvania, and served in World War II. He entered the foreign service in 1947 and served in Teheran and Jiddah. He was principal officer in Aden and second secretary in Sanaa; second secretary, consul, and chief of the political section in Iraq from 1954 to 1956; first secretary in London from 1962 to 1964; and counselor and deputy chief of mission in Tripoli in 1964–1965. He was ambassador to Saudi Arabia from 1965 to 1970, diplomatic adviser at the U.S. Army War College from 1970 to 1973, and ambassador to Egypt from 1973 to 1979. He played an active role in Henry Kissinger's* shuttle diplomacy in 1974–1975, and was later involved in President Anwar el-Sadat's peace initiative. Eilts became professor of international relations at Boston University in 1979. *References*: *BRDS*; *DADH*; *MENA*; *NYT*, January 28, 1978; *WWA*; and *WWAP*.

EINSTEIN, LEWIS DAVID (1877–1967). Diplomat and historian, born March 15, 1877, in New York City. Einstein graduated from Columbia University, entered the diplomatic service in 1903, and served as third secretary in Paris and London until 1906. From 1906 to 1909 he was second secretary and then first secretary in Constantinople as well as chargé d'affaires. He was secretary of legation in Peking from 1909 to 1911 and minister to Costa Rica in 1911. In

1915 he was a special agent at Constantinople and wrote *Inside Constantinople: A Diplomatist's Diary During the Dardanelles Expedition, April-September 1915* (London, 1915). In 1915–1916 he was a special agent to Sofia, assisting in caring for British interests in Bulgaria. From 1921 until his retirement in 1930, he was minister to Czechoslovakia. Died December 4, 1967, in Paris. His autobiography, *A Diplomat Looks Back*, ed. Lawrence E. Gelfand (New Haven, Conn., 1968), was published after his death. *References*: Papers, University of Wyoming Library; *DADH*; *NYT*, December 5, 1967; and *WWWA*.

EISEN, GUSTAVUS A(UGUSTUS) (1847–1940). Archaeologist and biologist, born August 2, 1847, in Stockholm, Sweden. Eisen graduated from the University of Uppsala, came to the United States in 1872, settled in Fresno, California, and was naturalized in 1887. As a horticulturist, he was particularly concerned with the Smyrna fig, was responsible for the introduction of the blastophaga to California in 1891, and conducted a variety of biological studies. He was the originator of the Sequoia National Park in California in 1890, and curator at the California Academy of Sciences from 1892 to 1900. In 1903 he became interested in Christian and Jewish archaeology and antique glass, and from 1903 to 1915, he explored Algeria, Tunis, Morocco, and Egypt. He wrote *The Great Chalice of Antioch* (New York, 1923). Died October 29, 1940, in New York City. *References*: E. O. Essig, *A History of Entomology* (New York, 1931), 615–617; *NYT*, October 30, 1940; and *WWWA*.

EISENHOWER DOCTRINE. On January 5, 1957 President Dwight D. Eisenhower asked Congress for a joint resolution endorsing the president's use of force in the Middle East to prevent the Soviet Union from expanding its influence in the region. The United States was prepared to provide military assistance to any nation desiring such assistance and use its armed forces to assist any nation requiring assistance against armed Communist aggression. The resolution was enacted on March 9, 1957. The only application of the doctrine occured in 1958, when President Eisenhower ordered marines to Lebanon*. *References*: *DADH*; *Encyclopedia of American Foreign Policy* (New York, 1978), 1:292–301; and Stephen J. Genco, "The Eisenhower Doctrine: Deterrence in the Middle East, 1957–1958," in Alexander George and Richard Smoke, eds., *Deterrence in American Foreign Policy: Theory and Practice* (New York, 1974), pp. 309–362.

ELDER, EARL E(DGAR) (1887–1973). Missionary educator and administrator, born March 23, 1887, in Albia, Iowa. Elder graduated from Monmouth College (Ill.) and Princeton Theological Seminary, and was ordained in 1914. He was a teacher in Assiut College* from 1908 to 1911, returned as a missionary to Egypt in 1915, was head of a boys' day and boarding school in Cairo, and taught at the theological seminary of the Synod of the Nile. In 1925 he began teaching Arabic at the School of Oriental Studies of the American University in

Cairo,* served as secretary of the Egypt mission, and treasurer of the Cairo station and the Delta Presbytery. After retirement, Elder was named coordinator of religious activities at Temple University, Philadelphia. He edited *Egyptian Colloquial Arabic Reader* (London, 1927), and wrote *Arabic Grammar, Inductive Method* (Cairo, 1937), and *Vindicating a Vision: The Story of the American Mission in Egypt 1854–1954* (Philadelphia, 1958). Died April 11, 1973. *Reference*: PrincetonTS.

ELDERKIN, GEORGE WICKER (1879–1965). Archaeologist, born October 5, 1879, in Chicago. Elderkin graduated from Dartmouth College and Johns Hopkins University, studied at the American School of Classical Studies in Athens, and served in the Army Ambulance Service in World War I. He joined the Princeton University faculty in 1910, was associate professor of art and architecture from 1921 to 1928, and professor from 1928 until his retirement in 1948. He was editor-in-chief of the *American Journal of Archaeology* from 1924 to 1931. In the 1930s he directed the archaeological expedition that excavated Antioch on the Orontes in southern Turkey, and edited *Antioch on the Orontes* (Princeton, N.J., 1934–1941). Died December 19, 1965, in Venice, Florida. *References*: *NYT*, December 20, 1965; *WWWA*.

ELKUS, ABRAHAM ISAAC (1867–1947). Lawyer and diplomat, born August 6, 1867, in New York City. Elkus graduated from the College of the City of New York and Columbia University, was admitted to the bar in 1888, and began to practice in New York City in 1888. He was ambassador to Turkey from 1916 to 1919, although he was forced to leave Turkey in 1917. He was involved in relief work to refugees and prisoners of war, and was president of the Red Cross Relief Commission and the American Jewish Relief in Turkey. In 1920 he was a member of the commission that decided the Aaland Islands dispute between Finland and Sweden. Died October 15, 1947, in Red Bank, New Jersey. *References*: *EJ*; *NCAB* 38:47; and *WWWA*.

ELLIOTT, JESSE DUNCAN (1782–1845). Naval officer, born July 14, 1782, in Hagerstown, Maryland. Elliott was commissioned lieutenant in the U.S. Navy in 1810 and served in the War of 1812. In 1815 he was a member of Stephen Decatur's* squadron against Algiers. He later commanded the West Indian Squadron, was commandant of the Boston Navy Yard, commanded the *Constitution*, was commander-in-chief of the Mediterranean Squadron from 1835 to 1837, and was named commandant of the Philadelphia Navy Yard in 1844. Died December 10, 1845, in Philadelphia. *References*: *ACAB*; *DAB*; *NCAB* 7:39; *WAMB*; and *WWWA*.

ELLIOTT, MABEL EVELYN (1881–1968). Physician and medical missionary, born February 8, 1881, in Tottenham, England, and grew up in St. Augustine, Florida. Elliott graduated from the University of Chicago and Rush

Medical College, and practiced medicine in Benton Harbor, Michigan. She served as relief doctor in France during World War I, and in 1919 she became a member of the American Women's Hospitals* group in the Middle East. She operated a hospital in Marash, Turkey, in 1919, and in Izmid, in 1920; was medical director for Near East Relief* in Armenia from 1921 to 1923; and took charge of an orphanage in Alexandropol. She returned to the United States in 1923 and wrote *Beginning Again in Ararat* (New York, 1924). She practiced medicine in Philadelphia in 1924–1925, and was medical missionary under the Episcopal Church in Japan from 1925 until her retirement in 1941. She later served on the staff of Penney Farms Memorial Community, Florida. Died June 13, 1968, in West Palm Beach, Florida. *References*: *Encyclopedia of American Biography* (West Palm Beach, Fla., 1970), n.s. 40:198; Esther P. Lovejoy, *Women Doctors of the World* (New York, 1957), pp. 325–332.

ELLIS, HARRY B(EARSE) (1921–   ). Journalist and author, born December 9, 1921, in Springfield, Massachusetts. Ellis graduated from Wesleyan University, became staff member of the *Christian Science Monitor* in 1947, was Middle East correspondent in Beirut from 1952 to 1954, and Mediterranean correspondent in Beirut from 1959 to 1960. He was also assistant overseas news editor from 1955 to 1958, chief of the Paris Bureau from 1961 to 1964, and correspondent for Germany in Bonn from 1965 to 1972, when he became a correspondent in Washington, D.C. He wrote *Heritage in the Desert, the Arabs and the Middle East* (New York, 1956), *Israel and the Middle East* (New York, 1957), *Challenge in the Middle East: Communist Influence and American Policy* (New York, 1960), and *Israel: One Land, Two People* (New York, 1972). *References*: *CA*; *WWA*.

ELLIS, WILLIAM THOMAS (1873–1950). Religious columnist, born October 25, 1873, in Allegheny, Pennsylvania. Ellis was editor of religious magazines from 1894 to 1902. He toured the world, investigating social, religious, and political conditions for a syndicate of American newspapers in 1906–1907 and in 1910–1911. He interviewed King Ibn Saud and the last Sultan of Turkey, and he was an early writer about Lawrence of Arabia. He reported from Russia in 1917 and from the various fronts in 1917–1918; was special correspondent for the *New York Herald* and other newspapers in the Balkans, Turkey, and Egypt in 1919; and was again in the Middle East in 1923 as reporter for the *Saturday Evening Post* and other magazines. He made a tour of Palestine in 1925–1926, identifying the site of Kadesh Barnea in the Sinai. He revisited Sinai and Petra in 1930, and returned to Palestine and the Middle East in 1938, as correspondent for the *New York Herald Tribune*. He wrote *Bible Lands To-day* (New York, 1927). Died August 14, 1950, In Lyndhurst, Ontario. *References*: *NYT*, August 16, 1950; *WWWA*.

ELMENDORF, DWIGHT LATHROP (1859–1929). Lecturer and photographer, born March 13, 1859, in Brooklyn, New York. Elmendorf graduated from Princeton University. He was teacher of the deaf from 1885 to 1897, and a lecturer after 1897, using lantern slides. He traveled in the Middle East in 1901, took photographs with which he illustrated his books and lectures, and wrote *A Camera Crusade Through the Holy Land* (New York, 1912). Died May 7, 1929, in New York City. *References*: *MBEP*; *WWWA*.

ELY, CHARLOTTE ELIZABETH (1839–1915) and **ELY, MARY ANN CAROLINE** (1841–1913). Missionary educators, Charlotte Elizabeth born July 2, 1839, in Philadelphia, and Mary Ann Caroline June 2, 1841, in Wilmington, Delaware. The sisters graduated from Mount Holyoke College. Financially independent and motivated by religious convictions, they came to Turkey in 1868, founded and operated a girls' school at Bitlis, near the Persian frontier, which they named "The Mount Holyoke Seminary of Kurdistan." Mary Ann Caroline died May 5, 1913, in Bitlis, and Charlotte Elizabeth on July 11, 1915, also in Bitlis. *References*: *Mount Holyoke*; Frank A. Stone, "Mt. Holyoke's Impact on the Land of Ararat," *MW* 66 (1976): 44–57.

ENGERT, CORNELIUS VAN H(EMERT) (1887–1985). Diplomat, born December 31, 1887 in Vienna, Austria, and brought to the United States as a child. He graduated from the University of California and its law school and Harvard University. He was attaché in Constantinople from 1912 to 1916, and represented the embassy at Chanak during the Dardanelles campaign in 1914–1915. He went on a special mission to Syria and Palestine in 1916–1917, and was interned by the Turks in 1917. He was third secretary in the Hague from 1917 to 1919, assistant to the U.S. High Commissioner in Constantinople in 1919–1920, and second secretary in Teheran from 1920 to 1922. He was sent to Kabul, Afghanistan, in 1922, was the first U.S. diplomatic officer to visit Kabul, and wrote *A Report on Afghanistan* (Washington, D.C., 1924). He was first secretary in Havana and San Salvador; first secretary in Santiago, Caracas, and Peking; first secretary in Cairo from 1933 to 1935; minister and consul general in Addis Ababa from 1935 to 1937; chargé d'affaires in Teheran from 1937 to 1940; and consul general in Beirut and Damascus from 1940 to 1942. Engert served as an intermediary in the negotiations between the British and Free French forces and the Vichy French garrisons in Syria and Lebanon during World War II. He was the first minister to reside in Kabul from 1942 to 1945. In 1945 he traveled from Kabul to Moscow via Bukhara and Samarkand, and in 1945 he visited Katmandu, Nepal. He was assistant and acting diplomatic adviser to the United Nations Relief and Rehabilitation Administration in 1946–1947, went on a special mission to the Middle East in 1947, and was the representative of the World Bank in the Middle East from 1948 to 1951. He was later a business consultant in Belgium. Died May 12, 1985, in Washington, D.C. *References*: *BRDS*; *NYT*, May 14, 1985; and *WWWA*.

ENGLISH, EARL (1824–1893). Naval officer, born February 18, 1824, in Crosswicks, Burlington County, Vermont. English entered the navy in 1840 and graduated from the U.S. Naval Academy in 1846. He was attached to the *Dolphin* and engaged in deep sea soundings in the Atlantic Ocean. He served in the Civil War and in the East India station. English commanded the *Congress* on the European station after 1874, was in Tripoli in 1875, and settled a triffe dispute between the pasha of Tripoli and the U.S. consul there, Michel Vidal,* using "gunboat diplomacy" threatening to bombard the city unless the pasha apologized to the consul, which he did. He was commander of the Portsmouth, New Hampshire, naval station and of the European station from 1884 until his retirement in 1886, with the rank of rear admiral. Died July 16, 1893, in Washington, D.C. *References*: *ACAB*; *NCAB* 5:394.

ENGLISH, GEORGE BETHUNE (1787–1828). Adventurer, born March 7, 1787, in Cambridge, Massachusetts. English graduated from Harvard College and Harvard Divinity School. He was unsuccessful as a minister and as editor of a newspaper, and was then commissioned a lieutenant in the marines and was sent to the Mediterranean. He left his ship in Alexandria, Egypt, in 1820, resigned his commission, became a Muslim, changed his name to Mohammed Effendy, and became an officer in the Turkish Army. He was appointed general of artillery in the Ismail Pasha's military expedition to Sennar in the Sudan in 1820–1821, and wrote an account of the campaign in *A Narrative of the Expedition to Dongola and Sennaer* (Boston, 1823). He resigned from the Turkish service in 1821 because he did receive the expected rewards and returned to the United States. He was appointed by secretary of state John Quincy Adams a secret agent to discover Ottoman attitudes toward a possible commercial treaty and allowing American ships to trade in the Black Sea. He conducted negotiations between 1823 and 1826, but they failed. He was left broke, unemployed and distrusted. Died September 20, 1828, in Washington, D.C. *References*: *ACAB*; *DAB*; *NCAB* 13:552; *WWWA*; and *WWWE*.

ERIM, KENAN TEVFIK (1929–   ). Archaeologist, born February 13, 1929, in Istanbul, came to the United States in 1947, and graduated from New York and Princeton universities. Erim was assistant professor of classics at New York University from 1958 to 1962, associate professor from 1962 to 1971, and professor after 1971. In 1967 he became director of the archaeological excavations in Aphrodisias, in southwest Turkey. He wrote *Aphrodisias: City of Venus Aphrodite* (New York, 1986). *References*: *DAS*; *WWA*.

ESCADRILLE CHERIFIENNE. Special squadron of volunteer flyers, composed mainly of Americans, set up by the French in 1925 to fight in the Rif Rebellion against French and Spanish colonial rule led by Abd-el-Krim. Its commanding officer was Colonel Charles Sweeney,* who was hired to organize the unit. It was formed in Paris in June 1925 and contained seventeen Americans, twelve of whom were pilots. It flew 470 bombing and observation missions in Morocco, but the bombing of Chaouen, which was defenseless and which was declared an open city, was criticized all over the world, and the French disbanded it in November 1925. *References*: "American Bombers and Riff Babies," *Literary Digest* 87 (October 31, 1925): 29–30; "Our Flying Fighters in Morocco," *Literary Digest* 87 (October 3, 1925): 10.

ESSELSTYN, LEWIS F(ILLMORE) (1863–1918). Missionary, born April 13, 1863, in Clayton, New York. Esselstyn graduated from Alma (Mich.) and Carroll colleges and Auburn Theological Seminary, and was ordained in 1887. He was missionary under the Presbyterian Church in the USA Board of Foreign Missions* in Persia from 1887 until his death. He served in Teheran from 1887 to 1911 and in 1911 became the first American missionary in Meshed, Persia. Died May 30, 1918, in Meshed. *Reference*: *AuburnTS*.

ESSEX. Ship of Salem under command of Captain Joseph Orne. The *Essex* was captured by Arab pirates in 1806 on a trip to Mocha, and all hands, except one, were murdered. *References*: J. D. Phillips, "Loss of the Ship Essex in 1806," *Essex Institute Historical Collections* 77 (1941): 299–305.

ETHRIDGE, MARK FOSTER (1896–1981). Editor and publisher, born April 22, 1896, in Meridian, Mississippi. Ethridge graduated from the University of Mississippi and served in the navy in World War I. From 1919 to 1936 he was editor of newspapers in Meridian, Columbus and Macon, Georgia, Washington, D.C., and Richmond, Virginia. In 1936 he became vice president and general manager, publisher, and chairman of the board of the *Louisville Courier-Journal and Louisville Times*, was vice president and editor of *Newsday* in 1963–1964, and began teaching journalism at the University of North Carolina in 1968. He was special envoy to Bulgaria in 1945 and chief U.S. delegate to the U.N. commission of inquiry concerning Greek frontier incidents. Ethridge became head of the U.S. delegation and U.S. representative on the Palestine Conciliation Commission (PCC) in 1948. Died April 5, 1981, in Moncure, North Carolina. His wife, **WILLIE SNOW ETHRIDGE (1900–1982)**, historian and author, was born December 10, 1900, in Savannah, Georgia. She was a reporter on the *Macon Telegraph* and later became a travel writer and historian. She accompanied her husband to the Middle East and wrote *Going to Jerusalem* (New York, 1950), and *There's Yeast in the Middle East* (New York, 1963). Died December 14, 1982, in Key West, Florida. *References*: *Biography News* 1 (1974): 276; *CA*; *CB* 1946; *NCAB* G:119; *NYT*, April 7, 1981; *PolProf: Truman*; and *WWWA*.

EUPHRATES COLLEGE. A co-educational college founded by Crosby Howard Wheeler* in Harput, Turkey, in 1878 and financed by the American Board of Commissioners for Foreign Missions (ABCFM).* It was initially named Armenia College, but the name was officially changed in 1888 as it proved offensive to the Turkish government. It was closed in 1915 after several Armenian faculty members were killed in the pogrom against the Armenians, and the others went into exile. *References*: Hapet M. Philibosian, ed. *Memoranda of Euphrates College (Formerly Armenia College) 1878–1915* (Boston, 1942); *Stone*, ch. 8.

EVANGELICAL SEMINARY, CAIRO. Founded in Cairo in 1863 by the United Presbyterian Church of North America Board of Foreign Missions.* The seminary was transferred to Assiut for twenty years and then returned to Cairo. It later became the responsibility of the Coptic Evangelical Church of the Nile Valley. *References*: Yorke Allen, Jr., *A Seminary Survey* (New York, 1960), pp. 22–23.

EVELAND, WILBUR (CRANE) (1918–   ). Intelligence officer, born July 1, 1918, in Spokane, Washington. Eveland served in the Marine Corps Reserve from 1936 to 1940, and in the army from 1941 to 1945. He was special agent for the Counter Intelligence Corps from 1941 to 1948; attaché in Baghdad from 1949 to 1952; member of the General Staff in 1952–1953; and head of the Office of the Assistant Secretary of Defense in the Middle East in 1953–1954. He was covert associate for the Central Intelligence Agency in the Middle East and Africa from 1955 to 1960; vice president of Vinnell Corporation in Rome, Washington, and Beirut from 1960 to 1966; freelance consultant to oil companies from 1966 to 1974; head of a petroleum support company from 1967 to 1974; and vice president of Fluor Arabia Ltd. in the Middle East in 1974–1975. Eveland became a writer in 1975 and wrote *Ropes of Sands: America's Failure in the Middle East* (New York, 1980). *Reference*: CA.

EXPEDITION TO THE DEAD SEA AND THE RIVER JORDAN, 1848. A naval expedition to explore the River Jordan and the Dead Sea, headed by Lieutenant William Francis Lynch,* which traveled in 1848 to the Sea of Galilee, down the Jordan River to the Dead Sea and around the Dead Sea. It was the first scientific survey of the Dead Sea and produced maps, drawings, and scientific reports. Lynch published the reports of the expedition in the *Official Report of the United States Expedition to the River Jordan-and the Dead Sea* (Philadelphia, 1849), and *Narrative of the United States Expedition to the River Jordan and the Dead Sea* (Philadelphia, 1849). *References*: Yehoshua Ben-Arieh, "William F. Lynch's Expedition to the Dead Sea, 1847–8," *Prologue* 5 (1973): 15–21; Vincent Ponko, Jr., *Ships, Seas, and Scientists: U.S. Naval Exploration and Discovery in the Nineteenth Century* (Annapolis, Md., 1974), ch. 4.

F

FAIRCHILD, DAVID GRANDISON (1869–1954). Plant explorer, born April 7, 1869, in Lansing, Michigan. Fairchild graduated from Kansas State College of Agriculture. Between 1895 and 1903, he went on expeditions in search of plants for introduction to the United States. He explored Egypt and the Persian Gulf in 1901–1902 and wrote *Persian Gulf Dates and Their Introduction into America* (Washington, D.C., 1903). He then organized the Plant Introduction Section of the Department of Agriculture, serving as its first chief from 1904 to 1928. He directed the Allison V. Armour expeditions from 1925 to 1927 and in 1932–1933, which included trips to Algeria and Morocco. He wrote *Exploring for Plants; from Notes of the Allison Vincent Armour Expeditions for the United States Department of Agriculture, 1925, 1926 and 1927* (New York, 1930). Fairchild was later in charge of the scientific work of the Fairchild Garden expedition to the Philippines and Dutch East Indies and collected plants in Central and South America. He wrote *The World Was My Garden: Travels of a Plant Explorer* (New York, 1938). Died August 2, 1954, in Coconut Grove, Florida. *References*: *DAB S5*; Marjory S. Douglas, *Aventures in Green World: The Story of David Fairchild and Barbour Lathrop* (Coconut Grove, Fla., 1973); *NCAB* C:253; *NYT*, August 7, 1954; Beryl Williams and Samuel Epstein, *Plant Explorer: David Fairchild* (New York, 1961); and *WWWA*.

FAIRSERVIS, WALTER A(SHLIN), JR. (1921–   ). Anthropologist, born in Brooklyn, New York. Fairservis graduated from the universities of Chicago and Michigan, and Columbia and Harvard universities. He was research assistant and research associate of the American Museum of Natural History and directed expeditions to the Kandahar and Seistan areas of Iran in 1949, to Seistan again in 1950, and to Hierakonpolis in Egypt, and wrote of his experiences in *Collier's* Magazine in 1951–1952. He was director of the Thomas Burke Memorial Washington State Museum and associate professor at the University of Washington, and became professor of anthropology at Vassar College in 1968. He wrote *Archaeological Studies in the Seistan Basin of Southwestern Afghanistan and*

Iran (New York, 1961), and *The Ancient Kingdoms of the Nile and the Doomed Monuments of Nubia* (New York, 1962). He was the scientific authority and the principal organizer of the Hall of Asian People at the American Museum of Natural History. *Reference*: *Daily News* [Poughkeepsie, N.Y.], May 15, 1974.

FARMAN, ELBERT ELI (1831–1911). Judge, born April 23, 1831, in New Haven, New York. Farman attended Genesee College, graduated from Amherst College, and was admitted to the bar in 1858. He traveled in Europe, studied at the universities of Berlin and Heidelberg from 1865 to 1867, practiced law in Warsaw, New York, from 1858 to 1876, and was district attorney of Warsaw County, New York, from 1868 to 1875. He was agent and consul general in Egypt from 1876 to 1881, accompanied ex-President Ulysses S. Grant up the Nile in 1878, and in 1879 secured an obelisk as a gift from the khedive to New York City (which was transported to the United States by Henry Honeychurch Gorringe*). He was a member of the international commission to revise the judicial codes of Egypt for the use of the Mixed Courts of Egypt* in 1880–1881 and judge of the Mixed Courts from 1881 until 1884. He had a large collection of ancient coins and Egyptian antiquities, now in the Metropolitan Museum of Art. He practiced law in the United States from 1884 to 1911, and wrote *Along the Nile with General Grant* (New York, 1904), and *Egypt and Its Betrayal* (New York, 1908). Died December 30, 1911, in Warsaw, New York. *References*: *ACAB*; *DAB*; *NCAB* 6:508; *NYT*, January 1, 1912; and *WWWA*.

FARNSWORTH, (WILSON) AMOS (1822–1912). Missionary, born August 29, 1822, in Greene, New York. Farnsworth graduated from Middlebury College and Andover Theological Seminary, and was ordained in 1852. He was a missionary under the American Board of Commissioners for Foreign Missions (ABCFM)* in Kayseri, Turkey, from 1852 to 1903. He imported wagon wheels and axles and made Kayseri a center for the Anatolian wagon industry. He climbed Erciyas Dage, second highest peak in Turkey, and succeeded in reaching its summit in 1874. Died June 5, 1912, in Glen Ridge, New Jersey. *References*: *AndoverTS*; *NYT*, June 7, 1912; and *WWWA*.

FECHET, EUGENE OSCAR (1846–1925). Soldier, born March 14, 1846, in Michigan. Fechet served in the Union Army in the Civil War, graduated from the U.S. Military Academy in 1868, and was commissioned in the artillery. In 1872 he joined the Egyptian General Staff under General Charles Pomeroy Stone.* In 1873–1874 he surveyed the route from Aswan through the Nubian Desert to Abu Hamad and Berber, and prepared *Journal of the March of an Expedition in Nubia, Between Assouan and Abouhamid* (Cairo, 1878). He resigned from the Egyptian Army and left Egypt in 1874. Fechet was later engaged in mining in Venezuela and served as consul at Piedras Negras, Mexico, until 1898. He served in the army again during the Spanish-American War. He retired in 1910 with the rank of lieutenant-colonel. Died January 15, 1925, in Eustis,

Florida. *References*: "Diary," Ms., U.S. Military Academy Library, West Point, New York; *Hesseltine*; *Hill*; and *RAGMA*, 1925.

FENN, HARRY (1838–1911). Illustrator, born September 14, 1838, in Richmond, Surrey, England. Fenn was apprenticed to a wood carving firm, came to the United States at nineteen, and became an illustrator for the publishing house of D. Appleton and Company, providing many of the illustrations for their books and magazines. He spent fourteen months in 1878–1879 in the Middle East with the American illustrator John Douglas Woodward,* drawing the illustrations for *Picturesque Palestine, Sinai and Egypt* (New York, 1881). He later established a studio in Montclair, New Jersey. Died April 22, 1911, in Montclair. *References*: *ACAB*; *NCAB* 6:368; *NYT*, April 23, 1911; and *WWWA*.

FENZI, EMANUELE ORAZIO (1843–1924). Botanist and horticulturist, known from 1893 to 1913 as **DR. FRANCESCO FRANCESCHI**, born March 12, 1843, in Florence, Italy. Fenzi studied at the University of Pisa, concentrating on botany and horticulture, and also managed a bank and an estate. He came to the United States in 1893 and settled in Santa Barbara where he established a nursery business. He went to Libya in 1912 to develop a plant introduction garden in the Italian colony, directing the enterprise until his death. Died November 5, 1924, in Tripoli, Libya. *References*: *Journal of Heredity* 22 (1928): 122–128; John M. Tucker, *Francesco Francheschi, Botanist and Horticulturist* (Santa Barbara, Calif., 1945).

FERNEA, ROBERT ALAN (1932–   ). Anthropologist, born January 25, 1932, in Vancouver, Washington. Fernea graduated from Reed College and the University of Chicago. He taught anthropology at the American University of Cairo* from 1959 to 1965, was director of the Nubian Ethnological Survey from 1961 to 1965, and became professor of anthropology at the University of Texas in Austin in 1966. He wrote *Shaykh and Effendi: Changing Patterns of Authority Among the El Shabana of Southern Iraq* (Cambridge, Mass., 1970), *Nubians in Egypt: Peaceful People* (Austin, Tex., 1973), and edited *Contemporary Egyptian Nubia* (New Haven, Conn., 1966). His wife, **ELIZABETH WARNOCK FERNEA (1927–   )**, anthropologist, born October 21, 1927, in Milwaukee, and graduated from Reed and Mount Holyoke colleges and the University of Chicago. She was on the public relations staff of Reed College from 1950 until 1954, and at the University of Chicago until 1956. She spent two years with her husband in a small village in Iraq, and wrote of her experiences in *Guests of the Sheik* (New York, 1965). From 1956 to 1958, she was contract reporter and writer for the Agency for International Development in Baghdad, and after 1973, a member of the Center for Middle Eastern Studies at the University of Texas at Austin. She wrote *A View of the Nile* (Garden City, N.Y., 1970), *A Street in Marakech* (New York, 1975), and coedited *Middle Eastern Muslim Women Speak* (Austin, Tex., 1977). She also made several films about the Middle East. Together they wrote *The Arab World; Personal Encounters* (Garden City, N.Y., 1985). *References*: *AMWS*; *CA*; *MENA*; and *WWA*.

FIELD, CHARLES WILLIAM (1828–1892). Soldier, born April 6, 1828, in Woodford County, Kentucky. Field graduated from the U.S. Military Academy in 1849, was commissioned second lieutenant in the Dragoons, and was an instructor in the academy from 1855 to 1860. He joined the Confederate Army and was seriously wounded in the second battle of Bull Run. After the war, he was involved in business in Baltimore and Georgia. In 1875 he was appointed a colonel in the Egyptian Army engineers and was inspector general during the Egyptian-AbyssinianWar of 1875–1876. He returned to the United States in 1877 and was appointed doorkeeper of the U.S. House of Representatives in the 46th Congress. He was a government civil engineer from 1881 to 1885 and superintendent of the Hot Springs (Ark.) Reservation from 1885 to 1889. Died April 9, 1892, in Washington, D.C. *References*: *BDC*; *CWD*; *DAB*; and *Hesseltine*.

FIELD, HENRY (1902–1986). Anthropologist, born December 15, 1902, in Chicago. Field graduated from New College, Oxford University. He was assistant curator of physical anthropology at the Field Museum of Natural History in Chicago from 1926 to 1931, and curator from 1931 to 1941, and conducted the Field Museum's expeditions to the Middle East in 1925–1926, 1927–1928, and 1934. He was engaged in government research in Washington from 1941 to 1945, and was special anthropological adviser to Presidents Roosevelt and Truman. He did research on anthropology in South West Asia in 1946–1947, was a member of the University of California African Expedition in 1947–1948 and the Peabody Museum-Harvard University Expedition to the Near East in 1950, and was research fellow at Harvard University from 1950 to 1953. He wrote *Arabs of Central Iraq: Their History, Ethnology and Physical Characters* (Chicago, 1935), *Contributions to the Anthropology of Iran* (Chicago, 1939), *The Anthropology of Iraq* (Chicago, 1940–1952), *Contributions to the Anthropology of the Faiyum, Sinai, Sudan, Kenya* (Berkeley, Calif., 1952), *An Anthropological Reconnaissance in the Near East 1950* (Cambridge, Mass., 1956), *Ancient and Modern Man in Southwestern Asia* (Coral Gables, Fla., 1956), *North Arabian Desert Archaeological Survey 1925–60* (Cambridge, Mass., 1960), and *Contributions to the Anthropology of Saudi Arabia* (Miami, 1972). He also wrote an autobiography, *The Track of Man: Adventures of an Anthropologist* (Garden City, N.Y., 1953), *The Track of Man, Vol. 2: The White House Years 1941–1945* (Miami, 1962), and *Arab Desert Tales: Between the Two Wars* (Santa Fe, N.M., 1976). Died January 4, 1986, in Coral Gables, Florida. *References*: Papers, Franklin D. Roosevelt Library; *AMWS*; *CA*; *CB* 1955; *Biography News* 2 (November 1975): 1219–1221; *MENA*; *NYT*, January 7, 1986; and *WWA*.

FIELD, HENRY MARTYN (1822–1907). Clergyman and author, born April 3, 1822, in Stockbridge, Massachusetts. Field graduated from Williams College and the Theological Seminary at East Windsor, Connecticut. He was pastor in St. Louis, West Springfield, Massachusetts, and New York City, and was editor and owner of the *Evangelist*. Field made a trip around the world in 1875–1876, and visited the Middle East in 1882 which he described in *Among the Holy Hills* (New York, 1884), *The Greek Islands and Turkey After the War* (New York, 1885), and *On the Desert with a Brief Review of Recent Events in Egypt* (New York, 1883). He again traveled in the Mediterranean in 1886–1887 and wrote *The Barbary Coast* (New York, 1893). Died January 26, 1907, in Stockbridge, Massachusetts. *References*: *ACAB*; *DAB*; *NCAB* 5:360; *NYT*, January 27, 1907; and *WWWA*.

FINCH, JOHN WELLINGTON (1873–1951). Geologist and engineer, born November 3, 1873, in Lebanon, New York. Finch graduated from Colgate University and the University of Chicago, was state geologist of Colorado in 1901–1902, consulting engineer for various companies, and vice president and general manager of New York Orient Mines Company from 1916 to 1922. He did exploration work in China, Siam, and India from 1916 to 1920, explored Turkey and the Middle East in 1922, and is said to have been one of the ten men to enter the tomb of King Tutankamen. He was industrial adviser to the government of the Yunnan Province, China, from 1922 to 1925; professor of geology at the Colorado School of Mines from 1926 to 1930; dean of the School of Mines of the University of Idaho from 1930 to 1934; and director of the U.S. Bureau of Mines from 1934 to 1940. From 1940 to 1945 he was a consulting engineer in New York City. Died February 22, 1951, in Denver. *References*: *NCAB* 39:619; *PGSA* for 1952 (1953): 97–100; and *WWWA*.

FINLEY, JOHN HUSTON (1863–1940). Editor and educator, born October 19, 1863, in Grand Ridge, Illinois. Finley graduated from Knox College and studied at Johns Hopkins University; was secretary of the State Charities Aid Association in New York; editor of the *Charities Review* from 1889 to 1892; president of Knox College from 1892 to 1899; editor of *Harper's Weekly* in 1899; and professor of political science at Princeton University from 1900 to 1903. He was president of the City College of New York from 1903 to 1913; commissioner of education for the state of New York and chairman of the University of the State of New York from 1913 to 1921; associate editor of the *New York Times* from 1921 to 1937; and editor-in-chief in 1937–1938. He was head of the American Red Cross* in Palestine and the Near East in 1918–1919, and went to Palestine with the Red Cross Relief Commission. He was later vice chairman of Near East Relief.* He wrote an account of his adventures, *A Pilgrim in Palestine; Being an Account of a Journey on Foot by the First American Pilgrim After General Allenby's Recovery of the Holy Land* (New York, 1919). Died March 7, 1940, in New York City. *References*: Papers, New York Public

Library; *DAB S2*; Marvin E. Gettleman, *An Elusive Presence: The Discovery of John H. Finley and His America* (Chicago, 1979); *NCAB* 30:90; *NYT*, March 8, 1940; and *WWWA*.

FISH, BERT (1875–1943). Judge and diplomat, born October 8, 1875, in Bedford, Indiana. Fish graduated from John B. Stetson University, was admitted to the bar in 1902, practiced at DeLand, Florida, and engaged in the citrus industry. He was a judge of the criminal court at Volusia County, Florida, until his retirement in 1926. Fish was minister to Egypt from 1933 to 1939, the first American minister to Saudi Arabia from 1939 to 1941, and chairman of the U.S. delegation to the Montreux Conference in 1937 which resulted in ending the system of capitulations in Egypt which exempted foreigners living there from local jurisdiction. From 1941 until his death he was minister to Portugal. Died July 21, 1943, in Lisbon, Portugal. *References*: *NCAB* 33:225; *NYT*, July 22, 1943; and *WWWA*.

FISHER, CLARENCE STANLEY (1876–1941). Archaeologist, born August 17, 1876, in Philadelphia. Fisher graduated from the University of Pennsylvania. He was archaeological architect with the University of Pennsylvania Babylonian Expedition to Nippur in 1899–1900; a member of the Harvard University Expedition to Samaria, Palestine, from 1908 to 1910; chief archaeologist and Egyptologist of the University Museum in Philadelphia from 1914 to 1925; and worked in Egypt during World War I for Near East Relief.* He directed the University Museum expedition to Beth-Shan, Palestine, from 1921 to 1923, and served as architect for excavations at Giza, Girga, Thebes, and Memphis in Egypt. He directed the Oriental Institute excavation of Megiddo and the Haverford College excavations at Beth-Shemesh in Palestine, in 1928–1929, and was professor of archaeology at the American Schools of Oriental Research (ASOR)* from 1925 until his death. Fisher founded a home for homeless children in Jerusalem. He was co-author of *Excavations at Nippur* (Philadelphia, 1905–1906) and *Harvard Excavations at Samaria* (Cambridge, Mass., 1924). He wrote *The Excavation at Armageddon* (Chicago, 1929). Died July 20, 1941, in Jerusalem. *References*: Papers, Bodleian Library, Oxford; *BASOR* 83 (1941): 1–4; *DAB S3*; *NCAB* 40:286; *NYT*, July 22, 1941; *WWWA*; and *WWWE*.

FISHER, EDGAR JACOB (1885–1968). Educator, born September 28, 1885, in Rochester, New York. Fisher graduated from the University of Rochester and Columbia University, and was a teacher and principal of high schools in Roselle Park and Summit, New Jersey. He was assistant professor of history at Robert College* from 1913 to 1915, professor from 1915 to 1933, and dean from 1917 to 1919 and in 1922–1923. He was expelled from Turkey in 1934 because of his involvement in the translation into English of the official Turkish history which led to the publication of a critical review of it. He was assistant director of the Institute of International Education in New York City from 1935 to 1948,

and professor of history at Sweet Briar (Va.) College from 1948 until his retirement in 1953. He was associated with American Friends of the Middle East
from 1953 until 1957. Died November 19, 1968, in Lynchburg, Virginia. *References*: "Diary," Ms., Ohio State University Library; *NCAB* 55:187; *NYT*,
November 20, 1968; and *WWWA*.

FISK, PLINY (1792–1825). Missionary, born June 24, 1792, in Shelbourne,
Massachusetts. Fisk graduated from Middlebury College and Andover Theological Seminary, and was ordained in 1818. He conducted a missionary tour in
the South in 1818–1819, and became a missionary under the American Board
of Commissioners of Foreign Missions (ABCFM)* in Palestine in 1819. He
traveled in the Middle East and was transferred to Syria in 1825. Died October
23, 1825, in Beirut, Syria. *References*: *ACAB*; *AndoverTS*; and Alvan Bond,
Memoir of the Rev. Pliny Fisk, A M: Late Missionary to Palestine (Boston,
1828).

FISKE, FIDELIA (1816–1864). Missionary, educator, niece of Pliny Fisk,*
born Fidelia Fisk, May 1, 1816, in Shelburne, Massachusetts, but adopted the
ancestral name Fiske. Fiske graduated from Mount Holyoke Seminary. She was
a missionary under the American Board of Commissioners for Foreign Missions
(ABCFM)* to the Nestorians from 1843 to 1858, stationed in Urmia, Persia,
where she established a boarding school for girls in 1843. She returned to the
United States in 1858 and served as unofficial chaplain at Mount Holyoke College. Thomas Laurie's *Woman and Her Saviour in Persia* (Boston, 1863) is
based on material which she supplied. Died July 26, 1864, in Shelburne, Massachusetts. *References*: *DAB*; *EM*; *NAW*; and *NCAB* 3:525.

FLOYD, ROLLA (1837?–1911). Travel agent and tourist guide, born in Mitten
Mountain, Centerville, Maine. Floyd's family was among the founders of the
American Colony* in Jaffa, and remained in Palestine. He settled in Jerusalem
and was one of that area's first travel agents and tourist guides. From 1874 to
1881 he was the representative for Thomas Cook and Son, a worldwide travel
agency, in Palestine. Later he was an independent tourist agent and established
the American Tourist Agency. He was co-author of *Bible Witnesses from Bible
Lands; Verified in the Researches of the Explorers and Correspondents of the
American Holy Land Exploration* (New York, 1874), and published *A General
Programme and Itinerary for Palestine and Syria* (New York, 1884). Died in
Jerusalem. *Reference*: *Letters from Palestine: 1868–1912*, ed. Helen Palmer
Parsons (n.p., 1981).

FLUOR CORPORATION. An engineering-construction firm, founded in 1912
in Santa Ana, California. In 1925 the firm began to specialize in oil refinery
construction and later in petrochemical construction. It began construction work
in the Middle East in 1947, working for the Arabian American Oil Company

(ARAMCO) in Saudi Arabia. It was also employed by the U.S. Air Force in construction work in the Dhahran air base. *Reference:* J. Robert Fluor, *Fluor Corporation: A 65-Year History* (New York, 1978).

FOHS, FERDINAND JULIUS (1884–1965). Petroleum geologist, born March 1, 1884, in New York City. Fohs graduated from Columbia University; worked for a mining company in Kentucky from 1900 to 1905; was assistant state geologist in Kentucky from 1902 to 1912; became a partner in a firm of consulting geologists from 1912 to 1916; and was a consulting geologist in 1916. He traveled to Palestine in 1919 on behalf of the World Zionist Organization to investigate oil possibilities and irrigation potentials. He made maps and a report to the British War Office in 1919, which led to the development of a cement plant and the Dead Sea's potash and bromine plant. Fohs also investigated the natural and water resources of Palestine, and directed water development in 1930, 1936, and 1937. He later worked in East Texas, Oklahoma, and Louisiana, was president of Fohs Oil Company from 1932 to 1945, and vice president and managing director of the Dakamont Exploration Corporation from 1952 to 1958. Died January 19, 1965, in Houston, Texas. *References*: BAAPG 49 (1965): 1009–1011; *GSAB* 76S (September 1965): 121–124; *NYT*, January 2, 1965; and *WWWA*.

FORBES, ROBERT HUMPHREY (1867–1968). Agriculturist, born May 15, 1867, near Cobden, Illinois. Forbes graduated from the University of Illinois and the University of California. He was professor of chemistry at the University of Arizona and chemist at the Arizona Agricultural Experiment Station from 1894 to 1899; director of the Arizona Agricultural Experiment Station from 1899 to 1915; agricultural instructor at the University of Arizona from 1912 to 1915; and dean of the College of Agriculture and director of the University of Arizona Agricultural Experiment Station from 1915 to 1918. He was agronomist to the Société Sultanienne d'Agriculture in Cairo from 1918 to 1922, working on problems of cotton production and irrigation. Later he was chief engineer for the agricultural mission in Niger, French West Africa, counselor to the technical office of Niger from 1922 to 1927 and again from 1929 to 1938, and director of experimental stations for Haiti from 1927 to 1929. He was a member of the Arizona House of Representatives from 1938 to 1952, and led the fight for the Colorado River Compact. Died April 26, 1968, in Tucson, Arizona. *References*: Papers, Arizona Historical Society; Charles C. Colley, *The Century of Robert H. Forbes: The Career of a Pioneer Agriculturist, Agronomist, Environmentalist, Conservationist and Water Specialist in Arizona and Abroad* (Tucson, Ariz., 1977); and *WWWA*.

FORD, GEORGE ALFRED (1851–1928). Missionary, son of Joshua Edwards Ford,* born May 31, 1851, in Aleppo. Ford graduated from Williams College and Union Theological Seminary, and was ordained in 1876. He was a pastor in Ramapo, New York, from 1876 to 1880, and a missionary under the Presbyterian Church in the USA Board of Foreign Missions* in Syria from 1880 to 1928. He was superintendent of Gerard Institute, Sidon, from 1894 to 1911, and became associate professor in the theological seminary of the Syria Mission* at Beirut in 1911. In 1914 he was acting consular agent for the Sidon district to care for the interests of subjects of governments whose consuls had been expelled from Syria. He prepared various textbooks in Arabic. Died May 18, 1928, in Sidon, Lebanon. *References*: *Hewitt*; *UnionTS*; and *WWWA*.

FORD, JOSHUA EDWARDS (1825–1866). Missionary, born August 3, 1825, in Ogdensburg, New York. Ford graduated from Williams College and Union Theological Seminary, and was ordained in 1847. He became a missionary under the American Board of Commissioners for Foreign Missions (ABCFM)* in Syria in 1847, was stationed at Aleppo, and served as a forwarding agent, postmaster, and banker for several stations in the interior of Syria. He was transferred to Beirut in 1855, joined William Woodbridge Eddy* in 1858 at the Sidon and Hasbeiya stations, and was involved with the Anglo-American Relief Committee for the relief of refugees from the massacres of Christian Maronites by Muslim Druzes in 1860 in Lebanon following a conflict between the two groups. In 1864 he moved to Deir Mimas, a village on the eastern side of the Sidon district. He returned to the United States in 1865. Died April 3, 1866, in Geneseo, Illinois. *References*: *ACAB*; *EM*; *Hewitt*; and *UnionTS*.

FOREIGN CHRISTIAN MISSIONARY SOCIETY. Established in 1875 by the churches of the Disciples of Christ in Louisville, Kentucky, to conduct a mission to non-Christians. The society entered the field in Turkey in 1879 and began work in Constantinople with a Turkish-born Armenian who was educated in the United States. It later opened stations in Marsovan and in Marash in Turkey. The work in Turkey was discontinued in 1905, and it merged with other societies to form the United Christian Missionary Society. *References*: *EM*; Archibald McLean, *The History of the Foreign Christian Missionary Society* (New York, 1919).

FOREIGN ECONOMIC ADMINISTRATION MISSION IN THE MIDDLE EAST. Established in 1942 in Cairo and lasted until the end of World War II. The mission conducted economic negotiations with officials of Middle Eastern governments, supervised the delivery and payment for civilian Lend-Lease materials, and planned postwar economic activities in the Middle East. *Reference*: *FRWW*.

FORT, JOSEPH MARSTAIN (1828– ?). Physician, born January 11, 1828, in Madison County, Tennessee. In 1836 Fort moved with his family to Texas. He studied at Jefferson Medical College in Philadelphia, practiced medicine in Bowie County, Texas, until 1868, and later in Paris, Texas, until his retirement in 1887. He traveled in the Middle East in 1891 and wrote *The Texas Doctor and the Arab Donkey, or Palestine and Egypt as Viewed by Modern Eyes* (Chicago, 1893). *References*: *Biographical Souvenir of the State of Texas* (Chicago, 1889); George P. Red, *The Medicine Man in Texas* (Houston, Tex., 1930).

FOSDICK, HARRY EMERSON (1878–1969). Clergyman and educator, born May 24, 1878, in Buffalo, New York. Fosdick graduated from Colgate University, attended Colgate-Rochester Divinity School, graduated from Union Theological Seminary, and Columbia University, and was ordained in 1903. He was Baptist minister to Montclair, New Jersey, from 1904 to 1915, and in New York City from 1915 until his death. He was instructor and professor of practical theology at Union Theological Seminary from 1908 until 1934. He visited Palestine in 1926 to write articles for the *Ladies' Home Journal* which were also published as *A Pilgrimage to Palestine* (New York, 1927). He wrote *The Living of These Days: An Autobiography* (New York, 1956). Died October 5, 1969, in Bronxville, New York. *References*: "Holy Land Diary 1926," Ms., Riverside Church Archives, New York City; *CA*; *CB* 1940; *DARB*; Robert M. Miller, *Harry Emerson Fosdick, Preacher, Pastor, Prophet* (New York, 1985); *NCAB* 55:13; and *NYT*, October 6, 1969.

FOSSUM, LUDVIG OLSEN (1879–1920). Missionary, born June 5, 1879, in Wallingford, Iowa. Fossum graduated from St. Ansgar (Iowa) Seminary and United Church Seminary (St. Paul, Minn.), and was ordained in 1902. He was a paster in Stayton, Minnesota, from 1902 to 1905, and a missionary of the Lutheran Orient Mission to the Nestorian Chaldeans in Urmia, Persia, from 1902 to 1905. He was a pastor in Chicago in 1909–1910 and returned to the Middle East as missionary to the Kurds in Sonjbulak, Kurdistan, from 1911 to 1916. He was a member of the American Red Cross* in Armenia from 1916 to 1919, and district commander of the Near East Relief* at Erivan, Armenia, in 1919–1920. He reduced the Kurdish language to writing, wrote *A Practical Kurdish Grammar* (Minneapolis, 1919), and also *Lutheran Evangelization Work in Persia and Kurdistan* (Berwyn, Ill., 1910). Died October 10, 1920. *Reference*: *Lutheran Cyclopedia*, rev. ed. (St. Louis, 1975).

FOWLE, LUTHER R(ICHARDSON) (1886–1973). Missionary, born July 30, 1886, in Kayseri, Turkey, to American parents. Fowle graduated from Williams College and Union Theological Seminary. He served at the American Board of Commissioners for Foreign Missions (ABCFM)* mission in Turkey from 1912 to 1946. In 1912 he was assigned to the mission station at Aintab, and became acquainted with Leonard Wooley and T. E. Lawrence who were excavating in Carchemish. His account of Lawrence was published in *Asia Magazine*. Fowle returned to Istanbul as assistant treasurer, and spent most of his time as mission treasurer and business manager of the ABCFM in Turkey, and assistant to William Wheelock Peet.* He was a member of the committee formed in 1915 to organize aid for Armenian refugees from northeastern Turkey, and he served as an attaché at the Swedish legation in Constantinople which was charged with the protection of U.S. interests in Turkey during the war. He later became known as an interpreter of things American to the Turks, and was a founder of the Admiral Bristol Hospital in Istanbul. Died April 5, 1973, in Stamford, Connecticut. *References*: *NYT*, April 6, 1973; *WWWA*.

FOX, ERNEST FRANKLIN (1902–   ). Mining and geology engineer. Fox explored in Northern Rhodesia from 1929 to 1932. With two other American geologists, he was commissioned in 1937 by an American company to explore in Afghanistan for oil and minerals. He explored Afghanistan in 1937–1938, searching for mineral deposits, and went to the remote northeastern and south central parts of the country. His book *Travels in Afghanistan 1937–1938* (New York, 1943) was based on his diary and travel notes.

FOX, WILLIAM CARLTON (1855–1924). Diplomat, born May 20, 1855, in St. Louis. Fox graduated from Washington University and Pennsylvania Military College (Chester). He was consul at Brunswick, Germany, from 1876 to 1888, and vice consul general in Teheran in 1891–1892. He was in charge of the legation during the cholera epidemic of 1892, and organized and financed the American missionary hospital and dispensary. He was secretary of legation in Athens in 1892–1893, established the *Diplomatic and Consular Review in 1894*, was chief clerk of the International Bureau of the American Republics from 1898 to 1905, became its director in 1905, and was minister to Ecuador from 1907 until his retirement in 1911. Died January 20, 1924, in New York City. *References*: *NCAB* 14:114; *WWWA*.

FREASE, EDWIN FIELD (1862–1938). Missionary, born December 28, 1862, in Canton, Ohio. Frease graduated from Taylor University and studied law, but in 1885 he became a Methodist clergyman. He was a missionary to India from 1888 until 1909, and served in Bombay and Baroda. He was the leader of the Methodist Episcopal Church Mission in North Africa from 1909 to 1932, becoming superintendent of the North Africa Mission in 1910, and supervising missionary work in Algeria and Tunis. He retired in 1932. Died April 22, 1938, in Canton, Ohio. *References*: *The Canton Repository*, April 23, 1938; *NYT*, April 23, 1938.

FREE, JOSEPH PAUL (1911–1974). Archaeologist, born October 1, 1911, in Cleveland. Free graduated from Princeton University and the Oriental Institute, and was assistant professor, associate professor, and professor of archaeology at Wheaton College from 1935 to 1966. He was a staff member of the American Schools of Oriental Research (ASOR)* excavation at Dhibon, Jordan, in 1951 and 1952, and director of the Wheaton archaeological expedition to Dothan,

Jordan, from 1953 to 1960 and from 1962 to 1964. He was executive director of the Near East School of Archaeology in Jerusalem in 1960, 1962, and 1964, and professor of archaeology and history at Bemidji State College (Minn.), from 1966 to 1974. He wrote *Archaeology and Bible History* (Wheaton, Ill., 1950). Died October 12, 1974, in Park Rapids, Minnesota. *References*: *DAS*; *WWWA*.

FREEDMAN, DAVID NOEL (1922–   ). Orientalist, born May 12, 1922, in New York City. Freedman graduated from the City College of New York, the University of California at Los Angeles, Princeton Theological Seminary, and Johns Hopkins University, and was ordained in 1944. He was assistant professor and professor of Hebrew and Old Testament literature at Western Theological Seminary (Pittsburgh) from 1948 to 1951; professor at Pittsburgh Theological Seminary from 1960 to 1964; professor of Old Testament at San Francisco Theological Seminary (San Anselmo, Calif.) from 1964 to 1970; and professor of Middle Eastern studies at the University of Michigan after 1971. He was director of the Ashdod Excavation Project in Israel from 1962 to 1964, and co-author of *Ashdod I: The First Season of Excavations, 1962* (Jerusalem, 1967), and director of the American Schools of Oriental Research (ASOR)* in Jerusalem in 1976–1977. He was co-author of the biography of William Foxwell Albright.* *References*: *The Word of the Lord Shall Go Forth: Essays in Honor of the Sixtieth Birthday of David Noel Freedman* (Winona Lake, Ind., 1983); *CA*; *DAS*; and *WWA*.

FREEMAN, GEORGE FOUCHE (1876–1930). Plant geneticist, born November 4, 1876, in Maple Grove, Alabama. Freeman graduated from Alabama Polytechnic and Harvard University. He taught at the Massachusetts College of Agriculture and the Kansas State Agricultural College from 1903 to 1906, was plant breeder at the Arizona Agricultural Experimental Station from 1906 to 1918, its director in 1915–1916, and acting dean of the College of Agriculture in 1915–1916. He was chief of plant breeding of the Société Sultanienne d'Agriculture in Cairo from 1918 to 1922, chief of the Department of Cotton Breeding at the Texas Agricultural Experimental Station in 1922–1923, agriculturist and economist on a mission for the French government to Indochina in 1923, and director general of the Service Technique d'Agriculture et de l'Enseignement Professional in Haiti from 1923. Died October 1930, in Puerto Rico. *Reference*: *WWWA*.

FRIEDENWALD, HARRY (1864–1950). Ophthalmologist, born September 21, 1864, in Baltimore. Friedenwald graduated from Baltimore City College, Johns Hopkins University, and the College of Physicians and Surgeons (Baltimore), and studied at the universities of Berlin and Vienna. He was associate professor of ophthalmology and otology at the College of Physicians and Surgeons in Baltimore (later the University of Maryland) from 1894 to 1902, professor from 1902 to 1929, and served as ophthalmic surgeon in various hospitals.

He was a member of the first Zionist society in America and president of the Federation of American Zionists from 1904 to 1918. In 1911 and 1912 he went to Palestine and served as a consultant for eye diseases in several hospitals in Jerusalem. He was again in Palestine in 1919–1920 as chairman of the Zionist Commission to Palestine. Died April 8, 1950, in Baltimore. *References*: Papers, Central Zionist Archives; *EJ*; Alexander L. Levin, *Vision: a Biography of Harry Friedenwald* (Philadelphia, 1964); *NCAB* 37:165; *NYT*, April 11, 1950; and *WWWA*.

FRIENDS MISSION. Founded by Eli and Sybil Jones* in 1869 when they established a girls' training home in Ramallah, Palestine. It continued at their own expense until 1874. In 1888 the mission was adopted by the New England Yearly Meeting. The mission has maintained girls' and boys' schools in Ramallah and has carried relief work among Arab refugees. *References*: Papers, Friends United Meeting, World Ministeries Commission, Richmond, Indiana; Christina Jones, *Friends in Palestine* (Richmond, Ind., 1981).

FROM THE MANGER TO THE CROSS. The first major American film produced "on location" in the Middle East in 1912 by the Kalem Company and filmed in Palestine and Egypt, together with several short films. *Reference*: Patrick G. Loughney, "The First American Film Spectacular: From the Manger to the Cross," *Quarterly Journal of the Library of Congress* 40 (1983): 57–69.

FRYE, RICHARD N(ELSON) (1920–   ). Orientalist, born January 10, 1920. Frye graduated from the University of Illinois and Harvard University, and studied at the School of Oriental and African Studies in London. He was a research analyst in the Near East Section of Research and Analysis of the Office of Strategic Services in World War II, executive secretary of the Near East Committee of the American Council of Learned Societies from 1948 to 1950, assistant professor, associate professor, and professor of Iranian at Harvard University, and director of the Asia Institute at the Pahlavi University of Iran from 1969 to 1974. He traveled in the central deserts of Iran and Baluchistan in 1951–1952. He was co-author of *The United States and Turkey and Iran* (Cambridge, Mass., 1951), and wrote *Iran* (New York, 1956), *The Heritage of Persia* (Cleveland, 1962), and *Persia* (New York, 1969). *References*: *CA*; *DAS*; *MENA*; and *WWA*.

FULTON, JOHN (1834–1907). Clergyman, born April 2, 1834, in Glasgow, Scotland. Fulton was educated at Aberdeen, came to the United States in 1853, and was ordained in 1858. He was professor of canon law at the Divinity School in Philadelphia and editor of *The Church Standard*. He traveled in Palestine and wrote *The Beautiful Land: Palestine As It Was and As It Now Is* (Chicago, 1891), and its abridged edition, *Palestine, the Holy Land As It Was and As It Is*

(Philadelphia, 1900). Died in Philadelphia. *References*: *ACAB*; *DAA*; and *WWWA*.

FURLONG, CHARLES WELLINGTON (1874–1967). Explorer and army officer, born December 13, 1874, in Cambridge, Massachusetts. Furlong graduated from Harvard and Cornell universities, and studied art in Paris. In 1904 he began a career of exploration. He underwrote and led the first American expedition into the unexplored regions of the Tripolitanian Sahara in 1904, discovered the wreck of the U.S. frigate *Philadelphia** in Tripoli Harbor, and wrote *The Gateway to the Sahara: Adventures and Observations in Tripoli* (New York, 1909; 2nd ed., 1912). He led expeditions to Turkey and the Middle East, and the first scientific expedition to Tierra del Fuego in 1907–1908. He was military observer and intelligence officer in the Balkans and the Middle East in 1919. He again visited the Middle East in 1929–1930. Died October 9, 1967, in Hanover, New Hampshire. *References*: *NCAB* 54:292; *NYT*, October 11, 1967; and *WWWA*.

G

GAGE, FRANCES COUSENS (1863–1917). Young Women's Christian Association (YWCA)* executive, born October 14, 1863, in Quincy, Massachusetts. Gage graduated from Carleton College and served as a missionary under the American Board of Commissioners for Foreign Missions (ABCFM)* in Marsovan, Turkey, from 1893 to 1898. She was later YWCA secretary in Oregon, Washington, Idaho, and Montana, but returned to Turkey in 1913, and became the first secretary of the YWCA in Turkey. Died July 15, 1917, in Marsovan, Turkey. *Reference*: Elizabeth Wilson, *The Road Ahead, Experiences in the Life of Frances C. Gage* (New York, 1918).

GAGE, WILLIAM LEONARD (1832–1889). Clergyman, born in Loudon, New Hampshire. Gage graduated from Harvard University, and was a pastor in Hartford from 1868 to 1884. In 1866–1867 he traveled in the Middle East, and wrote *The Home of God's People* (Hartford, Conn., 1872), *The Land of Sacred Mystery; or, the Bible Read in the Light of Its Own Scenery* (Hartford, Conn., 1871), and *Studies in Bible Land* (Boston, 1869). Died May 31, 1889, in Philadelphia. *Reference*: DAA.

GALLAGHER, CHARLES F(REDERICK) (1923–   ). Educator, born January 5, 1923, in San Francisco. Gallagher graduated from Harvard University, served in the navy during World War II, and was cultural property adviser in Tokyo from 1946 to 1949. He was staff associate of the American Universities Field Staff in North Africa and the Middle East from 1956 to 1965, senior staff associate on Islamic affairs from 1966 to 1968, and director of studies at the American Universities Field Staff after 1968. He wrote *The United States and North Africa* (Cambridge, Mass., 1963). *Reference*: DFAF.

GALLIER, JAMES, SR. (1798–1868). Architect, born July 24, 1798, in Ravensdale, County Louth, Ireland. Gallier attended a school of fine arts in Dublin, came to the United States in 1832, worked as a draftsman in New York City in

1832–1833, and was a partner in an architectural firm there in 1833–1834. He went to New Orleans in 1835, practiced architecture from 1836 to 1850, was the owner of a building firm, and speculated in real estate. After 1850, he traveled in Europe, North Africa, and Egypt, and much of his *Autobiography of James Gallier Architect* (Paris, 1864; reprinted, with new introduction by Samuel Wilson, Jr., New York, 1973) is devoted to his travels in North Africa. Drowned May 16, 1868, in a shipwreck near Cape Hatteras. *References: DAB S1; MEA;* and *WWWA.*

GALLMAN, WALDEMAR J(OHN) (1899–1980). Diplomat, born April 27, 1899, in Wellsville, New York. Gallman graduated from Cornell and Georgetown universities, entered the foreign service in 1922, and served in Havana, Cuba, San Jose, Costa Rica, Quito, Ecuador, Riga, Latvia, and Warsaw. He was consul general in Danzig from 1935 to 1938, deputy chief of mission in London during World War II, ambassador to Poland from 1948 to 1950, deputy commandant for foreign affairs at the National War College in 1950, and ambassador to the Union of South Africa in 1951. He was ambassador to Iraq from 1954 to 1959 and reported on his experiences in *Iraq Under General Nuri: My Recollections of Nuri al-Said, 1954–1958* (Baltimore, 1964). He was director general of the foreign service from 1959 until his retirement in 1961, and later consultant to the Asia Foundation and adviser to the governments of South Vietnam and Korea. Died June 29, 1980, in Washington, D.C. *References: CA; NYT,* June 30, 1980; and *WWWA.*

GALT, RUSSELL (1889–1959). Educator, born March 3, 1889, in Philadelphia. Galt graduated from Muskingum College (New Concord, Ohio) and Columbia University. He was associate professor of the American University in Cairo* from 1920 to 1924, acting dean and dean of the education department from 1924 to 1928, and dean of the college of arts and sciences from 1928 to 1938. He was dean of Susquehanna University (Selinsgrove, Pa.) from 1938 until his death. He wrote *The Effects of Centralization on Education in Modern Egypt* (Cairo, 1936). Died March 18, 1959, in Danville, Pennsylvania. *References: NYT,* March 17, 1959; *LE;* and *WWWA.*

GARRETT, ROBERT (1875–1961). Banker, philanthropist, and collector, born June 24, 1875, in Baltimore. Garrett graduated from Princeton and Johns Hopkins universities, and was general partner in the investment banking firm of Robert Garrett and Sons in Baltimore until 1947, and a limited partner until his retirement in 1957. He traveled in Europe and the Middle East from 1889 to 1891, competed in 1896 in the first modern Olympiad in Greece, and was in Syria in 1899–1900 as a member of the American archaeological expedition to Syria. He prepared *Topography and Itinerary* (New York, 1914), the first part of the publications of the expedition. He collected Arabic and other Middle Eastern manuscripts, and described his activities as a collector in the April 1949 issue of *Princeton Library Chronicle*. Died April 25, 1961, in Baltimore. *References*: *BDABL*; Donald C. Dickinson, *Dictionary of American Book Collectors* (Westport, Conn., 1986), pp. 133–134; *NCAB* 48:574; *NYT*, April 26, 1961; and *WWWA*.

GARY, HAMPSON (1873–1952). Diplomat, born April 23, 1873, in Tyler, Texas. Gary studied at the University of Virginia, and was admitted to the bar in 1894. He served in the Spanish-American War, was a member of the Texas House of Representatives in 1901–1902, and practiced law in Tyler until he moved to Washington in 1914. He was special counsel to the State Department in 1914 and solicitor in 1915. He was diplomatic agent and consul general with the rank of minister to Egypt from 1917 to 1920. He was also in charge of American interests in Palestine, Syria, and Arabia, and was with General Edmund Allenby at the front beyond Jerusalem in 1918. He served with the American Commission to Negotiate Peace in 1918, and was minister to Switzerland in 1920–1921. He practiced law in Washington until 1931 and in New York City from 1931 to 1934. He was a member of the Federal Communications Commission in 1934–1935, counsel from 1935 to 1938, and solicitor of the U.S. Export-Import Bank from 1938 until his retirement in 1946. Died April 18, 1952, in Palm Beach, Florida. *References*: Papers, University of Virginia Library; *ACAB*; *NCAB* 41:332; *NYT*, April 19, 1952; and *WWWA*.

GATES, CALEB FRANK (1857–1946). Missionary and educator, born October 18, 1857, in Chicago. Gates graduated from Beloit College and the Chicago Theological Seminary, and was ordained in 1881. He was a missionary under the American Board of Commissioners for Foreign Missions (ABCFM)* in Mardin, Turkey, from 1891 to 1894; president of Euphrates College* from 1894 to 1902; and president of Robert College* from 1903 to 1932. He overhauled the preparatory school and established commercial and engineering schools. He was chairman of the Near East Relief Commission in Constantinople from 1917 to 1919. He wrote an autobiography, *Not to Me Only* (Princeton, N.J., 1940). Died April 9, 1946, in Denver, Colorado. *References*: *DAB S4*; *NCAB* C:167; *NYT*, April 11, 1946; and *WWWA*.

GAY, W(INCKWORTH) ALLAN (1821–1910). Painter, born August 18, 1821, in West Hingham, Massachusetts. Gay began studying art in 1838 and went to Paris in 1847 for further training. Returning to the United States in 1850, he opened a studio in Boston. He spent the winter of 1874 in Egypt on the Nile and visited Palestine. In 1877 he had an exhibition in Boston of the landscapes he had painted in Egypt. He later traveled to the Far East and resided in Japan, China, and India. Died February 23, 1910, in West Hingham, Massachusetts. *References*: Papers, Columbia University Library; W. Craven, ''Winckworth Allan Gay, Boston Painter of the White Mountains, Paris, the Nile, and Mount

Fujiyama," *Antiques* 120 (1981): 1222–1232; *DAB*; *NCAB* 11:296; *NYHSD*; *NYT*, February 23, 1910; and *WWWA*.

GELB, IGNACE J(AY) (1907–1985). Assyriologist and linguist, born October 14, 1907, in Tarnow, Poland. Gelb graduated from the universities of Florence and Rome, came to the United States in 1929, joined the Oriental Institute, and was traveling fellow and instructor until 1941. He was involved in the decipherment of the Hittite hieroglyphs, wrote *Hittite Hieroglyphs* (Chicago, 1931–1942), and studied the development of writing. He was assistant professor of Assyriology from 1941 to 1943, associate professor from 1943 to 1947, and professor from 1947 until his retirement in 1976. He was a member of archaeological expeditions to the Middle East in 1932, 1935, 1947, 1963, and 1966. He served in army intelligence during World War II. From 1947 to 1954 he was also editor-in-chief of the *Assyrian Dictionary*. He was co-author of *Joint Expedition with the Iraqi Museum at Nuzi* (Paris, 1927–1939), and wrote *Hurrians and Subarians* (Chicago, 1944), and *Inscriptions from Alishar and Vicinity* (Chicago, 1935). He was an early user of the computer to study ancient writing, and he wrote *Computer-aided Analysis of Amorite* (Chicago, 1980). Died December 22, 1985, in Chicago. *References*: *CA*; *DAS*; *MENA*; *NYT*, December 24, 1985; and *WWA*.

GERARD INSTITUTE, SIDON. Founded in 1881 by the Syria Mission* as a vocational training school. Renamed Gerard, the National Evangelical Institute, it is now a school covering all grades from kindergarten to high school. *References*: *Survey*; *Schools*.

GETTY OIL COMPANY. Company incorporated as the Pacific Western Oil Corporation in 1928; name changed to Getty Oil Company in 1956. In 1949 it acquired oil exploration rights for sixty years to Saudi Arabia's interest in the Neutral Zone, the desert land between Saudi Arabia and Kuwait in which both countries had equal rights. It struck oil in 1953, and oil production was shared equally with the American Independent Oil Company (AMINOIL).* The company was taken over by Texaco in 1984. *Reference*: *IPE*.

GIBBONS, HELEN DAVENPORT (BROWN) (1882–1960). Author, born December 2, 1882, in Philadelphia, wife of Herbert Adams Gibbons.* Helen Gibbons graduated from Bryn Mawr and Simmons colleges. She wrote and translated books and wrote articles for *Century*, *Harper's*, and *The Pictorial Review*. In 1908 she traveled in the Middle East and wrote *The Red Rugs of Tarsus: A Woman's Record of the Armenian Massacres of 1909* (New York, 1917). In World War I she founded a relief organization for war orphans in France, was a Young Men's Christian Association (YMCA)* lecturer with the army in France in 1917–1918, and a correspondent of *Century Magazine* to the Paris Peace Conference. She later toured the United States on behalf of American colleges in the Middle East. Died September 1, 1960, in Princeton, New Jersey. *References*: *NYT*, September 2, 1960; and *WWWA*.

GIBBONS, HERBERT ADAMS (1880–1934). Author, born April 9, 1880, in Annapolis, Maryland. Gibbons graduated from the University of Pennsylvania, Princeton University, and Princeton Theological Seminary, and was ordained in 1908. He taught at St. Paul's College in Tarsus, Turkey, in 1909, and was professor of history and political science at Robert College* from 1910 to 1913. He was a correspondent for the *New York Herald Tribune* in Turkey, Egypt, the Balkans, and France from 1908 to 1918; wrote *The Blackest Page of Modern History: Events in Armenia in 1915, the Facts and the Responsibilities* (New York, 1916); and reported on the Turco-Italian War in Libya and on the Balkan Wars of 1912 and 1913. During part of World War I, he was a correspondent in Egypt and the Sudan, and later a correspondent for *Century*, *Harper's*, and the *Christian Science Monitor*. He wrote *The Reconstruction of Poland and the Near East: Problems of Peace* (New York, 1917). He was literary adviser for Century Company from 1925 to 1933. Died August 7, 1934, in Groundslee, Austria. *References*: Papers, Princeton University Library; *DAB S1*; *NCAB* 49:231; and *WWWA*.

GIBSON, CHARLES DANA (1867–1944). Illustrator, born September 14, 1867, in Roxbury, Massachusetts. Gibson grew up in Flushing, New York. He studied art in New York City and went to Europe in 1888. He was an illustrator for *Harper's*, *Scribner's*, and *Century* magazines, and won recognition in the 1890s for his creation of the "Gibson Girl." He traveled in Egypt in 1898 and wrote *Sketches in Egypt* (New York, 1899). He was owner and editor-in-chief of *Life* from 1920 to 1932. Died December 23, 1944, in New York City. *References*: *DAB S3*; Fairfax C. Downey, *Portrait of an Era as Drawn by C. D. Gibson: A Biography* (New York, 1936); Susan E. Meyer, *America's Great Illustrators* (New York, 1978); *NCAB* 11:290; *NYT*, December 24, 1944; and *WWWA*.

GIFFEN, J(OHN) KELLY (1853–1932). Missionary, born June 3, 1853, in St. Clairsville, Ohio. Giffen graduated from Franklin College (Ohio) and the United Presbyterian Theological Seminary (Allegheny, Pa.), and was ordained in 1881. He served as a missionary under the United Presbyterian Church of North America Board of Foreign Missions* in Egypt from 1881 to 1899; assistant in the training college from 1881 to 1888; superintendent in Upper Egypt from 1888 to 1891; and superintendent in other districts after 1891. He went to the Sudan in 1900 and worked in Khartoum, except for the years 1902–1903 which he spent at Doleib Hill, near the mouth of the River Sobat, where he founded a mission station. He was the first Protestant missionary to serve in the Sudan south of Khartoum after the Mahadist times. He was secretary of the mission in Egypt from 1883 to 1891, and became general secretary and treasurer of the

Sudan Mission in 1905. He wrote *The Egyptian Soudan* (New York, 1905). Died April 6, 1932, in Khartoum, the Sudan. *References: Hill; OAB;* and *WWWA.*

GIFFORD, R(OBERT) SWAIN (1840–1905). Painter, born December 23, 1840, on the Island of Naushon, Massachusetts. Gifford grew up in New Bedford, Massachusetts. He studied art and opened a studio in Boston in 1864 and moved to New York in 1866. He went to Oregon, California, and Washington in 1869, and to Europe in 1870 where he stayed two years. He visited Morocco and Egypt in 1870, and Algiers and parts of North Africa which tourists seldom visited in 1874. In 1884 he returned to the Middle East for a third visit. He later divided his time between a studio in New York and a summer home in Nonquit, Massachusetts. Died January 15, 1905, in New York City. *References: ACAB; DAB; NCAB* 2:482; *NYHSD; NYT,* January 16, 1905; *R. Swain Gifford 1840–1905* (New Bedford, Mass., 1974); and *WWWA.*

GIFFORD, SANFORD ROBINSON (1823–1880). Painter, born July 10, 1823, in Greenfield, Saratoga County, New York. Gifford graduated from Brown University and studied art in New York. He went to Europe in 1855–1857, and again in 1859, and returned to serve in the Civil War. In 1868–1869 he traveled in Europe and the Middle East. He toured and painted in Egypt, Palestine, Syria, and Turkey. He later made painting trips in the Rocky Mountains and in Alaska. Died August 29, 1880, in New York City. *References:* "Journal," Ms., Archives of American Art, Washington, D.C.; Nikolai Cikovsky, Jr., *Sanford Robinson Gifford, 1828–1880* (Austin, Tex., 1970); *DAB; NCAB* 2:443; *NYHSD; NYT,* August 30, 1880; Ila Joyce Weiss, *Sanford R. Gifford* (New York, 1977); and *WWWA.*

GILLESPIE, JULIAN EDGEWORTH (1893–1939). Commercial attaché, born June 20, 1893, in Brownwood, Texas. Gillespie graduated from the University of Texas, studied at the University of Chicago Law School, obtained a law degree from Georgetown University, and was admitted to the bar in 1915. He practiced in Dallas and served in the army during World War I. He was assistant trade commissioner for the U.S. Department of Commerce for the Near East and the Balkans from 1920 to 1922 with headquarters in Constantinople; trade commissioner from 1922 to 1926; and commercial attaché to Turkey from 1926 until his death. He served as an economic and financial adviser to the American delegation to the Lausanne Conference in 1922–1923, and as a delegate to negotiate a treaty of commerce and navigation between Turkey and the United States in 1929. Died June 23, 1939, in Istanbul. *References: NYT,* June 24, 1939; and *WWWA.*

GILLMAN, HENRY (1833–1915). Scientist and consul, born November 16, 1833, in Kinsale, Ireland, and came to the U.S. in 1850. Gillman was first assistant in the U.S. Geodetic Survey of the Great Lakes from 1851 to 1869;

assistant superintendent of construction for the lighthouse districts of the northern lakes from 1870 to 1876; and superintendent and librarian of the Detroit Public Library from 1880 to 1885. He was consul in Jerusalem from 1886 to 1891, and later traveled in Egypt and Asia Minor. Gillman did research in archaeology and botany, procured and published photograph facsimiles of early Christian manuscripts, wrote a series of illustrated articles on "The Wild Flowers and Gardens of Jerusalem and Palestine" in 1894, and *Hassan: A Fallah; a Romance of Palestine* (Boston, 1898). Died July 30, 1915, in Detroit. *References*: Papers in private hands; *DAB*; *NCAB* 7:359; and *WWWA*.

GILMORE, ALBERT FIELD (1868–1943). Editor, born February 15, 1868, in Turner, Maine. Gilmore graduated from Bates College. He was a principal of a high school in Kennebunk, superintendent of schools in Turner, and principal of Litchfield Academy. He was with the American Book Company from 1897 to 1917, the Christian Science Committee on Publications from 1917 to 1922, president of The Mother Church in 1922–1923, and editor of the Christian Science weekly and monthly magazines from 1922 to 1929. He traveled to the Middle East to study nature, particularly birds, and wrote *East and West of Jordan* (Boston, 1929). Died June 8, 1943, in Boston. *References*: *NCAB* 42:390; *NYT*, June 9, 1943; and *WWWA*.

GLAZEBROOK, OTIS ALLAN (1845–1931). Consul, born October 13, 1845, in Richmond, Virginia. Glazebrook graduated from Randolph-Macon College and the Episcopal Theological Seminary in Virginia, and was ordained in 1869. He served as a missionary in Virginia, a rector in Baltimore, Macon, Georgia, and Elizabeth, New Jersey, and a chaplain at the University of Virginia and during the Spanish-American War. He was consul in Jerusalem from 1914 to 1920, and became involved in the relief operations of foreigners in Palestine after the outbreak of World War I. He was later consul in Nice, France. Died April 26, 1931. *References*: *NCAB* 2:375; and *WWWA*.

GLIDDEN, CHARLES JASPER (1857–1927). Telephone pioneer, motorist, and aviator, born August 29, 1857, in Lowell, Massachusetts. In 1878 Glidden became involved in developing telephone systems, first in Lowell and later in other towns in New England and in other states. In 1902 he became involved in motoring, organized the first round-the-world motor tour, and brought the first motor car to Palestine in 1908, traveling from Haifa to Jerusalem and to other points of interest to tourists. He was later active in the development of commercial aviation. Died September 11, 1927, in Brookline, Massachusetts. *References*: *DAB*; *NCAB* 5:415; *NYT*, September 12, 1927; *With Eyes Toward Zion*, ed. Moshe Davis (New York, 1977), pp. 240–242; and *WWWA*.

GLIDDON, GEORGE ROBINS (1809–1857). Egyptologist, born in Devonshire. Gliddon's father, John Gliddon, was U.S. consul in Alexandria from 1835 to 1848, and he grew up in Egypt. He was consul in Cairo from 1837 to 1841. In 1842 he came to the United States and lectured on Egyptian archaeology until 1844. He published several works on Egypt which established his reputation as the first writer on ancient Egypt in the United States. He wrote *Otia Aegyptiaca. Discourses on Egyptian Archaeology and Hieroglyphical Discoveries* (New York, 1849), a study of mummification, *Ancient Egypt. Her Monuments, Hieroglyphics, History and Archaeology* (New York, 1843), *A Memoir on the Cotton of Egypt* (London, 1841), and *An Appeal to the Antiquaries of Europe on the Destruction of the Monuments of Egypt* (London, 1849), perhaps the first expression of archaeological concern in print. Died in Panama. *References*: *ACAB*; *WWWE*.

GLUECK, NELSON (1900–1971). Archaeologist and educator, born June 4, 1900, in Cincinnati, Ohio. Glueck graduated from Hebrew Union College and studied at the universities of Cincinnati, Berlin, Heidelberg, and Jena. He was instructor at the Hebrew Union College from 1929 to 1931, assistant professor from 1931 to 1934, associate professor from 1934 to 1936, and professor of Bible and Biblical archaeology in 1936. He became president of Hebrew Union College in 1947 and of the Jewish Institute of Religion in 1949. He was annual professor at the American Schools of Oriental Research (ASOR)* in Baghdad in 1933–1934, field director of ASOR in Jerusalem, and agent of the Office of Strategic Services there from 1942 to 1947. From 1932 to 1947 he made a complete survey of sites in Transjordan, excavated Tell el-Kheleifeh and Khirbet Tannur, and wrote *Explorations in Eastern Palestine* (Baltimore, 1934–1952), *The Other Side of the Jordan* (New Haven, Conn., 1940), and *The River Jordan* (Philadelphia, 1946). From 1952 to 1959 he conducted archaeological explorations of the Negev and wrote *Rivers in the Desert: A History of the Negev* (New York, 1949). He also wrote *DateLine: Jerusalem; a Diary* (Cincinnati, 1968). Died February 12, 1971, in Cincinnati. *References*: Papers, American Jewish Archives; *Near Eastern Archaeology in the Twentieth Century: Essays in Honor of Nelson Glueck*, ed. James A. Sanders (Garden City, N.Y., 1970); *BA* 34 (February 1971): 39–40; *BASOR* 202 (1971): 2–6; *CB* 1948, 1969; *NCAB* 56:170; *NYT*, February 14, 1971; *OAB*; and Ellen N. Stern, *Dreamer in the Desert: A Profile of Nelson Glueck* (New York, 1980).

GOETZE, ALBRECHT E(RNST) R(UDOLF) (1897–1971). Assyriologist and archaeologist, born January 11, 1897, in Leipzig, Germany. Goetze studied at the universities of Munich, Leipzig, Berlin, and Heidelberg, and served in the German Army in World War I. He was docent at the University of Heidelberg from 1923 to 1930, and professor at the University of Marburg from 1930 to 1933. Dismissed by the Nazi government, he left Germany in 1934, came to the United States in 1937, and was naturalized in 1940. He was professor of

Assyriology and Babylonian literature at Yale University from 1937 until his retirement in 1965. He was director of the American Schools of Oriental Research (ASOR)* at Baghdad from 1947 to 1956, and served as epigraphist in Nippur in 1956. Died August 15, 1971, in New Haven, Connecticut. *References*: Papers, Yale University Library; *BASOR* 206 (1972): 3–6; *CA*; *JAOS* 92 (1972): 197–203; *NYT*, August 18, 1971; and *WWWA*.

GOLDMAN, HETTY (1881–1972). Archaeologist, born December 19, 1881, in New York City. Goldman graduated from Bryn Mawr College, Columbia University, and Radcliffe College, and studied at the American School of Classical Studies in Athens. She excavated in Halae, Greece, from 1911 to 1914 and in 1921 and 1931, and directed excavations for the Fogg Museum of Harvard University at Colophon, Asia Minor, in 1922 and 1925, and in Eutresis, Greece, from 1924 to 1927. She was a member of the archaeological expedition to Yugoslavia in 1932, made an archaeological reconnaissance for Bryn Mawr College in ancient Cilicia in Turkey in 1934, and directed the excavations at Gozlo Kule, Tarsus, for Bryn Mawr College, Harverford College, the Fogg Museum of Harvard University, and the Archaeological Institute of America from 1936 to 1947. She edited and was co-author of *Excavations at Gozlu Kule, Tarsus* (Princeton, N.J., 1950–1983). Died May 4, 1972, in Princeton, New Jersey. *References*: *The Aegean and the Near East: Studies Presented to Hetty Goldman on the Occasion of Her Seventy-fifth Birthday*, ed. Saul S. Weinberg (Locust Valley, N.Y., 1956); Papers, Bryn Mawr College Archives; *NAW*; *NCAB* 56:510; *NYT*, May 6, 1972; and *WWWA*.

GOODELL, WILLIAM (1792–1867). Missionary, born February 14, 1792, in Templeton, Massachusetts. Goodell graduated from Dartmouth College and Andover Theological Seminary, and was ordained in 1822. He served as a missionary under the American Board of Commissioners for Foreign Missions (ABCFM)* in the Middle East from 1823 to 1851 and from 1853 to 1865. He helped establish the mission in Beirut in 1823, was superintendent of the mission press in Malta from 1828 to 1831, and established the mission in Constantinople in 1831. He translated the Bible into Armeno-Turkish, completing the work in 1841, and continued to revise it until 1863. He wrote *The Old and the New; or the Change of Thirty Years in the East* (New York, 1853). He returned to the United States in 1865. Died February 18, 1867, in Philadelphia. *Forty Years in the Turkish Empire; or, Memoirs of Rev. William Goodell. . . . Late Missionary of the A.B.C.F.M. at Constantinople*, ed. by Edward D. G. Prime (New York, 1875), was published after his death. *References*: *ACAB*; *DAB*; *EM*; *NCAB* 5:198; and *WWWA*.

GOODRICH, CASPAR FREDERICK (1847–1925). Naval Officer, born January 7, 1847, in Philadelphia. Goodrich graduated from the U.S. Naval Academy in 1864. He served on the European, Brazil, and China stations between 1868 and 1877, and again on the European station during 1881–1884. In 1882 he was naval attaché on the staff of General Garnet Joseph Wolseley during the Tel el-Kebir campaign in Egypt. In July 1882, after the British bombardment of Alexandria, he commanded a detachment of 150 sailors and marines which entered the city to restore order, put out fires, prevent looting, and repair the water system. He prepared a detailed report of the campaign, *Report of the British Naval and Military Operations in Egypt, 1882* (Washington, D.C., 1883). He later served in the Spanish-American War and was commander of the Navy Yard in Portsmouth, New Hampshire. He retired in 1909 with the rank of rear admiral. Died December 26, 1925, in Princeton, New Jersey. His reminiscences, *Rope Yarns from the Old Navy* (New York, 1931), were published after his death. *References*: Papers, New York Historical Society; *DI*; *NCAB* 13:76; *NYT*, December 27, 1925; and *WWWA*.

GOODSELL, FRED FIELD (1880–1976). Missionary educator and administrator, born September 21, 1880, in Montevideo, Minnesota. Goodsell graduated from the University of California and the Pacific School of Religion, studied at the universities of Marburg and Berlin, and was ordained in 1905. He was a missionary under the American Board of Commissioners for Foreign Missions (ABCFM)* in Turkey from 1905 to 1930; served in Aintab from 1907 to 1911; was president of the Central Turkey College at Aintab from 1908 to 1910; and was principal of the Marash Theological Seminary from 1911 to 1914. He served with the Young Men's Christian Association (YMCA)* in Rumania and Siberia from 1916 to 1919. Goodsell was the executive vice president of the ABCFM from 1930 to 1949, and lecturer in missions at the Boston University School of Theology from 1952 to 1955. He wrote *Inductive Turkish Lessons* (London, 1927), *You Shall Be My Witness* (Boston, 1959), and *They Lived Their Faith: An Almanac of Faith, Hope and Love* (Boston, 1961). He was later executive director of the Division of Foreign Missions of the National Council of Churches of Christ in the United States. Died August 13, 1976, in Auburndale, Massachusetts. *References*: *CA*; *NCAB* 60:69; *NYT*, August 14, 1976; and *WWWA*.

GOODYEAR, WILLIAM HENRY (1846–1923). Archaeologist, born April 21, 1846, in New Haven, Connecticut. Goodyear graduated from Yale, Heidelberg, and Berlin universities. He was curator in the Metropolitan Museum of Art, New York, from 1882 to 1888, and curator of fine arts at the Brooklyn Institute of Arts and Sciences from 1899 to 1923. He visited Cyprus and Syria in 1869–1970, and Egypt in 1891–1892 to study lotus ornaments, and wrote *Grammar of the Lotus* (London, 1891). Died February 19, 1923, in Brooklyn, New York. *References*: *DAB*; *NCAB* 19:455; *NYT*, February 20, 1923; *WWWA*; and *WWWE*.

GORHAM, JOHN WARREN (1813–1893). Physician, born November 9, 1813, in Boston. Gorham graduated from Harvard College. Soon after that, he went to Europe and practiced medicine in Italy until 1861. He was the first resident consul in Jerusalem from 1856 to 1860 and raised the U.S. flag in Jerusalem for the first time on July 4, 1857. He became involved in the Walter Dickson* affair in which the American colonist in Jaffa and his family were attacked by Arab burglars, and coerced the Turkish governer to arrest and punish the burglars. He returned to the United States in 1861, settled in Westerly, Rhode Island, with Charles Saunders,* who was a Seventh-Day Baptist missionary in Palestine, and was a teacher of languages. Died April 19, 1893, in Westerly. *Reference*: *Boston Evening Transcript*, April 20, 1893.

GORRINGE, HENRY HONEYCHURCH (1841–1885). Naval officer, born August 11, 1841, in Barbados, West Indies. Gorringe entered the U.S. Navy in 1862 and served in the Civil War. As an employee of the Hydrographic Office in Washington, he prepared several volumes of sailing directions for the South Atlantic from 1871 to 1874. He was in charge of bringing an Egyptian obelisk, secured by Elbert Eli Farman,* from Alexandria to New York City in 1880, and wrote *Egyptian Obelisks* (New York, 1882). He resigned his commission in 1883, whereupon he organized and managed the American Shipbuilding Company. Died July 6, 1885, in New York City. *References*: *ACAB*; *DAB*; *NCAB* 6:439; *NYT*, July 7, 1885; Peter Tompkins, *The Magic of Obelisks* (New York, 1981), ch. 14; *WWWA*; and *WWWE*.

GOSPEL MISSIONARY UNION. Established in 1892 as the World's Gospel Union in Topeka, Kansas, and changed its name in 1901. The organization began missionary work in Morocco in 1895 and established several inland stations. It celebrated its diamond anniversary in Morocco in 1967, the same year it ceased to function. *References*: George W. Collins, *Missionaries and Muslims: The Gospel Missionary Union in Morocco, 1895–1912* (Wichita, Kan., 1975); Dennis H. Phillips, "The American Missionary in Morocco," *MW* 65 (1975): 1–20.

GOTSHALL, WILLIAM CHARLES (1870–1935). Engineer, born May 9, 1870, in St. Louis, Missouri. Gotshall was an electrical expert for the Missouri Electric Light and Power Company, and government engineer in charge of the work to protect the Mississippi River. He built electric railways in St. Louis, New Orleans, and New York, was president and chief engineer of the New York and Port Chester Railroad Company, and did pioneer work in the design and development of high speed electric traction. In 1912 he began the design of a railroad from Cairo to Helouan in Egypt. He served as an engineer in World War I. In 1925, with William Frederic Badè,* he organized and directed the archaeological exploration and excavation at Tell en-Nasbeh in Palestine. Died August 20, 1935, in New York City. *References*: *DAB S1*; *NCAB* 26:138; *NYT*, August 21, 1935; and *WWWA*.

GOULD, WALTER (1829–1893). Painter, born July 10, 1829, in Philadelphia. Gould learned painting in Philadelphia, and had studios in Philadelphia and Fredericksburg, Virginia. He went to Europe in 1849 and resided in Florence until his death. He made frequent trips to the Middle East. He painted oriental subjects and scenes, particularly the habits and customs of the Turks. These pictures brought him an invitation to paint the Sultan. He went to Constantinople in 1851 and painted there. Died January 18, 1893, in Florence, Italy. *References*: *ACAB*; *NYHSD*.

GRABAR, OLEG (1929–   ). Archaeologist, born November 3, 1929, in Strasbourg, France. Grabar came to the United States in 1948 and was naturalized in 1960. He graduated from Harvard University, the University of Paris, and Princeton University. He was instructor, assistant professor, associate professor, and professor of the history of art at the University of Michigan from 1954 to 1969, and professor of fine arts at Harvard University after 1969. He was director of the American Schools of Oriental Research (ASOR)* in Jerusalem in 1960–1961, and secretary of the American Research Institute in Turkey (ARIT) from 1964 to 1968. He was director of the Michigan-Harvard excavations in Syria from 1964 to 1971. Grabar wrote *Formation of Islamic Art* (New Haven, Conn., 1973), *The Alhambra* (Cambridge, Mass., 1978), and was the co-author of *City in the Desert: Qasr al Hayr East* (Cambridge, Mass., 1978). *References*: *CA*; *DAS*; and *WWA*.

GRAFFAM, MARY LOUISE (1871–1922). Missionary, born May 11, 1871, in Monson, Maine. Graffam graduated from Oberlin College, and taught school in New Jersey and Washington, D.C. She became a missionary under the American Board of Commissioners for Foreign Missions (ABCFM)* in Turkey in 1901, served in Sivas as a teacher, and was principal of a girls' school. She volunteered in 1914 to go to the Erzurum front, serving as matron and head nurse. She aided Armenian refugees and started a factory that employed women to manufacture clothing. Died August 17, 1922, in Sivas, Turkey. *References*: Paul Geren, *New Voices Old Worlds* (New York, 1958), pp. 53–62; Ernest C. Partridge, "Mary Louise Graffam," *Armenian Affairs* 1 (1949–1950): 62–65.

GRANT, ASAHEL (1807–1844). Medical missionary, born August 17, 1807, in Marshall, New York. Grant graduated from Hamilton College, studied medicine in Clinton, New York, and practiced medicine in Braintrim, Pennsylvania, and Utica, New York. He was a missionary under the American Board of Commissioners for Foreign Missions (ABCFM)* to the Nestorians from 1835 until 1844. He established a mission and a dispensary at Urmia, made a journey into Kurdistan in 1839, and established a station among the mountain Nestorians in Ashitha in 1841. He traveled among the tribes and wrote *The Nestorians; or, The Lost Tribes. Containing Evidence of Their Identity; an Account of Their Manners, Customs and Ceremonies; together with Sketches of Travel in Ancient*

Assyria, Armenia, Media, and Mesopotamia (London, 1841). Following a massacre of the Nestorians, he escaped to Mosul in 1843 and ministered to the refugees. Died April 24, 1844, in Mosul, Mesopotamia. *References*: "Life in Kurdistan." Ms., Archives of ABCFM; *DAB*; *EM*; *NCAB* 4:457; and *WWWA*.

GRANT, ELIHU (1873–1942). Educator, born July 12, 1873, in Stevensville, Bradford County, Pennsylvania. Grant graduated from Boston University, was in business in Boston from 1889 to 1894, and was ordained in 1900. He was superintendent of the American Friends' Schools in Ramallah, Palestine, from 1901 to 1904, and a pastor in East Saugus, Massachusetts, from 1904 to 1907. He was associate professor and professor of Biblical literature at Smith College from 1907 to 1917, and professor of Biblical literature at Haverford College from 1917 to 1938. He participated in the archaeological expedition to Tell el Nasbeh in 1927 and was director of the Haverford expedition to Ain Shems, Palestine, from 1928 to 1933. Grant was president of the American Friends of the Arabs and chairman of the Palestine Relief Commission. He wrote *The Peasantry of Palestine: Life, Manners and Customs of the Village* (Boston, 1907), *Beth Shemesh (Palestine); Progress of the Haverford Archaeological Expedition* (Haverford, Pa., 1929), *Ain Shems Excavations (Palestine)* (Haverford, Pa., 1931), *Rumeileh; Being Ain Shems Excavations (Palestine), Part III* (Haverford, Pa., 1931), and *Palestine Today* (Baltimore, 1938). Died November 2, 1942, in New York City. *References*: *NYT*, November 4, 1942; *WWWA*.

GRAVES, CHARLES IVERSON (1838–1896). Naval officer, born July 26, 1838, in Longwood, Newton County, Georgia. Graves graduated from the U.S. Naval Academy in 1857, served in the Confederate Navy during the Civil War, and became an instructor in seamanship at the Confederate Naval Academy in Richmond, Virginia, in 1863. He joined the Egyptian service in 1875 and was port officer at Massawa during the Egyptian-Abyssinian War of 1875–1876. Afterwards he was sent on scientific duties to the Somali coast. He resigned from the Egyptian Army in 1878, although he was offered a high position in the Sudan. He settled in Rome, Georgia, and was civil engineer on construction for various railroads from 1881 to 1884. Died November 5, 1896, in Rome, Georgia. *References*: "Reminiscences," Ms., Southern Historical Collection, University of North Carolina Library; *Hesseltine*.

GRAY, ALBERT ZABRISIE (1840–1889). Clergyman, born March 2, 1840, in New York City. Gray graduated from the University of New York and General Theological Seminary, and served as chaplain in the Civil War. He was pastor in various places, and became warden of Racine (Wis.) College in 1882. He visited Palestine in 1877 and wrote *The Land and the Life: Sketches and Studies in Palestine* (New York, 1877). Died February 11, 1889, in Chicago. *References*: *ACAB*; *DAA*.

GREELY, JOHN N(ESMITH) (1885–1965). Army officer, born June 6, 1885, in Washington, D.C. Greely graduated from Yale University and was commissioned second lieutenant in 1908. He was chief of staff of the Hawaiian Division from 1932 to 1935, military attaché in Madrid in 1939–1940, and commanding officer of the Second Division in 1941. Based on his experiments as chief of the American Military Mission to Iran in 1941–1942, he wrote a travelogue on Iran in the August 1943 issue of the *National Geographic Magazine*. He was military observer in Brazil and Italy in 1944, retiring with the rank of major general. Died June 13, 1965, in Washington, D.C. *Reference*: *WWWA*.

GREENE, HARVEY B(ARTLETT) (1864–1949). Florist, born September 21, 1864, in Hatfield, Massachusetts. Greene graduated from Colorado College (Colorado Springs) and Yale Divinity School. He became pastor in Fairhaven, Massachusetts, in 1892 but left the ministry in 1895, and began to study botany. Beginning in 1892, he visited Palestine three times, traveling throughout the area and collecting several million specimens of wild flowers. He pressed them and mounted them on cards and in books that appeared in several editions, including *Wild Flowers from the Holy Land* (New York, 1895), *Pressed Flowers from the Holy Land* (Lowell, 1896), *Wild Flowers from Palestine* (Lowell, 1898), and *Floral Voices from the Bible Land* (Lowell, 1903). In Palestine he also collected rare types of farm implements and other utensils which he gave to the Field Museum of Natural History in Chicago. He settled in Lowell, Massachusetts, and entering the florist business, engaged in it until his death. Died April 11, 1949, in Lowell. *Reference*: *The Lowell Sun*, April 12, 1949.

GREENE, JOHN BULKLEY (ca. 1832–1856). Archaeologist and photographer. Greene grew up in Paris where his father managed a branch of a banking firm. He made his first photographic expedition in 1853–1854 on a trip to the Upper Nile and Nubia, and his photographs were published in *Le Nil-Monuments-Paysages-Explorations Photographiques* (Lille, 1854). In 1854 he went back to Egypt, excavating at Deir-el-Bahari and Thebes. In 1855 he went to Algeria and worked at the coastal town of Cherchell, and in 1856 he returned to Egypt. Died November 1856 in Egypt. *References*: Albums in the collection of the Institute de France; Bruno Jammes, "John B. Greene, an American Calotypist," *History of Photography* 5 (1981): 305–324; *MBEPA*; and *WWWE*.

GREENE, JOSEPH K(INGSBURY) (1834–1917). Missionary, born April 10, 1834, in Auburn, Maine. Greene graduated from Bowdoin College and Union Theological Seminary, and was ordained in 1858. He was a missionary under the American Board of Commissioners for Foreign Missions (ABCFM)* in Turkey from 1859 until 1912. He served in Nicomedia from 1859 to 1862, in Brusa from 1862 to 1868, in Manissa in 1871–1872, and in Constantinople from 1872 to 1912. He returned to the United States in 1912 and wrote *Leavening the Levant* (Boston, 1916). Died February 10, 1917, in Oberlin, Ohio. *Reference*: *UnionTS*.

GREENE, OLIVE (1883–1966). Missionary educator, born October 28, 1883, in Crossville, New York, and grew up in Ogden, Utah. Greene graduated from Wellesley College, and studied at Radcliffe College and Kennedy School of Missions of the Hartford Seminary Foundation. She taught at the American Collegiate Institute for Girls* in Smyrna in 1912–1913; did relief work in Petras and Athens in 1922–1923; reopened the American Collegiate Institute in 1923 after the burning of Smyrna in 1922; and experimented with methods of teaching English to Turks. She was the principal of the institute from 1944 until her retirement in 1953, continuing as volunteer worker until 1959. Died December 14, 1966, in Brunswick, Maine. *Reference*: *Townsman* (Wellesley, Mass.), December 29, 1966.

GREW, JOSEPH C(LARK) (1880–1965). Diplomat, born May 27, 1880, in Boston. Grew graduated from Harvard University, entered the foreign service in 1904, and served in Cairo, Mexico City, St. Petersburg, Berlin, and Vienna. He was minister to Denmark from 1920 to 1921, minister to Switzerland from 1921 to 1924, and an observer at the Lausanne Conference of 1922–1923 which negotiated the peace treaty between the Allies and Turkey. He negotiated the Turkish-American treaty of 1923 which regularized relations between the United States and Turkey (but was not ratified by the Senate). He was undersecretary of state from 1924 to 1927. As ambassador to Turkey from 1927 to 1932, he improved relations between the United States and Turkey. He was ambassador to Japan from 1932 to 1941, and undersecretary of state from 1941 until his retirement in 1945. He was later chairman of the board of the Free Europe Committee. He wrote his memoirs, *Turbulent Era: A Diplomatic Record of Forty Years, 1904–1945*, ed. Walter Johnson (Boston, 1952). Died May 25, 1965, in Manchester, Massachusetts. *References*: *CB* 1941; *DADH*; Waldo H. Heinrich, Jr., *American Ambassador: Joseph C. Grew and the Development of the U.S. Diplomatic Tradition* (Boston, 1966); *NCAB* 55:163; *NYT*, May 27, 1965; Roger R. Trask, "Joseph C. Grew and Turco-American Rapprochement, 1927–1932," *Studies on Asia*, 1967, ed. Sidney D. Brown (Lincoln, Neb., 1968), pp. 139–170; and *WWWA*.

GRIDLEY, ELNATHAN (1796–1827). Missionary, born August 3, 1796, in Farmington, Connecticut. Gridley graduated from Yale College and Andover Theological Seminary, and was ordained in 1825. He served as a missionary under the American Board of Commissioners for Foreign Missions (ABCFM)* in Asia Minor in 1826–1827. In 1826 he was in Smyrna to establish a mission to the Greeks, and in 1827 he went to Cappadocia to acquaint himself with that area. Died September 27, 1827, in Kayseri, Turkey. *Reference*: *UnionTS*.

GRIFFIS, STANTON (1887–1974). Banker and diplomat, born May 2, 1887, in Boston. Griffis graduated from Cornell University. He became a partner at the investment banking firm of Hemphill, Noyes and Company in 1919; chairman of the board and largest shareholder of Madison Square Garden; chairman of the board of Brentano; and chairman of the executive committee of Paramount Pictures. He was chief of the Motion Picture Bureau of the Office of War Information in 1943–1944, and American Red Cross* commissioner for the Pacific in 1944–1945. He was ambassador to Poland in 1947–1948, ambassador to Egypt in 1948–1949, ambassador to Argentina in 1949–1950, and ambassador to Spain in 1951–1952. He was involved in relief work for the Palestinian refugees. He wrote an autobiography *Lying in State* (Garden City, N.Y., 1952). Died August 29, 1974, in New York City. *References*: Papers, Harry S Truman Library; *CB* 1944; *MENA*; *NYT*, August 30, 1974; and *WWWA*.

GRISCOM, LLOYD CARPENTER (1872–1959). Diplomat, born November 4, 1872, in Riverton, New Jersey. Griscom graduated from the University of Pennsylvania and the New York Law School and was admitted to the bar in 1896. He was assistant district attorney in New York City in 1897 and in Arizona in 1897–1898, and served in the Spanish-American War. He entered the foreign service in 1899 and was first secretary and chargé d'affaires in Constantinople. Using threat of force, he succeeded in collecting from the Turkish government payment of the claims of U.S. citizens. He was minister to Persia in 1901–1902, minister to Japan from 1902 to 1906, minister to Brazil in 1906–1907, and minister to Italy from 1907 to 1909. After 1909 he practiced law in New York City. He wrote *Diplomatically Speaking: Memoirs of Constantinople and Persia* (New York, 1940). Died February 9, 1959, in Thomasville, Georgia. *References*: Papers, Harry S Truman Library; *DADH*; *DAB S6*; *NCAB* 12:196; *NYT*, February 9, 1959; and *WWWA*.

GROFF, WILLIAM N. (1857–1901). Egyptologist, born May 4, 1857, in Cincinnati. Groff went to Paris in 1878, and studied at the College de France, the Ecole des Hautes Etudes, and the Ecole du Louvre. He was attaché in the consulate in Algiers in 1890–1891, lived in Cairo from 1891 to 1899, and in Athens from 1900 until his death. Died November 4, 1901, in Athens. His papers were collected in *Oeuvres Egyptologiques le William N. Groff* (Paris, 1908). *References*: *OAB*; and *WWWE*.

GROSECLOSE, ELGIN (EARL) (1899–1983). Economist and author, born November 25, 1899, in Waukomis, Oklahoma. Groseclose graduated from the University of Oklahoma and American University. He taught at the mission school in Teheran, was secretary of the Persia Relief Commission from 1920 to 1923, and based his novel *Ararat* (New York, 1939) on his experiences in Armenia. He was special agent for the Department of Commerce from 1923 to 1926, and assistant trade commissioner in 1926. He was employed by the Guaranty Trust Company of New York City from 1927 to 1930; was associate editor of *Fortune* from 1930 to 1932; assistant professor at the University of Oklahoma from 1932 to 1935; economist with the Federal Communications Commission from 1935 to 1938; and economist with the Treasury Department from 1938 to 1943. He was a special assistant in the Arthur Chester Millspaugh* mission, was appointed treasurer-general of Iran by the Iranian Parliament in 1943, and served until 1944. In 1944 he became a financial and economic consultant and head of his own consulting firm. He wrote *The Persian Journey of the Reverend Ashley Wishard and His Servant Fathi* (Indianapolis, 1937), *Introduction to Iran* (New York, 1947), *The Carmelite, a Novel* (New York, 1955), and *The Scimitar of Saladin* (New York, 1956). Died April 3, 1983, in Washington, D.C. *References*: *AMWS*; *CA*; *NYT*, April 7, 1983; and *WWA*.

GROSVENOR, EDWIN AUGUSTUS (1845–1936). Educator and author, born on August 30, 1845, in West Newburyport, Massachusetts. Grosvenor graduated from Amherst College and Andover Theological Seminary, and was ordained in 1872. He was tutor at Robert College* from 1867 to 1871, and professor of Latin and history from 1873 to 1890. He was professor of history and government at Amherst College from 1892 until his retirement in 1914. He wrote *The Hippodrome of Constantinople and Its Still Existing Monuments* (London, 1889), and *Constantinople* (Boston, 1895), the first scholarly book to be profusely illustrated with photoengravings. Died September 15, 1936, in Amherst, Massachusetts. *References*: *Amherst*; *AndoverTS*; *NCAB* 10:493; *NYT*, September 16, 1936; and *WWWA*.

GUERIN, JULES (1866–1946). Artist, born November 18, 1866, in St. Louis, Missouri. Guerin studied at the Ecole des Beaux-arts in Paris and lived in Chicago from 1880 to 1896. With British author Robert Smyth Hichens, he went to the Middle East on a commission from *Century Magazine*. His illustrations appeared in the magazine and later in Hitchen's books *The Holy Land* (New York, 1910), *Egypt and Its Monuments* (New York, 1910), and *The Near East: Dalmatia, Greece and Constantinople* (New York, 1913). A collection of Guerin's prints, *Views of Palestine and Egypt*, was published in 1917. He established a studio in New York City in 1914 and gained a reputation through his murals in the Lincoln Memorial, the Pennsylvania Railroad Station in New York City, and in other buildings. Died June 13, 1946, in New York City. *References*: *ACAB*; *NYT*, June 15, 1946; and *WWWA*.

GULICK, JOHN (1924–   ). Anthropologist and educator, born April 18, 1924, in Newton, Massachusetts. Gulick graduated from Harvard University. In 1943 he was a volunteer ambulance driver for the American Field Service and spent six months in the Middle East. He did field research in Lebanon in 1951–1952 and 1961–1962, in Baghdad in 1965, and in Isfahan in 1970–1971. He was instructor at Adelphi College from 1953 to 1955, and then assistant professor, associate professor, and professor at the University of North Carolina at Chapel Hill. He wrote *Social Structure and Culture Change in a Lebanese Village* (New York, 1955), *Tripoli: A Modern Arab City* (Cambridge, Mass.,

1967), *The Middle East: An Anthropological Perspective* (Pacific Palisades, Calif., 1976), and edited *Dimensions of Cultural Change in the Middle East* (Ithaca, N.Y., 1965). *References*: *AMWS*; *CA*; and *WWA*.

GUMMERÉ, SAMUEL RENE (1849–1920). Diplomat, born February 19, 1849, in Trenton, New Jersey. Gummeré graduated from Princeton University, studied law, was admitted to the bar in 1874, and practiced in Trenton. He was secretary to the minister at the Hague from 1881 to 1884, consul general to Morocco from 1898 to 1905, first minister to Morocco from 1905 to 1909, and a member of the commission which represented the United States at the Algeciras Conference of 1906 which tried, unsuccessfully, to reduce French and Spanish influence in Morocco. He was involved in the Perdicaris affair,* when Ion Perdicaris was kidnapped, and forced the Moroccan Sultan to accept the kidnapper's terms to release Perdicaris. He resigned in 1909 and lived in England. Died May 28, 1920, in Wimbledon, England. *References*: George W. Collins, "Mission to Morocco," *New Jersey History* 89 (1971): 37–50; *DAB*; *DADH*; *NCAB* 13:521; *NYT*, May 29, 1920; and *WWWA*.

GUNTER, JOHN W(ADSWORTH) (1914–   ). Economist, born February 17, 1914, in Sanford, North Carolina. Gunter graduated from the University of North Carolina. He was an economist in the Office of International Finance of the Treasury Department from 1941 to 1948 and its deputy director in 1947–1948. He was the department's representative in Cairo from 1943 to 1944 and went to Saudi Arabia in 1943 to study Ibn Saud's finances. He was the department's representative in London in 1946–1947; associate professor of international trade at the University of Texas at Austin in 1948–1949; member of the Greek Currency Commission from 1949 to 1951; and alternate member of the Commission on German Debts from 1951 to 1953. He was assistant director of the Middle Eastern Department of the International Monetary Fund from 1953 to 1958 and its director after 1958. *References*: *Who's Who in the United Nations and Related Agencies* (New York, 1975).

GUNTHER, C(HARLES) GODFREY (1880–1929). Mining engineer, born September 4, 1880, in Bath, Long Island. Gunther graduated from Columbia University School of Mines. He was involved in various mining operations in the West and in Mexico. In 1912 he prospected unsuccessfully for copper in the Sinai peninsula, but discovered ancient copper mines in Cyprus. He acquired the properties and developed them for the Cyprus Mines Corporation, which he established in 1916. Forced to resign, he left Cyprus in 1925. Died December 26, 1929, while on a holiday in Zweiseimmer, Switzerland. *References*: David S. Lavender, *The Story of the Cyprus Mines Corporation* (San Marino, Calif., 1962).

H

HAAS, CYRIL H(ERBERT) (1876–1961). Medical missionary, born May 10, 1876. Haas graduated from Susquehanna University and the University of Michigan Medical School, and practiced for two years as company physician in the Virginia mountains. He served in Turkey under the American Board of Commissioners for Foreign Missions (ABCFM)* from 1910 to 1951. He was stationed first in the American Hospital at Adana, Turkey, about which he wrote *Eight Months Work in a Turkish Hospital* (New York, 1912?), and later established his own clinic in Adana. Died January 9, 1961, in Pleasant Hill, Tennessee. *Reference*: *NYT*, January 12, 1961.

HABIB, PHILIP C(HARLES) (1920–   ). Diplomat, born February 25, 1920, in Brooklyn, New York. Habib graduated from the universities of Idaho and California at Berkeley, entered the foreign service in 1949, and served as secretary in Ottawa and Wellington and consul general in Trinidad. He was counselor for political affairs in Seoul from 1962 to 1965, chief political adviser in Saigon, and the highest ranking career diplomat in the American delegation to the Vietnam peace talks in Paris from 1968 to 1971. He was ambassador to South Korea from 1971 to 1974, assistant secretary of state for East Asian and Pacific Affairs from 1974 to 1976, and undersecretary of state for political affairs from 1974 until his retirement in 1978. He was recalled from retirement in 1981 as special envoy to the Middle East to negotiate a cease-fire between Israel and the Palestine Liberation Organization (PLO), and to defuse the crisis between Syria and Israel over the placement of Syrian missiles in Lebanon. He was recalled again in 1982 following Israel's invasion of Lebanon. He practiced shuttle diplomacy, which achieved a cease-fire and the evacuation of the PLO from Lebanon, but he did not succeed in removing all foreign forces from Lebanon. *References*: *BRDS*; *CB 1981*; *NYT*, May 28, 1981; *MENA*; *PolProf: Johnson*; *WWA*; and *WWAP*.

HADASSAH, THE WOMEN'S ZIONIST ORGANIZATION OF AMER-ICA. Founded in 1912. Hadassah sponsored medical care, training and research, and special education in Palestine and Israel. It sent two visiting nurses to Palestine in 1913 and organized the American Zionist Medical Unit* which was sent to Palestine in 1918. It later became the Hadassah Medical Organization, set up a variety of services for infants, children, and the sick, and established a school for nurses. *References*: Archives, Central Files and Records Division, Hadassah, New York City; *EJ*; and Marlin Levin, *Balm in Gilead: The Story of Hadassah* (New York, 1973).

HAINES, RICHARD CARLTON (1904–1977). Archaeologist and architect, born December 22, 1904, in Tabernackle, New Jersey. Haines graduated from Carnegie Institute of Technology. He was a draftsman in various architectural offices from 1928 to 1930 and again from 1945 to 1949. He was field architect for the Oriental Institute from 1930 to 1942 and from 1949 to 1972; participated in archaeological excavations in Turkey, Syria, Iran, Israel, and Iraq from 1930 to 1940 and from 1949 to 1965; and was field director of the joint University Museum and Oriental Institute expedition to Nippur from 1956 to 1964. He was a member of the faculty of the University of Chicago from 1959 to 1971. He wrote *Excavations in the Plain of Antioch II* (Chicago, 1971), and *A Byzantine Church at Khirbet at-Karak* (Chicago, 1960), and was co-author of *Soundings at Tel Fakhariyeh* (Chicago, 1958), and *Nippur I* (Chicago, 1968). Died February 15, 1977, in Cape May Court House, New Jersey. *Reference*: WWWA.

HALABY, ELIZABETH. *See* Nur el Hussein.

HALE, CHARLES (1831–1882). Editor and diplomat, born June 7, 1831, in Boston. Hale graduated from Harvard College. He was a reporter and editor for the *Boston Daily Advertiser* from 1850 until 1865. Between 1855 and 1860 he served as a representative in the Massachusetts legislature and as speaker in 1859. In 1861 he traveled abroad. He was agent and consul general in Egypt from 1864 to 1871, and wrote an article on his experiences in the *Atlantic Monthly* in 1877. He served as state senator in 1871–1872 and as assistant secretary of state from 1872 to 1874, and was again a representive in the state legislature from 1875 to 1879. Died March 1, 1882, in Boston. *References*: ACAB; *DAB*; and *WWWA*.

HALE, SUSAN (1838–1910). Artist and author, sister of Charles Hale,* born on December 5, 1838, in Boston. Hale received a private education, was a teacher, and then devoted herself to art, traveling extensively. She went to Egypt in 1867 to visit her brother, and later associated with him in the publication of the ''Family Flight'' series of travel books for young people about the countries she had visited, including *A Family Flight Over Egypt and Syria* (Boston, 1882). Died September 17, 1910, in Matunuck, Rhode Island. *References*: Papers,

Sophia Smith College, Smith College Library; *ACAB*; *NAW*; *NYHSD*; *NYT*, September 18, 1910; and *WWWA*.

HALKIN, SHIMON (1898–   ). Poet and educator, born October 30, 1898, in Dobvk near Mohilev, Russia, and came to the United States in 1914. Halkin graduated from New York University. He taught Hebrew and Hebrew literature at the Hebrew Union College School for Teachers in New York City from 1925 to 1932, settled in Palestine in 1932, and taught English at a high school in Tel Aviv. He returned to the United States in 1939 and was lecturer at the College of Jewish Studies in Chicago from 1940 to 1943, and professor of Hebrew literature at the Jewish Institute of Religion in New York City from 1943 to 1949. He returned to Israel in 1949, serving as professor of modern Hebrew literature at the Hebrew University in Jerusalem until his retirement in 1968. *References*: *CA*; *EJ*; J. Kabakoff, ''Simon Halkin—Man of Letters,'' *Jewish Book Annual* 31 (1973–74): 62–70; *MENA*; and *WWAJ*.

HALL, GEORGE HENRY (1825–1913). Painter, born September 21, 1825, in Manchester, New Hampshire, and grew up in Boston. Hall began to paint in 1842, went to Europe in 1849, and studied in Dusseldorf and Paris. He returned to the United States and opened a studio in New York City. In 1860 and 1866 he visited Spain and Rome, in 1872 he was in Italy, and in 1875 he toured Egypt, making studies of bazaar scenes in Cairo, from which he afterwards painted pictures. Died February 17, 1913, in New York City. *References*: *ACAB*; *DAB*; *NCAB* 15:170; *NYHSD*; *NYT*, February 19, 1913; and *WWWA*.

HALL, HARVEY PORTER (1909–1975). Organization official, born November 16, 1909, in Beirut. Hall graduated from Union College and Harvard University. He taught at the American University of Beirut* from 1930 to 1933 and at Robert College* from 1936 to 1941, and was research analyst in Turkey with the Office of Strategic Services from 1942 to 1945. He was director of publications for the Middle East Institute and editor of the *Middle East Journal* from 1946 to 1956. He wrote *American Interests in the Middle East* (New York, 1948). He became an officer of the Ford Foundation in 1956, serving as its representative in the Beirut Field Office from 1967 to 1971. Died June 18, 1975, in Orford, New Hampshire. *References*: *MEJ* 29 (1975): 433; *MENA*.

HALL, ISAAC HOLLISTER (1837–1896). Orientalist, born December 12, 1837, in Norwalk, Connecticut. Hall graduated from Hamilton College and the Law Department of Columbia University, and practiced law from 1865 to 1875. In 1875 he went to Syria and was professor at the Syrian Protestant College until 1877. In 1876 he discovered a Syriac manuscript of the New Testament from ca. 800 A.D. He was on the editorial staff of the *Sunday School Times* from 1877 to 1884, and then joined the staff of the Metropolitan Museum of Art and became curator of the department of sculpture in 1886. He helped prepare catalogues of

Cypriote art, was one of the first scholars to read an entire Cypriote inscription, and published articles on Cypriote writing and language. He was also a student of Himyaritic and Phoenician. Died July 2, 1896, at Mount Vernon, New York. *References*: *ACAB*; *DAB*; *NCAB* 12:143; *NYT*, July 3, 1896; and *WWWA*.

HALL, LINDSLEY FOOTE (1883–1969). Surveyor and archaeological draftsman, born in Portland, Oregon. Hall graduated from the Massachusetts Institute of Technology. He joined the Metropolitan Museum of Art in 1905 and took part in eight archaeological expeditions to Egypt beginning in 1913. He was loaned by the Metropolitan Museum to the British expedition which discovered the tomb of Tutankhamen in 1923, and he helped Howard Carter record the contents of the tomb. Hall took part in the museum's excavations in Nishapur, Persia. He retired in 1940. Died February 3, 1969, in Portland, Oregon. *References*: Papers and diaries, Oregon Historical Society Library; *NYT*, February 7, 1969; *Oregon Journal*, February 4, 1969; and Jack Pement, "A Portlander's Legacy Records Discovery of Tut's Tomb," *Oregon Journal*, June 30, 1978.

HALL, MELVIN ADAMS (1889–1962). Military aviator, born April 14, 1889, in Bellows Falls, Vermont. Hall graduated from Princeton University, joined the British Army in 1914, transferred to the U.S. Army in 1918 as a flying officer, and served as the first assistant military attaché for aviation in London from 1920 to 1922. He was a member of the first Arthur Chester Millspaugh* mission from 1923 to 1927, and resided in Teheran, Meshed, and Shiraz. He was a financial expert for the Persian government, and one of his duties was guarding the Shah's collection of crown jewels. He also negotiated peace treaties with several nomadic tribes. He was recommissioned in the Naval Reserve in 1939, and served as assistant acting naval attaché in Turkey, Bulgaria, and Rumania until 1942. He was assistant chief of staff to the Ninth Air Force in 1943–1944. He retired in 1945. He wrote *Journey to the End of an Era: An Informal Autobiography* (New York, 1947), and his reminiscences, *Bird of Time* (New York, 1949). Died November 23, 1962, in New York City. *Reference*: *NYT*, November 25, 1962.

HALL, WILBURN BRIGGS (1838–1912). Naval officer, born September 20, 1838, in Fairfield district, South Carolina. Hall graduated from the U.S. Naval Academy in 1859, served in the West African Squadron, and in 1860 on the *Niagra*, returning to Japan the first Japanese embassy to the United States. He served in the Confederate Navy during the Civil War. In 1874 he was appointed major of engineers in Egypt, being placed in charge of the survey of Lower Egypt. He was later adjutant general and chief of the first section of the Ministry of War, and chief of military construction until 1880. In Baltimore he organized an institution for the preparation of cadets and was consul in Nice from 1894 until 1898. Died November 18, 1912, in Baltimore. *References*: *Hesseltine*; *NCAB* 8:269.

HALL, WILLIAM H. (1877?–1927). Educator, born in Biddleford, Maine. Hall graduated from Union College and McCormick Theological Seminary. He became a professor at the Syrian Protestant College in 1896, and associate principal and principal of the preparatory school of the college from 1903 until his death. He was secretary of a committee appointed by the American Committee for Armenian and Syrian Relief to collect data on the reconstruction of the Ottoman Empire, and published its report, *Reconstruction in Turkey* (New York, 1918). He also wrote articles for the *National Geographic Magazine*. Died January 8, 1927, in Beirut, Syria. *Reference*: *New York World*, January 12, 1927.

HALLOCK, HOMAN (1803–1894). Printer, born May 24, 1803, in Plainfield, Massachusetts. Hallock graduated from Amherst College. Sent to Smyrna in 1826 by the American Board of Commissioners for Foreign Missions (ABCFM),* he designed and cast Arabic type, making seven different fonts in different sizes. Died October 28, 1894. *References*: *Amherst*; *NCAB* 11:193.

HAMERSLEY, JOHN WILLIAM (1808–1889). Lawyer and author, born May 24, 1808, in New York City. Hamersley graduated from Columbia College, was admitted to the bar, and practiced law in New York City. He traveled to the Middle East in 1833. While in Egypt he accumulated a collection of antiquities which were later given to Columbia College. He met Lady Hester Stanhope, an English eccentric living in Mount Lebanon and known as the "Mad Nun of Lebanon," and wrote of their meeting in the November 1843 issue of *The United States Magazine and Democratic Review*. *References*: *ACAB*; *DAA*; and *NCAB* 7:298.

HAMILTON, LLOYD N(ELSON) (1891?–1945). Lawyer, born in San Francisco. Hamilton graduated from the University of California and was admitted to the bar. He joined Standard Oil Company of California (Socal) in 1921 and was sent to London in 1933. He was the company's representative to Saudi Arabia. In 1933 he accompanied Karl Saben Twitchell* to Jidda to negotiate a petroleum concession with the Saudi government, lived in Jidda for over a year, and completed negotiations for the oil drilling and refining concession granted to Socal and the Texas Company. He was president of Standard Oil of British Columbia in 1941 and chairman of the board of Bahrain Petroleum Company* in 1943. Died December 23, 1945, in New York City. *References*: "A Mission to Jiddah," *AWM* 13 (December 1962): 19–21; *NYT*, December 24, 1945.

HAMLIN, CYRUS (1811–1900). Educator, born January 5, 1811, in Waterford, Maine. Hamlin graduated from Bowdoin College and Bangor Theological Seminary. He was a missionary under the American Board of Commissioners for Foreign Missions (ABCFM)* in Turkey from 1837 to 1860. He founded Bebek Seminary in 1840 in a suburb near Constantinople, and Robert College* in 1863 in Constantinople, and was its first president from 1863 to 1877. He was later professor of theology at Bangor Theological Seminary from 1877 to 1880, and president of Middlebury (Vt.) College from 1880 until his retirement in 1885. He wrote *Among the Turks* (New York, 1878) and his autobiography, *My Life and Times* (Boston, 1893), and was co-author of *Turkey and the Armenian Atrocities* (Philadelphia, 1896). Died August 8, 1900, in Lexington, Massachusetts. *References*: Papers, Bowdoin College Library; *ACAB*; *DAB*; *BDAE*; *NCAB* 10:491; and *WWWA*.

HAMMOND, PHILIP (1924–   ). Archaeologist, born May 5, 1924, in Brooklyn, New York. Hammond graduated from Drew University, Drew Theological Seminary, and Yale University, and served in the infantry in World War II. He was a Methodist pastor in Martinsville, New Jersey, from 1950 to 1955; assistant professor of religion at Lycoming College (Williamsport, Pa.) from 1957 to 1960; assistant professor of Old Testament at Princeton Theological Seminary from 1960 to 1966, and at Brandeis University from 1966 to 1974; and professor of Old Testament at the University of Utah after 1974. He excavated at Jericho, Dhiban, and at Hebron in Jordan, from 1963 to 1966, and at Petra in 1954 and in 1961–1962. He wrote *The Excavation of the Main Theater at Petra, 1961–62* (London, 1965), *The Crusader Fort at El-Habis at Petra* (Salt Lake City, 1970), and *The Nabataeans—Their History, Culture and Archaeology* (Gothenburg, 1973). *References*: *CA*; *DAS*.

HANFMANN, GEORGE M(AXIM) A(NOSSOV) (1911–1986). Archaeologist, born November 20, 1911, in St. Petersburg, Russia, came to the United States in 1934, and was naturalized in 1940. Hanfmann studied at the universities of Jena, Munich, and Berlin and at Johns Hopkins University. He was a member of the Harvard University faculty in 1935, professor of archaeology in 1956, and curator of classical art at the Fogg Art Museum from 1946 to 1974. He was director of the Harvard-Cornell archaeological expedition to Sardis from 1958 to 1978. He wrote *Sardis: From Prehistoric to Roman Times: Results of the Archaeological Exploration of Sardis 1958–1975* (Cambridge, Mass., 1983), and *Letters from Sardis* (Cambridge, Mass., 1972). Died March 13, 1986, in Cambridge, Massachusetts. *Studies Presented to George M. A. Hanfmann*, ed. David Mitten et al. (Cambridge, Mass., 1971). *References*: *DAS*; *NYT*, March 15, 1986; and *WWWA*.

HARBORD, JAMES GUTHRIE (1866–1947). Army officer, born March 21, 1866, in Bloomington, Illinois. Harbord graduated from Kansas State Agricultural College (Manhattan, Kan.), enlisted as a private in the U.S. Army in 1889, and was commissioned a second lieutenant in 1891. He was assistant chief of the Philippines Constabulary from 1903 to 1914, and chief of staff of the American Expeditionary Force to France. He published *Leaves from a War Diary* (New York, 1925). In 1919 he was head of a mission to Armenia to collect data needed to understand what responsibilities a mandate on Armenia would entail on the United States, and traveled in Armenia and Transcaucasia. The report of his mission was published as a Senate document in 1920. He published his own impressions in the June 1920 issue of *International Conciliation*. He was later deputy chief of staff of the U.S. Army in 1921–1922, and retired in 1922 with the rank of major general. He was president of the Radio Corporation of America from 1923 to 1930, and chairman of the board from 1930 to 1947. Died August 20, 1947, in New York City. *References*: *CB* 1945; *DAB S4*; *NCAB* 36:493; *NYT*, August 21, 1947; Charles Penrose, *James G. Harbord (1866–1947) Lieutenant General: USA, Chairman of the Board: RCA* (New York, 1956); *WAMB*; and *WWWA*.

HARBORD MISSION. A mission headed by General James Guthrie Harbord* sent in 1919 to Armenia to collect information and to look into the consequences of a decision as to whether the United States should accept and undertake a mandate on Armenia. *Reference*: James H. Tashjian, "The American Military Mission to Armenia," *Armenian Review*, May 1949 through March 1952.

HARE, RAYMOND ARTHUR (1901–   ). Diplomat, born April 3, 1901, in Martinsburg, West Virginia. Hare graduated from Grinnell College. He was an instructor at Robert College* from 1924 to 1927 and executive secretary of the American Chamber of Commerce for the Levant in 1926–1927. He entered the foreign service in 1927 and served in Constantinople, Paris, Cairo, Beirut, Teheran, Jidda, and London. He was ambassador to Saudi Arabia and minister to Yemen from 1950 to 1953; ambassador to Lebanon in 1953–1954; director general of the foreign service from 1954 to 1956; ambassador to Egypt from 1956 to 1958; ambassador to the United Arab Republic in 1958–1959; and minister to Yemen in 1959. He was involved in the negotiations following Egypt's nationalization of the Suez Canal and the Suez War of 1956. He was deputy undersecretary of state for political affairs in 1960–1961, ambassador to Turkey from 1961 to 1965, and assistant secretary of state for Near Eastern and South Asian Affairs in 1965–1966. Hare retired in 1966 and was president of the Middle East Institute from 1966 to 1969. *References*: Papers, Middle East Institute Library, Washington, D.C.; slide collection, Freer Gallery of Art Library, Washington, D.C.; *CB* 1957; *BRDS*; *MENA*; and *NCAB* I:211.

HARLAN, JACK RODNEY (1917–   ). Agronomist and geneticist, born June 7, 1917, in Washington, D.C. Harlan graduated from George Washington University and the University of California. He was an agronomist in the Division of Forage Crops and Diseases of the Department of Agriculture from 1942 to 1951; professor of agronomy at Oklahoma State University and the Agricultural Experiment Station from 1951 to 1966; and professor of agronomy at the University of Illinois after 1966. He explored for plants for the U.S. Department of Agriculture in Turkey, Syria, Iraq, and Lebanon in 1948, and in Iran and Afghanistan in 1960–1961; made collecting trips to Israel and Turkey in 1964; was a senior staff member of the Iranian prehistoric project of the Oriental Institute in 1960 and of the Turkish prehistoric project in 1964; and a member of the Dead Sea archaeological project in 1977, 1979, and 1983. *References*: *Agronomy Journal* 69 (1977): 137; *AMWS*; *BDAE*; and *WWA*.

HARLAN, JOSIAH (1799–1871). Soldier and adventurer, born June 12, 1799, in Newlin Township, Chester County, Pennsylvania. In 1823 Harlan traveled to India, entered the employ of the East India Company as assistant surgeon, and served during the First Burmese War. He resigned in 1826, went to northern India, and became attached to Shah Shuja-ul-Mulk, the deposed King of Afghanistan, became a secret agent for him, and in 1828 went to Kabul disguised as a dervish. He then entered the service of Maharajah Ranjit Singh of the Punjab in Lahore. Later he returned to Kabul and became aide-de-camp to Amir Dost Mohammed of Afghanistan and general of the Afghan Army, and trained Afghan troops in European military tactics. In 1838–1839 he made a military expedition to the area of Balkh in North Afghanistan. He lost his position in 1839 following the British invasion of Afghanistan and returned to the United States in 1841. He wrote *A Memoir of India and Avghanistaun, with Observations on the Present Exciting and Critical State and Future Prospects of Those Countries* (Philadelphia, 1842) and an article on the fruits of Cabul and vicinity. He also wrote *Central Asia: Personal Narrative of General Josiah Harlan, 1823–1841*, ed. Frank E. Ross (London, 1939). Died October 1871 in San Francisco. *References*: P. E. Caspani, "The First American in Afghanistan," *Afghanistan* 2 (1947): 37–42; *DAB*; Charles Grey, *European Adventurers in Northern India, 1785–1849* (Lahore, India, 1929), ch. xii; and *WWWA*.

HARLAND, MARION (1830--1922). Author, pseudonym of Mary Virginia Terhune, born December 21, 1830, in Amelia County, Virginia. Harland began to write at age fourteen. She was sent to Palestine in 1893 by the *Christian Herald*, and her letters later appeared as *The Home of the Bible: A Woman's Vision of the Master's Land* (Baltimore, 1895). She also wrote *Under the Flag of the Orient* (Philadelphia, 1897), and *Marion Harland's Autobiography: The Story of a Long Life* (New York, 1910). Died June 3, 1922, in New York City. *References*: *DAB*; *NAW*; *NCAB* 34:102; and *WWWA*.

HARLOW, S(AMUEL) RALPH (1885–1972). Missionary educator, born July 20, 1885, in Boston. Harlow graduated from Harvard and Columbia universities and Union and Hartford theological seminaries, was ordained in 1912, and was a minister in New York City in 1909. He was a missionary under the American Board of Commissioners for Foreign Missions (ABCFM)* in Turkey from 1912 to 1922, and was chaplain and head of the Department of Sociology at the International College, Smyrna. In 1916–1917 he was a traveling secretary of the

Student Volunteers Movement, worked for the Young Men's Christian Association (YMCA)* with the American army in France during World War I, and was field secretary of ABCFM in 1922–1923. He became professor of religion and social ethics at Smith College in 1923, and was a member of the United Nations Relief and Rehabilitation Administration (UNRRA) mission to Greece in 1945–1946. Died August 21, 1972, in Oak Bluffs, Massachusetts. *References*: Papers, Tulane University Library, New Orleans; *CA*; *NYT*, August 23, 1972; and *WWWA*.

HARMON, ARTHUR LOOMIS (1878–1958). Architect, born June 13, 1878, in Chicago. Harmon studied at the Art Institute of Chicago and Columbia University School of Architecture. He was a designer with McKim, Mead and White, New York City, from 1902 to 1911, and with Wallis and Goodwillie from 1911 to 1913. He practiced under his own name from 1913 to 1928, and was a partner in Shreve, Lamb and Harmon of New York City after 1928. He designed and built the Young Men's Christian Association (YMCA)* building in Jerusalem, completed in 1933, considered one of the most significant buildings in Jerusalem, and called "the most beautiful Y in the world." He also built battle monuments in France and the Juilliard School of Music. Died on October 17, 1958, in White Plains, New York. *References*: *NYT*, October 18, 1958; and *WWWA*.

HARPER, ROBERT FRANCIS (1864–1914). Assyriologist, born October 18, 1864, in New Concord, Ohio. Harper graduated from Denison and Muskingum colleges and the universities of Chicago and Leipzig. He was instructor of Assyriology at Yale University from 1886 to 1891, and a member of the University of Pennsylvania archaeological expedition to Nippur in 1888–1889. He became associate professor at the University of Chicago in 1892, and professor of Semitic languages and literatures and curator of the Babylonian collection at the Haskell Oriental Museum in 1900. He was director of the University of Chicago expedition to Bismya, Iraq, from 1902 to 1906, and director of the American Schools of Oriental Research (ASOR)* in Jerusalem in 1908–1909. Died August 6, 1914, in London. *References*: *DAB*; *NCAB* 22:98; and *WWWA*.

HARRIS, FRANKLIN STEWART (1884–1960). Agriculturist, born August 29, 1884, in Benjamin, Utah. Harris graduated from Brigham Young University, Utah Agricultural College, and Cornell University. He was professor of agronomy at Utah Agricultural College from 1911 to 1916, director of the School of Agricultural Engineering from 1912 to 1916; director of the Utah Experimental Station from 1916 to 1921; president of Brigham Young University from 1921 to 1945; and president of Utah State Agricultural College from 1945 to 1950. He was chairman of a commission sent by the Jewish Colonization Society to the Soviet Union to investigate the attempt to establish a Jewish agricultural colony in Birobidzhan; was an adviser on economic and agricultural problems to the Iranian government in 1939–1940; organized the department of agriculture there; and established a forest and a weather bureau. He was chairman of the U. S. agricultural mission to the Middle East in 1946, of the Food and Agriculture Organization mission to Greece in 1947, of the mission on technical collaboration between the governments of Iran and the United States in 1950, and a member of the third agricultural mission to Saudi Arabia. Died April 18, 1960, in Salt Lake City. *References*: *Agronomy Journal* 52 (1960): 736; *BDAE*; *MENA*; *NCAB* 53:67; *NYT*, April 20, 1960; *Science* 132 (August 26, 1960): 533–534; and *WWWA*.

HARRIS, JAMES E(DWARD) (1928–   ). Orthodontist, born August 25, 1928, in Ann Arbor, Michigan. Harris graduated from the University of Michigan. He was assistant and associate professor of orthodontics and human genetics at the University of Michigan from 1964 to 1969, and professor of orthodontics from 1969 until his retirement in 1982. In 1965 he was director of the University of Michigan School of Dentistry expedition to Gebel Adda in Nubia, Egypt, to study teeth in ancient Nubian skulls and in modern Nubian children, and from 1966 to 1970 he was director of the expedition to the Egyptian Museum in Cairo to conduct x-ray investigations of the royal mummies. He was coauthor of *X-Raying the Pharoahs* (New York, 1973), and co-editor of *An X-Ray Atlas of the Royal Mummies* (Chicago, 1980). *References*: *AMWS*; and *CA*.

HARRISON, MARGUERITE E(LTON) (BAKER) (1879–1967). Journalist, born Marguerite Elton Baker, October 1879 near Baltimore. Harrison graduated from Radcliffe College. After her husband's death in 1915, she became a journalist for the *Baltimore Sun*. In 1918 she joined the Military Intelligence Division, was sent to Europe, and was stationed in Berlin until 1919. In 1920 she was sent to Russia, was arrested, and remained in prison ten months. In 1922–1923 she made a journey around the world, and in 1924–1925, she completed an overland journey from Istanbul to Persia and joined the Bakhtiari tribe in its annual spring migration route. She wrote articles for the *New York Times* and several magazines and an autobiography, *There's Always Tomorrow: The Story of a Checkered Life* (New York, 1935). Died July 16, 1967, in Baltimore. *References*: Elizabeth F. Olds, *Women of the Four Winds: The Adventures of Four of America's First Women Explorers* (Boston, 1985), pt. 3.

HARRISON, PAUL WILBERFORCE (1883–1962). Medical missionary, born January 12, 1883, in Scribner, Nebraska. Harrison graduated from Doane College, the University of Nebraska, and Johns Hopkins University Medical College. He served in the Arabian Mission* from 1909 to 1954, first in Kuwait and later in the Muscat, Oman, and Bahrain, running clinics and hospitals. He visited Riyadh in 1917 and 1919. He wrote *The Arab at Home* (New York, 1924) and his memoirs, *Doctor in Arabia* (New York, 1940). He retired in 1954 but in 1957 became medical director of a residential development for elderly missionaries in Penney Farms. Died November 30, 1962, in Penney Farms,

Florida. *References*: Jerome Beatty, *Americans All Over* (New York, 1940), pp. 219–230; Ann M. Harrison, *A Tool in His Hand* (New York, 1958); *MW* 53 (1963): 263–264; and *NYT*, December 1, 1962.

HARRISON, THOMAS SKELTON (1837–1919). Manufacturer, born September 19, 1837, in Philadelphia. Harrison attended a business college and served in the navy during the Civil War. He was a member of Harrison Bros. and Company from 1864 to 1897, vice president from 1897 to 1899, and president from 1899 to 1902. He traveled widely and made several trips to Egypt. He was diplomatic agent and consul general to Egypt from 1897 until 1899, and wrote *The Homely Diary of a Diplomat in the East, 1897–1899* (Boston, 1917). He later became prominent in the Philadelphia political reform movement. Died May 3, 1919, in Philadelphia. *References*: *NCAB* 27:99; and *WWWA*.

HART, CHARLES CALMER (1878–1956). Journalist and diplomat, born in Bryant, Indiana. Hart learned the printer's trade, was a reporter for the *San Francisco Call*, city editor on the Geneva (Ind.) *Herald*, reporter for the Muncie (Ind.) *Star* and the Indianapolis *Star*, and city editor on *The Spokesman Review* (Spokane, Wash.). He was the Washington correspondent of the *Portland Oregonian* and other newspapers. He was minister to Albania from 1925 to 1929 and minister to Persia from 1929 to 1933. In 1936 he was sent to Persia by the Amiranian Oil Company of New York, subsidiary of Seabord Oil Company, as their representative, to negotiate with the Persian government for petroleum and pipeline concessions, and obtained a concession in 1937. Died November 17, 1956, in Los Angeles. *Reference*: *NYT*, November 26, 1956.

HART, DAVID MONTGOMERY (1927–   ). Anthropologist, born May 18, 1927, in Chestnut Hill, Pennsylvania. Hart graduated from Princeton University and the University of Pennsylvania. He conducted fieldwork in Spanish Morocco and Tangier from 1952 to 1955, and for the American Museum of Natural History in Morocco from 1959 to 1966. He was a staff member of the Local Government Relation Department of Arabian American Oil Company (ARAMCO)* in 1956, station relations representative for Trans-Arabian Pipeline Company (TAPLINE)* in 1956–1957, and taught at the Institute of Sociology of the University Mohammed V in Rabat. He wrote *The Aith Waryaghar of the Moroccan Rif: An Ethnography and History* (Tucson, Ariz., 1976), *Dadd 'Atta and His Forty Grandsons: The Socio-Political Organization of the Ait 'Atta of Southern Morocco* (Cambridge, England, 1981), and *The Ait 'Atta of Southern Morocco: Daily Life & Recent History* (Cambridge, England, 1984). *Reference*: *DFAF*.

HART, PARKER T(HOMPSON) (WILLIAM) (1910–   ). Diplomat, born September 28, 1910, in Medford, Massachusetts. Hart graduated from Dartmouth College and Harvard and Georgetown universities, and studied in Geneva. He entered the foreign service in 1938, serving in Vienna, in Para, Brazil, in Cairo, and in Jidda, and opened the consulate in Dhahran in 1944. He later served in Damascus; was director of the Office of Near Eastern Affairs in 1952–1953; deputy chief of mission and counselor in Cairo from 1955 to 1958; deputy assistant secretary of state for Near Eastern and South Asian Affairs from 1958 to 1961; ambassador to Saudi Arabia from 1961 to 1965 and to Yemen in 1961–1962; ambassador to Kuwait in 1962–1963; ambassador to Turkey from 1965 to 1968; and assistant secretary of state for Near Eastern and South Asian Affairs in 1968–1969. He retired in 1969, was president of the Middle East Institute from 1969 to 1973, special representative for Middle East and North Africa for the Bechtel Corporation from 1973 to 1975, and consultant after 1976. *References*: *MENA*; *WWA*; and *WWAP*.

HARTE, ARCHIBALD CLINTON (1865–1946). Young Men's Christian Association (YMCA)* worker, born June 26, 1865, in Allentown, Pennsylvania. Harte graduated from Wesleyan University. Harte was secretary of the YMCA in Huntsville and Mobile, Alabama, from 1892 to 1907, served as chaplain in the Spanish-American War, was secretary of the YMCA in Ceylon, India, and Burma from 1907 to 1914, and directed YMCA service to prisoners of war in Europe from 1915 to 1919. He assumed leadership of the YMCA in Palestine in 1919 and was national general secretary of the YMCA in Jerusalem from 1920 to 1930. He expanded its interracial and interreligious work among the youth of Jerusalem, and was instrumental in creating the YMCA building in Jerusalem, designed by Arthur Loomis Harmon* and completed in 1933. He retired in 1930 and remained in Palestine. Died April 14, 1946, at Tiberias, the shore of Lake Galilee, Palestine. *Reference*: *NYT*, April 15, 1946.

HARZA ENGINEERING COMPANY. Water engineering company, established in Chicago in 1920. In 1953 it prepared the master plan for the development of the Jordan and Yarmouk rivers for the Kingdom of Jordan, began to implement the plan, and constructed the East Ghor Canal. From 1953 to 1963 it worked on the development of the Tigris River in Iraq and engineered the Derbendi Khan Dam, and between 1955 and 1979 it engineered three major dams in Iran, including the Reza Shah Kabir Dam. *Reference*: Richard D. Harza, *Harza Engineering Company: Developing Water Resources Worldwide 1920–1984* (New York, 1984).

HASKELL, EARL STANLEY (1886–1965). Agricultural economist, born October 5, 1886, in Des Moines, Iowa. Haskell graduated from the Iowa State College of Agriculture and Mechanical Arts. He served with the Bureau of Agriculture of the Philippines from 1909 to 1912, taking charge of the Baguio experimental station from 1901 to 1911; worked for the Farm Management Office of the U. S. Department of Agriculture from 1913 to 1920; was an economist in Ecuador in 1920–1921; and served as a consulting specialist in the Department of Agriculture in 1921–1922 and in Mexico in 1925. He was director general of agriculture and the public domains in Persia from 1926 to 1928. He was agricultural economist for the Federal Farm Board from 1930 to 1933, with the Agricultural Adjustment Administration from 1933 to 1938, with the Department of Agriculture from 1938 to 1942, with the U.S. Forest Service from 1942 to 1947, and again with the Department of Agriculture after 1947. Died April 16, 1965, in Washington, D.C. *Reference*: WWWA.

HASKELL, WILLIAM NAFEW (1878–1952). Army officer, born August 13, 1878, in Albany, New York. Haskell graduated from the U.S. Military Academy in 1901; served in the Philippine Islands, on the Mexican border, and in France during World War I; and was detailed as head of the American Relief Administration mission to Rumania. In 1919 he was appointed Allied High Commissioner to Armenia and was also charged with the coordination of all foreign relief measures there. He was in charge of American Relief Administration work in Russia from 1921 to 1923, and supervised relief work among Greek refugees from Turkey in 1922. He retired in 1924 with the rank of brigadier general, and was commander of the New York National Guard from 1926 to 1940. He returned to active duty in 1940 and retired in 1942. In 1947 he became vice president of Save the Children Federation. Died August 13, 1952, in Greenwich, Connecticut. *References*: *CB* 1947; *NCAB* 40:516; and *WWWA*.

HAUSER, WALTER (1893–1959). Archaeologist and architect, born May 22, 1893, in Middlefield, Massachusetts. Hauser graduated from the Massachusetts Institute of Technology, teaching there from 1914 to 1919. He joined Metropolitan Museum of Art Egyptian expeditions and worked mainly on the excavations at Deir el-Bahari and the Kharga Oasis, and prepared the master plan of the Malkata Palace of Amenhotep III at West Thebes. In 1931 he went to Iraq as a member of the Joint expedition of the Metropolitan Museum of Art and the Islamic Art Department of the German State Museums and excavated Ctesiphon, and later worked at Nishapur in Persia. He became curator of the Metropolitan Museum of Art Library in 1946 and was research curator of Near Eastern archaeology from 1954 to 1958. He retired in 1958. He was co-author of *The Monasteries of Wadi 'n Natrun* (New York, 1926–1933). Died July 13, 1959, in New York City. *References*: *AJA* 64 (1960): 85; *NYT*, July 15, 1959; *WWWA*; and *WWWE*.

HAWKES, JAMES WOODS (1853–1932). Missionary, born August 13, 1853, in Montezuma, Indiana. Hawkes graduated from the Princeton University and Union Theological Seminary, and was ordained in 1880. He served as a missionary under the Presbyterian Church in the USA Board of Foreign Missions* in Persia from 1880 to 1932. He was stationed in Teheran in 1880–1881, established a station in Hamadan in 1881, and served there until 1932. He assisted in the translation of the Bible into Persian and produced the first Bible dictionary in Persian. He wrote of his experiences in *The Moslem World* in 1923. Died

April 21, 1932, in Hamadan, Iran. The papers of his wife, **SARAH BELKNAP (SHERWOOD) HAWKES (1854–1919)**, missionary in Hamadan from 1883 to 1919, are in the Presbyterian Historical Society Collections, Philadelphia. *Reference*: *UnionTS*.

HAYDEN, LYLE JOHNSON (1903–   ). Agriculturist and administrator, born September 26, 1903, in Pittsfield, Illinois. Hayden graduated from the University of Illinois, Pennsylvania State College, and Cornell University. He was an instructor and a principal in vocational schools in New Park and Wellsboro, Pennsylvania, and served in the navy during World War II. In 1945 he became area director in Iran for the Near East Foundation,* was head of the Overseas Territories of the Agricultural Division of the Economic Cooperation Administration in Paris from 1949 to 1951, and overseas program director of the Near East Foundation with headquarters in Beirut from 1952 to 1958. He became executive director of the Near East Foundation in 1958 and its chief administrative officer in 1961. *References*: H. B. Allen, *Rural Reconstruction in Action* (Ithaca, N. Y., 1953), ch. 1; B. Clark, "Lyle Hayden, Shirt-Sleeve Ambassador," *Reader's Digest* 55 (December 1949): 117–121.

HAYES, WILLIAM CHRISTOPHER (1903–1963). Egyptologist, born March 21, 1903, in Hempstead, Long Island. Hayes graduated from Princeton University. In 1927 he joined the Metropolitan Museum of Art expedition to Deir el-Bahari in Egypt and served nine years in Egypt in excavations at Lisht and Thebes sponsored by other museums. He became assistant curator of Egyptian art at the Metropolitan Museum of Art in 1936 and curator in 1952. He served in the navy in World War II. In 1959 he became the American representative on the International Committee for the Preservation of the Nubian monuments. Died July 10, 1963, in New York City. *References*: *Nature* 200 (December 14, 1963): 1048–1049; *NCAB* 51:6; *NYT* July 11, 1963; and *WWWE*.

HAYNES, HENRY WILLIAMSON (1831–1912). Prehistoric archaeologist, born September 20, 1831, in Bangor, Maine. Haynes graduated from Harvard University, studied law, and was admitted to the bar. He taught and practiced law, and was professor of Latin and Greek at the University of Vermont from 1867 to 1873. After 1873, he devoted his time to prehistoric archaeology, conducted research in Egypt in 1877–1878, discovered stone implements, and wrote *Discovery of Palaeolithic Flint Implements in Upper Egypt* (Cambridge, Mass., 1882). He also made archaeological investigations in Europe and North America. Died April 16, 1912, in Boston. *References*: *ACAB*; *NCAB* 8:154; and *WWWA*.

HAYNES, JOHN HENRY (1849–1910). Archaeologist, born June 27, 1849, in Rowe, Massachusetts. Haynes graduated from Williams College. He was principal of a high school in Williamstown from 1876 to 1880, went with W.J.F. Stillman on an expedition to Crete in 1880, and was a member of the archaeological expedition to Assos in 1881–1882. He tutored in Robert College* from 1882 to 1884; was business manager and photographer of the Wolfe expedition to Mesopotamia in 1884–1885 to select an excavation site in Babylonia; taught at Aintab from 1885 to 1888; and in 1888 was business manager of the first expedition of the University of Pennsylvania to excavate Nippur. He became the first U. S. consul in Baghdad in 1888, and from 1888 to 1890 he was continuously in Mesopotamia. He assisted John Punnett Peters* in his excavations at Nippur. From 1893 to 1895 Haynes was field director and excavator, and from 1896 to 1900 he was again almost continuously in Nippur. Died June 29, 1910, in North Adams, Massachusetts. *Reference*: *DAB*.

HAYS, JAMES B(UCHANAN) (1889–1953). Engineer specializing in irrigation projects. Hays graduated from the University of Idaho. Associated for many years with Morrison Knudsen Company, he was employed in a project of irrigation and hydroelectrification in parts of Afghanistan. He was a consulting engineer with the Tennessee Valley Authority (TVA) and chief engineer of the commission in Israel that prepared plans for irrigation and power; based on the TVA, he prepared the Hays-Savage engineering plan for implementing the Lowdermilk* plan, 1948; and he was co-author of *T.V.A. on the Jordan: Proposals for Irrigation and Hydro-electric Development in Palestine* (Washington, D.C., 1948). Died October 24, 1953, in Summit, New Jersey. *References*: *Civil Engineering* 17 (January 1947): 40–42; *NYT*, October 26, 1953.

HEADLEE, WILLIAM HUGH (1907–   ). Specialist in medical parasitology, born June 15, 1907, in Morristown, Indiana. Headlee graduated from Earlham College, the University of Illinois Medical School, and Tulane University. He was an instructor in biology at the American University in Cairo* from 1929 to 1931, served as assistant in the International Health Division of the Rockefeller Foundation in Cairo from 1930 to 1932, and conducted research on the epidemiology of human helminth infections in Egypt. He also conducted research on human parasites in New Orleans, Indiana, and Venezuela, was instructor and assistant professor of zoology at Purdue University from 1935 to 1942, and after 1943, professor of parasitic diseases at the Indiana University School of Medicine in Indianapolis. *References*: *AMWS*; and *WWM*.

HEAP, GWINN HARRIS (1817–1887). Topographical artist and consul, son of Samuel Davies Heap,* born March 23, 1817, in Chester, Pennsylvania. Heap was vice consul and acting consul in Tunis in 1839–1840, where his father was consul. He was a government clerk in Washington from 1846 to 1855, and in 1855 the War Department sent him to Turkey to purchase camels. He drew the sketches that accompanied Henry Constantine Wayne's* report on the expedition sent in 1855 to the Middle East to purchase camels. After his return to the United States, he was clerk in the Navy Department, served in the U.S. Secret Service during the Civil War, was consul in Belfast in 1866 and in Tunis from 1867 to

1878, and was secretary of legation and consul general in Constantinople from 1878 until 1887. Died March 6, 1887, in Constantinople. *References*: *ACAB*; *NYHSD*.

HEAP, SAMUEL DAVIES (1781–1853). Naval officer and consul, born October 8, 1781, in Carlisle, Pennsylvania. Heap was commissioned a surgeon mate in the U.S. Navy in 1804 and was promoted to surgeon in 1808. From 1808 to 1817 he was stationed in New Orleans, Norfolk, Boston, and Philadelphia. He was in charge of the hospital of the Mediterranean Squadron from 1817 to 1823, chargé d'affaires in Tunis in 1823–1824, and consul in Tunis from 1824 until 1853. In 1824 he negotiated and signed a treaty of peace and friendship with Tunis. Died October 2, 1853, in Tunis. *References*: *DAB*; *WWWA*.

HENCKEN, HUGH O'NEILL (1902–1981). Prehistorian, born January 8, 1902, in New York City. Hencken graduated from Princeton and Cambridge universities. He was curator of European archaeology at the Peabody Museum of Harvard University from 1932 until 1972, director of the American School of Prehistoric Research from 1945 to 1972, and chairman from 1959 to 1972. He conducted archaeological excavations in England in 1928, 1930, and 1931, directed the Harvard Archaeological Expedition to Ireland from 1932 to 1936, and conducted excavations in Morocco and Tangier in 1947 and in Algeria in 1949. Died September 31, 1981, in Cape Cod, Massachusetts. *References*: *Ancient Europe and the Mediterranean: Studies Presented to Hugh Hencken*, ed. Vladimir Marktic (Westminster, England, 1977); *AMWS*; *NYT*, September 4, 1981; and *WWWA*.

HENDERSON, LOY WESLEY (1892–1986). Diplomat, born June 28, 1892, near Rogers, Arkansas. Henderson graduated from Northwestern University and Denver University Law School, and served in World War I with the Red Cross* in France. He entered the foreign service in 1922, serving in Dublin, Queenstown, Australia, and Riga, Kaunas, and Tallin in the Baltic States. He was second secretary and first secretary in Moscow from 1934 to 1938, and counselor in 1942–1943. He was minister to Iraq from 1943 to 1945, chief of Near Eastern and African Affairs in the State Department from 1945 to 1948, ambassador to India from 1948 to 1951, and ambassador to Iran from 1951 to 1955. He was deputy undersecretary of state for administration from 1955 until his retirement in 1961. He later taught at American University and worked with the Washington Institute of Foreign Affairs. Died March 24, 1986, in Bethesda, Maryland. *References*: *CB*, 1948; *DADH*; *MENA*; *NYT*, March 26, 1986; Allen H. Podet, "Anti-Zionism in a Key U.S. Diplomat: Loy Henderson at the End of World War II," *American Jewish Archives* 30 (1978): 155–187; and *WWA*.

HENRY, SCHUYLER B. ("KRUG") (1897–1981). Petroleum geologist, born June 18, 1897. Henry graduated from the University of California and began working for Standard Oil Company of California in 1924. He went with Robert Perry Miller* to Bahrain in 1932. They were the first two American geologists to land on the Arabian Peninsula in 1933 and to make a geological reconnaissance of the coast of al-Hasa. He retired in 1957. Died August 7, 1981.

HENRY, VELLORA MEEK (1854–1942). Medical missionary. Henry practiced medicine in Idana, Kansas. He was a missionary under the United Presbyterian Church of North America Board of Foreign Missions* and served in the Assiut Hospital in Assiut, Egypt, from 1891 until his retirement in 1927. He remained in Egypt until 1939. Died October 3, 1942. *Reference*: Anna A. Milligan, *Dr. Henry of Assiut, Pioneer Medical Missionary in Egypt* (Philadelphia, 1945).

HEPBURN, ARTHUR J(APY) (1877–1964). Naval officer, born October 15, 1877, in Carlisle, Pennsylvania. Hepburn attended Dickinson College and graduated from the U.S. Naval Academy in 1897. He served in the Spanish-American War and in World War I. He was assistant chief of the Bureau of Engineering and chief of staff of the U.S. Naval Forces in Turkey from 1921 to 1924. He led the evacuation of Americans from Smyrna and negotiated the evacuation of the Greeks in 1922. He was commander-in-chief of the U.S. Fleet from 1936 to 1938 and commandant of the 12th Naval District in San Francisco from 1938 to 1941. He retired in 1941 with the rank of admiral. That same year he was recalled, and he was director of public relations for the navy and chairman of the Navy General Board from 1942 to 1945 when he retired a second time. Died May 31, 1964, in Washington, D.C. *References*: *NCAB* 49:128; *NYT*, June 1, 1964; and *WWWA*.

HEPWORTH, GEORGE HUGHES (1833–1902). Clergyman and journalist, born February 4, 1833, in Boston. Hepworth graduated from Harvard Divinity School. He was a pastor in Nuntucket and Boston from 1855 to 1870, served as a chaplain in the Civil War, and was later a pastor in New York and Newark. In 1885 he became an editor on the staff of *New York Herald and Telegram*. In 1897 he was sent to Armenia by James Gordon Bennet as a special reporter, and wrote *Through Armenia on Horseback* (New York, 1898). Died June 7, 1902, in New York City. *References*: *ACAB*; *DAB*; *NCAB* 4:320; *NYT*, June 9, 1902; and *WWWA*.

HERRICK, GEORGE FREDERICK (1834–1926). Missionary, born April 19, 1834, in Milton, Vermont. Herrick graduated from the University of Vermont and Andover Theological Seminary, and was ordained in 1859. He became a missionary under the American Board of Commissioners for Foreign Missions (ABCFM)* in Turkey in 1859, was instructor in the mission's theological seminary from 1870 to 1873 and from 1876 to 1893, and was acting president of Anatolia College* from 1886 to 1893. He revised the translation of the Bible into Turkish. He retired in 1911. Died October 28, 1926, in New York City. *References*: *ACAB*; *AndoverTS*; and *WWWA*.

HEXTER, MAURICE B(ECK) (1891–   ). Welfare executive, born June 30, 1891, in Cincinnati. Hexter graduated from the University of Cincinnati and Harvard University. He was superintendent of the United Jewish Charities of Cincinnati from 1917 to 1919, and executive director of the Federation of Jewish Charities of Boston from 1919 to 1929. He was a member of the Jewish Agency Executive in Jerusalem from 1928 to 1938. He became assistant to the executive vice president of the Federation for the Support of Jewish Philanthropic Societies in New York in 1938 and was executive vice president from 1941 until his retirement in 1966. *References*: *OAB*; *WWA*; and *WWWJ*.

HIDDEN, WARREN H. (1812–1888). Machinist, born in Great Britain, and grew up in New York City. Hidden went to Constantinople in 1831 as an assistant to Henry Eckford,* American shipbuilder who was in charge of naval construction in Turkey, and remained in Constantinople after the others were ousted in 1839 as the result of intrigue by other powers who were unhappy about the extent of American influence in naval matters. He became chief machinist of the Imperial Ottoman Mint in 1840, remaining there for over forty years. He perfected new ways to stamp coins and print currency, devised a variety of guns, and invented special explosives for use in the Crimea. His reminiscences were published in the March 1895 issue of *The Scientific American Supplement*.

HIJACKING OF AIRPLANES (1970–1985). Several American commercial airliners were hijacked to the Middle East. On September 6, 1970, members of the Popular Front for the Liberation of Palestine (PFLP) hijacked TWA flight 741 and Pan Am flight 93. The TWA plane was diverted to a landing strip near Zarka, Jordan. The plane was destroyed by the terrorists on September 12, and the last hostage was released on September 29. The Pan Am plane was diverted to Cairo, where the passengers were released and the plane was blown up the next day. On June 14, 1985, Lebanese Shiite Moslems hijacked TWA flight 847 to Beirut. One American sailor was killed by the hijackers. The other passengers were held hostage for 17 days, then released. *References*: *Dictionary of American History*, rev. ed. (New York, 1976), 3: 276–278. Edward F. Mickolus, *International Terrorism: A Chronology of Events, 1968–1979* (Westport, Conn., 1980), 208–212. John Testrake (with David Wimbish), *Triumph Over Terror on Flight 847* (Old Tappan, N.J., 1987).

HILPRECHT, HERMANN VOLRATH (1859–1925). Assyriologist, born July 28, 1859, in Hohenerxleben, Germany. Hilprecht graduated from the universities of Leipzig and Erlangen, and came to the United States in 1886. He was professor of Assyriology at the University of Pennsylvania from 1886 until 1911 and curator of the Babylonian collection of the University Museum from 1887 until 1911. He was a member of the University of Pennsylvania expedition to Nippur in 1888–1889, became scientific director of the expedition in 1895, and went to Nippur a second time in 1900. From 1893 to 1909 he was also involved in the reorganization of the Imperial Ottoman Museum in Constantinople. He wrote *Exploration in Bible Lands During the Nineteenth Century* (Philadelphia, 1903). He resigned in 1911 and lived in Germany for several years. He returned to the United States after World War I and was naturalized. Died March 19, 1925, in Philadelphia. *References*: *ACAB*; *DAB*; *NCAB* 10:380; *NYT*, March 20, 1925; and *WWWA*.

HINES, WALKER DOWNER (1870–1934). Lawyer, born February 2, 1870, in Russelville, Logan County, Kentucky. Hines graduated from Ogden College (Bowling Green, Ky.) and the University of Virginia. He worked for the Louisville and Nashville Railroad Company from 1890 until 1904; was general counsel of the Atchison, Topeka and Santa Fe Railroad Company from 1906 to 1918; assistant to the director general of railroads from 1917 to 1919; and the director until 1920. He became the arbitrator of the Danuba River questions in 1920–21, returned there in 1925 to make a study of the river for the League of Nations, and became president of the Cotton Textile Institute in 1926. He headed a mission to Turkey in 1933 to survey its economic development and to advise the Turkish government. Died January 14, 1934, in Merano, Italy, on his way a second time to Turkey. *References*: *ACAB*; *BDABL*; *DAB S1*; *NCAB* 24:30; *NYT*, January 15, 1934; and *WWWA*.

HODGSON, WILLIAM BROWN (1801–1871). Consul and Orientalist, born September 1, 1801, in Georgetown, D.C. From 1826 to 1829 Hodgson was the first language student in the consulate in Algiers and acting consul. He made important studies on the Berber language. He published a grammatical sketch and specimen of the Berber language in the *Transactions of the American Philosopohical Society* in 1832, and *Linguistic and Ethnographic Material in Notes on Northern Africa, the Sahara and Soudan* (New York, 1844). He served in the State Department in Washington from 1829 to 1932 and was translator in the legation in Constantinople from 1832 to 1834. In 1834 he was sent to Egypt on a secret mission on the basis of which he wrote *Biographic Sketch of Muhammad Ali, Pacha of Egypt, Syria, and Arabia* (Washington, D.C., 1837). In 1835 he was sent on a diplomatic mission to Tangier, and later on diplomatic missions to Peru and Germany. He was consul general in Tunis from 1841 to 1842 after which he returned to the United States in 1842. He spent the rest of his life in Savannah, Georgia. Died June 26, 1871, in Savannah. *References*: Papers in the Telfair family papers, Georgia Historical Society Collections; Thomas A. Bryson, *William Brown Hodgson, 1801–1871: A Biography of an*

American Foreign Service Officer in the Middle East (Atlanta, 1970); *DAB S1*; and *WWWA*.

HOLE, FRANK (1931–). Anthropologist, born November 13, 1931, in Oak Park, Illinois. Hole graduated from Cornell (Iowa) College and the University of Chicago. He was assistant professor, associate professor, and professor of anthropology at Rice University (Houston) from 1961 to 1979, and professor of anthropology at Yale University after 1980. He conducted excavations in Iran from 1959 until 1977, was co-author of *Studies in the Archaeological History of the Deh Luran Plain: The Excavation of Chagha Sefid* (Ann Arbor, Mich., 1977), and edited *The Archaeology of Western Iran: Settlement and Society from Prehistory to the Islamic Conquest* (Washington, D.C., 1986). *Reference*: *WWA*.

HOLLIS, W(ILLIAM) STANLEY (1866–1930). Consul, born April 4, 1866, in Chelsea, Massachusetts. Hollis attended the U.S. Naval Academy but did not graduate. He was clerk in the consulate in Cape Town, consular agent in Durban, and consul in Mozambique, Laurenco Marquez, and Dundee, Scotland. He was consul general in Beirut from 1911 to 1917 and, after the entrance of Turkey into World War I, was in charge of the interests of the Allied Powers. He was head of the American Red Cross* in Beirut, distributed great quantities of relief, and assisted many to escape. He served in London from 1918 to 1920 and in Portugal from 1920 to 1928. Died June 8, 1930, in Washington, D.C. *Reference*: *WWWA*.

HOLLISTER, MARY GUILLAUME (? –1917). Missionary, born in South Glastonbury, Connecticut. Hollister graduated from Mount Holyoke College. She served as a missionary under the American Board of Commissioners for Foreign Missions (ABCFM)* in Turkey, was teacher in the girls' school in Aintab, and in 1880 ran a printing press that was her personal creation. She returned to the United States in 1886. Died October 26, 1917, in South Glastonbury, Connecticut. *Reference*: *Mount Holyoke*.

HOLMES, GEORGE WASHINGTON (1841–1910). Medical missionary, born February 22, 1841, in Crawfordsville, Indiana. Holmes served in Persia under the Presbyterian Church in the U.S.A. Board of Foreign Missions from 1874 to 1899, first in Urmia and after 1881 in Teheran, and was personal physician to the Crown Prince of Persia from 1886 to 1888, and a medical educator. Died May 10, 1910. *Reference*: *Assembly Herald*, October 1910.

HOLMES, JOHN HAYNES (1879–1964). Clergyman, editor, and author, born November 29, 1879, in Philadelphia. Holmes graduated from Harvard University and was ordained in 1904. He served as a Unitarian minister in Dorchester, Massachusetts, and in New York City; became president of the All World Gandhi Fellowship in 1929; and was active in local and national sociological and civic improvement committees and commissions. In 1929 he went on a special mission to Palestine and wrote *Palestine To-day and To-morrow; A Gentile's Survey of Zionism* (New York, 1929). Died April 3, 1964, in New York City. *References*: *CA*; *CB*, 1941; *DARB*; *NCAB* 15:273; *NYT*, April 4, 1964; and *WWWA*.

HOLMES, MARY CAROLINE (1859–1927). Missionary and author, born in Deposit, New York. Holmes went to Syria as a missionary in 1883. She was director of relief work in Urfa from 1919 to 1922, and served as intermediary during the siege of Urfa by Turkish troops in 1920. After the massacre of the French garrison, she continued to be in charge of foreign interests for two years. She was later a national speaker for the Near East Relief.* She wrote *"Who Follows in Their Train": A Syrian Romance* (New York, 1917), and *Between Lines in Asia Minor* (New York, 1923). Died March 3, 1927, in New York City. *Reference*: *WWWA*.

HOMES, HENRY AUGUSTUS (1812–1887). Missionary, born March 10, 1812, in Boston. Homes graduated from Amherst College, Andover Theological Seminary, and Yale University, and was ordained in 1835. He was a missionary under the American Board of Commissioners for Foreign Missions (ABCFM)* in Turkey from 1830 to 1850, and interpreter and chargé d'affaires in the legation in Constantinople from 1851 to 1853. He returned to the United States in 1854, becoming assistant librarian and later chief librarian of the New York State Library until his death. Died November 3, 1887, in Albany, New York. *References*: *ACAB*; *Amherst*; *AndoverTS*; *DAB*; *NCAB* 13:42; and *WWWA*.

HOOGSTRAAL, HARRY (1917–   ). Biologist, born February 24, 1917, in Chicago. Hoogstraal graduated from the universities of Illinois and London. He was assistant entomologist and curator of insects in the University of Illinois from 1938 to 1942; head of the Philippine Islands zoological expedition of the Chicago Museum of Natural History and the Philippines government in 1946–1947; and medical zoologist of the University of California African expedition in 1948–1949. He became head of the Department of Medical Zoology at the U.S. Navy Medical Research Unit No. 3 in Cairo in 1949. He was also a visiting lecturer at Cairo and Alexandria universities and field associate in zoology of the Chicago Natural History Museum. He was a member of medical research expeditions to Yemen and Sudan and described his experiences in the February 1952 and February 1953 issues of the *National Geographic Magazine*. *Reference*: *AMWS*.

HOPKINS, CLARK (1895–1976). Archaeologist, born September 16, 1895, in New York City, and grew up in New Haven, Connecticut. Hopkins served in the army in World War I and graduated from Yale University and Balliol College, Oxford. He taught classics at Yale University from 1924 to 1931, became associate professor of Latin and Greek at the University of Michigan in 1935, and was professor of classical art and archaeology from 1946 until his retirement in 1965. He was an assistant in the Yale University excavations at Dura Europos, Syria, in 1928 and 1929; its field director from 1931 until 1935; and director of the University of Michigan excavations at Seleucia-on-the-Tigris in 1936 and 1937, and of the excavations at Apollonia, Libya, in 1964 and 1965. He was co-author of various reports on the excavations in Dura Europos, wrote *The Christian Church at Dura-Europos* (New Haven, Conn., 1934), and *Topography and Architecture of Seleucia on the Tigris* (Ann Arbor, Mich., 1972). Died May 21, 1976, in Ann Arbor, Michigan. His book, *The Discovery of Dura Europos*, ed. Bernard Goldman (New Haven, Conn., 1979) was published posthumously. *References*: *CA*; *DAS*; and *NCAB* 59:175.

HOPPIN, AUGUSTUS (1828–1896). Illustrator, born July 13, 1828, in Providence, Rhode Island. Hoppin attended Brown University, studied at the Harvard Law School, and was admitted to the bar in 1850. He abandoned law in the early 1850s and began his career as illustrator for magazine and book publishers. He traveled in Europe and Egypt in 1854–1855 and wrote *On the Nile* (Boston, 1874) which includes his original illustrations of the trip. Died April 1, 1896, in Flushing, Long Island, New York. *References*: *DAB*; Sinclair Hamilton, *Early American Book Illustrators and Wood Engravers, 1670–1870* (Princeton, N.J., 1950), pp. 318–324; and *NYHSD*.

HORTON, ALAN W(ILLIAMS) (1921–   ). Educator, born July 31, 1921, in Middletown, Connecticut. Horton graduated from Princeton and Harvard universities and the American University in Cairo,* and served in the navy during World War II. He was a member of the Gaza unit of the American Friends Service Committee in 1949–1950, senior area office of the Gaza district for the United Nations Relief and Works Agency (UNRWA) in 1950, and deputy chief district officer in Lebanon in 1950–1951. He was director of the School of Oriental Studies of the American University in Cairo and dean of the graduate faculty from 1956 to 1962; Middle East associate of the American Universities Field Staff (AUFS) in Cairo* and dean of the graduate faculty from 1956 to 1962; Middle East associate of the Aemrican Universities field staff (AUFS) in Cairo from 1962 to 1968; and executive director of the AUFS from 1968 to 1978, when he became director of the Center for Mediterranean Studies in Rome. *Reference*: *WWA*.

HORTON, GEORGE (1859–1942). Consul and author, born October 11, 1859, in Fairville, New York. Horton graduated from the University of Michigan. He was consul at Athens from 1893 to 1888, literary editor of the *Chicago Times-Herald* from 1899 to 1901, and editor of the literary supplement of the *Chicago American* from 1901 to 1903. In 1903 he was consul in Athens and consul general from 1906 to 1910. He was consul in Salonika in 1910–1911, consul general in Smyrna from 1911 to 1917 and again in 1919. He was in charge of the interests of the Allied Powers in Asia Minor from the outbreak of World

War I until April 1917, and he distributed relief among civilians and prisoners of war. He was consul in Salonika from 1917 to 1919, delegate to the American High Commission to Turkey in 1920–1921, and consul in Budapest in 1923–1924. Horton retired in 1924 and wrote *The Blight of Asia* (Indianapolis, 1926), and *Story of a Mediterranean Consul* (Indianapolis, 1927). From 1936 to 1942 he traveled in France, Greece, and Italy, and resided in Rapallo, Italy, from 1940 to 1942. Died January 5, 1942, on Staten Island on his return to the United States. *References*: *NYT*, June 10, 1942; and *WWWA*.

HOSKINS, FRANKLIN EVANS (1858–1920). Missionary, born September 28, 1858, in Rockdale, Pennsylvania. Hoskins graduated from Princeton University, Union Theological Seminary, and Yale University, and was ordained in 1888. He was the principal of the Preparatory Department of the Syrian Protestant College from 1883 to 1886, became editor of the American Press* in Beirut in 1900, and was president of the theological faculty in 1911. He conducted journeys of exploration in Transjordan and Arabia from 1888 to 1890, and, with William Libbey,* wrote *The Jordan Valley and Petra* (New York, 1905). He traveled in Sinai and Palestine in 1912, and wrote *From the Nile to Nebo: A Discussion of the Problem and the Route of the Exodus* (Philadelphia, 1912). He was commissioner of the Syria and Palestine Relief from 1914 to 1918. Died November 12, 1920, in Beirut, Syria. *Reference*: *WWWA*.

HOSKINS, HAROLD B(OIES) (1895–1977). Business executive and diplomat, born May 19, 1895, in Beirut to American parents. Hoskins graduated from Princeton University and served in the marines in World War I. He was manager of the foreign department of an engineering and textile manufacturing company from 1920 to 1925, and merchandising manager and vice president in charge of sales for textile companies from 1925 to 1941. During World War II he was the representative of the Middle East Supply Center* in Iran, economic counselor for the Middle East area, and the last American representative to the Middle East Supply Center in 1945. He made a survey trip to the Middle East in 1942–1943 and in 1943 was sent on a mission to Saudi Arabia to discuss with King Ibn Saud the problem of Palestine. He was vice president of Cannon Mills from 1947 to 1953, in charge of sales and merchandising, and director of the Foreign Service Institute of the State Department from 1955 to 1961. He retired in 1962, was a business consultant on the Middle East, and president of the Near East College Association. Died April 23, 1977, in New York City. *References*: *MENA*; *NYT*, April 25, 1977.

HOSMON, SARAH LONGWORTH (1883–1964). Medical missionary, born September 16, 1883, in Henderson County, Kentucky. Hosmon graduated from the Medical Department of the University of Illinois. She served in the Arabian Mission* from 1911 to 1938 and was head of the Women's Hospital in Muscat. From 1938 to 1962 she was an independent Presbyterian missionary on the

Trucial Coast and operated a woman's clinic in Sahan, a small seaport in Oman. Died July 25, 1964. *Reference*: *HDRCA*.

HOSTAGES IN THE BARBARY STATES (1784–1796). The first American merchant ship captured by Barbary warships was the *Betsy*, which was captured by Morocco on October 1, 1784. Its crew was held hostage until July 1785 when they were released after the intervention of the Spanish government. Warships of Algiers captured *Maria* on July 25, 1785 and *Dauphin* on August 4, and seized some twenty-one Americans, several of whom were held hostage in Algiers for over eleven years. Between October and December 1793, Algierian warships captured twelve additional American merchant ships and seized more than one hundred Americans, who were held as prisoners in Algiers and treated as slaves. The U.S. government did little to rescue the hostages for a long time, and several diplomatic missions failed; but some prisoners were ransomed by their families and some by foreign governments. Several hostages died in captivity, mostly from the bubonic plague. In 1795 Joseph Donaldson Jr.* negotiated with Algiers the payment of a ransom of over $700,000, and the remaining eighty-nine Americans left Algiers on July 12, 1796. *References*: H. F. Barnaby, *The Prisoners of Algiers: An Account of Forgotten American-Algerian War 1785–1797* (London, 1966). Gray E. Wilson, "American Hostages in Moslem Nations, 1784–1796: the Public Response," *Journal of the Early Republic* 2 (1982): 123–41; "The First American Hostages in Moslem Nations, 1784–1789," *American Neptune* 41 (1981): 208–23.

HOSTAGES IN IRAN (1979–1981). In January 1979 the Shah left Iran and the Iranian Revolutionary Republic was established. The Shah came to a hospital in New York on October 23, 1979, and on November 4, 1979, Iranian militants seized the American embassy in Teheran and took 66 Americans hostage. The Iranians demanded, in exchange for the release of the hostages, the return of the Shah for trial and the handing over of his fortune. Even when the Shah left the U.S., the hostages continued to be held, but thirteen hostages were released on November 18 and 19. American military efforts to release the hostages failed; diplomatic negotiations, mediated by Algeria, were concluded in January 1981. The hostages were released on January 20, 1981, in exchange for the release of the Iranian frozen assets in the U.S. *References*: *American Hostages in Iran: The Conduct of a Crisis* (New Haven, Conn., 1985). Clyde R. Mark, *The Iran Hostage Crisis: A Chronology of Daily Developments* (Washington, D.C., 1981). Robert D. McFadden et al., *No Hiding Place: The New York Times Inside Report on the Hostage Crisis* (New York, 1981). Pierre Salinger, *American Held Hostage* (Garden City, N.Y., 1981).

HOSTAGES IN LEBANON (1984–   ). Since February 10, 1984, several Americans have been kidnapped in Beirut and held as hostages. The majority of the kidnapped were connected with the American University of Beirut* as administrators and faculty members. Most of the hostages were held by Hiz-ballah, a fundamentalist Shiite terrorist group with links to Iran, in order to obtain the release of Shiite terrorists jailed in Kuwait prison. While several of the hostages have been released, two were killed, and the others still remain hostage. *Newsweek*, October 20, 1986.

HOWE, BRUCE (1912–   ). Archaeologist, born November 20, 1912, in Washington, D.C. Howe graduated from Yale and Harvard universities. He was honorary research fellow in paleolithic archaeology at the Peabody Museum of Harvard University from 1952 to 1976, research associate of the Oriental Institute from 1976 to 1980, and annual professor at the American Schools of Oriental Research (ASOR)* in Baghdad in 1954–1955. He excavated in Morocco, explored northeastern Iraq in search of the remains of early village life, and excavated in Kurdistan. He was co-author of *Prehistoric Investigations in Iraqi Kurdistan* (Chicago, 1960), and *The Palaeolithic of Tangier, Morocco: Excavations at Cape Ashkar, 1939–1947* (Cambridge, Mass., 1967). *Reference: DAS.*

HOWELL, J(OSEPH) MORTON (1863–1937). Diplomat, born March 17, 1863, in Uniopolis, Ohio. Howell graduated from Starling Medical College (Columbus, Ohio) and Ohio Northern University and studied in Europe. He practiced medicine in Dayton from 1885 to 1921, was diplomatic agent and consul general in Egypt in 1921, and the first minister to Egypt from 1922 to 1927. He wrote *Egypt's Past, Present and Future* (Dayton, Ohio, 1929). Died December 27, 1937, in Oakland, California. *References: NCAB* 27:429; *NYT*, December 28, 1937; *OAB*; and *WWWA*.

HUFFMAN, ARTHUR VINCENT (1912–   ). Criminologist, born February 7, 1912, in New Holland, Illinois. Huffman graduated from McKendree College and the University of Illinois. He was educational adviser to the Royal Afghan Ministry of Education in Kabul from 1942 to 1949, and prepared a pocket guide to Afghanistan in 1945. He was supervising sociologist in the Division of State Criminologists, Department of Public Safety, in Joliet, Illinois, from 1949 to 1961; state criminologist of Illinois from 1961 to 1970; and chief of professional services in the Illinois Department of Corrections, Springfield, from 1970 until his retirement. *References: AWMS*; and *WWW*.

HULL, BURTON E(LIAS) (1884–1958). Oil engineer, born May 23, 1884, in Navasota, Texas. Hull graduated from Texas A & M College. He was employed by the Texas Company and was involved in building major pipelines, was vice president of Texas Company, president of the Texas Pipeline Company, and president of Trans-Arabian Pipeline Company (TAPLINE).* During World War II, he was vice president and general manager of War Emergency Pipelines, Inc. He was in charge of the construction of the Tapline from the Persian Gulf to the Mediterranean Sea and its terminal and loading dock in Sidon, Lebanon. He retired in 1951. Died November 8, 1958, in Dallas, Texas. *References*: *NYT*, November 9, 1958; *Oil and Gas Journal* 56 (November 17, 1958): 141; and Eric G. Schroeder, "Meet Mr. Pipelines," *World Oil* 135 (November 1952): 284–288.

HULL, ISAAC (1773–1843). Naval officer, born March 9, 1773, in Huntington, Connecticut. Hull was commissioned a lieutenant in the navy in 1798 and served in the quasi-war with France. He commanded the ships *Enterprise* and *Argus* during the war with Tripoli, and assisted William Eaton* in the attack on Derna in Tripoli in 1805. He served in the War of 1812, and later commanded the Boston, Portsmouth, and Washington, D.C., navy yards. From 1839 to 1841 he was commander of the Mediterranean station. Died February 13, 1843, in Philadelphia. *References*: Papers, USS Constitution Museum, Boston; New York Historical Society; Franklin D. Roosevelt Library; *ACAB*; Linda M. Maloney, *The Captain from Connecticut: The Life and Naval Times of Isaac Hull* (Boston, 1986); Let T. Molloy, comp., *Commodore Isaac Hull, U.S.N., His Life and Times* (Derby, Conn., 1964); *WAMB*; and *WWWA*.

HUNT, LEIGH SMITH JOHN (1855–1933). Irrigation and mining pioneer, born August 11, 1855, in Larwill, Indiana. Hunt received unsystematic education, and was teacher, school administrator, president of the State Agricultural College at Ames, Iowa, in 1885–1886, and in 1886, became owner and editor of the Seattle (Wash.) *Post-Intelligencer*. In 1893 he traveled in China and Japan, and organized a mining company in Korea where he developed gold mines. He visited Egypt and the Sudan in 1903. Becoming convinced that cotton could be grown in the Sudan by using irrigation from the Nile, he acquired land in al-Zaidab in 1904 and formed the Sudan Plantations Company. His enterprise was called "Hunt's folly," but he succeeded in demonstrating the possibility of growing cotton commercially in the Sudan. He returned to the United States in 1910. Died October 5, 1933, in Las Vegas, Nevada. *References*: *Hill*; *NCAB* 24:14; and *WWWA*.

HUNT, RICHARD MORRIS (1827–1895). Architect, born October 31, 1827, in Brattleboro, Vermont. Hunt graduated from Harvard University, went to Europe in 1843, and studied at the Ecole des Beaux-Arts in Paris. He traveled in the Middle East in 1852–1853 with his brother **LEAVITT HUNT (1830–1907)** who photographed their trip. Richard returned to the United States in 1855 and practiced in New York City. Died July 31, 1895, in Newport, Rhode Island. *References*: "Nile diary." Ms., American Architectural Archive, Greenwich, Connecticut; Records, American Institute of Architects Foundation, Washington, D.C.; Leavitt Hunt's photograph collection, Division of Prints and Photographs, Library of Congress; Paul R. Baker, *Richard Morris Hunt* (Cambridge, Mass., 1980); *DAB*; *MEA*; *NCAB* 6:430; *NYT*, August 1, 1895; and *WWWA*.

HUNTINGTON, ELLSWORTH (1876–1947). Geographer, born September 16, 1876, in Galesburg, Illinois. Huntington graduated from Beloit College and went to Harput, Turkey, in 1897 as assistant to the president of Euphrates College.* He did fieldwork in Turkey, mapped the area around Harput, and journeyed down the Euphrates River on a raft in 1901. He returned to the United States in 1901 and studied at Harvard University. In 1903 he was a member of the Pumpelly expedition to Transcaucasia, remained in Turkestan and Persia, and made a journey through the Himalayas to Inner Asia in 1906. In 1907 he became instructor in geography at Yale University and was assistant professor from 1910 to 1915 and research associate from 1919 until his death. He also traveled in Palestine in 1910, and he wrote *Palestine and Its Transformation* (Boston, 1911). Died October 17, 1947, in New Haven, Connecticut. *References*: Papers, Yale University Library; *DAB S4*; *NCAB* 37:43; *NYT*, October 18, 1947; and *WWWA*.

HUNTINGTON, GEORGE HERBERT (1878–1953). Educator, brother of Ellsworth Huntington,* born April 12, 1878, in Gorham, Maine. Huntington graduated from Williams College, Hartford and Union theological seminaries, and Columbia University Teachers College. He was professor at Robert College* from 1907 to 1937, principal of the preparatory school from 1907 to 1927, vice president of Robert College from 1917 to 1937, and acting president in 1919–1920. He was also president of the board of managers of the Constantinople Young Men's Christian Association (YMCA)* from 1915 to 1924. Stricken with polio, he returned to the United States in 1933. Died August 2, 1953, in Portland, Maine. His wife, **ELIZABETH DODGE HUNTINGTON CLARKE (1884–1976)**, sister of Bayard Dodge,* lived in Turkey from 1916 to 1953, and wrote her memoirs (with Elspeth M. Clarke and Court C. Walters), *The Joy of Service* (New York, 1979). *References*: Diaries and papers, YWCA Archives; *NCAB* 42:316; *NYT*, August 4, 1953; and *WWWA*.

HUSS, GEORGE MOREHOUSE (1857–1947). Civil engineer, born July 14, 1857, in Tiffin, Ohio. Huss graduated from Heidelberg College (Tiffin, Ohio), Ohio Business College (Sandusky), and Cornell University. He was a civil engineer and railway builder in the West and in Mexico until 1894. In 1894 he was a consulting engineer for the Basrah to Baghdad Railway and the Beira Railway in East Africa, and in 1895–1896, he built the railway from Haifa to Damascus. Later, he built railways and towns in Ohio and Wisconsin, served with the U.S. Railroad Administration from 1918 to 1922, and was in consulting practice and in farming. Died February 15, 1947, in La Grange, Illinois. *References*: *NYT*, February 20, 1947; and *WWWA*.

HUTCHISON, ELMO H(ARRISON) (1910–1964). Soldier, born May 4, 1910. Hutchison graduated from the University of Utah. He served in the navy during World War II. He became military observer with the United Nations Truce Supervision Organization in 1951 and chairman of the Israel-Jordan Mixed

Armistice Commission from 1952 to 1956. He wrote *Violent Truce: A Military Observer Looks at the Arab-Israeli Conflict, 1951–1955* (New York, 1956). In 1956 he became Middle East director of the American Friends of the Middle East in charge of the Cairo office. Drowned June 24, 1964, in the Red Sea coast of Saudi Arabia. *Reference*: *NYT*, June 26, 1964.

HUTCHISON, RALPH COOPER (1898–1966). Educator, born February 27, 1898, in Florissant, Colorado. Hutchison graduated from Lafayette College, Harvard University, Princeton Theological Seminary, and the University of Pennsylvania. He was director of publicity and literature for the Young Men's Christian Association (YMCA)* in Constantinople in 1919, director of religious education of the Presbyterian Church in Norristown, Pennsylvania, from 1922 to 1924, and secretary of young people's work for the Presbyterian Board of Education in Philadelphia in 1924–1925. He was dean of the American College in Teheran from 1925 to 1931; president of Washington and Jefferson College from 1931 to 1945; president of Lafayette College from 1945 to 1957; chancellor of the Abadan Institute of Technology; educational adviser to the National Iranian Oil Company in Teheran from 1957 to 1960; and president and director of Studies in Higher Education in Philadelphia from 1960 until his death. Died March 15, 1966, in Bryn Mawr, Pennsylvania. *References*: *NCAB* 52:593; *NYT*, March 16, 1966; and *WWWA*.

HUYSER MISSION. Mission of General Robert E. ("Dutch") Huyser (1924–), air force officer and deputy commander of U.S. Forces in Europe, who had contacts with Iranian military leaders, to Iran in January-February 1979 to determine whether Shah Muhammad Reza's regime could be saved or whether a military successor could be arranged. The mission was unsuccessful because the military were unwilling to confront Ayatollah Khomeini's Revolution. *Reference*: Robert E. Huyser, *Mission to Teheran* (New York, 1986).

HYDE, ORSON (1805–1878). Missionary, born January 8, 1805, in Oxford, New Haven County, Connecticut, and moved with his family to Kirtland, Ohio, in 1818. Hyde became a member of the Church of Jesus Christ of Latter-day Saints, being baptized in 1831. He became a missionary and in 1835 was selected as one of the Apostles. In 1837–1838 he went on a mission to England, and in 1841, he went to Palestine and prayed on the Mount of Olives. He wrote *A Voice from Jerusalem; or, Sketch of the Travels and Ministry of Elder Orson Hyde* (Boston, 1842). In 1846–1847 he went on a second mission to England. In 1852 he moved to Utah, became a pioneer colonizer, a Utah state senator, and the Senate president in 1870. Died November 28, 1878, in Spring City, Utah. *Reference*: Howard H. Barron, *Orson Hyde: Missionary, Apostle, Colonizer* (Bountiful, Utah, 1977).

I

IMBRIE, ROBERT WHITNEY (1883–1924). Consul, born April 23, 1883, in Washington, D.C. Imbrie graduated from George Washington and Yale universities and the New York Nautical College. He was attorney for the Legal Aid Society in New York in 1907–1908, and practiced law in Baltimore from 1909 to 1915. In 1911 he accompanied the Garner Expedition to the Belgian Congo. He enlisted in the American Ambulance Service in 1915, and served in France and the Balkans, writing of his experiences in *Behind the Wheel of a War Ambulance* (New York, 1918). He was chargé d'affaires in Russia in 1918–1919 and consul in Viborg, Finland, from 1919 to 1922. He became vice consul in Therean in 1923. Murdered July 18, 1924, by a mob in Teheran, Persia for taking pictures of a religious celebration. *References* : Bruce Hardcastle, "Death in Teheran," *New Republic* 181 (December 29, 1979): 10–12; *NCAB* 53:123; M. Zirinsky, "Blood, Power, and Hypocrisy: The Murder of Robert Imbrie and American Relations with Pahlavi Iran, 1924," *International Journal of Middle Eastern Studies* 8 (1986): 275–292.

INGRAHAM, DUNCAN NATHANIEL (1802–1891). Naval officer, born December 6, 1802, in Charleston, South Carolina. Ingraham was appointed a midshipman in 1812, and served in the War of 1812 and in the Mexican War. In 1853 he commanded the sloop-of-war *St Louis* in the Mediterranean. He was involved in the Koszta affair in Smyrna, when Martin Koszta, a Hungarian revolutionary who fled to the United States after the 1848 revolution and took out first citizenship papers, returned to Turkey, was kidnapped by the Austrians, and was held a prisoner in Smyrna. With the support of John Porter Brown,* Ingraham presented an ultimatum to the Austrians and forced them to surrender Koszta. Ingraham was chief of the Bureau of Ordnance from 1856 to 1860 and served in the Confederate Navy during the Civil War. Died October 16, 1891, in Charleston, South Carolina. *References*: *ACAB*; *DAB*; *NCAB* 8:336; and *WWWA*.

INTERNATIONAL COLLEGE, SMYRNA AND BEIRUT. Founded in Smyrna in 1891 as a junior college in order to provide college preparatory training, and chartered in 1903 by the Commonwealth of Massachusetts. The college was transferred to Beirut in 1936 and was combined with the preparatory department of the American University of Beirut* which was established in 1872. It provided education from kindergarten through the sophomore year of college. The affiliation with the American University of Beirut ended in 1957, and it continued as a college preparatory school. *References*: *Schools*; *Stone*, ch. 12; and *Survey*.

IRAN ARMS AFFAIR (1985–1986). Beginning in August 1985, the United States made indirect (through Israel) and direct shipments of military equipment to Iran in order to obtain the release of the American hostages* held by Hizballah in Lebanon, and as a good-faith gesture to establish contact with moderate elements in Iran. The equipment included TOW anti-tank and Hawk anti-aircraft missiles and Hawk parts. The United States also gave Iran intelligence information. Three American hostages held by Hizballah in Lebanon were released before the affair was revealed in the media. *References*: *Congressional Quarterly Weekly Report*, February 14, 1987; April 25, 1987. *Report of the President's Special Review Board* (Washington, D.C., 1987).

IRAN MISSION. Established in 1870 by the Presbyterian Church of the U.S.A Board of Foreign Missions,* which took over missionary work in Persia from the American Board of Commissioners of Foreign Missions (ABCFM).* The work was transferred to the Evangelical Church of Iran in 1965, and the American missionaries were expelled from Iran in 1969. *References*: *A Century of Mission Work in Iran (Persia) 1834–1934. A Record of One Hundred Years of the Work of the Iran (Persia) Mission of the Board of Missions of the Presbyterian Church in the USA* (Beirut, 1936); John Elder, *History of the American Presbyterian Mission to Iran, 1834–1960* (Teheran, n.d.).

IRANIAN RESCUE MISSION. A military mission to rescue the American hostages in Teheran in April 1980. Several units were supposed to rendezvous at Desert I, an airstrip some 500 miles inland in Iran, proceed to Desert II, an abandoned airfield near Teheran, and then assault the embassy compound in Teheran and rescue the hostages (see Hostages in Iran). Several helicopters malfunctioned on the way to Desert I, and the mission was aborted. *References*: Gary Sick, "Military Options and Constraints," in *American Hostages in Iran: The Conduct of a Crisis* (New Haven, Conn., 1985), 144–72. Paul B. Ryan, *The Iranian Rescue Mission: Why It Failed* (Annapolis, Md., 1985).

ISENBERGER, NATHAN PERRY (1896–1956). Petroleum geologist, born February 9, 1896, in Albany, Indiana. Isenberger graduated from Kansas University and served in the navy in World War I. He worked as a geologist in

Venezuela, Colombia, Kansas, Texas, Louisiana, Oklahoma, Ecuador, Mexico, Chile, Peru, Bolivia, and the Middle East for a variety of companies. He became a geologist for Phillips Petroleum Company in 1933, and its foreign consultant and adviser in 1944. He played a major role in the negotiations in Kuwait which culminated in obtaining the oil concession for the Neutral Zone between Kuwait and Saudi Arabia for the American Independent Oil Corporation. Died December 21, 1956, in Bartlesville, Oklahoma. *Reference*: *BAAPG* 42 (1958): 225–228.

J

JACKSON, A(BRAHAM) V(ALENTINE) W(ILLIAMS) (1862–1937). Orientalist and philologist, born February 9, 1862, in New York City. Jackson graduated from Columbia University and studied at the University of Halle. An authority on Iranian religion, he was professor of Indo-Iranian languages at Columbia University from 1886 until 1935. He made four trips to Iran and India between 1901 and 1910, and in 1903 he ascended the Bisitun Rock to read the inscription of Darius. He recorded his travels in *Persia, Past and Present: A Book of Travel and Research* (New York, 1906), and *From Constantinople to the Home of Omar Khayyam; Travels in Transcaucasia and Northern Persia for Historic and Literary Research* (New York, 1911). He returned to Persia in 1918 as a member of the American Persian Relief Commission, and made another journey of research in Afghanistan, Baluchistan, and Eastern Persia in 1926. Died August 8, 1937, in New York City. *References*: *DAB S2*; *NCAB* 13:550; *NYT*, August 9, 1937; and *WWWA*.

JACKSON, CHARLES DOUGLAS (1902–1964). Publishing executive, born March 16, 1902, in New York City. Jackson graduated from Princeton University, was president of C. D. Jackson and Company from 1924 to 1931, vice president of Time, Inc. from 1931 until his death, and publisher of *Life* magazine from 1960 to 1964. In 1942–1943 he went to Turkey on a special mission for the State Department and the Bureau of Economic Welfare and was special assistant to the ambassador for the purpose of retaining access to Turkish chrome. He was deputy chief of psychological warfare from 1943 to 1945, president of the Free Europe Committee in 1951–1952, and special assistant to the president in 1952–1953. Died September 18, 1964, in New York City. *References*: *DAB S7*; *NCAB* 51:501; *NYT*, September 20, 1964; *PolProf: Eisenhower*; and *WWWA*.

JACKSON, ELMORE (1910–   ). Quaker leader, born April 9, 1910, in Marengo, Ohio. Jackson graduated from Pacific College (now George Fox College) and Yale University. He became a staff member of the American Friends

Service Committee in Philadelphia in 1936, was assistant executive secretary from 1946 to 1948, director of the Quaker Program at the United Nations from 1948 to 1961, and special assistant for policy making to the assistant secretary of state for international organization affairs from 1961 to 1965. He was vice president for policy studies of the U.N. Association of the United States, consultant to the Rockefeller Foundation, and special adviser to the Aspen Institute for Humanistic Studies. In 1955 he undertook a major mediation effort in the Middle East, which he described in *Middle East Mission: The Story of a Major Bid for Peace in the Time of Nasser & Ben Gurion* (New York, 1983). He was later director of the American Friends Service Committee project survey of the Middle East from 1957 to 1959. *References*: *AMWS*; *CA*; and *WWA*.

JACKSON, JESSE BENJAMIN (1871–1947). Consul, born November 17, 1871, in Paulding, Ohio. Jackson served in the Spanish-American War, was clerk of the Ohio House of Representatives in 1900–1901, and engaged in real estate and other businesses until 1905. He was consul at Alexandretta from 1905 to 1908 and at Aleppo from 1909 to 1923, representing Allied and neutral countries during World War I. He was later consul in Leghorn, Italy, and in Fort William and Fort Arthur, Ontario, Canada. He retired in 1935. Died December 4, 1947, in Columbus, Ohio. *References*: *NYT*, December 6, 1947; *WWWA*.

JACKSON, JOHN BRINCKERHOFF (1862–1920). Diplomat, born August 19, 1862, in Newark, New Jersey. Jackson graduated from the U.S. Naval Academy in 1883, served in the navy until 1886, studied law, and was admitted to the bar in 1889. He served in the legation in Berlin from 1900 to 1902, and was minister to Greece and representative to other Balkan countries from 1902 to 1907. He was minister to Persia from 1907 to 1909, and became involved in the Persian Revolution. He was minister to Cuba from 1909 to 1911, minister to Rumania, Serbia, and Bulgaria from 1911 to 1913, and special agent in the embassy in Berlin from 1915 to 1917. He retired in 1913 and lived in Switzerland. Died December 20, 1920, in Switzerland. *References*: *DAB*; *DADH*; *NYT*, December 21, 1920; *NCAB* 12:250; and *WWWA*.

JACOBSEN, THORKILD (1904–   ). Assyriologist, born June 7, 1904, in Copenhagen, Denmark. Jacobsen graduated from the universities of Copenhagen and Chicago. He was field Assyriologist for the Iraq expedition of the Oriental Institute from 1929 to 1937. He joined the faculty of the University of Chicago in 1937, became professor in 1946, was director of the Oriental Institute from 1946 to 1948, and professor of Assyriology at Harvard University from 1963 until his retirement in 1974. He was annual professor at the American Schools of Oriental Research (ASOR)* in Baghdad in 1953–1954, conducted a survey of ancient mounds in southern Iraq, and was director of the Diyala Basin Archacological Project. *References*: *Sumerological Studies in Honor of Thorkild Jacobsen on His Seventieth Birthday* (Chicago, 1975); *CA*; *DAS*; and *WWA*.

JAQUITH, HAROLD CLARENCE (1888–1943). Educator, born May 25, 1888, in Nashua, New Hampshire. Jaquith graduated from Trinity College (Conn.), Columbia University, and Hartford and Union theological seminaries, was ordained in 1915, and was an assistant pastor in New York City from 1912 to 1917. He was assistant secretary of Near East Relief* from 1917 to 1919, and managing director of Near East Relief in Istanbul from 1920 to 1923, and in Athens from 1924 to 1929. He was associate general secretary of Near East Relief and the Near East Foundation* in New York City from 1930 to 1933, and president of Illinois College from 1933 until his death. Died April 20, 1943, in West Hartford, Connecticut. *References*: *NYT*, April 21, 1943; *UnionTS*; and *WWWA*.

JARDINE, WILLIAM MARION (1879–1955). Educator and diplomat, born January 16, 1879, in Oneida County, Idaho. Jardine graduated from the Agricultural College of Utah. He was in charge of dry land grain investigations from 1907 to 1910, director of the experimental station, and dean of agriculture at the Kansas State Agricultural College from 1913 to 1918, president of the college from 1918 to 1925, and secretary of agriculture from 1925 to 1929. He was minister to Egypt from 1930 to 1933 and was particularly interested in Egyptian agriculture. He was later state treasurer of Kansas in 1933–1934, and president of the University of Wichita from 1934 to 1949. Died January 17, 1955, in San Antonio, Texas. *References*: Papers, Manuscript Division, Library of Congress; Wichita State University Library; *DAB S5*; *NCAB* A:14; *NYT*, January 18, 1955; and *WWWA*.

JENNINGS, ASA KENT (1877–1933). Clergyman and social worker, born September 20, 1877, in Ontario, Wayne County, New York. Jennings graduated from Syracuse University. He was director of religious work at the Utica Young Men's Christian Association (YMCA)* and held pastorates in northern New York from 1907 until 1917. During World War I he was secretary of the YMCA in the army, and from 1917 until his death he was secretary of the International Committee of the YMCA. He was in France in 1918, assisted in organizing the YMCA in Czechoslovakia, and was YMCA national boys' work secretary for Turkey. In September 1922 he organized and directed the evacuation of more than a quarter of a million Greek refugees out of Smyrna. In 1923 Turkish officials requested his help in developing welfare work for youth, and he organized the Smyrna Community Welfare Council, which was reorganized in 1928. He was the moving force behind the American Friends of Turkey, organized local Turkish-American clubs, and served as educational and social welfare adviser in Turkey from 1930 to 1933. Died January 27, 1933, in Washington, D.C. *References*: *NCAB* 23:229; *NYT*, January 28, 1933.

JESSUP, HENRY HARRIS (1832–1910). Missionary, born April 19, 1832, in Montrose, Pennsylvania. Jessup graduated from Yale College and Union Theological Seminary, and was ordained in 1855. He served as a missionary under the American Board of Commissioners for Foreign Missions (ABCFM)* in Syria. He was stationed in Tripoli in 1856, remaining there until 1860, when he moved to Beirut. He was editor of the Arabic journal *El-Neshrah*, acting pastor of the Syrian Church of Beirut, secretary of the Asfuriyeh Hospital for the Insane, and one of the founders of the Syrian Protestant College. In 1883 he declined the post of minister to Persia. He wrote many illustrated Arabic books for children and *The Woman of the Arabs* (New York, 1873), *Syrian Home Life* (New York, 1874), and his memoirs, *Fifty-three Years in Syria* (New York, 1910). Died April 28, 1910, in Beirut. *References*: Papers, Yale University Divinity School Library; *ACAB*; *DAB*; *NCAB* 10:144; *NYT*, April 29, 1910; *Union*; and *WWWA*.

JESSUP, SAMUEL (1833–1912). Missionary, brother of Henry Harris Jessup,* born December 21, 1833, in Montrose, Pennsylvania. Jessup graduated from Yale College and Union Theological Seminary, was ordained in 1861, and served as a chaplain during the Civil War. He was a missionary under the Presbyterian Church in the USA Board of Foreign Missions* in Syria from 1862 until his death. He was editor of an Arabic weekly from 1883 to 1896, manager of the Arabic publishing house in Beirut, and principal of the Gerard Institute in Sidon from 1903 to 1907. From 1880 to 1890, while on furlough, he was acting secretary of the Presbyterian Board of Foreign Missions. Died July 15, 1912, in Sidon, Syria. *References*: *ACAB*; *NCAB* 10:144; *NYT*, July 17, 1912; *UnionTS*; and *WWWA*.

JEWETT, ALBERT C. (1870?–1926). Electrical engineer. Jewett installed the first electric street railway in San Francisco, as well as other street railways and power plants in California, was foreign installation engineer for the General Electric Company, and installed power plants in Mysore and Srinagar, India, and in Brazil. He was chief engineer for the Amir Habibullah Khan of Afghanistan from 1911 to 1919, in charge of installing a hydroelectric plant in Kabul. After 1919 he spent part of his time in the Society Islands and settled in Papeete in 1923. Died February 3, 1926, in Papeete. His memoir, *An American Engineer in Afghanistan; From the Letters and Notes*, ed. Marjorie Jewett Bell (Minneapolis, 1948), was published after his death.

JEWISH LEGION. Military units formed by Jewish volunteers to fight with the British Army in World War I to liberate Palestine from Turkish rule. One-third of the volunteers came from the United States to join the 39th Battalion. The volunteers reached Palestine when the war was already over. By 1920 most American volunteers were discharged and returned to the United States, but several remained permanently in Palestine. *References*: *EJ*; Elias Gilner, *War and Hope: A History of the Jewish Legion* (New York, 1969).

JOHNSON, J(EREMIAH) AUGUSTUS (1836–1914). Lawyer and consul, born June 3, 1836, in Boston. Johnson studied law and was admitted to the bar in 1867. He was consul in Beirut from 1858 to 1867 and consul general from 1867 to 1870. He discovered the Hamath Stone in Syria and Hittite inscriptions, and wrote accounts of them in 1870. He also wrote an account of the colonization of Palestine for the *Century Magazine* in 1886. He returned to the United States in 1870, resumed the practice of law, and was employed as counsel for railroads and other corporations. He was married to Sarah Barclay Johnson, an author who wrote about the Middle East. Died February 28, 1914, in South Orange, New Jersey. *Reference*: *WWWA*.

JOHNSON PLAN. A plan for the resolution of the Palestine refugee problem proposed by Joseph E. Johnson (1906–   ), president of the Carnegie Endowment for International Peace, who was appointed U.S. special representative on the U.N. Conciliation Commission for Palestine in 1961. He conducted fact finding missions to the Middle East in 1961 and 1962. His plan was rejected by Israel and the Arab states and his mission failed in December 1962. *References*: David P. Forsyth, *United Nations Peacemaking: The Conciliation Commission for Palestine* (Baltimore, 1972); Steven L. Spiegel, *The Other Arab-Israeli Conflict: Making America's Middle East Policy from Truman to Reagan* (Chicago, 1985), 110–117.

JOHNSON, SARAH (BARCLAY) (1837–1885). Author, daughter of James Turner Barclay,* born in Albermale County, Virginia. Barclay accompanied her father in his mission to Jerusalem and drew most of the illustrations in his book *The City of the Great King*. She wrote *The Hadji in Syria; or, Three Years in Jerusalem* (Philadelphia, 1858). In 1856 she married Jeremiah Augustus Johnson* and lived in Syria until 1870, when she returned with him to the United States. She resided in New York City and, after 1883, in Greenwich, Connecticut. Died April 21, 1885, in Greenwich, after having been shot by her son who then committed suicide. *Reference*: *NCAB* 11:189.

JOHNSON, THOMAS DICKSON (1842–1918). Physician, born January 21, 1842, at Farmers Hill, Robertson County, Tennessee. Johnson served in the Civil War and later graduated from the medical department of the University of Virginia and from the College of Physicians and Surgeons (Baltimore). He practiced medicine at Clarksville, Tennessee, from 1869 to 1875. In 1875 he was appointed staff surgeon in the Egyptian Army and served in the Egyptian-Abyssinian War of 1876. He was wounded at Gura, and was captured and held prisoner by the Ethiopians. He resigned in 1877, whereupon he returned to the United States and resumed his medical practice in Clarksville until his death.

Died March 6, 1918, in Clarksville. *References*: *Tennessee the Volunteer State 1769–1923* (Chicago, 1923), 3:921–922.

JOHNSTON, CLARENCE T(HOMAS) (1872–1970). Civil engineer, born October 23, 1872, in Littleton, Colorado. Johnston graduated from the University of Michigan. From 1890 to 1911 he was involved in irrigation work, was assistant state engineer of Wyoming from 1895 to 1899, and state engineer from 1903 to 1911. He worked for the U.S. Geological Survey from 1896 to 1898 and for the U.S. Department of Agriculture from 1899 to 1903. He made a trip to Egypt in 1903 and reported on Egyptian irrigation in *Egyptian Irrigation: A Study of Irrigation Methods and Administration in Egypt* (Washington, D.C., 1903). He was professor of surveying and geodesy at the University of Michigan from 1911 until his retirement in 1941. Died January 17, 1970, in Ann Arbor, Michigan. *References*: *Ann Arbor News*, January 19, 1970; *WWWA*.

JOHNSTON, ERIC ALLEN (1896–1963). Businessman and motion picture executive, born December 21, 1896, in Washington, D.C. Johnston graduated from the University of Washington and served in the marines from 1917 to 1922. In 1923 he organized an electrical retail business in Spokane, Washington, and in 1933 he organized the Columbia Electric and Manufacturing Company, serving as its president until 1949. He became president of the Motion Picture Association of America in 1945. From 1953 to 1955, he was special representative of the president with personal rank of ambassador on a diplomatic mission to the Middle East to mediate a comprehensive plan for regional development of the Jordan River system. In 1955 he presented the Jordan Valley Unified Plan known as the Johnston Plan. Died August 22, 1963, in Washington, D.C. *References*: *BDABL*; Michael Brecher, *Decisions in Israel's Foreign Policy* (London, 1974), pp. 173–224; *CB* 1943, 1955; *DAB S7*; *NCAB* H:98; *NYT*, August 23, 1963; *PolProf: Truman*; and *WWWA*.

JOINT AMERICAN MILITARY MISSION FOR AID TO TURKEY (JAM-MAT). Established in late 1947 by the U.S. Army, Navy, and Air Force to provide American military personnel to serve as advisers to the Turkish armed forces; to supervise and instruct the Turks in the use of American equipment, and to give them specialized training. In 1949 the name of the mission was changed to Joint United States Military Mission for Aid to Turkey (JUSMMAT), and in 1951 it was the largest American military advisory group abroad. The JUSMMAT helped transform the Turkish army into a professional organization, but eventually its role declined. *References*: Charlotte Wolfe, *Garrison Community: A Study of an Overseas American Military Colony* (Westport, Conn., 1969).

JONES, A(RLEIGH) WILLARD (1894–1973). Educator, born September 6, 1894, in Richland, Iowa. Jones graduated from William Penn College (Oskaloosa, Ia.), the University of Chicago, and Yale Divinity School. He was principal of the Friends boys' school in Ramallah, Palestine, from 1924 until 1930. From 1930 to 1940, he taught in schools in North Carolina and Pennsylvania and in a boys' school in Kisumu, Kenya. He returned to Ramallah in 1944 as principal and served until 1954. He was executive secretary of the Near East Christian Council Committee for Refugee Relief from 1953 until his retirement in 1962. Died May 29, 1973, in Waverly, Ohio. His wife, **CHRISTINA (HENDRY) JONES (1896–1984)**, educator, was born November 8, 1896, in Scotland. She graduated from William Penn College. She served as a teacher in the American Friends Mission's school in Ramallah from 1922 to 1930 and from 1943 to 1954. She wrote a memoir, *The Untempered Wind: Forty Years in Palestine* (London, 1975), and *Friends in Palestine* (Richmond, Ind., 1981). Died March 25, 1984, in Lebanon, Ohio.

JONES, ELI (1807–1890) and **JONES, SYBIL** (1808–1873). Preachers and missionaries, Eli born in 1807 in China Lake, near Augusta, Maine and Sybil born February 28, 1808 in Brunswick, Maine. They were married in 1833, became preachers for the Society of Friends, and preached in the United States, Europe, Liberia, and the West Indies. They went to the Middle East in 1867–1868, visited Syria and Palestine again in 1869, and founded the Friends mission and a girls' training home in Ramallah. Sybil died December 4, 1873, in Dirigo, near Augusta, Maine. *References*: Papers of Sybil Jones, Quaker Collection, Haverford College, Haverford, Pennsylvania; *DAB*; *NAW*; and *NCAB* 2:480–481.

JONES, GEORGE (1800–1870). Naval chaplain and author, born July 30, 1800, near York, Pennsylvania. Jones graduated from Yale College. He served as secretary to Commodore Charles Morris on the frigate *Brandywine* and cruised Mediterranean ports in the frigate *Constitution* as a schoolmaster in the navy, and accompanied Josiah Brewer* on a tour of Constantinople. He described his travels in *Sketches of Naval Life, With Notices of Men, Manners and Scenery, on the Shores of the Mediterranean* (New York, 1829). In 1832 he became a chaplain on the *United States* and in 1834 on the *Delaware* in which he made a second cruise to the Middle East and wrote his account in *Excursions to Cairo, Jerusalem, Damascus, and Balbec, from the United States Ship Delaware* (New York, 1836). He continued as chaplain on various ships, traveled to China with Commodore Matthew C. Perry, and served in the Naval Academy until his retirement in 1862. Died January 22, 1870, in Philadelphia. *References*: *ACAB*; *DAB*; and *WWWA*.

JONES, H(UGH) BOLTON (1848–1927). Landscape painter, born October 20, 1848, in Baltimore, Maryland. Jones trained at the Maryland Institute. In 1876 he went to France and worked at Pont-Aven in Brittany. He made a sketching tour of North Africa in 1877; "Tangiers" was one of his more famous paintings. He returned to the United States in 1880 and established himself as a painter in New York. Died September 24, 1927, in New York City. *References*: *ACAB*; *DAB*; *NCAB* 27:343; and *WWWA*.

JONES, JACOB (1768–1850). Naval officer, born March 1768, near Smyrna, Delaware. Jones studied medicine and practiced it in Kent County, Delaware, and was clerk of the Delaware Supreme Court. He enlisted in the navy as a midshipman in 1799, and was second lieutenant on the *Philadelphia** when it was grounded and captured off Tripoli. He was a captive in Tripoli for twenty months and was released at the end of the Barbary Wars. He served in the War of 1812 and was in command of the *Macedonian* in Stephen Decatur's* squadron against Algiers in 1815. He commanded the Mediterranean Squadron from 1821 to 1823 and the Pacific squadron from 1826 to 1829, and served on shore duty until his death. Died August 3, 1850, in Philadelphia. *References*: *DAB*; *NCAB* 2:233; *WAMB*; and *WWWA*.

JONES, QUILL (1875–1954). Oriental rug connoisseur, born February 28, 1875, in Indianapolis. Jones had various business concerns in Indianapolis until 1905. He made ten trips to the Middle East after 1905, studying and collecting rugs and antiquities. He traveled in Arabia in 1929 and was the first American archaeological collector to enter Yemen. The Sabean and Himyaritic antiquities he collected were placed in the University Museum of the University of Pennsylvania. He also loaned exhibits to various institutions. Died July 27, 1954, in New York City. *References*: NYT, July 21, 1954; *WWWA*.

JONES, WILLIAM M(EAD) (1818–1895). Missionary, born May 2, 1818, in Fort Ann, Washington County, New York. Jones graduated from Madison University (Hamilton, N.Y.). He was a Baptist missionary to Haiti from 1845 to 1850, and a Seventh Day Baptist missionary to Palestine from 1854 to 1860, stationed in Jerusalem. He was a pastor in Walwoth, Wisconsin, Scott, New York, and London, England, from 1872 until his death. He was also professor of Arabic and Hebrew at the City of London College. Died February 22, 1895, in London. *References*: *Seventh Day Baptists in Europe and America* (Plainfield, N.J., 1910).

JORDAN, SAMUEL MARTIN (1871–1952). Missionary and educator, born January 6, 1871, in Stewartstown, Pennsylvania. Jordan graduated from Lafayette College and Princeton Theological Seminary, and was ordained in 1898. He served as a missionary under the Presbyterian Church in the U.S.A. Board of Foreign Missions in Persia from 1898 until 1941. He was professor of history and social sciences and principal of the American school for boys in Teheran from 1895 to 1925. He developed the school into the American College (later Alborz College),* and was its president from 1925 until his retirement in 1941. He returned to Iran in 1944 on a special mission. Died June 21, 1952, in Hollywood, California. *References*: Arthur C. Boyce, "Alborz College of Teheran and Dr. Samuel Martin Jordan Founder and President," in Ali Pasah Saleh, *Cultural Ties Between Iran and the United States* (Teheran, 1976), pp. 155–234; *NCAB* 41:146; *NYT*, June 25, 1952; and *WWWA*.

JUDSON, HARRY PRATT (1849–1927). Educator, born December 20, 1849, Jamestown, New York. Judson graduated from Williams College. He was teacher and school principal of a high school in Troy, New York, professor of history at the University of Minnesota, professor of history and political science at the University of Chicago, and president of the University of Chicago from 1906 until his retirement in 1923. He traveled in the Middle East in 1918 as director of the Persian Commission of the American Committee for Relief in the Near East. Died March 4, 1927, in Chicago. *References*: Papers, University of Chicago Library; *DAB*; *NCAB* 20:24; *NYT*, March 5, 1927; and *WWWA*.

K

KAPLAN, ROSE (1867–1917). Nurse, born September 1867, in Petrograd, Russia, and came to the United States in 1892. Kaplan graduated from Mount Sinai Hospital Training School for Nurses and worked in Mount Sinai Hospital in New York City. She went to Palestine in 1913 when Hadassah* established a nursing settlement in Jerusalem. She took over midwife service in Jerusalem and helped establish an anti-Trachoma campaign in Palestine. She was head nurse of a Jewish refugee camp in Alexandria, Egypt, during World War I. Died August 3, 1917, in Alexandria, Egypt. *Reference*: *NYT*, August 8, 1917.

KATHERINA FIELD STATION. Following inspection tours conducted in 1931, a solar radiation station established in 1933 on Gebel Katherina (Mount Catherine) in the Sinai Peninsula by the Smithsonian Astrophysical Observatory. The station was closed down in 1938 when sufficient data were collected. *References*: Records, Smithsonian Institution Archives, Washington, D.C.; Bessie. Z. Jones, *Lighthouse of the Skies: The Smithsonian Astrophysical Observatory: Background and History 1846–1955* (Washington, D.C., 1965), ch. 10.

KEARNEY, THOMAS HENRY (1874–1956). Botanist and plant explorer, born June 27, 1874, in Cincinnati. Kearney graduated from the University of Tennessee and Columbia University. In 1894 he joined the Bureau of Plant Industry of the Department of Agriculture, was physiologist from 1902 to 1924, senior physiologist from 1924 to 1929, and principal physiologist from 1929 until his retirement in 1944. In 1899 he was an assistant on the Harriman Alaska Expedition. In 1902 he was in North Africa studying alkali soils and crop growth on such soils in Algeria and cotton cultivation in Egypt, and in 1903 he began breeding Egyptian-style cotton in Arizona. He was again in Algeria and Tunisia in 1904–1905, investigating olives and studying date culture, and obtaining offshoots for planting in the desert region of southern California. He was co-author of *Agricultural Explorations in Algeria* (Washington, D.C., 1905), and *Egyptian Cotton in the Southwestern United States* (Washington, D.C., 1908).

Died October 19, 1956, in San Francisco. *References*: *NCAB* 45:565; *NYT*, October 22, 1956; and *WWWA*.

KEITH, AGENS (NEWTON) (1901–   ). Author, born July 6, 1901, in Oak Park, Illinois. Keith graduated from the University of California. She became a reporter for the *San Francisco Examiner* in 1924, lived in Borneo from 1934 to 1952, and was in the Philippines for the Food and Agriculture Organization in 1952. She lived in Libya from 1955 to 1964, and wrote and illustrated *Children of Allah* (Boston, 1965). *References*: *American Women Writers*, ed. by Lina Mainiero (New York, 1980), 2:432–34; *CA*; and *WWAW*.

KELLOGG, MINER KILBOURNE (1814–1889). Painter, born August 22, 1814, in Manlius Square, New York, and grew up in New Harmony, Indiana, and in Cincinnati. Kellogg became a painter in 1831 and went to Europe in 1841. In 1843–1844, he traveled to Egypt, Palestine, Syria, and Turkey. He visited Turkey again in 1844, maintained a studio in Constantinople, and visited North Africa in 1846 and again in the 1850s. After 1855 he lived in Paris and London, and returned to the United States in 1865. He wrote several articles about Mount Sinai. Died February 17, 1889, in Toledo, Ohio. *Texas Journal, 1872*, ed. Llerena Friend (Austin, Tex., 1967). *References*: Papers, Archives of American Art, Washington, D.C.; Indiana Historical Society Library, Indianapolis; Richard J. Boyle, "Miner Kilbourne Kellogg," *The Cincinnati Art Museum Bulletin* 8 (1966): 17–23; *OAB*; and *NYHSD*.

KELLY, C(ALEB) GUYER (1887–1960). Missionary, born August 14, 1887, in Baltimore. Kelly graduated from Johns Hopkins University. He was a missionary in Tunisia under the Board of Missions of the Methodist Church from 1918 to 1953 and was stationed in Tunis. In 1921 he formed the baseball club "Carthage-Orioles," reputedly the first baseball club in Africa. He organized 160 baseball clubs in North Africa and became known as "the baseball missionary of North Africa." He wrote of his experiences in the January 1941 issue of *The Moslem World*. Died January 11, 1960, in Casablanca, Morocco. *Reference*: *NYT*, January 31, 1960.

KELSEY, FRANCIS WILLEY (1858–1927). Classicist and archaeologist, born May 23, 1858, in Ogden, New York. Kelsey graduated from the University of Rochester and studied in Europe. He taught classics at Lake Forest University (Lake Forest, Ill.) and was professor of Latin language and literature at the University of Michigan from 1881 until his death. In 1893 he studied archaeological sites in the Mediterranean, was director of the American School of Classical Studies in Rome in 1900–1901, and headed the University of Michigan expeditions to Antioch of Pisidia, Syria, and to Karanis, Egypt, in 1919 and 1924. In 1924 he discovered the ruins of an ancient Christian church. In 1925–1926 Kelsey led the University of Michigan excavations at Carthage in cooperation with French archaeologists, and wrote *Excavations at Carthage, 1925: A Preliminary Report* (New York, 1926). Died May 14, 1927, in Ann Arbor, Michigan. *References*: *DAB*; *NCAB*, 26:461; *NYT*, May 15, 1927; and *WWWA*.

KELSO, JAMES ANDERSON (1873–1951). Theologian, born June 6, 1873, in Rawalpindi, India, to American parents. Kelso graduated from Washington and Jefferson College and Western Theological Seminary, studied at the universities of Berlin and Leipzig, and was ordained in 1898. He was an instructor at Western Theological Seminary in Pittsburgh from 1897 to 1900, was professor of Hebrew and Old Testament literature after 1901, and served as president from 1909 until 1943. He was annual professor at the American Schools of Oriental Research (ASOR)* in Jerusalem in 1922–1923. He directed the excavations at Jericho in 1950, reputedly discovering the remains of the winter palace of Herod the Great. Died November 3, 1951, in Pittsburgh, Pennsylvania. *References*: *AJA* 56 (July 1952): 182; *BASOR* 124 (1951): 11–12; *NYT*, November 5, 1951; and *WWWA*.

KEMMERER, EDWIN WALTER (1875–1945). Economist, born June 29, 1875, in Scranton, Pennsylvania. Kemmerer graduated from Wesleyan and Cornell universities. He served as financial adviser to the U.S. Philippine Commission in 1903 and was chief of the Division of Currency of the Philippines from 1904 to 1906. In 1906 he studied the Agricultural Bank of Egypt and wrote *Report on the Agricultural Bank of Egypt* (Manila, 1906). He was professor of economics and finance at Cornell University from 1906 to 1912 and at Princeton University from 1912 until 1928, and professor of international finance there until his retirement in 1943. He was financial adviser to foreign governments, served on commissions as adviser for financial matters, and in 1934 was co-chairman of the Hines-Kemmerer Commission which made an economic survey of Turkey. Died December 16, 1945, in Princeton, New Jersey. *References*: "Autobiography of a Money Doctor," Ms.; Papers, Princeton University Library; *American Economic Review* 36 (1946): 219–222; *DAB S3*; *NCAB* E:406; *NYT*, December 17, 1945; and *WWWA*.

KENITRA (PORT LYAUTY). American naval and air base in Morocco obtained in 1950 through agreement with France and terminated by an agreement with Morocco in 1959. It was the staging point for the U-2 flights. The base was closed down in 1963, but a secret radio communication center belonging to the Sixth Fleet continued until it was closed down in 1978. *Reference*: I. William Zartman, "The Moroccan-American Base Negotiations," *MEJ* 18 (1964): 27–40.

KERR, MALCOLM H(OOPER) (1931–1984). Educator, son of Stanley E. Kerr,* born October 8, 1931, in Beirut. Kerr graduated from Princeton and Johns Hopkins universities and the American University of Beirut,* and taught in Beirut until 1961. He became professor of political science at the University of California at Los Angeles in 1967 and director of the Von Gruenbaum Center for Near Eastern Studies. He was professor of political science at the American University of Beirut from 1979 to 1981 and its president from 1982 until his death. He wrote *The Arab Cold War, 1958–1965* (London, 1965), co-authored *The Economics and Politics of the Middle East* (New York, 1975), edited *The Elusive Peace in the Middle East* (Albany, N.Y., 1975), and *Rich and Poor States in the Middle East; Egypt and the New Arab Order* (Boulder, Colo., 1982). Killed by pro-Iranian gunmen January 18, 1984, in Beirut. *References*: *CA*; *NYT* January 19, 1984; and *WWWA*.

KERR, RICHARD CALDWELL (1896–1972). Oil explorer and aerial mapping specialist, born in Selma, California. Kerr graduated from the University of California at Berkeley and was a naval aviator in World War I. He was a partner in Continental Air Map Company, performed aerial photographic work and air reconnaissance for California Arabian Standard Oil Company (CASOC)* in Saudi Arabia, and flew the first airplane into Dhahran. During World War II he was engaged in logistics research for the Army Engineer Corps, and after his retirement in 1957 was consultant on transportation research and chief scientist for the Transportation Corps from 1959 to 1961. Died January 2, 1972, in Coalinga, California. *References*: Papers, Petroleum History and Research Collection Center, University of Wyoming, Laramee, Wyoming; *AWM* 35 (May-June 1984): 14.

KERR, STANLEY E(LPHINSTONE) (1894–1976). Biochemist, born March 30, 1894, in Princeton, New Jersey. Kerr graduated from the University of Pennsylvania. He was an officer in the U.S. Army Sanitary Corps and an instructor at the University of Pennsylvania from 1918 to 1921. From 1919 to 1922 he was involved with relief operations in Turkey and Syria which formed the basis of his memoir, *The Lions of Marash: Personal Experiences with American Near East Relief, 1912–1922* (Albany, N.Y., 1973). He was adjunct professor, associate professor, and professor of biochemistry at the American University of Beirut* from 1925 until his retirement in 1964. Died December 15, 1976, in Princeton, New Jersey. *References*: Papers, Hoover Institution Archives; *CA*; and *NYT*, December 15, 1976.

KERWOOD, CHARLES W. ("CHUCK") (1897–1976). Pilot, born in Bryn Mawr, Pennsylvania. Kerwood served in the Foreign Legion during World War I and was later a member of the Lafayette Flying Corps of the French Army. He was shot down by the Germans in 1918 and was a prisoner of war. He was one of the first barnstormers, served as colonel in the Greek Royal Air Force during the Greek-Turkish War, and helped organize the Escadrille Cherifienne,* a volunteer American squadron during the French-Spanish expedition against Berber tribes in the Rif in 1925. During World War II he served in the intelligence division of the U.S. Army Air Corps, was later a special investigator for the U.S. Senate aircraft safety committee, helped plan the airport in Rio de Janeiro, and was an executive in the Civil Aviation Division of the International Cooperation Administration. Died December 15, 1976, in Washington, D.C. *Reference*: *Washington Post*, December 17, 1976.

KHALIL AGHA (fl. 1820–1821). Adventurer, born in New York. Original name unknown. Khalil Agha accompanied Ismail, son of Muhammad Ali, on the Egyptian expedition to Sennar in Eastern Sudan in 1820–1821 and was probably the first individual to travel the whole distance from Rosetta, in the Nile's delta, to Sennar, on the Blue Nile, by water. *Reference*: *Hill*.

KILBURN, BENJAMIN WEST (1827–1909). Photographer, born December 10, 1827, in Littleton, New Hampshire. Kilburn and his brother formed a partnership in 1867 for the production and distribution of stereographs, for which Benjamin did the photography. He made a prolonged visit to the Middle East in 1873 in which he took stereoviews from which he later made stereographs. He bought his brother's interests in 1877, renamed the firm B. W. Kilburn and Company, and was its manager. The company was dissolved after his death. Died January 15, 1909, in Littleton, New Hampshire. *Reference*: Dorothy H. Cummings, "Watch the Birdie," *New Hampshire Profiles* 1 (July 1952): 22–24.

KIMBALL, GRACE N(IEBUHR) (1855–1942). Medical missionary, born in Dover, New Hampshire. Kimball served as a missionary under the American Board of Commissioners for Foreign Missions (ABCFM)* in Van, Turkey, from 1882 to 1888, when she returned to the United States, and studied at the Woman's Medical College of the New York Infirmary. She returned to Van as a medical missionary and served there from 1892 to 1896. During the Armenian massacres of 1895–1896, she conducted extensive industrial relief work in eastern Turkey. She was assistant physician at Vassar College from 1896 to 1900 and began to practice medicine in Poughkeepsie, New York, from 1898 until her retirement in 1941. She also served on the Board of Health and was a leader in the women's suffrage movement. Died November 18, 1942, in Poughkeepsie. *Reference*: *Poughkeepsie New Yorker*, November 19, 1942.

KING, HENRY CHURCHILL (1858–1934). Clergyman and educator, born September 18, 1858, in Hillsdale, Michigan. King graduated from Oberlin College and Oberlin Theological Seminary. He became a member of the faculty of Oberlin College in 1884, was professor of philosophy from 1891 to 1897, professor of theology from 1897 to 1925, and president from 1902 to 1927. He was director of the religious work department of the Young Men's Christian Association (YMCA)* for France in 1918–1919. He was a member of the Inter-Allied Commission on Mandates (King-Crane Commission*) in Turkey in 1919. Died February 27, 1934, in Oberlin, Ohio. *References*: Papers, Oberlin College

Library; *DAB S1*; Donald M. Love, *Henry Churchill King of Oberlin* (New Haven, Conn., 1956); *NCAB* 13:296; *NYT*, February 28, 1934; and *WWWA*.

KING, JONAS (1792–1869). Missionary, born July 29, 1792, at Hawley, Massachusetts. King graduated from Williams College and Andover Theological Seminary. He worked as a city missionary in Charleston, South Carolina, was ordained in 1819, and studied Arabic in Paris in 1821–1822. He became a missionary under the American Board of Commissioners for Foreign Missions (ABCFM)* in 1822, served in Jerusalem from 1822 to 1825, and was transferred to Greece in 1828. He established a teachers' school, leading to the organization of a free school system in Greece, and was consular agent in Athens from 1851 to 1858. When he planned a Greek Protestant Church, he came into conflict with the Greek Orthodox Church and was tried in Athens in 1852 on the charge of reviling the Greek Church. He was sentenced to fifteen days' imprisonment and exile from Greece, but served only one day in prison and the sentence of exile was reversed. The case was investigated by George Perkins Marsh* in 1852–1853 who found the charges to be unjustified. King's journal was published in the *Missionary Herald*. Died May 22, 1869, in Athens. *References*: *ACAB*; *AndoverTS*; *DAB*; *EM*; *Hewitt*; and *WWWA*.

KING-CRANE COMMISSION (1919). Formally named the American Section of the Inter-Allied Commission on Mandates in Turkey. This body was appointed by President Woodrow Wilson to gather information about the Middle East for the purpose of creating a stable peace in that part of the world. Its members were Henry Churchill King* and Charles Richard Crane.* The commission spent two and a half months in the Middle East and submitted a report with recommendations for an active American mandatory role in the area which had little impact on U.S. foreign policy. *References*: *DADH*; M. Thomas Davis, "The King-Crane Commission and the American Abandonment of Self-Determination," *American-Arab Affairs* 9 (Summer 1984): 55–66; Harry N. Howard, *The King-Crane Commission: An American Inquiry in the Middle East* (Beirut, 1963); Stuart E. Knee, "The King-Crane Commission of 1919: The Articulation of Political Anti-Zionism," *American Jewish Archives* 29 (1977): 22–52.

KIRK, HOWARD M. ("HOWDIE") (1899–   ). Petroleum geologist, born May 9, 1899, in Gallatin Gateway, Montana. Kirk served in the navy in World War I and graduated from Stanford University. He was geologist with the Henry L. Doherty Company in Mexico, Canada, and Venezuela from 1926 to 1933, and geologist in charge of foundation studies at Fort Peck Dam, Montana, for the U.S. Army Engineers. From 1934 to 1937 he was employed by the Turkish government to conduct a reconnaissance geological study over a large portion of Turkey, and in 1937–1938 he was employed in a reconnaissance of Afghanistan and Baluchistan with Henry Carter Rea* for Seabord Oil Company, investigating oil possibilities. His account of the Afghanistan reconnaissance appeared in Edgar W. Owen, *Trek of the Oil Finders: A History of Exploration for Petroleum* (Tulsa, Okla., 1975). From 1940 to 1961 he was employed by the Atlantic Refining Company (now Atlantic-Richfield) in geological and managerial assignments in Haiti, the Dominican Republic, Cuba, Guatemala, and Canada, and from 1961 to 1964, he was manager of the Foreign Exploration Division of its Foreign Department. He was consultant with John W. Mecom from 1964 to 1966, and a petroleum consultant after 1966.

KIRKLAND, ELIZABETH CABOT (1785–?). Traveler, born in Beverly, Massachusetts. Kirkland traveled in the Middle East in 1832 with her husband, **JOHN THORNTON KIRKLAND (1770–1840)**, Unitarian clergyman and president of Harvard University from 1810 to 1828. She was perhaps the first American woman tourist in the Middle East. Her letters were published in the *Proceedings of the Massachusetts Historical Society* for 1906.

KIRKWOOD, SAMUEL BROWN (1907–   ). Physician and educator, born May 2, 1907, in Seattle. Kirkwood graduated from Macalester College and Harvard University and served in the army medical corps during World War II. He was assistant professor in obstetrics and maternal health at Harvard University from 1946 to 1953, and clinical professor in 1953. He practiced medicine in Boston from 1938 to 1953. He was state commissioner of public health in Massachusetts from 1953 to 1958, chief of the division of public health of the U.S. foreign aid program in Iran from 1959 to 1961, professor of obstetrics and dean of faculties of medical sciences of the American University of Beirut* from 1962 to 1965, and president of the American University of Beirut from 1965 until his retirement in 1976. *References*: *AMWS*; *WWA*.

KISSINGER, HENRY ALFRED (1923–   ). Government official, born May 27, 1923, in Furth, Bavaria, Germany, came to the U.S. in 1938, and served in the army in World War II. Kissinger graduated from Harvard University, became a member of the faculty of Harvard in 1954, was research director of the Council on Foreign Resources from 1954 to 1956, and consultant to the State Department from 1965 to 1969. In 1969, under the Nixon administration, he became special assistant to the president for national security affairs, and negotiated a cease-fire agreement with North Vietnam. Following the October 1973 Israel-Arab War, Kissinger conducted personal "shuttle diplomacy" months between Jerusalem, Cairo, and Demascus from 1973 to 1975, and his mediation efforts led to the conclusion of five agreements, including cease-fire agreement between Israel and Egypt, and disengagement agreements between Egypt and Israel and Syria and Israel in 1975. He was secretary of state from 1973 to 1977. He published his memoirs, *Years of Upheaval* (Boston, 1982). *References: DADH; Dynamics of Third Party Intervention: Kissinger in the Middle East*, ed. Jeffrey Z. Rubin (New York, 1981); Ishaq I. Ghanayem and Alden H. Voth, *The Kissinger Legacy: American-Middle East Policy* (New York, 1984); Matti

Golan, *The Secret Conversations of Henry Kissinger; Step-by-step Diplomacy in the Middle East* (New York, 1976); Edward F. Sheehan, *The Arabs, Israelis, and Kissinger: A Secret History of American Diplomacy in the Middle East* (New York, 1976); *Touval*, ch. 9; and *WWA*.

KLIGLER, ISRAEL JACOB (1889–1944). Bacteriologist, born April 24, 1889, in Kamenets-Podolsky, Russia, and came to the United States in 1901. Kligler graduated from Columbia University and was fellow of the Rockefeller Institute for Medical Research from 1916 to 1920. He was a member of malaria and yellow fever commissions to Mexico, Africa, Peru, and Palestine. He was chief bacteriologist at Hadassah Medical Organization* in Palestine in 1921–1922 and head of the Malaria Research Unit in Palestine from 1923 to 1926. He was director of the Department of Hygiene at the Hebrew University of Jerusalem from 1926 until his death. He also founded the Microbiological Society and the Malaria Research Station at Rosh Pinnah, Palestine. He wrote *The Epidemiology and Control of Malaria in Palestine* (Chicago, 1930). Died September 24, 1944, in Palestine. *References*: *EJ*; Solomon R. Kagan, *Modern Medical World* (Boston, 1945).

KNABENSHUE, PAUL (1883–1942). Diplomat, born October 31, 1883, in Toledo, Ohio. Knabenshue was partner and general manager of Geroe and Knabenshue, Brokers, in Toledo from 1903 to 1904. He entered the consular service in 1906, becoming vice consul in Belfast from 1906 to 1911; vice consul, deputy consul, and deputy consul general in Cairo from 1911 to 1915; consul in Beirut from 1915 to 1928; consul general in Jerusalem from 1928 to 1932; and minister and consul general in Baghdad from 1932 until his death. In 1933 he was special envoy to the Sultan of Muscat and Oman on the one hundredth anniversary of the signing of the Treaty of Amity and Commerce, and in the same year concluded the first commercial treaty between the United States and Iraq. Died February 1, 1942, in Baghdad. *References*: *NYT*, February 2, 1942; *WWWA*.

KNAPP, GEORGE CUSHING (1829–1895). Missionary, born October 30, 1829, in Lyndon, Vermont. Knapp graduated from Middlebury College and Andover Theological Seminary, and was ordained in 1855. He became a missionary under the American Board of Commissioners for Foreign Missions (ABCFM)* in Turkey in 1856, was stationed in Diyarbekir from 1856 to 1858, and was transferred to Bitlis in 1858. Died March 12, 1895, in Bitlis, Turkey. His son, **GEORGE P. KNAPP**, was a missionary stationed in Bitlis, Turkey. He became associated with an organization of Armenian revolutionaries known as the "Joint Committee Against Turkey," and was caught circulating messages among them. As a result, the Ottoman government expelled him from Bitlis in March 1896 on the charge of sedition. He was the only American actually implicated in Armenian revolutionary schemes. *Reference*: *AndoverTS*.

KNAPP, GRACE HIGELY (1870–1953). Missionary, daughter of George Cushing Knapp,* born November 21, 1870, in Bitlis, Turkey. Knapp graduated from Mount Holyoke College. She was a missionary in Turkey under the Women's Board of Missions of the Congregational Church from 1893 to 1902 and from 1910 to 1915. She wrote *The Mission at Van* (New York, 1915), co-authored *An American Physician in Turkey, a Narrative of Adventures in Peace and War* (Boston, 1917), and wrote *The Tragedy of Bitlis* (New York, 1919). She served with Near East Relief* in New York from 1918 to 1922, and was on the editorial staff of the American Board of Commissioners for Foreign Missions (ABCFM)* from 1922 to 1940 as managing editor of *The Missionary Herald at Home and Abroad*. Died March 14, 1953, in Newton, Massachusetts. *References*: *Mount Holyoke*; *WWWA*.

KNIGHT, EDGAR WALLACE (1886–1953). Educator, born April 9, 1886, in Northampton County, North Carolina. Knight graduated from Trinity College and Columbia University. From 1913 to 1916 he was assistant professor and professor of education at Trinity College, and from 1919 until his death, professor of education at the University of North Carolina. He was a member of the research staff of the Layman's Foreign Missions' inquiry on education to China in 1930–1931, and a member of the educational commission to Iraq in 1931–1932 which helped prepare the public school system for Iraq. Died August 7, 1953, in Chapel Hill, North Carolina. *References*: *BDAE*; *NCAB* 40:77; and *NYT* August 8, 1953.

KNOX, THOMAS WALLACE (1835–1896). Traveler and journalist, born June 26, 1835, in Pembroke, New Hampshire. Knox was war correspondent during the Civil War. He traveled in the Middle East in 1873–1874 and again in 1878, and wrote *Backsheesh! or Life and Adventures in the Orient* (Hartford, Conn., 1875), and *The Boy Travellers in the Far East; Part Fourth, Adventures of Two Youth in a Journey to Egypt and the Holy Land* (New York, 1883). Died January 6, 1896, in New York City. *References*: *ACAB*; *DAB*; *NCAB* 7:89; and *WWWA*.

KOELZ, WALTER NORMAN (1895–   ). Zoologist and botanist, born September 11, 1895, in Waterloo, Michigan. Koelz graduated from Olivet College and the University of Michigan. In 1919 he became curator of fishes at the Museum of Zoology of the University of Michigan and worked for the U.S. Bureau of Fisheries from 1919 to 1927 and again in 1930. In 1925 he was naturalist with the Macmillan Arctic expedition; from 1930 to 1932 a biologist for the Himalayan Research Institute of the Roerich Museum in Kulu, India; and in 1932–1933 a collector of Indian and Tibetan materials for the Museum of Anthropology and Natural History. From 1936 to 1941 and from 1947 to 1949, he was plant explorer for the Department of Agriculture, and from 1939 to 1941, he explored Afghanistan and Iran. His record of this trip was published as *Persian Diary, 1939–1941* (Ann Arbor, Mich., 1983). *Reference*: AMWS.

KOLLEL AMERICA TIFERETH YERUSHALAYIM, JERUSALEM. [The American Congregation, The Pride of Jerusalem]. Founded in 1897 by a group of American Jewish immigrants living in Jerusalem who received financial aid from their fellow countrymen. The importance of the group decreased continuously after World War I, and it continued for a time as a charitable society. *References*: Papers, Jewish Theological Seminary Library; Simcha Fishbane, "The Founding of Kollel America Tifereth Yerushalayim," *American Jewish Historical Quarterly* 64 (1974): 120–136.

KOSZTA AFFAIR. The Hungarian revolutionary Martin Koszta fled to the United States following the unsuccessful Hungarian Revolution of 1848, and took out first citizenship papers. He came to Smyrna in 1853, was kidnapped by the Austrians and was held a prisoner in an Austrian naval vessel in Smyrna harbor. Duncan Daniel Ingraham,* in command of the U.S.S. *St Louis*, with the support of John Porter Brown,* chargé d'affaires in Constantinople, presented an ultimatum to the Austrians and forced them to surrender Koszta to the French consul general in Smyrna, who later released him. *References*: *Dictionary of American History*, rev. ed. (New York, 1976), 4:57; Andor Klay, *Daring Diplomacy: The Case of the First American Ultimatum* (Minneapolis, 1957).

KRAELING, CARL H(ERMAN) (1897–1966). Educator and archaeologist, born March 10, 1897, in Brooklyn, New York. Kraeling graduated from Columbia University, Lutheran Theological Seminary (Philadelphia), and the universities of Pennsylvania and Heidelberg, and was ordained in 1920. He was fellow, instructor, and assistant professor at Lutheran Theological Seminary from 1920 to 1928; assistant and associate professor and professor of New Testament criticism and interpretation at Yale Divinity School from 1929 to 1950; and professor of Oriental archaeology at the University of Chicago from 1950 to 1962. He was also director of the Oriental Institute from 1950 to 1960; annual professor at the American Schools of Oriental Research (ASOR)* in Jerusalem in 1934–1935; and president of the ASOR from 1948 to 1954. He directed the Yale University-British School of Archaeology in Jerusalem expedition to Gerasa (Jerash), Jordan from 1928 to 1930; studied the synagogue at Dura-Europos; and directed the excavations in Ptolemais in the Cyrenaica. Kraeling co-authored and edited *Gerasa, City of the Decapolis* (New Haven, Conn., 1938), wrote *Excavations at Dura Europos VIII. The Synagogue* (New Haven, Conn., 1956), and co-authored *Ptolemais, City of the Libyan Pentapolis* (Chicago, 1962). Died November 14, 1966, in New Haven, Connecticut. *References*: BASOR 198 (1970): 4–7; *NYT*, November 15, 1966; and *WWWA*.

KRAMER, SAMUEL NOAH (1897–). Sumerologist, born September 28, 1897, in Russia and came to the United States in 1906. Kramer graduated from Temple and Dropsie colleges and the University of Pennsylvania. He was a member of the University of Pennsylvania expeditions to Billah, Tepe Gawra, and also Fara in Iraq in 1930–1931. He was on the staff of the Oriental Institute, University of Chicago, from 1932 to 1942; was research associate, associate curator, and curator of the Babylonian collection at the University Museum; and was professor of Assyriology from 1948 until his retirement in 1968. He was annual professor at the American Schools of Oriental Research (ASOR)* in Baghdad in 1946–1947, studied in Istanbul in 1951–1952, and wrote *A "Fulbright" in Turkey* (Philadelphia, 1952), an account of his research there. He wrote *In the World of Sumer: An Autobiography* (Detroit, 1986). *References*: *CA*; *DAS*; *EJ*; *MENA*; and *WWA*.

KRUM, JOHN HARRY (1866–1949). Missionary, born November 18, 1866, in Reamstown, Lancaster County, Pennsylvania. Krum graduated from Union College (Lincoln, Neb.) and Baltimore Medical College. In 1898 he went to Palestine as a Seventh Day Adventist missionary and opened a mission in Jaffa, opened a medical clinic in Jerusalem in 1901, and traveled in Asia Minor in 1902. He returned to the United States in 1904 and served as a pastor in Oklahoma, Texas, Arkansas, Tennessee, and Florida. Died November 4, 1949, in Smyrna Beach, Florida. *Reference*: *Seventh Day Adventists Encyclopedia* (Washington, D.C., 1976).

KUWAIT OIL COMPANY. Incorporated in 1934 to hold exclusive oil exploration and production rights within the Sheikhdom of Kuwait. The company was originally owned equally by Gulf Exploration Company (a subsidiary of Gulf Oil Corporation) and D'Arcy Exploration Company (a subsidiary of Anglo-American Oil Company). Oil was struck in 1938, and shipment began in 1946. In 1975 the Kuwaiti government acquired 100 percent of the company's properties. *References*: *IPE*; *Survey*.

KYLE, MELVIN GROVE (1858–1933). Archaeologist and educator, born May 7, 1858, near Cadiz, Ohio. Kyle graduated from Muskingum College and Allegheny Theological Seminary. He was a lecturer on Biblical theology and archaeology at Xenia Theological Seminary (now Pittsburg Theological Seminary) from 1908 until 1915, professor of Biblical theology and archaeology from 1915, and president from 1922 until 1930. He was annual professor at the American Schools of Oriental Research (ASOR)* in Jerusalem in 1921, conducted an expedition into the land of Moab, east of the Jordan River, and made an exploration of Sodom and Gomorrah in 1924, and of Kirjath Sefer, Palestine, from 1926 to 1928. He wrote *Excavating Kirjath-Sepher's Ten Cities* (Grand

Rapids, Mich., 1934), and *Explorations at Sodom: The Story of Ancient Sodom in the Light of Modern Research* (New York, 1928), letters of the expedition organized by Xenia Theological Seminary and ASOR. Died May 25, 1933, in Pittsburgh. *References*: *OAB*; *NYT*, May 26, 1933; and *WWWA*.

L

LABAREE, BENJAMIN (1834–1906). Missionary, born March 21, 1834, in Columbia, Tennessee. Labaree graduated from Middlebury College and Andover Theological Seminary, studied at Harvard Medical School, and was ordained in 1860. He became a missionary under the American Board of Commissioners for Foreign Missions (ABCFM)* to the Nestorians in Persia in 1860, and was stationed in Seir from 1860 to 1862 and in Urmia from 1862 until 1906. He was superintendent of the mission press, translated the Gospels into Azerbaijan Turkish, and edited a revision of the Bible in modern Syriac. Died May 14, 1906, at sea on the way to the United States. His son, **BENJAMIN W(OODS) LABAREE (1871–1904)**, missionary, was born March 21, 1871, in Newcastle, Indiana. He became a missionary under the Presbyterian Church in the USA Board of Foreign Missions* in Persia in 1893. He was murdered by Kurds near Mount Ararat in northwestern Persia, on March 9, 1904. His death caused the first incident of consequence between the United States and Persia in which the consul William F. Doty,* played a major role. *References*: *AndoverTS*; *NYT*, May 19, 1906; *WWWA*; and Abraham Yeselson, *United States-Persian Diplomatic Relations 1883–1921* (New Brunswick, N.J., 1956), ch. 3.

LADD, DANIEL (1804–1872). Missionary, born January 22, 1804, in Unity, New Hampshire. Ladd graduated from Middlebury College and Andover Theological seminary, and was ordained in 1836. He served as a missionary under the American Board of Commissioners for Foreign Missions (ABCFM)* in Cyprus from 1836 to 1842, when the mission in Cyprus was discontinued. He served in Brusa, Turkey, from 1841 to 1850, in Smyrna from 1850 to 1865, and in Constantinople from 1865 to 1867, when he returned to the United States. Died October 11, 1872, in Middlebury, New Hampshire. *References*: *AndoverTS*; *EM*.

LAING, FREDERIC WILLIAMS (1906–1959). Naval officer, born December 10, 1906, in Savannah, Georgia. Laing graduated from the U.S. Naval Academy in 1930, was involved in the salvage operations of the submarine *Squalos*, and served in World War II as a navigator in a submarine, aboard submarine rescue vessels, and as assistant operations officer of a submarine task force. He was associate professor of naval science at Brown University from 1948 to 1950, and later commander of Brown University's training unit. In 1956 he was the commander of Transport Amphibious Squadron Six and the task force that went to Alexandria, Egypt, to rescue Americans during the Suez War. Died July 14, 1959, in New York City. *References*: Thomas A. Bryson, *Tars, Turks, and Tankers: The Role of the United States Navy in the Middle East, 1800–1979* (Metuchen, N.J., 1980), ch. 6; *NYT*, July 15, 1959.

LAKE, KIRSOPP (1872–1946). New Testament scholar, born April 7, 1872, in Southampton, England. Lake was educated at Lincoln College, Oxford, and St. Andrew University, and was ordained in 1896. He was a cataloguer of Greek manuscripts at the Bodleian Library from 1897 to 1900, curate in Oxford from 1897 to 1904, and professor of early Christian literature and New Testament exegesis at the University of Leyden, Holland, from 1904 to 1913. He came to the United States in 1913, was professor of early Christian literature at Harvard Divinity School from 1913 to 1919, lecturer in New Testament at Union Theological Seminary from 1915 to 1919, and professor of ecclesiastical history at Harvard University until 1932. He visited libraries in the Middle East to investigate Greek manuscripts, was director of the archaeological expedition to the Sinai Peninsula investigating the inscriptions at Serabit el-Khadem in 1927, and director of the archaeological expedition to Samaria, Palestine, from 1932 to 1934, and to Lake Van, Turkey, in 1938–39. Died November 10, 1946, in Haverford, Pennsylvania. *References*: *DAB S4*; *DNB*; *NYT*, November 12, 1946; and *WWWA*.

LAMB, JOHN (fl. 1785–1797). Sea captain from Norwich, Connecticut. Lamb was sent to Europe in 1785 by Congress and was appointed agent to Algiers. He went to Algiers in 1786 on a mission to ransom the American hostages in Algiers. (See Hostages in Barbary States). He reached an agreement with the Dey of Algiers but Congress could not raise the required amount. He returned to the United States in 1787. *Reference*: Frank E. Ross, "The Mission of John Lamb to Algiers, 1795–97," *Americana* 28 (July 1934): 287–294.

LAMBERG-KARLOVSKY, CLIFFORD CHARLES (1937–   ). Anthropologist and archaeologist, born October 2, 1937, in Prague, Czechoslovakia, and came to the United States in 1939. Lamberg-Karlovsky graduated from Dartmouth College and the University of Pennsylvania. He was assistant professor of anthropology at Harvard University from 1965 and 1969, became professor and curator of Near Eastern archaeology at the Peabody Museum of

Archaeology and Ethnology in 1969, and director of the museum in 1977. He was director of archaeological surveys in Syria in 1965; and director of the Peabody Museum expedition to Tepe Yahya, Iran, from 1967 to 1975 and of an archaeological survey in Saudi Arabia from 1977 to 1980. He wrote *Excavations at Tepe Yahya, Iran* (Cambridge, Mass., 1970). *References*: *AMWS*; *CA*; and *WWA*.

LAMBERT, ROSE (1878–1974). Missionary nurse, born in Vera Cruz, Pennsylvania. Lambert graduated from Deaconess Hospital in Cleveland. She served as missionary under the United Missionary Church* and from 1899 until 1910 was stationed in Hadjin, Turkey, where she established an orphanage. She returned to the United States in 1910, wrote *Hadjin and the Armenian Massacre* (New York, 1911), and later lived in Texas. *References*: Mary L. Hammack, *A Dictionary of Women in Church History* (Chicago, 1984).

LAMBIE, THOMAS ALEXANDER (1885–1954). Medical missionary, born in Pittsburgh. Lambie graduated from the University of Pennsylvania and Western Pennsylvania Medical College. He served as a missionary under the United Presbyterian Church of North America Board of Foreign Missions in the Sudan, first at Dolieb Hill, at the confluence of the Sobat and the White Nile rivers, and later in Khartoum, at the upper Sobat River and at Nasir. In 1919 he was transferred to Ethiopia and built George Memorial Hospital in Addis Ababa, becoming its director. During the war with Italy, he was the executive secretary of the Ethiopian Red Cross and physician to Emperor Haile Selassie. After the Italian conquest Lambie returned to the Sudan. He went to Palestine in 1946 under the Independent Board of Presbyterian Foreign Missions, built Berachah Tuberculosis Sanatorium in Ain Arrub, near Bethlehem, and was also one of the custodians of the Garden Tomb in Jerusalem. He wrote several books of memoirs, *A Doctor Without a Country* (New York, 1939), *A Doctor Carries on* (New York, 1942), *Boot and Saddle in Africa* (Philadelphia, 1943) and *A Doctor's Great Commission* (Wheaton, Ill., 1954), which was published after his death. Died April 14, 1954, in Ain Arrub, Jordan. *References*: Dorothy Haskin, *Medical Missionaries You Would Like to Know* (Grand Rapids, Mich., 1957), pp. 66–73; *NYT*, April 17, 1954.

LAMSON, ROBERT S(CHUYLER) (?–1876). Mining engineer. Lamson served in the Egyptian Army from 1875 until 1876 and was a member of the staff of the commander of the Egyptian Army which was defeated by the Abyssinians at Gura in March 1876. He was then sent on a mission to Darfur in the Sudan. Died in November 1876 near al-Fashar in the Sudan. *References*: *Hesseltine*; *Hill*.

LANCE, H(UBERT) DARRELL (1935–   ). Archaeologist, born June 8, 1935, in Indianapolis. Lance graduated from Wabash College, Colgate Rochester Divinity School, and Harvard University, and was ordained in 1961. He joined the faculty of Colgate Rochester/ Bexley/ Crozer Theological Seminary in 1965 and became professor of Old Testament in 1975. He was associate director of the Hebrew Union College Biblical and Archaeological School and Harvard University's excavations at Tell Gezer from 1966 to 1971. In 1973–1974 he was professor at the Albright Institute of Archaeology in Jerusalem. He co-authored *Gezer I–II* (Jerusalem, 1970–1974), co-edited *A Manual of Field Excavation: A Manual for Field Archaeologists* (Cincinnati, 1978), and wrote *The Old Testament and the Archaeologist* (Philadelphia, 1981). *Reference*: *DAS*.

LANDIS, JAMES MCCAULEY (1899–1964). Lawyer and federal administrator, born September 25, 1899, in Tokyo, Japan, to American parents, and came to the United States at thirteen. Landis graduated from Princeton University and Harvard University Law School. He joined Harvard's law faculty in 1926 and became dean of the Harvard Law School in 1937. He served on the Federal Trade Commission in 1933, became a member of the Securities and Exchange Commission in 1934, and was its chairman from 1934 to 1937. From 1941 to 1943 he was director of the Office of Civilian Defense, and in 1943 he became minister for economic affairs to the Middle East, director of economic operations in the Middle East, and principal American civilian representative to the Middle East Supply Centre* with personal rank of minister. He also represented the Lend-Lease Administration and the Board of Economic Warfare. He returned to the United States in 1945. In 1946–1947 Landis was chairman of the Civil Aeronautics Board and began to practice law in 1949. Drowned July 30, 1964, in Harrison, New York. *References*: Papers, Library of Congress; *DAB S7*; *NCAB* F:402; *NYT*, November 1, 1968; *PolProf: Truman*; *PolProf: Kennedy*; and Donald A. Ritchie, *James M. Landis: Dean of the Regulators* (Cambridge, Mass., 1980).

LANE, JAMES CRANDALL (1823–1888). Engineer, born July 23, 1823, in New York City. Lane was employed in railroad construction until 1852, served in the U.S. Coast Survey from 1852 to 1856, commanding expeditions to New Grenada and Nicaragua, and was engaged in a private survey in the Caribbean Islands from 1857 to 1860. He served in the Civil War, was later engaged in minerological surveys in California and the Southwest, and was chief engineer for the South Side Railroad of Long Island from 1870 to 1875. In 1875–1876 he was chief of the American Palestine Exploration Society's* archaeological survey of the area east of the River Jordan. After his return, he was chief engineer for several railroads and in 1884 began to survey new parks in New York. Died December 12, 1888, in New York City. *Reference*: *NCAB* 4:294.

LANE, ROSE WILDER (1886–1968). Journalist and author, born December 5, 1886, in De Smet, South Dakota. Lane was a telegrapher for Western Union Telegraph Company, real estate agent in California from 1910 to 1913, and reporter for the *San Francisco Bulletin* from 1914 to 1918. From 1918 to 1921 she worked for the Red Cross in Europe and the Middle East and for Near East Relief.* She traveled again in the Middle East in 1924, driving a car across the Syrian desert from Damascus to Baghdad. Her journal appeared in the *Atlantic Monthly* from September to November 1925. She was a freelance writer and editor of the Economic Council *Review of Books* from 1945 to 1950. Died October 30, 1968, in Danbury, Connecticut. *Rose Wilder Lane: Her Story* (New York, 1977) by Roger L. MacBride is a fictional autobiography based on her letters and diaries. *References*: Papers, Herbert Hoover Presidential Library, West Branch, Iowa; *CA*; William Holtz, "The Little House on - the Desert," *AWM* 35 (November-December 1984): 28–33; *NAW*; *NCAB* 54:522; *NYT*, November 1, 1968; and *WWWA*.

LANGDON, STEPHEN HERBERT (1876–1937). Assyriologist and archaeologist, born May 8, 1876, in Ida, Michigan. Langdon graduated from the University of Michigan, Union Theological Seminary, and Columbia University. He also studied at the universities of Paris, Berlin, and Leipzig. He was reader in Assyriology and Semitic philology at the University of Oxford from 1908 to 1918 and became professor of Assyriology in 1918. He was director of the Oxford University and the Field Museum expedition in Mesopotamia from 1923 to 1932 and directed the excavations at Kish in 1923 and 1925. He was co-author of *Excavations at Kish* (Paris, 1924–1934). Died May 19, 1937, in Oxford, England. *References*: *DNB*; *NYT*, May 20, 1937; and *WWWA*.

LANSING, AMBROSE (1891–1959). Egyptologist and museum curator, born September 20, 1891, in Cairo, son of Elmer Ellsworth Lansing (see Gulian Lansing). Lansing came to the United States in 1904, and graduated from Washington and Jefferson College and the University of Leipzig. He began working in the Metropolitan Museum of Art in 1911 and finally rose to curator in 1939. He participated in fieldwork in Egypt between 1911 and 1922 and was connected with many projects, particularly the work at the Malkata palace of Amenhotep III. Died May 28, 1959, near Apache Junction, Arizona. *References*: *NYT*, May 29, 1959; *WWWA*; and *WWWE*.

LANSING, GULIAN (1825–1892). Missionary, born February 1, 1825, at Lishaskill, Albany county, New York. Lansing graduated from Union College and the Associated Reformed Church Seminary (Newburgh, N.Y.), and was ordained in 1850. In 1850 the Associate Reformed Church sent him to Damascus to serve as a missionary in the mission to the Jews. He moved to Egypt in 1856 and remained there for the rest of his life, first in Alexandria and, after 1860, in Cairo. He was involved with the United Presbyterian mission to the Copts, became leader of the American Mission,* established several missionary stations, and conducted many journeys on the Nile which he described in his book *Egypt's Princes: A Narrative of Missionary Labour in the Valley of the Nile* (New York, 1864). He was married to a missionary, Sarah B. Dales.* He also taught at the mission's theological school. Died September 12, 1892, in Cairo. His son, **ELMER ELLSWORTH LANSING (1861–1893)**, a physician, was born August 16, 1861, in Cairo, came to the United States in 1873, and graduated from Albany Medical College. He was a medical missionary in Egypt from 1884 to 1888, practicing in Assiut. He left the mission in 1889 but continued to practice in Cairo. Died June 1, 1893, while returning to Cairo from a trip to Kusseir on the Red Sea. *References*: *DAB*; *WWWA*; and *WWWE*.

LAPP, PAUL W(ILBERT) (1930–1970). Archaeologist, born August 5, 1930, in Sacramento, California. Lapp graduated from California Concordia College (Oakland, Calif.), Concordia Seminary, Washington University, and the University of California at Berkeley. He taught at American University (Washington, D.C.), was annual professor at the American Schools of Oriental Research (ASOR)* in Jerusalem in 1960–1961, director of the ASOR from 1961 to 1965, and professor of ancient Near Eastern history and archaeology from 1965 to 1968. In 1957 he began fieldwork in Tell Balatah, Jordan. He directed excavations at 'Araq el-Emir in 1961–1962, Ta'anach from 1963 to 1968, Tell er-Rumeith in 1967, and Bab edh-Dhra' from 1965 to 1967, as well as in Dhahr Mirzbaneh, Wadi ed-Daliyeh, Tell el-Ful, and Tell Ta'annek in Jordan. He wrote *The Dhar Mirzb'aneh Tombs; Three Bronze Age Cemeteries in Jordan* (New Haven, Conn., 1966) and *Biblical Archaeology and History* (New York, 1969). In 1968 he became a professor at Pittsburgh Theological Seminary. Drowned April 26, 1970, off Cyprus. Lapp wrote *Arabic for the Beginner in Archaeology* (Pittsburgh, 1971), and edited *Discoveries in the Wadi ed-Daliyeh* (Cambridge, Mass., 1974), and *The Tale of the Tell: Archaeological Studies* (Pittsburgh, 1975), which were edited by his wife and published after his death. *References*: *BASOR* 199 (1970): 2–4; *Harvard Theological Review* 64 (1971): 129–134.

LAURIE, THOMAS (1821–1897). Missionary, born May 19, 1821, in Craigleith, Scotland, and came to the United States in 1830 with his parents who settled near Jacksonville, Illinois. Laurie graduated from Illinois College and Andover Theological Seminary, and was ordained in 1842. He served as a missionary under the American Board of Commissioners for Foreign Missions (ABCFM)* in Persia—to the Nestorians from 1842 to 1844, and to the Syrians from 1844 to 1846. He returned to the United States in 1846 because of impaired health. He was pastor at Charleston, South Hadley, West Roxbury, and Arlington, Massachusetts, and Providence, Rhode Island, until his retirement in 1885. He wrote *Dr. Grant and the Mountain Nestorians* (Boston, 1853), *Woman and Her Saviour in Persia* (Boston, 1863), *The Ely Volume; or the Contributions of*

Our Foreign Missions to Science and Human Well-being (Boston, 1881), and *Assyrian Echoes of the Word* (New York, 1894). Died October 10, 1897, in Providence, Rhode Island. *Reference*: AndoverTS.

LAY, JOHN LOUIS (1832–1899). Inventor, born January 14, 1832, in Buffalo, New York. Lay was commissioned second assistant engineer in the U.S. Navy in 1862 and served in the Civil War. From 1865 to 1867 he worked as a naval engineer for the Peruvian government. He invented an automatic torpedo suspension mine and a self-propelled submarine torpedo which was adopted by the U.S. Navy. He served in the Egyptian Army from 1871 to 1874, surveying the Egyptian coast to prepare coastal defenses, surveying the Nile from Cairo to its mouth, and experimenting with torpedo-mines at Aboukir Bay. He sold the right to his torpedoes to the Russian and Turkish governments and resided in Europe after 1870. He lost his fortune and returned to the United States in 1897. Died April 17, 1899, in New York City. *References*: Frederick J. Cox, "The American Naval Mission to Egypt," *Journal of Modern History* 26 (1954): 173–178; "Colonel John Lay's Naval Mission in Egypt," *Cahiers d'Histoire Egyptienne* 5 (1953): 36–46; *DAB*; *NCAB* 7:528; *NYT*, April 21, 1899; and *WWWA*.

LEAR, TOBIAS (1762–1816). Consular official, born September 19, 1762, in Portsmouth, New Hampshire. Lear graduated from Harvard College, traveled and studied in Europe, was George Washington's private secretary and tutor to his children from 1786 to 1792, president of the Potomac Canal Company, and military secretary to George Washington in 1798–1799. He was consul in Santo Domingo in 1801–1802 and consul general in Algiers from 1803 to 1812. In 1805 he signed an accord with the Pasha of Tripoli agreeing to ransom the American hostages. He was forced to leave Algiers in 1812, after which he became an accountant in the War Department. Committed suicide October 11, 1816, in Washington, D.C. *References*: Papers, New York Historical Society; Ray Brighton, *The Checkered Career of Tobias Lear* (Portsmouth, N.H., 1985); *DAB*; *DADH*; *NCAB* 13:466; and *WWWA*.

LEARY, LEWIS GASTON (1877–1951). Clergyman, born August 3, 1877, in Elizabeth, New Jersey. Leary graduated from Rutgers and New York universities, Union and McCormick theological seminaries, and was ordained in 1900. He was an instructor at the Syrian Protestant College from 1900 to 1903, and later a pastor in Blauvelt and Pelham Manor, New York, and West Milford, New Jersey. He wrote *The Real Palestine of To-day* (Philadelphia, 1911) and *Syria: the Land of Lebanon* (New York, 1913). In 1921–1922 he was professor of biblical literature at Vassar College. Died May 27, 1951, in Paterson, New Jersey. *References*: *NYT*, May 28, 1951; *UnionTS*; and *WWWA*.

LEAVITT, LESLIE W(ESTBROOK) (1895–   ). Educator, born July 29, 1895, in Moreno, California. Leavitt graduated from Dartmouth College, Union Theological Seminary, and Columbia University Teachers college. He was an instructor at the Syrian Protestant College from 1916 to 1919 and served in the Syria Mission* from 1922 to 1926 as principal of the boys' school in Tripoli. He was associate principal of International College, Beirut, from 1928 to 1934, and principal from 1934 until his retirement in 1960. He wrote his memoirs, *With Youth on Phoenician Shores* (Wellesley, Mass., 1968). *Reference*: *UnionTS*.

LEBANON, MARINES IN (1958). In July 1958, Camille Chamoun, president of Lebanon, appealed to the United States for military forces to help maintain order in Lebanon. In the only application of the Eisenhower doctrine,* some 8500 U.S. Marines landed in Beirut on July 15 and 16, 1958, to assist the Lebanese government in preserving its sovereignty and integrity and to help restore peace. They left Lebanon by October 25, 1958. *References*: Robert McClintock, *The Meaning of Limited War* (Boston, 1967), ch. 7. Jack Shulimson, *Marines in Lebanon 1958* (Washington, D.C., 1966). Roger J. Spiller, *"Not War But Like War": The American Intervention in Lebanon* (Fort Leavenworth, Kan., 1981).

LEBANON, MARINES IN (1982–1984). On August 25, 1982, U.S. Marines landed in the Beirut port as part of the Multinational Force (MNF), with French and Italian forces, to oversee the evacuation from Beirut of members of the Palestine Liberation Organization (PLO). They left Beirut port on September 10. They returned to Beirut on September 27, following the massacres of Palestinians in the Sabra and Shatila refugee camps. Some 1300 marines were positioned near the Beirut International Airport "to establish a presence." On October 23, 1983 a suicide terrorist attack on the marine compound at the airport killed 241 marines. The United States carried out no reprisals for the bombing. The marines left Lebanon by February 27, 1984. *References*: Eric Hammel, *The Root: The Marines in Beirut August 1982 - February 1984* (New York, 1985). *NYT Magazine*, April 8, 1984.

LEDYARD, JOHN (1751–1789). Explorer, born November 1751 in Groton, Connecticut. Ledyard attended Dartmouth College but left to become a sailor in 1773–1774. He participated as a marine in the voyage of Captain Cook to the North Pacific from 1776 to 1780, and published his journal of the voyage in 1783. In 1787–1788 he embarked on a trip attempting to reach the northwest coast of America by way of Siberia but was arrested by the Russian authorities in Irkutsk and forced to turn back. After his return to London, the Association for Promoting the Discovery of the Interior Parts of Africa hired him to conduct an expedition to explore the Niger River. He arrived in Alexandria in 1788 and then moved to Cairo, becoming the first American traveler in Egypt. His Cairo journal was published in the *Proceedings of the African Association*. Died January 10, 1789, in Cairo. *References*: *Journey Through Siberia 1787–1788*, ed. Stephen W. Watrous (Madison, Wis., 1966); Helen Augur, *Passage to Glory: John Ledyard's America* (Garden City, N.Y., 1946); John Brinton, "Footsore and Fancy-free," *AWM* 31 (November–December 1980): 28–33; *DAB*; and *WWWA*.

LEE, JAMES WIDEMAN (1849–1919). Clergyman and editor, born November 28, 1849, in Rockbridge, Georgia. Lee graduated from Emory College, was ordained in 1874, and held pastorates in St. Louis and Atlanta. He edited *The Earthly Footprints of the Man from Galilee* (New York, 1894), containing photographs made in Palestine under his personal direction by Robert Edward Mather Bain* in 1894. He also wrote *The Romance of Palestine: A History for Young People Containing Over One Hundred and Fifty Original Photographs and Pen Pictures* (St. Louis, 1897) and was the editor of *The Self-Interpreting Bible* (St. Louis, 1895–1896). Died October 4, 1919, in St. Louis. *References*: *DAB*; *NCAB* 9:506; *NYT*, October 5, 1919; and *WWWA*.

LEIGHTON-FLOYD, MARY (CLARK) (1859–1934). Colonist, sister of Herbert Edgar Clarke,* born April 6, 1859, in Rochester, New York. Leighton-Floyd went to Palestine in 1866 with her family who were members of the American Colony* in Jaffa. She married Rolla Floyd* in 1900 and came to the United States in 1911 but later returned to Palestine and lived in Jaffa. Died October 18, 1934, in Jerusalem, the last member of the American Colony. Her son, **ALBERT W. LEIGHTON-FLOYD (1890–1954)**, a businessman, born in Jerusalem, was brought back to the United States in 1911 and lived in the Fort Peck Indian Reservation in Montana from 1914 to 1930. He returned to Palestine in 1930, built the first cinema in Jerusalem in 1931, and lived there until 1936 and again from 1939 until 1954. Died in Independence, Missouri. *Reference*: Ralph Leighton-Floyd, "Remembrances from Missouri of Mainer-founded Jaffa Colony," *Bangor Daily News*, December 29–30, 1973.

LEISHMAN, JOHN G. A. (1857–1924). Steel manufacturer and diplomat, born March 25, 1857, in Pittsburgh, Pennsylvania. Leishman grew up in an orphanage and was an office boy in an iron and steel work. He helped establish and became a senior member of an iron and steel brokerage firm from 1881 to 1886. In 1886 he became vice president of Carnegie Brothers and Company and president of Carnegie Steel Company. He was minister to Switzerland from 1897 to 1901 and minister to Turkey from 1901 until 1906. In 1906 he became the first ambassador to Turkey, serving until 1909. He was particularly concerned with the protection of American schools and property in Turkey. He was ambassador to Italy from 1909 to 1911 and ambassador to Germany from 1911 to 1913. Died March 27, 1924, in Pittsburgh. *References*: *DAB*; *DADH*; *NCAB* 13:598; *NYT*, March 28, 1924; and *WWWA*.

LELAND, CHARLES GODFREY (1824–1903). Author, born August 15, 1824, in Philadelphia. Leland graduated from Princeton University and studied at the universities of Heidelberg, Munich, and Paris. He practiced law in Philadelphia from 1849 until 1853 and then was editor of the *New York Times*, the Philadelphia *Evening Press*, *Vanity Fair*, the Philadelphia *Press*, the *Knickerbocker Magazine*, and the *Continental Magazine*. After 1869 he devoted his time mainly to writing and was a student of the occult and of gypsy lore. He lived in London from 1869 to 1880 and later again in London and in Florence. He went to Egypt in 1872 to visit the land from which the gypsies ostensibly originated and wrote *The Egyptian Sketch Book* (New York, 1874). In 1876 he visited Russia and in 1889 was chairman of the first European folklore congress in Paris. He wrote his *Memoirs* (New York, 1893). Died March 20, 1903, in Florence, Italy. *References*: Van Wyck Brooks, *Fenollosa and His Circle* (New York, 1962), pp. 217–247; *NCAB* 5:356; *NYT*, March 21, 1903; and *WWWA*.

LEONARD, J(OHN) PAUL (1901–   ). Educator, born December 2, 1901, in Lockwood, Missouri. Leonard graduated from Drury College (Springfield, Mo.) and Columbia University. He was associate professor and professor of education at William and Mary College from 1929 to 1937, associate professor and professor of education at Stanford University from 1937 to 1945, and president of San Francisco State College from 1945 to 1957. He was president of the American University of Beirut* from 1957 until 1961. During his term, the university adopted its first ten-year plan for development and established graduate programs. He was professor of education at the Institute of International Studies of Colombia University from 1961 to 1967, when he retired. *Reference*: *NYT*, July 2, 1957.

LEVY, JOSEPH M. (1901–1965). Reporter, born in New Brunswick, New Jersey. Levy was taken to Jerusalem as a child and grew up there. He graduated from the American University of Beirut,* was private and political secretary to Sir Ronald Storrs, governor of Jerusalem, and spent seven months with a bedouin tribe. He became foreign correspondent for the *New York Times* in 1928, with headquarters in Jerusalem; was later based in Cairo and traveled to Damascus, Baghdad, and Amman; was correspondent in North Africa during World War II; and was transferred to Ankara in 1943. He retired in 1947 and served as public relations counsel to the French embassy in Washington and as press spokesman for the House Judiciary Committee. Died April 19, 1965, in New York City. *References*: Papers, Israel State Archives; *NYT*, April 20, 1965.

LEWIS, EDWIN RUFUS (1839–1907). Physician, born April 2, 1839, in Madison, Indiana. Lewis graduated from Wabash College, Amherst College, and Union Theological Seminary, served in the Civil War, and later studied medicine in Cleveland and at the Harvard Medical School. He practiced medicine in Amherst in 1867–1868 and was ordained in 1870. He was professor of chemistry and geology at the Syrian Protestant College from 1871 to 1883, but was forced to resign because of his pro-Darwinian views, causing a student rebellion at the college. He practiced medicine in Wabash, Indiana, and was professor of chemistry and geology at Wabash College from 1883 to 1887. He practiced in Indianapolis from 1887 to 1896 and resided in Washington, D.C. from 1896 to 1906. Died January 31, 1907, in Indianapolis. *References*: *Amherst*; Nadia Farag, "The Lewis Affair and the Fortunes of *al-Muqtataf*," *Middle Eastern Studies* 8 (1972): 73–86; Donald M. Leavitt, "Darwinism in the Arab World: The Lewis Affair at the Syrian Protestant College," *MW* 71 (1981): 85–98; and *UnionTS*.

LEWIS, SAMUEL WINFIELD (1930–   ). Diplomat, born October 1, 1930, in Houston. Lewis graduated from Yale and Johns Hopkins universities, entered the diplomatic service in 1954, and served in Naples and Florence, Italy. He was senior staff member on the National Security Council and special assistant to the director general of the Foreign Service in 1970. From 1971 to 1974 he was deputy chief of mission and counselor in Kabul. From 1974 to 1977 he was deputy director of the policy planning staff at the State Department. He was ambassador to Israel from 1977 until 1985. He established close relations with Israeli political leaders, played an important role in the Israeli-Egyptian peace negotiations, and was involved in the negotiations about the implementation of the peace treaty. *References*: *DADH*; *NYT*, January 28, 1978; *MENA*; *WWA*; and *WWAP*.

LIBBEY, WILLIAM (1855–1927). Geologist, born March 27, 1855, in Jersey City, New Jersey. Libbey graduated from Princeton University. In 1880 he became assistant professor of physical geography and director of the Museum of Geology and Archaeology at Princeton, and was professor from 1883 until 1923. He participated in an expedition to Moscow in 1887, to Mount Saint Elias, Alaska, in 1888, to Hawaii in 1893, and to Greenland in 1894 and 1899. He traveled in the Middle East with Franklin Evans Hoskins* in 1902, and they wrote *The Jordan Valley and Petra* (New York, 1905). Died September 6, 1927, in Princeton, New Jersey. *References*: *BGSA* 39 (1928): 35–40; *NCAB* 10:401; and *WWWA*.

LIBERTY, U.S.S. (AGTR–5). An intelligence-gathering ship, commanded by Commander William McGonagle, which was attacked on June 8, 1967, during the six-day war, by Israeli aircraft and motor torpedo boats while cruising in international waters north of the Sinai Peninsula. Thirty-four Americans were killed. Israel claimed that her forces mistook the *Liberty* for an Egyptian ship, and paid compensation for the loss of life. *References*: Anthony Pearson, *Conspiracy of Silence: The Attack on the USS Liberty* (London, 1978); Richard K. Smith, "The Violation of the *Liberty*," *USNIP* 104 (June 1978): 62–70.

LIBYA, RAID ON. *See* Raid on Libya (1986).

LINDHEIM, IRMA LEVY (1886–1978). Zionist leader, born December 9, 1886, in New York City. Lindheim graduated from Columbia University and the Jewish Institute of Religion, and served as ambulance driver in World War I. She visited Palestine in 1925 and wrote an account of her travels in *The Immortal Adventure* (New York, 1928), was national president of Hadassah,* and vice president of the Zionist Organization of America from 1926 to 1928. Although she settled in kibbutz Mishmar Ha-'emek in Palestine in 1933, she divided her time between Palestine (and later Israel) and the United States. She helped organize the League of Labor in Palestine. Lindheim wrote an autobiography, *Parallel Quest: A Search of a Person and a People* (New York, 1962). Died April 10, 1978, in Berkeley, California. *References*: *CA*; *EJ*; and *NYT*, April 11, 1978.

LINDSEY, ROBERT L(ISLE) (1917–   ). Missionary, born August 16, 1917, in Norman, Oklahoma. Lindsey graduated from the University of Oklahoma, Princeton Theological Seminary, and Southern Baptist Theological Seminary. He visited Palestine in 1939–1940 as a member of the Palestine Biblical Institute and studied at Hebrew University. He returned as a missionary under the Southern Baptist Foreign Mission Board in 1944 and has been the Southern Baptist representative to Israel, stationed in Jerusalem. He translated the *Gospel of Mark* into Hebrew (Jerusalem, 1969).

LIVERMORE, HARRIET (1788–1868). Evangelist, born April 14, 1788, in Concord, New Hampshire. Livermore began to travel and preach in 1821. She went to Palestine in 1837 believing herself sent out by heaven on a special mission to Jerusalem. She conducted several additional pilgrimages, the last one from 1858 to 1862, when the Anglican Bishop of Jerusalem, tired of supporting her, convinced her to leave Jerusalem, and she returned to the United States. Died March 30, 1868, in Philadelphia. *References*: Elizabeth F. Hoxie, "Harriet Livermore: 'Vixen and Devotee'," *New England Quarterly* 18 (145): 39–50; *NAW*.

LOBDELL, HENRY (1827–1855). Medical missionary, born January 25, 1827, in Danbury, Connecticut. Lobdell graduated from Amherst College, Yale Medical School, and Auburn Theological Seminary, and was ordained in 1851. He was a missionary under the American Board of Commissioners for Foreign Missions (ABCFM)* in Mosul, Iraq, from 1852 until his death, and opened a dispensary there. In 1852 he journeyed to Sheikh Ali, the seat of the Yezidees, or devil worshipers and reported his observations. A journal of his journey was published in *The New York Tribune* in 1852. He also made a journey to Tabriz. Died March 25, 1855, in Mosul. *References*: *Memoir of the Rev. Henry Lobdell*,

M.D., *Late Missionary of the American Board in Mosul*, ed. by William S. Tyler (Boston, 1859); *AuburnTS*; and *EM*.

LOCKETT, SAMUEL HENRY (1837–1891). Soldier, born July 6, 1837, in Mecklenburg County, Virginia. Lockett graduated from the U.S. Military Academy in 1859, was commissioned second lieutenant in the Corps of Engineers, and was assistant professor in the U.S. Military Academy. He served in the Confederate Army in the Civil War, and was professor of mechanics and engineering at the State University of Louisiana from 1867 to 1873. He joined the Egyptian Army in 1875 as a colonel of engineers and became chief of the Topographical Bureau of the Egyptian Army. He was sent to Masawwa in the Sudan in order to make a topographical survey of the country inland of that town in preparation for the Egyptian campaign against Abyssinia, and was chief engineer of the Egyptian Army in the Egyptian-Abyssinian war of 1875–1876. In 1877 he directed the preparation of the great map of Africa by officers of the Egyptian General Staff. He resigned in 1877, returned to the United States in 1878, and became professor of engineering and mechanics at the University of Tennessee. He was principal construction engineer in the construction of the pedestal of the Statute of Liberty and was involved in the construction of water works and gas works. Lockett went to Chile in 1888 and then to Colombia. Died October 12, 1891, in Bogotá, Colombia. *References*: Papers, Southern Historical Collections, University of North Carolina; *Hill*; *Hesseltine*; and *RAGMA*, 1892.

LONGFELLOW, ERNEST WADSWORTH (1845–1921). Painter, son of Henry Wadsworth Longfellow, born November 23, 1845, in Cambridge, Massachusetts. Longfellow graduated from Lawrence Scientific School of Harvard University and studied art in Paris. In 1866 he opened a studio in Boston and spent his professional life there, making frequent visits to Europe. He visited Turkey and Egypt, made sketches there and wrote of his impressions in his memoirs, *Random Memories* (Boston, 1922). Died November 24, 1921, in Boston. *References*: *DAB*; *NCAB* 21:363; *NYT*, November 25, 1921; and *WWWA*.

LORING, CHARLES GREELY (1828–1902). Soldier and museum curator, born July 22, 1828, in Boston. Loring graduated from Harvard University and traveled abroad in the 1850s, visiting Egypt, Arabia, and Palestine. He served in the Civil War reaching the rank of brevetted major general of volunteers. He visited Egypt again in 1868–1869 and began the study of Egyptology. In 1876 he became curator of the Museum of Fine Arts in Boston and was its director from 1886 to 1902. He bequeathed his extensive Egyptological library to the museum. Died August 18, 1902, in Beverly, Massachusetts. *References*: *NCAB* 25:301; *WWWA*.

LORING, WILLIAM WING (1818–1886). Soldier, born December 4, 1818, in Wilmington, North Carolina, and grew up in Florida. Loring attended Georgetown College, studied law, was admitted to the bar, and served in the Florida legislature. He fought as a volunteer in the Seminole War and became a captain in the regular army. He served in the Mexican War and later in the Southwest and the West. In 1859 he traveled to Europe and the Middle East studying foreign armies. He served in the Confederate Army in the Civil War, and after the war was a petty banking consultant in New York City. He joined the Egyptian Army in 1869 and was appointed inspector general. In 1870 he assumed command of the Egyptian coast defenses. He was appointed second-in-command and chief of staff in the Egyptian campaign of 1875–1876 against Abyssinia and participated in the battle of Kaya-Khor. Loring left the Egyptian service in 1879 and returned to the United States. He wrote *A Confederate Soldier in Egypt* (New York, 1884). Died December 30, 1886, in New York City. *References*: *DAB*; *NCAB* 4:364; *NYT*, December 31, 1886; William L. Wessels, *Born to Be a Soldier: The Military Career of William Wing Loring of St. Augustine, Florida* (Fort Worth, Tex., 1971); and *WWWA*.

LOUD, GORDON (1900–1971). Archaeologist, born November 5, 1900, in Place du Sable, Michigan. Loud graduated from the Harvard School of Architecture and was field architect on the University of Michigan Fayum expedition in Egypt. In 1929 he became field architect for the Iraq expedition of the Oriental Institute. He later directed the excavations at Khorsabad in Iraq and at Megiddo in Palestine. He was co-author of *Khorsabad* (Chicago, 1936–1938) and *Megiddo* (Chicago, 1939–1948). He resigned from the Oriental Institute in 1946. Died March 3, 1971, in Washington, D.C. *References*: *The Oriental Institute Annual Report for 1970/71*.

LOVE, IRIS (CORNELIA) (1933–   ). Archaeologist and educator, born August 1, 1933, in New York City. Love graduated from Smith College and New York University and studied at the University of Florence. She was assistant professor of art history and archaeology at C. W. Post College of Long Island University in 1966–1967 and became research assistant professor in 1967. She was a staff member of the archaeological expedition to the Greek island of Samothrace from 1955 to 1966, and director of the archaeological expedition of Long Island University to Knidos in southwestern Turkey from 1967 to 1978. *References*: *CA*; *CB 1982*; C. T. Buckley, "Profiles: Iris Love," *Architectural Digest* 43 (August 1986); 90–97; and *WWAW*.

LOWDERMILK, WALTER CLAY (1888–1974). Irrigation engineer, born July 1, 1888, in Liberty, North Carolina. Lowdermilk graduated from Park College (Mo.) and the universities of Arizona and California. He was a Rhodes scholar at Oxford University and served in World War I in France in the Lumberjack division of the Corps of Engineers. He was employed by the U.S. Forest

Service from 1915 to 1917 and 1919 to 1922; was research professor of forestry at the American Union University in Nanking, China, 1922 to 1927; and project leader for the U.S. Forest Service's California Forest and Range Experiment Station, 1927 to 1933. From 1933 to 1947 he was associate chief, chief of research, and assistant chief of the Soil Conservation Service of the Department of Agriculture. In 1938–1939 he made a survey of land use, soil and water conservation, and flood control in North Africa and the Middle East. He was in Palestine, suggested a Jordan valley authority, and wrote *Palestine, Land of Promise* (New York, 1944). From 1942 to 1944 Lowdermilk worked for the Chinese government in Chunking. In 1948 he was consultant to the French colonial governments in Algeria, Morocco, and Tunisia. From 1955 to 1957 under the auspices of the Food and Agricultural Organization he developed a soil and water conservation program in Israel and the curriculum in agricultural engineering in the Israel Institute of Technology (later renamed the Lowdermilk School of Agricultural Engineering). He wrote a memoir, *Soil, Forest, and Water Conservation Reclamation in China, Israel, Africa, United States* (Berkeley, Calif., 1969). Died May 6, 1974, in Berkeley, California. *References*: Papers, American Heritage Center, University of Wyoming; *NCAB* 63:295; and *NYT*, May 9, 1974.

LOWELL, JOHN (1799–1836). Traveler, born May 11, 1799, in Boston. Lowell attended Harvard University and traveled to India in 1816–1817. He began a business career in Boston, but, after the death of his wife and two children in 1832, he set out on a voyage around the world. He arrived in Egypt in 1834, traveled to Nubia, and visited Meroe and Khartoum. He was the first American to collect both ancient and Graeco-Roman Egyptian antiquities which were sent to the United States (and given in 1875 to the Museum of Fine Arts, Boston). He embarked at Massawa for the coast of Arabia, but was shipwrecked in the Red Sea and reached Mocha. He again set out for India but became sick. Died March 4, 1836, in Bombay, India. *References*: *DAB*; Ferris Greenslet, *The Lowells and Their Seven Worlds* (Boston, 1946); *NCAB* 7:195; Nancy S. Newhouse, "From Rome to Khartoum: Gleyre, Lowell, and the Evidence of the Boston Watercolors and Drawings," in *Charles Gleyre 1806–1874* (New York, 1980), pp. 79–117; and *WWWE*.

LOWTHER, WILLIAM E(RNEST) (1879–1953). Missionary and clergyman, born January 19, 1879, in Cardington, Ohio. Lowther served as a missionary under the Methodist Episcopal Church in Ipoh, Federated Malay States from 1902 until 1906, and was pastor in Rosedale and South Bend, Wisconsin, from 1906 to 1911. He was the first American Methodist missionary in North Africa. He went to Algeria in 1910, and established the mission station in Oran in 1911. He left Algeria in 1914, served in the Nevada mission in Reno from 1914 to 1919, and held pastorates in Morgantown, West Virginia, Newark, New Jersey, Lincoln, Nebraska, Manchester, New Hampshire, Norwich, Connecticut, and

Essex, Massachusetts. Died July 21, 1953, in Essex, Massachusetts. *References*: Stefanie R. Lowther, *A Traveling Minister and His Family* (n.p., ca. 1962). *NYT*, July 23, 1953. *Salem Evening News*, July 22, 1953.

LUCKENBILL, DANIEL DAVID (1881–1927). Assyriologist, born June 21, 1881, near Hamburg, Pennsylvania. Luckenbill graduated from the universities of Pennsylvania and Chicago and studied at the University of Berlin. He was instructor, assistant professor, and associate professor at the University of Chicago from 1909 to 1923 and became professor of Semitic languages and literatures in 1923. He was also curator of the Assyrian collections in the Haskell Oriental Museum. He was annual professor at the American Schools of Oriental Research (ASOR)* in 1908–1909, and excavated in Palestine in that year. He was a member of the American Scientific Expedition to the Middle East in 1919–1920. Died June 5, 1927, in London. *References*: *NCAB* 21:224; *WWWA*.

LUTHERAN ORIENT MISSION. Also known as the Kurdish Mission, founded in 1910, when Kurdistan was awarded as a missionary field to American Lutherans in the World Missionary Conference in 1910. The first mission was established in Soujbulak, Iraq, in 1911. The mission was abandoned in World War I but returned to Soujbulak in 1921 for a short time. It resumed work again in 1924, but the Iranian government forced it to leave. It relocated in Arbil, Iraq, in 1938 and left in 1958. *References*: *EMCM*; C.A.A. Jensen, "Lutheran Orient Mission," in Andrew S. Burgess, ed., *Lutheran World Mission: Foreign Missions of the Lutheran Church in America* (Minneapolis, 1954), pp. 224–227.

LYNCH, WILLIAM FRANCIS (1801–1865). Naval officer, born April 1, 1801, in Norfolk, Virginia. Lynch was appointed a midshipman in the navy in 1819, and served in various stations and in the Mexican War. He headed the expedition to the River Jordan and the Dead Sea* in 1848. He launched metal boats which he brought with him in the Lake of Galilee, descended the Jordan River, and made a voyage around the coast of the Dead Sea, surveying it. Lynch also explored parts of Palestine and Syria. He wrote the *Narrative of the United States Expedition to the River Jordan and the Dead Sea* (Philadelphia, 1849) and the *Official Report of the United States Expedition to the River Jordan and the Dead Sea* (Philadelphia, 1849). He also wrote *Naval Life; or, Observations Afloat and on Shore* (New York, 1851) which is partly autobiographical. He served in the Confederate Navy during the Civil War. Died October 17, 1865, in Baltimore. *References*: Yehoshua Ben-Arieh, "William F. Lynch's Expedition to the Dead Sea, 1847–8," *Prologue* 5 (Spring 1973): 15–21; *DAB*; and *NCAB* 13:172.

LYON, DAVID GORDON (1852–1935). Orientalist, born May 24, 1852, in Benton, Alabama. Lyon graduated from Howard College (Ala.), Southern Baptist Theological Seminary (Louisville, Ky.), and the University of Leipzig. He inaugurated the teaching of Assyriology in the United States at Harvard University in 1882–1883, was professor of divinity at Harvard University from 1882 to 1910, and professor of Hebrew and other Oriental languages from 1910 to 1922. He was also the founder of the Semitic Museum and its director from 1891 to 1922. He made visits to Palestine in 1902, in 1906–1907 as director of the American Schools of Oriental Research (ASOR),* and in 1908 as joint director of the excavations at Samaria. He was co-author of *Harvard Excavations at Samaria, 1908–10* (Cambridge, Mass., 1924). Died December 4, 1935, in Cambridge, Massachusetts. *References*: "Journal." Ms., Harvard University Archives; *DAB S1*; *NYT*, December 5, 1935; and *WWWA*.

LYTHGOE, ALBERT MORTON (1868–1934). Egyptologist, born March 15, 1868, in Providence, Rhode Island. Lythgoe graduated from Harvard College and studied at the American School of Classical Studies at Athens and the University of Bonn. From 1899 to 1904 he excavated in Egypt as a member of the Hearst Egyptian Expedition of the University of California. He became instructor in Egyptology in Harvard in 1898 and curator of the Egyptian Department at the Boston Museum of Fine Arts in 1904. In 1904–1905 he organized the Joint Harvard-Boston Museum Egyptian expedition, and in 1905 he excavated at the Pyramids at Gizeh. From 1906 until his retirement in 1926 he was curator of the Egyptian Department at the Metropolitan Museum of Art, organized and directed the Egyptian expeditions of the museum, and conducted excavations at Lisht, Thebes, Kargeh Oasis, and other sites. He was present at the opening of the inner chamber of the tomb of Tutankhamen and of his sarcophagus in 1923. Lythgoe co-authored *The Early Dynastic Cemeteries of Naga-ed-D'er* (Leipzig, 1908) and *The Tomb of Perneb* (New York, 1916). Died January 29, 1934, in Boston. *References*: *BMMA* 29 (1934): 42–43; *NYT*, January 30, 1934; and *WWWE*.

M

MACCORMACK, DANIEL WILLIAM (1880–1937). Banker, born April 9, 1880, in Wick, Scotland, and came to the United States in 1889. MacCormack studied at Boston College, Robert Gordon's College (Aberdeen), and St. Laurent's College (Montreal). He enlisted in the U.S. Army in 1899, served in the Philippine insurrection, and was with the Panama Canal organization from 1905 to 1917. In World War I he served in the Transportation Corps and was inspector general in charge of the reorganization of the Army Transport Service in France. He was sent on a mission to Russia in connection with the Paris peace conference in 1919. Resigned from the army in 1922. He was a member of the American financial mission to Persia from 1922 to 1927, serving as director of internal revenue of the Persian government, director of alimentation during the famine of 1925 to 1927, and member of the Russo-Persian Tariff Commission. MacCormack studied opium control, and represented Persia on the council and assembly of the League of Nations in 1927. He organized and administered the receivership department of the Irving Trust Company in New York City in 1929–1930; was founder and president of the Fiduciary Trust Company and the Fiduciary Corporation of New York from 1930 to 1933; and was commissioner of immigration and naturalization from 1933 until his death. Died January 1, 1937, in Washington, D.C. *References*: *NCAB* 28:295; *NYT*, January 1, 1937; and *WWWA*.

MACMURRAY, JOHN VAN ANTWERP (1881–1960). Diplomat, born October 6, 1881, in Schenectady, New York. MacMurray graduated from Princeton University; entered the foreign service in 1907; was secretary of legation and consul general in Bangkok, Siam; and served in St. Petersburg, Tokyo, and Peking. He was assistant secretary of state in 1924–1925; minister to China from 1925 to 1929; minister to Estonia, Latvia, and Lithuania from 1933 to 1936; and ambassador to Turkey from 1936 to 1941. He helped arrange a reciprocal trade agreement between the United States and Turkey in 1939. Died September

25, 1960, in Norfolk, Connecticut. *References*: Papers, Princeton University Library; *BRDS*; and *NYT*, September 26, 1960.

MAGNES, JUDAH LEON (1877–1948). Rabbi and educator, born July 5, 1877, in San Francisco. Magnes graduated from the University of Cincinnati and Hebrew Union College, and studied at the universities of Berlin and Heidelberg. He was a rabbi in Brooklyn and in New York City from 1904 to 1912, and chairman of the executive committee of the Jewish Community (Kehilla) of New York City from 1909 to 1922. He went to Palestine in 1922, was chancellor of the Hebrew University in Jerusalem from 1925 to 1935, and its president from 1935 until his death. A pacifist, he was concerned with improving relations with the Arabs and was involved with the *Ihud* (Unity) Association for Jewish-Arab Rapprochement. Died October 27, 1948, in New York City. His wife, **BEATRICE L. MAGNES**, wrote *Episodes, a Memoir* (Berkeley, Calif., 1977). *References*: *Dissenter in Zion: from the Writings of Judah L. Magnes*, ed. Arthur A. Goren (Cambridge, Mass., 1982); Papers, Central Archives for the History of the Jewish People, Jerusalem; David Biale, *Judah L. Magnes, Pioneer & Prophet on Two Continents: A Pictorial Biography* (Berkeley, Calif., 1977); *DAB S4*; *EJ*; Yohai Goell, "Aliyah in the Zionism of an American Oleh: Judah L. Magnes," *AJHQ* 65 (1975–1976); 99–120; *NCAB* 35:27; *NYT*, October 28, 1948; and *WWWA*.

MAHAL. Acronym for *Mitnadvey hutz la'aertz* [Volunteers from Outside the Country]. Residents of the United States and other English-speaking and Western European countries who came to Israel as volunteers during the 1948 war. Mahal included some 1,300 Americans. *Reference*: A. Joseph Heckelman, *American Volunteers and Israel's War of Independence* (New York, 1974).

MARCH, FREDERICK WILLIAM (1847–1935). Missionary, born March 6, 1847, in Cheshire, Connecticut. March graduated from Amherst College and Princeton Theological Seminary. He was a missionary under the Presbyterian Board of Missions in Syria, serving in Zahleh from 1873 to 1883, in Tripoli from 1883 to 1905, and in Beirut from 1905 until his retirement in 1927. Died September 28, 1935, at Suk-ul Gharb, Syria. *Reference*: *Amherst*.

MARCUS, DAVID ("MICKEY") (1901–1948). Army officer, born February 22, 1901, in Brooklyn, New York. Marcus graduated from the U.S. Military Academy in 1924, left the army in 1926, studied law in the Brooklyn Law School, and was admitted to the bar. He was assistant U.S. district attorney for the southern district of New York, joined the New York Department of Corrections in 1934, and was commissioner of corrections in 1940. He returned to active service in 1940, served in the army during World War II, and was head of the War Crimes Branch in 1945–1946. He retired in 1947 with the rank of colonel. Marcus came to Palestine in 1948, served with the Jewish forces, and led the forces in the Jerusalem front. Killed accidently by a sentry outside his headquarters, June 10, 1948, near Jerusalem. *References*: Papers, U.S. Military Academy Library, West Point, New York; Ted Berkman, *Cast a Giant Shadow: The Story of Mickey Marcus Who Died to Save Jerusalem* (New York, 1962); *EJ*; and *NYT*, June 12, 1948.

MARDEN, HENRY (1837–1890). Missionary, born December 9, 1837, in New Boston, New Hampshire. Marden graduated from Dartmouth College and Andover Theological Seminary, and was ordained in 1869. He served as a missionary under the American Board of Commissioners for Foreign Missions (ABCFM)* in Turkey, and was stationed at Aintab from 1869 to 1875, and at Marash from 1878 until 1890. Died May 13, 1890, in Athens, Greece, on his way back to the United States. *References*: *AndoverTS*. *EM*.

MARDEN, JESSE KREKORE (1872–1949). Medical missionary, born March 10, 1872, in Aintab, Turkey, son of Henry Marden,* and came to the United States in 1888. Marden graduated from Dartmouth College and the University of Michigan Medical School, and studied in Vienna. He became a medical missionary under the American Board of Commissioners for Foreign Missions (ABCFM)* in Turkey in 1898. He was placed in charge of the Anatolia Hospital at Marsovan in 1903. He was a member of the Red Cross expedition to Palestine in 1918–1919 and medical director of Near East Relief* in Constantinople in 1921–1922 and in the Caucasus in 1922–1923. He served in Greece from 1923 until 1941. Died March 21, 1949, in Claremont, California. *References*: Lucy H. M. Marden and Bertha B. Morley, *Jesse Krekore Marden, 1872–1949, Missionary Physician* (Claremont, Calif., 1950); and *WWWA*.

MARDEN, PHILIP SANFORD (1874–1963). Editor and author, born January 12, 1874, in Lowell, Massachusetts. Marden graduated from Dartmouth College and Harvard Law School. In 1901 he became managing editor of the *Lowell Courier-Citizen* and later editor-in-chief of the newspaper until 1941. In 1906 he also became president of the Courier-Citizen Company, commercial printers. An extensive traveler, he traveled in Egypt and wrote *Egyptian Days* (Boston, 1912). Died July 20, 1963, in Lowell, Massachusetts. *References*: *NYT*, July 22, 1963; *WWWA*.

MARINES IN LEBANON. *See* Lebanon, Marines in (1958); (1982–1984).

MARSH, DWIGHT WHITNEY (1823–1896). Missionary, born November 5, 1823, in Dalton, Massachusetts. Marsh graduated from Williams College, Andover and Union theological seminaries, and was ordained in 1849. He became a missionary under the American Board of Commissioners for Foreign Missions (ABCFM)* in Mosul, Iraq, in 1850. He reached Mosul by floating down the Tigris River from Diyarbekir. In 1851 he made a journey with the American clergyman Leonard Bacon to the mountains of Kurdistan, where they were detained in a Kurdish castle, robbed, and their lives threatened. He described the incident in the *Missionary Herald* for 1851. In 1852 he sent Williams College the first Assyrian reliefs to be displayed in the United States. He returned to the United States in 1860 and was a pastor in Hinsdale, Amherst, Haydenville, Massachusetts, Whitney's Point, and Oswego, New York. He wrote a biography of Samuel Audley Rhea.* Died June 16, 1896, in Amherst, Massachusetts. *Reference*: Hewitt.

MARSH, GEORGE PERKINS (1801–1882). Lawyer and diplomat, born March 15, 1801, in Woodstock, Vermont. Marsh graduated from Dartmouth College, practiced law in Vermont from 1825 to 1849, and served in the U.S. House of Representatives from 1835 to 1839. He was minister to Turkey from 1849 to 1853. He aided the refugees from the 1848 revolutions in Europe, investigated the charges against the missionary Jonas King* and was involved in a diplomatic dispute with the Austrian ambassador in Constantinople over the Kostza case,* and later wrote *The Camel: His Organization, Habits and Uses, Considered with Reference to His Introduction into the United States* (Boston, 1856). He was fish commissioner in Vermont and lecturer at Columbia University from 1854 to 1861, and the first minister to the Kingdom of Italy from 1862 until 1882. Died July 23, 1882, in Vallombrosa, Italy. *References*: Papers, Bailey/Howe Library, University of Vermont; *BDAS*; *DAB*; *DADH*; D. W. Gade, "The Growing Recognition of George Perkins Marsh," *Geographical Review* 73 (1983): 341–344; David Lowenthal, *George Perkins Marsh: Versatile Vermonter* (New York, 1958); and *WWWA*.

MARSHALL, S(AMUEL) L(YMAN) A(TWOOD) (1900–1977). Military historian, born July 18, 1900, in Catskill, New York, and grew up in El Paso, Texas. Marshall graduated from Texas College of Mines and served in the army in World War I. He was a reporter for *The El Paso Herald* from 1922 to 1927, and later editorial writer, military critic, and foreign correspondent for the *Detroit News* and the North American Newspaper Alliance. He became chief of orientation for the army in 1942, chief combat historian in the Pacific, and chief historian of the European theater. He left the army in 1946 but was recalled in 1948. He reported on several wars in the Middle East and wrote *Sinai Victory: Command Decisions in History's Shortest War* (New York, 1958), and *Swift Sword: The Historical Record of Israel's Victory, June, 1967* (New York, 1967). He retired in 1960 with the rank of brigadier general. Died December 17, 1977, in Fort Bliss, El Paso, Texas. His memoirs, *Bringing Up the Rear: A Memoir*, ed. Cate Marshall (San Rafael, Calif., 1979), appeared after his death. *References*: Papers, U.S. Army Military History Institute, Carlisle Barracks, Pennsylvania; *DAMIB*; and *NYT*, December 18, 1977.

MASON, ALEXANDER MCCOMB (1841–1897). Naval officer, born November 10, 1841, in Washington, D.C. Mason attended the U.S. Naval Academy and served in the Confederate Navy during the Civil War. Later he also served in Chile and Cuba. He entered the service of the Egyptian government in 1870 and was employed as an officer in the Khedival steamer service plying between Alexandria and Constantinople. He was then appointed to the Egyptian General Staff and worked with Erastus Sparrow Purdy* on surveys of the White Nile between Dufile and Lake Albert. In 1877 he made a reconnaissance of Lake Albert. In 1878 Mason resigned from the army and was given a position in the Survey Department of the Egyptian government. He surveyed the country between Wadi Halfa and Berber in the Sudan, and compiled a map of this area. In 1878 he was appointed chief of the anti-slave trade organization on the Red Sea coast. He was in Fayyum during the revolt of Ahmad Arabi Pasha in 1882. In 1883 Mason was a member of the commission to consider the future of the Sudan railway and was appointed governor of Masawwa in 1884. He retired in 1885. Died March 17, 1897, in Washington, D.C. *References*: Papers, Manuscript Division, Library of Congress; *ACAB*; Betty P. Greene, "The Bey from Virginia," *AWM* 25 (March-April 1974): 24–25; *Hesseltine*; and *Hill*.

MASON, SHIRLEY LOWELL (1893–1975). Petroleum geologist, born July 4, 1893, in Gloucester, Massachusetts. Mason graduated from Harvard University and the University of Pittsburgh. He was entomologist for the U.S. Department of Agriculture and served as pilot in World War I. He did appraisals and fieldwork in Kansas, Oklahoma, and Bolivia from 1919 to 1922, and fieldwork in Colombia from 1922 to 1924. He was a member of the International Geological Party and field geologist in Iraq for the Iraq Petroleum Company in 1925–1926. His recollections of the expedition to Iraq were published in Edgar W. Owen, *Trek of the Oil Finders: A History of Exploration for Petroleum* (Tulsa, Okla., 1975). From 1926 to 1930, he was a partner in a consulting firm and did appraisals and fieldwork in several states and countries, including Turkey, and wrote on the geology of oil fields in Turkey. He was in Angola in 1930–1931, and in Venezuela in 1934, and was geologist for Stanolind Oil and Gas Company (later Amoco Oil Company) from 1936 to 1948. He retired in 1958. Died May 10, 1975, in Houston, Texas. *Reference*: *BAAPG* 60 (1976): 462–463.

MASON, SILAS CHEEVER (1857–1935). Horticulturist, born April 19, 1857, in East Greensboro, Vermont. Mason graduated from Kansas State Agricultural College and was a member of its faculty from 1890 to 1897, professor from 1894 to 1897, and professor of horticulture and forestry at Berea College from 1897 to 1906. From 1907 to 1931 he was with the U.S. Department of Agriculture, and in 1913–1914 was detailed to study date palm culture in Egypt and the Sudan, and to secure offshoots of valuable varieties. He was again in Egypt in 1920 and in Algeria in 1921–1922, and was consulting expert on date culture to the Sudan government in 1924–1925. He discovered the identity, history, and geographical range of the Saidy date of the oases in the Libyan Desert, securing 7,000 offshoots for the U.S. Department of Agriculture for planting in southern California. He wrote *Dates of Egypt and the Sudan* (Washington, D.C., 1915). Died October 19, 1935, in Riverside, California. *Reference*: *WWWA*.

MATTHEWS, RODERIC D(ONALD) (1899–1982). Educator, born April 8, 1899, in Clear Lake, Iowa. Matthews graduated from Grinnell College and the University of Pennsylvania. He was an instructor at the American University in Cairo* from 1920 to 1923 and a high school teacher at Clear Lake in 1923–1924, and at Woodbury, New Jersey, from 1924 to 1927. In 1927 he became instructor, associate professor, and after 1947, professor of education at the University of Pennsylvania. He was the director of the American Council of Education's commission to study education in the Arab-speaking countries of the Middle East in 1945–1946 and was the co-author of *Education in Arab Countries of the Near East* (Washington, D.C., 1949). Died January 3, 1982. *Reference*: *WWWA*.

MAXWELL, RUSSELL LAMONTE (1890–1968). Army officer, born December 28, 1890, in Oakdale, Illinois. Maxwell graduated from the U.S. Military Academy in 1912, was commissioned second lieutenant in field artillery, was transferred to ordnance, and served as an ordnance officer in various units. From 1935 to 1938 he was chief ordnance officer in the General Headquarters of the Army Air Force, was later chief of the planning and equipment section of the Supply division of the War Department General Staff, and in 1940 was appointed administrator of export control. In 1941 he headed the military mission in Cairo and was commander of the U.S. Army Forces in the Middle East with headquarters in Cairo in 1942–1943. He was assistant chief of staff from 1943 to 1946. He retired in 1946 with the rank of major general. Maxwell was vice president of American Machine and Foundry Company until his retirement in 1958. Died November 24, 1968, in Washington, D.C. *References*: Papers, U.S. Army Military History Institute, Carlisle Barracks, Pennsylvania. *NCAB* 54:450; *NYT*, November 25, 1968.

MAYO, WILLIAM STARBUCK (1811–1895). Physician and author, born April 15, 1811, in Ogdensburg, New York. Mayo graduated from the College of Physicians and Surgeons in New York City and practiced medicine in Ogdensburg. He traveled to Spain and North Africa in about 1835, and wrote two novels based on his impressions of North Africa, *Kaloolah, or Journeyings to the Djebel Kumri* (New York, 1849), which went through no less than nine editions, and *The Berber; or, the Mountaineer of the Atlas* (New York, 1850). He later practiced medicine in New York City. Died November 22, 1895, in New York City. *References*: *ACAB*; *DAB*; *NCAB* 8:483; and *WWWA*.

MCCAGUE, THOMAS (1825–1914). Missionary, born December 25, 1825, in Ripley, Brown County, Ohio. McCague graduated from Jefferson College (Pa.) and Oxford Seminary (Oxford, Ohio). He was a missionary under the Associate Reformed Church in Cairo from 1854 until 1861. Died June 7, 1914. *References*: "Adventures in Faith as Described in the Letters of the First American Missionaries to Egypt," with Biographical Material and Notes by Lydia S. McCague (1941), Ms.; McCague Family Papers, Presbyterian Historical Society; Lydia S. McCague, "Egypt in 1857–1861," *MW* 9 (1919): 363–338.

MCCASKEY, CHARLES I(RVING) (1877–1954). Financial administrator, born August 7, 1877, in Fort Snelling, Minnesota. McCaskey graduated from A. and M. College of the University of Kansas. He was examiner, chief clerk, chief of the inspection division, deputy surveyor, acting surveyor of customs at Manila, Philippine Islands, inspector and acting deputy surveyor of customs in New York City, collector of customs at Corinto, Nicaragua, and manager of branches for Banco Mercantil Americano de Colombia and for the Compañía Mercantil de Ultramar in Colombia. He was assistant to William Morgan Shuster* in Iran in 1911–1912; accompanied Arthur Chester Millspaugh* to Persia in 1922; was treasurer general of Persia from 1922 to 1927; director of the Imperial Persian Mint from 1923 to 1927; director of Bank-i-Iran in 1923–1924; director of the General Supply Service of the Persian Government in 1926–1927; and director of the Imperial Persian Government pawnbroking institution in 1927. He was superintendent of internal revenue and customs in Liberia from 1928 to 1932, acting financial adviser from 1930 to 1932, and financial adviser from 1935 to 1938. In 1934–1935 McCaskey was secretary to the governor of Puerto Rico. Died March 16, 1954, in San Rafael, California. *References*: Papers in private hands; *WWWA*.

MCCAULEY, DANIEL SMITH (?–1852). Consul. McCauley was a naval lieutenant. He was consul in Tripoli from 1831 to 1848, became consul general in Alexandria, Egypt, in 1848, and was first diplomatic agent and consul general in Egypt from 1848 until his death. Died October 24, 1852, in Alexandria. His son, **EDWARD YORKE MCCAULEY (1827–1894)**, born November 2, 1827, in Philadelphia and raised in Tripoli, Libya, was a naval officer and Egyptologist, and published a dictionary of Egyptian hieroglyphics. Died September 14, 1894, on Canonicut Island, Narragansett Bay, Rhode Island. *References*: *DAB*; *NCAB* 13:131; *WWWA*; and *WWWE*.

MCCLENAHAN, ROBERT S(TEWART) (1871–1949). Missionary educator, born in Wyoming, Iowa. McClenahan graduated from Tarkio College (Mo.) and Yale University. He taught at the mission college in Norfolk, Virginia, and at Phillips Academy in Andover, Massachusetts. He went to Egypt as professor of religion and ethics at Assiut College* and was president of the college from 1910 to 1918. He joined the faculty of the American University in Cairo* in

1918, and was its dean from 1928 to 1932. He was also chairman of the Committee on Missions and Government of the Egypt Inter-Mission Council from 1921 to 1939. He returned to the United States in 1939. Died on November 8, 1949, in Philadelphia. His son, **WILLIAM U. MCCLENAHAN (1889–   )** wrote *G.P.*, ed. by Tom L. McClenahan (Philadelphia, 1974), which deals partly with his childhood in Egypt. *References*: *NYT*, November 9, 1949; *WWWA*.

MCCLINTOCK, ROBERT (MILLS) (1909–1976). Diplomat, born August 30, 1909, in Seattle, Washington. McClintock graduated from Stanford University, entered the foreign service in 1931, and served in Panama City, Kobe, Japan, Santiago, Chile, Ciudad Trujillo, Dominican Republic, Helsinki, Finland, and Stockholm. He was special assistant to the director of the Office of Special Affairs at the State Department in 1946–1947, and the Office of U.N. Affairs in 1948 and adviser to the delegation to the United Nations from 1946 to 1948. He was secretary in Belgium from 1949 to 1951; deputy chief of mission and counselor in Egypt in 1952–1953; deputy chief of mission in Vietnam in 1953–1954, ambassador to Cambodia from 1954 to 1956; and ambassador to Lebanon from 1957 to 1961. He played the role of mediator during the Lebanese crisis of 1958 in which American marines landed in Lebanon (see Lebanon, Marines in) and provided eyewitness account in his book *The Meaning of Limited War* (Boston, 1967). He was ambassador to Argentina from 1962 to 1964, foreign service inspector from 1966 to 1968, and ambassador to Venezuela from 1970 to 1975. Killed in an automobile accident, November 1, 1976, in Beaune, France. *References*: *CB* 1955; *NCAB* I:298; *NYT*, November 3, 1976; Charles W. Thayer, *Diplomat* (New York, 1959), chs. 1–3; and *WWWA*.

MCCLURE, ROBERT ALEXIS (1897–1957). Army officer, born March 4, 1897, in Mattoon, Illinois. McClure graduated from the Kentucky Military Institute (Lyndon) and was commissioned second lieutenant in 1916. He served in the Philippines constabulary, was assigned to China, and was instructor in the Infantry School from 1926 to 1930 and in the Army War College from 1935 to 1940. He was military attaché in London in 1941–1942, chief of intelligence in the European theater from 1942 to 1943, and chief of the Psychological Warfare Division in Supreme Headquarters Allied Expeditionary Forces in 1944–1945. He was director of the Information Control Division of the military government in Germany from 1945 to 1947 and first chief of the Psychological Warfare Branch of the U.S. Army from 1950 to 1953. He served as chief of the U.S. military mission with the Iranian armed forces from 1953 to 1956, and started a literacy and vocational training program for the Iranian Army. He retired in 1956 with the rank of major general. Died January 1, 1957, in Fort Huachuca, near Tucson, Arizona. *References*: Papers, U.S. Army Military History Institute, Carlisle Barracks, Pennsylvania; *DAB S6*; *NYT*, January 5, 1957; and *WWWA*.

MCCOWN, CHESTER CHARLTON (1877–1958). Archaeologist, born November 26, 1877, in Orion, Illinois. McCown graduated from DePauw University, Garrett Biblical Institute, and studied at the universities of Heidelberg, Berlin, and Chicago. He was principal of the American Methodist Institute in Calcutta from 1902 to 1908; professor at Wesley College (N.D.) from 1909 to 1912; professor of New Testament theology at the Pacific School of Religion (Berkeley) from 1914 to 1942; dean of the school from 1928 to 1936 and in 1945–1946; and director of the Palestine Institute of the Pacific School of Religion from 1936 to 1947. He was director of the American Schools of Oriental Research (ASOR)* in Jerusalem from 1919 to 1931, annual professor and acting director in 1935–1936, and joint director of the ASOR excavation of Jerash, Jordan. He wrote *The Ladder of Progress in Palestine: A Story of Archaeological Adventure* (New York, 1943), and *Tell en-Nasbeh Excavated Under the Direction of the Late William Frederick Bade* (Berkeley, Calif., 1947). McCown was technical adviser for the film *David and Bathsheba* (1950–1951). Died January 9, 1958. *References*: *BASOR* 149 (1958): 3–4; *Journal of Biblical Literature* 78 (March 1959): x–xi; and *WWWA*.

MCCOWN, DONALD E(UGENE) (1910–1985). Archaeologist, son of Chester Charlton McCown,* born August 13, 1910, in Grand Rapids, North Dakota. McCown graduated from the universities of California and Chicago. He was an archaeological assistant in excavations of Jericho in 1930–1931, in Jerash and Athlit, Palestine, in 1930, and in the Persepolis expedition of the Oriental Institute from 1933 to 1938. He served in the Signal Corps during World War II. He was field director for the Iranian project in 1947–1948, and of the joint expedition of the University Museum and the Oriental Institute to Nippur from 1948 until 1954. He was research assistant at the Oriental Institute from 1939 to 1948 and associate professor of archaeology at the Oriental Institute from 1948 until 1955. He was co-author of *Tall-i-Bakun A: Season of 1932* (Chicago, 1942), *The Comparative Stratigraphy of Early Iran* (Chicago, 1942), *Nippur I: Temple of Enlil, Scribal Quarter and Soundings* (Chicago, 1967), and *Nippur II: The North Temple and Sounding E* (Chicago, 1955). He was later employed by the U.S. government. Died January 19, 1985, in Silver Spring, Maryland. *References*: *The Oriental Institute News & Notes*, No. 98 (March–April 1985).

MCCOWN, THEODORE DONEY (1908–1969). Anthropologist, son of Chester Charlton McCown, born June 18, 1908, in McComb, Illinois. McCown graduated from the University of California. He became a member of the faculty of the University of California in 1929 and professor of physical anthropology in 1951. He was a member of the Joint Expedition of the British School of Archaeology in Jerusalem and the American School of Prehistoric Research to the caves of Mount Carmel in Palestine in 1931; discovered skeletons from the Mousterian period of the Stone Age; was joint leader of the expedition in 1932; and co-authored *The Stone Age of Mount Carmel*, Vol. 2 (Oxford, 1939). Died

August 17, 1969, in Berkeley, California. *References*: Kenneth A. R. Kennedy and Sheilagh T. Brooks, "Theodore D. McCown: A Perspective on a Physical Anthropologist," *Current Anthropology* 25 (1984): 99–103; *NYT*, August 20, 1969; and *WWWA*.

MCCRACKEN, WILLIAM DENNISON (1864–1923). Historian and author, born February 12, 1864, in Munich, Germany, to American parents and came to the United States in 1878. He graduated from Trinity College (Hartford), traveled abroad, and wrote articles and books on a variety of topics, particularly about Switzerland and Swiss political institutions. He went to Palestine in 1919 as a member of a delegation under the auspices of the Anglo-American Society and was engaged in educational and relief work in Palestine for the British military administration. In 1919–1920 he was editor of the *Palestine News*, the first daily newspaper in the English language in Jerusalem, founded by Elizabeth Lippincott McQueen.* McCracken returned to the United States in 1920 and wrote *The New Palestine* (Boston, 1922). Died June 12, 1923, in New York City. His memoirs, *An American Abroad and at Home: Recollections of W. D. McCracken* (New York, 1924), appeared posthumously. *Reference*: *NCAB* 19:146.

MCCREERY, ELBERT L. (1877–1955). Missionary, born May 18, 1877, in Loveland, Colorado. McCreery graduated from Colorado Agricultural College, Monmouth (Ill.) College, and Xenia Theological Seminary. He was a teacher at Assiut College* from 1901 to 1903, a teacher of Hebrew at Xenia Theological Seminary from 1904 to 1906, and was ordained in 1906. He was a missionary in the Sudan from 1906 to 1913. He reduced to writing the Shulla and Nuer languages and translated the Gospel of John into Shulla. He was field secretary of the Laymen's Missionary Movement from 1914 to 1918; a pastor in Mission Creek, Nebraska, from 1920 to 1922; professor of New Testament Greek and phonetics and director of a pastors' course at Moody Bible Institute in Chicago from 1922 to 1927; a pastor at Fort Morgan, Colorado, from 1927 to 1929; and dean of the Bible Missionary Institute of the Western Bible College in Los Angeles from 1937 to 1940. *Reference*: *WWWA*.

MCDONALD, JAMES GROVER (1886–1964). Internationalist and diplomat, born November 29, 1886, in Coldwater, Ohio. McDonald graduated from Indiana and Harvard universities. He served on the staff of the Civil Service Reform Association in New York and was chairman of the board and president of the League of Free Nations Association (renamed the Foreign Policy Association) from 1919 to 1933. He was the League of Nations' high commissioner for refugees from Germany from 1933 to 1935; member of the editorial staff of the *New York Times* from 1936 to 1938; president of the Brooklyn Institute of Art and Sciences from 1938 to 1942; and news analyst for NBC Radio from 1942 to 1944. He was a member of the Anglo-American Committee of Inquiry* on Palestine in 1945–1946, U.S. Special representative, and the first ambassador to Israel from 1948 to 1951. He wrote *My Mission to Israel, 1948–1951* (New York, 1952). McDonald retired in 1952 and was consultant on European and Middle Eastern affairs. Died September 26, 1964, in New York City. *References*: Papers, School of International Affairs Library, Columbia University; *CB* 1949; *DAB S7*; *DADH*; *DI*; *NYT*, September 27, 1964; *NCAB* F:174; and *WWWA*.

MCDOWELL, EDMUND WILSON (1857–1939). Missionary, born March 13, 1857, in Altoona, Pennsylvania. McDowell graduated from Wooster (Ohio) College and Western Theological Seminary (Allegheny, Pa.), and was ordained in 1887. He was a missionary under the Presbyterian Board of Missions in Persia from 1887 to 1897 and from 1902 to 1922. He organized a chain of village schools and churches, wrote about the Nestorians, was involved in relief work in Urmia from 1915 to 1917, and represented Near East Relief* in Mesopotamia in 1918. He served in Mosul for the United Mission to Mesopotamia from 1922 until his retirement in 1928. Died March 1, 1939, in Fort Collins, Colorado. His wife was **MARGARET DEAN MCDOWELL (1872–1927)**, missionary educator, born March 12, 1872. She attended Mount Holyoke College and taught in Kansas from 1892 to 1902. She taught missionary children in Urmia, Persia, from 1902 to 1905, and in Harper, Kansas, and Chicago from 1905 to 1915. She was also head of the Persian mission in Chicago from 1907 to 1915. She returned to Urmia in 1918, served as relief worker in Baghdad, from 1919 to 1922, and as a teacher in Mosul, Iraq, from 1922 until her death. Died December 13, 1927, in Mosul. Her letters were published in *In the Land of Jonah and His Gourd: Home Letters of Margaret Dean McDowell*, ed. by Elizabeth D. Fickett and Edmund W. McDowell (n.p., 192-?). *References*: *NYT*, April 10, 1939; and *WWWA*.

MCEWAN, CALVIN WELLS (1906–1950). Archaeologist, born in Pittsburgh. McEwan graduated from Washington and Jefferson College and the universities of Pittsburgh and Chicago. A member of the staff of the Oriental Institute, he spent much of his time in the Middle East, serving as field director of several expeditions sent by the institute. In 1931–1932 he was on the staff of the Anatolian expedition and in 1932–1933 on the staff of the Iraq expedition. In 1933 he became field director of the Syrian-Hittite expedition which excavated at Chatel Hutuk, Tell Jedeideh, and Tell Tayanot, and in 1941 he was director of the Theodore Marriner Memorial Expedition of the Oriental Institute and the Boston Museum of Fine Arts to Tell Fakharieth (Mitanni) in Syria. McEwan was co-author of *Soundings at Tell Fakhariyah* (Chicago, 1958). He was stationed in the Middle East in World War II, serving British military intelligence and then the U.S. Military Intelligence Service. Died January 12, 1950, in St. Paul, Minnesota. *References*: *AJA* 55 (1951): 101–102; *NYT*, January 15, 1950.

MCFARLANE, ROBERT C(ARL) (1937–   ). Government official, born July 12, 1937, in Washington, D.C., and grew up in Graham, Texas. McFarlane graduated from the U.S. Naval Academy in 1958 and was commissioned second lieutenant in the Marine Corps. He served in Vietnam, Japan, and Korea and studied at the Graduate Institute of International Studies at the University of Geneva. He was military assistant to Henry Alfred Kissinger* from 1973 to 1975, and special assistant to the president for national security affairs in 1975–1976. He resigned from the Marine Corps in 1979. He became counselor in the State Department in 1981 and was deputy assistant for national security affairs in 1982–1983. In 1983 he became special envoy to the Middle East, but his mission was unsuccessful. McFarlane was national security adviser from 1983 to 1985. In May 1986 he made a secret trip to Iran and was involved in secret talks with the Iranian government. *References*: *CB* 1984; *NYT*, October 18, 1982; July 23, 1983; October 18, 1983; *NYT Magazine*, May 26, 1985; *WWA* and *WWAP*.

MCGARVEY, JOHN WILLIAM (1829–1911). Clergyman and writer, born March 1, 1829, in Hopkinsville, Kentucky. McGarvey graduated from Bethany College and was ordained in 1851. He served as minister of the Disciples of Christ in Missouri from 1853 to 1862, and in 1865 he became professor of sacred history in the College of Bible affiliated with Kentucky University. He was dismissed in 1873 because he insisted on larger support for the college but was reinstated in 1875. From 1895 until his death he was president of the college. In 1879 he made a tour of the Middle East; his book, *Lands of the Bible: A Geographical and Topographical Description of Palestine, with Letters of Travel in Egypt, Syria, Asia Minor and Greece* (Cincinnati, 1880), had considerable circulation. Died October 6, 1911, in Lexington, Kentucky. His *Autobiography of J. W. McGarvey (1829–1911)* (Lexington, Ky., 1960) was published after his death. *References: ACAB*; *DAB*; *NCAB* 4:517; and *WWWA*.

MCGHEE, GEORGE CREWS (1912–   ). Diplomat, born March 10, 1912, in Waco, Texas. McGhee graduated from Southern Methodist University and the University of Oklahoma and was Rhodes scholar at Oxford University. In the early 1930s he was employed as a geologist by various petroleum companies, and in 1940 he established his own oil-producing firm. He served with the War Petroleum Board during World War II and was deputy executive secretary of the U.S.-U.K. Combined Raw Material Board. He served in the navy in World War II. In 1946 he became special assistant to the undersecretary of state for economic affairs and coordinator of the Greek-Turkish Aid Program. He was assistant secretary of state for Near Eastern, South Asian and African Affairs from 1949 to 1951 and ambassador to Turkey from 1951 to 1953. In 1961 he became counselor in the State Department's Policy Planning Council and undersecretary of state for political affairs. He was ambassador to West Germany from 1963 to 1968 and ambassador-at-large in 1968–1969. McGhee retired in

1969 and wrote *Envoy to the Middle World: Adventures in Diplomacy* (New York, 1983). *References*: Papers, Georgetown University Library; *CB* 1950; *DADH*; and *WWA*.

MCKOWN, MARTHA J. (1834–1897). Missionary, born March 22, 1834, in Elizabeth, Pennsylvania. McKown graduated from Menmouth College. She went to Egypt in 1860 as a missionary under the United Presbyterian Church of North America Board of Foreign Missions,* serving in Alexandria until 1865 when she was transferred to Assiut. She was a pioneer of woman's work in Upper Egypt, opening a school in 1866 and a boarding school in 1874. In 1881 she established a girls' college, later renamed Pressly Memorial Institute. Becoming blind in 1890, she returned to the United States in 1894. Died January 30, 1897, in Pittsburgh. *Reference*: *In the King's Service* (Philadelphia, 1905), pp. 43–80.

MCLAIN, RAYMOND FRANCIS (1905–   ). Educator, born February 9, 1905, in Lancaster, Ohio. McLain graduated from Mount Union College and Columbia University, and was ordained in 1924. He was director of religious education for the Ohio Christian Missionary Society from 1932 to 1936, president of Eureka College (Ill.) from 1936 to 1939, and president of Transylvania College (Ky.) from 1939 to 1951. He served in the navy in World War II. From 1951 to 1954 he was general director of higher education for the National Council of Churches. He was president of the American University in Cairo* from 1955 to 1963; chancellor of American University (Washington, D.C.) from 1963 to 1966; dean of international programs; dean of the College of Arts and Sciences; vice president of academic affairs; and professor at the University of Alabama from 1966 until his retirement in 1976. *References*: *Christian Scholar* 38 (1955): 165–167; *MENA*; and *WWA*.

MCMAHON, THOMAS J(OHN) (1909–1956). Clergyman, born April 5, 1909, in Tuxedo Park, New York. McMahon graduated from St. Joseph's Seminary (Yonkers), Propaganda and Gregorian universities in Rome, and Fordham University, and was ordained in 1933. He was professor of church history at St. Joseph's Seminary from 1936 to 1943 and became national secretary of the Catholic Near East Welfare Association in 1943. He was made papal chamberlain in 1945 and apostolic prelate in 1948. In 1949 he became president of the Pontifical Mission for Palestine which Pope Pius XII established in 1949 for the care of Palestinian refugees, and he spent much of his time in the Middle East. McMahon resigned in 1954 and returned to the United States. Died December 6, 1956, in New York City. *Reference*: *DACB*; *WWWA*.

MCQUEEN, ELIZABETH LIPPINCOTT (1878–?). Author, born September 26, 1878, in Pennington, New Jersey. In 1918 McQueen founded and directed the Anglo-American Society of America in Boston. She was in Palestine in 1918–1919 and directed the relief work in Jerusalem. She founded the *Jerusalem*

News in 1919 and financed it with the help of American and British friends. In 1922–1923 she toured the world on behalf of Anglo-American friendship. She later became involved with aviation, organized several women's aeronautical associations, and was a lecturer on aviation. She wrote *Palestine Problem* (Riverside, Calif., 1948). *References*: *NCAB* A:495; *WWWA*.

MEAD, ELWOOD (1858–1936). Irrigation engineer, born January 16, 1858, near Patriot, Switzerland County, Indiana. Mead graduated from Purdue University and Iowa State College. He was professor at the Colorado State Agricultural College in 1883–1884 and from 1886 to 1888; territorial and state engineer of Wyoming from 1888 to 1899; and chief of irrigation and drainage investigation for the U.S. Department of Agriculture from 1897 to 1907. From 1901 to 1907 he was also head of the department of irrigation at the University of California. He was chairman of the State Rivers and Water Supply Commission of Victoria, Australia, from 1907 to 1915; professor of rural institutions at the University of California; chairman of California's Land Settlement Board; head of the Bureau of Reclamation from 1924 until his death; and consulting engineer for various irrigation and water works companies. He made a trip to Palestine in 1923 as a consulting engineer for the Zionist Organization of America, and in 1927 he headed a commission that surveyed Palestine and produced the *Report of the Experts Submitted to the Joint Palestine Survey Commission* (Boston, 1928). Died January 26, 1936, in Boston. *References*: Papers, Colorado State University Library, Fort Collins; *DAB S2*; *IAB*; *NCAB* 26:44; and *WWWA*.

MEARS, ELIOT GRINNELL (1889–1946). Economist and author, born February 1, 1889, in Worcester, Massachusetts. Mears graduated from Harvard University, and was an instructor and secretary in the Harvard Graduate School of Business Administration from 1912 to 1916. He served with the U.S. Bureau of Foreign and Domestic commerce from 1916 to 1920, organizing the American Trade Commissioners Service, and from 1917 to 1919 was chief of the American Commercial Attaché Service which was engaged primarily in economic intelligence. He was acting chief of the European division and American Trade Commissioner to the Near East, opened the Department of Commerce office in Athens and Constantinople in 1919, was commercial attaché to the American High Commissioner in Turkey in 1919–1920, and was economist to the Harbord Mission.* He edited *Modern Turkey* (New York, 1924). Mears was acting professor and lecturer on economics at Stanford University from 1921 to 1925, and professor of geography and international trade in its graduate school of business after 1925. He served in the War Shipping Administration in 1942. Died May 27, 1946, in Middlebury, Vermont. *References*: Papers, Hoover Institution Archives; *NCAB* 35:2886; *NYT*, May 29, 1946; and *WWWA*.

MELLINK, MACHTED J(OHANNA) (1917–   ). Archaeologist, born October 26, 1917, in Amsterdam, the Netherlands. Mellink graduated from the universities of Amsterdam and Utrecht, and came to the United States in 1949. She was professor of classical and Near East archaeology at Bryn Mawr College and became research associate at the University Museum in 1955. She was a staff member of the Tarsus expedition from 1947 to 1949 and the University Museum excavation at Gordion in 1950, and field director of the excavations at Karatas-Semayuk in Lycia, Turkey, in 1963. She wrote *A Hittite Cemetery at Gordion* (Philadelphia, 1956). *References*: *Ancient Anatolia: Aspects of Change and Cultural Development: Essays in Honor of Machted J. Mellink*, ed. Jeanny V. Canby et al. (Madison, Wis., 1986); *DAS*; *MENA*; *WWA*; and *WWAW*.

MELVILLE, HERMAN (1819–1891). Author, born August 1, 1819, in New York City. Melville went to sea in 1837 and traveled extensively afterwards. He was crew member of a whaler and jumped ship in the Marquesas Islands. His first book appeared in 1846, and he later lived in Pittsfield, Massachusetts and New York City. In 1856 he toured Turkey and Palestine. His diary was published as *Journal of a Visit to Europe and the Levant: October 11, 1856– May 6, 1857*, ed. Howard C. Horsford (Princeton, N.J., 1955). The narrative poem *Clarel*, which was published in 1876, is based on his impressions from this trip: *Clarel, a Poem and Pilgrimage in the Holy Land*, ed. Walter E. Bezanson (New York, 1960). He was customs inspector in New York City from 1866 to 1885. Died September 28, 1891, in New York City. *References*: *ACAB*; *DAB*; Vincent Kenny, *Herman Melville's Clarel* (Hamden, Conn., 1973); Milton Konvitz, "Herman Melville in the Holy Land," *Midstream* 25 (December 1979): 50–57; *NCAB* 4:59; Franklin Walker, *Irreverent Pilgrims: Melville, Browne and Mark Twain in the Holy Land* (Seattle, 1974), chs. 5–6; and *WWWA*.

MERRICK, JAMES LYMAN (1803–1866). Missionary, born December 17, 1803, in Monson, Massachusetts. Merrick attended Amherst College and Princeton and Columbia (S.C.) theological seminaries, and was ordained in 1834. The American Board of Commissioners for Foreign Missions (ABCFM)* sent him to Persia in 1834 to investigate the possibility of beginning mission work there, and he visited Teheran, Isfahan, and Shiraz. He returned to Tabriz in 1835 as a missionary, moved to Shiraz in 1836, and served at the Nestorian mission at Urmia from 1841 until 1845. He returned to the United States in 1845, was a pastor at Amherst from 1849 to 1864, and an instructor in Oriental literature in Amherst College from 1852 to 1857. He translated several works from Persian and into Persian. Died June 18, 1866, in South Amherst, Massachusetts. *References*: *ACAB*; *Amherst*; and *EM*.

MERRILL, JOHN ERNEST (1872–1960). Educational missionary, born May 9, 1872, in Medina, New York. Merrill graduated from the University of Minnesota and Hartford Theological Seminary. He became a missionary under the

American Board of Commissioners for Foreign Missions (ABCFM)* in Turkey in 1898, taught at Central Turkey College in Aintab, and became president of the college in 1905. He saved the college from extinction during World War I and was involved in relief work. In 1924 he transferred the operations of the college to Aleppo. He retired in 1937. Died September 22, 1960, in Bellows Falls, Vermont. *References*: Papers, Case Memorial Library, Hartford Theological Foundation; *MW* 51 (1961): 53–54; and *NYT*, September 24, 1960.

MERRILL, SELAH (1837–1909). Clergyman, archaeologist, and consul, born May 2, 1837, in Canton Centre, Connecticut. Merrill graduated from Yale University and Yale Divinity School, and was ordained in 1864. He served as a chaplain in the Civil War, was a preacher in Leroy, New York, San Francisco, and Salmon Falls, New Hampshire, studied in Germany, and taught Hebrew at Andover Theological Seminary. He made an extended tour of Egypt, Palestine, and Syria in 1869, served as an archaeologist with the American Palestine Exploration Society* from 1874 to 1877, explored the area east of the Jordan River in 1876–1877, and wrote *East of the Jordan: A Record of Travel and Observation in the Countries of Moab, Gilead and Bashan* (New York, 1881). Merrill was consul in Jerusalem from 1882 to 1885, from 1891 to 1893, and from 1898 to 1907. He discovered and excavated the second wall of Jerusalem. He wrote *The Site of Calvary* (Jerusalem, 1885) and *Ancient Jerusalem* (New York, 1906). He was later consul at Georgetown, British Guiana. Died January 22, 1909, near East Oakland, California. *References*: Papers, Case Memorial Library, Hartford Seminary Foundation; *ACAB*; *DAB*; *NCAB* 13:218; and *WWWA*.

METCALF, WILLARD LEROY (1858–1925). Painter, born July 1, 1858, in Lowell, Massachusetts. Metcalf went to Europe in 1883 and studied art in Paris. He made several trips to North Africa between 1883 and 1888, and in 1889 exhibited paintings from Tunis and Biskra, Algeria. From 1890 to 1898 he was magazine and book illustrator for Scribner's. Died March 9, 1925, in New York City. *References*: "Diary," Ms., American Archives of Art; *DAB*; *NCAB* 31:417; *NYT*, March 10, 1925; *Willard Leroy Metcalf: A Retrospective* (Springfield, Mass., 1976); and *WWWA*.

METHODIST EPISCOPAL CHURCH. BOARD OF FOREIGN MISSIONS. Began missionary work in North Africa in 1910, and opened stations in Algeria and later in Tunis. Rapid expansion followed until the 1930s, when work was curtailed. After 1939 the name was changed to the Board of Global Ministries of the United Methodist Church, Archives of the Board of Missions of the Methodist Church, New York City. *Reference*: J. Tremayne Copplestone, *History of Methodist Missions, Vol. IV: Twentieth Century Perspectives* (New York, 1973).

MEYER, ALBERT JULIUS (1919–1983). Educator and economist, born May 14, 1919, in Hawarden, Iowa. Meyer graduated from the University of California at Los Angeles and Johns Hopkins University, and served in the navy during World War II. He was associate professor of economics and executive assistant to the president at the American University of Beirut* from 1947 to 1955, became a member of the faculty of Harvard University in 1955, and professor of Middle East Studies in 1956. He wrote *Middle East Capitalism* (Cambridge, Mass., 1959) and *The Economics of Cyprus* (Cambridge, Mass., 1962). He was head of the special economic mission to Saudi Arabia in 1962. Died October 31, 1983, in Boston. *References: NYT*, November 4, 1983; *WWA*.

MEYERS, ERIC MARK (1940–   ). Archaeologist, born June 5, 1940, in Norwich, Connecticut. Meyers graduated from Dartmouth College and Brandeis and Harvard universities. He joined the faculty of Drew University in 1969, becoming associate professor and professor of religion. He was area supervisor of the joint expedition to Tell Gezer from 1964 to 1969 and director of the joint expeditions to Khirbet Shema', Meiron, Gush Halav, and En-Nabratein in Israel for the American Schools of Oriental Research (ASOR)* from 1970 to 1982. He was co-author of *Ancient Synagogue Excavations at Khirbet Shema', Upper Galilee, Israel, 1970–1972* (Durham, N.C., 1976) and *Excavations at Ancient Meiron, Upper Galilee, Israel, 1971–72, 1974–75, 1977* (Cambridge, Mass., 1981). He was named director of the Albright Institute in 1976–1977. *Reference: DAS*.

MICHENER, JAMES A(LBERT) (1907–   ). Novelist, born February 3, 1907, in New York City. Michener attended Swarthmore College and the University of North Colorado. He was a teacher from 1929 to 1931 and from 1933 to 1936, professor at Colorado State College of Education from 1936 to 1941, and associate editor at Macmillan Company from 1941 to 1949. He served in the navy during World War II. His first novel, *Tales of the South Pacific*, won the Pulitzer Prize in 1947. Two of his novels dealt with the Middle East: *Caravans* (New York, 1963), based on his travels in Afghanistan in 1955; and *The Source* (New York, 1964), based on his travels in Israel. *References: CA; Contemporary Novelists*, ed. James Vinson (New York, 1975); *DLB*; John P. Hayes, *James A. Michener: A Biography* (Indianapolis, 1984); and *WWA*.

MIDDLE EAST COLLEGE. Coeducational four-year college, located in DeKouame, a suburb of Beirut. It was founded in 1939 by the Seventh Day Adventist Church as the Adventist College of Beirut, a two-year training program. It was reorganized in 1946 and renamed Middle East College. *References: Boardman; Qubain,* 359; and *Seventh Day Adventist Encyclopedia*, rev. ed. (Washington, D.C., 1976).

MIDDLE EAST SUPPLY CENTER. World War II agency, established in Cairo by the British government in 1941. Americans joined the staff in 1942. The agency was established in order to control imports and to eliminate shipping of nonessential goods, to provide civilians in the Middle East with the minimum requirements of essential commodities, and to stimulate the production locally of as much of the area's requirements as possible. It also served as a regional planning agency and was involved with economic development operations. *References*: Martin W. Wilmington, *The Middle East Supply Center* (Albany, N.Y., 1971).

MIKESELL, RAYMOND FRENCH (1913–   ). Economist, born February 13, 1913, in Eaton, Ohio. Mikesell graduated from Carnegie Institute of Technology (now Carnegie-Mellon University) and Ohio State University. He was assistant professor at the University of Washington from 1937 to 1941 and government economist from 1941 to 1947. He served in the Department of the Treasury from 1942 to 1947 and was its representative in the Middle East, with headquarters in Cairo. He was co-author of *Arabian Oil: America's Stake in the Middle East* (Chapel, Hill, N.C., 1949). Mikesell was professor at the University of Virginia from 1946 to 1957, and served on the Foreign Economic Policy Commission in 1953–1954 and on the Council of Economic Advisers in 1955–1956. From 1956 to 1968 he was acting and associate director of the Institute of International Studies and Overseas Administration at the University of Oregon, and became professor of economics in 1957. *References*: *AMWS*; *CA*; *WWA*; and *Who's Who in Economics*, ed. Mark Blaug and Paul Surges (London, 1983).

MILLARD, DAVID (1794–1873). Clergyman, born November 24, 1794, in Ballston, New York. Millard was a pastor in West Bloomfield, New York, from 1818 to 1832, and in Portsmouth, New Hampshire, from 1837 to 1841. He journeyed to the Middle East in 1841 and wrote *A Journal of Travels in Egypt, Arabia Petraea and the Holy Land* (Rochester, 1843). He was later professor of Bible antiquities and sacred geography at Meadville (Pa.) Theological Seminary. Died August 3, 1873, in Jackson, Michigan. *References*: *Memoir of Rev. David Millard, with Selections from His Writings*, ed. David E. Millard (Dayton, Ohio, 1847); *ACAB*; and *DAA*.

MILLER, ALVAH L(ESLIE) (1884–1966). Young Men's Christian Association (YMCA)* executive, born in Marcus, Iowa. Miller graduated from Morningside College (Sioux City, Iowa). He was YMCA executive in India from 1912 to 1935 and chief executive of YMCA in Jerusalem from 1935 to 1951, when the YMCA provided social, cultural, and religious amenities for both Arabs and Jews in Jerusalem. In 1939 he acted to ransom an American clergyman who was kidnapped by Arabs in Palestine. He later lived in Brookfield Center, Connecticut. Died January 4, 1966, in Newtown, Connecticut. *Reference*: *NYT*, January 12, 1966.

MILLER, BARNETTE (1875–1956). Educator, born November 1, 1875, in Charlotte, North Carolina. Miller graduated from Columbia University. She taught briefly at Mount Holyoke, Vassar, and Smith colleges, was professor at the Constantinople College for Girls from 1909 to 1913 and from 1916 to 1919, and was chairman of the Constantinople chapter of the American Red Cross.* Between 1909 and 1913 she conducted four trips through Asia Minor, and again traveled in the Middle East in 1927–1928. She was associate professor and professor of history at Wellesley College from 1920 until her retirement in 1943. She wrote *Beyond the Sublime Porte* (New Haven, Conn., 1931). Died April 23, 1956, in South Natick, Massachusetts. *Reference*: *Boston Herald*, April 25, 1956.

MILLER, DANIEL LONG (1841–1921). Writer and editor, born October 5, 1841, in Goose Creek, near Hagerstown, Maryland. Miller was engaged in the grain and grocery business in Polo, Illinois, became part owner and business manager of Mount Morris College in 1879, its president from 1881 to 1883, and president of the board of trustees from 1893 until 1913. He became involved in publishing in 1882, was the managing editor of *The Gospel Messenger* from 1885 to 1891, and was editor-in-chief from 1891 until his death. He was ordained a bishop in the Church of the Brethren in 1890. He traveled in Asia Minor in 1883–1884 and again in the early 1890s, and described his travels in *The Seven Churches of Asia: Ephesus, Smyrna, Pergamos, Thyatira, Sardis, Philadelphia, Laodicea. Notes of Travel in Asia Minor* (Mount Morris, Ill., 1894), and in *Letters from Europe and Bible Lands* (Mount Morris, Ill., 1884). Died June 8, 1921, in Huntingdon, Pennsylvania. *References*: Bess R. Bates, *Life of D. L. Miller* (Elgin, Ill., 1921); *The Brethren Encyclopedia* (Philadelphia, 1983); *NCAB* 19:32; and *WWWA*.

MILLER, ROBERT P(ERRY) ("BERT") (1891–1984). Petroleum geologist, born July 29, 1891, in Bringhurst, Indiana. Miller graduated from the universities of Alberta (Edmonton) and California at Berkeley. He joined Standard Oil Company of California in 1924 and worked in the Arctic Circle, Sicily, Spain, Colombia, and Venezuela, Ethiopia and Somalia, and India. He came to Bahrein in 1932 with Schuyler B. ("Krug") Henry.* They were the first American geologists to conduct a geologic reconnaissance of the coast of al-Hasa in Saudi Arabia in 1933. Miller was one of the first Americans to cross Arabia in the same year. He later worked in Italy, India, and Colombia, and was an executive of Standard Oil Company of California until his retirement in 1956. Died January 14, 1984, in Sonoma County, California. *Reference*: *AWM* 35 (May–June 1984): 17.

MILLER, WILLIAM MCELWEE (1892–   ). Missionary, born December 12, 1892, in Middleboro, Kentucky. Miller graduated from Washington and Lee University and Princeton Theological Seminary, and was ordained in 1916. He served as a missionary under the Presbyterian Church in the USA Board of Foreign Missions in Iran from 1919 to 1962. He wrote *How the Revivals Came to Persia* (New York, 1933) and *Tales of Persia, a Book for Children* (Philadelphia, 1971). Reference: *CA*.

MILLSPAUGH, ARTHUR C(HESTER) (1883–1955). Political scientist, born March 1, 1883, in Augusta, Michigan. Millspaugh graduated from Albion College, the University of Illinois and Johns Hopkins University, and served in the State Department from 1918 to 1922. He headed a financial mission to Persia between 1922 and 1927, and was the Administrator General of Finances for Persia. He received a virtual veto over all expenditures of the Persian government, and succeeded in achieving control over government expenditures, improving the government's taxation and financial structure, and putting the Persian economy on a sound basis. Millspaugh left Persia in August 1927, when Reza Shah demanded that his authority be reduced. He was financial adviser and general receiver in Haiti from 1927 to 1929, and member of the staff of Brookings Institution from 1929 to 1942 and again from 1946 to 1948. In 1943 he again headed a financial mission to Iran, in order to effect reforms in its financial administration, and to ensure adequate food supplies in Iran during the war. Because of wide opposition to his reforms within Iran, his second mission failed, and he resigned in 1944. He wrote *The Financial and Economic Situation of Persia* (Boston, 1926), and described his experiences in *The American Task Force in Persia* (New York, 1925), and *Americans in Persia* (Washington, D.C. 1946). Died September 24, 1955, in Kalamazoo, Michigan. *References*: Hassan Mojedhi, 'Arthur C. Millspaugh's Two Missions to Iran and Their Impact on American-Iranian Relations.'' Ph.D. diss., Ball State University, 1975; *NYT*, September 26, 1955; Douglas L. Smith, "The Millspaugh Mission and American Corporate Diplomacy in Persia, 1922–1927," *Southern Quarterly* 14 (1976): 151–72; James Thorpe, "The Mission of Arthur C. Millspaugh to Iran, 1943–1945." Ph.D. diss., University of Wisconsin, 1973; and *WWWA*.

MINOR, CLORINDA S. (1808–1855). Religious zealot, born in Philadelphia. Minor became a Millerite in 1842. She went on a pilgrimage to Palestine in 1849–1850 and wrote *Meshullam: or, Tidings from Jerusalem* (Philadelphia, 1851). In 1851 she led a group of American Millerite settlers to Palestine. She settled first in Urtas, near Bethlehem, and in 1853 she transferred her colony to Jaffa. In 1855 she bought a large garden plot near Jaffa and called it Mount Hope.* Died November 6, 1855, in Mount Hope, Palestine. *Reference*: Ruth Kark, "Millenarism and Agricultural Settlement in the Holy Land in the Nineteenth Century," *Journal of Historical Geography* 9 (1983): 47–62.

MISSOURI, **U.S.S.** Battleship which traveled in the eastern Mediterranean and visited Turkey in 1946 as a symbol of U.S. interest in preserving Turkey's liberty. *Reference*: David J. Alvarez, "The Missouri Visit to Turkey: An Alternative Perspective to Cold War Diplomacy," *Balkan Studies* 15 (1974): 225–236.

MITCHELL, BRUCE (HANDYSIDE) (1908–1963). Illustrator, born January 27, 1908, in Tayport, Scotland, brought to the United States in 1916, and naturalized in 1942. Mitchell studied art at the Art Students League in New York City. From 1943 to 1945 he served in Iran as an artist correspondent for the U.S. Army Corps of Engineers and for *Life* magazine, illustrating the work of the Persian Gulf Command. He was resident artist at Bucknell University from 1947 to 1962 and exhibited his work in various exhibits. Died September 12, 1963, in Langhorne, Pennsylvania. *References*: *DAS*; *NCAB* 47:540; *NYT*, September 14, 1963; and *WWWA*.

MITCHELL, HINCKLEY GILBERT (THOMAS) (1846–1920). Clergyman and scholar, born February 22, 1846, in Lee, Oneida County, New York. Mitchell graduated from Wesleyan University, Boston University School of Theology, and the University of Leipzig. He taught Latin and Hebrew at Wesleyan University from 1880 to 1883, and Hebrew at Boston University School of Theology from 1883 to 1905. He visited Palestine in 1888 and was the second director of the American Schools of Oriental Research (ASOR)* in Jerusalem in 1901–1902. From 1909 until his death he was professor of Hebrew and later of New Testament as well at Tufts College. His unfinished autobiography, *For the Benefits of My Creditors* (Boston, 1922) was published after his death. Died May 19, 1920, in Boston. *References*: *ACAB*; *DAB*; *NCAB* 11:183; and *WWWA*.

MITCHELL, LEBBENS H. (1834–?). Mining engineer, born in Boston. Mitchell served in the Union Army in the Civil War, employed as a topographical engineer. He resigned his commission in 1864 and joined the Egyptian General Staff in a scientific capacity. He made a geological survey of the country between the Nile and the Red Sea in 1874. In 1877 he conducted a geological and mineralogical survey of the country between Massawa and the Ethiopian highlands. He and his party were captured by Ethiopians and taken to the interior. After great suffering, he was released and returned to Massawa. He wrote an account of his adventures in *Report on the Seizure by the Abyssinians of the Geological and Mineralogical Reconnaissance Expedition Attached to the General Staff of the Egyptian Army Containing an Account of the Subsequent Treatment of the Prisoners and Final Release of the Commander* (Cairo, 1878). He made a survey of the Red Sea Coast region in 1886, and in *Ras Gemsah & Gebel Zeit. Report on Their Geology & Petroleum* (Cairo, 1887) he reported extensive evidence of oil on the surface and convinced the Egyptian government that it possessed substantial deposits of petroleum. *Reference*: *Hill*.

MIXED COURTS OF EGYPT. Established in 1875, with exclusive jurisdiction over all litigation between Egyptians as well as the Egyptian government and foreigners and between foreigners of different nationalities. In addition, the courts had to give approval to laws affecting foreigners. Sixteen Americans served on the three district courts of the first instance (in Cairo, Alexandria, and Al-Mansura), and six (four of whom served previously on district courts) served on the Court of Appeals (in Alexandria). Jasper Yeates Brinton* was the only American to serve as president of the Court of Appeals (1943–1948). The court was closed down in 1949. *Reference*: Jasper Y. Brinton, *The Mixed Courts of Egypt*, rev. ed. (New Haven, Conn., 1968).

MOHR, EMANUEL NEHEMIAH (1883–1956). Engineer and economist, born in Russia. Mohr studied at Cooper Union in New York City. He was managing director of the Palestine Economic Company in Palestine from 1921 until 1933, co-founder and managing director of the Loan Bank in Jerusalem and the Palestine Mortgage and Credit Bank, and co-founder and president of the Palestine and Near East Water Development Corporation. His wife, **SOPHIE BERGER MOHR (1882–1958)**, was a social worker, born in La Crosse, Wisconsin. She graduated from the University of Chicago. She was executive director of The Young Women's Hebrew Association from 1909 to 1917, founder and first treasurer of Hadassah,* and volunteer with the American Red Cross* in France during World War I. She came to Palestine in 1918 and was executive director of the Palestine Orphan Committee of the Joint Distribution Committee from 1920 to 1928. She founded a branch of the American Association of University Women in Palestine. She returned to the United States in 1941. Died June 22, 1958, in Haifa, Israel. *Reference*: *NYT*, July 2, 1958.

MONROE, PAUL (1869–1947). Educator, born June 7, 1869, in North Madison, Indiana. Monroe graduated from Hanover and Baptist Franklin colleges and the University of Chicago. He was a high school principal from 1891 to 1894, and became an instructor of history at Columbia University Teachers' College in 1897. He became professor of the history of education in 1902 and professor of education in 1925. In 1923 he founded the International Institute of Education at Teachers College and directed it until 1938. He headed an educational survey team sent to the Middle East by the Near East Relief* in 1923, and in 1932 conducted an educational survey of Iraq commissioned by the Iraqi government. He was president of the Istanbul Woman's College and Robert College* from 1932 to 1935. Died December 6, 1947, in Goshen, New York. *References*: *DAB S4*; *DAEB*; *IAB*; *NCAB* 36:336; and *NYT*, December 7, 1947.

MONTGOMERY, GILES FOSTER (1835–1888). Missionary, born November 8, 1835, in Walden, Vermont. Montgomery graduated from Middlebury College and Lane Theological Seminary. He became a missionary under the

American Board of Commissioners for Foreign Missions (ABCFM)* at Aintab, Turkey, in 1863. He was the first missionary to enter Marash in 1865 and was later stationed in Adana. Died December 4, 1888, in Adana, Turkey. *Reference*: *EM*.

MONTGOMERY, JAMES ALAN (1866–1949). Biblical scholar and clergyman, born June 13, 1866, in Germantown, Pennsylvania. Montgomery graduated from the University of Pennsylvania and the Philadelphia Divinity School, studied at the universities of Greifswald and Berlin, and was ordained in 1893. He served as a pastor in Philadelphia from 1893 until 1907, and was professor at the Philadelphia Divinity School from 1899 until his retirement in 1935. He was director of the American Schools of Oriental Research (ASOR)* in Jerusalem in 1914–1915 and president of the ASOR from 1921 to 1934. Died February 6, 1949, in Philadelphia. *References*: *DAB S4*; Cyrus H. Gordon, "A Scholar and Gentleman: James Alan Montgomery," *BA* 46 (1983): 187–189; *NYT*, February 8, 1949; and *WWWA*.

MOOSE, JAMES SAYLE, JR. (1903–   ). Diplomat, born October 2, 1903, in Morrillton, Arkansas. Moose graduated from Kentucky Military Institute and the University of Missouri, and studied at L'Ecole Libre des Sciences Politiques and L'Ecole Nationale des Langues Orientales Vivantes in Paris. He entered the foreign service in 1928 and served in Salonika, Greece, Paris, Beirut, and Baghdad. He was second secretary and consul in Baghdad from 1933 to 1936, second secretary and consul in Teheran from 1936 to 1942 and second secretary in Kabul from 1940 to 1942. In 1934 he accompanied Paul Knabenshue* on a special diplomatic mission to Muscat. He became second secretary and consul in Jidda in 1942, opened the legation there, and was minister and counselor until 1944. He was counselor in Damascus from 1945 to 1947, director of the Office of African and Near Eastern Affairs from 1949 to 1952, minister to Syria in 1952, the first ambassador to Syria from 1952 until 1957, and ambassador to the Sudan from 1958 until his retirement in 1962. *Reference*: *BRDS*.

MORGAN, ORA S(HERMAN) (1877–1961). Agricultural economist and educator, born August 11, 1877, in Hampshire, Illinois. Morgan graduated from Illinois State University (Normal), the University of Illinois, and Cornell University. He was first president of the New York State University Agricultural and Technical Institute at Alfred, New York, from 1908 to 1911, and professor of agricultural economics at Columbia University from 1911 to 1943. He made agricultural surveys for the Near East Relief* in southern Russia and in Greece in 1926 and 1927, was director of education for the Near East Relief in Armenia in 1927, and made a survey of agriculture in the Near East in 1926–1927. In 1942–1943 he conducted an agricultural survey of the Middle East for the U.S. Board of Economic Warfare and the Near East Foundation.* From 1946 to 1948 he was in charge of United Nations Relief and Rehabilitation Administration work in Chekiang province, China. Died August 14, 1961, near Chico, California. *References*: *NCAB* 50:248; *NYT*, August 16, 1961; and *WWWA*.

MORGENTHAU, HENRY (1856–1946). Lawyer and diplomat, born April 26, 1856, in Mannheim, Germany, and came to the United States in 1866. Morgenthau graduated from the City College of New York and Columbia Law School, and was admitted to the bar in 1877. He practiced law in New York City until 1899, and established a real estate company in 1899 and another in 1905 which he headed until 1913. He was ambassador to Turkey from 1913 until 1916, and after the beginning of World War I became involved in relief work and in representing the interests of the Allied Powers in Turkey. In 1917 he was sent on a mission to mediate a separate peace between Turkey and the Allies, but the mission was called off. He wrote an account of his diplomatic work, *Ambassador Morgenthau's Story* (New York, 1918). He later served as adviser at the Paris Peace Conference, was a member of the Harbord Mission,* and in 1923 chairman of the League of Nations refugee Resettlement Commission in Greece. He wrote an autobiography, *All in a Lifetime* (New York, 1922). Died November 25, 1946, in New York City. *References*: Papers, Manuscript Division, Library of Congress; *ACAB*; J. Adler, "Morgenthau's Mission of 1917," *Herzel Year Book* 5 (1963): 249–281; *DAB S4*; *EJ*; Richard N. Lebow, "The Morgenthau Peace Mission of 1917," *Jewish Social Studies* 32 (October 1970): 267–228; *NCAB* 36:24; *NYT*, November 26, 1946; Barbara W. Tuchman, "The Assimilationist Dilemma: Ambassador Morgenthau's Story," *Commentary* 63 (May 1977): 58–62; *WWWA*; and William Yale, "Ambassador Henry Morgenthau's Special Mission in 1917," *World Politics* 1 (1949): 308–320.

MORRIS, EDWARD JOY (1815–1881). Lawyer and diplomat, born July 16, 1815, in Philadelphia. Morris graduated from the University of Pennsylvania and Harvard University, studied law in Philadelphia, and was admitted to the bar in 1842. He traveled in the Middle East in 1838, and wrote *Notes on a Tour Through Turkey, Greece, Egypt, Arabia Petraea, to the Holy Land* (Boston, 1842). He was congressman from Pennsylvania in 1843–1845 and 1857–1861; chargé d'affaires to the Two Sicilies from 1850 to 1853; and minister to Turkey from 1861 to 1870. Morris negotiated a treaty of commerce and navigation between the United States and Turkey in 1862. Died December 31, 1881, in Philadelphia. *References*: *ACAB*; *DAB*; Harry N. Howard, "President Lincoln's Minister Resident to the Sublime Porte: Edward Joy Morris (1861–1870)," *Balkan Studies* 5 (1964): 205–220; *NCAB* 13:25; and *WWWA*.

MORRIS, LELAND BURNETTE (1886–1950). Diplomat, born February 7, 1886, in Fort Clark, Texas. Morris graduated from the University of Pennsylvania. He was appointed student interpreter in Turkey in 1910; served in Salonika and Smyrna from 1912 to 1917; was consul in Montreal in 1918–1919; was detailed to the American High Commission in Constantinople in 1919; and was consul in Salonika from 1919 to 1924 and in Cologne from 1924 to 1926. He became consul in Athens in 1929, first secretary in 1932, and chargé d'affaires in 1932–1933. He was consul general in Jerusalem in 1936 and in Alexandria from 1936 to 1938, and chargé d'affaires in Cairo in 1937–1938. Morris was sent to Jidda in 1936–1937 to investigate the practicability of initiating official U.S. representation in Saudi Arabia. He was consul general in Vienna from 1938 to 1940, chargé d'affaires ad interim in Germany in 1940–1941, minister to Iceland from 1942 to 1944, and ambassador to Iran in 1944–1945. He retired in 1948. Died July 2, 1950, in Washington, D.C. *References*: *NCAB* 39:288; *NYT*, July 5, 1950; and *WWWA*.

MORRIS, RICHARD VALENTINE (1768–1815). Naval officer and diplomat, born March 8, 1768, in Morrisania, New York. Morris was commissioned a captain in the navy in 1798. In 1802–1803 he commanded the Mediterranean squadron sent to operate against Tripoli and later to superintend all negotiations with the Barbary States, but was an unsuccessful negotiator. His commission was revoked following a court of inquiry. He retired to Morrisania. Died May 13, 1815, in Morrisania. *References*: *ACAB*; *DAB*; *DADH*; and *WWWA*.

MORRIS, ROBERT (1818–1888). Masonic writer and lecturer, born August 31, 1818, near Boston. Morris moved to Mississippi and later to Kentucky. He visited the Middle East in 1868 and wrote *Freemasonary in the Holy Land . . . Embracing Notes Made During a Series of Masonic Researchers, in 1868, in Asia Minor, Syria, Palestine, Egypt and Europe* (New York, 1872). He founded the Order of the Eastern Star and produced many publications about freemasonry. Died July 31, 1888, in La Grange, Kentucky. His *Letters of Rob Morris, LL.D. to Wife and Children from the Holy Land in 1868* were edited by John K. Lacock (Boston, 1931). *References*: Papers, Grand Lodge Library, Boston; *ACAB*; *DAB*; Beulah H. Malone, *He Belongs to the Ages* (Tulsa, Okla., 1967); *NCAB* 25:394; and *WWWA*.

MORRISON KNUDSEN CORPORATION. Engineering and constructing firm, also involved in shipbuilding and manufacturing, founded in 1912 and incorporated in 1932. This company was involved with several large construction projects in Afghanistan, Iran, and Saudi Arabia, including the construction of the Karadj Dam near Teheran and the King Khalid Military City project in Saudi Arabia. *References*: "Anniversary Issue," *The eMKayan* [Boise, Id.] 46 (March 1987); *Time*, May 3, 1954.

MOSER, CHARLES KROTH (1877–1968). Consul, born August 27, 1877, in Marion, Smythe County, Virginia. Moser graduated from the University of California. He was sports writer and reporter for the *San Francisco Chronicle* from 1900 to 1904, was admitted to the bar, practiced law in San Francisco from 1902 to 1904, was magazine writer from 1904 to 1907, and associate editor of the *Washington Post* from 1907 to 1909. He entered the foreign service in 1909 and was consul in Aden from 1909 to 1911. He was the first American official to visit Yemen when he went there in 1910 to investigate the death of an American missionary. He also visited the island of Sokotra and reported his experiences in the *National Geographic Magazine*. Moser was later consul in Colombo, Ceylon, Harbin, Manchuria, and Tiflis, the Georgia Republic. He retired from the foreign service in 1922 and joined the Bureau of Foreign and Domestic Commerce of the Department of Commerce, ultimately becoming chief of the Far Eastern Division, and retired in 1947. Died September 23, 1968, in Washington, D.C. *References*: *Foreign Commerce Weekly*, October 11, 1947; *WWWA*.

MOTT, JOHN R(ALEIGH) (1865–1955). Ecumenical pioneer and Young Men's Christian Association (YMCA)* official, born May 25, 1865, near Purvis (later Livingston Manor), Sullivan County, New York, and grew up in Pottsville, Iowa. Mott attended Upper Iowa University (Fayette, Ia.) and graduated from Cornell University. He became affiliated with the YMCA in 1886, became its senior student secretary in 1890, the national executive for the American YMCA from 1915 to 1928, and president of the World YMCA in 1926. He was chairman of the Student Volunteer Movement for Foreign Missions from 1888 to 1920 and one of the founders of the World's Student Christian Federation in 1895, becoming its general secretary until 1920 and its chairman from 1920 until 1928. He was chairman of the International Missionary Council from 1921 to 1940 and was instrumental in convening it in Jerusalem in 1928. He traveled widely throughout the world. Mott first visited Palestine in 1895, returning in 1911 when he was involved in ecumenical work there, and again in 1924, 1928, 1933, and 1937. He shared in the Nobel Peace Prize in 1946. Died January 31, 1955, in Orlando, Florida. *References*: Archives, Yale Divinity School Library, New Haven, Connecticut; *CB* 1947; *DAB S5*; *DARB*; Robert T. Handy, "Holy Land Experiences of Two Pioneers of Christian Ecumenism: Schaff and Mott," in *Contemporary Jewry: Studies in Honor of Moshe Davis*, ed. Geoffrey Wigodor (Jerusalem, 1984), pp. 65–78; C. Howard Hopkins, *John R. Mott, 1865–1955: A Biography* (Grand Rapids, Mich., 1979); *NCAB* 44:346; *NYT*, February 1, 1955; and *WWWA*.

MOTT, THADDEUS P(HELPS) (1831–1894). Army officer, son of Valentine Mott,* born December 7, 1831, in New York City. Mott attended the University of New York. He accompanied his father to Constantinople in 1838, served in the Mexican War, and fought during the Revolts of 1848–1849. He married the daughter of a wealthy Turkish landowner, shipped as an officer on clipper ships from 1850 to 1855, and commanded Mott's Battery in the Civil War. He went to Turkey in 1868, met Khedive Ismail of Egypt, was appointed a major general in the Egyptian Army in 1869, and was aide-de-camp to the Khedive in 1870. In 1870 he escorted the first American recruits to Egypt, and in 1871 he was sent to the United States as an agent of the Khedive to recruit veterans of the American Civil War for the Egyptian Army. Mott retired to Turkey in 1875, remaining there until 1879, when he settled in Toulon, France. Died November 23, 1894, in Toulon. *References*: *ACAB*; *Hesseltine*; and *NYT*, November 27, 1894.

MOTT, VALENTINE (1785–1865). Surgeon, born August 20, 1785, in Glen Cove, Long Island, New York. Mott graduated from Columbia University, and studied at London and Edinburgh. He taught surgery at Columbia College, New York College of Physicians and Surgeons, Rutgers Medical College, and the University of the City of New York (now New York University). He lived in Europe from 1835 to 1841, visited the Middle East in 1838 with his family, and went to Constantinople to remove a tumor from the head of the Sultan Abdul Mecid. He wrote *Travels in Europe and the East* (New York, 1842). Died April 26, 1865, in New York City. *References*: *ACAB*; *DAB*; *DAMB*; *NCAB* 6:281; and *WWWA*.

MOULTON, WARREN JOSEPH (1865–1947). Theologian, born August 30, 1865, in Sandwich, New Hampshire. Moulton graduated from Boston University, Amherst College, Yale University, and the University of Gottingen, and was ordained in 1899. He was a pastor at Athol, Massachusetts, from 1903 to 1905, professor of New Testament language and literature at Bangor Theological Seminary from 1908 to 1933, and president of the seminary from 1921 to 1933. He traveled in the Middle East in 1902–1903, was resident director of the American Schools of Oriental Research (ASOR)* in Jerusalem in 1912–1913, and excavated in Palestine. He returned to Palestine in 1935–1936 as lecturer at the ASOR. Died May 7, 1947, in Bangor, Maine. *References*: *AJA* 51 (1947): 307; *NYT*, May 8, 1947; and *WWWA*.

MOUNT HOPE COLONY, JAFFA. The first American colony in Palestine, established near Jaffa in 1853 by Clorinda S. Minor* and a group of American Millerites. In 1855 Minor bought a plot of land north of Jaffa and called it Mount Hope. After her death, the colony was run by John Steinbeck, son-in-law of Walter Dickson,* until 1858 when it was attacked by Arabs, and the colony ended. In 1869 the land was acquired by German Templars.

MULLER, W(ILHELM) MAX (1862–1919). Orientalist, born May 15, 1862, in Gliessenberg, Bavaria, Germany. Muller studied at the universities of Erlangen, Leipzig, Berlin, and Munich, and came to the United States in 1888. The Carnegie Institution sent him to Egypt on archaeological researches in 1904, 1906, and 1910, and the results of his expeditions were published in *Egyptological Researchers* (Washington, D.C., 1906–1920). He was professor of ancient languages and Old and New Testament exegesis at the Reformed Episcopal Theological Seminary in Philadelphia, and then assistant professor of Egyptology at the University of Pennsylvania. Drowned July 12, 1919, in Wildwood, New Jersey. *References*: *DAB*; *NCAB* 21:413; *WWWA*; and *WWWE*.

MULTINATIONAL FORCE AND OBSERVERS (MFO). A multinational agency, established by the protocol signed by the governments of Egypt and Israel in 1981, which took peacekeeping responsibilities in the Sinai on April 25, 1982, when Israel completed its withdrawal from the Sinai in accordance with the 1979 peace treaty with Egypt. About half of the MFO is manned by the United States. The agency's mission is to supervise the implementation of the peace treaty and to prevent violations of its provisions. *Reference*: Mala Tabory, *The Multinational Force and Observers in the Sinai: Organization, Structure, and Function* (Boulder, Colo., 1986).

MURCH, CHAUNCEY (1856–1907). Missionary, Egyptologist, and collector, born January 1, 1856, in Alexander, Pennsylvania. Murch graduated from Muskingum College and Xenia (Ohio) and Allegheny (Pa.) theological seminaries, and was ordained in 1882. He became a missionary under the United Presbyterian Church in North America Board of Foreign Missions* in 1883, and served in Luxor, Egypt. He collected antiquities, part of which he sold to the Metropolitan Museum of Art and the Art Institute of Chicago. Died October 16, 1907, in Luxor, Egypt. *References*: *NYT*, October 21, 1907; *WWWA*; and *WWWE*.

MURPHY, ROBERT DANIEL (1894–1978). Diplomat, born October 28, 1894, in Milwaukee. Murphy graduated from Marquette and George Washington universities, and was admitted to the bar. He entered the diplomatic service in 1917, and served in Zurich, Munich, and Seville. He was consul in Paris from 1930 to 1936, first secretary from 1936 to 1939, counselor from 1939 to 1941, and chargé d'affaires from 1940 to 1941. He was detailed to investigate conditions in French North Africa in 1940; involved in the preparations for the Allied landings in North Africa in 1942. He was then appointed the president's personal representative with the rank of minister to French North Africa and chief civil affairs officer on the staff of the supreme Allied commander of the Mediterranean theater, and co-chairman of the North African Economic board; and political adviser with the rank of ambassador in 1943. He was political adviser for Germany in 1944, director of the Office of German and Austrian Affairs in 1949, ambassador to Belgium from 1949 to 1952, ambassador to Japan from 1952 to 1953, and deputy undersecretary of state from 1954 to 1959. He was President Dwight Eisenhower's special representative in Lebanon in 1958 and helped in the negotiations between France and Tunisia which led to Tunisia's freedom. He was undersecretary of state for political affairs in 1959. He wrote his memoirs, *Diplomat Among Warriors* (Garden City, N.Y., 1964). Died January 9, 1978, in New York City. *References*: *CA*; *CB* 1943; *DADH*; David Kahn, "Robert Murphy: Codebreakers' Delight," *Nation* 222 (March 20, 1976): 325–326;

NCAB 60:258; *NYT* January 11, 1978; *PolProf: Truman*; *PolProf: Eisenhower*; and *WWWA*.

MURPHY, U.S.S. Destroyer. In 1945, commanded by Commander Bernard A. Smith, the *Murphy* escorted the U.S.S. *Quincy*, carrying President Franklin D. Roosevelt from Norfolk, Virginia, to Yalta and then to the Great Bitter Lake in the Suez Canal, and then transported King Ibn Saud of Saudi Arabia from Jidda to the conference with the president regarding the Palestine problem and the Jewish refugees. *References*: John S. Keating, ''Mission to Mecca: The Cruise of the Murphy,'' *USNIP* 102 (January 1976): 54–63; *Life*, March 19, 1945.

N

NATHAN, ALBERT J. (fl. 1895–1899). Missionary, born in Hamburg, Germany. Nathan was converted to Christianity in New York City and served as a pastor in Oklahoma. He went to Morocco in 1895, leading the first missionary party of the Gospel Missionary Union. He established a mission station in Tangiers and later in Meknes. He withdrew from the mission and terminated his relationship with the Gospel Missionary Union in 1899, but remained in Morocco, acting as informal adviser, private investigator, interpreter, and attaché for the U.S. consul in Tangier. He later founded the Nathan Missionary Society of Butler, Pennsylvania, and returned to Tangier as missionary to the Jews.

NEAR EAST FOUNDATION Not-for-profit organization, incorporated in 1930 in the state of New York to continue the work of Near East Relief.* Its objectives were to improve the economic and agricultural conditions among the rural populations of the Middle East through education, demonstrations, and training by technical experts, and to help initiate agricultural extension services, rural education, public health projects, and rural recreation. *References*: *Bread from Stones: Fifty Years of Technical Assistance*, ed.. John S. Badeau and Georgiana G. Stevens (Englewood Cliffs, N.J., 1966); Robert L. Daniel, *American Philanthropy in the Near East 1820–1960* (Athens, Ga., 1970), chs. 9, 11.

NEAR EAST RELIEF (NER). Relief organization, incorporated by the U.S. Congress in 1917 as a permanent organization providing relief and assisting in the repatriation and rehabitation of refugees in the Near East, by providing food, shelter, medical care, and educational, and social programs during and after World War I. In 1922–1923 it was in charge of feeding and housing repatriated Greeks and Turks, and it continued to operate orphanages and provide limited disaster relief work. It was replaced in 1930 by the Near East Foundation.* *References*: James L. Barton, *Story of Near East Relief (1915–1930): An Interpretation* (New York, 1930); Robert L. Daniel, *American Philanthropy in the Near East 1920–1960* (Athens, Ga., 1970), ch. 7.

NEAR EAST SCHOOL OF THEOLOGY, BEIRUT. Established as a seminary in Beirut in 1882, and moved in 1883 to the campus of the Syrian Protestant College. It reopened in 1905, and in 1926 the name was changed from the Beirut Theological Seminary to the School for Religious Workers. In 1932 it merged with the School of Religion in Athens, and the name was changed to the Near East School of Theology. It offers theological education and pastoral training. *References*: Yorke Allen, Jr., *A Seminary Survey* (New York, 1960), pp. 88–92; W. Semaann, "The First Protestant Theological Seminary in Lebanon," *Theological Review* 7 (1986): 8–22.

NELSON, HAROLD HAYDEN (1878–1954). Egyptologist, born November 25, 1878, in New Orleans. Nelson graduated from the University of Chicago. He was an instructor at the Syrian Protestant College from 1904 to 1908, professor of history from 1904 to 1927, chairman of the History Department from 1924 to 1927, and editor of *Al Kulliyah*, the college magazine. He was professor of Egyptology and field director of the Oriental Institute's epigraphic and architectural survey at Luxor, Egypt, from 1924 until 1947, directed the studies of the temples at Medinet Habu and Karnak, and was responsible for six volumes of copied temple inscriptions, including *Epigraphic Survey of the Great Temple of Medinet Habu* (Chicago, 1929), *Medinet Habu* (Chicago, 1930–1940), *Work in Western Thebes, 1931–33* (Chicago, 1934), and *Reliefs and Inscriptions at Karnak* (Chicago, 1936). Died January 24, 1954, in Chicago. *References*: *JNES* 13 (1954): 119; *NYT* January 25, 1954; *WWWA*; and *WWWE*.

NELSON, WILLIAM S(HEDD) (1860–1934). Missionary, born January 25, 1860, in St. Louis, Missouri. Nelson graduated from Hamilton and Amherst colleges and Lane Theological Seminary, and was ordained in 1881. He was professor of mathematics and natural science at Park College (Mo.) from 1881 to 1884, and a missionary under the Presbyterian Church in the USA Board of Foreign Missions* in Tripoli, Syria, from 1888 until 1904. He was consular agent in Tripoli in 1916 and was involved in relief work under the American Red Cross* in Syria from 1919 to 1929. Nelson retired in 1930. He wrote *Habeeb the Beloved: A Tale of Life in Modern Syria* (Philadelphia, 1913), and *Silver Chimes in Syria: Glimpses of a Missionary's Experiences* (Philadelphia, 1914). *Reference*: Amherst.

NESTORIAN MISSION. Mission to the Nestorian Christians in northwestern Persia (now West Azerbaijan Province of Iran), established in 1934 by the American Commissioners for Foreign Missions (ABCFM).* The mission was transferred to the Presbyterian Church in the USA Board of Foreign Missions* in 1870 and was renamed the Iran Mission.* The mission was closed down in 1934. *References*: John Joseph, *The Nestorians and Their Muslim Neighbors: A Study of Western Influence on Their Relations* (Princeton, N.J., 1961); Richard M. Schwartz, "Missionaries on the Rezaiyeh Plain, Iran," *MW* 69 (1979): 77–100.

NEUMANN, EMANUEL (1893–1980). Communal leader and organization executive, born July 2, 1893, in Libau, Latvia, and came to the United States as an infant. Neumann graduated from Columbia and New York universities; was educational director of the Zionist Organization of America from 1918 to 1920; co-founder of Keren Hayesod in the United States in 1921 and its first national director from 1921 to 1925; chairman of the executive committee of the United Palestine Appeal from 1925 to 1928; and president of the Jewish National Fund in the United States in 1929–1930. He was a member of the Jewish Agency Executive in Jerusalem from 1931 to 1939, political representative of the Jewish Agency in Washington from 1940 to 1946, president of the Zionist Organization of America from 1947 to 1949 and from 1956 to 1958, and chairman of the executive of the Jewish Agency from 1953 to 1971. He wrote *In the Arena: An Autobiographical Memoir* (New York, 1976). Died October 26, 1980, in Tel Aviv, Israel. *References*: *CA*; *CB* 1967; *EJ*; *NYT*, October 27, 1980; and *WWWA*.

NEUMANN, ROBERT GERHARD (1916–   ). Political scientist, born January 2, 1916, in Vienna, Austria. Neumann studied at the universities of Rennes and Vienna, Amherst College, and the University of Minnesota. He was a prisoner in a Nazi concentration camp. He was a member of the faculty of Wisconsin State Teachers College (Oshkosh) in 1941–1942, and the University of Wisconsin in 1946–1947, assistant professor, associate professor, and professor of political science at the University of California at Los Angeles from 1947 to 1967, and director of the Institute of International and Foreign Studies from 1958 to 1967. He served as consultant on international security affairs to the secretary of defense from 1962 to 1966, and on the policy planning council of the State Department from 1963 to 1966. He was ambassador to Afghanistan from 1966 to 1973, and ambassador to Morocco from 1973 to 1976. In 1977 he became a staff member of the Institute for the Study of Diplomacy (renamed Center for Strategic and International Studies) at Georgetown University. He became ambassador to Saudi Arabia in 1981. He was forced to resign by secretary of state Alexander Haig, Jr. the same year because he disagreed with and criticized United States policy regarding Israel. *References*: *AMWS*; *NYT*, July 30, 1981; and *WWA*.

NEWMAN, HENRY RODERICK (1843–1917). Painter, born March 1943 in Easton, New York, and grew up in New York City. In 1861 Newman began to study art and to paint. In 1869 he went to study in France, and in 1870 he settled in Florence, remaining there until his death. From 1885 until World War I, he would paint in Egypt during the winter, rent a houseboat, live on the Nile, and paint Egyptian temples and tombs along the Nile. He visited Japan in the late 1890s. Died in Florence in December 1917. *References*: Kent Ahrens, "Pioneer Abroad: Henry R. Newman (1843–1917), Watercolorist and Friend of Ruskin,"

American Art Journal 8 (November 1976): 85–98; *DAB*; *NYHSD*; *NYT*, January 31, 1918; and *WWWA*.

NEWMAN, JOHN PHILIP (1826–1899). Clergyman, born September 1, 1826, in New York City. Newman graduated from Cazenovia (N.Y.) Seminary, and began preaching in Albany and later in New York City. He went to Palestine and wrote *From Dan to Beersheba; or, the Land of Promise as It Now Appears* (New York, 1864). He was in New Orleans from 1864 to 1869, establishing the Methodist Episcopal Church in the Southwest. In 1869 he became a pastor in Washington, D.C., and from 1869 to 1874 he was also a chaplain to the Senate. He was created "Inspector of United States Consulates," made a trip around the world, visited the Middle East, and wrote *The Thrones and Palaces of Babylon and Nineveh from Sea to Sea: A Thousand Miles on Horseback* (New York, 1876). He was again pastor in Washington until 1879 and in New York City from 1879 until 1882. In 1888 he was elected bishop and resided in Omaha and San Francisco. Died July 5, 1899, in Saratoga, New York. *References*: *ACAB*; *DAB*; *EWM*; *NCAB* 6:431; and *WWWA*.

NEWSOM, DAVID D(UNLAP) (1918–   ). Diplomat, born January 6, 1918, in Richmond, California. Newsom graduated from the University of California and Columbia University Graduate School of Journalism, was newspaper reporter from 1938 to 1941, and served in the army in World War II. He was publisher of the Walnut Creek (Calif.) *Courier-Journal* in 1946–1947, entered the foreign service in 1947, was third secretary in Karachi, second secretary and vice consul in Oslo and in Baghdad, officer in charge of Arabian Peninsula affairs from 1955 to 1959, first secretary in London from 1960 to 1962, and director of the Office of North Africa Affairs from 1963 to 1965. He was ambassador to Libya from 1965 to 1969, assistant secretary of state for African affairs from 1969 to 1974, ambassador to Indonesia from 1973 to 1977 and ambassador to the Philippines in 1977–1978, and undersecretary of state for political affairs from 1978 to 1981. In 1981 he became director of the Institute for the Study of Diplomacy and associate dean of the School of Foreign Service of Georgetown University. *References*: *BRDS*; *MENA*; *PolProf: Nixon/Ford*; Robert Shaplen, "Profiles (David Newsom)," *New Yorker*, June 2, June 9, June 16, 1980; and *WWA*.

NICHOLSON, JAMES WILLIAM AUGUSTUS (1821–1887). Naval officer, born March 10, 1821, in Dedham, Massachusetts. Nicholson was appointed a midshipman in 1838, served in the West India Squadron, in a cruise to the Mediterranean, and in the Pacific. In 1852 he served on one of Commodore Perry's ships sent to Japan and was stationed in Shanghai. Nicholson later served in the African Squadron, in the Civil War, and in the Pacific Squadron, and was commandant of the New York Navy Yard from 1876 to 1880. He was commander of the European station in 1881. He visited Alexandria, Egypt, in 1882 when that city was bombarded by the British fleet, rescuing the archives of the consulate and landing a detachment of marines which put out fires, buried the dead, and restored order. He retired in 1883 with the rank of rear admiral. Died October 28, 1887, in New York City. *References*: *DAB*; *NCAB* 2:112; and *WWWA*.

NICOL, JAMES HOUDEN (1875–1962). Missionary, born October 11, 1875, in Dubuque, Iowa. Nocol graduated from the University of Minnesota and Auburn Theological Seminary, and was ordained in 1904. He became a missionary under the Presbyterian Church in the U.S. A. Board of Foreign Missions in Tripoli, Syria, in 1905. In 1918–1919 he directed relief work in Syria and Palestine. He was later secretary of the Syria Mission* until his retirement in 1945. He was interim secretary of the Near East Christian Council in Beirut from 1945 until 1949. Died September 1962 in Trumansburg, New York. His autobiographical account of his early years, *The Autobiography of an Ordinary Soul* (Trumansburg, N.Y., 1963) appeared after his death. *Reference: AuburnTS*.

NIELSEN, FRED(ERICK) KENELM (1879–1963). Lawyer and diplomat, born April 22, 1979, in Slagelse, Denmark, came to the United States in 1880 and grew up in Audubon, Iowa. Nielsen graduated from the University of Nebraska and Georgetown University, was admitted to the bar in 1904, and served in the army in World War I. He was an attorney in the legal department of the State Department from 1904 to 1913, assistant solicitor and acting solicitor from 1913 to 1920, and solicitor from 1920 to 1924. He was professor of international law at Georgetown University from 1924 until his retirement in 1953, but continued to represent the United States. He headed the American delegation to the American-Turkish Claims Commission in 1933–1934, and prepared the *American-Turkish Claims Settlement* (Washington, D.C., 1937). Died January 12, 1963, in Washington, D.C. *References*: Papers, Manuscript Division, Library of Congress; *NCAB* 50:393; and *WWWA*.

NIES, JAMES BUCHANAN (1856–1922). Clergyman and archaeologist, born November 22, 1856, in Newark, New Jersey. Nies graduated from Columbia College and General Theological Seminary, and was ordained in 1886. He served as a pastor in New York City, Tuckahoe, Upper New Rochelle, and Brooklyn, New York, until his retirement in 1898. He then devoted himself to travel and archaeology. He endowed the American Schools of Oriental Research (ASOR)* in Jerusalem, of which he was field director in 1901. In 1922 he donated his collection of Babylonian clay tablets to Yale University. Died June 19, 1922, in Jerusalem. *References*: *DAB*; *NCAB* 20:257; and *WWA*.

***NIMROD SPAR*, OPERATION.** The salvage operation conducted in 1974–1975, in which units of the U.S. Navy, commanded by Captain J. Huntly Boyd, Jr., supervised the removal of vessels sunk in the Suez Canal during the Six Day War of 1967 and the October 1973 War. The actual salvage work was done by the Murphy Pacific Marine Salvage Company of New York. *Reference*: J.

Huntley Boyd, Jr., "Nimrod Spar: Clearing the Suez Canal," *USNIP* 102 (February 1976): 18–26.

NIXON, ROY W(ESLEY) (1895–   ). Horticulturist, born August 15, 1895, in Dade City, Florida. Nixon graduated from the University of Arizona. He rose from junior horticulturist to research horticulturist in date investigation for the U.S. Department of Agriculture from 1923 to 1965, and was a collaborator from 1965 to 1975. In 1938–1939 he explored Iraq and West Iran for varieties of dates, was in North Africa in 1948–1949, and served as date consultant to Saudi Arabia in 1953, to Libya in 1959, and to the Sudan in 1965–1966. *Reference*: *AMWS*.

NOAH, MORDECAI MANUEL (1785–1851). Lawyer and journalist, born July 19, 1785, in Philadelphia. Noah was engaged in politics in Charleston, South Carolina, and in 1813 became consul to Tunis with a special mission to Algeria. His commission was revoked in 1815, he returned to the United States in 1816, and wrote *Correspondence and Documents Relative to the Attempt to Negotiate for the Release of the American Captives at Algiers; Including Remarks on Our Relations with That Regency* (Washington, D.C., 1816), and *Travels in England, France, Spain and the Barbary States in the Years 1813–14 and 15* (New York, 1819). After 1816 he was involved in journalism, became editor of the *National Advocate* in 1817, tried to establish Ararat, a Jewish colony, wrote plays, was admitted to the bar in 1823, established the *New York Enquirer* in 1826, and was surveyor of the Port of New York from 1829 to 1833. He was later editor of several other newspapers including *Noah's Times and Weekly Messenger*, which he edited until his death. Died March 22, 1851, in New York City. *References*: *ACAB*; *DAB*; *EJ*; Issac Goldberg, *Major Noah: American Jewish Pioneer* (Philadelphia, 1938); *NCAB* 9:200; Jonathan D. Sarna, *Jacksonian Jew: The Two Worlds of Mordecai Noah* (New York, 1981); and *WWWA*.

NOEL, CLEO ALLEN, JR. (1918–1973). Diplomat, born August 6, 1918, in Oklahoma City, Oklahoma. Noel graduated from the University of Oklahoma and Harvard University, and served in the navy during World War II. He entered the foreign service in 1949; was vice consul in Genoa and Dhahran, and consul in Marseille; second secretary in Jidda in 1957–1958 and in Khartoum from 1958 to 1961; officer in charge of Sudanese affairs from 1961 to 1963; and counselor in the Hague from 1965 to 1967 and in Khartoum from 1967 to 1972. He was ambassador to the Sudan in 1972–1973. Executed by Palestinian terrorists, March 1, 1973, in Khartoum, the Sudan. *References*: *NYT*, March 3, 1973; *WWWA*.

NOLTE, RICHARD HENRY (1920–). Consultant, born December 27, 1920, in Duluth, Minnesota. Nolte graduated from Yale University and was a Rhodes scholar at Oxford University. He was a fellow of the Institute of Current World

Affairs from 1948 to 1954, an associate of the American Universities Field Staff in the Middle East from 1953 to 1958, and executive director of the Institute of Current World Affairs from 1959 to 1978. He edited *The Modern Middle East* (New York, 1963). He was appointed ambassador to the United Arab Republic in 1967 but left when it severed diplomatic relations with the United States after the Six Days War. He became consultant on the Middle East to Dillon, Read and Company, and general partner of the Washburn Island Research Ltd. in 1981. *Reference*: *WWA*.

NORTH, ROBERT GRADY (1916–   ). Archaeologist, born March 25, 1916, in Iowa City, Iowa. North graduated from St. Louis University and the Pontifical Biblical Institute in Rome, and became a member of the Society of Jesus. He was a teacher at Marquette University High School from 1939 to 1941, professor of archaeology and Arabic at the Pontifical Biblical Institute in Rome from 1951 to 1956, professor of archaeology, Arabic, and Hebrew, and director of the Pontifical Biblical Institute in Jerusalem from 1956 to 1959. He participated in excavations in Lebanon in 1952, in Turkey and Iraq in 1955, and was director of the excavations at Telilat Ghassul, Jericho, in 1959–1960. He was associate professor and professor of theology at Marquette University from 1961 to 1972, and professor of Old Testament and archaeology at the Pontifical Biblical Institute in Rome after 1973. He wrote *Guide to Biblical Iran* (Rome, 1956), *Stratigraphia Palestinae* (Rome, 1956), revised as *Stratigraphia Geobiblica: Biblical Near East Archaeology and Geography* (Rome, 1970), and *Ghassul 1960 Excavation Report* (Rome, 1961). *Reference*: *CA*.

NORTH AFRICA AMERICAN CEMETERY AND MEMORIAL. Situated 10 miles northeast of the city of Tunis, Tunisia, established in 1948, and completed in 1960. In this cemetery rest 2,840 military dead from North Africa and Iran. The Wall of the Missing records 3,724 missing. *Reference*: American Battle Monuments Commission, *North Africa American Cemetery and Memorial* (Washington, D.C., 1971).

NORTH CAROLINA, **U.S.S.** Armored cruiser. The *North Carolina* cruised the eastern Mediterranean Sea in 1909 to protect Americans threatened by military conflict in the Ottoman Empire, and to provide food, shelter, supplies, and medicines to Armenian refugees. It was again sent to the Middle East in August 1914 to protect Americans, and it cruised constantly between Jaffa, Beirut, and Alexandria until June 1915. *Reference*: *DANES*.

NORTON, RICHARD (1872–1918). Archaeologist, born February 9, 1872, in Dresden, Germany, to American parents. Norton graduated from Harvard University and studied at the American School of Classical Studies at Athens and the University of Munich. He was lecturer at Bryn Mawr College from 1895 to 1897. He was assistant director of the American School of Classical Studies at Rome from 1897 to 1907 and director after 1899. In 1903 he visited Central Asia as a member of the Pumpelly archaeological expedition, and he returned there in 1909. He was director of the American expedition to Cyrene in Cyrenaica, Libya. Norton made a survey of the place and began excavations in 1910, which were aborted in 1911 after the murder of Herbert Fletcher De Cou.* He was chief of the American Volunteer Motor Ambulance Corps and later of the American Red Cross* Ambulance Sections in France from 1914 to 1917, and served in the Naval Intelligence Department in Paris in 1917–1918. Died August 1, 1918. *References*: *AJA* 22 (1918): 343–344; *WWWA*.

NORTON, ROY (1869–1942). Explorer and author, born September 30, 1869, in Kewanee, Illinois. Norton graduated from the Denver School of Mines. He practiced law in Ogden, Utah, and prospected for gold in the western states and Alaska. In 1901 he crossed Alaska diagonally from Nome to the Arctic Ocean with a dog team. He founded the *San Bernardino* (Calif.) *Sun* in 1892, was editor of the *San Jose Herald* in 1899, and worked on the editorial staff of the *Seattle Star*, *Portland* (Ore.) *Journal*, and the *San Francisco Chronicle*. He was managing director of the Golconda Mine in Oregon from 1903 to 1905, and chief engineer for the construction of the Cuban railroad in 1905–1906. For the next twenty years he lived in England, traveled in Turkey and North Africa, and served in the British Army intelligence in France in World War I. In 1920 he led an exploration party through the Sinai Peninsula and northern Arabia, and directed engineering work in the Sahara Desert for the French government from 1922 to 1926, constructing golf courses at Biskra, Algeria, and Tunis. He wrote articles for British and American newspapers and magazines as well as westerns and science fiction novels. Norton returned to the United States in 1926. Died June 28, 1942, in Freeport, Long Island, New York. *References*: *NYT*, June 30, 1942; *WWWA*.

NORTON, THOMAS (HERBERT) (1851–1941). Chemist, editor, and consul, born June 30, 1851, in Rushford, New York. Norton graduated from Hamilton College and studied at the universities of Heidelberg, Berlin, and Paris. He was a chemist and manager of chemical works in Paris from 1878 to 1883, and professor of chemistry at the University of Cincinnati from 1883 to 1900. He was the first to travel on foot in Syria in 1873 and demonstrated the feasibility of doing so alone. In 1900 he was appointed consular representative to establish the consulate in Harput, Turkey. He made a voyage down the Euphrates River on a native raft of inflated goatskins with Ellsworth Huntington,* was sent by the government to investigate conditions in Armenia in 1904 and on a special mission to Persia in 1904–1905, was consul to Smyrna in 1905–1906, and in Chemintz, Saxony, from 1906 to 1914. He was editor of *Chemical Engineer* in 1917–1918, chemist with E. I du Pont de Nemours & Co. from 1917 to 1920, editor of *Chemicals* from 1920 to 1929, and became a research chemist with American Cyanamid Co. in 1930. He wrote *Reflections, Retrospective, Intros-*

pective, Prospective: At the Seventieth Milestone (New York, 1921). Died December 2, 1941, in White Plains, New York. *References: ACAB. NCAB* 13:478. *NYT*, December 3, 1941. *WWWA*.

NOTESTEIN, FRANK B. (1885–1973). Petroleum geologist, born in Wooster, Ohio. He graduated from the College of Wooster, Yale School of Forestry, and the University of Minnesota. He was employed by the U.S. Forestry Service, conducted geologic field work for Texaco in western U.S. in 1917, and made one of the earliest oil-reconnaissance trips to the upper Amazon in Peru in 1919. He was employed by Whitehall Petroleum Company of London from 1919 to 1926, explored in Egypt from 1920 to 1922, prospected in northern Sinai and the Red Sea, and then in India until 1926. In 1926 he returned to Texaco and explored in Santo Domingo, Colombia, and Argentina. He served with the Petroleum Administration for War in World War II, and was later geological consultant in Arabia and Turkey. Died November 30, 1973, in Wooster, Ohio. His memoirs, *A Wandering Rockhound*, ed. Lucy L. Notestein and Sallie P. McClenahan (Wooster, Ohio, 1980), were published posthumously. *Reference: BAAPG* 58 (September 1974): 1864–1865.

NOYES, JAMES OSCAR (1829–1872). Author and physician, born June 14, 1829, in Niles, Cayuga County, New York. Noyes graduated from Hamilton College and studied medicine at the University of Vienna. He was appointed to the medical staff of the commander of Turkish forces and became a surgeon in the Ottoman Army. He saw service in the Russo-Turkish War of 1853–1855, and wrote *Roumania: The Border Land of the Christian and the Turk, Comprising Adventures of Travel in Eastern Europe and Western Asia* (New York, 1857). He was later a correspondent in Turkey, Palestine, and he became proprietor and chief editor of *Knickerbocker Magazine*. He was a newspaper correspondent in the Civil War, engaged in army contracts and in planting, and was commissioner of immigration for the state of Louisiana. Died September 11, 1872, in New Orleans. *References: ACAB; DAA*.

NUR EL HUSSEIN (1951?–   ). Consort of the King of Jordan, born Elizabeth Halaby in Washington, D.C. Halaby graduated from Princeton University and worked for Alia, the Royal Jordanian Airlines. In June 1978 she was married to King Hussein of Jordan and was proclaimed Queen Nur al Hussein [Light of Hussein]. *References: NYT*, November 7, 1978; June 21, 1980; R. Flick, ''A Royal Pain: From American Princess to Jordanian Queen,'' *New Republic* 193 (August 26, 1985): 16–18.

O

O'BANNON, PRESLEY NEVILLE (1784–1850). Marine officer, born in Fauquier County, Virginia. O'Bannon was commissioned second lieutenant in the marines in 1801. During the Barbary Wars (1801–1805)* he served with the Mediterranean Squadron, and in 1804 he was in command of the marines aboard the *Argus*. Commanding a marine detachment, he went with William Eaton* to assist in the expedition against Darna in Tripoli and functioned as Eaton's second-in-command. He was wounded in the attack on Darna but raised the first American flag over foreign soil. He retired in 1807 and lived in Kentucky. Died September 12, 1850, in Logan County, Kentucky. *References*: Charles L. Lewis, *Famous American Marines* (Boston, 1950), pp. 39–54; *WAMB*.

O'BRIEN, RICHARD (1758–1824). Sailor and diplomat, born in Maine. O'Brien was a privateer during the Revolutionary War. Master of the brig *Dauphin*, he was captured by Algerian pirates. In 1797 he was appointed an agent to conclude a treaty of peace with Tripoli, and was consul general in Algiers from 1797 to 1803. In 1808 he was a member of the Pennsylvania legislature. Died February 14, 1824, in Washington, D.C. *References*: *ACAB*; *DAB*; and *WWWA*.

O'CALLAGHAN, ROGER (TIMOTHY) (1912–1954). Orientalist and archaeologist, born October 12, 1912, in New York City. O'Callaghan joined the Society of Jesus in 1929, studied at Toronto and Rome, and attended Johns Hopkins University and the Oriental Institute. He taught at the Pontifical Biblical Institute in Rome, was involved with archaeological work in Byblos, Lebanon, from 1946 until 1950, and took part in the excavation of Nippur, Iraq. Killed March 5, 1954, in a car accident in Baghdad. *References*: *BASOR* 134 (1954): 3–4; *DACB*; and *WWWE*.

OCCIDENTAL PETROLEUM CORPORATION. Incorporated in California in 1920. Occidental obtained oil concessions in Libya in 1966, struck oil in the same year, and began production in 1968. In 1973 it sold 51 percent of its Libyan assets to the Libyan government. *References*: Stanley H. Brown, "Dr. Hammer's Magic Tingle," *Fortune* 78 (July 1968): 98–101, 138–140; Milton Moskowitz et al., *Everybody's Business: An Almanac* (New York, 1980), pp. 517–521; and *IPE*.

ODENHEIMER, WILLIAM HENRY (1817–1879). Clergyman, born August 11, 1817, in Philadelphia. Odenheimer graduated from the University of Pennsylvania and General Theological Seminary, and was ordained in 1841. He was assistant rector in Philadelphia from 1841 to 1859, bishop of New Jersey for the Protestant Episcopal Church from 1859 to 1874, and of the Northern Diocese of New Jersey from 1874 to 1879. He traveled in Palestine in 1851–1852 and wrote *Jerusalem and Its Vicinity* (Philadelphia, 1855). Died August 14, 1879, in Burlington, New Jersey. *References*: *ACAB*; *DAB*; *NCAB* 3:473; and *WWWA*.

OFFLEY, DAVID (fl. 1811–1838). Merchant and consul. Offley went to Smyrna in 1811 with a cargo of merchandise and founded the first American commercial house in the Middle East. In 1823 he was appointed consular commercial agent, served as adviser to Commodore John Rodgers* in the 1826 negotiations with the Turkish authorities, and together with Commodore William M. Crane,* negotiated with them again. In 1829 he, James Biddle,* and Charles Rhind* were members of the commission that concluded a treaty with Turkey in 1830. In 1832 Offley was appointed consul in Smyrna, a position he held until his death. Died October 4, 1838, in Smyrna. *References*: *DAB*; *WWWA*.

OHLIGER, FLOYD W(ILLIAM) (1902–   ). Petroleum geologist and oil executive, born February 14, 1902, in Pittsburgh. Ohliger graduated from the University of Pittsburgh and Stanford University. He was a petroleum geologist with the Venezuela Gulf Oil Company and South American Gulf Company (Colombia) in 1926–1927, and production engineer for Standard Oil Company of California from 1929 to 1933. He was a petroleum engineer for California Arabian Standard Oil Company (CASOC) in Saudi Arabia from 1934 to 1937, and resident manager of CASOC, and later of Arabian American Oil Company (ARAMCO)* in Saudi Arabia from 1937 to 1945. He was vice president of ARAMCO from 1947 until his retirement in 1957. *References*: *AWM* 35 (May–June 1984): 30.

OLIN, STEPHEN (1797–1851). Clergyman, born March 2, 1797, in Liecester, Vermont. Olin graduated from Middlebury College. He was a preacher of the Methodist Episcopal Church, professor of ethics and belles-letters at Franklin College (Athens, Ga.) from 1826 to 1833, the first president of Randolph-Macon

College from 1834 to 1837, and president of Wesleyan University (Middletown, Conn.) from 1842 to 1851. He traveled in the Middle East and wrote *Travels in Egypt, Arabia Petraea, and the Holy Land* (New York, 1843), and *Greece and the Golden Horn* (New York, 1854). Died August 16, 1851, in Middletown, Connecticut. *References*: *ACAB*; *DAB*; *EWM*; *NCAB* 9:429; and *WWWA*.

OLMSTEAD, ALBERT TENEYCK (1880–1945). Orientalist, born March 23, 1880, in Troy, New York. Olmstead graduated from Cornell University. He was director of the Cornell University expedition to Asia Minor and Mesopotamia in 1907–1908, and the co-author of *Travel and Studies in the Nearer East* (Ithaca, N.Y., 1911). He was a member of the faculty of the University of Missouri from 1909 to 1917, professor of history and curator of the Oriental Museum at the University of Illinois from 1917 to 1929, and professor of Oriental history at the University of Chicago after 1929. He was annual professor of the American Schools of Oriental Research (ASOR)* in Baghdad in 1936–1937. Died April 11, 1945, in Chicago. *References*: *DAB S3*; *NYT*, April 12, 1945; and *WWWA*.

OSBORN, HENRY STAFFORD (1823–1894). Clergyman, mapmaker, and metallurgist, born August 17, 1823, in Philadelphia. Osborn graduated from the University of Pennsylvania and Union Theological Seminary and was ordained in 1848. He was a pastor in Richmond and Liberty, Virginia, and Belvidere, New Jersey, professor of chemistry at Lafayette College from 1866 to 1870, and professor of natural science at Miami University (Oxford, Ohio) from 1870 to 1873. After 1873 he was a lecturer and wrote on the sciences. He visited Palestine in 1857, wrote *Palestine Past and Present* (Philadelphia, 1859), *New Descriptive Geography of Palestine* (Oxford, Ohio, 1877), and *Plants of the Holy Land, with Their Fruits, and Flowers. Beautifully Illustrated by Original Drawings, Colored from Nature* (Philadelphia, 1859). He also prepared maps of Palestine and the Middle East. Died February 2, 1894, in Oxford, Ohio. *References*: *ACAB*, *DAB*; *NCAB* 11:495, and *WWWA*.

OSGOOD, JOHN FELT (1825–1894). Merchant, born December 18, 1825, in Salem, Massachusetts. Osgood was an employee of the Bertram-Shepard concern, supercargo of the bark *Emily Wilder*, and resident agent in Arabian ports. He later published his diary, *Notes on Travel; or Recollections of Majunga, Zanzibar, Muscat, Aden, Mocha and Other Eastern Ports* (Salem, Mass., 1845). Died in Salem, Massachusetts. *References*: Sketches and diary, Essex Institute, Essex, Massachusetts.

OSTER, JOHN FREDERICK (1881–1960). Missionary, born July 12, 1881, in Switzerland, and came to the United States as a child. He graduated from Walla Walla College, was trained in Germany and Russia, and was ordained in 1920. In 1909 he went to Iran as a Seventh Day Adventist missionary. He was superintendent and secretary-treasurer of the Persian Mission from 1921 until

1938, and director of the Turkish Mission from 1938 until 1943. He returned to the United States in 1943, and worked in the Indiana Conference until his retirement in 1948. Died March 22, 1960, in San Diego, California. *Reference*: *Seventh-Day Adventists Encyclopedia*, rev. ed. (Washington, D.C., 1976).

OYLER, DAVID SMITH (1881–1934). Missionary, born January 11, 1881, in Mortonville, Kansas. Oyler graduated from Cooper College and Xenia Theological Seminary. He became a missionary under the United Presbyterian Church of North America Board of Foreign Missions* in the Sudan in 1909, and was stationed at Doleib Hill on the Sobat River until 1927, when he returned to the United States. He published several studies of the customs of the Shilluk people. He was later a pastor at Cutler, Illinois. Died November 19, 1934, in Cutler. *References*: *Hill*.

OZMUN, EDWARD HENRY (1857–1910). Consul, born August 6, 1857, in Rochester, Minnesota. Ozmun graduated from the universities of Wisconsin and Michigan, was admitted to the bar in 1881, and practiced in St. Paul from 1881 to 1897. He served as counsel for the Northern Pacific Railroad from 1882 to 1886, was a member of the Minnesota Senate from 1893 to 1897, consul at Stuttgart from 1897 to 1906, and consul general in Constantinople in 1906. He made journeys into the interior of Asia Minor and in Syria, Palestine, and Egypt, collecting data used in *Practical Suggestions for the Development of American Export Trade, with Directories of the Chief Cities of European and Asiatic Turkey* (Chicago, 1908) published by the National Business League of America. Died December 9, 1910. *Reference*: *WWWA*.

P

PACIFIC WESTERN OIL CORPORATION. *See* Getty Oil Company.

PADDOCK, GORDON (1865–1932). Consul and diplomat, born September 6, 1865, in New York City. Paddock graduated from Princeton University and Columbia University Law School, and practiced law in New York City. He was secretary of legation in Korea in 1901–1902, consul and later vice consul general in Seoul from 1902 to 1909, vice consul general and deputy consul general in Harbin in 1909–1910, consul general in Teheran, and consul in Tabriz from 1910 to 1920. He was in charge of the relief committee and protected Allied citizens in Persia during World War I. He was later first secretary in Belgrade, Copenhagen, and Paris, and retired in 1930. Died November 2, 1932, in Paris. *Reference*: *NYT*, November 4, 1932.

PAGE, RUFUS (1787–1870). Sea captain, born March 13, 1787, in Exeter, New Hampshire. Page was engaged in shipbuilding on the Kennebec River in Maine, was joint owner of the first line of steamers between Boston and the Kennebec, and later established a line of steamers to San Francisco. He brought the river paddle steamer *Bangor** to Constantinople in 1842, the first American steamer to enter the Black Sea. He sold it to the Turkish government which renamed it the *Sudaver*, and put it in service between Constantinople and the Princes' Island in the Sea of Marmara. His son was **WILLIAM RUFUS PAGE** (1820– ?), sea captain, born March 17, 1820, in Hallowell, Maine. He took the twin-screw steamer *Marmora* to Constantinople in 1845, but the ship was wrecked on the coast of Morocco. He was consul in Jerusalem in 1860–1861, and consul in Port Said after 1870. *References*: William A. Baker, *A Maritime History of Bath, Maine and the Kennebeck River Region* (Bath, Me., 1973); Emma H. Nason, *Old Hallowell on the Kennebec* (Augusta, Me., 1909).

PAIGE, SIDNEY (1880–1968). Engineering geologist, born November 2, 1880, in Washington, D.C. Paige graduated from the University of Michigan and Yale University. He was employed by the Nicaragua Canal Commission, the U.S. Geological Survey, and the Panama Canal Commission. He was adviser to the Bureau of Mines of the Department of Economy of the Government of Turkey from 1933 to 1935, studying the gold mining industry of Turkey. From 1935 to 1946 he was principal geologist of the North Atlantic division of the Army Corps of Engineers. He was later director and executive secretary of the Committee on Geographical Explorations for the Joint Research and Development Board in Washington. Died February 4, 1968, in New York City. *References*: *NYT*, February 5, 1968; *WWWA*.

PAINE, JOHN ALSOP (1840–1912). Archaeologist, born January 14, 1840, in Newark, New Jersey. Paine graduated from Hamilton College, Andover Theological Seminary, Sheffield Scientific School of Yale University, and the School of Mines of Columbia University, studied at the universities of Leipzig and Halle, and was ordained in 1867. He was professor of natural history at Robert College* from 1867 to 1869, professor of natural history and German at Lake Forest (Ill.) University in 1870–1871, and associate editor of *The Independent* in 1871–1872. He was archaeologist for the first expedition of the Palestine Exploration Society in the area east of the Jordan and the Dead Sea from 1872 to 1874. He later edited and published the *Journal of Christian Philosophy*, was on the staff of *The Century Dictionary*, and was curator of the Metropolitan Museum of Art from 1889 to 1906. Died July 24, 1912, in Tarrytown, New York. *References*: *ACAB*; *DAB*; *NCAB* 13:456; *NYT*, July 25, 1912; and *WWWA*.

PALMER, ELY ELIOT (1887–1977). Diplomat, born November 29, 1887, in Providence, Rhode Island. Palmer graduated from Brown and George Washington universities and studied at the University of Paris. He entered the foreign service in 1910, and served in Mexico City, Paris, Brussels, Madrid, Bucharest, and Vancouver. He was consul general in Jerusalem from 1933 to 1935, counselor and consul general in Ottawa from 1935 to 1937; consul general in Beirut from 1937 to 1940 and in Sydney from 1940 to 1945; minister to Afghanistan from 1944 to 1948; and the first ambassador to Afghanistan in 1948–1949. He was the U.S. representative to the U.N. Conciliation Committee for Palestine from 1949 to 1951. Palmer retired in 1952. Died August 12, 1977, in Highland, California. *References*: *BRDS*; *Washington Post*, August 28, 1977.

PALOS, U.S.S. Screw tug, converted to gunboat. In 1870, on its way from Boston to the Asiatic station, the *Palos* became the first American warship to transit the Suez Canal. *Reference*: *DANES*.

PARKER, BERYL (1893–   ). Educator, born December 29, 1893, in Se-
bree, Kentucky. Parker graduated from the University of Chicago and Columbia
University Teachers College. She was a teacher in St. Louis, Des Moines, Iowa,
Frostburg, Maryland, and Greenwich, Connecticut, from 1916 to 1926; supervisor of elementary schools in Norfolk, Virginia, from 1928 to 1930; and assistant
professor of elementary education at New York University from 1930 to 1938.
From 1932 to 1934 she was an adviser to the Turkish Ministry of education,
directed the development of an experimental kindergarten and primary school
in Turkey and in 1939 published a report on her work in Istanbul. She was editor
of elementary publications for D.C. Heath and Company from 1938 to 1945,
and lecturer in education and educational consultant at Fisk University from 1947
to 1951. *Reference: LE.*

PARKER, RICHARD A(NTHONY) (1905–   ). Egyptologist, born December 10, 1905, in Chicago. Parker graduated from Dartmouth College and the
University of Chicago. He was research assistant, research associate, and assistant professor of Egyptology at the Oriental Institute epigraphic and archaeological survey of Luxor, Egypt, from 1938 to 1940; assistant field director in
1946–1947 and field director from 1947 to 1949; and professor of Egyptology
at Brown University from 1949 until his retirement in 1972. He was co-author
of *Medinet Habu IV. Festival Scenes of Rameses III* (Chicago, 1940), *Medinet
Habu V: The Tempel Proper* (Chicago, 1957–1963), and *The Edifice of Taharqa
by the Sacred Lake of Karnak* (Providence, R.I., 1979). *References*: *Egyptological Studies in Honor of Richard A. Parker, Presented on the Occasion of
His 78th Birthday*, ed. Leonard H. Lesko (Hanover, N.H., 1986); *DAS*; and
WWA.

PARKER, RICHARD BORDEAUX (1923–   ). Diplomat, born July 3,
1923, in the Philippine Islands to American parents. Parker served in World
War II, and graduated from Kansas State and Princeton universities. He was
second secretary in Amman, first secretary in Beirut, counselor in Cairo from
1965 to 1967, country director for the United Arab Republic from 1967 to 1970,
minister counselor in Rabat from 1970 to 1974, ambassador to Algeria from
1974 to 1977, ambassador to Lebanon in 1977–1978, and ambassador to Morocco
in 1978–1979. He was Department of State adviser to the Air University (Maxwell Air Force Base, Alabama) in 1979–1980, diplomat in residence at the
University of Virginia from 1980 to 1982, and editor of the *Middle East Journal*
in 1981. He was co-author of *A Practical Guide to Islamic Monuments in Cairo*
(Cairo, 1974), and wrote *North Africa: Regional Tensions and Strategic Concerns* (New York, 1984). *References*: *MENA*; *WWA.*

PARMELEE, MOSES CHRISTOPHER (1834–1902). Medical missionary,
born May 4, 1834, in Westford, Vermont. Parmelee graduated from the University of Vermont and Union Theological Seminary. He went to Turkey in 1863

as a missionary under the American Board of Commissioners for Foreign Missions (ABCFM),* served in Erzurum from 1863 to 1878, and in Trebizond from 1878 until his death. He wrote *Life Scenes Among the Mountains of Ararat* (Boston, 1868), and *Home and Work by the Rivers of Eden* (New York, 1888). Died October 4, 1902, in Beirut, Syria. *References*: *Missionary Herald* 98 (1902): 512–15; *UnionTS*.

PARMELEE, RUTH A(ZNIV) (1885–1973). Physician, born April 3, 1885, in Trebizond, Turkey. Parmelee graduated from Oberlin College and the University of Illinois Medical School. She served under the American Board of Commissioners for Foreign Missions (ABCFM)* in cooperation with Near East Relief* as physician in Harput, Turkey, from 1914 to 1917 and from 1919 to 1922. She directed the American Women's Hospitals in Greece in 1922–1923, and was in charge of refugee relief and public health projects from 1923 to 1941, and founded the first school of nursing in Greece. In World War II she was senior medical officer for Greek refugees near Gaza in Palestine, and then for British and Americans in the Cyclades Islands. She worked with the United Nations Relief and Works Agency (UNRWA) as a relief worker in Turkey and Palestine. She wrote her memoirs, *A Pioneer in Euphrates Valley* (n.p., 1967). Died December 15, 1973, in Concord, New Hampshire. *Reference*: Papers, Hoover Institution Archives.

PARSONS, JUSTIN WRIGHT (1824–1880). Missionary, born April 26, 1824, in Westhampton, Massachusetts. Parsons graduated from Williams College and Union Theological Seminary, and was ordained in 1849. He became a missionary under the American Board of Commissioners for Foreign Missions (ABCFM)* in 1850, was stationed in Salonika and later in Smyrna as missionary to the Jews. He served in Bardezag from 1856 to 1858, in Nicomedia from 1858 to 1872, and after an extensive tour of Asia Minor returned to Bardezag where he opened a teachers' training school for girls. Murdered by robbers, July 28, 1880, on the road between Nice and Bardezag. *References*: *EM*; *Hewitt*.

PARSONS, LEVI (1792–1822). Missionary, born July 18, 1792, in Goshen, Massachusetts. Parsons graduated from Middlebury College and was ordained in 1817. In 1819 he went with Pliny Fisk* to Palestine as a missionary under the American Board of Commissioners for Foreign Missions (ABCFM).* He arrived in Jerusalem in 1820, the first Protestant missionary who entered that city to make it the permanent field of his work. In 1822 he sailed with Fisk to Egypt to restore his health. Died February 10, 1822, in Alexandria, Egypt. *References*: Daniel O. Morton, *Memoir of Rev. Levi Parsons, First Missionary to Palestine from the United States* (Burlington, Vt., 1830).

PARTRIDGE, ERNEST CROCKER (1870–1955). Missionary, born December 8, 1870, in Weybridge, Vermont. Partridge graduated from Oberlin College and Andover Theological Seminary, and was ordained in 1898. He was a pastor in Shoreham, Vermont, from 1898 to 1900, and became a missionary under the American Board of Commissioners for Foreign Missions (ABCFM)* in Turkey in 1900. He served in Sivas from 1900 to 1917 and was principal of the Sivas Normal school. He was the director of the Pensacola Party* in 1919. He again served in Sivas in 1921–1922; Erivan and Alexandropol, Armenian Republic, from 1922 to 1924; Beirut in 1926–1927; Aleppo from 1927 to 1929; and Izmir from 1931 to 1933. He was later pastor in Gentry, Arkansas, and Rootstown, Ohio. Died May 4, 1955, in Stow, Ohio. *Reference*: *AndoverTS*.

PARTRIDGE, WILLIAM ORDWAY (1861–1930). Sculptor, born April 11, 1861, in Paris, to American parents, grew up in Paris, and returned to the United States in 1870. Partridge studied art at the Adelphi Academy in Brooklyn and attended Columbia University. He was in Europe from 1882 to 1884, and studied in Paris and in Italy from 1887 to 1889. He traveled in Egypt and Palestine in 1900–1901, serving as a special correspondent for the *New York Herald* and collecting art objects. He returned to the United States in 1889 and settled in Milton, Massachusetts. Died May 22, 1930, in New York City. *References*: Papers in private hands; *ACAB*; Marjorie P. Balge, "William Ordway Partridge (1861–1930): American Art Critic and Sculptor," Ph.D. diss. University of Delaware, 1982; *NCAB* 23:12; *NYT*, May 24, 1930; and *WWWA*.

PATON, LOUIS BAYLES (1864–1932). Educator, born June 27, 1864, in New York City. Paton graduated from New York University, Princeton Theological Seminary, and the universities of Berlin and Marburg, and was ordained in 1890. He was an instructor of Old Testament exegesis and criticism at the Hartford Theological Seminary in 1892–1893, associate professor from 1893 to 1900, and professor after 1900. He was director of the American Schools of Oriental Research (ASOR)* in Jerusalem in 1903–1904, wrote *Jerusalem in Bible Times* (Chicago, 1908), and prepared the report on Palestine for the Inquiry, the organization set up in 1917 to conduct studies of the problems of peacemaking after World War I. Died January 24, 1932, in West Hartford, Connecticut. *References*: Papers, Case Memorial Library, Hartford Seminary Foundation; *DAB*; and *WWWA*.

PATRICK, MARY MILLS (1850–1940). Educator, born March 10, 1850, in Canterbury, New Hampshire. Patrick graduated from Lyon's Collegiate Institute (Iowa) and the State University of Iowa and studied at the universities of Heidelberg, Zurich, Leipzig, and Berne. She was a missionary under the American Board of Commissioners for Foreign Missions (ABCFM)* in Turkey, and was appointed a teacher in the American mission school for girls in Erzurum in 1871, traveling on horseback to the villages of the Ararat region to open schools. In

1875 she went to teach at the mission high school in Scutari and became its administrator in 1883. In 1890 it became the American College for Girls at Constantinople. She was its first president from 1890 to 1924, when she retired and returned to the United States. She wrote an autobiography, *Under Five Sultans* (New York, 1929), and a history of the college, *A Bosporus Adventure: Istanbul (Constantinople) Women's College, 1871–1924* (London, 1934). Died February 25, 1940, in Palo Alto, California. *References*: Papers, Hoover Institution Archives; *DAB S2*; *NAW*; *NCAB* A:482; *NYT*, February 27, 1940; and *WWWA*.

PAXTON, JOHN D. (1784–1868). Clergyman, born September 28, 1784, in The Forks, Rockbridge County, Virginia. Paxton graduated from Washington College (Lexington, Va.), taught at Hampden Sidney College (Prince Edward, Va.), and was ordained in 1812. He was pastor in Goochland, Virginia, went to Europe in 1834, resided in the Middle East from 1836 to 1838, served in the Syria Mission,* and wrote *Letters on Palestine and Egypt Written During Two Years Residence* (Lexington, Ky., 1839). He was pastor in Shelby County, Kentucky, from 1838 to 1855, in Princeton, Indiana, from 1855 to 1860, in Highland, Kansas, from 1860 to 1863, and again in Princeton, Indiana. *References*: *A Memoir of J. D. Paxton, D. D., Late of Princeton, Indiana*, comp. by Martha W.M.D. Paxton (Philadelphia, 1870).

PAYNE, JOHN HOWARD (1791–1852). Author and playwright, born June 9, 1791, in New York City. Payne graduated from Union College. He made his acting debut in 1809, went to England in 1813, and worked as an actor, playwright, and theater secretary. He amassed debts, however, and was held in debtors' prison in 1820–1821. He published a theatrical paper in London in 1826–1827 and returned to the United States in 1832. He served as consul in Tunis from 1842 to 1845 and again in 1851–1852. Died April 9, 1852, in Tunis. *References*: *ACAB*; *DAB*; *DLB*; *NCAB* 2:347; Grace Overmyer, *America's First Hamlet* (New York, 1959); and *WWWA*.

PEACE CORPS. U.S. government agency, created by President John F. Kennedy in 1961, which sent volunteers to many countries, several thousand of whom went to the countries of the Middle East. Volunteers have served in Afghanistan (1962–1979), Bahrain (1974–1979), Cyprus (1962–1964), Iran (1962–1976), Libya (1966–1970), Morocco (1962–   ), Oman (1974–   ), Tunisia (1962–1967, 1968–   ), Turkey (1962–1972), and Yemen (1974–   ). *References*: *Cultural Frontiers of the Peace Corps*, ed. Robert B. Textor (Cambridge, Mass., 1966); Kevin Lowther and C. Payne Lucas, *Keeping Kennedy's Promise: The Peace Corps* (Boulder, Colo., 1978); Coates Redmon, *Come as You Are: the Peace Corps Story* (New York, 1986); and Gerard T. Rice, *Twenty Years of Peace Corps* (Washington, D.C., 1981).

PEACOCK, **U.S.S.** Sloop-of-war. In 1832, with *Boxer* the *Peacock* sailed on a diplomatic mission to the Far East, carrying Edmund Roberts,* who negotiated a treaty with the Sultan of Muscat. In 1835, with the *Enterprise*, it went on a second voyage to the Far East in order to deliver the ratified treaties to Muscat. It was nearly wrecked on a coral reef in the mouth of the Persian Gulf but was pulled free after sixty-one hours. *Reference*: *DANES*.

PEARSON, THOMAS (1893–1963). Banker and economic adviser, born June 24, 1893, in Asheville, North Carolina. Pearson graduated from Princeton University and served in the army in World War I. He was employed by the American International Corporation of New York City from 1916 to 1920, and was foreign trade editor for the *New York Evening Post* in 1920–1921. He was a member of the financial commission invited by the government of Persia to reorganize and administer its finances from 1922 to 1924, and was director of the civil service administration under the Persian Ministry of Finance until 1927. He served in the U.S. Section of the International Chamber of Commerce from 1927 to 1936; was deputy general receiver and general receiver of customs in the Dominican Republic from 1937 to 1941; vice president in charge of the fiscal department in the National Bank of Haiti from 1941 to 1947; and director of economic research in the Central Bank of the Dominican Republic from 1947 until his retirement in 1951. Died April 16, 1963, in Asheville, North Carolina. *References*: Papers, Southern Historical Collection, University of North Carolina Library; *NCAB* 50:675; and *WWWA*.

PEASE, LORENZO WARRINER (1809–1839). Missionary, born May 20, 1809, in Hinsdale, Massachusetts. Pease graduated from Hamilton College and Auburn and Andover Theological seminaries, and was ordained in 1834. He went to Cyprus in 1834 as a missionary under the American Board of Commissioners for Foreign Missions (ABCFM)* and remained there until his death. He opened a station in Larnaca in 1835, explored Cyprus, and sent Cypriote antiquities to the Auburn Theological Seminary Museum. Died August 28, 1839, in Larnaca, Cyprus. *References*: Papers and diaries, Union Theological Seminary Library; *AndoverTS*; *AuburnTS*; and *EM*.

PEET, WILLIAM WHEELOCK (1851–1942). Missionary, born February 14, 1851, in Fall River, Massachusetts. Peet graduated from Grinnel College and the University of Vermont. He was with the Burlington and Missouri Railroad as tax agent, and assistant land commissioner and chief clerk in the general manager's office in Iowa and Nebraska from 1874 to 1881. He was treasurer and business manager of the American Board of Commissioners for Foreign Missions (ABCFM) mission in Turkey from 1881 to 1925; organized relief work after the massacre of 1895; conducted other relief work in Asia Minor and Thrace; and was in charge of the diplomatic relations of the Turkish Mission. He declined to serve as commissioner of the Supreme Council of the League of Nations in

Constantinople. He returned to the United States in 1926, and wrote an auto-biography, *No Less Honor, The Biography of William Wheelock Peet*, ed. Louise J. Peet (Chattanooga, Tenn., 1939). Died September 9, 1942, in Ames, Iowa. *References*: *NYT*, September 10, 1942; *WWWA*.

PENDAR, KENNETH W. (1906–1972). Consul, born December 22, 1906, in Sioux Falls, South Dakota. Pendar graduated from Harvard University and stud-ied in Paris. In 1938 he worked with Thomas Whittemore* in restoring the mosaics in the Mosque of Hagia Sophia in Istanbul, and in 1940–1941, he worked at Harvard University Library. He was sent to Vichy-occupied North Africa in June 1941 as one of the vice consuls to serve under Robert Daniel Murphy*, chief American diplomatic representative in North Africa. Pendar collected mil-itary and political intelligence and acted as an undercover agent. He wrote *Adventure in Diplomacy: Our French Dilemma* (New York, 1945). In 1947 he opened a Coca-Cola bottling plant in Casablanca and lived in Morocco and southern France. He was administrator of the Daniel Chester French Museum, Stockbridge, Massachusetts, from 1968 to 1970. Died December 5, 1972, in Tangier, Morocco. *References*: Leon B. Blair, "Amateurs in Diplomacy: The American Vice Consuls in North Africa 1941–1943," *Historian* 35 (1975): 607–620; *CA*; *NYT*, December 8, 1972.

PENFIELD, FREDERIC COURTLAND (1855–1922). Diplomat, born April 23, 1855, in East Haddam, Connecticut. Penfield graduated from Princeton University and studied in England and Germany. He worked for the Hartford *Courant* from 1880 to 1885, entered the foreign service in 1885, was vice consul general in London, and diplomatic agent and consul general in Egypt from 1893 until 1897. He then traveled and wrote books, including *Present Day Egypt* (New York, 1899). He was minister to Austria from 1913 until his retirement in 1917. Died June 19, 1922, in New York. *References*: *ACAB*; *DAB*; *DADH*; *NCAB* 15:311; *NYT*, June 20, 1922; and *WWWA*.

PENIEL MISSION. Founded in 1886 in Los Angeles. It opened a mission in Port Said in 1895 to provide services to British seamen and soldiers, distributing literature on ships waiting to go through the Suez Canal. In 1897 it established the first girls' school in Port Said, known as the Peniel American School, which continued until 1969. *Reference*: *EMCM*.

PENROSE, STEPHEN B(EASLEY) L(INNARD) (1908–1954). Educator, born March 19, 1908, in Walla Walla, Washington. Penrose graduated from Whitman College and Columbia University, and taught physics at the American University of Beirut* from 1928 to 1931. In 1938 he became assistant director of the Near East College Association in New York City, and wrote a history of the American University of Beirut, *That They May Have Life* (Beirut, 1941). During World War II he served as special assistant in the Office of Strategic

Services, was stationed in Cairo, and collected intelligence form the Arab world. He served as assistant secretary of defense in 1947–1948, was president of the American University of Beirut from 1948 until his death, and initiated an expansion program for the university, including the establishment of schools of engineering and architecture, agriculture, and public health. Died December 9, 1954, in Beirut. *References*: *MENA*; *NCAB* 16:429; *NYT*, December 10, 1954; and *WWWA*.

PENSACOLA PARTY *Pensacola* was a screw steamer placed by the government at the disposal of the American Committee for Relief in the Near East in early 1919. Ernest C. Partridge, an American Board of Commissioners for Foreign Missions (ABCFM)* missionary from Sivas, was the director. The steamer carried supplies and personnel for the relief of Armenians and other victims of World War I in the Ottoman Empire. *Reference*: Ernest C. Partridge, "The Pensacola Party and Relief Work in Turkey," *Armenian Affairs* 1 (1950):: 293–297.

PERDICARIS AFFAIR (1904). Ion Perdicaris, an American citizen, was kidnapped in Morocco in 1904 by the Moroccan bandit Raisuli. Following pressure from the U.S. government, the Sultan of Morocco paid a ransom, and Perdicaris was released. *References*: Harold E. Davis, "The Citizenship of Jon Perdicaris," *Journal of Modern History* 13 (1941): 517–526; Thomas H. Etzold, "Protection or Politics? 'Perdicaris Alive or Raisuli Dead'," *Historian* 37 (1975): 297–304; and Barbara W. Tuchman, "Perdicaris Alive or Raisuli Dead," *American Heritage* 10 (August 1959): 18–21, 98–101.

PERKINS, JUSTIN (1805–1869). Missionary, born March 12, 1805, in West Springfield, Massachusetts. Perkins graduated from Amherst College and Andover Theological Seminary. He was a missionary under the American Board of Commissioners for Foreign Missions (ABCFM)* in Persia from 1835 to 1869. He established the Nestorian Mission at Urmia, learned modern Syriac, and translated the Bible and several religious books into that language. He wrote *A Residence of Eight Years in Persia Among the Nestorian Christians* (New York, 1843) and *Missionary Life in Persia* (Boston, 1861). He returned to the United States in 1869. Died December 31, 1869, in Chicopee, Massachusetts. *References*: Papers, Amherst College Library; *ACAB*; *Amherst*; *AndoverTS*; *DAB*; *EM*; *NCAB* 10:46; and *WWWA*.

PERRY, AMOS (1812–1899). Diplomat and author, born August 12, 1812, in Natick, Massachusetts. Perry graduated from Harvard College. He taught school in Providence and New London, Connecticut, from 1837 to 1859, traveled abroad from 1852 to 1855, and was diplomatic agent and consul in Tunis from 1862 to 1867. He wrote *Carthage and Tunis, Past and Present* (Providence, R.I., 1891). He was later secretary and librarian of the Rhode Island Historical Society.

Died August 10, 1899, in New London, Connecticut. *References*: *ACAB*; *NCAB* 2:297.

PERRY, WALTER SCOTT (1855–1934). Educator and art director, born December 26, 1855, in Stoneham, Massachusetts. Perry graduated from the Massachusetts Normal Art School (later Massachusetts School of Art). He was director of drawing in the public schools in Fall River and Worcester, and was the first director of the School of Fine and Applied Art of Pratt Institute in Brooklyn from 1887 until his retirement in 1928. He traveled, sketched, and photographed in Egypt and Palestine, and wrote *Egypt, the Land of the Temple Builders* (Boston, 1898), and *With Azir Girges in Egypt* (Boston, 1913). Died August 22, 1934, at Stoneham, Massachusetts. *References*: *DAB S1*; *WWWA*.

PERSIA COMPANY. Founded in the late 1880s. The company sent Francis Hector Clergue* to Persia to obtain concessions to build railroads and establish industrial enterprises. In 1899 it received a sixty-year general electric concession for all of Persia. Ownership later passed to W. W. Torrence, but the concession was never implemented, and the company failed in 1894.

PERSIAN GULF COMMAND. Established in 1942 as the Iraq-Iran Service, renamed Persian Gulf Service Command in 1942–1943 and Persian Gulf Command from 1942 to 1945. This supply, transport, and service command planned, supervised, and implemented the movement of Lend-Lease material and supplies to Great Britain and the Soviet Union by way of ports on the Persian Gulf and transportation across Iran. It constructed and maintained roads, operated the Trans-Iranian Railway and port facilities, constructed and operated assembly plants, and operated a motor transport service. Headquarters were successively in Baghdad, Basra, and Teheran. *References*: "History of the Persian Gulf Command," Ms., U.S. Army Center of Military History, Washington, D.C.; T. H. Vail Motter, *The Persian Corridor and Aid to Russia* (Washington, D.C., 1952); and Joel Sayre, *Persian Gulf Command* (New York, 1945).

PETERS, JOHN PUNNETT (1852–1921). Clergyman and archaeologist, born December 16, 1852, in New York City. Peters graduated from Yale College, Yale Divinity School, and the universities of Berlin and Leipzig, and was ordained in 1877. He was professor of Old Testament languages and literatures at the Protestant Methodist Divinity School of Philadelphia from 1884 to 1891, and professor of Hebrew at the University of Pennsylvania from 1886 to 1893. He was director of the University of Pennsylvania expedition to Nippur from 1888 to 1890, excavated there, and wrote *Nippur; or, Explorations & Adventures on the Euphrates, the Narratives of the University of Pennsylvania Expedition to Babylonia in the Years 1888–1890* (New York, 1897). He was rector of St. Michael's Church in New York City from 1893 to 1919, traveled in Palestine in 1902, and wrote *Painted Tombs of the Necropolis of Marissa (Maresha)*

(London, 1905). He was professor of Old Testament exegesis at the University of the South (Sewanee, Tenn.) from 1920 until his death. Died November 10, 1921, at Sewanee. *References*: *ACAB*; *DAB*; *NCAB* 13:556; and *WWWA*.

PETERSON, ENOCH E(RNEST) (1891–1978). Archaeologist, born September 24, 1891, in Liberty Pole, Wisconsin, and grew up in Fargo, North Dakota. Peterson graduated from Luther College (Debortah, Ia.) and the University of Michigan, and studied at Edinburgh. He was a member of the University of Michigan archaeological expeditions to Antioch in Psidia, Turkey, in 1924–1925; Carthage, Tunisia, 1925; Karanis, Egypt, 1925–1926; and director of the expeditions to Karanis, Dime, and Terenouthis in Egypt, from 1927 to 1935. He was co-author of *Karanis, Topographical and Architectural Report of Excavations During the Seasons 1924–28* (Ann Arbor, Mich., 1931), and *Saknopaiou Nesos: The University of Michigan Excavations at Dime in 1931–32* (Ann Arbor, Mich., 1935). He was Egyptian curator at the Kelsey Museum of Archaeology of the University of Michigan from 1938 to 1950, and museum director from 1950 until 1961. Died September 1978 in Fargo, North Dakota. *References*: Elinor M. Husselman, *Karanis Excavations of the University of Michigan in Egypt, 1928–1935: Topography and Architecture: A Summary of the Reports of the Director, Enoch E. Peterson* (Ann Arbor, Mich., 1979); Papers, Kelsey Museum, University of Michigan, Ann Arbor; and *DAS*.

PFEIFFER, ROBERT HENRY (1892–1958). Archaeologist, born February 14, 1892, in Bologna, Italy, to American parents. Pfeiffer studied at the universities of Geneva, Berlin, Tubingen, and Harvard University, and was ordained in 1916. He was a pastor in Sanborn, New York, from 1916 to 1919, instructor and lecturer at Harvard University from 1922 to 1930, assistant professor of Semitic languages and history, professor of Hebrew and Oriental languages until 1958, and curator of the Semitic Museum after 1931. He served as field director of the Harvard-American Schools of Oriental Research (ASOR)* expedition to Nuzi, Iraq, from 1928 to 1933, and was co-author of *Excavations at Nuzi* (Cambridge, Mass., 1929–1932). Died March 16, 1958, in Cambridge, Massachusetts. *References*: *BASOR* 150 (1928): 1–6; *Journal of Biblical Literature* 78 (1959): xi–xii; *NCAB* 43:511; *NYT*, March 17, 1958; and *WWWA*.

PHILADELPHIA, U.S.S. Frigate. The *Philadelphia* served in the quasi-war with France in the West Indies, was in the Mediterranean in 1801–1802, and returned again in 1803, commanded by Captain William Bainbridge.* It cruised off Tripoli and ran aground in October 1803 on an uncharted reef off Tripoli Harbor. All efforts to refloat the ship failed; it surrendered and its officers and men became prisoners. The ship was boarded in February 1804 by a party of officers, led by Stephen Decatur, Jr.,* and burned. *Reference*: *DANES*.

PHILIP, (HERMAN) HOFFMAN (1872–1951). Diplomat, born July 13, 1872, in Washington, D.C. Philip studied at Magdalene College, Cambridge University, and Columbia University Law School. He was a Rough Rider during the Spanish-American War, became vice consul in Tangier in 1901, and then secretary of legation and consul general. He was the first minister and consul general to Abyssinia (Ethiopia) from 1908 to 1910, and secretary, counselor, and chargé d'affaires in Constantinople from 1910 to 1916, representing the interests of the Allied Powers at war with Turkey, and directing the delivery of relief supplies to Syria. He was minister to Colombia from 1919 to 1922, minister to Persia from 1925 to 1928, minister to Norway from 1930 to 1935, and ambassador to Chile from 1935 until his retirement in 1937. Died October 31, 1951, in Santa Barbara, California. *References*: Van Ness-Philip Family Papers, New York Historical Society; *DADH*; *NCAB* 44:410; *NYT*, November 1, 1951; and *WWWA*.

PHILLIPS, WENDELL (1921–1975). Explorer, born September 25, 1921, in Oakland, California. Phillips graduated from the University of California. He was a member of the University of California Museum of Paleontology expedition to Northern Arizona in 1940 and to Monument Valley in Southern Utah and Grand Canyon, Arizona, in 1942; and served in the merchant marine during World War II. He organized and led the University of California African expedition from 1947 to 1949, organized the American Foundation for the Study of Man in 1949, and was its president until 1975. With the Library of Congress, he organized and led the foundation's Mount Sinai expedition to microfilm manuscripts in 1949–1950, and with the Carnegie Museum, the Arabian expedition in 1949. He was leader of the Yemen expedition in 1951–1952, the Oman expedition in 1952–1953, and the Oman-Sohar expedition in 1958. He wrote of the Arabian expeditions in *Qataban and Sheba: Exploring the Ancient Kingdoms on the Biblical Spice Routes of Arabia* (New York, 1955). He was president and director of Philryor Corporation from 1951 to 1958, obtained oil concessions in Dhofar in Oman, and organized the Middle East American Oil Company in Libya in 1954. He was director general of antiquities for the Sultanate of Oman from 1953 to 1970, economic adviser to the Sultan of Oman from 1956 to 1970, and leader of the archaeological expedition to Oman-Dhofar from 1958 to 1960. He wrote *Unknown Oman* (New York, 1966) and *Oman: A History* (New York, 1967). Died December 4, 1975, in Arlington, Virginia. *References*: *CA*; *CB* 1958; *DAS*; Elmer G. Leterman and T. W. Carlin, *They Dare to Be Different* (New York, 1968), pp. 125–132; *NYT*, August 18, 1975; Herbert Solow, "The Drillings and Diggings of Dr. Phillips," *Fortune* 55 (February 1957): 146–148, 222–230; and *WWWA*.

PICKERING, CHARLES (1805–1878). Physician and naturalist, born November 10, 1805, in Susquehanna County, Pennsylvania. Pickering graduated from Harvard College, began to practice medicine in Philadelphia in 1827, was librarian and curator of the Academy of Natural Sciences of Philadelphia, and chief zoologist with the U.S. Exploring Expedition from 1838 to 1842. He visited Egypt, Arabia, and the Red Sea in 1843 to study the races of men, brought back specimens of mummy and papyri, and wrote *Races of Men and Their Geographical Distributions* (Philadelphia, 1848). After 1843, he lived in Boston. Died March 17, 1878, in Boston. *References*: Papers, Academy of Natural History, Philadelphia; *ACAB*; *DAB*; *DAMB*; *NCAB* 13:176; and *WWWA*.

PIER, GARRETT CHATFIELD (1875–1943). Archaeologist, born October 30, 1875, in London, England. Pier graduated from Columbia University and the University of Chicago, and studied in museums in Europe and the Middle East. He was assistant curator of decorative arts at the Metropolitan Museum of Art from 1907 to 1910, and from 1911 to 1914, he traveled to Japan, China, and the Orient to buy antiques for the museum. He formed a considerable collection of Egyptian antiquities, which he described in *Egyptian Antiquities in the Pier Collection* (Chicago, 1906). He wrote *Inscriptions of the Nile Monuments: A Book of Reference for Tourists* (New York, 1908) and *Pottery of the Near East* (New York, 1909). He served in the Spanish-American War and in World War I, and was attached to the State Department and the Commission to Negotiate Peace. He also wrote two works of fiction with a Middle Eastern background: *Hanit, the Enchantress* (New York, 1921), and *The Jeweled Tree, an Egyptian Dramatic Fantasy* (New York, 1927). Died December 30, 1943, in St. Petersburg, Florida. *References*: *NYT*, December 31, 1943; *WWWA*; and *WWWE*.

PIERCE COLLEGE FOR GIRLS. *See* American Collegiate Institute for Girls, Smyrna.

POLAND, WILLIAM BABCOCK (1868–1950). Civil engineer, born May 16, 1868, in West Point, New York. Poland graduated from the Massachusetts Institute of Technology. He was engineer for the Baltimore and Ohio Railroad from 1899 to 1904, vice president and chief engineer of the Philippine Railway Company in Manila from 1907 to 1911, chief engineer and general manager of the Alaska Central Railway Company from 1911 to 1914, and of J. G. White & Company of New York from 1914 to 1917. In 1915 he became associated with the Belgian Relief Commission, went to Europe in 1916 as assistant to Herbert Hoover and subsequently replaced him as food director for Europe. In 1920 he became a consulting engineer in New York City; after 1935, in Washington, D.C. In 1926 he organized the railway system in Persia, was director general of railways, and laid the railroad line from the Caspian Sea to the Persian Gulf. He was later U.S. Rivers and Harbors engineer, director general of railway and port construction in Yugoslavia, adviser to the Ministry of Railways in China, and chief economic consultant to the Board of Economic Warfare during

World War II. Died June 27, 1950, in Washington, D.C. *Reference: NYT*, June 28, 1950.

POLK, JUDD KNOX (1912–1975). Economist, born July 3, 1912, in Toledo, Ohio. Polk graduated from the University of Michigan. He was an intelligence officer in the army air force in World War II and later a representative of the Treasury Department in the Middle East, with headquarters in Cairo. He visited Saudi Arabia in 1948. He was economic adviser on Middle Eastern and European affairs with the California Texas Oil Company and with the Federal Reserve Bank of New York, economist and director of programs and studies with the U.S. Council of the International Chamber of Commerce from 1966 until his retirement in 1974. Died April 31, 1975, in New York City. *Reference: NYT* May 1, 1975.

POLK, WILLIAM ROE (1929–   ). Educator, born March 7, 1929, in Fort Worth, Texas. Polk studied at the University of Chile, Harvard University, the American University of Beirut,* and Oxford University. He was assistant professor of Middle Eastern studies at Harvard University from 1955 to 1962, member of the Policy Planning Council of the State Department from 1961 to 1965, and professor of Middle Eastern Studies at the University of Chicago from 1965 to 1975. He became president of Rabia Ltd. in 1975. He made a 1,200-mile camel-back journey across the Arabian desert from Riyadh to Jordan and co-authored the account of this trip in *Passing Brave* (New York, 1973). He also wrote *The United States and the Arab World* (Cambridge, Mass., 1965), was co-author of *Backdrop to Tragedy: The Struggle for Palestine* (Boston, 1957), and edited *Perspective of the Arab World* (New York, 1956). *References: CA; WWA.*

POPE, ARTHUR UPHAM (1881–1969). Authority on Persian art, born February 7, 1881, in Phoenix, New York. Pope graduated from Harvard, Brown, and Cornell universities. He taught philosophy at the University of California from 1910 to 1917, served in the army in World War I, and was director of the California Art Museum in San Francisco. Between 1925 and 1939, he made many trips of study and research and led several archaeological expeditions to Persia. He organized the first exhibition of Persian art in Philadelphia in 1926, founded the American Institute for Iranian Art and Archaeology in New York City in 1928 (it became the Asia Institute in 1947), and edited the monumental *A Survey of Persian Art* (Oxford, 1938–1939). Died September 3, 1969, in Shiraz, Iran. *References:* Papers, New York Public Library; *CA; CB* 1947; *NYT*, September 4, 1969; Robert L. Taylor, *Doctor, Lawyer, Merchant, Chief* (Garden City, N.Y., 1948), pp. 204–226; and *WWWA.*

POPENOE, PAUL (BOWMAN) (1888–   ). Plant explorer and family relations specialist, born October 16, 1888, in Topeka, Kansas. Popenoe graduated from Occidental College and Stanford University. He was city editor of the *Pasadena Star* from 1908 to 1911 and agricultural explorer for the West India Gardens in Altadena, California, from 1911 to 1913. He made trips to Northern India, the Persian Gulf, and twice to North Africa to collect varieties of date palms. His book *Date Growing in the Old and New Worlds* (Altadona, Calif., 1913) is largely about his travels in the date-growing areas. He brought 16,000 offshoots of date palms back to the United States and was a date grower in Coachella Valley in California from 1920 to 1926. He was editor of the *Journal of Heredity* from 1913 to 1918, served in the sanitary corps in World War I, worked for the American Breeders Association (renamed American Genetic Association), was secretary of the Human Betterment Foundation in Pasadena from 1926 to 1934, and was the founder of the American Institute of Family Relations and its general director from 1930 to 1960. *References*: *AMWS*; *CA*; *CB* 1946; and *WWA*.

PORTER, DAVID (1780–1843). Naval officer, born February 1, 1780, in Boston. Porter went to sea at sixteen, entered the navy in 1798, and became a lieutenant in 1799. He served during the war with Tripoli as first lieutenant and later commander of the *Enterprise*. He was captured with the frigate *Philadelphia** and was imprisoned in Tripoli. He commanded the New Orleans naval station and served in the War of 1812. He was commissioner of the Navy Board from 1815 to 1823 and commander of the West Indies Squadron from 1823 to 1825. He resigned in 1826 and was commander-in-chief of the Mexican Navy from 1826 to 1829. In 1830–1831 he was consul general in Algiers. From 1831 to 1839 he was chargé d'affaires to Turkey and, from 1839 until his death, the first minister to Turkey. He wrote *Constantinople and Its Environs* (New York, 1835). Died March 3, 1843, in Constantinople. *References*: Papers, Manuscript Division Library of Congress; *ACAB*; *DAB*; *DAMIB*; David F. Long, *Nothing Too Daring: A Biography of Commodore David Porter 1780–1843* (Annapolis, Md., 1970); *NCAB* 2:98; *WAMB*; and *WWWA*.

PORTER, DAVID DIXON (1813–1891). Naval officer, son of David Porter,* born June 8, 1813, in Chester, Pennsylvania. Porter went to sea at ten and entered the Mexican Navy as midshipman. He was appointed a midshipman in the U.S. Navy in 1835 and was assigned to the Coast Survey. He served in the Mexican War, served again in the Coast Survey, and took a leave of absence to command merchant ships. In 1855 he was commander of the steamship *Supply** which made two voyages to the Middle East for camels. He served in the Civil War, was commander of the U.S. Naval Academy, and from 1877 until his death was head of the Board of Inspection. Died February 13, 1891, in Washington, D.C. *References*: Papers, Manuscript Division, Library of Congress; *ACAB*; Malcolm W. Cagle, "Lieutenant David Dixon Porter and His Camels,"

USNIP 83 (1957): 1327–1333; *DAB*; *DAMIB*; Paul Lewis, *Yankee Admiral: A Biography of David Dixon Porter* (New York, 1968); *NCAB* 2:97; *WAMB*; Richard S. West, Jr., *The Second Admiral: A Life of David Dixon Porter, 1813–1891* (New York, 1937); and *WWWA*.

PORTER, HARVEY (1844–1923). Missionary, born July 27, 1844, in Shelbourne Falls, Massachusetts. Porter graduated from Amherst College and served in the Civil War. He was principal of Amherst High School in 1869–1870 and was ordained in 1880. He was a tutor at Syrian Protestant College from 1870 to 1872, and professor of mental science and history from 1872 until his retirement in 1914. He prepared an Arabic-English and English-Arabic dictionary for the use of schools, and wrote articles on archaeology and nunismatics. Died January 12, 1923, in Beirut, Syria. *Reference*: Amherst.

PORTER, PAUL A(LDERMANDT) (1904–1975). Lawyer, born October 6, 1904, in Joplin, Missouri. Porter graduated from Kentucky Wesleyan College and the University of Kentucky Law School. He was a reporter and city editor for the Lexington (Ky.) *Herald* from 1923 to 1928, attorney in Oklahoma from 1929 to 1931, editor and publisher of the Magnum (Ok.) *Daily Star* from 1930 to 1932, and the LaGrange (Ga.) *Daily News* in 1932–1933. From 1933 to 1946 he served with several federal agencies, with the exception of the years 1937 to 1942, when he was Washington counsel for the Columbia Broadcasting Corporation. He was chairman of the Federal Communications Commission from 1944 to 1946, chief of the American economic mission to Greece in 1946–1947, and head of the U.S. delegation to the Conciliation Commission for Palestine in 1950–1951. He practiced law in Washington after 1947 and founded the law firm of Arnold, Fortas, and Palmer. *References*: Papers, Harry S Truman Library; *CB* 1945; *NCAB* 60:75; *NYT*, November 27, 1975; *PolProf: Truman*; and *WWWA*.

POST, GEORGE EDWARD (1838–1909). Physician and missionary, born December 17, 1838, in New York City. Post studied at the New York Free Academy (later College of the City of New York), Medical School of New York University, Union Theological Seminary, and the Baltimore College of Dentistry. He became a missionary under the American Board of Commissioners for Foreign Missions (ABCFM)* in Syria in 1867, and was stationed in Tripoli. In 1868 he became professor of surgery and diseases of the eye and ear at the Syrian Protestant College, and dean of the medical department until shortly before his death. He held clinics at the German Johanniter Hospital in Beirut, translated a number of medical and scientific texts into Arabic, was editor of the Arabic medical journal *Al-Tabib*, and wrote *Plantae Postianae* (Lausanne and Geneva, 1890–1900), *Flora of Syria, Palestine, and Egypt: A Handbook of the Flowering Plants and Ferns, Native and Naturalized form the Taurus to Ras Muhammad and from the Mediterranean Sea to the Syrian Desert* (Beirut, 1884), and articles in scientific journals. With Cornelius Van Alen Dyck* he composed a concord-ance to the Arab version of the Bible. *References*: *DAB*; *DAMB*; *NCAB* 13:416; Lutfi M. Sa'di, "The Life and Works of George Edward Post (1838–1909)," *Isis* 28 (1938): 385–417; and Frans A. Stafleu and Richard S. Cowan, *Taxonomic Literature* (Utrecht, 1983), 4:351–352.

POTTER, HENRY CODMAN (1835–1908). Clergyman, born May 25, 1835, in Schenectady, New York. Potter graduated from the Theological Seminary in Virginia and was ordained in 1858. He served as a pastor in Greensburg, Penn-sylvania, Troy, Boston, and New York City; was secretary of the House of Bishops of the General Convention of the Protestant Episcopal Church from 1863 to 1883; assistant to the bishop of New York from 1883 to 1887; and bishop of New York from 1887 until his death. He traveled in the Middle East in 1876 and wrote *The Gates of the East: A Winter in Egypt and Syria* (New York, 1877). Died July 21, 1908, in Cooperstown, New York. *References*: *ACAB*; *DAB*; *NCAB* 14:35; and *WWWA*.

POWELL, ADAM CLAYTON, SR. (1865–1953). Clergyman, born May 5, 1865, in Soak Creek, Franklin County, Virginia. Powell graduated from Wayland Seminary and College (Washington, D.C.). He was a pastor in New Haven, Connecticut, and from 1908 to 1937, pastor of the Abyssinian Baptist Church in New York City. He traveled in the Middle East in 1924, and wrote *Palestine and Saints in Caesar's Household* (New York, 1939), and *Against the Tide: An Autobiography* (New York, 1938). Died June 12, 1953, in New York City. *References*: *CA*; *DAB*; and *DANB*.

POWELL, E(DWARD) ALEXANDER (1879–1957). Traveler and author, born August 16, 1879, in Syracuse, New York. Powell graduated from Syracuse University and Oberlin College. He was a correspondent for British and American publications in the Middle East, and a consular official in Beirut and Alexandria from 1906 to 1908. He went on a special mission to Central Asia for the Department of Agriculture, and toured the Caucasus and the Sudan in 1909. He was a war correspondent and served in the army in World War I. In 1919 he went on a special mission to the Balkans, and in 1922 he traveled overland from Paris to Persia, and wrote *By Camel and Car to the Peacock Throne* (New York, 1923), and *The Struggle for Power in Moslem Asia* (New York, 1923). He traveled to Morocco and the Sahara in 1925–1926, and wrote *In Barbary: Tunisia, Algeria, Morocco and the Sahara* (New York, 1926). He served in World War II in the Office of Naval Intelligence and the Office of Censorship. He wrote an autobiography, *Adventure Road* (Garden City, N.Y., 1954). Died November 13, 1957, in Fall Village, near Camden, Connecticut. *References*: *NCAB* 46:308; *NYT*, November 14, 1957; and *WWWA*.

POWELL, LUCIEN WHITING (1846–1930). Painter, born December 13, 1846, near Upperville, Virginia. Powell served in the Civil War, and studied at the Pennsylvania Academy of Fine Arts, and in London, Rome, Venice, and Paris. He established a studio in Washington, D.C., in 1885, and was the first artist to hold an exhibition on an ocean liner. He traveled in Egypt and Palestine in 1910, and the trip resulted in many oil paintings of Middle Eastern scenes. Died December 27, 1930, in Washington, D.C. *References*: *DAB*; *NCAB* 23:137; and *WWWA*.

POWERS, PHILANDER O(LIVER) (1805–1872). Missionary, born August 19, 1805, in Phillipston, Massachusetts. Powers graduated from Amherst College and Andover Theological Seminary, and was ordained in 1834. He was a missionary under the American Board of Commissioners for Foreign Missions (ABCFM)* in Turkey, served in Brusa from 1834 until 1845, and in Trebizond from 1845 to 1861, when he was released by the ABCFM. He was a pastor in Oneida Lake, New York, and South Windsor, Connecticut, from 1862 to 1866. He was reappointed a missionary in 1865 and was stationed at Antioch, Turkey, from 1866 until his death. He wrote many hymns in Turkish. Died October 2, 1872, at Kessab, an outstation of Antioch. *References*: *EM*; *Hewitt*.

PRATT, ANDREW T(ULLY) (1826–1872). Medical missionary, born February 22, 1826, in Black Rock, near Buffalo, New York. Pratt graduated from Yale College, Union Theological Seminary, Yale Divinity School, and the College of Physicians and Surgeons in New York, and was ordained in 1852. He became a missionary under the American Board of Commissioners for Foreign Missions (ABCFM)* in Turkey in 1852, was stationed at Aintab from 1858 to 1860, at Antioch in 1861–1862, in Aleppo in 1862–1863, in Marash from 1863 to 1868, and in Constantinople from 1868 until his death. He helped translate and revise the Armeno-Turkish Bible and prepared a grammar of Armeno-Turkish. Died December 5, 1872, in Constantinople. *References*: *EM*; George F. Herrick, *An Intensive Life: A Sketch of the Life and Work of Rev. Andrew T. Pratt, M.D., Missionary of the A.B.C.F.M. in Turkey 1852–1872* (New York, 1890).

PREBLE, EDWARD (1761–1807). Naval officer, born August 15, 1761, in Falmouth (now Portland), Maine. Preble ran away to sea at sixteen, and in 1779 he was appointed a midshipman in the Massachusetts navy. After the Revolutionary War, he served in the merchant marine until 1798 when he became a lieutenant in the navy. In 1799 he commanded the frigate *Essex*, the first American warship to sail beyond the Cape of Good Hope. He was in command of the third squadron sent to the Mediterranean, maintaining a blockade on Tripoli and attacking Tripoli several times in 1804 but failing to capture the city, and was superseded by Samuel Barron.* Preble was later employed to build gunboats for the navy. Died August 25, 1807, in Falmouth, Maine. *References*: Papers,

Manuscript Division, Library of Congress; *ACAB*; *DAB*; *DAMIB*; Christopher McKee, *Edward Preble: A Naval Biography, 1761–1807* (Annapolis, Md., 1972); *NCAB* 8:92; *WAMB*; and *WWWA*.

PRESBYTERIAN CHURCH IN THE U.S.A.: BOARD OF FOREIGN MISSIONS. Founded in 1837 and established missions in Iran, Syria, Lebanon, and Iraq. It merged in 1958 with the Board of Foreign Missions of North America to form the Commission on Ecumenical Missions and Relations of the United Presbyterian Church in the United States of America. *References*: Manuscript collection, Presbyterian Historical Society, Philadelphia; Arthur J. Brown, *One Hundred Years: A History of the Foreign Missionary Work of the Presbyterian Church in the U.S.A.* (New York, 1936); *The Crisis Decade: A History of the Foreign Missionary Work of the Presbyterian Church in the U.S.A. 1937–1947*, ed. W. Reginald Wheeler (New York, 1951).

PRIME, WILLIAM COWPER (1825–1905). Journalist and author, born October 31, 1825, in Cambridge, New York, and grew up in Sing Sing (now Ossining), New York. Prime graduated from the College of New Jersey, was admitted to the bar in 1846, and practiced in New York City. From 1861 to 1869 he was editor of the *New York Journal of Commerce*. He visited the Middle East in 1855, and wrote *Boat life In Egypt and Nubia* (New York, 1857), and *Tent Life in the Holy Land* (New York, 1857). He was professor of art at Princeton University after 1884. Died February 13, 1905, in New York City. *References*: *ACAB*; *DAB*; *NCAB* 13:254; and *WWWA*.

PRITCHARD, JAMES BENNETT (1909–   ). Archaeologist, born October 4, 1909, in Louisville, Kentucky. Pritchard graduated from Asbury College, Drew University, the University of Pennsylvania, and the Philadelphia Divinity School. He was acting professor of Old Testament Literature at Crozer Theological Seminary (Chester, Pa.) from 1942 to 1944, professor from 1944 to 1954, professor of Old Testament Literature at the Church Divinity School of the Pacific from 1954 to 1962, professor of religious thought at the University of Pennsylvania, and curator of biblical archaeology at the University Museum from 1962 to 1978. He was a member of the Kyle memorial expedition to Palestine in 1935, the American Schools of Oriental Research (ASOR)* expedition to Dhiban in 1950, annual professor of the ASOR in 1950–1951, field director of the ASOR expedition to Tulul Abu el-'Alayiq in 1950–1951, and the University Museum expeditions to el-Jib in 1956–1957, 1959, 1960, 1962. In 1964, 1965, and 1966 he led expeditions to Tell es-Sa'idiyeh. He wrote *The Excavation at Herodian Jericho, 1951* (New Haven, Conn., 1958), *Archaeology and the Old Testament* (Princeton, N.J., 1958), *The Water System at Gibeon* (Philadelphia, 1961), *Gibeon, Where the Sun Stood Still: The Discovery of the Biblical City* (Princeton, N.J., 1962), *The Bronze Age Cemetery at Gibeon* (Philadelphia, 1963), *Recovering Sarepta, a Phoenician City: Excavations at Sarafand, Lebanon 1969–*

1974) (Princeton, N.J., 1978), and *The Cemetery at Tell es-Sa'idiyeh, Jordan* (Philadelphia, 1980). *References*: *CA*; *DAS*; *MENA*; and *WWWA*.

PROCTOR, MYRA ALLEN (1834–1914). Missionary educator, born October 12, 1834, in Townsend, Massachusetts. Proctor graduated from State Normal School (Framingham, Mass.). She served under the American Board of Commissioners for Foreign Mission (ABCFM)* in Turkey, was principal of a girls' boarding school in Aintab from 1859 to 1878, and superintendent of schools connected with the Aintab Mission from 1878 to 1882, when she was transferred to Kessab. She returned to the United States in 1883 and resigned in 1885. Died September 12, 1914, in Stoneham, Massachusetts. *References*: *Woman's Who's Who in America 1914–1915* (New York, 1914).

PROTESTANT EPISCOPAL CHURCH IN THE UNITED STATES OF AMERICA: BOARD OF MISSIONS. The Domestic and Foreign Missionary Society of the Protestant Episcopal Church was established in 1835 and sent Horatio Southgate, Jr.,* to study the possibility for missionary work among the Muslims in Persia. It established a mission in Turkey in 1839, and the first missionary went to Constantinople in 1840. It ended the mission in 1950. It later appointed a priest to serve on the staff of the Anglican archbishop in Jerusalem. *References*: Records, Historical Society of the Episcopal Church, Austin, Texas; Charles T. Bridgeman, *The Episcopal Church and the Middle East* (New York, 1958); Karen M. Booth, "The Domestic and Foreign Missionary Society Papers: The Constantinople Papers: 1835–1850," *Historical Magazine of the Protestant Episcopal Church* 40 (1971), 104–108.

PROTHRO, EDWIN TERRY (1919–   ). Psychologist, born December 11, 1919, in Robeline, Louisiana. Prothro graduated from Louisiana College and Louisiana State University, and served in World War II. He was assistant professor of psychology at Louisiana State University from 1946 to 1949; associate professor at the University of Tennessee from 1949 to 1951; associate professor of psychology at the American University of Beirut* from 1951 to 1955; professor of psychology in 1955; dean of the faculty of arts and sciences from 1965 to 1973; and director of the Center for Behavioral Research after 1965. He wrote *Child Rearing in Lebanon* (Cambridge, Mass., 1961) and was co-author of *Changing Family Patterns in the Arab East* (Beirut, 1974). *References*: *AMWS*; *CA*.

PROUT, HENRY GOSLEE (1845–1927). Engineer, born in Fairfax County, Virginia, and grew up in Berkshire, Massachusetts. Prout served in the Union Army during the Civil War and graduated from the University of Michigan. He joined the Egyptian Army in 1872 and was chief of the Bureau of Engineering in the General Staff. He was second-in-command to Raleigh Edward Colston* on a reconnaissance of Kordofan in 1875, and took over command after Colston became an invalid at al-Ubaiyad. He then led the expedition into Darfur. He was governor of the Equatoria Province in 1876. He resigned in 1878 and returned to the United States. He settled in Nutley, New Jersey, was editor of *The Railroad Gazette* from 1887 to 1903, and vice president and general manager of the Union Switch and Signal Company from 1903 until 1914. Died in Nutley, New Jersey. *References*: *Hesseltine*; *Hill*; *Scannell's New Jersey's First Citizens* (Paterson, N.J., 1918), 1:415–17; and *WWWA*.

PURDY, ERASTUS SPARROW (1838–1881). Soldier, born in New York and grew up in California. Purdy served in the Union Army in the Civil War. In 1870 he joined the Egyptian General Staff and led a scientific expedition to survey the Upper Egypt between the Nile and the Red Sea. In 1873 he surveyed the country between Berenice and Berber, and from 1874 to 1876, he was in command of a party that surveyed the Egyptian province of Darfur. Parts of his reports were published in the publications of the Egyptian Geographical Society of Cairo. He was sued for debt in Cairo in 1874, discharged from the army in 1878, and reemployed as a cadastral inspector from 1879 to 1881 when he was finally discharged. Died in Cairo. *References*: *Hesseltine*; *Hill*.

Q

QUAKER CITY. Paddle-wheel steamship. The first American cruise boat to make a cruise to the Middle East in 1867 with seventy-five American tourists on board. The cruise became famous because Mark Twain* was one of the passengers and his book, *Innocents Abroad* (Hartford, Conn., 1869), which described the trip, became very popular. The letters of two other passengers were also published: Mrs. Stephen M. Griswold, *A Woman's Pilgrimage to the Holy Land; or, Pleasant Days Abroad* (Hartford, Conn., 1871), and Emily Severance, *Journal Letters of Emily A. Severance*, ed. Julia S. Millikan (Cleveland, 1938). *References*: "Captain log," Ms., Patten Free Library, Bath, Maine; Dewey Ganzel, *Mark Twain Abroad: The Cruise of the "Quaker City"* (Chicago, 1968).

R

RAID ON LIBYA (1986). Following terrorist attacks on Rome and Vienna airports in December 1985, the United States accused Libya of training, arming and protecting Arab terrorists. In January the United States cut its economic ties with Libya and ordered Americans to leave Libya. It also began a war of nerves, and later conducted flight operations over the Gulf of Sidra. On March 24, 1986, Libya attacked American planes. On April 15, 1986, American warplanes attacked "terrorist-related targets" in Tripoli and Benghazi, Libya, in retaliation for Libyan-directed anti-American terrorist attacks, and to deter future Libyan-directed attacks. Four of the five main targets were hit and substantially damaged; one American plane was lost. *References*: *Newsweek*, April 28, 1986; *Time*, April 28, 1986.

RAPPLEYE, JULIA A. (1835–1881). Missionary educator, born November 18, 1835, in Seneca Castle, Ontario County, New York. Rappleye graduated from Oberlin College, and became a missionary under the American Board of Commissioners for Foreign Missions (ABCFM)* in Constantinople in 1871. In 1872 she started the home school (later the American College for Girls), and in 1876 she was transferred to Brusa. She returned to the United States in 1881. Died June 9, 1881, in Bernicia, California. *Reference*: *American Heroes on Mission Fields* (New York, 1890), No. 10.

RAU, WILLIAM H(ERMAN) (1855–1920). Photographer, born in Philadelphia. In 1874 Rau accompanied the expedition to observe the transit of Venus, he later traveled to the Rocky Mountains as a government survey photographer, and in 1878 he purchased the stereographic company established by his father-in-law. He traveled in Egypt and Palestine and prepared many stereographs during this trip which were later produced in his studio in Philadelphia, and were issued throughout the 1890s. He developed Robert Peary's photographs form the North Pole. Rau's company was purchased by Underwood and Underwood in 1901. Died in Philadelphia. *Reference*: *MBEP*.

RAVNDAL, GABRIEL BIE (1865–1950). Journalist and consul, born June 27, 1865, in Norway. Ravndal graduated from the Royal University of Norway and came to the United States in 1885. He was newspaper publisher in South Dakota from 1889 to 1898, and a member of the South Dakota House of Representatives from 1892 to 1894. He entered the foreign service in 1898, served in Beirut from 1898 to 1905, and at Dawson, Yukon Territory, in 1905–1906. He was consul general in Baghdad from 1906 to 1910 and consul in Constantinople in 1910. He served the Red Cross during the massacres in Eastern Turkey in 1909, was president of the Beirut Relief Committee during the Cilician disturbances in 1909, was founder and secretary of the Beirut chapter of the American Red Cross,* and founder and secretary of the Constantinople chapter. He was the founder of the American Chamber of Commerce for the Levant, and founder and president of the American Club of Constantinople. Ravndal was in charge of the consular interests of several countries at Constantinople from 1914 to 1917. He was consul general in Paris, St. Nazaire, and Nantes in 1917–1918, returned to Constantinople in 1919, and served until 1921. He was later consul general in Zurich, Hamburg, and Berlin until his retirement in 1930. He wrote *The Origins of the Capitulations and of the Consular Institution* (Washington, D.C., 1921), and *Turkey: A Commercial and Industrial Handbook* (Washington, D.C., 1926). Died March 24, 1950, in Orlando, Florida. *References*: *NCAB* 38:431; *NYT*, March 24, 1950; and *WWWA*.

RAWSON, ALBERT LEIGHTON (1829–1902). Artist and author, born October 15, 1828, in Chester, Vermont. Rawson studied law and medicine. He made several visits to the Middle East and claimed to have made a pilgrimage to Mecca in 1851–1852 with the annual caravan disguised as a Muslim medical student, to have been adopted as a brother by the Adwan Bedouins of Moab, and to be initiated by the Druses on Mount Lebanon. He wrote *Recent Explorations in Bible Lands* (Philadelphia, 1875). He met Madame Helena Blavatsky in Cairo in 1850, was later one of the founders of the Theosophical Society in America, organized the first American branch of the Theosophical Society at Rochester, New York, in 1882, and was one of the founders of the Nobles of the Mystic Shrine. Died November 1902 in New York City. *References*: *ACAB*; *NYHSD*; and *WWWA*.

RAY, WILLIAM (1771–1827). Sailor and author, born December 8, 1771, in Salisbury, Litchfield County, Connecticut. Failing in business, Ray joined the navy and was a sailor on the U.S.S. *Philadelphia** when it was grounded in Tripoli Harbor in 1803. He was held prisoner in Tripoli for some twenty months and described his experiences in *Horrors of Slavery or The American Tars in Tripoli* (Troy, N.Y. 1808). He later served in the War of 1812. Died in New York. *References*: *DAA*; *NCAB* 1:315.

RAYNOLDS, GEORGE COOK (1839–1920). Medical missionary, born February 25, 1839, in Longmeadow, Massachusetts. Raynolds graduated from Williams College and the Medical Department of New York University, and was an assistant surgeon in the Union Navy during the Civil War. He served in hospitals in Long Island, Manchester, Vermont, and Chicago until 1869. In 1869 he became a missionary under the American Board of Commissioners of Foreign Missions (ABCFM)*, and was stationed in Harput, Turkey, until 1871. He was ordained in 1871, and opened a station in Van in 1872, started a school which grew into a high school and a college, and became president of the college. Died February 14, 1920, in San Francisco. *Reference*: Hewitt.

REA, HENRY CARTER (1900–1963). Petroleum geologist, born March 23, 1900, in Brooklyn, New York. Rea served in the navy in World War I and graduated from the University of California at Berkley. He was employed by various oil companies and conducted oil exploration work in Italy, Borneo, Java, India, Afghanistan, Pakistan, Canada, and the United States. He was a member of the survey team that investigated oil possibilities in Afghanistan in 1937–1938 and in Iran. He was later a consulting geologist for an exploration company in Littleton, Colorado. Died December 9, 1963, in Albuquerque, New Mexico. *References*: *BAAPG* 48 (September 1964): 1601–1603; *WWWA*.

RECOVERY. Ship from Salem under captain Joseph Ropes.* The first American ship to call at Mocha in 1798, and to enter the Red Sea. *References*: ''Journal,'' Peabody Museum, Salem, Massachusetts; Eric Macro, ''The First Americans at Mocha,'' *Geographical Journal* 130 (1964): 183–184.

REDHOUSE PRESS, ISTANBUL. The American Board of Commissioners for Foreign Missions* (ABCFM) began operating the press in Malta in 1822. It was removed in part to Beirut in 1823 and in part to Smyrna in 1833, and from there to Constantinople in 1853. It published Bibles and books in Armenian, Judeo-Spanish, and Armeno-Turkish, periodicals in Armenian and Turkish, and several editions of the English-Turkish dictionary prepared by the English scholar James William Redhouse. It was known until 1960 as the American Board Publications Department, and after 1960, as the Redhouse Press. In the 1960s the press began to specialize in the publication of children's books and reading material for newly literate adults. *Reference*: Robert Avery, *Ink on Their Thumbs: The Antecedents of the Redhouse Press* (Istanbul, 1970).

REED, CASS ARTHUR (1884–1949). Educator, born November 25, 1884, in Port Huron, Michigan. Reed graduated from Pomona College, Union Theological Seminary, and Columbia and Harvard universities, and was ordained in 1911. He was a teacher in Yamaguchi, Japan, from 1906 to 1908, and assistant pastor in New York City from 1908 to 1911. He was professor of education and English at the International College in Smyrna from 1912 to 1914, dean of the college from 1914 to 1926, and its president from 1926 until his retirement in 1936. He did relief work in Turkey during World War I, served as director of the relief unit in Western Turkey in 1919–1920 for the American Committee for Relief in the Near East, and was a member of the disaster relief committee in Smyrna in 1922–1923 which evacuated 240,000 refugees From Smyrna in six days. He was pastor in Pomona, California, from 1937 to 1944, chief finance officer of the United Nations Relief and Rehabilitation Administration's (UNRRA) mission to Greece in 1945–1946, and co-pastor in Whittier, California, from 1947 until his death. Died August 22, 1949, in Redondo Beach, California. *References*: *AndoverTS*; *NCAB* 49:261; and *WWWA*.

REED, CHARLES A(LLEN) (1912–   ). Anthropologist, born June 6, 1912, in Portland, Oregon. Reed graduated from Whitman College and the universities of Oregon and California at Berkley. He was a member of the faculty of Reed College from 1943 to 1946, the University of Arizona from 1946 to 1949, and the University of Illinois School of Pharmacy from 1949 to 1961. He was curator of mammals and reptiles at the Peabody Museum of Yale University from 1961 to 1966, and professor of anthropology at the University of Illinois at Chicago after 1967. He was a member of the Iraq-Jarmo archaeological expedition of the Oriental Institute in 1954–1955, the Iranian prehistoric project of the Oriental Institute in 1960, the joint University of Istanbul and the Chicago Prehistoric Project in Turkey in 1970, and director of the Yale prehistoric expedition to Nubia from 1962 to 1965. *References*: *AMWS*; *WWA*

REED, GEORGE C(LINTON) (1872–1966). Missionary, born in Weeping Water, Nebraska. Reed graduated from Oberlin College. He served as a missionary under the Gospel Missionary Union in Morocco from 1897 until 1917 and was stationed at Meknes. He translated part of the New Testament into Arabic. He left for Bamako, French Sudan (now Mali Republic), in 1919 and served there until his retirement in 1951. Died January 21, 1966. *References*: "Memoirs of Morocco, 1897–1914," Ms., Gospel Missionary Union, Kansas City, Missouri.

REED, HORATIO BLAKE (1837–1888). Army officer, born January 22, 1837, in Rockaway, Long Island. Reed was educated at Troy Polytechnic Institute, was commissioned second lieutenant in 1861, and served in the Union Army in the Civil War. He resigned from the army in 1870 and was a civil engineer in the employ of a railroad in New York. He was an officer on the Egyptian General Staff and was appointed second-in-command to Raleigh E. Colston* who was charged with a survey mission in Kordofan in 1874. Reed collected antiquities on this expedition. Before the mission reached Dongola, however, he became an invalid and was replaced in 1875 with Henry Goslee Prout.* Died March 7, 1888, in Togus, Kennebec County, Maine. *References*: *ACAB*; *Hesseltine*.

REED, WILLIAM LAFOREST (1912–   ). Archaeologist, born January 9, 1912, in Defiance, Ohio. Reed graduated from Hiram College and Yale University, and was ordained in 1939. He was pastor from 1939 to 1942; a chaplain in World War II; member of the faculty of Brite Bible College from 1948 to 1956; professor of Old Testament at the Lexington Theological Seminary from 1956 to 1968; and professor of religion at the Texas Christian University from 1968 until his retirement in 1980. He was director of the American Schools of Oriental Research (ASOR)* in Jerusalem in 1951–52, director of the excavations at Dibon, Moab, in 1951–1952, co-director of the Qumran Caves Expedition in 1952, and senior archaeologist for the Agency for International Development in Amman in 1964. He also participated in the excavations of Gibeon in 1959 and 1962, of Elealeh in 1962, in Saudi Arabia in 1962 and 1967, and in Yemen in 1972, and was the co-author of *The Excavation at Dibon (Dhiban) in Moab* (New Haven, Conn., 1964), and *Ancient Records From North Acobia* (Toronto, 1969). *Reference*: *DAS*; *WWA*.

REES, THOMAS (1850–1933). Newspaper publisher, born May 13, 1850, in Pittsburgh, and grew up in Iowa. Rees learned the printer's trade and engaged in this trade until 1876. He was publisher of the *Keokuk Constitution* from 1876 to 1881 and the *Illinois State Register* after 1881, and member of the Illinois Assembly from 1902 to 1906. He visited Egypt and Palestine, and wrote *Egypt and the Holy Land Today* (Springfield, Ill., 1922). Died September 9, 1933, in Springfield, Illinois. *Reference*: *WWWA*.

REFORMED CHURCH IN AMERICA: BOARD OF WORLD MISSIONS. The Board of Foreign Missions was organized in 1832. Missionary work in the Arabian Peninsula began in 1889, and it took over responsibility for the Arabian Mission* in 1894. In 1924 it joined in the United Mission in Iraq,* and in 1948 it began work among the Nilotic tribes in Southern Sudan from which it was expelled in 1964 by the Sudanese government because the missionaries were suspected of helping the nationalist rebellion in southern Sudan. *References*: Peter N. VandenBerge, *Historical Directory of the Reformed Church in America 1628–1798* (Grand Rapids, Mich., 1978).

REFORMED PRESBYTERIAN CHURCH OF NORTH AMERICA: BOARD OF FOREIGN MISSIONS. Began missionary work in Syria in 1856 which was centered in the Latakia district chiefly among the *Nusairiyeh* and in Cyprus in 1895. The Syrian government expelled the mission in 1958. *Reference*: Andrew J. McFarland, *Eight Decades in Syria* (Topeka, Kan., 1937).

REISNER, GEORGE ANDREW (1867–1942). Egyptologist, born November 5, 1867, in Indianapolis. Reisner graduated from Harvard University and studied in Berlin. He was instructor in Semitics at Harvard University in 1896–1897, and a member of the international commission to catalogue the

Cairo Museum from 1897 to 1898. He was director of the Hearst Egyptian Expedition of the University of California from 1898 to 1905, excavating at Quft in Upper Egypt; archaeological director of the Nubian Archaeological Survey for the Egyptian government from 1907 to 1909; director of the Harvard excavations in Samaria, Palestine, in 1909–1910; and director of the Harvard University-Boston Museum of Fine Arts Egyptian Expedition from 1905 to 1942, excavating at Giza. He led excavations at Deir el-Ballas, Naga-ed-Der, the Giza Pyramids, Zawiyat el-Aryan Pyramids, Kerma, Jebel Barkal, Nuri, Kurru, Semna, and Begarawiya. Reisner was assistant professor of Semitic archaeology from 1905 to 1910, assistant professor of Egyptology from 1910 to 1914, professor of Egyptology at Harvard University from 1914 to 1942, and curator of the Department of Egyptian Art at the Boston Museum of Fine Arts from 1910 to 1942. Reisner wrote *The Archaeological Survey of Nubia* (Cairo, 1910–1927), *The Early Dynastic Cemeteries of Naga-ed-Der* (Leipzig, 1908), *Excavations at Kerma* (Cambridge, Mass., 1923), *Harvard Excavations at Samaria* (Cambridge, Mass., 1924), *Mycerinus: The Temples of the Third Pyramid of Giza* (Cambridge, Mass., 1931), *A Provincial Cemetery of the Pyramid-Age: Naga-ed-Der* (Berkeley, Calif., 1932), *The Development of the Egyptian Tomb Down to the Accession of Cheops* (Cambridge, Mass., 1936), and *A History of the Giza Necropolis* (Cambridge, Mass., 1942). Died June 6, 1942, in his camp at the Pyramids of al-Jiza, Cairo. *References*: "The Adventures of an Archaeologist," Ms., Harvard University Archives; Dows Dunham, *The Egyptian Department and Its Excavations* (Boston, 1958); "The Egyptian Expedition Under George A. Reisner," *Apollo* 91 (January 1970): 16–21. *DAB*; *IAB*; *WWWA*; and *WWWE*.

REYNOLDS, ALEXANDER WELCH (1817–1876). Soldier, born August 1817 in Clarke County, Virginia. Reynolds graduated from the U.S. Military Academy in 1838 and was commissioned first lieutenant in 1839. He served in the Seminole War, on frontier duty, in the Mexican War, and in the Confederate Army in the Civil War. He went to Egypt in 1869, served in the Egyptian Army in various capacities, and was chief of staff to William Wing Loring* in 1875. Died May 26, 1876; in Alexandria, Egypt. *References*: *CWD*; *DAB*; *Hesseltine*; and *WWWA*.

RHEA, SAMUEL AUDLEY (1827–1865). Missionary, born January 23, 1827, in Blountville, Tennessee. Rhea graduated from Knoxville College and Union Theological Seminary, and was ordained in 1851. He became a missionary under the American Board of Commissioners for Foreign Missions (ABCFM),* and served in the Nestorian Mission. In 1851 he opened a new station at Gawar, in the Kurdish Mountains, and was stationed in Urmia from 1860 until his death. He prepared a grammar and a vocabulary of the Kurdish language. Died September 2, 1865, near Urmia while traveling in Kurdistan. *References*: *EM*;

Dwight W. Marsh, *The Tennesseean in Persia and Koordistan, Being Scenes and Incidents in the Life of Samuel Audley Rhea* (Philadelphia, 1869).

RHETT, THOMAS GRIMKÉ (ca. 1825–1878). Soldier, born in South Carolina. Rhett graduated from the U.S. Military Academy in 1845, was assigned to the Ordnance Corps, transferred to the mounted rifles, and served in the Mexican War and in the Civil War in the Confederate Army. From 1870 to 1873 he was a colonel of ordnance in the Egyptian Army. In 1873 he had a paralytic stroke and had to resign but remained abroad until 1876. Died July 28, 1878, in Baltimore. *References*: *ACAB*; *Hesseltine*; and *NCAB* 4:167.

RHIND, CHARLES (fl. 1810–1845). Merchant and diplomatic agent, born in Aberdeen, Scotland, and came to the United States in 1810. Rhind was a merchant in New York City, engaged in business with Smyrna after 1810, was agent of the North River Steam Boat Company in 1822, and first consul in Odessa in 1829. He was member of a commission, with David Offley* and James Biddle,* to negotiate a treaty of commerce and navigation with the Ottoman Empire. On the instructions of Secretary of State Martin Van Buren, Rhind went to Constantinople in 1830, and negotiated a treaty without his fellow commissioners. He then coerced them to sign the treaty. He returned to the United States with the treaty. In 1831 he returned to Constantinople with Henry Eckford* but left for the United States in 1832, and resumed his commercial activities in New York City. Died in New York City. *References*: *DAB*; *WWWA*.

RHOADES, RALPH OMER (1895–1961). Geologist and petroleum executive, born July 30, 1895, in Urich, Missouri. Rhodes graduated from the University of Kansas and Stanford University, and served in the marines in World War I. He conducted geological explorations in South America, Europe, the Middle East, and the Far East for Gulf Oil Corporation from 1926 to 1940. In 1928 he made the first complete geological survey of Bahrain, and in 1935, he carried out geological explorations in Kuwait that led to the discovery of a large oil field. He was successively geologist, staff geologist, executive assistant to the vice president in charge of production, senior vice president, executive vice president, and chairman of the board of Gulf Oil Corporation, until his retirement in 1960. Died July 19, 1961, in Pittsburgh. *References*: *NCAB* 52:253; *WWWA*.

RHODES, ALBERT (1830– ?). Author, born February 1, 1840, in Pittsburgh. Rhodes spent most his life abroad. He was consul in Jerusalem from 1863 to 1865, and wrote *Jerusalem as It Is* (London, 1865). He was later chargé d'affaires at the Hague, and consul in Rouen and Eberfeld, Germany. He lived in Paris after 1885. *References*: *ACAB*, *DAA*.

RHODES, FOSTER (fl.   −1839). Shipbuilder, native of Long Island, New York. Rhodes was Henry Eckford's* assistant in Turkey, where Eckford was in charge of a Ottoman Navy's shipyard. After Eckford's death he succeeded to the position of director of the Turkish naval shipyard and supervised the construction of several ships for the Ottoman Navy. He remained in Turkey until 1839.

RICE, WILLIAM A. (1892?−1946). Clergyman, born in Framingham, Massachusetts. Rice graduated from the College of the Sacred Heart (Woodstock, Md.), became a member of the Society of Jesus, and was ordained in 1925. He was vice president of Boston College from 1927 to 1929, and rector of the Jesuit novitiate in Lenox, Massachusetts, from 1929 to 1931. He was sent to Baghdad in 1931 by an association of American Jesuit universities and colleges to establish a secondary school there, and from 1932 to 1939, he was rector of the Jesuit mission in Baghdad and of Baghdad College. He was vicar apostolic of Belize, British Honduras, from 1939 until his death. Died February 28, 1946, in Belize. *References*: *NYT*, March 2, 1946.

RICHARDS, A(LEXANDER) KEENE (1827−1881). Horse breeder, born October 10, 1827. Richards graduated from Bethany College. He made several trips to the Middle East to buy Arabian horses for his stock farms, the most important of which was "Blue Grass Park" in Georgetown, Kentucky. He made his first trip to the Middle East between 1851 and 1853, accompanied by Professor Joseph Desha Pickett of Bethany College, and received permission from Sultan Abdulmecid to export Arabian stallions to the United States. He wrote *The Arabian Horses Mokhladi and Massoud-and-Sacklowie Imported by A. Keene Richards* (Lexington, Ky., 1857). Between 1855 and 1857 he made another extended tour of the Middle East, accompanied by the painter Edward Troye.* Died in Georgetown, Kentucky. *References*: Alexander Mackay-Smith, *The Race Horses of America 1832–1872: Portraits and Other Paintings by Edward Troye* (Saratoga Springs, N.Y., 1981).

RICHARDS MISSION. Mission to the Middle East in 1957, headed by James P(riouleu) Richards (1894–1979), former congressman from South Carolina and chairman of the House Foreign Affairs Committee. Richards was appointed special assistant to President Dwight Eisenhower in 1957 on problems of the Middle Eastern area. Richards was instructed to explain the terms of the Eisenhower Doctrine, which established a policy of U.S. resistance to any Communist aggression in the Middle East. *References*: *NYT*, February 24, 1979.

RIDGAWAY, HENRY BASCOM (1830–1895). Clergyman, born September 7, 1830, in Talbot County, Maryland. Ridgaway graduated from Dickinson College (Carlisle, Pa.). He was a pastor in Maryland, Portland, Maine, New York City, and Cincinnati; professor of theology at Garret Bible Institute, Evanston, Illinois, from 1882–1889; professor of practical theology from 1884 to 1895; and president from 1885 to 1892. He traveled in Palestine in 1873–1874, and wrote *The Lord's-Land: A Narrative of Travels in Sinai, Arabia Petraea, and Palestine, from the Red Sea to the Entering In of Hamath* (New York, 1876). Died March 30, 1895, in Evanston, Illinois. *References*: *ACAB*; *DAB*; *NCAB* 9:287; and *WWWA*.

RIDLEY, CLARENCE SELF (1883–1969). Army officer, born June 22, 1883, in Croydon, Indiana. Ridley graduated from the U.S. Military Academy in 1905 and was commissioned a second lieutenant in the Corps of Engineers. He was military aide to President Woodrow Wilson from 1917 to 1921, governor of the Panama Canal, and president and director of the Panama Railroad Company from 1936 to 1940. He served with the 3rd Division in 1940–1941 and the 6th Division in 1941. He was chief of the military mission to Iran from 1942 to 1946, and was inspector general of the Iranian Army. He retired in 1947 with the rank of major general. Died July 26, 1969, in Carmel, California. *Reference*: *WWWA*.

RIGGS, CHARLES TROWBRIDGE (1871–1953). Missionary, born September 1, 1871, in Sivas, Turkey. Riggs graduated from Princeton University and Auburn Theological Seminary, and was ordained in 1903. He was a missionary in Turkey under the American Board of Commissioners for Foreign Missions (ABCFM),* instructor at Robert College* from 1893 to 1897, and instructor at Anatolia College from 1900 to 1903. He was secretary of the West Turkey Mission on Constantinople in 1903 and checked the revision of the Redhouse Turkish-English dictionary. He retired in 1946 and lived in Middlebury, Vermont, but after the death of his wife in 1948, he returned to Turkey. Died February 12, 1953, in Istanbul. *References*: "Diary, 1918–1922," Ms. in private hands; *AuburnTS*; and *NYT*, February 15, 1953.

RIGGS, EDWARD (1844–1914). Missionary, son of Elias Riggs,* born June 30, 1844, in Smyrna, Turkey. Riggs graduated from Princeton University and Union Theological Seminary, and was ordained in 1869. He became a missionary under the American Board of Commissioners for Foreign Missions (ABCFM)* in Turkey in 1869, and served in Sivas from 1869 to 1876 and in Marsovan from 1876 until 1914. He became a teacher at Anatolia College in 1886 and president of Marsovan Theological Seminary in 1901. Died February 16, 1914, in Smyrna. *Reference*: *UnionTS*; *WWWA*.

RIGGS, ELIAS (1810–1901). Missionary, born November 19, 1810, in New Providence, New Jersey. Riggs graduated from Amherst and Hanover colleges and Andover Theological Seminary, and was ordained in 1832. He became a missionary under the American Board of Commissioners for Foreign Missions (ABCFM)* in 1832 and served in Athens until 1834, in Argos from 1834 to 1838, and in Smyrna from 1838 to 1853. He was engaged in translating the Bible into modern Armenian, and wrote *A Manual of the Chaldee Language: Containing a Chaldee Grammar* (Boston, 1832) and *Brief Grammar of the Modern Armenian Language* (Smyrna, 1847). He moved to Constantinople in 1853 and was involved with the publishing activities of the mission. He taught at Bebek Seminary from 1853 to 1856, as well as at a girls' school, and after 1859 was involved in translating the Bible into Bulgarian. Riggs wrote *A Grammar of the Modern Armenian Language as Spoken in Constantinople and Asia Minor* (Constantinople, 1856) and *Outline of a Grammar of the Turkish Language as Written in the Armenian Character* (Constantinople, 1856). After 1873, he helped prepare the standard Turkish text of the Bible, and in 1884 he prepared a Bulgarian Bible dictionary. From 1885 to 1888 he served in Aintab. Died January 17, 1901, in Constantinople. *References*: ACAB; *Amherst*; DAB; NCAB 3:120; and *WWWA*.

RIGGS, ERNEST WILSON (1881–1952). Missionary, son of Edward Riggs,* Riggs graduated from Princeton University and Auburn Theological Seminary, and was ordained in 1910. He was vice consul in Harput, Turkey, from 1904 to 1907; president of Euphrates College* from 1910 to 1921; child welfare director of the Near East Relief* in 1920–1921; and associate secretary and corresponding secretary of the American Board of Commissioners for Foreign Missions (ABCFM)* from 1921 to 1932. He was president of Anatolia College* in Thessaloniki from 1933 to 1950, and director of the Greek Office of Relief in Thessaloniki in 1940–1941. He escaped hours before the Germans made the college their headquarters for operations in the Balkans. He returned and reopened the college in 1945. Died March 25, 1952, in Dallas, Texas. *References*: Papers, Hoover Institution Library; *AuburnTS*; *NYT*, March 26, 1952; and *WWWA*.

RIGGS, HENRY HARRISON (1875–1943). Missionary, grandson of Elias Riggs,* Riggs graduated from Carleton College and Auburn Theological Seminary, and was ordained in 1902. He was a teacher at Anatolia College* from 1896 to 1899, and became a missionary under the American Board of Commissioners for Foreign Missions (ABCFM)* in Kayseri, Turkey, in 1902. He was president of Euphrates College* from 1903 to 1910, served in Harput from 1912 to 1915, and did relief and rescue work in Armenia from 1915 to 1917, in Turkey in 1919–1920, and missionary work in Constantinople and Beirut from 1920 until his death. Died August 17, 1943. *References*: *AuburnTS*; *WWWA*.

RIGHTER, CHESTER NEWELL (1824–1856). Missionary, born September 25, 1824, in Parsippany, Morris County, New York. Righter graduated from Yale College and New Haven and Andover theological seminaries, and was ordained in 1954. In 1854 he went to the Middle East as an agent of the American

Bible Society. Died December 16, 1856, in Diyarbekir, Turkey. *References*: *ACAB*; *AndoverTS*; and Samuel I. Prime, *The Bible in the Levant; or, the life and Letters of Rev. C. N. Righter, Agent of the American Bible Society in the Levant* (New York, 1859).

RIHANI, AMEEN (FARES) (1876–1940). Author, poet, and translator, born November 24, 1876, in Freike, Mount Lebanon, brought to the United States in 1888, and naturalized in 1903. Rihani left school and began writing for Arabic papers in New York. He lived in Lebanon from 1905 to 1910. In 1922 he traveled to Arabia, Yemen, Saudi Arabia, and Kuwait, served as King Ibn Saud's personal adviser, and was involved in oil negotiations in 1924. He wrote *Maker of Modern Arabia* (Boston, 1928), *Around the Coasts of Arabia* (Boston, 1930), and *Arabian Peak and Desert, Travels in al-Yeman* (Boston, 1930). He visited Iraq in 1932 and Morocco in 1939. Died September 13, 1940, in Freike, Lebanon. *References*: Nadeem Naimy, *The Lebanese Prophets of New York* (Beirut, 1985); *WWWA*.

RILEY, JAMES (1777–1840). Sea captain, born in Middletown, Connecticut. Riley served in the War of 1812, and was master and supercargo of the brig *Commerce*, which was shipwrecked off the western coast of North Africa in 1915. He was captured with several crewmen as slaves by the Arabs, and was forced to wander north into Morocco, until ransomed by the British consul general in Mogador. His *Sufferings in Africa: Captain Riley's Narrative* (1817; edited with an introduction by Gordon E. Evans, New York, 1965) went through several editions. He was later state senator in Ohio. *References*: *ACAB*; *OAB*.

RILEY, WILLIAM E(DWARD) (1897–1970). Army officer, born February 2, 1897, in Minneapolis. Riley graduated from the College of St. Thomas (St. Paul, Minn.), and was commissioned second lieutenant in the Marine Corps in 1917. He served in World War I, and later in Haiti, Puerto Rico, Santo Domingo, and Cuba. He was assistant chief of staff for war plans in the south and central Pacific, and commanding general of the Third Marine Division during World War II. In 1948 he became commander of American military personnel in Palestine and senior military observer under the United Nations. He was chief of staff of the U.S. Truce Supervision Organization (UNTSO) in Palestine from 1946 to 1953, with headquarters in Jerusalem. He retired in 1951 with the rank of lieutenant general. Died April 28, 1970, in Annapolis, Maryland. *References*: *CB* 1951.

ROBERT COLLEGE. Founded in 1863 in Constantinople as a private American institution, the first American institution of higher learning abroad, and chartered by the Board of Regents of the State of New York. In 1871 it consolidated with the American College for Girls* into one campus and continued to function as a preparatory school and high school. The college was renamed Boğaziçi (Boshporus) University, a Turkish state university. *References*: *Board-*

man; Franklin Burroughs, "Robert College and Turkish Advancement," *MW* 54 (October 1964): 288–291; Keith M. Greenwood, "Robert College: The American Founders," Ph.D. diss., Johns Hopkins University, 1965; Malcolm P. and Marcia R. Stevens, "A College on the Bosporus," *AWM* 35 (1984): 16–21; and *Survey*.

ROBERTS, EDMUND (1784–1836). Merchant and diplomat, born June 29, 1784, in Portsmouth, New Hampshire. In business from 1808, Roberts went on the brig *Mary Ann* to Zanzibar in 1831 and visited parts of India. In 1832 he was sent on a diplomatic mission to negotiate treaties with Muscat, Siam, and Cochin, China, and signed the first American treaty with the Sultan of Muscat in 1833. In 1835 he returned to Muscat to exchange ratified treaties. Died June 12, 1836, at Macao. His diary was published as *Embassy to the Eastern Courts of Cochin-China, Siam and Muscat; in the U. S. Sloop-of-war Peacock, David Geisinger, Commander, During the Years 1832–3–4* (New York, 1837). *References*: Papers, Manuscript Division, Library of Congress; New Hampshire Historical Society; *ACAB*; *DAB*; Frederic A. Greenhut, "Edmund Roberts: Early American Diplomat," *Manuscripts* 35 (1983): 273–280; and *WWWA*.

ROBERTSON, WILLIAM BRYAN (1893–1943). Aviation executive, born October 8, 1893, in Nashville, Tennessee. Robertson served in the aviation section of the U.S. Special Corps in World War I, established a flying field in Forest Park, St. Louis, in 1919, organized the Robertson Aircraft Corporation in 1920, and sold it in 1928, and in 1926 was awarded the air mail contract for service between St. Louis and Chicago. In 1928 he organized Curtiss-Robertson Airplane Manufacturing Company, and was its president and chairman of the board. He was in China in 1929 and organized China National Airways; in Turkey in 1932, he organized the Turkish national airline. Died August 1, 1943, in a crash of an army glider. *References*: *NCAB* 36:268; *WWWA*.

ROBINSON, EDWARD (1794–1863). Philologist, geographer, and biblical scholar, born April 10, 1794, in Southington, Connecticut. Robinson graduated from Hamilton College and studied in Gottingen, Halle, and Berlin. He was an instructor of Hebrew at Andover Theological Seminary from 1823 to 1826, and professor of biblical literature at Union Theological Seminary from 1837 until his death. He founded the *American Biblical Repository* in 1831 and *Bibliotheca Sacra* in 1843. In 1838 he traveled in Sinai, Palestine and Syria with Eli Smith* and conducted the first scholarly exploration of Palestine. His book *Biblical Researchers in Palestine, Mount Sinai and Arabia Petraea* (New York, 1841) was published simultaneously in England, Germany, and the United States and established him as the leading biblical geographer. He revisited Palestine and Syria in 1852, and later wrote *Biblical Researchers in Palestine and Adjacent Regions* (New York, 1856). Died January 27, 1863, in New York City. *References*: F. M. Abel, "Edward Robinson and the Identification of Biblical Sites,"

The Journal of Biblical Literature 58 (1939): 365–372. ACAB; Albrecht Alt, "Edward Robinson and the Historical Geography of Palestine," The Journal of Biblical Literature 58 (1939): 373–377; Jerry W. Brown, The Rise of Biblical Criticism in America, 1800–1870: The New England Scholars (Middletown, Conn., 1969), ch. 7; DAB; Philip J. King, "Edward Robinson: Biblical Scholar," BA 46 (1983): 230–232; NCAB 2:242; and WWWA.

ROBINSON, GEORGE LIVINGSTONE (1864–1958). Archaeologist, born August 19, 1864, near West Hebron, New York. Robinson graduated from Princeton University and Princeton Theological Seminary, and studied at the universities of Berlin and Leipzig. He was an instructor at Syrian Protestant College from 1887 to 1890, professor of Old Testament literature and exegesis at Knox College (Toronto) from 1896 to 1898 and at McCormick Theological Seminary from 1898 until 1915, and then professor of biblical literature and English Bible until his retirement in 1939. He explored the Sinai Peninsula and Kadesh-Barnea and discovered the "High Place" at Petra in 1900, was director of the American Schools of Oriental Research (ASOR)* in Jerusalem in 1913–1914, returned to Petra in 1928, and wrote The Sarcophagus of an Ancient Civilization (New York, 1930). He also wrote Autobiography of George L. Robinson: A Short Story of a Long Life (Grand Rapids, Mich., 1957). Died December 17, 1958, in Chicago. References: From the Pyramids to Paul; Studies in Theology, Archaeology and Related Subjects, Prepared in Honor of the Seventieth Birthday of George Livingstone Robinson, ed. Lewis G. Leary (New York, 1935); NCAB 43:552; NYT, December 18, 1958; and WWWA.

ROBINSON, PASCHAL (1870–1948). Archbishop and diplomat, born April 26, 1870, in Dublin, Ireland, and brought to the United States as an infant. Robinson studied law, became a journalist, and was associate editor of the North American Review. He then studied at St. Bonaventure College, joined the Franciscan Order in 1896, and was ordained in 1901. He taught at Catholic University from 1901 to 1919, and in 1919 he assisted the U.S. Educational and Economic Commission at the Versailles Peace Conference. From 1920 to 1921 he was apostolic visitor to the Custody of the Holy Land and, from 1925 to 1928, to the Latin Patriarchate in Jerusalem and the Uniate Churches in Palestine, Transjordan, and Cyprus. In 1927 he was appointed titular bishop of Tyana. Robinson became the first papal nuncio to Ireland in 1929 and remained there until his death. Died August 27, 1948, in Dublin. References: DACB; NYT, August 28, 1948.

ROCKHILL, WILLIAM WOODVILLE (1854–1914). Diplomat, born April 1854, in Philadelphia. Rockhill graduated from St. Cyr Military School in France in 1873 and served in the French Army in Algiers. He entered the foreign service, serving in Peking and Seoul from 1884 to 1888. From 1888 to 1893 he traveled in Mongolia and Tibet for the Smithsonian Institution. He was chief clerk in the State Department in 1893–1894; third assistant secretary of state in 1894–1895; assistant secretary of state in 1896–1897; minister to Greece, Rumania, and Serbia from 1897 to 1899; director of the Bureau of the American Republics from 1899 to 1905; minister to China from 1905 to 1909; and minister to Russia from 1909 to 1911. He was minister to Turkey from 1911 until his retirement in 1913, and became involved in the negotiations for the Chester Project.* Died December 8, 1914, in Honolulu en route to China. *References*: Papers, Houghton Library, Harvard University; *DAB*; *DADH*; *NYT*, December 9, 1914; *NCAB* 8:129; Paul A. Varg, *Open Door Diplomat: The Life of W. W. Rockhill* (Champaign, Ill., 1952); and *WWWA*.

RODGERS, JOHN (1773–1838). Naval officer, born near Lower Susquehanna Ferry (now Havre de Grace), Maryland. Rodgers served in the merchant marine until 1798 when he was appointed second lieutenant in the navy, served in the Mediterranean from 1802 to 1808, and participated in the war with Tripoli. He traveled to the Middle East in the *North Carolina* in 1825 in order to obtain information on commercial activities. Died August 1, 1838, in Philadelphia. *References*: Papers, Rodgers Family Papers, Naval Historical Foundation, Library of Congress; New York Historical Society, Historical Society of Pennsylvania; K. Jack Bauer, "John Rodgers: The Stalwart Conservative," in *Command Under Sail: Makers of the American Naval Tradition 1775–1850*, James C. Bradford (Annapolis, Md., 1985), pp. 220–247; *DAB*; *DAMIB*; *WAMB*; and *WWWA*.

ROEDING, GEORGE CHRISTIAN (1868–1928). Nurseryman and horticulturist, born February 4, 1868, in San Francisco. In 1885 Roeding began working in a nursery in Fresno, and later established nurseries and operated orchards. He introduced the fig wasp to California in 1899, visited Smyrna in 1901 to study the fig industry, and wrote *The Smyrna Fig at Home and Abroad* (Fresno, Calif., 1903) which includes an account of his trip. Died July 23, 1928, in Livermore, California. *References*: *DAB*; *NCAB* 40:498.

ROGERS PLAN. A plan proposed in December 1969 by Secretary of State William Rogers to settle the Arab-Israeli conflict. It called for Israel to withdraw from the Arab territories occupied in the June 1967 war in exchange for a formal peace settlement between the Arab states and Israel. The plan was rejected by Israel and the Arab states. *References*; *DADH*; Ishaq I. Ghanayem and Aden H. Voth, *The Kissinger Legacy: American-Middle East Policy* (New York, 1984), ch. 4; and Steven L. Spiegel, *The Other Arab-Israeli Conflict: Making America's Middle East Policy from Truman to Reagan* (Chicago, 1985), 181–209.

ROLSHOVEN, JULIUS (1858–1930). Painter, born October 28, 1858, in Detroit. Rolshoven studied at the Cooper Union Art School in New York City, and in Dusseldorf, Munich, Venice, and Paris. He lived in London in 1896 and moved to Florence, Italy, in 1897. In 1910 he made a trip to North Africa and gathered material for a large series of Tunisian paintings which were exhibited in 1912 in Detroit. He returned to the United States in 1914, and established a studio in Taos, New Mexico. Returning to Florence in 1919, he resided there until the year of his death. Died December 7, 1930, in New York City. *References*: Van Deren Coke, "Julius Rolshoven," *University of New Mexico Art Museum Bulletin*, no. 1 (Winter 1965–1966): 4–15; *DAB*; *NCAB* 26:292; *NYT*, December 8, 1930; and *WWWA*.

ROOSEVELT, ARCHIBALD BULLOCH ("ARCHIE"), Jr. (1918–   ). Diplomat, born February 18, 1918, in Boston. Roosevelt graduated from Harvard University. He was a reporter from 1939 to 1942 and served in the army in World War II. He was assistant military attaché in Teheran in 1946–1947 and was one of four Americans to visit the Kurdish Republic of Mahabad during its brief existence. He wrote of his experiences in the July 1947 issue of the *Middle East Journal*. He entered the foreign service in 1947 and served in Beirut, Istanbul, Madrid, and London. In 1975 he became vice president and director of international relations for Chase Manhattan Bank. *Reference*: *WWA*.

ROOSEVELT, KERMIT (1889–1943). Explorer, army officer, and shipping executive, son of President Theodore Roosevelt, born October 10, 1889, in Oyster Bay, New York. Roosevelt graduated from Harvard University and accompanied his father on a hunting trip in Africa in 1909–1910 as well as an exploring expedition to the "River of Doubt" in Brazil in 1914. He was engaged in engineering and banking in South America from 1911 to 1916, and was president of Roosevelt Steamship Company and vice president of U.S. Lines Company. In 1917 he served in the British Army with Motor Machine Guns in Mesopotamia, which he later described in *War in the Garden of Eden* (New York, 1919). He then transferred to the U.S. Army and served in France. With his brother Theodore he led exploring expeditions in Eastern Turkestan in 1925 and in western China in 1928–1929. He served with the British Army from 1939 to 1941 and in the U.S. Army after 1942. Died on active service on June 4, 1943, in Alaska. *References*: Papers, Manuscript Division, Library of Congress; *DAB S3*; *NCAB* 33:10; and *WWWA*.

ROOSEVELT, KERMIT (1916–   ). Intelligence officer, son of Kermit Roosevelt (1889–1943) and grandson of President Theodore Roosevelt, born February 16, 1916, in Buenos Aires, Argentina. Roosevelt graduated from Harvard University. He served in the Office of Strategic Services during World War II, joined the Central Intelligence Agency, and became an expert in Middle Eastern affairs. He played a role in the 1953 coup that overthrew Iranian premier

Mohammed Mussadeqh and restored the Shah, and was involved in the Suez crisis of 1956. He was later government relations director for Gulf Oil Corporation and became its vice president in 1960. In 1964 he formed Roosevelt and Associates. He wrote *Arabs, Oil, and History: The Story of the Middle East* (New York, 1949) and *Countercoup: The Struggle for the Control of Iran* (New York, 1979). *References*: Nancy E. Gallagher and Dunning S. Wilson, "The CIA and a Variant Edition," *AB Bookman's Weekly* 67 (1981): 1171–1174; *PolProf: Eisenhower*; and Thomas Powell, "A Book Held Hostage," *Nation* 230 (1980): 437–440.

ROPES, JOSEPH (1770–1850). Merchant, born December 15, 1770, in Salem, Massachusetts. Ropes commanded the ship *Recovery** in 1794 and the ship *John* in 1797, and made voyages to China, the East Indies, and Arabia. He commanded in the ship *America* in 1809 and made a voyage to the Mediterranean. He was the first American merchant to visit Constantinople and to be received by the Sultan. Ropes was a privateer in the War of 1812, served as selectman of Salem and member of the Massachusetts legislature, and was a founder of the East India Marine Society. Died September 29, 1850, in Salem, Massachusetts. *References*: *DAB*; *WWWA*.

ROSENAU, M(ILTON) J(OSEPH) (1869–1946). Epidemiologist, born January 1, 1869, in Philadelphia. Rosenau graduated from the University of Pennsylvania and studied at the universities of Berlin, Paris, and Vienna. He was a surgeon at the U.S. Public Health and Marine Hospital Service from 1890 to 1909, director of its hygienic laboratory from 1899 to 1909, professor of preventive medicine and hygiene at Harvard Medical School from 1909 to 1935, and professor of epidemiology at Harvard School of Public Health from 1922 to 1935. In 1927 he was a member of the Palestine Survey Commission and prepared a sanitary survey of Palestine. His report is part of the *Reports of the Experts Submitted to the Joint Palestine Survey Commission* (Boston, 1928). After 1936 he was dean of the School of Public Health at the University of North Carolina. Died April 9, 1946, in Chapel Hill, North Carolina. *References*: *DAB S4*; *NCAB* 42: 690; and *WWWA*.

ROSENBERG, ADAM (fl. 1886–1895). Zionist. Rosenberg came to the United States in about 1886. He was sent to Palestine in 1891–1892 by a New York Zionist society to purchase land to found a settlement for American immigrants. He purchased land on the Golan Heights. He returned to Palestine in 1895, building a house near Sahem el-Gaulan and planting vines and raspberry bushes, but he was expelled by the Turkish governor. *References*: Israel Klausner, "Adam Rosenberg: One of the Earliest American Zionists," *Herzl Year Book* 1 (1958): 232–287.

ROSENBLATT, BERNARD ABRAHAM (1886–1969). Zionist leader, born June 15, 1886, in Poland, and brought to the United States in 1891. Rosenblatt graduated from Columbia University and Columbia University Law School, practiced law, and was a justice in the New York City Magistrates Court in 1921. In 1915 he organized the American Zionist Commonwealth, a land development and settlement firm that established several communities in Palestine, and was its first president. He was vice president and a member of the executive committee of the Zionist Organization of America from 1920 to 1946, and from 1921 to 1923, he was the first American representative to the World Zionist Executive in Jerusalem. He floated the first Palestinian Jewish bonds and was active in developing business enterprises in Palestine in the 1920s and 1930s. He was president of the Jewish National Fund and Keren Hayesod of America. He wrote an autobiography, *Two Generations of Zionism: Historical Recollections of an American Zionist* (New York, 1967). Died October 14, 1969, in New York City. *References*: *CA*; *EJ*; and *NYT*, October 15, 1967.

ROSS, FRANK ALEXANDER (1888–1968). Sociologist and educator, born January 23, 1888, in New York City. Ross graduated from Yale and Columbia universities. He was an instructor and assistant professor at Columbia University from 1914 to 1916 and from 1919 to 1926. He served in the army in World War I and was professor of sociology at Syracuse University from 1926 to 1941. In 1926 he was director of an economic and social survey of several countries in the Middle East for the Near East Relief* and other philanthropies and was co-author of *The Near East and American Philanthropy* (New York, 1929). He served in various positions in the U.S. government, including the Federal Emergency Administration in 1934–1935. Died June 30, 1968, in Thetford, Vermont. *References*: *NCAB* 55:415; *NYT*, August 13, 1966; and *WWWA*.

ROSSOW, ROBERT JR. (1918–   ). Diplomat, born September 19, 1918, in Bloomington, Indiana. Rossow graduated from Georgetown University and the University of Michigan Law School, entered the foreign service in 1940, and served in Vancouver, Panama, and Colon. He was vice consul in Teheran in 1945 and in Tabriz in 1945–1946. He wrote of his experiences in Tabriz in the Winter 1956 issue of *Middle East Journal*. He later served in Sofia, Madras, Constantinople, New Delhi, and Katmandu. He was consul in Calcutta in 1952–1953 and counselor for political affairs in Kabul from 1958 to 1960. He was deputy director of the Office of International Economic and Social Affairs from 1962 to 1964, and counselor for the Food and Agriculture Organization in the embassy in Rome from 1964 until his retirement in 1969. *References*: "Diary" in private hands; Peter Lisager and Marguerite Higgins, *Overtime in Heaven: Adventures in the Foreign Service* (Garden City, N.Y., 1964), ch. 7.

ROSTOVTZEV, MIKHAIL IVANOVITCH (1870–1952). Historian and archaeologist, born November 10, 1870, in Zhitomir, Ukraine. Rostovtzev graduated from the universities of Kiev and St. Petersburg and studied abroad. He taught at St. Petersburg University from 1903 to 1918 and later at Oxford University; was professor of ancient history at the University of Wisconsin from 1920 to 1925; professor of ancient history and archaeology at Yale University from 1925 to 1939; and director of archaeological research there until 1944. He was organizer and supervisor of the Yale expedition at Dura-Europos on the Euphrates from 1928 to 1938, and edited its reports. He wrote *Caravan Cities* (Oxford, 1932), his impressions of a journey in Syria, Arabia, and Palestine. Died October 20, 1952, in New Haven, Connecticut. *References*: *AJA* 58 (1954): 55; *DAB S5*; *NCAB* 39:558; *NYT*, October 21, 1952; and *WWWA*.

ROUNTREE, WILLIAM MANNING (1917–   ). Diplomat, born March 28, 1917, in Swainsboro, Georgia. Rountree graduated from Columbia University, was an accountant-auditor in the Treasury Department from 1935 to 1941, budget officer in the Office of the Lend Lease Administration in 1941–1942, and assistant to the director of the American Economic Operations in the Middle East from 1942 to 1945. He entered the foreign service in 1946; was economic adviser in the Bureau of Near Eastern, South Asian, and African Affairs in 1946–1947; special assistant to the ambassador to Greece from 1947 to 1949; deputy director and director of the Office of Greek, Turkish, and Iranian Affairs from 1949 to 1952; counselor in Turkey in 1952–1953; and minister-counselor in Iran from 1953 to 1955. He was deputy assistant secretary of state for Near Eastern, South Asian, and African Affairs in 1955–1956 and assistant secretary from 1956 to 1959. In 1958 he conducted a fact-finding tour of the Middle East and was threatened by violent demonstrations in Baghdad. He was ambassador to Pakistan from 1959 to 1962, ambassador to the Sudan from 1962 to 1965, ambassador to South Africa from 1965 to 1970, and ambassador to Brazil from 1970 to 1973. He retired in 1974. *References*: *BRDS*; *CB* 1959; *Time*, December 29, 1958; and *WWAP*.

ROWE, L(OUIS) EARLE (1882–1937). Archaeologist, born June 19, 1882, in Providence, Rhode Island. Rowe graduated from Brown University and studied at the American School of Classical Studies in Athens. He was assistant in charge of the Egyptian Department at the Boston Museum of Fine Arts from 1909 to 1912 and assistant in history at the Massachusetts Institute of Technology from 1910 to 1912. He was a member of the Harvard University-Museum of Fine Arts Egyptian expedition of 1912. He was director of the Rhode Island School of Design from 1918 to 1928 and of its museum from 1928 until his death. Died February 17, 1937, in Providence, Rhode island. *References*: *NCAB* 28:308; *WWWA*.

ROWLAND, JOSEPH MEDLEY (1880–1938). Clergyman and editor, born January 9, 1880, in Rowland, North Carolina. Rowland graduated from Weaverville and Randolph-Macon colleges, and was ordained. He was a pastor in Richmond, Norfolk, and Lynchburg, Virginia, and became editor of the *Richmond Christian Advocate* in 1921. He managed Pilgrimage Tours of Nashville, Tennessee, conducted tours abroad, and wrote *A Pilgrimage to Palestine* (Richmond, 1915), and *Travels in the Old World* (Richmond, 1923). Died August 17, 1938, in Richmond, Virginia. *References*: *WWWA*.

RUBIN, GAIL (1938–1978). Photographer, born April 12, 1939, in New York City. Rubin studied at the University of Michigan and Finch College. She was editor for several publishers, went to Israel in 1969, and began professional photography in 1972. She served as a war photographer in the 1973 war and then specialized in nature photography. Killed by Palestinian terrorists March 11, 1978, in Maagan Michael, Israel. Her photographs were published in *Psalmist with a Camera: Photographs of a Biblical Safari* (New York, 1979). *Reference*: *NYT*, March 13, 1978.

RUBINOW, ISAAC MAX (1875–1936). Physician and social worker, born April 19, 1875, in Grodno, Russia, and came to the United States in 1893. Rubinow graduated from New York Medical College and practiced medicine in New York City, but abandoned it in favor of statistics and social work. He conducted research for several U.S. government agencies, specializing in social insurance. During 1919–1922 he served in Palestine as director of the American Zionist Medical Unit*, and helped develop modern medical services and hospital care in Palestine. After his return to the United States, he was active in Jewish social welfare and Zionist activities. Died April 19, 1936, in New York City. *References*: *DAB S2*; *DAMB*; *EJ*; *NYT*, September 3, 1936; and *WWWA*.

RUE, (LARS) LARRY (1893–1965). Reporter, born March 10, 1893, in Fosston, Minnesota. Rue graduated from the University of North Dakota. He became a reporter in 1913, working first on newspapers in Minnesota and, from 1919 to 1932, with the *Chicago Tribune*. He covered the Middle East during the 1920s and 1930s, interviewing most of its leaders. From 1932 to 1939 he was with the *New York Daily News*, and after 1939, again with the *Tribune*. He wrote *I Fly for News* (New York, 1932). Died July 13, 1965. *References*: *NYT*, July 13, 1965; *WWWA*.

RUSCHENBERGER, WILLIAM SAMUEL WAITMAN (1807–1895). Surgeon, born September 4, 1807 in Cumberland County, New Jersey. Ruschenberger attended the University of Pennsylvania medical department and was commissioned a surgeon in the navy in 1831. He was fleet surgeon in the East India Squadron from 1835 to 1837 and again from 1847 to 1850, was ship's doctor on the *Peacock** on Edmund Roberts'* second diplomatic trip to Muscat, and described the voyage in *A Voyage Around the World: Including an Embassy to Muscat and Siam, in 1835, 1836, and 1837* (Philadelphia, 1838). He was on shore duty from 1851 to 1857, was fleet surgeon in the Pacific fleet from 1854 to 1857 and in the Mediterranean fleet in 1860–1861, and chief surgeon of the Boston Navy Yard during the Civil War. He retired in 1869. Died in New York City. *References*: *ACAB*; *DAMB*; *NCAB* 13:369; and *WWWA*.

RUSSELL, CHARLES WELLS (1856–1927). Diplomat, born March 16, 1856, in Wheeling, West Virginia. Russell attended Georgetown Law School. He worked for the Justice Department and investigated the French spoliation claims from 1886 to 1893. He investigated conditions in Cuba in 1897 and was later involved with the U.S.-Spanish Claims Commission. In 1902 he investigated the French Panama Canal Company title. From 1905 to 1909 he was assistant attorney general. He was minister to Persia from 1909 to 1914 and was involved closely with the William Morgan Shuster* mission. Died April 5, 1927, in Washington, D.C. *References*: *DAB*; *DADH*; *NCAB* 15:358; and *WWWA*.

RYAN, ARTHUR CLAYTON (1879–1927). Missionary, born December 28, 1879, in Grandview, Louisa County, Iowa. Ryan attended Oberlin College. He graduated from Grinnel College and Oberlin Theological Seminary and was ordained in 1911. He became a missionary under the American Board of Commissioners for Foreign Missions (ABCFM)* in 1911, served in Talas, Turkey, but in 1912 traveled through central and southern Anatolia. He was assigned to relief work in Constantinople in 1912, served as agent of the British and American Red Cross* in 1913–1914, and was secretary of the Constantinople chapter of the American Red Cross until 1916. From 1916 to 1919 he was involved in raising funds in the United States for the Near East Relief,* returned to Turkey in 1919, and was secretary of the Levant Agency of the American Bible Society* from 1920 to 1924. He was general secretary of the American Bible Society in New York City from 1924 until his death. Died June 22, 1927 in Scarsdale, New York. *References*: *DAB*; *NYT*, June 24, 1927.

RYERSON, KNOWLES AUGUSTUS (1892–   ). Agriculturist, born October 17, 1892, in Seattle and grew up in California. Ryerson graduated from the College of Agriculture of the University of California in Berkeley and served in World War I. From 1919 to 1925 he served in the Agricultural Extension Service, becoming Los Angeles County farm adviser in 1924, and he was horticulturist in the Agricultural Experiment Station in Haiti from 1925 to 1927. He was a member of the Joint Survey Commission of Palestine and Transjordan in 1927 and contributed a report on horticultural possibilities in the *Reports of the Experts Submitted to the Joint Palestine Survey Commission* (Boston, 1928). He was in charge of the Division of Foreign Plant Introduction in the Department of Agriculture from 1928 to 1934, and chief of the Division of Plant Industry from 1934 to 1937. In 1930 he traveled to Algeria and Morocco and studied the apricot. He became professor of horticulture in the College of Agriculture of the University of California at Davis in 1937, and was dean of the College of Agriculture in Berkeley from 1952 until his retirement in 1960. He wrote a memoir, *The World Is My Campus* (Davis, Calif., 1977). *References*: *AMWS*; *Journal of Heredity* 59 (1968): 338; and *WWA*.

S

SACKS, MENDES (1907–   ). Citrus grower and company executive, born November 17, 1907, in Baltimore. Sacks graduated from the University of Maryland, Harvard University, and the University of California. He settled in Palestine in 1931, and became involved in citrus growing in Gan Chaim. He became manager of Pardess Syndicate, a cooperative of private citrus growers, in 1945, general manager of Mehadrin in 1951, and general manager of Israel's Citrus Marketing Board in 1963. *Reference*: Yaakov Morris, *On the Soil of Israel: Americans and Canadians in Agriculture* (Tel Aviv, 1965), ch. 3.

ST. AUBIN, WILFRID DE (1902–1980). Executive of the American Red Cross,* born November 24, 1902, in Chicago. St. Aubin graduated from Notre Dame University and Chicago-Kent College of Law. He worked for relief organizations in India and Washington, D.C., became a representative of the American Red Cross in 1943, and served in Europe until 1948. The League of Red Cross Societys appointed him as their delegate to the Middle East in 1948. He surveyed and advised national Red Cross and Red Crescent societies in the Middle East and helped reestablish these societies, was director of the U.N. emergency relief program in Palestine, and conducted a survey of the humanitarian problems resulting from the 1948 war. He was later supervisor for international agency relations of the American National Red Cross, and executive director of the Washtenaw County chapter of the American Red Cross from 1955 until his retirement in 1969. Died November 2, 1980. *Reference*: Papers, Michigan Historical Collection, Bentley Historical Library, Ann Arbor.

ST. PAUL'S INSTITUTE Founded in 1889 in Tarsus, Turkey. The institute came under the care of the American Board of Commissioners for Foreign Missions (ABCFM) and served as the preparatory school for Central Turkey College. Under the name Tarsus American School, it continues to offer a college preparatory curriculum. *References*: *Schools*; *Stone*, ch. 10.

SALLER, SYLVESTER JOHN (1895–1976). Archaeologist, born September 25, 1895, in Petoskey, Michigan. Saller graduated from St. Joseph College (Teutopolis, Mich.) and studied in several Franciscan monasteries, in St. Anthony's College, Rome, and in the Franciscan Biblical Institute in Jerusalem, and was ordained in 1922. He was professor of classical languages at St. Joseph's College from 1922 to 1927, became professor of archaeology at the Franciscan Biblical Institute in Jerusalem in 1932, was its president from 1945 to 1950, and the president of the Franciscan Monastery of Transfiguration on Mount Tabor in 1943–1944. He directed the excavations at Mount Nebo, Jordan, in 1933, the excavations within the Church Dominus Flevit on the Mount of Olives, the excavations in St. John's Ein Kerem Franciscan Monastery from 1941 to 1944, and in Bethany from 1949 to 1953. He wrote *The Memorial of Moses on Mount Nebo* (Jerusalem, 1950) and *Discoveries at St. John's Ein Karim, 1941–44* (Jerusalem, 1946); was co-author of *The Town of Nebo: Khirbet el-Mekhayyat* (Jerusalem, 1949); wrote *Excavations at Bethany (1949–53)* (Jerusalem, 1957) and *The Archaeological Setting of the Shrine of Beth Phage* (Jerusalem, 1961); and prepared *A Catalogue of the Ancient Synagogues of the Holy Land* (Jerusalem, 1962; 2nd rev. ed. Jerusalem, 1972). Died in Jerusalem. *References*: *ACWW*; *WWA*.

SAMPTER, JESSIE (ETHEL) (1883–1938). Author, born March 22, 1883, in New York City. Sampter was one of the early leaders of Hadassah,* moved to Palestine in 1919, and lived in Jerusalem and Rehovot until 1933 when she joined kibbutz Givat Brenner, where she built a rest home. She published her first book in 1908 and continued to publish in Palestine in both Hebrew and English, including *The Emek* (New York, 1927). She also edited *Modern Palestine* (New York, 1933). Died November 11, 1938, in Givat Brenner, Palestine. *References*: Papers, Central Zionist Archives, Jerusalem; *EJ*; *NAW*; and *NYT*, November 26, 1938.

SANBORN, (CYRUS) ASHTON (ROLLINGS) (1882–1970). Archaeologist, born March 13, 1882, in Rochester, New Hampshire. Sanborn graduated from Harvard University and studied at the American School of Classical Studies in Athens and the University of Munich. He studied and excavated in Greece from 1909 to 1911. From 1915 to 1920 he was assistant curator of the Egyptian section of the Boston Museum of Fine Arts. He did archaeological work in Egypt at Gizeh, Memphis, and Denderah as a member of the Egyptian expedition of the University Museum. He was executive secretary of the American Red Cross Commission in Palestine in 1918–1919, and assisted George A. Reisner in explorations and excavations in Egypt and the Sudan in 1920–1921. He was librarian of the Boston Museum of Fine Arts from 1922 to 1952, secretary of the museum from 1925 to 1952, and supervisor of the museum's educational work from 1934 to 1942. He retired in 1952 and was actively associated with the establishment of the American Research Center in Egypt. Died June 21,

1970, in Boston. *References*: *BMFA* 68 (1970): 215–217; *The Boston Globe*, June 22, 1970; and *NCAB* A:404.

SANGER, RICHARD HARLANKENDEN (1905–1979). Diplomat, born July 22, 1905, in Sangerfield, New York. Sanger graduated from Harvard University and Harvard Business School. He visited the Arabian Peninsula in 1928 and made several other trips to the Middle East between World War I and World War II. He served in the Department of Commerce in 1931–1932, was a reporter from 1932 to 1936, and served on the staff of the Republican National Committee from 1936 to 1940. He was an economic analyst for the Board of Economic Welfare in 1941–1942, member of the Economic Mission to Algiers in 1943, member of the first diplomatic mission to Yemen in 1946, and deputy chief of mission and counselor in Jordan from 1955 to 1958. He wrote *The Arabian Peninsula* (Ithaca, N.Y., 1954) and *Where the Jordan Flows* (Washington, D.C., 1963). Died March 20, 1979, in Washington, D.C. *References*: Papers, American Heritage Center, University of Wyoming Archives; *CA*; and *WWWA*.

SARGENT, JOHN SINGER (1856–1925). Painter, born January 12, 1856, in Florence, Italy, to American parents. Sargent studied art in Rome, Florence, and Paris. He established a studio in Paris in 1875, but moved to London in 1885 and became famous as a portrait painter. He visited Egypt and Palestine in 1891–1892 and returned to Palestine in 1905–1906 to collect material for the wall paintings in the Boston Public Library on which he worked for the next twenty-five years. Died April 15, 1925, in London. *References*: *DAB*; Patricia Hills et al., *John Singer Sargent* (New York, 1986); Donelson F. Hoopes, *Sargent Watercolors* (New York, 1970); Charles M. Mount, *John Singer Sargent, A Biography* (New York, 1955); *NCAB* 11:291; Stanley Olson, *John Singer Sargent: His Portrait* (New York, 1986); Carter Ratcliff, *John Singer Sargent* (New York, 1982); Joy Wilson, "The Unknown Sargents," *AWM* 29 (July-August 1978): 7–13; and *WWWA*.

SARTAIN, WILLIAM (1843–1924). Painter, born November 21, 1843, in Philadelphia. Sartain studied at the Pennsylvania Academy of Fine Arts in Philadelphia, went abroad in 1868, and studied in Paris. He sketched in several European countries and spent the year 1874 in Algiers. The French government bought his painting "Nubian Sheikh" (1879–1880) for the Luxembourg Gallery. He returned to the United States in 1877 and settled in New York City. Died October 25, 1924, in New York City. *References*: *ACAB*; *DAB*; *NCAB* 13:326; *NYT*, October 24, 1924; and *WWWA*.

SAUNDERS, CHARLES (1812–1876) and **MARTHA CHASE (BURDICK)** (1813–1883). Missionaries, Charles born May 27, 1812, and Martha June 14, 1813, in Westerly, Rhode Island. Martha acquired a knowledge of medicine. They served as agricultural missionaries to Palestine under the auspices of the

Seventh Day Baptist Church from 1854 to 1860. They settled near Jaffa and tried to introduce modern agricultural practices among the Arabs and the Jews. He was also vice consul in Jaffa. They were recalled in 1860, and the mission was discontinued. He later worked in a machine shop. Charles died April 8, 1876, and Martha May 30, 1883, in Westerly, Rhode Island. *References*: *The Narragansett Weekly* [Westerly, R.I.], April 13, 1876; *Seventh Day Baptists in Europe and America* (Plainfield, N.J., 1910).

SAUNDERS, DANIEL, JR. (1772– ?). Sailor, born March 4, 1772, in Salem, Massachusetts. Saunders shipped on vessels bound for India and was shipwrecked near Cape Murabat in the Arabian Peninsula in 1792. He wrote *A Journal of the Travels and Sufferings of D. Saunders, Jun. a Mariner on Board the Ship Commerce, of Boston, Samuel Johnson, Commander, which was Cast Away Near Cape Morebet on the Coast of Arabia, July 10, 1792* (Salem, 1794), which included information on the manners and customs of the Bedouins. It was reprinted several times and is the earliest American account of first-hand experience in Arabia. He returned to the United States in 1793 and continued in the profession of mariner. *Reference*: Sara S. Smith, *The Founders of Massachusetts Bay Colony* (Pittsfield, Mass., 1897).

SAVAGE, RICHARD HENRY (1846–1903). Author, born June 12, 1846, in Utica, New York. Savage graduated from the U.S. Military Academy in 1868 and served as second lieutenant in the Corps of Engineers from 1868 to 1871. From 1871 to 1872 he served in the Egyptian Army. He was later vice consul in Marseille and Rome. He was a joint commissioner of the Texan-Mexican Frontier Commission in 1873–1874 and an engineer on a railway in the South from 1874 to 1884. He traveled in Turkey, Russia, Siberia, and the Far East from 1884 to 1891. After 1891 he practiced law in New York City and served in the Spanish-American War. He wrote *In the Shadow of the Pyramids: The Last Days of Ismail Khedive, 1879, a Novel* (Chicago, 1898) and *In the Esbekieyeh Gardens: and Other Stories* (New York, 1900). Died October 11, 1903, in New York City. *Reference*: *ACAB; and WWWA*.

SAYRE, JOEL (GROVER) (1901–1979). Reporter and war correspondent, born December 13, 1900, in Marion, Indiana, and grew up in Columbus, Ohio. Sayre served with Canadian Expeditionary Forces in Siberia in 1917, was crime reporter for the *New York Herald*, and a screenwriter. He was correspondent for the *New Yorker* in the Persian Gulf Command during World War II, and his reports were published as *Persian Gulf Command: Some Marvels on the Road to Kazvin* (New York, 1945). He was later a staff writer and correspondent for the *New Yorker*. Died September 9, 1979, in Taftsville, Indiana. *References*: *CA; EAJ*; and *NYT*, September 14, 1979.

SCHAFF, PHILIP (1819–1893). Church historian, born January 1, 1819, in Chur, Grisons, Switzerland. Schaff studied at the universities of Tubingen, Halle, and Berlin, and was ordained in 1844. He came to the United States in 1843 and served on the theological faculty of Mercersburg (Pa.) Seminary until 1864. From 1864 to 1869 he was secretary of the Sabbath Committee in New York City, became a member of the faculty of Union Theological Seminary in 1870, and was professor of church history from 1887 until his death. He visited the Middle East in 1877 and wrote *Through Bible Lands: Notes of Travels in Egypt, the Desert, and Palestine* (New York, 1878). Died October 20, 1893, in New York City. *References*: *ACAB*; *DAB*; Robert T. Handy, "Holy Land Experiences of Two Pioneers of Christian Ecumenism: Schaff and Mott," in *Contemporary Jewry: Studies in Honor of Moshe Davis*, ed. Geoffrey Wigodor (Jerusalem, 1984), pp. 65–78; *NCAB* 3:76; and *WWWA*.

SCHAUFFLER, WILLIAM GOTTLIEB (1798–1883). Missionary, born August 22, 1798, in Stuttgart, Germany, grew up in Odessa, Russia, and came to the United States in 1826. Schauffler graduated from Andover Theological Seminary, studied in Paris, and was ordained in 1831. He served as a missionary to the Jews under the American Board of Commissions for Foreign Missions (ABCFM)* in Constantinople from 1832 until 1855 and as a missionary among the Armenians and the Turks from 1855 to 1861. He translated the Bible into Hebrew-Spanish and Osmanli-Turkish, and prepared a grammar and lexicon of Hebrew-Spanish. He resided in Austria from 1874 until his retirement in 1877, when he returned to the United States. He wrote *Autobiography of William G. Schauffler, for Forty-Nine Years a Missionary in the Orient*, ed. by his Sons (New York, 1877). Died January 27, 1883, in New York City. His son, **ADOLPH FREDERICK SCHAUFFLER (1845–1919)**, was born in Constantinople and grew up there, and later wrote *Memoirs of a Happy Boyhood* (New York, 1919). *References*: *ACAB*; *DAB*; *EM*; *NCAB* 18:280; and *WWWA*.

SCHMIDT, DANA ADAMS (1915–   ). Foreign correspondent, born September 15, 1915, in Bay Village, Ohio. Schmidt graduated from Pomona College and Columbia University. He was a foreign correspondent for the United Press from 1938 to 1944, and for the *New York Times* after 1944. He was based in Lebanon from 1961 to 1966, and again from 1968 to 1970. He wrote *Journey Among Brave Men* (Boston, 1964), *Yemen, the Unknown War* (New York, 1968), and *Armageddon in the Middle East* (New York, 1974). *Reference*: *CA*.

SCHMIDT, ERICH FRIEDRICH (1897–1964). Archaeologist, born September 13, 1897, in Baden Baden, Germany. Schmidt graduated from Friedrich Wilhelm University (Berlin) and Columbia University, served in the German Army during World War I, and came to the United States in 1923. He was assistant in archaeology at the American Museum of Natural History from 1924 to 1927 and became assistant in archaeology at the Oriental Institute in 1927.

He was co-director of the Anatolian expedition, was in charge of the Hittite expedition at Alishar, Central Turkey, from 1927 to 1929, and wrote *Anatolia Through the Ages: Discoveries at the Alishar Mound 1927–29* (Chicago, 1931). He conducted excavations at Fara, Iraq, and at Tepe Issar, Persia, from 1930 to 1933, and directed the archaeological expedition to Persepolis from 1935 until 1939. He was also field director of the University Museum and the Boston Museum of Fine Arts expedition to Ray, Iran, from 1934 to 1936, and wrote *Excavations at Tepe Hissar Damghan* (Philadelphia, 1937), and *Persepolis* (Chicago, 1953–1970). He used aircraft extensively in his work and described it in *Flights Over Ancient Cities of Iran* (Chicago, 1940). He was associate professor in the Oriental Institute from 1954 to 1962 and professor from 1962 until his death. Died October 4, 1964, in Santa Barbara, California. *References*: *Journal of Near East Studies* 24 (1965): 145–148; *NCAB* 51:671; *NYT*, October 5, 1964; and *WWWA*.

SCHMIDT, NATHANIEL (1862–1939). Orientalist, born May 22, 1862, in Hudiksvall, Sweden. Schmidt graduated from Stockholm University, Madison (now Colgate) University, and the University of Berlin. He was professor of Semitic languages and literature at Colgate University from 1888 to 1896, and professor of Semitic languages and Oriental history at Cornell University from 1896 to 1932. He was director of the American Schools of Oriental Research (ASOR)* in Jerusalem in 1904–1905, traveled in the Middle East, and excavated in Palestine. Died June 29, 1939, in Ithaca, New York. *References*: *BASOR* 75 (1929): 7–8; *DAB S2*; and *WWWA*.

SCHNEIDER, BENJAMIN (1807–1877). Missionary, born January 18, 1807, in Hanover, Pennsylvania. Schneider graduated from Amherst College and Andover Theological Seminary, and was ordained in 1833. He served as a missionary under the American Board of Commissioners for Foreign Missions (ABCFM)* in Bursa, Turkey, from 1833 to 1849 and again from 1868 to 1872. He served in Constantinople from 1834 until 1849 and in Aintab from 1849 until 1868, and taught at the Marsovan Theological Seminary in 1874–1875. He returned to the United States in 1875 because of illness. Died September 14, 1877, in Boston. His wife, **ELIZA CHENEY (ABBOTT) SCHNEIDER (1809–1856)**, published *Letters from Broosa, Asia Minor* (Chamberburg, Pa., 1846). *References: DAB*; *EM*; and *WWWA*.

SCHOEDSACK, ERNEST BEAUMONT ("SHORTY") (1893–). Photographer and motion picture director, born June 8, 1893, in Council Bluffs, Iowa. At twelve Schoedsack ran away to California, became cameraman for Keystone Studios in 1914, served in the photographic section of the Signal Corps during World War I, and remained as a freelance photographer in Europe. With Merian C. Cooper* and Marguerite Elton Baker Harrison* he went to Persia in 1925 to photograph the annual migration of the Bekhtiari tribe and produced the first full-length documentary film, *Grass*. In 1927 he went to Siam with Cooper, and they directed *Chang* (1927) and *King Kong* (1933). He later directed other movies. *References*: Richard Koszarski, *Hollywood Directors, 1914–1940* (New York, 1976), pp. 260–269; *Cinema, a Critical Dictionary*, ed. Rochard Roud (New York, 1980), 2: 910–917.

SCHUMACHER, GOTTLIEB S. (1857–1824). Architect, cartographer, and archaeologist, born November 21, 1857, in Zanesville, Ohio. Schumacher came to Palestine with his parents in 1869 to join the German Templar colony and settled in Haifa. He studied in the technical college in Stuttgart. He was involved in construction and planning for a railroad from Haifa to Damascus, traveled in the Golan in 1885, in western Hauran and north Adjlun in 1886, and in East Jordan in 1891 and in 1894 to 1902. He wrote *Abila of the Decapolis* (London, 1889), *Across the Jordan: Being an Exploration and Survey of Part of Hauran and Jaulan* (New York, 1886), *The Jaulan* (London, 1888), *Northern 'Ajlun, "Within the Decapolis"* (London, 1890), and *Pella* (London, 1888). He also prepared maps. He served as vice consul until 1905. He excavated in Tell Taanach in 1902–1903, and was involved in the excavations of Tell el-Mutesellim from 1903 to 1905 and in Baalbeck in 1903–1904. He participated in the excavations of Harvard University in Samaria in 1908. In World War I he was chief engineer for the fourth Ottoman Army, and after the war he continued preparing the map of East Jordan which was completed in 1924. Died November 26, 1924, in Haifa, Palestine. *Reference*: *EJ*.

SCHUYLER, EUGENE (1840–1890). Author and diplomat, born February 26, 1840, in Ithaca, New York. Schuyler graduated from Yale University and Columbia University Law School, and was admitted to the bar. He practiced law in New York City until 1867, was consul general in Moscow from 1867 to 1869, in Revel (now Tallinn), Estonia, and secretary of legation in St. Petersburg. He was secretary of legation and consul general in Constantinople from 1876 to 1878, and in 1876 he published a report on Turkish atrocities in Bulgaria. He was minister to Greece, Rumania, and Serbia from 1882 to 1884, lived in Italy from 1886 to 1889, and was diplomatic agent and consul general in Egypt from 1889 to 1890. Died July 16, 1980, in Alassio, Italy. *References*: Papers, Manuscript Division, Library of Congress; *ACAB*; *DAB; DADH*; *NCAB* 8:339; *NYT*, July 19, 1910; and *WWWA*.

SCHWARZKOPF, H(ERBERT) NORMAN (1895–1958). Policeman, born August 28, 1895, in Newark, New Jersey. Schwarzkopf graduated from the U.S. Military Academy in 1917, was commissioned second lieutenant in the cavalry, and served in the army until 1920. He became the first superintendent of the New Jersey State Police in 1921, serving until 1936. He then managed a trucking system and was announcer on the radio show "Gangbusters." Recalled to active duty in 1940, he was sent to Iran in 1942 to advise the Gendarmerie, the national rural police force. He reorganized the police force, trained it, and was commander of the Imperial Iranian Gendarmerie from 1942 to 1948. He was later sent to occupied Germany and reorganized its criminal investigations division. From 1951 to 1953, he was administrative director of the New Jersey Department of Law and Public Safety. He retired in 1955. Died November 25, 1958, in West Orange, New Jersey. *References*: Leo J. Coakley, *Jersey Troopers: A Fifty Year History of the New Jersey State Police* (New Brunswick, N.J., 1971); *NYT*, November 27, 1958.

SCIPIO, LYNN ADOLPHUS (1876–1963). Mechanical engineer and educator, born October 20, 1876, in White County, Indiana. Scipio graduated from Tri-State College (Angola, Ind.), Armour Institute of Technology, and Purdue University. He was a teacher, principal, and superintendent of public schools in Indiana, and assistant professor of mechanical engineering at the University of Nebraska from 1908 to 1912. He founded the engineering school at Robert College* in 1912, serving as its dean until 1920 and again from 1921 until 1943. He was head engineer of the War Production Board in 1943–1944 and industrial rehabilitation specialist for United Nations Relief and Rehabilitation Administration from 1945 to 1947. He prepared an *English-Turkish Technical Dictionary* (Istanbul, 1939) and wrote his memoirs, *My Thirty Years in Turkey* (Rindge, N.Y., 1955). Died June 10, 1963, in Washington, Ohio. *References*: *Mechanical Engineering* 85 (November 1963): 113; *WWWA*.

SCORPION U.S.S. Converted steam yacht. The *Scorpion* served in the Spanish-American War in Cuban waters and was on various duties until 1908. It arrived in Constantinople in 1908 and took up duties as a station ship. The yacht later assumed the duties of the flagship of Admiral Mark Lambert Bristol.* It returned to the United States in 1927. *References*: *DANES*; William N. Still, Jr., *American Sea Power in the Old World: The United States Navy in European and Near Eastern Waters, 1865–1917* (Westport, Conn., 1980), ch. 10.

SEABROOK, WILLIAM BUEHLER (1886–1945). Author, born February 22, 1886, in Westminster, Maryland. Seabrook graduated from Roanoke (Salem, Va.) and Newberry (S.C.) colleges and the University of Geneva. He was a reporter and city editor for the *Augusta Chronicle* in 1906; tramped through Europe as a freelance writer in 1907–1908; was a reporter for the *Atlanta Journal* in 1909–1910; partner in an advertising agency in Atlanta from 1911 to 1915; served in the French Army in World War I; and was a feature writer for newspaper syndicates from 1917 to 1924. After 1924 he was involved in travel, exploration, and writing. He lived in the Middle East and wrote *Adventures in Arabia Among the Bedouins, Druses, Whirling Dervishes, & Yezidee Devil Worshippers* (New York, 1927). He later lived in Haiti and West Africa and crossed the Sahara by airplane. He wrote *No Hiding Place, an Autobiography* (New York, 1942). Died September 20, 1945, in New York City. *References*: *CB*, 1940; *WWWA*.

SEELE, KEITH C(EDRIC) (1898–1971). Egyptologist, born February 13, 1898, in Warsaw, Indiana. Seele graduated from the College of Wooster and McCormick Theological Seminary and studied at the universities of Berlin and Chicago. He was a teacher at Assiut College* in 1922–1923 and a member of the epigraphic survey expedition of the Oriental Institute at Luxor and Sakkara, Egypt, from 1929 to 1936. He was a member of the faculty of the University of Chicago from 1936 to 1964, and was professor of Egyptology after 1950. He was director of the Oriental Institute's Egyptian Assuan High Dam Program from 1960 to 1971, and excavated in the Babkalabsha area of Nubia in 1960–1961 and at Qustul, Ballana, and Arminna in Nubia from 1962 to 1964. Died July 23, 1971, in Chicago. *References*: *IAB*; *NYT*, July 27, 1971; and *WWWA*.

SEGER, JOE D(ICK) (1935–   ). Archaeologist, born October 15, 1935, in Eau Claire, Wisconsin. Seger graduated from Elmhurst College, Eden Theological Seminary, and Harvard University. He was assistant professor and associate professor of Old Testament and archaeology at the Hartford Seminary Foundation from 1964 to 1971, and curator of its museum from 1965 to 1970, archaeological director of the Nelson Glueck School of Biblical Archaeology in Jerusalem from 1971 to 1974, and professor of archaeology and religion at the University of Nebraska at Omaha. He was a member of the Hebrew Union College archaeological expedition at Gezer from 1966 to 1970, director of the excavations from 1971 to 1974, and field director of the Drew-McCormick excavations at Tell Balatah, Shechem, in 1969 and of the Lahav Research Project excavations at Tell Halif in 1973 and 1976–1977. He wrote *Handbook for Field Operations* (Jerusalem, 1971), and *Tomb Offerings from Gezer* (New York, 1972). *Reference*: *DAS*.

SELIGSBERG, ALICE LILLIE (1873–1940). Social worker and civic leader, born August 8, 1873, in New York City. Seligsberg graduated from Barnard College and Columbia University and studied at the University of Berlin. She founded the Fellowship House and served as its president from 1913 to 1918, was one of the founders of Hadassah* in 1912, and headed the American Zionist Medical Unit* in Palestine in 1918. She helped lay the foundations for Hadassah's medical program in Palestine and was executive director of the Palestine Orphan Committee of the Joint Distribution Committee in 1919. She returned to the United States in 1920, was president of Hadassah in 1920–1921, senior adviser to the Junior Hadassah from 1924 to 1940, and executive director of the Jewish Children's Clearing House Bureau in New York City from 1922 to 1936. Died August 27, 1940, in New York City. *References*: Papers, Zionist Archives and Library, New York City; *American Jewish Year Book* 43 (1941–1942): 431–436; and *EJ*.

SELLERS, OVID R(OGERS) (1884–1975). Archaeologist, born August 12, 1884, in Waco, Texas. Sellers graduated from the University of Chicago, McCormick Theological Seminary, and Johns Hopkins University, and was ordained in 1915. He was a chaplain in World War I, instructor and headmaster at the Wentworth Military Academy in Lexington, Missouri, and editor of the *Lexington Intelligencer* until 1921. He was professor of Old Testament at the McCormick Theological Seminary from 1922 to 1954 and dean from 1940 to 1954. He retired in 1957. He participated in the excavation at Tell Beit Mirsim in 1930, at Bethel in 1934, and at Shechem in 1957, 1960, 1962, 1964, and 1966; was director of the excavations at Beth-Zur in 1931 and 1957 and at Silet edh-Dhahr in 1949; and director of the American Schools of Oriental Research (ASOR)* in Jerusalem in 1948–1949. He suffered severe burns on a flight from Beirut to Jerusalem in September 1948 when his aircraft was shot down. He wrote *The Citadel of Beth-zur: A Preliminary Report of the First Excavation Conducted by the Presbyterian Theological Seminary, Chicago, and American School of Oriental Research, Jerusalem in 1931 at Khirbet-et Tubeiqa* (Philadelphia, 1933), and co-authored *A Roman-Byzantine Burial Cave in Northern Palestine* (New Haven, Conn., 1953) and *The 1957 Excavation at Beth-zur, Conducted by McCormick Theological Seminary and the American School of Oriental Research in Jerusalem* (Cambridge, Mass., 1968). Died July 6, 1975, in Lexington, Missouri. His wife, **KATHERINE W(ILSON) SELLERS (1892–1979)**, church worker, was born September 11, 1892, in Lexington, Missouri, and graduated from Vassar College. She visited Palestine several times after 1928 and was actively engaged in reviving local crafts. She was an instructor at the Beirut College for Women in 1948, director of the Midwest area of the American Friends of the Middle East from 1952 to 1954, and correspondent for *The Christian Century* from Jerusalem in 1957–1958. She was later vice president and secretary of the International Folk Art Foundation in Santa Fe, New Mexico. Died December 25, 1979, in Lexington, Missouri. *References*: *DAS*; *The New Mexican* [Santa Fe], January 1, 1980; *WWAW*; and *WWWA*.

SHALER, WILLIAM (1773–1833). Sea captain and consul, born in Bridgeport, Connecticut. From 1797 to 1815 Shaler was engaged in trade in South America and the Pacific, and lived in Mauritius for several months. He was consul in Havana in 1810, a representative in Louisiana to report on Mexican revolutionary activities in 1812, and an observer at the Ghent Peace Conference of 1814. In 1815 he was appointed commissioner to negotiate a settlement with Algiers. With Stephen Decatur* he negotiated the treaty of 1815, and he was consul general in Algiers from 1915 to 1928. Shaler wrote *Sketches of Algiers, Political, Historical and Civil* (Boston, 1826). He was again consul in Havana from 1830 to 1833. Died March 29, 1833, in Havana. *References*: Papers, Historical Society of Pennsylvania, Manuscript Division, Library of Congress, and New York Historical Society; *ACAB*; *DAB*; Aurie H. Miller, "One Man's View: William Shaler and Algiers," in *Through Foreign Eyes: Western Attitudes Toward North*

Africa, ed. Alf Andrew Heggoy (Lanham, Md., 1982), pp. 7–55; *NCAB* 4:532; Roy F. Nichols, *Advance Agents of American Destiny* (Philadelphia, 1956); and *WWWA*.

SHATTUCK, CORINNA (1848–1910). Missionary educator, born April 21, 1848, in Louisville, Kentucky. Shattuck graduated from State Normal School (Framingham, Mass.). In 1873 she joined Myra Allen Proctor* as assistant in the girls' boarding school in Aintab and was placed in charge in 1874. In 1876–1877 she opened a high school for girls in Urfa and helped the Armenians after the Urfa massacre. She returned to the United States in 1910. Died May 23, 1910, in Boston. *References*: *NYT*, May 24, 1910; Emily C. Peabody, *Corinna Shattuck, Missionary Heroine* (Chicago, 1913).

SHAW, GARDINER ROWLAND (1893–1965). Diplomat, born June 15, 1893, in Boston. Shaw graduated from Harvard University. He entered the foreign service in 1917, served with the High Commission to Turkey from 1921 to 1924, was first secretary in Turkey from 1924 to 1926, chief of the Division of Near Eastern Affairs from 1926 to 1929, counselor of the embassy in Turkey from 1930 to 1937, and member of the American-Turkish Claims Commission in 1933. He was chief of the Division of Foreign Service Personnel from 1937 to 1941 and assistant secretary of state from 1941 to 1944. He retired in 1945 and became a specialist in the field of criminal rehabilitation, juvenile delinquency, and youth problems. Died August 15, 1965, in Washington, D.C. *References*: *NCAB* G:423; *NYT*, August 17, 1965; and *WWWA*.

SHEDD, JOHN HASKELL (1833–1895). Missionary, born July 9, 1833, in Mount Gilead, Ohio. Shedd graduated from Ohio Western University, Marietta College, and Lane and Andover theological seminaries, and was ordained in 1859. He served as a missionary to the Nestorians under the American Board of Commissioners for Foreign Missions (ABCFM)* from 1859 to 1870, was professor at Biddle University (N.C.) from 1872 to 1878, when he returned to Persia, and was president of Urmia College and Theological Seminary from 1878 until 1895. He wrote *A Sketch of the Persia Mission* (New York, 1871). Died April 12, 1895, in Urmia, Persia. *References*: *AndoverTS*; *EM*.

SHEDD, WILLIAM AMBROSE (1865–1918). Missionary, son of John Haskell Shedd,* born January 24, 1865, in Mount Seir, Urmia, Persia. Shedd graduated from Marietta College and Princeton Theological Seminary, and was ordained in 1892. He became a missionary under the Presbyterian Church in the U.S.A. Board of Foreign Missions* in Urmia in 1892. He was treasurer of the mission, superintendent of schools, teacher of theology, and editor of a paper in Syriac. He was active in relief work during World War I, was chairman of the Urmia Relief Committee, and member of the food committee. He wrote *Islam and the Oriental Churches* (New York, 1908). Died August 7, 1918, in

Sain Kaleh, Persia. His wife, **MARY (EDNA) (LEWIS) SHEDD**, wrote *The Urumia Exodus; More Leaves from the War Journal of a Missionary in Persia* (New York, 1918?) and a biography of her husband, *The Measure of a Man: The Life of William Ambrose Shedd, Missionary to Persia* (New York, 1922). *References*: *DAB*; Paul Geren, *New Voices, Old Worlds* (New York, 1958), pp. 33–50.

SHEEAN, (JAMES) VINCENT (1899–1975). Foreign correspondent, born December 5, 1899, in Pana, Illinois. Sheean graduated from the University of Chicago. He began reporting for the *Chicago Daily News* and the *New York Daily News*, moved to Paris, and was foreign correspondent for the *Chicago Tribune* from 1922 to 1925. In 1925 he penetrated the French and Spanish lines in Morocco and interviewed Abd al-Krim. He became a freelance reporter and reported the 1929 riots in Jerusalem and the Spanish Civil War. He recorded his experiences in *An American Among the Riffi* (New York, 1925), *The New Persia* (New York, 1927), and in his autobiography, *Personal History* (New York, 1953). During World War II he served in the Army Air Corps intelligence in North Africa and Italy. He later lived near Lago Maggiore in northern Italy. Died March 15, 1975, in Arolo, Italy. *References*: *CA*; *EAJ*; *NYT*, March 17, 1975; and *WWWA*.

SHELTON, WILLIAM ARTHUR (1875–1959). Clergyman and educator, born September 6, 1875, in Azusa, California, and grew up in Texas and Oklahoma. Shelton graduated from Hargrove College (Ardmore, Okla.) and Yale University, studied at the University of Chicago, and was ordained in 1899. He was pastor in Oklahoma from 1899 to 1905 and from 1908 to 1911, president of Oklahoma Wesleyan College from 1911 to 1914, professor of Old Testament and Semitic languages at Emory University from 1914 to 1930, pastor in Washington, D.C., Atlanta, Birmingham, and Gadsden, (Ala.). He traveled in the Middle East in 1919–1920 as member of the American Scientific Mission, collecting material for the Emory University archaeological museum which he founded, and wrote of his experiences in *Dust and Ashes of Empires* (Nashville, Tenn., 1922). Died February 22, 1959, in Atlanta. *References*: Boone M. Bowen, *The Chandler School of Theology: Sixty Years of Service* (Atlanta, Ga., 1974), pp. 172–173; *WWWA*.

SHEPARD, FRED(ERICK) D(OUGLAS) (1855–1915). Medical missionary, born September 11, 1855, in Ellenburg, New York. Shepard graduated from Cornell University and the University of Michigan Medical School and also studied in New York. In 1882 the American Board of Commissioners for Foreign Missions (ABCFM)* asked him to organize and develop the medical department of Central Turkey College in Aintab, Turkey. Shepard was professor of surgery at Central Turkey College from 1882 to 1888 and acting president of the college in 1884–1885 and 1895–1896. He also became surgeon and director of the

Azariah Smith Memorial Hospital in 1883. Died December 18, 1915, in Aintab, Turkey. *References*: *DAB*; *NYT* January 11, 1916; and *WWWA*.

SHEPARD, LORRIN ANDREWS (1890–1983). Medical missionary, born March 24, 1890, in Aintab, Turkey, son of Frederick Douglas Shepard,* and grew up in East Orange, New Jersey. Shepard graduated from Yale University and Columbia College of Physicians and Surgeons. He became a missionary under the American Board of Commissions for Foreign Missions (ABCFM)* in 1919 and served as director of the American hospital in Istanbul from 1927 to 1957. Died July 16, 1983, in Haverhill, Massachusetts. *Reference*: *NYT*, July 21, 1983.

SHERRILL, CHARLES HITCHCOCK, JR. (1867–1936). Lawyer and diplomat, born April 13, 1867, in Washington, D.C. Sherrill graduated from Yale University and practiced law in New York City from 1891 to 1909. He was minister to Argentina from 1909 to 1911 but retired from the diplomatic service and resumed the practice of law in 1912. He was ambassador to Turkey from 1932 to 1933. He wrote *Mosaics in Italy, Palestine, Syria, Turkey and Greece* (London, 1933) and a memoir of his ambassadorship, *A Year's Embassy to Mustafa Kemal* (New York, 1934). Died June 25, 1936, in Paris. *References*: *NCAB* 37:20; *NYT*, June 26, 1936; and *WWWA*.

SHIELDS, FLOYD F(FRANCIS) (1901–   ). Lawyer, born September 9, 1901, in Wathena, Kansas. Shields graduated from the University of Kansas and Washburne University, and was admitted to the bar in 1932. He was general counsel to General Expressways in Chicago from 1937 to 1943 and again from 1946 to 1951. He was transport adviser in the Arthur Chester Millspaugh* mission to Iran, and director of the Iranian Road Transport Department of the Persian Gulf Command from 1943 to 1945. In 1945 he became transportation specialist in the Office of Inter-American Affairs, and after 1958 he practiced law in Mission, Kansas. *Reference*: *WWM*.

SHIELDS, REID F(RAMPTON) (1893–   ). Missionary, born March 1, 1893, in Allerton, Iowa. Shields graduated from Tarkio College and Pittsburgh Theological Seminary, and was ordained in 1917. He was a missionary under the United Presbyterian Church of North America Board of Foreign Missions* in the Sudan from 1917 until 1958, and served at Khartoum and Omdurman. He was also general secretary and treasurer of the Sudan Mission, and wrote *Behind the Garden of Allah* (Philadelphia, 1937), a history of the American mission in the Sudan.

SHINGLER, DON G(ILMORE) (1896–1963). Army officer, born October 25, 1896, in Perry Center, Wyoming County, New York. Shingler attended the University of Wyoming, graduated from the U.S. Military Academy in 1919, studied at the Massachusetts Institute of Technology, and was commissioned second lieutenant in the army in 1918. He served in the Corps of Engineers, was an instructor and assistant professor of mathematics at West Point from 1925 to 1930, and served in the Panama Canal. In 1941 he became chief of staff of the U.S. Military Mission to Iran and Iraq, and in 1942–1943 he was chief of the Iranian Mission with headquarters in Basra. In 1944 he became chief of the amphibious section of the First Army and from 1946 to 1949, chief engineer of U.S. forces in Europe. He was later division engineer in various posts in the United States. He retired in 1954 with the rank of brigadier general. Died October 29, 1963, in Washington, D.C. *References*: *NCAB* 50:440; *NYT*, November 1, 1963.

SHOEMAKER, MICHAEL MYERS (1853–1924). Traveler and author, born June 26, 1853, in Covington, Kentucky. Shoemaker attended Cornell University. He spent part of his life in Cincinnati where he established the Ohio Society of Colonial Wars. He traveled all over the world, including the Middle East, and wrote *The Heart of the Orient: Saunterings Through Georgia, Armenia, Persia, Turkomania and Turkestan to the Vale of Paradise* (New York, 1903), and *Islam Lands: Nubia, the Sudan, Tunisia, and Algeria* (New York, 1910). After 1915 he lived in Bennington, Vermont. Died August 11, 1924, in Paris. *References*: *NYT*, August 12, 1924; *OAB*; and *WWWA*.

SHUBRICK, JOHN TEMPLER (1788–1815). Naval officer, born September 12, 1788, in Bull's Island, South Carolina. Shubrick was commissioned a midshipman in the navy in 1806 and first lieutenant in 1812, and served in the War of 1812. He was first lieutenant in Stephen Decatur's* flagship *Guerriere* against Algiers in 1815. Commanding the *Epervier*, Shubrick was lost at sea in July 1815 on his way home with the treaty. *References*: *ACAB*; *DAB*; *NCAB* 8:98; *WAMB*; and *WWWA*.

SHUFELDT, ROBERT WILSON (1822–1895). Naval officer, born February 21, 1822, in Red Hook, New York. Shufeldt was appointed a midshipman in 1839, resigned in 1854, and was captain of a steamship in the merchant service, consul to Cuba from 1861 to 1863, and a special agent to Mexico in 1862. He was recommissioned in the navy in 1862 and served in the Civil War. From 1878 to 1880 he went on a combined diplomatic and commercial mission to the East, commanding the *Ticonderoga*.* He visited the Persian Gulf in December 1879 and described the opportunities for American trade in the area. He returned to China in 1881 as naval attaché and negotiated a treaty with China in 1882. From 1882 to 1884 he was president of the Naval Advisory Board and superintendent of the Naval Observatory. He retired in 1884 with the rank of rear admiral. Died November 7, 1895, in Washington, D.C. *References*: *ACAB*; *DAB*; *DADH*; Frederick C. Drake, *The Empire of the Seas: A Biography of Admiral*

Robert Wilson Shufeldt, USN (Honolulu, 1984); *NCAB* 4:293; *NYT*, November 8, 1895; *WAMB*; and *WWWA*.

SHUSTER, W(ILLIAM) P. MORGAN (1877–1960). Financier, lawyer, and publisher, born February 23, 1877, in Washington, D.C. Shuster graduated from Columbia University and its Law School. In 1898 he worked as a stenographer in Cuba for the War Department; was collector of customs in Cuba from 1899 to 1901; organized the customs service in the Philippine Islands, becoming collector of customs from 1901 to 1906; and was secretary of public instruction in the Philippines Commission from 1906 to 1909. He went to Persia in 1911 to help it out of its financial difficulties and to reorganize its financial structure. However, he was soon embroiled in conflicts between British and Russian interests and was dismissed. He wrote of his experiences in *The Strangling of Persia: Story of the European Diplomacy and Oriental Intrigue That Resulted in the Denationalization of Twelve Million Mohammedans—A Personal Narrative* (New York, 1912). In 1915 he became president of Century (later Appleton-Century, and still later Appleton-Century-Crofts), and chairman of the board from 1952 until his death. Died May 26, 1960, in New York City. *References*: Papers, Manuscript Division, Library of Congress; Robert A. McDaniel, *The Shuster Mission and the Persian Constitutional Revolution* (Minneapolis, 1974); *DAB S6*; *NCAB* 47:618; *NYT*, May 27, 1960; and *WWWA*.

SIBLEY, HENRY HOPKINS (1816–1886). Soldier, born May 25, 1816, in Nachitoches, Louisiana. Sibley graduated from the U.S. Military Academy in 1838, was commissioned in the 2nd Dragoons, and served in the Seminole War in Florida, in the Mexican War, in Texas and Kansas, and in the Confederate Army during the Civil War. He entered the Egyptian Army in 1869, became chief of artillery, and was assigned the duty of constructing seacoast and river defenses. He returned to the United States in 1874 and later lectured on the conditions in Egypt. Died August 23, 1886, in Fredericksburg, Virginia. *References*: *ACAB*; *CWD*; *Hesseltine*; *NCAB* 2:365; and *WAMB*.

SIMPSON, WILLIAM KELLY (1928–   ). Archaeologist, born January 3, 1928, in New York City. Simpson graduated from Yale University. He was an assistant in Egyptian art at the Metropolitan Museum of Art from 1948 to 1954, became assistant professor at Yale University in 1958, professor of Egyptology in 1965, curator of Egyptian and ancient Near Eastern art at the Boston Museum of Fine Arts in 1970, and director of the University Museum-Yale University expedition to Nubia in 1960. He wrote *The Terrace of the Great God at Abydos* (New Haven, Conn., 1974), *The Mastabas of Qar and Idu, Giza Mastabas* (New Haven, Conn., 1976), and *The Offering Chapel of Shekem-ankh-ptah* (New Haven, Conn., 1976), and co-authored *Ancient Egypt; Discovering Its Splendors* (Washington, D.C., 1978). *References*: *CA*; *DAS*; and *WWA*.

SINAI FIELD MISSION (SFM). Following the Sinai agreements of 1975 between Israel and Egypt, an electronic early warning system was installed and began operating in 1976. It was monitored by the Sinai Field Mission in order to alert all parties to any apparent violation of the agreement for Israel's withdrawal from the Sinai. It was manned by unarmed civilian volunteers, and its base camp was in Umm Khusheib. *References*: U.S. Department of State, *The United States Sinai Support Mission: Watch in the Sinai* (Washington, D.C., 1980); U.S. Department of State, *The United States Sinai Support Mission: Peace in Sinai* (Washington, D.C., 1983).

SMITH, AZARIAH (1817–1851). Medical missionary, born February 16, 1817, in Manlius, New York. Smith graduated from Yale College, Geneva (N.Y.) Medical College, and New Haven Divinity School, and was ordained in 1842. He was a missionary under the American Board of Commissioners for Foreign Missions (ABCFM)* in Turkey from 1842 until his death, practiced medicine throughout Turkey from 1843 to 1845, and was assigned to Aintab in 1847. He made numerous journeys to the interior of Anatolia, was a traveling companion of Sir Austin Henry Layard, and reported on the discoveries made in Nineveh in 1843 and 1844 in the *American Journal of Science and Arts* in 1845. He also wrote papers on meteorology and Syrian antiquities. Died June 3, 1851, at Aintab, Turkey. *References*: *ACAB*; *DAB*; *EM*; and *WWWA*.

SMITH, EDWIN (1822–1906). Adventurer and dealer, born in Connecticut. Smith settled in Egypt in 1858 and resided there, chiefly in Thebes, until 1876, as a moneylender and antiquities dealer. He had considerable knowledge of hieroglyphic and hieratic writing, and owned the Edwin Smith Surgical Papyrus (presented in 1906 by his daughter to the New York Historical Society). He lived in Italy from 1876 until his death. *References*: James H. Breasted, *The Edwin Smith Surgical Papyrus* (Chicago, 1930); Caroline R. Wilson, "The Place of the New York Historical Society in the Growth of American Interest in Egyptology," *New York Historical Society Quarterly Bulletin* 4 (1920): 3–20; and *WWWE*.

SMITH, ELI (1801–1857). Missionary, born September 13, 1801, at Northford, Connecticut. Smith graduated from Yale College and Andover Theological Seminary, and was ordained in 1826. In 1826 the American Board of Commissioners for Foreign Missions (ABCFM)* sent him to Malta as associate editor at the publishing house and to oversee the printing press. He was transferred to Syria in 1833. He continued his involvement with the press and went to Germany in 1838 to arrange for the casting of fonts of Arabic type. He traveled throughout Asia Minor, Armenia, Georgia, and Persia with Harrison Gray Otis Dwight* in 1830–1831 and wrote *Researches of the Rev. E. Smith and Rev. H.G.O. Dwight in Armenia; Including a Journey Trough Asia Minor and into Georgia and Persia, with a Visit to the Nestorian and Chaldean Christians of Oormiaah and Salmas*

(Boston, 1833). He accompanied Edward Robinson* in the exploration of Palestine, Sinai, and Syria in 1838, and on Robinson's second trip in 1852. From 1847 until his death, he was involved in the translation of the Bible into Arabic. He also prepared a treatise on Arabic music. Died January 11, 1857, in Beirut. *References*: Papers, Yale University Divinity School Library; *ACAB*; *AndoverTS*; *CAB*; *EM*; *NCAB* 8:15; and *WWWA*.

SMITH, EUSTACE JOHN (1908–1975). Clergyman, born August 22, 1908, in Medford, Massachusetts. Smith studied in several seminaries, joined the Franciscan order, was ordained in 1934, and later studied in Rome and Jerusalem. He returned to the United States in 1939, was vice rector at Christ the King Seminary (Allegheny, N.Y.)., and went to Rome in 1946 as secretary at the headquarters of the orders of Friars Minor. He was back in the United States in 1951 as professor of scripture at Christ the King Seminary. In 1955 he became titular bishop of Cibotus and vicar apostolic of Beirut for the Latin Rites Catholics in Lebanon, was consecrated in 1956, and served until 1973 when he returned to the United States. Died June 13, 1975, in Boston. *References*: *NYT*, June 15, 1975.

SMITH, FREDERICK G(EORGE) (1880–1947). Evangelist and missionary, born November 12, 1880, near Lacota, Michigan. Smith began working for the Gospel Trumpet Company in 1897 and became minister of the Church of God in 1898. He was missionary to Syria from 1912 to 1914 and wrote *Missionary Journey Through Bible Lands; Including a Description of Religious and Social Conditions in Palestine and Syria, Personal Missionary Experiences* (Anderson, Ind., 1915). He was editor of *The Gospel Trumpet* from 1916 to 1930 and pastor in Akron, Ohio, from 1930 to 1946. Died April 24, 1947, in Anderson, Indiana. *References*: *IAB*; John W.V. Smith, *Heralds of a Bright Day: Biographical Sketches of Early Leaders in the Church of God Reformation Movement* (Anderson, Ind., 1955), pp. 100–122.

SMITH, F(RANCIS) HOPKINSON (1838–1915). Engineer, artist, and author, born October 23, 1838, in Baltimore. Self-educated, Smith moved to New York, worked in a foundry, set himself up as an engineer, and was engaged in construction work for about thirty years, including the Race Rock lighthouse and the foundations for the Statue of Liberty. He was a successful novelist and turned his hobby of painting into a profession. He spent a summer in Constantinople and Palestine, and published his impressions in the September 1891 issue of *Harper's Monthly*. Died April 7, 1915, in New York City. *References*: *ACAB*; *DAB*; *NCAB* 5:326; *NYT*, April 8, 1915; *Summers Abroad: The European Watercolors of Francis Hopkinson Smith* (New York, 1985); and *WWWA*.

SMITH, GEORGE ALBERT (1817–1875). Mormon leader, born June 26, 1817, in Pottsdam, New York. Smith joined the Church of Jesus Christ of Latter-Day Saints in 1832 and was ordained as an apostle in 1839. He went on a mission to England in 1839–1841, settled in Nauvoo, Illinois, and moved to Utah in 1847. From 1864 to 1870 he was president of the church's Council and was in charge of organizing work south of Salt Lake City. He went on a mission to Palestine in 1872–1873, and his letters were included in *Correspondence of Palestine Tourists* (Salt Lake City, 1875). Died September 1, 1875, in Salt Lake City. *References*: Journal, Archives Division, The Church of Jesus Christ of Latter-Day Saints, Salt Lake City; *NCAB* 16:18; and Merlo J. Pusey, *Builders of the Kingdom: George A. Smith, John Henry Smith, George Albert Smith* (Provo, Utah, 1982).

SMITH, JEROME VANCROWNINSHIELD (1800–1879). Physician, born July 20, 1800, in Conway, New Jersey. Smith studied at the medical department of Brown University and at Berkshire Medical School. He was port physician in Boston from 1826 to 1849, and mayor of Boston in 1854. He was professor of anatomy and physiology at the New York Medical College, established and edited the *Boston Medical Intelligencer* in 1823, edited the *Boston Medical and Surgical Journal* from 1828 to 1856, and the *Medical World* from 1857 to 1859. He went to the Middle East in 1852 and wrote *Pilgrimage to Palestine* (Boston, 1851), *Pilgrimage to Egypt, Embracing a Diary of the Explorations on the Nile* (Boston, 1852), and *Turkey and the Turks* (Boston, 1852). Died August 21, 1879, in New York City. *References*: *ACAB*; *DAMB*.

SMITH, J(OHN) LAWRENCE (1818–1883). Chemist and mineralogist, born December 17, 1818, near Charleston, South Carolina. Smith graduated from the University of Virginia and the Medical College of South Carolina and studied abroad. He began to practice medicine in Charleston in 1844 and was co-founder of the *Southern Journal of Medicine and Pharmacy* in 1846. He was sent to Turkey in 1846 as an adviser on cotton culture, became an adviser on the mineral resources of Turkey, was engaged as a mining engineer by the Ottoman government, and discovered emery and coal deposits. He returned to the United States in 1850, was professor of chemistry at the University of Virginia in 1852–1853, and professor of medical chemistry and toxicology at the University of Louisville from 1854 until 1866. He published *Original Researches in Mineralogy and Chemistry* (Louisville, Ky., 1884). Died October 12, 1883, in Louisville. *References*: *ACAB*; *BDAS*; *BMNAS* 2 (1886): 217–248; *DAB*; *NCAB* 6:54; John R. Sampey, "J. Lawrence Smith," *Journal of Chemical Education* 5 (1928): 123–128; and *WWWA*.

SMITH, JOSEPH (1790–1877). Naval officer, born March 30, 1790, in Hanover, Massachusetts. Smith was commissioned in the U.S. Navy in 1809, served in the War of 1812, and participated in the war with Algiers in 1815. He aided in fitting out the U.S. Exploring Expedition. He brought the Mediterranean Squadron, with his flagship *Plymouth*, to Beirut in 1845, at the time of a conflict between the Druzes and the Maronite Christians. From 1846 to 1869 he was chief of the Bureau of Navy Yards and Docks. Died January 17, 1877, in Washington, D.C. *References*: *ACAB*; *DAB*; *NCAB* 4:381; and *WWWA*.

SMITH, JOSEPH ALLEN (1769–1828). Traveler, born in Charleston, South Carolina. Smith spent the years 1793 to 1807 in adventurous travels. He went to Portugal, Spain, and England in 1793, and was in Italy from 1793 to 1796, in Poland in 1797, in France in 1801, and in Russia from 1802 to 1805. In 1803 he went on a journey to Astrakhan, visited Tiflis, returned through much of the Turkish Empire, and wintered in Constantinople. He returned to the United States in 1807. *Reference*: E. P. Richardson, ''Allen Smith, Collector and Benefactor,'' *American Art Journal* 1 (1969): 5–19.

SMITH, JOSEPH LINDON (1863–1950). Artist and copyist, born October 11, 1863, in Pawtucket, Rhode Island. Smith studied at the Museum of Fine Arts in Boston and in Paris, and devoted much of his life to painting replicas in oil of ancient works of art. He traveled widely and painted scenes in Iraq, Iran, Syria, and Lebanon, the Far East, Cambodia, and the Mayalands, but particularly in Egypt and Nubia. He visited Egypt for the first time in 1898, became involved with the explorations in the Valley of the Kings in Luxor and with the Harvard University-Boston Museum of Fine Arts expedition to the Pyramids of Giza, and was also employed by the Egyptian government to teach his techniques of art reproduction to Egyptian students. Died October 18, 1950, in Dublin, New Hampshire. His account of his life, *Tombs, Temples & Ancient Art* (Norman, Okla., 1956), was edited by his wife, **CORINNA HAVEN (PUT-NAM) SMITH** (1876–1965), who also wrote her memoirs, *Interesting People: Eighty Years with the Great and Near Great* (Norman, Okla., 1962). *References*: *AJA* 55 (1951): 269; *NCAB* 39:32; *NYT*, October 20, 1950; *WWWA*; and *WWWE*.

SMITH, MYRON BEMENT (1897–1970). Archaeologist, born January 19, 1897, in Newark Valley, New York. Smith graduated from Yale, Harvard, Johns Hopkins, and Columbia universities, studied in Italy, and served in the medical corps in World War I. From 1919 to 1929 he was a draftsman and designer in several architectural offices. He was executive secretary of the American Institute of Persian Art and Archaeology from 1930 to 1933, directed an expedition to Iran to study Islamic architecture from 1933 to 1937, and was honorary consultant to the Library of Congress from 1938 to 1940 and from 1948 until his death. During World War II, he was a consultant on Persian roads and transport facilities to the U.S. Army Corps of Engineers and to other governmental agencies. Died March 21, 1970, in Washington, D.C. His Islamic archives are in the Freer Gallery of Art Library, Washington, D.C. *References*: *Archeology* 23 (1970): 257; *NCAB* 55:539.

SMITH, RAY WINFIELD (1897–1982). Archaeologist, born June 4, 1897, in Marlboro, New Hampshire. Smith graduated from Dartmouth College and served in ordnance during World War I. He was employed by American oil companies in Belgium, the Netherlands, and Germany from 1922 to 1936, and owned an import-export firm in Houston from 1936 to 1942. He was economic adviser to the U.S. commandant in Berlin in 1951–1952, was U.S. commissioner to the Military Security Board in Germany from 1952 to 1955, and served as president of the Ray Winfield Smith Foundation from 1955 to 1973. He was director of the Akhenaten Temple project in Egypt from 1965 to 1972, and director of the research project on the City of Isfahan in Iran. Died April 17, 1982, in Houston, Texas. *References*: *NYT*, April 19, 1982; *Journal of Glass Studies* 26 (1984): 160–161; and *WWA*.

SMITH, ROBERT H(OUSTON) (1931–   ). Archaeologist, born February 13, 1931, in McAlester, Oklahoma. Smith graduated from the University of Tulsa and Yale University. He was a member of the faculty of the College of Wooster and was professor of religion after 1960. He was a member of the University Museum archaeological expeditions to El Jib in 1959 and to Tell es-Saidiyeh, Jordan, in 1964, and became director of the Wooster expedition to Pella, Jordan, in 1965. He wrote *Pella of the Decapolis* (Wooster, Ohio, 1973). *References*: *CA*; *DAS*.

SMITH, WALTER GEORGE (1854–1924). Lawyer, born November 24, 1854, in Logan County, Ohio, and moved to Philadelphia in 1865. Smith graduated from the University of Pennsylvania and its law school, and began practicing law in Philadelphia in 1877. He was a member of the relief commission to the Middle East in 1919 and was involved with the Armenia-America Society and Near East Relief.* He was a member of the advisory committee to the American delegation to the Washington Naval Conference and later a member of the Board of Indian Commissioners. Died April 4, 1924, in Philadelphia. *References*: "Journal of a Journey to the Near East," ed. Thomas A. Bryson, *Armenian Review* 24 (1971) and 25 (1972); Papers, Archive of the American Catholic Historical Society, St. Charles Seminary, Philadelphia; Thomas A. Bryson, *Walter George Smith* (Washington, D.C., 1977); *NCAB* 21:43; *NYT*, April 5, 1924; and *WWWA*.

SMITH, WILBERT B. (1883–1962). Young Men's Christian Association (YMCA)* official, born in Camden, New York. Smith graduated from the University of Pennsylvania and New York University, and was employed by the International Committee of the YMCA. He went to India in 1914, was student secretary of the YMCA in Poona, and YMCA secretary in the army in World War I. He served in Bombay from 1917 to 1920 and went to Cairo in 1920 to establish YMCA work in Egypt. He then served in the New York headquarters but returned to Cairo, staying there until 1942, and was also senior secretary for the YMCA in Palestine. Smith again served in the New York headquarters from 1942 until his retirement in 1945 and was executive secretary of the Council of Churches in Wilmington, Delaware, until 1954. Died June 19, 1962, in Wilmington.

SMITH, WILLIAM STEVENSON (1907–1969). Egyptologist, born February 7, 1907, in Indianapolis. Smith graduated from the University of Chicago and Harvard University. In 1928 he joined the staff of the Boston Museum of Fine Arts. He was a member of the joint expedition of Harvard University and the Boston Museum of Fine Arts to Egypt, excavating at the Giza Pyramids under George A. Reisner from 1930 to 1939, and returned in 1946–1947 to close down the expedition. He served in the navy during World War II. In 1941 he became an assistant, associate, and, from 1956 until his death, curator in the Department of Egyptian Art at the Boston Museum of Fine Arts. From 1951 to 1966 he was director of the American Research Center in Cairo. Died January 13, 1969, in Cambridge, Massachusetts. *References*: *NYT*, January 14, 1969; *WWWA*; and *WWWE*.

SNODGRASS, C(ORNELIUS) STRIBLING (1900–1974). Consulting engineer, born August 9, 1900, in Martinsburg, West Virginia. Snodgrass graduated from the U.S. Naval Academy in 1922, was commissioned an ensign in the U.S. Navy in 1922, and resigned in 1927. He was European manager for C. F. Braun and Company from 1927 to 1934, and was later a consultant to independent refiners. He was director of the foreign refining division of the Petroleum Administration for War from 1941 to 1946 and a member of the Everette Lee deGolyer* mission to the Middle East. He was vice president for engineering and development for the Bechtel International Corporation from 1946 to 1951, in charge of directing the first Saudi Arabian development program, and director of the refining division of the Petroleum Administration for Defense in 1951–1952. He opened his own firm, Snodgrass Associates, in 1952; advised Saudi Arabia in establishing its first public works program; was technical consultant to Iran and Syria; became a consulting engineer and petroleum consultant to the Sultanate of Oman in 1972; and natural resources adviser to Jordan in 1973. Died in July 19, 1974, near Leesburg, Virginia. *Reference*: *Washington Post*, July 21, 1974.

SOLECKI, RALPH S(TEFAN) (1917–   ). Archaeologist, born October 15, 1917, in Brooklyn, New York. Solecki graduated from City College of New York and Columbia University. From 1948 to 1959 he was on the staff of the Smithsonian Institution, and in 1949 he made an archaeological reconnaissance in northwest Alaska for the U.S. Geological Survey. In 1950 he participated in George Glenn Cameron's* expedition to Iraq and visited Shanidar. He returned as field director of an archaeological expedition there in 1951, 1953, 1956–1957, 1960, and 1978. He also conducted archaeological expeditions to Sudanese Nubia in 1961, to Turkey and Syria in 1963 and 1964–1965, to Iran in 1968, and to

Lebanon from 1969 to 1973. He became a member of the faculty of Columbia University in 1959 and professor of anthropology in 1965. He wrote *Shanidar: The First Flower People* (New York, 1971) and prepared a record of *Kurdish Folk Songs and Dances* (New York, 1955). *References*: *AMWS*; *CA*; and *WWA*.

SOMERS, RICHARD (1778–1804). Naval officer, born September 15, 1778, in Somers Point, New Jersey, and grew up in Philadelphia and Burlington, New Jersey. Somers served in the merchant service and was commissioned a midshipman in the navy in 1798. He commanded a gunboat division in the attacks against Tripoli in 1804. He then commanded the ketch *Intrepid* which on September 4, 1804, filled with powder, tried to drift into Tripoli Harbor and blow it up. The plan did not succeed, and all aboard were killed. *References*: *ACAB*; *DAB*; *NCAB* 8:412; and *WAMB*.

SOMERVELL, BREHON BURKE (1892–1955). Army officer, born May 9, 1892, in Little Rock Arkansas, and moved with his family to Washington, D.C., in 1906. Somervell graduated from the U.S. Military Academy in 1914, was commissioned second lieutenant in the U.S. Army, and served on the Mexican border and in World War I. He assisted Walker Downer Hines* in the survey of the Rhine and Danube rivers for the League of Nations in 1925. He collaborated in the economic survey of Turkey in 1933–1934, was in charge of the field work and, after Hines's death, completed the report. Somervell was commanding general of the services of supply during World War II and retired in 1946 with the rank of major general. He became chairman and president of Koppers Company of Pittsburgh. Died February 13, 1955, in New York City. *References*: *CB*, 1942; *DAB S5*; *DAMIB*; *NCAB* F:548; *WAMB*; and *WWWA*.

SOUTHARD, ADDISON E. (1884–1970). Consul, born October 18, 1884, in Louisville, Kentucky. Southard graduated from Lebanon University and Santo Tomas University in Manila, Philippines. From 1908 to 1915 he was an officer of the Philippine government. He entered the consular service in 1916 and served in Aden, Abyssinia, Somaliland, and Eritrea. He did intelligence work in Persia in 1918, was consul in Jerusalem from 1920 to 1922, and prepared *Palestine, Its Commercial Resources with Particular Reference to American Trade* (Washington, D.C., 1922). He was chief of the Consular Commercial Office from 1922 to 1926; consul general in Singapore in 1926; minister and consul general in Addis Ababa from 1927 to 1934; consul general and counselor in Stockholm in 1934–1935 and in Paris in 1936–1937; and consul general in Hong Kong and Macao from 1938 to 1941. He was interned by the Japanese and returned to the United States in 1942. Died February 11, 1970. *Reference*: *BRDS*; *WWWA*.

SOUTHERN BAPTIST CONVENTION: FOREIGN MISSION BOARD. Founded in 1845, it began work in the Middle East in 1921 when it sent its first missionaries to Palestine. It established a permanent "Palestine and Syria Mission" in 1923. After 1948, it extended its missionary work to other countries of the Middle East. *Reference*: Baker J. Cauthen and Frank K. Means, *Advance to Bold-Mission Thrust, 1845–1980* (Richmond, 1981).

SOUTHGATE, HORATIO, JR. (1812–1894). Missionary, born July 5, 1812, in Portland, Maine. Southgate graduated from Bowdoin College and Andover Theological Seminary, and was ordained in 1839. In 1835, the Episcopal Missionary Society asked him to explore missionary possibilities in the Middle East. From 1836 to 1838 he visited Turkey and Persia, recommended a policy of cooperation with the Episcopal Church of the East, and wrote *Narrative of a Tour Through Armenia, Kurdistan, Persia and Mesopotamia, with an Introduction, and Occasional Observations Upon the Conditions of Mohammedanism and Christianity in Those Countries* (New York, 1840) and *Narrative of a Visit to the Syrian (Jacobite) Church of Mesopotamia, with Statements and Reflections Upon the Present State of Christianity in Turkey, and the Character and Prospects of the Eastern Churches* (New York, 1844). In 1840 Southgate returned to Constantinople as a missionary to the Jacobites in Syria, with headquarters at Mardin, established contacts with the eastern churches, and in 1844 was consecrated the Episcopal bishop of the Turkish Empire. He became involved in the controversies with the American Board of Commissioners for Foreign Missions (ABCFM)* missionaries, returned to the United States in 1849, and resigned in 1850. He served pastorates in Portland, Boston, and New York City, and later wrote *The Cross Above the Crescent: A Romance of Constantinople* (Philadelphia, 1878). Died April 12, 1894, in Astoria, New York. *References*: *ACAB*; Kenneth W. Cameron, "The Oriental Manuscripts of Horatio Southgate," *Historical Magazine of the Protestant Episcopal Church* 10 (1941): 57–61; *DAB S1*; *NCAB* 13:417; and *WWWA*.

SOUTHWORTH, ALVAN S. (1846–1901). Journalist and traveler, born in Lockport, New York. Southworth attended the U.S. Naval Academy. He became foreign correspondent for the *New York Herald*, reported on the Fenian uprising in Canada and on the Franco-Prussian War, and was in Paris during the Commune. In 1871 he was sent to Africa by James Gordon Bennett, publisher of the *New York Herald*, to investigate the rumors about the fate of Sir Samuel Baker, who was sent in 1870 by the Khedive Ismail to the Sudan in command of a military expedition to annex the Upper Nile to Egypt and to suppress the slave-trade there. Southworth left Cairo in December 1871, traveled to Khartoum in the Sudan, and continued 300 miles up the Nile. He then returned to Khartoum, traveled to the Red Sea coast and returned to Egypt. He described his travels in *Four Thousand Miles of African Travel: A Personal Record of a Journal Up the Nile and Through the Soudan to Central Africa* (New York, 1875). He returned to the United States in 1874, was secretary of the American Geographical Society in 1874–1875, and receiver for the Becker Street and Fulton Ferry Railroad

Company from 1875 until 1877. He had no regular occupation after 1877. Died January 7, 1901, in New York City. *Reference*: *NYT*, January 8, 1901.

SPAFFORD, HORATIO GATES (1828–1888). Religious zealot, born October 20, 1828, in North Troy, New York. Spafford was admitted to the bar, settled in Chicago in 1856, and practiced law. After a series of family tragedies, he moved with his family to Palestine and settled in Jerusalem in 1881. His group became known as the American Colony.* He introduced the potato and the eucalyptus tree to Palestine. Died in Jerusalem. His wife **ANNA (TUBENA) (LAWSON) SPAFFORD (1842–1923)**, was born March 16, 1842, in Stavanger, Norway, and came to the United States in 1846. She accompanied her husband to Palestine. Died April 17, 1923, in Jerusalem. *Reference*: Bertha S. Vester, *Our Jerusalem* (Garden City, N.Y., 1950).

SPAIN, JAMES W(ILLIAM) (1926–   ). Diplomat, born July 22, 1926, in Chicago. Spain graduated from the University of Chicago and Columbia University, entered the foreign service in 1951, but left in 1953 to teach at American University and Florida State University. He wrote *The Way of the Pathans* (London, 1962) and *Pathan Borderland* (The Hague, 1963). He rejoined the foreign service in 1963; was a member of the Policy Planning Council in the State Department in 1963–1964; director of the Office of Research and Analysis for Near Eastern and South Asian Affairs from 1964 to 1966; country director for Pakistan and Afghanistan from 1966 to 1969; vice consul in Karachi; chargé d'affaires at Islamabad; consul general in Istanbul from 1970 to 1972; deputy chief of mission and minister in Ankara from 1972 to 1974; ambassador to Tanzania from 1975 to 1981; and ambassador to Turkey from 1980 to 1981. He wrote *American Diplomacy in Turkey: Memoirs of an Ambassador Extraordinary and Plenipotentiary* (New York, 1984). *References*: *MENA*; *WWA*; and *WWAP*.

SPEISER, EPHRAIM AVIGDOR (1902–1965). Orientalist, born January 24, 1902, in Skalat, Galicia (then in Austria-Hungary), and came to the United States in 1920. Speiser graduated from the University of Pennsylvania and Dropsie College. He was annual professor at the American Schools of Oriental Research (ASOR)* in Baghdad in 1926–1927, surveyed southern Kurdistan, and discovered and made a preliminary excavation at Tepe Gawra. In 1930–1932 and 1936–1937 he was field director of the ASOR and the University Museum joint expedition to Tepe Gawra and Tell Billa, and was co-author of *Excavations at Tepe Gawra, Joint Expedition of the Baghdad School, the University Museum, and Dropsie College, 1935–50, to Mesopotamia* (Philadelphia, 1935–1950). He became a member of the faculty of the University of Pennsylvania in 1928 and professor of Semitics in 1931. During World War II he was chief of the Near East section of the Research and Analysis Branch of the Office of Strategic Services. He wrote *The United States and the Near East* (Cambridge, Mass., 1947; rev. ed., 1950). Died June 15, 1965, in Elkins Park, Pennsylvania. *Ref-*

erences: *Essays in Memory of E. A. Speiser*, ed. William M. Hallo (New Haven, Conn., 1968); *DAB S7*; and *NYT*, June 17, 1965.

SPENCE, CARROLL (1818–1896). Diplomat, born February 22, 1818, in Clare Mont, near Baltimore. Spence graduated from St. Mary and Dickinson colleges, practiced law in Baltimore, and served as a member of the Maryland legislature. From 1853 to 1857 he was minister to Turkey. In Constantinople in 1856 he negotiated the first treaty between the United States and Persia. Died August 9, 1896, in Baltimore. *References*: *NCAB* 12:318; and *Treaties and Other International Acts of the United States of America*, ed. Hunter Miller (Washington, D.C., 1942), 7: 429–489.

SPENCER, JESSE AMES (1816–1898). Clergyman and educator, born June 17, 1816, in Hyde Park, New York. Spencer graduated from Columbia University and General Theological Seminary, and was ordained in 1841. He was pastor and editor of *The Churchman's Miscellany*. He traveled to the Middle East in 1849 and wrote *The East—Sketches of Travels in Egypt and the Holy Land* (New York, 1850). He was editor and secretary of the General Protestant Episcopal Sunday School Union in New York from 1850 to 1857, and professor of Greek at the College of the City of New York from 1869 to 1879. In 1883 he was appointed custodian of the Standard Bible of the Episcopal Church. Died September 2, 1898, in New York City. *References*: *ACAB*; *DAB*; and *WWWA*.

SPOER, HANS HENRY (1873–1951). Clergyman and Orientalist, born August 1, 1873, in Krefeld, Germany. Spoer came to the United States after completing high school, studied at Bloomfield (N.J.) Theological Seminary, New York University, and New Brunswick and Union theological seminaries, and at the American Schools of Oriental Research (ASOR)* in Jerusalem. He was a lecturer on the Old Testament at Lichfield Theological Seminary in England in 1909–1910, was ordained in 1911, was assistant chaplain in Cairo from 1911 to 1913, and professor of English and German at University Salah-ed-Din in Jerusalem from 1915 to 1917, when he was deported by the Turkish authorities because he was an American. He was co-author of *Manual of Palestinian Arabic for Self-instruction* (Jerusalem, 1909). He was district commissioner for relief work in Russia and Armenia from 1919 to 1921, was imprisoned by the Bolsheviks in Baku and sentenced to be executed, but was reprieved. He was secretary of the Young Men's Christian Association (YMCA) in Istanbul in 1921–1922. Spoer gave his collection of Arabic and Hebrew manuscripts to Union Theological Seminary. He later served as a minister in the diocese of Michigan and in Sycamore, Illinois, was chaplain of the New York Mission Society, and a pastor in New York City until his retirement in 1951. Died October 2, 1951, in Woodbury, New Jersey. *References*: *NYT*, October 4, 1951; *UnionTS*.

SPURR, JOSIAH EDWARD (1870–1950). Geologist, born October 1, 1870, in Gloucester, Massachusetts. Spurr graduated from Harvard University. He joined the U.S. Geological Service in 1894 and in 1895 went on an expedition to Alaska. In 1900 he went to Turkey as geological adviser to Sultan Abdul Hamid, studied the gold gravel of Macedonia, and helped revise the mining laws of Turkey. He was again a geologist with the U.S. Geological Survey from 1902 to 1906, and chief geologist of the American Refining and Smelting Company from 1906 to 1908. He was a consulting specialist in mining from 1908 to 1911, employed by the Tonopah Mining Company from 1911 to 1917, and served with the U.S. Shipping Board in 1917–1918 and with the Bureau of Mines in 1918–1919. He was editor of the *Engineering and Mining Journal* from 1919 to 1927 and professor of geology at Rollins College from 1930 to 1932. Died January 12, 1950, in Winter Park, Florida. *References*: Papers, University of Wyoming Library. *DAB S4*; *NYT*, January 13, 1950; and *WWWA*.

STAGER, LAWRENCE E. (1943–   ). Archaeologist, born January 5, 1943, in Kenton, Ohio. Stager graduated from Harvard University. He became associate professor of Syro-Palestinian archaeology at the Oriental Institute, University of Chicago, in 1976. He was co-director of the American expedition to Idalion, Cyprus, from 1972 to 1974 and co-editor of *American Expedition to Idalion, Cyprus: First Preliminary Report, Seasons of 1971 and 1972* (Cambridge, Mass., 1974). Stager was director of the UNESCO Save Carthage project and the American Punic archaeological expedition to Carthage in Tunis, from 1975 to 1980, and excavated at Carthage from 1973 to 1979. *Reference*: *DAS*.

STAUDT, CALVIN K(LAPP) (1875?–1951). Clergyman and educator, born in Lower Heidelberg Township, Berks County, Pennsylvania. Staudt graduated from Franklin and Marshall College, the Reformed Theological Seminary, Lancaster, Pennsylvania, and the University of Chicago. He served several pastorates of the Evangelical and Reformed Church in the United States and taught at the American University of Beirut* from 1922 to 1925. He founded the American School for Boys in Baghdad in 1925 and was its headmaster from 1925 until his retirement in 1945, when he returned to the United States. Died April 3, 1951. *Reference*: *NYT*, April 4, 1951.

STEEVER, EDGAR Z(ELL) (1849–1920). Army officer, born August 20, 1849, in Philadelphia. Steever graduated from the U.S. Military Academy in 1871, was commissioned second lieutenant in the cavalry in 1871, and served in the Indian campaigns in the West. He was on special duty with the American Palestine Exploration Society* expedition to the area east of the Jordand River from 1872 to 1874. Later, he again served in the West on the Mexican border, and in 1891 he became engineer and secretary of the Intercontinental Railway Commission. He served in the Philippines during the Spanish-American War, was civil and military governor of the Sulu Archipelago, and from 1911 until his retirement in 1913 with the rank of brigadier general, served again on the Mexican border. Died January 19, 1920, in Washington, D.C. *References*: *Army and Navy Journal*, January 31, 1920; *RAGMA* 1920.

STEINEKE, MAX (1898–1952). Petroleum geologist, born in March 1898 in Brookings, Oregon. Steineke graduated from Stanford Univerisity. He joined Standard Oil Company of California in 1922 and explored in Colombia, California, and New Zealand. In 1933 he was transferred to Bahrain Petroleum Company (BAPCO)—later Arabian American Oil Company (ARAMCO), and became its chief geologist in 1936. In 1933 he went to Saudi Arabia, discovered oil in the Dammam Dome in 1936, and bought the first oil-producing well in Saudi Arabia in 1938. Died April 16, 1952, in Los Altos, California. *References*: *AWM* 35 (May-June 1984): 25; *BAAPS* 35 (1951): 1695–1696; and *NYT*, April 17, 1952.

STEINHARDT, LAWRENCE ADOLPH (1892–1950). Lawyer and diplomat, born October 6, 1892, in New York City. Steinhardt graduated from Columbia University, was admitted to the bar in 1916, and practiced law in New York City. He was minister to Sweden from 1933 to 1937, ambassador to Peru from 1937 to 1938, ambassador to the Soviet Union from 1939 to 1941, and ambassador to Turkey from 1942 to 1945. During World War II he played an important role in keeping Turkey from fulfilling its commitments to deliver chrome to Germany and in turning Turkey toward the Allies. He was ambassador to Czechoslovakia from 1945 to 1948 and ambassador to Canada in 1948. Killed March 28, 1950, in a plane crash near Ottawa, Canada. *References*: Papers, Manuscript Division, Library of Congress; *CB* 1941; *DAB S4*; *NCAB* 40:70; *NYT*, March 29, 1950; Ralph R. Stackman, "Lawrence A. Steinhardt: New Deal Diplomat, 1933–1945," Ph.D. diss., Michigan State University; and *WWWA*.

STEPHENS, JOHN LLOYD (1805–1852). Traveler and author, born November 28, 1805, in Shrewsbury, New Jersey. Stephens graduated from Columbia College, studied law, was admitted to the bar, and practiced law in New York City. He traveled in the Middle East and Eastern Europe from 1834 to 1836, and wrote *Incidents of Travel in Egypt, Arabia Petraea, and the Holy Land* (New York, 1837; modern edition, ed. Victor W. Van Hagen, Norman, Okla., 1970), and *Incidents of Travel in Greece, Turkey, Russia and Poland* (New York, 1838), and became known as "the American Traveler." In 1839 he was sent on a confidential diplomatic mission to Central America. With Frederick Catherwood, he explored the ruins of Honduras, Guatemala, and Yucatan, and wrote *Incidents of Travel in Central America, Chiapas, and Yucatan* (New York, 1841). He later promoted mail steamships, the Ocean Navigation Company, and the Panama Railroad. Died October 12, 1852, in New York City. *References*: *ACAB*; Van Wyck Brooks, *Fenollosa and His Circle* (New York, 1962), pp. 110–156; *DAB*; *DADH*; *NCAB* 5:424; and Victor W. Van Hagen, *John Lloyd*

Stephens and the Lost Cities of Central America and Yucatan (Norman, Okla., 1947).

STEVENS, HARLEY CRAWFORD (1900–1959). Lawyer, born August 11, 1900, in Porland, Oregon. Stevens graduated from the University of California at Berkeley and was admitted to the bar in 1924. He practiced law again until 1934. He was manager of the tax department of Standard Oil Company of California from 1934 until 1947, when he became vice president and special counsel of the American Independent Oil Company,* was vice president in charge of marketing from 1952 to 1959, and was involved in the negotiations leading to the grant of oil concessions in the Nuetral Zone between Kuwait and Saudi Arabia. He was lent to Trans-Arabian Pipeline* (TAPLINE) in 1946 and traveled in the Middle East, participating in the negotiations relating to TAPLINE concessions. In 1952 he conducted a survey of the Middle East for the Ford Foundation. From 1959 until his death, he was an international petroleum consultant. Died December 26, 1959, in San Francisco. *References:* Papers, Hoover Institution Archives; *NCAB* 48:84; and *NYT*, December 28, 1959.

STEWART, WILLIAM (fl. 1803). Philadelphia merchant. In 1802 Stewart was appointed the first consul in Smyrna. He arrived in 1803, but being refused recognition from the Turkish authories, he returned to the United States. He was probably the major informant to Philadelphia merchants, such as Benjamin Wilcocks about the possibility of shipping opium from Symrna.

STITH, GRIFFIN (ca. 1791–1838). Merchant, born in Virginia and settled in Baltimore. Stith established the firm of Issaverdes, Stith and Company in Smyrna in 1827, and was one of the principal American merchants there. His international partnership (the other two partners were Greek) imported coffee, tea, sugar, spices, cotton, and rum to Turkey and exported raisins, figs, sultanas, madder, opium, olive oil, sponges, and wool. *Reference*: Papers, Dallam Collection, Maryland Historical Society, Baltimore.

STODDARD, CHARLES WARREN (1843–1909). Author, born August 7, 1843, in Rochester, New York, and moved with his family to San Francisco in 1855. After 1867 Stoddard traveled widely, made two trips to Hawaii and one to Tahiti between 1868 and 1873, and traveled in Europe. He traveled in Egypt and Palestine in 1876–1877, and wrote *Mashallah! A Flight into Egypt* (New York, 1881) and *A Cruise Under the Crescent: From Suez to San Marco* (Chicago, 1898). Died April 23, 1909, in Monterey, California. *References*: *ACAB*; *DAB*; Robert L. Gale, *Charles Warren Stoddard* (Boise, Idaho, 1977); *NCAB* 7:116; *NYT*, April 25, 1909; and *WWWA*.

STODDARD, DAVID TAPPAN (1818–1857). Missionary, born December 2, 1818, in Northampton, Massachusetts. Stoddard graduated from Williams and Yale colleges and Andover Theological Seminary, and was ordained in 1843. He was a missionary under the American Board of Commissioners for Foreign Missions (ABCFM),* and served in the Nestorian Mission in Persia from 1843 until his death. He assisted Justin Perkins* in translating the Bible into modern Syriac and was head of a boys' school in Urmia. He prepared *Grammar of the Modern Syriac Language as Spoken in Oroomiah, Persia, and in Koordistan* (New Haven, Conn., 1855). He wrote *Narrative of the Revival of Religion Among the Nestorians of Persia* (Boston, 1848) and articles on meteorology. Died January 22, 1857, in Urmia, Persia. *References*: Briggs Family Papers, Schlesinger Library on the History of Women in America, Radcliffe College, Cambridge, Massachusetts; *ACAB*; *AndoverTS*; *DAB*; *EM*; and *NCAB* 4:292.

STONE, CHARLES POMEROY (1824–1887). Soldier, born September 30, 1824, in Greenfield, Massachusetts. Stone graduated from the U.S. Military Academy in 1845 and served in the Mexican War and in the Union Army during the Civil War. From 1865 to 1869 he was an engineer and superintendent of the Dover Mining Company in Goochland County, Virginia. He served in the Egyptian Army as chief of the General Staff and as lieutenant general from 1870 and 1883. He organized and collated many surveys of the Sudan and superintended the preparation of the great map of Africa published by the Egyptian General Staff in 1877. He was at the side of the Khedive Muhammad Tawfik throughout the revolt of 1882. He returned to the United States in 1883, and became managing and construction engineer for the laying of the foundations of the Statue of Liberty in New York Harbor. Died January 24, 1887, in New York City. His daughter, **FANNY**, wrote an account of life in Cairo during the 'Arabi Revolt in the June 1884 issue of *Century* Magazine. *References*: *ACAB*; Frank J. Cox, "The Suez Canal Incident of 1874," *Cahiers d'Histoire Egyptienne* 4 (1952): 193–204; "Arabi and Stone: Egypt's First Military Rebellion," *Cashiers d'Historie Egyptienne* 8 (1956): 155–175; *DAB*; *Hesseltine*; John Luther, "Stone of Egypt," *AWM* 23 (January-February 1972): 14–19; *NCAB* 11:216; *WAMB*; and *WWWA*.

STORM, WILLIAM HAROLD (1901–   ). Medical missionary, born in Hope, New Jersey. Storm graduated from the University of Pennsylvania and its medical school and served in the Arabian Mission* from 1926 to 1966. In 1935–1936 he made a 5,000-mile journey from Bahrein across Arabia via Riyadh to the Red Sea, toured Hadramaut in 1935, and made a survey of leprosy in the Arabian Peninsula. He wrote *Whither Arabia? A Survey of Missionary Opportunity* (London, 1938). His wife, **IDA ADAMS (PATERSON) STORM (1894–1971)**, a missionary nurse, was born November 27, 1894, in Belfast, Ireland, and studied at Randolph Macon Woman's College, the University of Virginia, Cornell University, and the Medical College of Virginia School of Nursing. She served as a teacher in the Southern Baptist Mission in China from 1921 to 1928 and was secretary of the Babtist Mission from 1928–1932. She served in the Arabian Mission from 1936 to 1966 and wrote *Highways in the Desert* (Nashville, Tenn., 1950). Died October 17, 1971, in Port Charlotte, Florida. *Reference*: *HDRCA*.

STRAUS, NATHAN (1848–1931). Businessman and philanthropist, born January 31, 1848, in Otterberg, Rhenish Bavaria, and brought to the United States in 1854. Straus joined his father's firm, became a partner in Macy's department store, and established Abraham and Sons department store. He visited Palestine five times. There he established a home economics school for girls in 1912, a health bureau, the Pasteur Institute, child-health welfare stations, and the Nathan and Lina Straus Health Centers. Died January 11, 1931, in New York City. His wife, **LINA GUTHERZ STRAUS** (1854–1930), philanthropist, was born April 20, 1854, in Mannheim, Germany, and came to the United States in 1875. She took an active part in her husband's many philanthropies, particularly in the preparation and distribution of pasteurized milk. They established soup kitchens in Jerusalem in 1912, took American-trained nurses to Jerusalem in 1913, and planned and built the Nathan and Lina Straus Health Centers in Palestine. Died May 4, 1930, in Mamaroneck, New York. *References*: Papers, New York Public Library; *ACAB*; *DAB*; *EJ*; *NCAB* 22:47; *NYT*, January 12, 1931; and *WWWA*.

STRAUS, OSCAR SOLOMON (1850–1926). Merchant, diplomat, and Jewish communal leader, born December 22, 1850, in Otterburg, Bavaria, and came to the United States in 1854. Straus graduated from Columbia College and Columbia Law School and practiced law in New York City from 1873 to 1881. In 1881 he became a partner in L. Straus and Sons, merchants. He was minister to Turkey from 1887 to 1890 and again from 1898 to 1900, and ambassador to Turkey from 1909 to 1910. He was involved in problems of missionary rights, protection of naturalized Americans, and issues of "dollar diplomacy." He was American representative to the International Court in the Hague from 1902 to 1926 and secretary of commerce and labor from 1906 to 1908. He was the Progressive candidate for governor of New York in 1912. Died May 3, 1926, in New York City. *References*: Papers, Manuscript Division, Library of Congress; *ACAB*; Naomi W. Cohen, "Ambassador Straus in Turkey, 1909–1910: A Note on Dollar Diplomacy," *Mississippi Valley Historical Review* 45 (1959): 632–642; *A Dual Heritage: The Public Career of Oscar S. Straus* (Philadelphia, 1969); *DAB*; *NCAB* 40:60; *NYT*, May 4, 1926; and *WWWA*.

SULLIVAN, WILLIAM H(EALY) (1922–   ). Diplomat, born October 12, 1922 in Cranston, Rhode Island. Sullivan graduated from Brown University and the Fletcher School of Law and Diplomacy, and served in the navy during World War II. He entered the foreign service in 1947; was political adviser to General Douglas MacArthur during the Korean War; U.N. adviser in the Bureau of Far

Eastern Affairs from 1960 to 1963; ambassador to Laos from 1964 to 1969; deputy in the final peace negotiations to end the Vietnam War; deputy assistant secretary of state for East Asia and Pacific Affairs from 1969 to 1973; ambassador to the Philippines from 1973 to 1977; and ambassador to Iran from 1977 to 1979. He wrote *Mission to Iran* (New York, 1981) and his autobiography, *Obligato 1939–1979; Notes on a Foreign Service Career* (New York, 1984). He was later president of the American Assembly. *References*: *MENA*; *WWA*.

SUPPLY, **U.S.S.** A ship-rigged sailing vessel. In 1847, under the command of Lieutenant William Francis Lynch,* it carried equipment and stores to be used in the expedition to explore the Dead Sea. The *Supply* cruised the eastern Mediterranean and returned to the United States in 1848. In 1855–1856, under the command of Lieutenant David Dixon Porter,* it was again in the Middle East and transported camels to the United States. It made a second trip to the Middle East for this purpose in 1857. *Reference*: *DANES*.

SUYDAM, JAMES AUGUSTUS (1819–1865). Painter, born March 27, 1819, in New York City. After a decade in business, Suydam turned to painting and studied under Miner Kilbourne Kellogg.* From 1842 to 1845 he traveled throughout Europe, and with Kellogg, he traveled in Greece, Turkey, and elsewhere in the Middle East. On his return to the United States, he established a studio in New York City. Died September 15, 1865, at North Conway, New Hampshire. *Reference*: John I. H. Baur, "A Tonal Realist: James Suydam," *The Art Quarterly* 13 (1950): 221–227.

SWEENEY, ZACHARY TAYLOR (1849–1926). Clergyman, lecturer, and educator, born February 10, 1849, in Liberty, Kentucky. Sweeney graduated from Eureka College and Indiana Asbury College (now Depauw University). He was a pastor in Kansas City and Paris, Illinois, and in Columbus, Indiana, from 1872 to 1897, chancellor at Butler College, editor-in-chief of *Central Christian*, and commissioner of fisheries, game and birds for Indiana. He traveled to the Middle East in 1886 and wrote of his experience in *Under Ten Flags* (Cincinnati, 1888). He was consul in Constantinople in 1890–1891, was Ottoman commissioner at the World's Columbia Exposition in 1893, and prepared a report on sheep and wool in Asiatic Turkey. Died February 4, 1926, in Columbus, Indiana. *References*: *IAB*; Lester G. McAllister, *Z. T. Sweeney: Preacher and Peacemaker* (St. Louis, 1968); *NCAB* 20:279; and *WWWA*.

SWEENY, CHARLES (1882–1963). Soldier of fortune, born January 26, 1882, in San Francisco. Sweeny studied at Notre Dame University and the U.S. Military Academy. He fought in the Spanish-American War and early in World War I joined the French Foreign Legion, becoming the first American ever to earn a commission in the legion. He later fought with the Polish Army and served with Ataturk in the Turkish revolution. In 1925 he was hired by the French government to organize a special squadron of volunteer flyers, the Escadrille Cherifienne,* to fight against Abd el Karim in Morocco. After several months, the squadron was disbanded. He fought for the loyalists in the Spanish Civil War, served in the French Foreign Legion during World War II, organized the "Eagle Squadron" in the Royal Air Force, and joined the U.S. Army Air Corps in 1942. He settled in Salt Lake City in 1944. Died February 27, 1963, in Salt Lake City. *Reference*: *The Salt Lake Tribune*, February 28, 1963.

SWEET, LOUIS E. ELIZABETH (1916–   ). Anthropologist, born October 1, 1916, in Ypsilanti, Michigan. Sweet graduated from Eastern Michigan University and the University of Michigan. She was associate professor at Indiana State College from 1960 to 1963 and at the State University of New York at Binghamton from 1963 to 1971, and was professor of anthropology at the University of Manitoba, Winnipeg, after 1971. She conducted ethnographic field research in Syria in 1953–1954, in the Arab States of the Persian Gulf in 1958–1959, and in Lebanon in 1964–1965. She wrote *Tell Toqaan: A Syrian Village* (Ann Arbor, Mich., 1960) and edited *Peoples and Cultures of the Middle East* (New York, 1970). *References*: AMWS.

SWIFT, JOHN FRANKLIN (1829–1891). Lawyer and diplomat, born February 28, 1829, in Bowling Green, Missouri, moved to San Francisco in 1852, studied law, and was admitted to the bar in 1857. Swift practiced law in San Francisco, became a member of the lower house of the legislature in 1863, and registrar of the land office in San Francisco from 1865 to 1867. He traveled to the Middle East in 1867–1868 and wrote *Going to Jericho* (New York, 1868). He was again a member of the state legislature, unsuccessful candidate for governor in 1880, member of a commission to renegotiate a treaty with China in 1880, and minister to Japan from 1889 until his death. Died March 10, 1891, in Tokyo. *References*: DAB; DADH; NCAB 18:405; and WWWA.

SWINGLE, WALTER TENNYSON (1871–1952). Botanist, born January 8, 1871, in Canaan, Wayne County, Pennsylvania. Swingle graduated from Kansas State Agricultural College, and studied in Bonn and Leipzig. He joined the U.S. Department of Agriculture in 1891, became an agricultural explorer in 1898, and was later senior and principal physiologist in the Bureau of Plant Industry. He studied date culture in Algeria, Tunis, and Morocco, and the culture of the Smyrna fig in Algeria and Asia Minor in 1899. He collected figs and supplied the fig wasps, and was largely responsible for the successful introduction of the date palm from Algeria to the United States in 1900. He explored for plants in other parts of Asia, particularly in China, and collected Chinese books for the Library of Congress. He retired from the Department of Agriculture in 1941 and was a consultant in tropical botany at the University of Miami until his death. Died January 19, 1952, in Washington, D.C. *References*: NCAB 54:13; *NYT*, January 20, 1952; *Science* 118 (September 11, 1953): 288–289; and WWWA.

SYRIA MISSION. Established in Beirut in 1824 by the American Board of Commissioners for Foreign Missions (ABCFM).* The work in Syria began in 1848. The mission was transferred to the Presbyterian Church in the USA Board of Foreign Missions* in 1870. U.S. missionaries were expelled from Syria in 1963, and the work was transferred to the National Evangelical Synod of Syria and Lebanon. *References*: Syria and Lebanon Mission records, 1834–1971, Presbyterian Historical Society Collections, Philadelphia; A. L. Tibawi, *American Interests in Syria, 1800–1901: A Study of Educational, Literary and Religious Work* (Oxford, 1966).

SYRIAN PROTESTANT COLLEGE. *See* American University of Beirut.

SZOLD, HENRIETTA (1860–1945). Zionist leader, born December 21, 1860, in Baltimore. Szold was involved in Jewish community work and was editorial secretary of the Jewish Publications Society from 1893 to 1916. One of the founders of Hadassah* in 1912, she went to Palestine in 1920 as the American representative on the American Zionist Medical Unit's* executive committee. She became its director in 1922, directed the Nurses' Training School, and supervised the health program in the Jewish schools until 1923. She returned to Palestine in 1927 as a member of the Palestine Executive Committee and supervisor of the department of health and education. She then took charge of Youth Aliyah to save the Jewish youth of Germany and continued to work for children and youth until her death. Died February 13, 1945, in Jerusalem. *References*: Papers, Central Zionist Archives, Jerusalem, and American Jewish Archives; *DAB*; Joan Dash, *Summoned to Jerusalem: The Life of Henrietta Szold* (New York, 1979); *EJ*; *NAW*; and *NYT*, February 14, 1945.

T

TALMAGE, T(HOMAS) DE WITT (1832–1902). Clergyman, born January 7, 1832, in Bound Brook, New Jersey. Talmage attended the University of the City of New York, graduated from New Brunswick Theological Seminary, and was ordained in 1856. He was a pastor in Belleville, New Jersey, Syracuse, New York, Philadelphia, Brooklyn, and Washington, D.C. He edited *The Christian Herald* from 1890 until his death. He traveled to Palestine in 1899, leading a group of pilgrims, and wrote *From Manger to Throne, Embracing a New life of Jesus Christ, and a History of Palestine and Its People, Including Dr. Talmage's Account of his Journey to, Through and from the Christland* (Philadelphia, 1890). Died April 12, 1902, in Washington, D.C. His autobiography, *T. De Witt Talmage as I Knew Him*, ed. Eleanor Talmage (New York, 1912), appeared after his death. *References*: Papers, Manuscript Division, Library of Congress; *ACAB*; *DAB*; *DARB*; *NCAB* 4:26; Ferenc M. Szasz, "T. DeWitt Talmage: Spiritual Tycoon of the Gilded Age," *Journal of Presbyterian History* 59 (1961): 18–32; and *WWWA*.

TANNER, HENRY OSAWA (1859–1937). Painter, born June 21, 1859, in Pittsburgh and grew up in Philadelphia. Tanner studied at the Pennsylvania Academy of Fine Arts, moved to Atlanta in 1887, and went to live in Paris in 1891. He remained in France for the rest of his life, specializing in paintings on biblical subjects. He visited Palestine in 1897 and wrote about his visit in the June and July 1909 issues of *World's Work*. He visited Palestine again in 1897. He served with the American Red Cross* in France during World War I. Died May 25, 1937, in Paris. *References*: *ACAB*; *DAB*; Carroll Greene, Jr., *The Art of Henry O. Tanner (1859–1937)* (Washington, D.C., 1969); Lynda R. Hartigan, *Sharing Traditions: Five Black Artists in Nineteenth-century America* (Washington, D.C., 1985), pp. 99–116; Marcia M. Mathews, *Henry Osawa Tanner: American Artist* (Chicago, 1969); *NCAB* 3:89; and *WWWA*.

TAPLINE. *See* Trans-Arabian Pipeline.

TARLER, G(EORGE) CORNELL (1879–1945). Diplomat, born October 4, 1876, in New York City. Tarler graduated from the City College of New York and Columbia University, and practiced law in New York City from 1899 to 1908. He was secretary of legation in Cuba, secretary of legation and consul general in Bangkok, Siam, and secretary of legation in Uruguay and Paraguay. He was secretary of embassy and then first secretary in Constantinople; in charge of diplomatic interests and nations of the Allied Powers in Turkey from 1914 to 1917; and chargé d'affaires at the time of the break of relations between the United States and Turkey in 1917. He was first secretary in Rio de Janiero, but resigned in 1922 and practiced law until 1939. Died December 26, 1945, in New York City. *References*: *NCAB* 37:173; *NYT*, December 28, 1945; and *WWWA*.

TARSUS COLLEGE. *See* St. Paul's College.

TAYLOR, BAYARD (JAMES) (1825–1878). Author, traveler, and diplomat, born January 11, 1825, at Kennett Square, Chester County, Pennsylvania. From 1844 to 1848 Taylor was apprenticed to a printer in West Chester. In 1847 he moved to New York City where he began to write, and in 1848 he began his association with the *New York Tribune*. He traveled in the Middle East in 1852 and wrote *The Land of the Saracens; or, Pictures of Palestine, Asia Minor, Sicily and Spain* (New York, 1854). He visited the Sudan, made a journey through Nubia to Khartoum, and continued 250 miles south to the island of Aba on the White Nile. He wrote *A Journey to Central Africa; or, Life and Landscapes from Egypt to the Negro Kingdoms of the White Nile* (New York, 1854). He accompanied Commodore Matthew C. Perry's expedition to Japan and visited Scandinavia, Greece, and Russia. In 1862–1863 he was secretary of legation in St. Petersburg. He wrote *Egypt and Iceland in the Year 1874* (New York, 1874). He was minister to Germany in 1878. Died December 19, 1878 in Berlin. *References*: *DAB*; *DADH*; Richmond C. Heatty, *Bayard Taylor: Laurette of the Gilded Age* (Norman, Okla., 1936); Paul C. Wermuth, *Bayard Taylor* (New York, 1973); *NCAB* 3:454; and *WWWA*.

TELEMACHUS. Brigantine belonging to John Crowninshield of Salem. The ship arrived in Constantinople in 1809 and was probably the first American merchant ship to drop anchor in the Golden Horn. *Reference*: Samuel E. Morison, "Forcing the Dardanelles in 1810, with Some Account of the Early Levant Trade of Massachusetts," *New England Quarterly* 1 (1928): 208–225.

TEMPLE, DANIEL. Missionary, born December 23, 1789, in Reading, Massachusetts. Temple graduated from Dartmouth College and Andover Theological Seminary, and was ordained in 1821. The American Board of Commissioners for Foreign Missions (ABCFM)* appointed him a missionary to Palestine, but he remained in Malta from 1822 until 1833. He prepared books and tracts that were printed on the printing press he brought with him. He was transferred to Smyrna in 1833 with the printing presses and printing materials, and in 1837 he began publishing a monthly magazine in Greek. He returned to the United States in 1844 and was a pastor in Concord, New Hampshire, and Phelps, New York. Died August 9, 1851, in Reading, Massachusetts. *References*: *ACAB*; *EM*; and Daniel H. Temple, *Life and Letters of Rev. Daniel Temple* (Boston, 1855).

TENNESSEE U.S.S. Armored cruiser. The ship arrived in Smyrna in November 1912 to protect American citizens and property during the First Balkan War. It left in May 1913. *Reference*: *DANES*.

TERHUNE, ALBERT PAYSON (1872–1942). Author, born December 31, 1872, in Newark, New Jersey, son of Marion Harland.* Terhune graduated from Columbia College. He traveled on horseback through Syria and Egypt in 1893–1894, and he wrote *Syria from the Saddle* (New York, 1896). In his novel *Najib* (New York, 1925), he used Syria for the setting. He served on the staff of the *New York Evening World* from 1894 to 1916, and he was park commissioner of the state of New Jersey from 1925. He was famous for his many dog books. He wrote an autobiography, *To the Best of My Memory* (New York, 1930). Died February 18, 1942, in Pompton Lakes, New Jersey. *References*: *CA*; *DLB*; *NCAB* 34:102; *NYT*, February 19, 1942; Kurt Unkelbach, *Albert Payson Terhune, the Master of Sunnybank* (New York, 1972); and *WWWA*.

TERHUNE, MARY VIRGINIA HAWES. *See* Harland, Marion.

TEVIS, CHARLES CARROL (1828–1900). Soldier of fortune, born Washington Carrol Tevis on February 22, 1828, in Philadelphia. Tevis graduated from the U.S. Military Academy in 1849 and was commissioned second lieutenant in the mounted rifles. He resigned in 1850, entered the Turkish Army under the name of Nessim Bey, served as a major in the Turkish irregular cavalry until 1854, and participated in the Crimean War. He lived in Paris from 1854 until 1862, when he returned to the United States and served in the Union Army during the Civil War. In 1868 he became secret Chamberlain of the Cloak and Sword to Pope Louis IX, and he served in the French Army during the Franco-Prussian War of 1870–1871. He served in the Egyptian Army from 1872 to 1873 as a commandant of a military school. He settled in Paris in 1875 but went back to Turkey in 1874 and 1877 to serve in the Turkish Army during its wars. Died September 19, 1900, in Paris. *References*: *CWD*; *Hesseltine*; and *RAGMA*, 1901.

THAYER, WILLIAM S(YDNEY) (1830–1864). Consul. Thayer served as consul general in Egypt from 1861 to 1864. Died on May 10, 1864, in Alexandria, Egypt. *References*: "Diary." Ms., New York Historical Society; Papers, Manuscript Division, Library of Congress; and Gordon Waterfield, *Lucie Duff Gordon in England, South Africa and Egypt* (London, 1937), ch. 30.

THOMAS, JOSEPH (1811–1891). Lexicographer, born September 23, 1811, in Ledyard, Cayuga County, New York. Thomas graduated from Rensselaer Polytechnic Institute, and attended Yale College and the School of Medicine of the University of Pennsylvania. From 1854 to 1871 he was associated with J. B. Lippincot and Company as compiler and editor of a series of reference books. In order to improve his knowledge of the pronunciation of Oriental proper and place names, he toured Egypt and Palestine in 1852–1853, and wrote *Travels in Egypt and Palestine* (Philadelphia, 1853). In 1857 he made a similar trip to India to study Sanskrit. He was later involved in the founding of Swarthmore College, serving as professor of English from 1874 to 1887. Died December 24, 1891, in Philadelphia. *References*: *ACAB*; *DAB*; *DAMB*; *NCAB* 11:53; and *WWWA*.

THOMAS, LOWELL (JACKSON) (1892–1981). Traveler and author, born April 6, 1892, in Woodington, Ohio, and grew up in Cripple Creek, Colorado. Thomas graduated from the University of Northern Indiana (now Valparaiso), Kent College of Law, and Princeton University. He was a reporter in Cripple Creek and Victor, Colorado, and in Chicago. He went to Egypt during World War I, was one of three reporters covering General Edmund Allenby's Palestine campaign, and the only reporter to accompany T. E. Lawrence. He wrote *With Lawrence in Arabia* (New York, 1924) and *With Allenby in the Holy Land* (London, 1938). He visited Afghanistan and wrote *Beyond the Khyber Pass into Forbidden Afghanistan* (New York, 1925). Thomas was a broadcaster and radio commentator on CBS Radio from 1930 until 1976. He wrote an autobiography, *Good Evening Everybody: From Cripple Creek to Samartkanad* (New York, 1976). Died August 29, 1981, in Pawling, New York. *References*: *Biography News* 1 (July 1974): 863; Norman R. Bowen, ed., *Lowell Thomas: The Stranger Everyone Knows* (Garden City, N.Y., 1968); *CA*; *NYT*, October 22, 1970, February 5, 1978, August 30, 1981; and *WWWA*.

THOMPSON, A(LFRED) WORDSWORTH (1840–1896). Painter, born May 26, 1840, in Baltimore. Thompson went to Paris in 1861 to study art and traveled in Europe. He returned to the United States in 1868 and settled in New York City. In 1882–1883 he traveled with his wife in North Africa. Some of his more famous paintings are of scenes in Morocco and Tangier. Died August 28, 1896, in Summit, New Jersey. His wife's diary of their travels is in the New York Historical Society. *References*: *ACAB*; *DAB*; *NYHSD*; and *WWWA*.

THOMPSON, JOSEPH PARRISH (1819–1879). Clergyman and editor, born August 7, 1819, in Philadelphia. Thompson graduated from Yale College and from Andover and New Haven theological seminaries, and was ordained in 1840. He was a pastor in New Haven and New York City from 1845 to 1871, helped edit *The Independent* from 1848 to 1852, and was a leader in home missionary work. He made a trip to Egypt and Palestine in 1853 and wrote *Photographic Views of Egypt, Past and Present* (Boston, 1854), which included the music of the Nile boatmen's chant. In 1871 he moved to Germany. Died September 20, 1879, in Berlin. *References: AndoverTS*; *DAB*; *NCAB* 10:132; and *WWWA*.

THOMPSON, LEANDER (1812–1896). Clergyman, born March 7, 1812, in Woburn, Massachusetts. Thompson graduated from Amherst College and Andover Theological Seminary, and was ordained in 1838. He was a missionary under the American Board of Commissioners for Foreign Missions (ABCFM)* in Syria from 1840 to 1843 and wrote about the sects in Syria in *Bibliotheca Sacra*. He was later a pastor in South Hadley Falls, Went Amesbury, and North Woburn, Massachusetts. Died October 18, 1896, in North Woburn, Massachusetts. *References: Amherst*; *AndoverTS*.

THOMS, JOHN SHARON (1871–1913). Medical missionary, born September 27, 1871, in Three Rivers, Michigan. Thoms graduated from the University of Michigan and its medical school. He served in the Arabian Mission* from 1898 to 1913 and opened the Matrah Hospital in Muscat in 1909. Died January 15, 1913, from injuries received in a fall in Matrah, Muscat. His son, **WILLIAM WELLS THOMS (1903–1971)**, medical missionary, was born December 13, 1903, at Garbutt, Genesee County, New York, and graduated from Hope and Kalamazoo colleges and the University of Michigan Medical School. He served in the Arabian Mission from 1930 to 1970, traveled in Qatar in 1934, and visited Riyadh in 1937. He went to Oman in 1939 and was head of the Knox Memorial Hospital in Matrah. Died October 25, 1971, in New Orleans. *Reference: HDRCA*.

THOMSON, WILLIAM MCCLURE (1806–1894). Missionary, born December 31, 1806, in Spring Dale, Ohio, near Cincinnati. Thomson graduated from Miami University and Princeton Theological Seminary, and was ordained in 1831. He came to Syria in 1833 as a missionary under the American Board of Commissioners for Foreign Missions (ABCFM).* In 1834 he moved to Jerusalem, was imprisoned as a spy, and returned to Beirut in the same year. He opened the first boys' boarding school in the Ottoman Empire in Beirut in 1835. In 1843 he was transferred to Abieh in Lebanon, and in 1850 he opened a mission station in Hasbeiyeh. He wrote *The Land and the Book; or, Biblical Illustrations Drawn from the Manners and Customs, Scenes and Scenery of the Holy Land* (New York, 1858), based on his extensive travels in Palestine and Syria. The book became a best seller. In 1858 he returned to Beirut, remaining there until 1876. He lived in New York City and published the second edition of his book in 1880–1885. In 1890 he moved to Denver. Died April 8, 1894, in Denver. *References*: *ACAB*; *DAB*; *NCAB* 11:57; *OAB*; and *WWWA*.

THORNBURG, MAX WESTON (1892–1967). Engineer, born October 3, 1892, in Los Angeles County, California. Thornburg graduated from the University of California, studied at the University of Grenoble, and served in the army in World War I. He joined Standard Oil Company of California in 1920, was chief engineer of the manufacturing department from 1924 to 1929, manager of the Richmond refinery from 1929 to 1931, and chairman of the board of engineers from 1931 to 1936. He went to the Middle East in 1936 as vice president of the Bahrain Petroleum Company (BAPCO)* in Bahrain. He was special assistant to the undersecretary of state and petroleum adviser to the State Department from 1941 to 1943. In 1947 he directed the economic survey of Turkey for the Twentieth Century Fund, was co-author of *Turkey: An Economic Appraisal* (New York, 1949), and assisted in the design of a Turkish petroleum law. From 1948 to 1951 he helped prepare Iran's first seven-year plan, and in 1954–1955 he helped Turkey prepare an industrial plan. He was later professor of political science at the University of California. He wrote *People and Policy in the Middle East: A Study of Social and Political Change as a Basis for United States Policy* (New York, 1964). *References*: *BRDS*; Linda W. Qain-Magami, "Max Thornburg and the Quest for Corporate Oil Policy: An Experiment in Cooperation," Ph.D. diss., Texas A&M University, 1986.

THURBER, CHRISTOPHER CARSON (1880–1930). Social worker, born May 19, 1880, in Norwich, Connecticut. Thurber graduated from Trinity College (Hartford). In 1900 he became a social worker in Danbury, New Hampshire, among lumbermen in Canada and soft coal miners in Pennsylvania and West Virginia. From 1912 to 1917 he was superintendent of a home for homeless boys in Covington, Virginia. He worked for the Red Cross in army camps from 1917 to 1919 and was social director of the U.S. Public Health Service in Greenville, South Carolina, from 1919 to 1921. He joined Near East Relief* in 1921, was head of an orphanage in Sivas, and later director of the Constantinople unit of Near East Relief until his return to the United States in 1924. From 1926 until his death, he was director of work for Near East Relief in Greece. Died May 31, 1930, in Athens. *Reference*: *DAB*.

TICONDEROGA, **U.S.S.** Screw sloop-of-war. In November 1878 the ship embarked on a cruise around the world, Commodore Robert Wilson Shufeldt* commanding. It was a commercial expedition, intended to expand existing trade relations and establish new ones. It was probably the first American man-of-war in the Persian Gulf. *Reference*: Kenneth J. Hagan, "Showing the Flag in the Indian Ocean," in *America Spreads Her Sails: U.S. Seapower in the 19th Century*, ed. Claytor R. Barrows, Jr. (Annapolis, Md., 1973), pp. 153–175.

TIDRICK, RALPH W. (1875–1914). Missionary, born April 13, 1875, in Bedford, Iowa. Tidrick graduated from Tarkio College and studied agriculture at Iowa State College. He became a missionary under the United Presbyterian Church of North America Board of Foreign Missions* in the Sudan in 1903, worked in the mission station on the Sobat River, and was in charge of industrial work at Doleib Hill, where he died after being mauled by a lion, April 21, 1914. *Reference*: Hill.

TIFFANY, LOUIS COMFORT (1848–1933). Painter, born February 18, 1848, in New York City. Tiffany began to study painting in 1866 and went to study in Paris in 1868. He traveled in North Africa in 1870, visited it again in 1875, and made a trip to Egypt in 1908, including a yacht trip up the Nile. He exhibited paintings from these travels, and he became famous for his paintings of eastern scenes. He founded Tiffany Glass Company in 1885 and designed stained glass, jewelry, furnishings, and interiors. Died January 17, 1933, in New York City. *References*: *ACAB*; *DAB*; *Louis Comfort Tiffany: The Paintings* (New York, 1979); *NCAB* 36:167; *NYT*, January 18, 1933; and *WWWA*.

TODD, MABEL LOOMIS (1856–1932). Author, born November 10, 1856, in Cambridge, Massachusetts. Mabel Loomis married the astronomer David Peck Todd, lived in Amherst after 1881, and edited Emily Dickinson's poems and letters. She accompanied her husband on his astronomical expeditions, including expeditions to Libya in 1900 and 1905, and wrote an account of the trips to Libya in *Tripoli the Mysterious* (Boston, 1912). Died October 14, 1932, in Hog Island, Muscongus, Maine. *References*: Papers, Sterling Library, Yale University, New Haven, Connecticut; *DAB*; *NAW*; *NCAB* 41:97; *WWWA*; and Polly Longsworth, *Austin and Mabel* (New York, 1984).

TORCH, OPERATION. Code name for the invasion of Northwest Africa on November 8, 1942. Some 80,000 Americans participated in the invasion which took place in three locations: Casablanca, Oran, and Algiers. Fighting lasted until November 11, 1942. *References*: William B. Breuer, *Operation Torch: The Allied Gamble to Invade North Africa* (New York, 1985); Arthur Layton Funk, *The Politics of Torch: The Allied Landings and the Algiers Putsch, 1942* (Lawrence, Kan. 1974); George F. Howe, *Northwest Africa: Seizing the Initiative in the West* (Washington, D.C., 1957); and Samuel E. Morison, *Operations in North African Waters October 1942–June 1943* (Boston, 1959).

TORREY, CHARLES CUTLER (1863–1956). Orientalist, born December 20, 1863, in East Hardwick, Vermont. Torrey graduated from Bowdoin College, Andover Theological Seminary, and the University of Strasbourg. He was an instructor and professor at Andover from 1892 until 1900, and professor of Semitic languages and literatures at Yale University from 1900 until his retirement in 1932. He established and was the first director of the American School of Archaeology (later the American Schools of Oriental Research*) in Jerusalem in 1900–1901. He conducted archaeological excavations in Sidon in 1901 and published his account in 1920. Died November 12, 1956, in Chicago. *References*: *AndoverTS*; *BASOR* 132 (1953):608; *DAB*; *NCAB* 42:92; and *NYT*, November 13, 1956.

TOULMIN, JOHN E(DWIN) (1902–1968). Banker, born November 1, 1902, in Brookline, Massachusetts. Toulmin graduated from Harvard University. He was employed by the First National Bank of Boston from 1925 to 1967, becoming vice president in 1932 and senior vice president in 1947. He was vice chairman of the board and head of the commercial loan division from 1959 until his retirement in 1967. From 1942 until 1945 he served as commanding officer of the Office of Strategic Services for the Balkans and the Middle East, with headquarters in Cairo. Died April 9, 1968, in Boston. *References*: *NYT*, April 12, 1968; *WWWA*.

TRACY, CHARLES CHAPIN (1838–1917). Missionary educator, born October 31, 1838, in East Smithfield, Bradford County, Pennsylvania. Tracy graduated from Williams College and Union Theological Seminary, and was ordained in 1867. He became a missionary under the American Board of Commissioners for Foreign Missions (ABCFM)* in Turkey in 1868, was stationed at Marsovan, and taught at the Marsovan Theological Seminary. In 1871 he was transferred to Constantinople, and was engaged in educational and literary work until 1873 when he returned to the seminary in Marsovan. He founded and developed Anatolia College* in 1866, becoming its first president until 1913. Tracy returned to the United States at the beginning of World War I. He wrote *Letters to Families* (Constantinople, 1872), *Myra; or, Child's Story of Missionary Life* (Boston, 1877), and *Talks on the Veranda in a Far-way Land* (Boston, 1893). Died April 19, 1917, in Los Angeles. *References*: *ACAB*; George E. White, *Charles Chapin Tracy, Missionary, Philanthropist, Educator, First President of Anatolia College, Marsovan, Turkey* (Boston, 1919); *NCAB*; 11:103; *NYT*, April 21, 1917; and *WWWA*.

TRANS-ARABIAN PIPELINE COMPANY (TAPLINE). Firm incorporated in Delaware in 1945 to obtain concessions for pipelines in Saudi Arabia, Jordan, Lebanon, and Syria. Owned by Texas Company, Standard Oil Company of California, Standard Oil Company (New Jersey), and Socony-Vacuum Oil Company, it built a 754-mile pipeline from Qaisumah in Saudi Arabia, to Sidon, Lebanon. The work began in 1947 and was completed in 1950. *References*: Gilbert Jenkins, *Oil Economists' Handbook*, 4th ed. (London, 1986).

TRASHER, LILLIAN (HUNT) (1887–1961). Missionary, born September 27, 1887, in Jacksonville, Florida. Trasher went to Egypt in 1910 and founded the Assiut Orphanage which she directed until her death. She became an Assemblies of God* missionary in 1919, and the orphanage was later supported and maintained by the Assemblies of God. She wrote *The Birth of Assiut Orphanage* (Springfield, Mo., 1951). Died December 17, 1961, in Assiut, Egypt. Her letters were excerpted in *Letters from Lillian* (Springfield, Mo., 1983). The orphanage was renamed the Lillian Trasher Memorial Orphanage. *References*: Jerome Beatty, *Americans All Over* (New York, 1940), pp. 219–230; Beth P. Howell, *Lady on a Donkey* (New York, 1960); and Lester F. Sumerall, *Lillian Trasher, the Nile Mother* (Springfield, Mo., 1951).

TREVER, JOHN CECIL (1915–   ). Biblical scholar, born November 26, 1915, in Milwaukee, Wisconsin. Trever graduated from the University of Southern California and Yale University. He was on the faculty of the College of the Bible at Drake University from 1944 to 1947; executive director of the Department of English Bible at the National Council of Churches, Chicago, from 1948 to 1953; professor of religion at Morris Harvey College from 1953 to 1959; and professor at Baldwin-Wallace College from 1959 to 1975. He photographed the Dead Sea Scrolls in Jerusalem in 1948, and he assisted Millar Burrows* in publishing *The Dead Sea Scrolls of St. Mark's Monastery* (New Haven, Conn., 1950). He became the director of the Dead Sea Scrolls Project at the School of Theology in Claremont College in 1975, and consultant on biblical flora for the *Interpreter's Dictionary of the Bible* (New York, 1962). He wrote *The Untold Story of Qumran* (Westwood, N.J., 1965), of which *The Dead Sea Scrolls: A Personal Account* (Grand Rapids, Mich., 1978) was a revised edition. *References*: CA; DAS.

TRIPOLITANIAN WAR. *See* Barbary Wars.

TROWBRIDGE, TILLMAN CONKLIN (1831–1888). Missionary, born January 28, 1831, in Michigan. Trowbridge graduated from the University of Michigan and Union Theological Seminary. He was a missionary under the American Board of Commissioners for Foreign Missions (ABCFM)* in Turkey from 1856 until his death. He made a long tour, with George Washington Dunmore,* through northern Armenia, and was then placed in charge of the city work of Constantinople until 1868, when he was transferred to Marash to teach in the theological seminary. In 1876 he became president of Central Turkey College at Aintab. He was a student of Turkish history and wrote *Occasional Papers in Regard to Turkey* (New York, 1874). Died July 20, 1888, in Marash, Turkey. *Reference*: EM.

TROYE, EDWARD (1808–1874). Painter, born Edouard de Troy July 12, 1808, in Lausanne, Switzerland, and came to the United States in 1828. Troye traveled in the southern states painting race horses, and was a professor of drawing and French at Spring Hill College (near Mobile, Alabama). In 1855 he accompanied Alexander Keene Richards* to the Middle East. After his return,

Troye exhibited his paintings in several cities and described them in *The Dead Sea and the Ruins of Sodom and Gomorrah* (New York, 1858). Died July 25, 1874, in Georgetown, Kentucky. *References*: "Journal in Europe and the Middle East, 1855–1856," Ms. in private hands; J. Winston Coleman, Jr., *Three Kentucky Artists: Hart, Prince, Troye* (Lexington, Ky., 1974); *DAB*; Alexander Mackay-Smith, *The Race Horses of America 1832–1872: Portraits and Other Paintings by Edward Troye* (Saratoga Springs, N.Y., 1981); *NYHSD*; and *WWWA*.

TRUMAN DOCTRINE. In March 1947 Britain notified the U.S. that it must relinquish its position in the Eastern Mediterranean. On March 12, 1947 President Harry Truman sent Congress a message promulgating his doctrine supporting nations that were resisting Soviet pressure and containing the spread of Communism. President Truman asked Congress for $400 million in economic and military assistance for Greece and Turkey to enable them to resist pressure or aggression from the outside. *References*: Cecil V. Crabb, Jr., *The Doctrines of American Foreign Policy: Their Meaning, Role, and Future* (Baton Rouge, La., 1982), ch. 3; *DADH*; *Encyclopedia of American Foreign Policy* (New York, 1978), 3:292–301; and John L. Gaddis, "Was the Truman Doctrine a Real Turning Point?" *Foreign Affairs* 52 (1974): 386–402.

TRUMBULL, HENRY CLAY (1830–1903). Clergyman and author, born June 8, 1830, in Stonington, Connecticut. Trumbull did not attend college and was involved in the railroad business until 1856. He became superintendent of a mission sunday school in 1852, was a missionary for the Connecticut State Sunday School Association from 1858 to 1862, and served as a chaplain in the Civil War. He was later secretary for New England for the American Sunday School Union from 1865 to 1875, and editor of *The Sunday School Times*. He visited Palestine in 1881, was particularly concerned with the location of Kadesh Barnea, and wrote *Kadesh-Barnea: Its Importance and Probable Site, with the Story of a Hunt for It* (New York, 1884), and *Studies in Oriental Social Life and Gleams from the East on the Sacred Page* (Philadelphia, 1894). Died December 9, 1903, in Philadelphia. *References*: *ACAB*; *DAB*; *NCAB* 9:383; and *WWWA*.

TUCK, SOMERVILLE, PINKNEY (1848–1923). Lawyer, born September 24, 1848, in Annapolis, Maryland. Tuck graduated from St. John's College, Annapolis, and the University of Virginia Law School, and practiced law in New York City. In 1882 he was appointed one of the commissioners of the court of the *Alabama* claims. As a special agent of the Department of Justice, he visited the maritime towns of France in 1885 to investigate French spoliation claims. In 1894 he became a judge of the Mixed Courts of Egypt* and in 1897 the presiding judge. In 1908 he became a judge of the court of appeals of the Mixed Courts in Alexandria, remaining there until his retirement in 1920. Died

April 14, 1923, in Mentone, France. *References*; *NCAB* 12:369; *NYT*, April 15, 1923; and *WWWA*.

TURNER, W(ILLIAM) MASON (1835–1877). Physician, born December 15, 1835, in Petersburg, Virginia. Turner graduated from Brown University and the University of Pennsylvania Medical School. He visited Syria and Egypt in 1859 and published his diary, *El-Kuds the Holy; or, Glimpses in the Orient* (Philadelphia, 1861). He practiced medicine in Petersburgh, Virginia, served in the Civil War as a Confederate naval surgeon, and later practiced in Philadelphia. Died October 13, 1877, in Philadelphia. *Reference*: Albert Johannsen, *The House of Beadle and Adams and Its Dime and Nickel Novels: The Story of a Vanished Literature* (Norman, Okla., 1950).

TWAIN, MARK (1935–1910). Author, born Samuel Langhorne Clemens on November 30, 1835, in Florida, Missouri, and grew up in Hannibal, Missouri. Twain was apprenticed to a printer at twelve and worked at a newspaper; he was apprenticed to a steamboat pilot on the Mississippi River from 1856 to 1861. In 1861 he moved to Nevada, worked on the Virginia City *Territorial Enterprise*, moved to San Francisco in 1864, and wrote for the *San Francisco Call* and other papers. In 1867 he went on a trip on the *Quaker City* to the Middle East and wrote letters for the *Alta California* which were later published in *Innocents Abroad* (Hartford, Conn., 1869) with great popular success. It was followed by many of his best known works. Died April 21, 1910, in Redding, Connecticut. *References*: *Traveling with the Innocents Abroad*, ed. Daniel McKeithan (Norman, Okla., 1958); *DAB*; Leon T. Dickinson, ''Marketing a Bestseller: Mark Twain's 'Innocents Abroad,' '' *Papers of the Bibliographical Society of America* 41 (1947): 107–122; Dewey Ganzel, *Mark Twain Abroad: The Cruise of the "Quaker City"* (Chicago, 1968); Steven G. Kellman, ''Mark Twain in the Middle East,'' *Texas Quarterly* 20 (1977): 35–41; *NCAB* 6:24; and Franklin Walker, *Irreverent Pilgrims: Melville, Browne, and Mark Twain in the Holy Land* (Seattle, Wash., 1974), chs. 7–8.

TWEDDLE, HERBERT W.C. (1832– ?). Chemist and oil driller, born in Liverpool, England, and came to the United States in 1853. Tweddle was involved in the refining of oils, soaps, and fats, and the production of cottonseed oil in New York, Providence, St. Louis, and New Orleans; developed a process for the distillation of oils; began to utilize his method in the distillation of petroleum in Pittsburgh in 1862; and took out several patents for distilling petroleum. In 1886 he went to the oil fields of Russia and later to Peru, and was contracted by the Egyptian government as an adviser and superviser of operations. The first American to drill for petroleum in the Middle East, he drilled five wells at Ras Gemsah and one at Jabal Zeit in the Red Sea region of Egypt, all of which were unproductive. *Reference*: *NCAB* 12:463.

TWITCHELL, KARL S(ABEN) (1885–1968). Engineer, born June 7, 1885, in St. Albans, Vermont. Twitchell graduated from the Kingston (Ont.) School of Mines of Queen's University. He was associated with mining operations in California and Idaho, and operated copper mines in Cyprus in support of the British war effort in World War I. He examined mines in Nevada, Idaho, Arizona, and California; was engaged in developing mineral and petroleum concessions; and explored for minerals and petroleum in Cyprus, Ethiopia, Saudi Arabia, Yemen, and Iran. Charles Richard Crane* sent him to Yemen in 1927, investigated water resources in and around the Red Sea coast near Jidda in Saudi Arabia in 1931, and organized the Saudi Arabia. In 1933 he was involved in negotiations with the Saudi Arabian government which led to the granting of the first concession for petroleum exploration in Saudi Arabia to Standard Oil Company of California. In World War II he headed the first U.S. agricultural mission to Saudi Arabia and prepared the report of the mission (Cairo, 1943). He also did advisory work in Iran. He wrote *Saudi Arabia, With an Account of the Development of Its Natural Resources* (Princeton, N.J., 1947; 3rd ed., New York, 1969) and *Keith Arnold in Mining Engineering* (New York, 1955). Died January 7, 1968, in Byron, Connecticut. *References*: Paul C. Merritt, "Karl S. Twitchell: An Interview," *Mining Engineering* 17 (September 1965): 78–83; *NYT*, January 10, 1968.

TYTUS, ROBB DE PEYSTER (1876–1913). Archaeologist, born February 2, 1876, in Asheville, North Carolina. Tytus graduated from Yale College and studied in London, Paris, and Munich. He went to Egypt in 1899–1900, worked at the site of the Palace of Amenopis III at Thebes in 1901–1902, obtained a concession to explore Luxor, and made a number of excavations. He later farmed and raised sheep in Massachusetts, and served in the Massachusetts House of Representatives in 1908 and 1909. Died August 14, 1913, in Saranac Lake, New York. *References*: *NCAB* 47:541; *NYT*, August 16, 1913; and *WWWE*.

U

ULEN AND COMPANY. Construction firm founded by Henry Charles Ulen (1871–1963) in Indianapolis, Indiana in 1901 as the American Light and Water Company. The name was changed in 1921. It was engaged in building and financing large projects in foreign countries. In 1927 it negotiated with the Turkish government for the construction of municipal improvements in Ankara and harbor installations at Samsum and Mersin. It was the major and managing partner in a syndicate which in 1928 contracted to build the Trans-Persian Railway from the Caspian Sea to the Persian Gulf and the port of Bandar Shapur. It carried the work nearly through Dezful, in southwest Persia, when it stopped for lack of funds. *Reference*: *NCAB* 53:49.

UNDERWOOD, BERT ELIAS (1862–1943) and **UNDERWOOD, ELMER JUDSON** (1859–1947). Photographers and businessmen. Bert was born April 29, 1862, in Oxford, Illinois, and graduated from Ottawa (Kan.) University. Elmer was born October 9, 1859, in Fulton County, Illinois, was apprenticed to a printer, and established a printing firm in Ottawa, Kansas, in 1877. Bert began selling stereoscopic views in 1882, and with his brother formed the partnership of Underwood and Underwood, later incorporated. Bert was president of the company until 1925, extended its activities to the Pacific states in 1884, and later opened offices on the East Coast and in many countries in Europe and Asia. The brothers traveled in Palestine and Egypt in 1891 taking stereoscopic pictures. They also worked as news photographers, covering the Greco-Turkish War of 1897 and taking the first war picture published as news. In World War I, Bert commanded the photographic division of the Signal Corps. Bert died December 23, 1943, in Tucson, Arizona, and Elmer died August 17, 1947, in St. Petersburg, Florida. *References*: *Life* 23 (September 8, 1947): 22–24; *MBEP*; *NCAB* 35:47; and *WWWA*.

UNITED CHURCH FOR WORLD MINISTRIES. *See* American Board of Commissioners for Foreign Missions.

UNITED MISSION IN IRAQ. Founded in 1924 as the United Mission in Mesopotamia, succeeding preliminary efforts by Reformed and Presbyterian missionaries in the region. The Reformed Church in America joined with the Presbyterian Church in the U.S.A.* and the Reformed Church in the United States to form the mission, combining personnel and finances. After 1958 the work was restricted to several schools, and in 1967 the mission ceased to function. *Reference*: Records 1920–1967, Presbyterian Historical Society Collections, Philadelphia. *EMCM*.

UNITED MISSION IN MESOPOTAMIA. *See* United Mission in Iraq.

UNITED MISSIONARY CHURCH. Sent its first missionaries to Turkey in 1898. It was reorganized as the United Missionary Society* in 1921, and it joined with the United Orphanage and Mission Society in 1932. *References*: Everek R. Storms, *What God-Hath-Wrought. The Story of the Foreign Missionary Efforts of the United Missionary Church* (Springfield, Ohio, 1948); *History of the United Missionary Church* (Elkhart, Ind., 1958).

UNITED MISSIONARY SOCIETY. The mission board of the United Missionary Church,* organized in 1921 to unite and enlarge the foreign mission work of the church. After World War I, it moved its work to Syria and Lebanon, and established a printing press in Aleppo. It withdrew from the Middle East in 1938 leaving an indigenous church, the Evangelical Spiritual Brotherhood. *Reference*: Everek R. Storms, *What God Hath Wrought. The Story of the Foreign Missionary Efforts of the United Missionary Church* (Springfield, Ohio, 1948).

UNITED PRESBYTERIAN CHURCH OF NORTH AMERICA BOARD OF FOREIGN MISSIONS. Organized in 1866, and began in the work of the Associate Reformed Presbyterian Church and the Associate Presbyterian Church which merged in 1858. The Associate Reformed Church established a mission in 1848 in Damascus, Syria (which was closed in 1878) and in Egypt in 1854. The mission in the Sudan was established in 1900. *References*: Walter N. Jamison, *The United Presbyterian Story: A Centennial Study 1858–1958* (Pittsburgh, 1958); Anna A. Milligan, *Facts and Folks in Our Fields Abroad* (Philadelphia, 1921).

U.S. ARMY FORCES IN THE MIDDLE EAST (USAFIME). Established in 1941 as the U.S. Military North African Mission, with headquarters in Cairo; name changed in 1942. The mission was concerned with the construction of bases and installations for facilitating the delivery, maintenance, and servicing of Lend-Lease material to the British in the Middle East. It ceased operations in 1946. *References*: "History of Africa—Middle East Theater, United States Army (including USMNAN and USAFIME) to 30 April 1946;" Ms., U.S. Army Center of Military History, Washington, D.C.; *FRWW*.

U.S. MILITARY MISSION WITH THE IRANIAN ARMY. Established in 1942, with headquarters in Teheran, to assist in the organization and training of the Iranian Army and to help in the transfer of military equipment to Iran under the Lend-Lease program. *Reference*: *FRWW*.

U.S. MILITARY NORTH AFRICAN MISSION. *See* U.S. Army Forces in the Middle East (USAFIME).

U.S. NAVAL DETACHMENT IN TURKISH WATERS, 1919–1924. A detachment of American warships stationed in Turkey and the Middle East from 1919 to 1924 which provided numerous services to American citizens and diplomats in that area. *Reference*: Henry P. Beers, *U.S. Naval Detachment in Turkish Waters, 1910–1924* (Washington, D.C., 1943).

U.S. NAVAL MEDICAL RESEARCH UNIT NO. 3 (NAMRU–3). Research unit of the U.S. Navy which began its activities in Egypt during World War II. It was established in 1946 at the invitation of the Egyptian government, and it expanded in 1948. It carries out studies in tropical medicine and conducts research on the ecology, epidemiology, and pathophysiology of infectious diseases of military importance prevalent in the Middle East. Scientists from this unit also carried out research and treatment expeditions to Arabia, Lebanon, Libya, Syria, the Sudan, and Yemen. *Reference*: W. Richard Whitaker, "MARU–3's New Cairo Lab opens for Business," *U.S. Navy Medicine* 74 (November-December 1983): 9–11.

UPHAM, THOMAS COGSWELL (1799–1872). Educator and author, born January 30, 1799, in Deerfield, New Hampshire. Upham graduated from Dartmouth College and Andover Theological Seminary, and was ordained in 1823. He was a pastor in Rochester, New Hampshire, in 1823–1824, and professor of mental and moral philosophy at Bowdoin College from 1824 to 1867. He visited the Middle East in 1852, and wrote *Letters, Aesthetic, Social, and Moral, Written from Europe, Egypt, and Palestine* (Brunswick, Me., 1855). Died April 2, 1872, in New York City. *References*: *ACAB*; AndoverTS; *DAB*; *NCAB* 13:171; and *WWWA*.

V

VAN BEEK, GUS WILLARD (1922–   ). Archaeologist, born March 22, 1922, in Tulsa, Oklahoma. Van Beek graduated from the University of Tulsa, McCormick Theological Seminary, and Johns Hopkins University. He was archaeologist in the Arabian Expedition of the American Foundation for Study of Man in 1951; research associate and assistant editor of the Arabian publication project at Johns Hopkins University from 1954 to 1959; associate curator; and, after 1967, curator of Old World archaeology at the Smithsonian Institution. He was director of the archaeological expeditions to Hadramaut in 1961–1962, and to Saudi Arabia in 1968, conducted an archaeological survey of Yemen in 1964, and was director of the Tell Jemmeh archaeological expedition from 1970 to 1982. He wrote *Hajar Bin Humeid: Investigations at a Pre-Islamic Site in Southern Arabia* (Baltimore, 1969). *Reference*: DAS.

VAN DYCK, CORNELIUS VAN ALEN (1818–1895). Medical missionary and Arabic scholar, born August 13, 1818, in Kinderhook, New York. Van Dyck graduated from the Jefferson Medical College in Philadelphia and became a missionary under the American Board of Commissioners for Foreign Missions (ABCFM)* in Syria in 1840. He accompanied William McClure Thompson,* on an extensive tour through northern Syria and visited Jerusalem. In 1841 Van Dyck was stationed in Beirut, moved to 'Abeih in 1843, and with Thompson conducted a high school for boys and prepared textbooks in Arabic. He was ordained in 1846, transferred to Sidon in 1849, and remained there until 1857 when he returned to Beirut. He continued the translation of the Bible into Arabic begun by Eli Smith.* When completed in 1865, Van Dyck spent two years in New York supervising the preparation of the electrotype plates. He returned to Beirut in 1867, became editor of the mission's weekly journal *al-Nashrah*, professor of pathology in the medical department of the Syrian Protestant College, professor of astronomy, and director of the astronomical and meteorological observatory. He also practiced medicine in Beirut and continued to write textbooks in Arabic. He resigned his professorship in 1883, but continued to practice in the Hospital of St. George until 1893. Died November 13, 1895, in Beirut. His son, **EDWARD ABBOTT VAN DYCK (1846–1939)**, was born in Beirut, and studied at the Union Theological Seminary. He was interpreter and vice consul at the consulates in Beirut and Cairo from 1873 to 1882, taught in Egyptian government schools in Cairo from 1885 to 1912, and wrote *Report on the Capitulations of the Ottoman Empire* (Washington, D.C., 1881). *References*: *DAB*; *NCAB* 5:560; *DAMB*; Lutfi M. Sa'di, "Al-Hakim Cornelius Van Alen Van Dyck (1815–1895)," *Isis* 27 (1937): 20–45; *UnionTS*; and *WWWA*.

VAN DYKE, HENRY (1852–1933). Author, born November 10, 1852, in Germantown, Pennsylvania. Van Dyke graduated from Princeton College and Princeton Theological Seminary, and was ordained in 1879. He was a pastor in Newport, Rhode Island, and New York City from 1879 to 1899, and professor of English literature at Princeton University from 1899 to 1923. He traveled in the Middle East in 1907 and wrote *Out-of-doors in the Holy Land: Impressions of Travel in Body and Spirit* (New York, 1908). From 1913 to 1917 he was minister to the Netherlands and Luxembourg and a chaplain in the U.S. Navy during World War I. Died April 10, 1933, in Avalon, New Jersey. *References*: *ACAB*; *DAB*; *DARB*; *NCAB* 25:10; *NYT*, April 11, 1933; Tertius Van Dyke, *Henry Van Dyke: A Biography* (New York, 1935); and *WWWA*.

VAN ESS, JOHN (1879–1949). Missionary, born August 10, 1879, in New Holland, Michigan. Van Ess graduated from Hope College and Princeton Theological Seminary, and was ordained in 1902. He served in the Arabian Mission* from 1903 to 1949, and founded the American School for Boys at Basra, Iraq, in 1912. He journeyed down the Euphrates River from Aleppo to Mosul on a raft. An Arabic scholar, he was the author of several language texts that were used by the British Army and oil companies, including *An Aid to the Spoken Arabic of Mesopotamia* (Oxford, 1918) which was often reprinted. He wrote *Meet the Arab* (New York, 1943). Died April 26, 1949, in Basra. His wife **DOROTHY (FIRMAN) VAN ESS (1885–1975)**, missionary educator, was born July 30, 1885, in Wakefield, Massachusetts. She graduated from Mount Holyoke and Wellesley colleges, and was an instructor at Carleton College in 1908–1909. She served in the Arabian Mission* from 1909 until 1955. She wrote *Fatima and Her Sisters* (New York, 1964), *History of the Arabian Mission, 1926–1957* (n.p., 195-), and *Pioneers in the Arab World* (Grand Rapids, Mich., 1974), an autobiography and a memoir of her husband. Died September 1, 1975, in Somers, New York. *References*: Jerome Beatty, *Americans All Over* (New York, 1940), pp. 60–69; Herman J. Bergman, "The Diplomatic Missionary: John Van Ess in Iraq," *MW* 72 (1982): 180–196; *CA*; Paul Geren, *New Voices Old Worlds* (New York, 1958), pp. 71–88; *HDRCA*; *NYT*, April 27, 1949; and *Washington Post*, September 5, 1975.

VAN LENNEP, HENRY JOHN (1815–1889). Missionary, born March 18, 1815, in Smyrna into a Dutch trading family and came to the United States at fifteen. Van Lennep graduated from Amherst College and Andover Theological Seminary, and was ordained in 1839. In 1839 he went to Turkey as a missionary under the American Board of Commissioners for Foreign Missions (ABCFM),* was stationed in Smyrna from 1839 to 1844 and in Constantinople from 1844 to 1854, and taught at Bebek Seminary. He visited Syria and Palestine in 1847 and wrote *Bible Lands, Their Modern Customs and Manners Illustrative of Scripture* (1875). In 1854 he was transferred to Tokat in North Central Anatolia, establishing a mission station and a theological seminary. In 1864 he made an archaeological tour of Asia Minor and wrote *Travels in Little-Known Parts of Asia Minor* (New York, 1870) in which he described archaeological remains. He was in Smyrna from 1863 until 1869, when he returned to the United States and taught at Ingham University (LeRoy, N.Y.). He published *Oriental Album: Twenty Illustrations, in Oil Colors of the People and Scenery of Turkey, with Exploratory and Descriptive Text* (New York, 1862). His books were illustrated with his own sketches. Died January 11, 1889, in Great Barrington, Massachusetts. *References*: *ACAB*; *Amherst*; *AndoverTS*; *DAB*; *EM*; and *WWWA*.

VAN SICLEN, MATTHEW (1880–1941). Mining engineer, born November 8, 1880, in New York City. Van Siclen graduated from Amherst College and Columbia University School of Mines. From 1907 to 1912 he was employed by various mines in Mexico, was superintendent of exploration at Rosevale, New Brunswick, and operator of mines in Webb City, Missouri. He served in the air service during World War I and was an examining engineer for the War Minerals Relief Commission from 1919 to 1921. In 1921 he was employed by the Bureau of Mines, and in 1926 he inspected metal and coal mines and mining methods in Europe. He was a mining engineer for the Turkish government from 1933 to 1935. Van Siclen returned to the U.S. Bureau of Mines in 1937 as chief engineer in the Coal Economics Division. Died March 3, 1941, in Arlington, Virginia. *References*: *Amherst*; *WWWA*.

VEDDER, ELIHU (1836–1923). Painter, born February 26, 1836, in New York City. From 1844 to 1849 Vedder lived in Cuba with his family, and in 1856 he went to Europe and studied in Paris. He lived in Florence from 1857 to 1861, when he returned to the United States and opened a studio in New York City; but he was back in Europe in 1865. In 1866 he went to live in Rome, which became his residence for the rest of his life. In 1884 he published a series of illustrations of the *Rubaiyat* of Omar Khayyam, and in 1889–1890 he visited and painted in Egypt. He wrote a memoir, *The Digressions of ''V''* (Boston, 1910). Died January 19, 1923, in Rome. *References*: *ACAB*; *DAB*; *NCAB* 6:328; *NYHSD*; *NYT*, January 30, 1923; Regina Soria, *Elihu Vedder, American Visionary Artist in Rome (1836–1923)* (Rutherford, N.J., 1970); and *WWWA*.

VELIOTES, NICHOLAS ALEXANDER (1928–   ). Diplomat, born October 28, 1928, in California. Veliotes graduated from the University of California at Berkeley and served in the U.S. Army from 1946 to 1948. He entered the foreign service in 1955, serving in Naples, Rome, New Delhi, and Vientien, Laos; became deputy chief of mission in Israel in 1973 and minister-counselor in 1974; ambassador to Jordan from 1978 to 1981; and assistant secretary of state for Near Eastern and South Asia Affairs from 1981 to 1983. He was ambassador to Egypt from 1983 to 1986 but resigned following a disagreement with secretary of state George P. Shulz after Veliotes clashed with the Egyptian authorities over his demand that Egypt prosecute the hijacker of the Italian liner *Achille Lauro*. He retired in 1986 and became president of the Association of American Publishers. *References*: *Newsweek*, February 16, 1981; *WWA*; and *WWAP*.

VESTER, BERTHA HEDGES (SPAFFORD) (1878–1968). Colonist, daughter of Horatio Spafford,* born March 24, 1878, in Chicago. Vester was brought to Jerusalem in 1881 by her parents, who established the American Colony in Jerusalem. She started a children's clinic in 1925 in the Old City of Jerusalem which later became the Anna Spafford Children's Hospital and administered it until 1965. She was a painter of wildflowers and wrote *Flowers of the Holy Land* (Kansas City, Mo., 1962), articles in the *National Geographic Magazine*, and her memoirs, *Our Jerusalem: An American Family in the Holy Land, 1881–1949* (Garden City, N.Y., 1950). Died June 27, 1968, in Jerusalem. Her son, **HORATIO VESTER** (1906–1985), lawyer and hotelkeeper, was born on August 25, 1906, in Jerusalem. He graduated from Columbia University and studied at the American University of Beirut* and Gray's Inn, London. He became barrister-in-law in 1935, and practiced commercial and industrial law in London from 1946 to 1962. After retirement he was chairman of the American Colony Ltd., the American Colony Hotels, Ltd., and several other enterprises in Jerusalem, and chairman of the Anna Spafford Memorial Children's Hospital, Jerusalem. Died November 28, 1985, in Jerusalem. *References*: *CA*; *NYT*, June 28, 1968; and Lowell Thomas, "My Most Unforgettable Character," *Reader's Digest* 40 (August 1962): 193–198.

VIDAL, MICHAEL (1824–   ?   ). Consul, born October 1, 1824, in Carcassonne, France, immigrated to Texas, and later moved to Louisiana. He was associate editor of several newspapers, served in the Civil War, was registrar for the city of New Orleans, and served in Congress in 1868–1869. He was consul at Tripoli from 1870 to 1876. He investigated the slave trade, traveled through Cyrenaica to the Egyptian border, and recommended the establishment of an American base there. *References*; *BDAC*; James A Field, Jr., "A Scheme in Regard to Cyrenaica," *Mississippi Valley Historical Review* 44 (1957): 445–468; and *WWWA*.

VILLARD, HENRY S(ERRANO) (1900–   ). Diplomat, born March 30, 1900, in New York City. Villard graduated from Harvard University, studied at Magdalen College, Oxford, drove an ambulance for the Italian Army in World War I, and from 1923 to 1927 he was employed in teaching, journalism, and real estate. He entered the foreign service in 1928, and served in Teheran, Rio de Janeiro, and Caracas; was assistant chief of the division of Near Eastern Affairs from 1940 to 1944; chief of the Division of African Affairs from 1944 to 1946; deputy director of the Office of Near Eastern and African Affairs in 1946–1947; counselor in Oslo from 1948 to 1950; and the first minister to Libya from 1952 to 1954. He wrote *Libya: The New Arab Kingdom of North Africa* (Ithaca, N.Y., 1956). He was special assistant to the secretary of state in 1957–1958, representative to the U.N. European Office from 1958 to 1960, and ambassador to Senegal and Mauritania in 1960–1961. He retired in 1961, was director of programs in the Washington Institute of Foreign Affairs from 1964 to 1967, and wrote a memoir, *Affairs at State* (New York, 1965). *References*: *CA*; *WWA*.

VINCENT, JOHN HEYL (1832–1920). Clergyman, born February 23, 1832, in Tuscaloosa, Alabama. Vincent graduated from Ohio Wesleyan University, held pastorates in several communities in Illinois, was bishop of the Methodist Episcopal Church, one of the founders of the Chautauqua movement, and a leader of the American Sunday School Movement. He visited Palestine in 1862–1863, 1887, and 1893, and he inspired and wrote the introduction to the largest American album of Holy Land photographs, *Earthly Footsteps of the Man of Galilee, Being Five Hundred Original Photographic Views and Descriptions of the Places Connected with the Earthly Life of Our Lord and His Apostles* (New York, 1894). He retired in 1904. Died May 9, 1920, in Chicago. *References*: *ACAB*; *BDAE*; *DAB*; C. R. Niker "Evangelists for Education," *Religious Education* 74 (January 1979): 72–86; *NCAB* 24:378; and *WWWA*.

W

WADSWORTH, GEORGE (1893–1958). Diplomat, born April 3, 1893, in Buffalo, New York. Wadsworth graduated from Union College, taught at the American University of Beirut* from 1914 to 1917, entered the foreign service in 1916 in Beirut, and served in Beirut, Nantes, Constantinople, Sofia, Alexandria, and again in Constantinople. He was consul in Cairo from 1922 to 1924, first secretary and consul in Cairo from 1928 to 1931, first secretary in Teheran from 1931 to 1933, first secretary, counselor, and consul general in Bucharest in 1935–1936, consul general in Jerusalem from 1936 to 1940, and counselor in Rome in 1941–1942. He was diplomatic agent and consul general to Syria and Lebanon from 1942 to 1944 and first minister to these countries from 1944 to 1947; first ambassador to Iraq from 1947 to 1948; ambassador to Turkey from 1948 to 1952; ambassador to Czechoslovakia from 1952 to 1953; and ambassador to Saudi Arabia and minister to Yemen from 1954 to 1958. Died March 5, 1958, in Bethesda, Maryland. *References*: *NCAB* G:439; *NYT*, March 6, 1958; *Saturday Evening Post*, August 11, 1951; and *WWWA*.

WAINWRIGHT, JONATHAN MAYHEW (1792–1854). Clergyman, born February 24, 1792, in Liverpool, England, to an American mother and came to the United States in 1793. Wainwright graduated from Harvard University and was ordained in 1817. He served as a pastor in Hartford, Boston, and New York from 1821 to 1852, and became bishop of the Protestant Episcopal Church in 1852. He traveled in the Middle East in 1848–1849 and wrote *The Pathways and Abiding-places of Our Lord: Illustrated in the Journal of a Tour Through the Land of Promise* (New York, 1851), and *The Land of Bondage; Its Ancient Monuments and Present Conditions: Being the Journal of a Tour in Egypt* (New York, 1852). Died September 21, 1854, in New York City. *References*: *DAB*; *NCAB* 1:515; J. N. Norton, *Life of Bishop Wainwright* (New York, 1858); and *WWWA*.

WALKER, CHARLES THOMAS (1858–1921). Clergyman, born February 5, 1858, in Hephzibah, Richmond County, Georgia. Walker graduated from Augusta (Ga.) Theological Institute (now Morehouse College). He was minister in the Missionary Baptist Church and served as a pastor in Augusta, Georgia, in New York City, and again in Augusta, founded the Colored Young Men's Christian Association (YMCA) in New York City, and served as chaplain in the Spanish-American War. He traveled in the Middle East in 1891 and wrote *The Colored Man Abroad: What He Saw in the Holy Land and Europe* (Augusta, Ga., 1892), the earliest account of a black making the pilgrimage to the Holy Land. Died July 29, 1921, in Augusta, Georgia. *References*: Silas X. Floyd, *Life of Charles T. Walker, D.D.* (Nashville, Tenn., 1902); *NCAB* 13:36; *NYT*, July 30, 1921; and *WWWA*.

WALLACE, EDWIN SHERMAN (1864–1960). Clergyman, born October 3, 1864, in Butler County, Pennsylvania. Wallace graduated from Washington and Jefferson College and Princeton Theological Seminary, and was ordained in 1889. He was a pastor in Aberdeen, South Dakota, from 1888 to 1893, and consul in Jerusalem from 1893 to 1898. He wrote *Jerusalem the Holy; a Brief History of Ancient Jerusalem; with an Account of the Modern City and Its Conditions Political, Religious and Social* (Edinburgh, 1898). He was later a pastor in Greensburg, Pennsylvania, in business in Pittsburgh from 1910 to 1931, and again became a pastor in Blawnox, Pennsylvania, in 1931. Died August 15, 1960, in Daytona Beach, Florida. *References*: *DAA*; *WWWA*.

WALLACE, LEWIS ("LEW") (1827–1905). General and author, born April 110, 1827, in Brookville, Indiana. Wallace was admitted to the bar and practiced law in Indianapolis, Covington, and Crawfordsville, Indiana. He was elected to the State Senate in 1856, was a Union general in the Civil War, went to Mexico after the war to help the forces of Benito Juarez, and was territorial governor of New Mexico from 1878 to 1881. He attained fame from his book *Ben Hur: A Tale of the Christ* (New York, 1880) which sold 300,000 copies within ten years. He was minister to Turkey from 1881 to 1885. He wrote *The Prince of India; or, Why Constantinople Fell* (New York, 1893), which was inspired by his stay in Constantinople. Died February 15, 1905, in Crawfordsville, Indiana. His autobiography, *Lew Wallace: An Autobiography* (New York, 1906) was completed by his wife and Mary H. Krout after his death. His wife, **SUSAN (ARNOLD) ELSTON WALLACE** (1830–1907), was born December 25, 1830, in Crawfordsvill, Indiana. She accompanied her husband to Turkey and wrote *Along the Bosporus, and Other Sketches* (Chicago, 1898), a journal in Turkey and Palestine in 1881–1882, *The City of the King; What the Child Jesus Saw and Heard* (Indianapolis, 1903), and *The Repose in Egypt: A Medly* (New York, 1888). Died October 2, 1907, in Crawfordsville, Indiana. *References*: Papers, Indiana State Historical Society Library; *ACAB*; *DAB*; *DADH*; *DAMIB*; *IAB*; Irving McKee, *"Ben-Hur" Wallace: The Life of General Lew Wallace* (Berkeley,

Calif., 1947); Robert E. and Katharine M. Morsberger, *Lew Wallace: Militant Romantic* (New York, 1980); *NCAB* 4:363 and 10:359; *NYHSD*; Lee S. Theisen, "The Public Career of General Lew Wallace, 1845–1905," Ph.D. diss., University of Arizona, 1973; and *WWWA*.

WALLER, FRANK (1842–1923). Painter, born June 12, 1842, in New York City. Trained as an architect, Waller went to Europe in 1870 and lived in Rome. In 1872 he visited Egypt with the American painter Edwin White (1817–1877), making many studies which Waller would later use in his more notable paintings. He returned to New York in 1874, practiced as an architect from 1885 to 1902, and made painting his full-time profession in 1903. Views of Egypt were his speciality. Died March 9, 1923, in Morristown, New Jersey. *References: ACAB*; *NCAB* 23:146; and *WWWA*.

WALSH, EDMUND A(LOYSIUS) (1885–1956). Educator, born October 10, 1885, in South Boston. Walsh studied at Woodstock (Md.) College, Georgetown University, and the universities of Dublin, London, and Innsbruck, joined the Society of Jesus in 1902, and was ordained in 1916. He taught at Georgetown University, was the founder and the first director of its School of Foreign Service in 1919, and was vice president of Georgetown University from 1924 until his death. He was the director of the papal relief mission for Russia and American Catholic representative on the American Relief Administration to Russia in 1922; president of the Catholic Near East Welfare Association from 1926 to 1930; and the Vatican representative to Mexico in 1928. He went to Iraq in 1931 to survey the educational needs of that country and in 1932 was granted permission to open Baghdad College, a secondary school. During World War II he was consultant to the War Department and civilian consultant to the U.S. chief counsel in the Nuremberg War Crimes Trial. He was Jesuit visitor to Japan in 1947–1948 and founded the Institute of Languages and Linguistics at Georgetown University in 1949. Died October 31, 1956, in Washington, D.C. *References*: Papers, College of the Holy Cross, Worcester, Massachusetts; *DAB S6*; *DACB*; *NCAB* 47:640; and *WWWA*.

WALTON, PAUL T(ALMAGE) (1914–   ). Petroleum geologist, born February 4, 1914, in Salt Lake City, Utah. Walton graduated from the University of Utah and the Massachusetts Institute of Technology. He was a district engineer of the Soil Conservation Service from 1935 to 1938, chief geophysicist in a prospecting party for the Standard Oil Company of California in 1938–1939, geologist for the Texas Company from 1942 to 1944, and chief geologist for the Rocky Mountain Division of the Pacific Western Oil Corporation from 1944 to 1949. He explored for oil in the Neutral Zone between Kuwait and Saudi Arabia in 1948, and negotiated with Saudi Arabia officials for an oil concession for that area. He was chief geologist and a partner in Morgan and Walton Oils from 1949 to 1952, private petroleum geologist and oil and gas producer from

1952 to 1955, partner in Walton-Kearns from 1955 to 1967, and later president and general director of American Geological Enterprises in Salt Lake City. *Reference*: *Who's Who in Frontiers of Science and Technology* (Chicago, 1985).

WARD, AARON (1790–1867). Congressman and soldier, born July 5, 1790, in Sing Sing (now Ossining), New York. Ward served in the War of 1812 and in the New York state militia, reaching the rank of major general. He studied law and was admitted to the bar. In 1826 he was elected to Congress and served six terms. He was an unsuccessful candidate for secretary of state of New York in 1855. He toured the Middle East in 1859–1860 and wrote *Around the Pyramids* (New York, 1863). Died March 2, 1867, in Georgetown, D.C. *References*: *ACAB*; *BDAC*; *NCAB* 10:212; and *WWWA*.

WARD, EDWIN ST. JOHN (1880–1951). Physician and educator, born March 31, 1880, in Brookline, Massachusetts. Ward graduated from Amherst College and Columbia University. The American Board of Commissioners for Foreign Missions named him to the Turkey Mission in 1906, and he began medical work at Diyarbekir in 1907. From 1910 to 1931 he was professor of surgery at the Syrian Protestant College and dean of the medical school from 1924 to 1931. He was a representative of the American Red Cross* in the Middle East during World War I; head of a hospital in the Suez Campaign; and head of the medical service at the Tash Kushla Barracks in Constantinople during the Gallipoli campaign. He was deputy commissioner and organizer of the Red Cross Commission to Palestine in 1918–1919. In 1926 and 1927 he organized two expeditions to explore Dog River Cave in Lebanon. He returned to the United States in 1931, and was superintendent and medical director of the Hospital Cottages for Children in Baldwinsville, Massachusetts, from 1933 until 1946. In 1947–1948 he returned to Turkey as an associate missionary under the ABCFM at Gaziantep, and from 1950 until his death he was a physician at the Memorial Home Community, Penney Farms, Florida. Died July 31, 1951, in Northampton, Massachusetts. *References*: *NCAB* 40:193.

WARD, HENRY AUGUSTUS (1834–1906). Naturalist, born March 8, 1834, in Rochester, New York. Ward attended Williams College, and studied and worked at Agassiz's museum in Cambridge, Massachusetts. From 1854 to 1858 he studied in Paris, and in 1855 he made a tour of Egypt, Nubia, Arabia, and Palestine, gathering fossils and minerals. From 1858 to 1860 he made a collecting and exploration trip to West Africa, and in 1876–1877 he again traveled in Egypt and the Red Sea region. He was professor of natural history at the University of Rochester from 1861 to 1875, and in 1862 he established Ward's Natural Science Establishment in Rochester. Killed July 4, 1906, by automobile in Buffalo, New York. *References*: Papers, University of Rochester Library; *ACAB*; *DAB*; *NCAB* 28:169; Sally G. Kohlstedt, "Henry A. Ward: The Merchant Naturalist and American Museum Development," *Journal of the Society for the*

Bibliography of Natural History 9 (April 1970): 647–661; Roswell Ward, *Henry A. Ward: Museum Builder to America* (Rochester, N.Y., 1948); and *WWWA*.

WARD, LAURISTON (1882–1960). Archaeologist, born May 15, 1882, in Andover, Massachusetts. Ward graduated from Harvard University. He was involved in commercial publicity activity in Chicago from 1904 to 1909, went to India as correspondent for the *Boston Transcript* in 1910, and was writer for that newspaper from 1910 to 1913. From 1913 to 1932 he was employed with a travel agency in Boston. He returned to Harvard in 1932 as a student of anthropology, joined the staff of the Peabody Museum of Archaeology and Ethnology in 1934, became associate curator in 1935, and was curator of Asian archaeology from 1937 until his death. In 1938–1939 he conducted an extensive field survey in Syria and Iraq. Died February 1, 1960, in Boston. *References*: *NCAB* 48:554; *NYT*, February 3, 1960.

WARD, WILLIAM HAYES (1835–1916). Clergyman, Orientalist, and journalist, born June 25, 1835, in Abington, Massachusetts. Ward graduated from Amherst College, attended Union and Andover theological seminaries, graduated from Yale Divinity School, and was ordained in 1860. He served as pastor in Oskaloosa, Kansas, teacher at Utica Free Academy, Easthampton, Massachusetts, and professor of Latin and sciences at Ripon College from 1865 until 1867. After 1868 he was associated with the *New York Independent* in various editorial capacities and was its editor from 1896 to 1913. He led the Wolfe expedition to Mesopotamia in 1884–1885, named after its benefactress, Catherine Lorillard Wolfe of New York, to select a good excavation site. He surveyed various sites there, wrote the *Report on the Wolfe Expedition to Babylonia, 1885–1885* (Boston, 1886), and recommended an expedition to Nippur. This survey led to the first American archaeological expedition to the Middle East and to the excavation of Nippur by the University of Pennsylvania expeditions. "Diary," in John P. Peters, *Nippur: or, Expedition and Adventures on the Euphrates* (New York, 1897), 1:318–375. Died August 28, 1916, in Berwick, Maine. *References*: *ACAB*; *Amherst*; *AndoverTS*; *DAB*; *NCAB* 8:147; *UnionTS*; and *WWWA*.

WARNE, WILLIAM E(LMO) (1905–   ). Government official, born September 2, 1905, in Seafield, Indiana. Warne graduated from the University of California at Berkeley. He was a correspondent for newspapers in California from 1925 to 1935, was employed by the Bureau of Reclamation from 1935 to 1947, and was assistant secretary of the interior from 1947 to 1951. He was minister in charge of technological cooperation for Iran from 1951 to 1955, and wrote *Mission for Peace: Point 4 in Iran* (Indianapolis, 1956). He was in charge of technological cooperation in Brazil in 1955–1956, and was minister and economic coordinator for Korea from 1956 to 1959. He directed various departments for the state of California from 1959 to 1967 and was consultant on water resources from 1967. *References*: Papers, University of Wyoming Library; *AMWS*; *CA*; *CB* 1952; *IAB*; and *WWA*.

WARNER, CHARLES DUDLEY (1829–1900). Author and editor, born September 12, 1829, in Plainfield, Massachusetts. Warner graduated from Hamilton College and studied law at the University of Pennsylvania. He began to practice law in Chicago in 1858, was assistant to the editor of the *Evening Press* in Hartford, Connecticut, in 1860 and editor from 1861 until 1867, and began to write essays. In 1868 he went on the first of five trips to Europe and the Middle East, and sent travel sketches to the *Hartford Courant*. Warner wrote two travel books about the Middle East, *In the Levant* (Boston, 1877), and *Mummies and Moslems* (Hartford, Conn., 1876), retitled *My Winter on the Nile* (Hartford, 1876). He was later contributing editor to *Harper's New Monthly*. Died October 20, 1900, in Hartford, Connecticut. *References*: *ACAB*; *DAB*; *NCAB* 2:116; and *WWWA*.

WARREN, EDWARD (1828–1893). Surgeon, born January 22, 1828, in Tyrrell County, North Carolina. Warren graduated from the University of Virginia and Jefferson Medical College, and studied medicine in Paris hospitals. He practiced in Edenton, North Carolina, from 1851 to 1860, was professor of materia medica and therapeutics at the University of Maryland in 1860–1861, and was medical director of the Department of Cape Fear, North Carolina, surgeon general of North Carolina, and medical inspector of the Army of Northern Virginia during the Civil War. He practiced medicine in Baltimore from 1865 to 1873 and was professor of surgery and director of the Washington University Medical School in Baltimore from 1867 to 1871. From 1873 to 1875 he was chief surgeon of the General Staff of the Egyptian Army, and from 1875 until his death, practiced medicine in Paris. He wrote an autobiography, *A Doctor's Experiences in Three Continents* (Baltimore, 1885). *References*: *BDC*; *DAMB*; *DAMB 1984*; *Hesseltine*; *NCAB* 33:169; and Hubert A. Royster, *Adventurous Life of Edward Warren Bey* (n.p., 1937?).

WARREN, EDWARD K(IRK) (1847–1919). Manufacturer, born April 7, 1847, in Ludlow, Vermont. In his youth Warren moved to Three Oaks, Michigan. In 1868 he organized a firm for the sale of general merchandise, invented a substitute for whalebone in 1882, organized a bank in 1902, and owned cattle ranches in Texas, New Mexico, and Mexico. He went to Palestine in 1901, where he met the Samaritans and formulated a plan by which the Samaritan community could gain financial security. He purchased many of their manuscripts and artifacts to hold in safekeeping. The plan never came to fruition, and when he died the materials were placed in the Three Oaks Museum and were later donated to Michigan State University. He returned to Jerusalem in 1904 as president of the International Sunday School Union, established schools for Samaritan boys and girls, and the American Samaritan Committee in 1913 to render aid to the Samaritans. (The Committee ceased to function after his death and its assets were distributed among the Samaritans in 1926.) Died January 16, 1919, in Evanston, Illinois. *References*: *ACAB*; Robert T. Anderson, *Studies in Samaritan Manuscripts and Artifacts: The Chamberlain-Warren Collection* (Cambridge, Mass., 1978); *NCAB* 17:235; *NYT*, January 17, 1919; and *WWWA*.

WASHBURN, GEORGE (1833–1915. Missionary and educator, born March 1, 1833, in Middleboro, Massachusetts. Washburn graduated from Amherst College and Andover Theological Seminary. He went to Turkey as treasurer of the American Board of Commissioners for Foreign Missions (ABCFM)* to the United States in 1862, and was ordained in 1863. He was a missionary under the ABCFM and became professor of philosophy at Robert College* in 1869. He was acting president of the college from 1870 to 1878, and as president from 1878 to 1903, he made innovations in the curriculum. He studied the geology of the Bosporus, was an authority on the politics of the Middle East, and served as counselor to the British ambassadors in Constantinople. He wrote many articles and an autobiography, *Fifty Years in Constantinople and Recollections of Robert College* (Boston, 1909). Died February 15, 1915, in Boston. *References*: *ACAB*; *Amherst*; *AndoverTS*; *DAB*; *NCAB* 16:102; and *WWWA*.

WASHINGTON, GEORGE THOMAS (1908–1971). Judge and government official, born June 24, 1908, in Cuyahoga Falls, Ohio. Washington graduated from Yale College, Oxford University, and Yale Law School, and practiced law in New York City from 1932 to 1938. He was a faculty member of Cornell University Law School from 1938 to 1942, and attorney in the Office of Emergency Management in 1942. He served as economic representative in Baghdad for the Foreign Economic Administration from 1942 to 1943, and was chief of the U.S. Lend-Lease Mission in Teheran in 1943–1944. He was special assistant to the attorney general and assistant solicitor general from 1944 to 1949, and judge of the U.S. Court of Appeals for the District of Columbia Circuit from 1949 until his retirement in 1965. Died August 21, 1971, in Santa Barbara, California. *References*: Papers, Manuscript Division, Library of Congress; *NYT*, August 25, 1971; and *WWWA*.

WASHINGTON, HENRY STEPHENS (1867–1934). Geologist, born January 15, 1867, in Newark, New Jersey. Washington graduated from Yale College and the University of Leipzig. He traveled extensively in Europe and Asia Minor, worked on igneous rock in Lydia, Turkey, studied a group of volcanoes in Asia Minor, and wrote *The Volcanoes of the Kula Basin in Lydia* (New York, 1894), as well as an article on the igneous rocks from Smyrna and Pergamon. He established a private laboratory at Locust, New Jersey, and conducted chemical and mineralogical investigations of igneous rocks; was a consulting and mining geologist from 1906 to 1912; became associated with the geophysical laboratory of the Carnegie Institute of Washington in 1912; and was scientific attaché in the embassy in Rome in 1918–1919. Died January 7, 1934, in Washington, D.C. *References*: *DAB*; *DSB*; *NCAB* C:520; *PGSA* for 1951 (1952): 165–178; and *WWWA*.

WASSON, THOMAS C(AMPBELL) (1896–1948). Consul, born February 8, 1896, in Great Falls, Montana. Wasson graduated from New Jersey Agricultural College and Cornell University, was a representative of a manufacturing company in France in 1919, and a plantation manager from 1920 to 1924. In 1924 he became clerk in the consulate in Melbourne, and later served as vice consul and consul in Adelaide, Australia; Puerto Cortes, Honduras; Naples; Lagos, Nigeria; Vigo, Spain; and Dakar, French West Africa. He was counselor in Athens in 1947–1948 and consul general in Jerusalem and U.S. representative on the U.N. Truce Commission in Palestine in 1948. Killed May 23, 1948, from a sniper's bullet in Jerusalem. *References*: *NYT*, May 24, 1948; *WWWA*.

WATERMAN, LEROY (1875–1972). Archaeologist, born July 4, 1875, in Pierpont, Ohio. Waterman studied at Hillsdale College, Oxford University, and at the universities of Berlin and Chicago. He was a member of the faculty of Hillsdale College Divinity School (Hillside, Mich.) from 1902 to 1910, Meadville (Pa.) Theological School from 1913 to 1915, and professor of Semitics at the University of Michigan from 1915 to 1945. He was annual professor of the American Schools of Oriental Research (ASOR) in Baghdad in 1928–1929; director of the archaeological expedition to Tel Umar, south of Baghdad, sponsored by the University of Michigan and the Toledo and Cleveland art museums, from 1928 to 1931; and director of the archaeological expedition at Sepphoris, Galilee, for the University of Michigan in 1931. He wrote *Preliminary Report Upon the Excavations at Tel Umar, Iraq* (Ann Arbor, Mich., 1931–1937), and *Preliminary Report of the University of Michigan Excavations at Sepphoris, Palestine, in 1931* (Ann Arbor, Mich., 1937). Died May 9, 1972, in Ann Arbor. *References*: Papers, Michigan Historical Collections, Bentley Historical Library, Ann Arbor; *CA*; *NCAB* 58:512; and *WWWA*.

WATERMAN, MARCUS (MARK) A. (1834–1914). Painter, born September 1, 1834, in Providence, Rhode island. Waterman graduated from Brown University. He had a studio in New York City from 1857 until 1874, when he moved to Boston. He made two trips to North Africa. The series of paintings for which he was best known was composed of scenes from the *Arabian Nights*, based on his Algerian experiences. In 1900 he moved to Europe permanently. Died April 2, 1914, in Moderno, Italy. *References*: *ACAB*; *NYHDS*; and *WWWA*.

WATERS, CLARA ERSKIŃE CLEMENT (1834–1916). Author and lecturer on art and travel, born Clara Erskine, August 28, 1834, in St. Louis, Missouri, and grew up in Milford, Massachusetts. Waters traveled extensively, visited Turkey and Palestine in 1868, and returned to the Middle East several times. At age sixty-six she climbed the Great Pyramid. She wrote *A Simple Story of What One of Your Lady Friends Saw in the East* (Boston, 1869), *Egypt* (Boston, 1880), and *Constantinople, the City of the Sultans* (Boston, 1895). Died February 20, 1916, in Brookline, Massachusetts. *References*: *NAW*, *WWWA*.

WATSON, ANDREW (1834–1916). Missionary, born February 15, 1834, in Oliverburn, Ferthshire, Scotland, and came to the United States in 1848. Watson graduated from Carroll College (Waukesha, Wis.), studied at Princeton and Allegheny theological seminaries and at Jefferson Medical College, and was ordained in 1861. He went to Egypt in 1861 as a missionary under the United Presbyterian Church of North America Board of Foreign Missions,* and served in Alexandria from 1861 to 1867, in Mansura from 1869 to 1873, and in Cairo from 1873 until his death. He established the theological seminary in Cairo in 1864, and was professor of systematic theology at the seminary after 1870, and head of the school from 1892 until his death. He was a member of the commission for surveying missionary conditions in Egyptian Sudan in 1889. He wrote *The American Mission in Egypt, 1854–1896* (Pittsburgh, 1897). Died December 9, 1916, in Cairo. *References: DAB; WWWA.*

WATSON, CHARLES ROGER (1873–1948). Educator, son of Andrew Watson,* born July 17, 1873, in Cairo. Watson graduated from Princeton University and Princeton and Allegheny theological seminaries, and was ordained in 1900. He was pastor in St. Louis from 1900 to 1902, and corresponding secretary of the Board of Foreign Missions of the United Presbyterian Church of North America from 1902 to 1916, visiting the mission fields of India, Egypt, and the Sudan in 1903–1904. In 1914 he became the secretary and president-elect of the American University in Cairo,* being named the first president of the university from 1922 until 1945. He conducted several studies of educational and missionary problems in Egypt and served as a member of the National Commission of Education in Egypt in 1931. He wrote *Egypt and the Christian Crusade* (Philadelphia, 1907), *In the Valley of the Nile: A Survey of Missionary Movement in Egypt* (New York, 1904), and *The Sorrow and the Hope of The Egyptian Sudan: A Survey of Missionary Conditions and Methods of Work in the Egyptian Sudan* (Philadelphia, 1913). Died January 10, 1948, in Philadelphia. *References: DAB S4; MW* 38 (1948): 151; *NYT,* January 12, 1948; and *WWWA.*

WAYNE, HENRY CONSTANTINE (1815–1883). Soldier, born September 8, 1815, in Savannah, Georgia. Wayne graduated from the U.S. Military Academy in 1838 and was appointed to the artillery. He was transferred to the Quartermaster Corps after the outbreak of the Mexican War and served in the Quartermaster General Office in Washington from 1848 to 1855. Converted to the idea of using camels in the American West, he succeeded in persuading Jefferson Davis of the soundness of that concept. When Davis became secretary of war, he appointed Wayne to direct the Camel Military Corps. In 1855 Wayne traveled to Turkey and Egypt on the *Supply** to procure camels, and succeeded in purchasing or obtaining thirty-two camels of several types, which were brought back to Texas. The report of his activity was published as a Senate executive document. The camels were used on mail and express routes through the deserts, but their use was soon discontinued and they later became extinct. He served in the Confederate Army during the Civil War. Died March 15, 1883, in Savannah, Georgia. *References*: *ACAB*; *DAA*; and Odie B. Faulk, *The U.S. Camel Corps: An Army Experiment* (New York, 1976).

WEEKS, EDWIN LORD (1849–1903). Painter, born in Boston. Weeks studied art in Paris. In 1869 he traveled to South America, and in 1870 he went to the Middle East. He visited Morocco, Palestine, and Syria in 1872, and resided in Tangier in 1878. In 1882 he traveled to India through Turkey, Kurdistan, and Persia, and wrote an account of the journey in *From the Black Sea Through Persia and India* (New York, 1896). He lived in Paris after 1883 and traveled again to Turkey and Persia in 1892. Died November 17, 1903, in Paris. *References*: *ACAB*; *DAB*; Kathleen D. Ganley and Leslie K. Paddock, *Art of Edwin Lord Weeks (1849–1903)* (Durham, N.H., 1976); *NCAB* 12:505; *NYT*, November 18, 1903; and *WWWA*.

WEISGAL, MEYER WOLF (1894–1977). Journalist and executive, born October 11, 1894, in Kikol, near Kipno, Poland, and came to the United States in 1905. Weisgal graduated from Columbia University, served in the army in World War I, was the national secretary of the Zionist Organization of America from 1921 to 1938, and editor of *The New Palestine* in New York from 1921 to 1930. He was the personal political representative of Chaim Weizmann, president of the World Zionist Organization (WZO) in the United States from 1940 to 1948, and organizer of the American section of the secretariat general of the Jewish Agency for Palestine from 1943 to 1946. He went to Israel in 1949; was organizer and executive vice chairman of the American committee of the Weizmann Institute from 1946 to 1959; chairman of the executive council of the Weizmann Institute of Science in Rehovot, Israel, from 1949 to 1966; president of the institute from 1966 to 1969; and chancellor from 1970 until his death. He wrote an autobiography, *Meyer Weisgal . . . So Far: Autobiography* (New York, 1971). Died September 29, 1977, in Tel Aviv, Israel. *References*: *EJ*; *MENA*; *NYT*, September 30, 1977; and *WWWJ*.

WEITZMANN, KURT (1904–   ). Art historian, born March 7, 1904, in Klein Almerode, Germany. Weitzmann studied at Munster, Wurzberg, Vienna, and Berlin universities, came to the United States in 1935, and was naturalized in 1940. He was a member of the Institute for Advanced Study at Princeton from 1953 to 1972, and associate professor and professor of art and archaeology at Princeton University from 1945 to 1972. He conducted expeditions to Mount Sinai in 1956, 1968, 1960, 1963, and 1965, and co-authored *The Monastery of Saint Catherine at Mount Sinai: The Church and Fortress of Justinian* (Ann Arbor, 1973) and *The Monastery of St. Catherine at Mount Sinai: The Icons* (Princeton, N.J., 1976). *References*: *CA*; *DAS*; and *WWA*.

WEST, HENRY SERGEANT (1827–1876). Medical missionary, born January 21, 1827, in Binghamton, New York. West graduated from Yale College and the College of Physicians and Surgeons of New York, and practiced medicine in Binghamton from 1850 to 1859. In 1859 he went to Turkey under the American Board of Commissioners for Foreign Missions (ABCFM),* was stationed in Sivas, and educated Armenians as physicians. He wrote about his medical and surgical experiences in Asia Minor in the *Transactions of the Medical Society of the State of New York* in 1869. Died April 1, 1876, in Sivas, Turkey. *References*: *DAB*; *DAMB*; *EM*; and *WWWA*.

WEST, MARIA ABIGAIL (1827–1894). Educational missionary, born March 27, 1827, in Palmyra, New York. West, under the auspices of the American Board of Commissioners for Foreign Missions (ABCFM),* went to Turkey in 1855 and was in charge of a girls' boarding school in Constantinople for about ten years. She was later stationed in Marsovan and Harput, was in charge of a girls' seminary in Harput, and wrote the first primer in Armenian for children in mission schools. After leaving the ABCFM, she organized coffee houses in Smyrna and Constantinople for sailors and others. She wrote *Romance of Missions; or, Inside Views of Life and Labor in the Land of Ararat* (New York, 1875). Died June 28, 1894, in London. *References*: *EM*.

WESTOVER, HARVEY LEROY (1879–1943). Plant explorer, born June 4, 1879, in Austerlitz, New York. Westover graduated from Cornell University. He became an agronomist at the Bureau of Plant Industry in the Department of Agriculture in 1906, was involved in foreign exploration and plant breeding, and collected wild and domesticated alfalfa in North Africa in 1930, in Turkey, Persia, and Afghanistan in 1934, and again in Turkey in 1936. Died January 2, 1943, in Washington, D.C. *Reference*: *NYT*, January 3, 1943.

WHARTON, EDITH (1862–1937). Author, born Edith Newbold Jones on January 24, 1862, in New York City. Wharton began publishing at sixteen, moved to France in 1907, and lived there until her death. In 1918 she traveled in Morocco under the protection of the French government and wrote *In Morocco* (New York, 1920). Died August 11, 1937, at St. Brice-sous-foret, near Paris. *References*: Papers, Yale University Library; *ACAB*; *DAB*; *DLB*; R.W.B. Lewis, *Edith Wharton: A Biography* (New York, 1975); *NAW*; *NCAB* 14:80; *NYT*, August 13, 1937; and *WWWA*.

WHEELER, CROSBY HOWARD (1823–1896). Missionary, born September 8, 1823, in Hampden, Maine. Wheeler graduated from Bowdoin College and Bangor Theological Seminary. He was a missionary under the American Board of Commissioners for Foreign Missions (ABCFM)* in Turkey from 1857 until 1895, served in Harput, and was the founder of Euphrates College and its president until 1893. He wrote *Ten Years on the Euphrates; or, Primitive Mis-*

sionary Policy Illustrated (Boston, 1868), *Letters from Eden; or, Reminiscences of Missionary Life in the East* (Boston, 1868) and *Odds and Ends; or, Gleanings from Missionary Life* (Boston, 1888). He returned to the United States in 1895. Died October 11, 1896, in Auburndale, Massachusetts. His wife, **SUSAN ANNA (BROOKINGS) WHEELER**, wrote *Missions in Eden: Glimpses of Life in the Valley of the Euphrates* (New York, 1899). *References*: *BangorTS*; Charles C. Creegan, *Pioneer Missionaries of the Church* (New York, 1903); *DAA*; and *EM*.

WHEELER, RAYMOND ALBERT (1885–1974). Military officer and engineer, born July 31, 1885, in Peoria, Illinois. Wheeler graduated from the U.S. Military Academy in 1911 and was commissioned second lieutenant in the Corps of Engineers. He served in the Panama Canal Zone, in the Vera Cruz expedition of 1914, and in World War I in France and Germany. From 1922 to 1940 he served in the District of Columbia, the Panama Canal Zone, Wilmington, North Carolina, and Rock Island, Illinois, in various capacities. He was chief of the U.S. Military Mission to the Persian Gulf area from 1941 to 1942. Later in the war he served in the China-Burma-India theater of operations and was chief of the U.S. Corps of Engineers from 1945 until his retirement in 1949. From 1949 to 1964 he was principal engineering adviser with the World Bank and special representative of the secretary general of the United Nations in the clearance operations of the Suez Canal in 1956–1957 after the Suez war. He reported on these operations in the January-February 1958 issue of *Military Engineer*. Died February 8, 1974, in Washington, D.C. *References*: *CB* 1957; *NCAB* 58:346; *NYT*, February 10, 1974; and *WWWA*.

WHEELUS FIELD, LIBYA. Air base outside Tripoli, Libya, leased to the United States by the Libyan government in 1954. The base served mainly as a training center. It was evacuated by the U.S. Air Force in 1970, following an agreement between the United States and the Republican Government of Libya.

WHITE, DONALD (1935–   ). Archaeologist, born April 2, 1935, in Boston. White graduated from Harvard and Princeton universities. He was instructor and associate professor of classical archaeology at the University of Michigan from 1963 to 1973, and became associate professor of classical archaeology and associate curator of the University Museum in 1973. He excavated in Sicily from 1963 to 1966, directed the preliminary investigation and excavation of Apollonia in Libya from 1965 to 1967, and became director of the excavations at Cyrene, Libya, in 1969. He was co-author of *Apollonia, the Port of Cyrene. Excavations by the University of Michigan 1965–1967* (Tripoli, 1977), and wrote *The Extramural Sanctuary of Demeter and Persephone at Cyrene, Libya* (Philadelphia, 1984). *Reference*: *DAS*.

WHITE, GEORGE EDWARD (1861–1946). Missionary educator, born October 14, 1861, in Marash, Turkey, to American parents, and came to the United States in 1863. White graduated from Iowa College, Hartford and Chicago theological seminaries, studied at Oxford University, and was ordained in 1887. He was a teacher at Hastings College (Neb.) from 1882 to 1884 and a pastor at Waverly, Iowa, from 1887 to 1890. He became a missionary under the American Board of Commissioners for Foreign Missions (ABCFM)* in 1890, was a member of the faculty of Anatolia College* and Marsovan Theological Seminary from 1890 to 1921, dean of the college from 1905 to 1913, and its president from 1913 to 1923. He sent Hittite artifacts from Bogazkoy to Grinnell College. He was director of Near East Relief* in Minneapolis from 1917 to 1919, and at Merzifon, Turkey, from 1919 to 1921, and again in Minneapolis from 1921 to 1923. After Anatolia College was relocated in Salonika, Greece, in 1925, he resumed its presidency. After he retired in 1934, he wrote a biography of the American missionary Charles Chapin Tracy* and his memoirs, *Adventuring with Anatolia College* (Grinnell, Ia., 1940). Died April 27, 1946, in Claremont, California. *References*: Hans G. Goeterbock, "'Hittite' at Grinnell," in *Ancient Anatolia: Aspects of Change and Cultural Development*, ed. Jeanny V. Canby et al. (Madison, Wis., 1986), pp. 70–76; *NYT*, May 4, 1946; and *WWWA*.

WHITEHOUSE, FREDERICK COPE (1842–1911). Lawyer and archaeologist, born November 9, 1842, in Rochester, New York. Whitehouse graduated from Columbia College and General Theological Seminary, studied in France, Germany, and Italy, and was admitted to the bar in 1871. He lived a great part of his life in Europe, made his first trip to Egypt in 1879, and afterwards had prolonged stays in Egypt. He explored the desert region, and in 1882 discovered Wadi Raiyan in the Faiyum which he identified with the ancient Lake Moeris, made a special study of this region, wrote *Moeris, the Wonder of the World* (New York, 1884), and prepared a plan for better irrigation of the Nile River. Died November 16, 1911, in New York City. *References*: *DAB*; *NYT*, November 17, 1911; *WWWA*; and *WWWE*.

WHITEHOUSE, WILLIAM E(DWIN) (1893–1982). Agriculturist, born in New Hampshire. Whitehouse graduated from Oregon Agricultural College, Iowa State University, and the University of Maryland, and served as a pilot training inspector in World War I. He was a member of the faculty of Iowa State University and the University of Maryland. In 1929 he joined the Plant Exploration Division of the U.S. Department of Agriculture as an agricultural explorer, and he made expeditions to Iran to collect onions, to study pistachio nut orchards, and to collect samples. He helped to develop the pistachio nut industry in California. He was assistant head of the Plant Introduction Section from 1956 to 1959 and head of the Crop Development Investigations Section of the New Crops Research Division of the Agricultural Research Service from 1959 until his retirement in 1963. Died October 17, 1982, in Riverdale, Maryland. *Reference*: *Journal of Heredity* 59 (1968): 338.

WHITING, GEORGE BACKUS (1801–1856). Missionary, born August 30, 1801, in Canaan, New York. Whiting graduated from Union College and Princeton Theological Seminary, and was ordained in 1829. He was a missionary under the American Board of Commissioners for Foreign Missions (ABCFM)* in Syria from 1830 until his death. He was stationed in Beirut until 1834, and was in Palestine in 1835–1836 and again in 1847. Died November 8, 1856, in Beirut. *References*: *EM*; *PrincetonTS*.

WHITING, JOHN D. (?   –1951). Member of the American Colony* in Jerusalem. Whiting was manager of the American Colony Stores at the American Colony Hotel in Jerusalem, representative of the American Samaritan Committee in Palestine, and vice consul in Jerusalem. He was involved in political intelligence work for the British Army during World War I. He collected costumes in Arab villages and contributed ten articles about the Middle East to the *National Geographic Magazine* between 1913 and 1940. *References*: Yedida K. Stillman, *Palestinian Costume and Jewelry* (Albuquerque, N.M., 1979).

WHITTEMORE, THOMAS (1871–1950). Archaeologist, born January 2, 1871, in Cambridge, Massachusetts. Whittemore graduated from Tufts College. He excavated for the Egypt Exploration Society at Balabish, El-Amarna, and elsewhere in Egypt. He was keeper of Byzantine coins in the Fogg Museum of Harvard University and director of the Byzantine Institute of America. In 1932 he began to work on the preservation of the mosaics in Haggia Sophia in Istanbul with the permission of the Turkish government. Died June 8, 1950, in Washington, D.C. *References*: *Archaeology* 3 (1950): 180–182; *DAB S4*; *NYT*, June 9, 1950; and *WWWE*.

WILBER, DONALD N(EWTON) (1907–   ). Author and government official, born November 14, 1907, in Madison, Wisconsin. Wilber graduated from Princeton University. He was a member of archaeological expeditions to Egypt, Syria, Iran, and Afghanistan from 1930 to 1939; was assistant professor and associate professor at the Asia Institute in New York City from 1939 to 1947; served in the Office of Strategig Services in Iran during World War II; and was consultant to the Central Intelligence Agency from 1948 to 1970. He wrote *Iran, Past and Present* (Princeton, N.J., 1948; 9th ed., Princeton, N.J., 1981), *The Architecture of Islamic Iran: The Il-Khanid Period* (Princeton, N.J., 1955), *Persian Gardens and Garden Pavilions* (Rutland, Vt., 1962), *Contemporary Iran* (New York, 1963), *Persepolis, the Archaeology of Parsa, Seat of the Persian Kings* (New York, 1969), and co-authored *Afghanistan: Its People, Its Society, Its Culture* (New Haven, Conn., 1962), *United Arab Republic, Egypt, Its People, Its Society, Its Culture* (New Haven, Conn., 1969), and *Riza Shah*

Pahlavi: The Resurrection and Reconstruction of Iran (Hicksville, N.Y., 1975). Wilber wrote his memoirs, *Adventures in the Middle East: Excursions and Incursions* (Princeton, N.J., 1986). *References*: *CA*; *WWE*.

WILBOUR, CHARLES EDWIN (1833–1896). Businessman and Egyptologist, born March 17, 1833, in Little Compton, Newport County, Rhode Island. Wilbour went to New York in 1854, served as a reporter for the *New York Tribune*, studied law, and was admitted to the bar in 1859. In 1872 he began to study Egyptian antiquities, and in 1874 he went abroad and studied Egyptology in Paris and Berlin. He spent the last twenty years of his life alternatively in Egypt and France, and accompanied Gaston Maspero, French Egyptologist and director general of the Service of Antiquities in Egypt, on five winter exploring expeditions up the Nile. Died December 17, 1896, in Paris. Wilbour's collection of antiquities and his library were bequeathed to the Brooklyn Museum. His letters were collected in *Travels in Egypt (December 1880 to May 1981): Letters of Charles Edwin Wilbour*, ed. Jean Capart (Brooklyn, 1936). *References*: *WWWE*.

WILCOCKS, BENJAMIN CHEW (1776–1845) and **WILCOCKS, JAMES**, (fl. 1804–1805). Merchants. The first figures of consequence in the American opium trade from Smyrna to China. Benjamin Chew was born December 13, 1776, in Philadelphia. He arrived in Smyrna in 1804 with James as supercargoes of the brig *Pennsylvania* and took opium for China. James returned to Smyrna in 1805 on the *Sylph* for more opium. Benjamin Chew became a resident commission agent and opium merchant in Canton, China, in 1811. He was consul in Canton from 1813 to 1922, and returned to the United States in 1827. Died December 1, 1845, in Philadelphia. *References*: Chew Family papers, Historical Society of Pennsylvania, Philadelphia; Jacques Downes, "American Merchants and the China Opium Trade, 1800–1840," *Business History Review* 42 (1968): 418–442; Jonathan Goldstein, *Philadelphia and the China Trade 1682–1846: Commercial, Cultural, and Attitudinal Effects* (University Park, Pa., 1978); and Jean Gordon Lee, *Philadelphians and the China Trade 1784–1844* (Philadelphia, 1986).

WILLARD, CHARLOTTE R(ICHARDS) (1860–1930). Missionary educator, born September 20, 1860, in Fairhaven, Massachusetts. Willard graduated from Smith College, taught at Auburndale, Massachusetts, and Clinton, Kentucky, studied at the Astronomical Observatory of Harvard University, and was a member of the faculty at Carleton College (Northfield, Minn.) from 1887 until 1897. She went to Turkey in 1895, serving as a missionary at Marsovan from 1897 to 1930. She was a teacher at the Anatolia School for Girls in Marsovan from 1895 to 1898, became its principal in 1898, and opened the King School for the Deaf in 1910. She returned to the United States in 1919, but went back to Turkey in 1922 as a Near East Relief* worker at Merzifon, where she directed relief work. She retired in 1930 and returned to the United States. Died October 1, 1930, in

Chicago. *Reference*: *Charlotte R. Willard, of Merzifon: Her Life and Times*, ed. Ernest Pye (New York, 1933).

WILLIAMS, GEORGE ST. JOHN (1888–1922). Soldier, born May 24, 1888, in Chefoo, North China, to American parents. Williams worked as accountant and typist in Chicago and served in the army in World War I. In 1922 he enlisted in Near East Relief* work in Turkey and was director of relief work at Marsovan. Died December 10, 1922, in Marsovan, Turkey. *Reference*: *NCAB* 20:490.

WILLIAMS, JAMES (1796–1869). Journalist and diplomat, born July 1, 1796, in Grainger County, Tennessee. Williams founded the Knoxville *Post* in 1841 and was its editor, and served in the Tennessee legislature in 1843. Around 1850 he moved to Nashville and was active in public affairs and politics. He was minister to Turkey from 1858 to 1861. He traveled in the Middle East and tried to get more protection for missionaries by extending consular protection over Americans to cover civil as well as criminal cases. He served as diplomatic agent for the Confederacy and remained in Europe after the Civil War. Died April 10, 1869, in Graz, Austria. *References*: *BDC*; *DAB*; *DADH*; and *WWWA*.

WILLIAMS, MAYNARD OWEN (1888–1963). Writer, born September 12, 1888, in Havana (now Montour Falls), New York. Williams graduated from Kalamazoo College, the University of Chicago, and Columbia University School of Journalism. He was an instructor at the Syrian Protestant College from 1911 to 1914 and at the Wayland Academy in Hangchow in 1914–1915. He was special correspondent for various American periodicals to many parts of the world from 1913 to 1919 and was in charge of relief work in Van, Turkey, in 1917–1918. He was on the editorial staff of the *National Geographic Magazine* from 1919 to 1953, and staff correspondent and chief of the foreign editorial staff from 1930 to 1953. He traveled extensively in the Middle East, writing a number of articles about this area to the *National Geographic Magazine*. Died June 26, 1963, in Antalya, Turkey. *References*: Photograph collection, Prints and Photographs Division, Library of Congress; *NCAB* 52:540; *NYT*, June 28, 1963; and *WWWA*.

WILLIAMS, TALCOTT (1849–1928). Journalist, son of William Frederic Williams,* born July 20, 1849, in Abeih, Syria. Williams graduated from Amherst College. He was on the staff of the *New York World* from 1873 to 1877; Washington correspondent for the *New York Sun* and the *San Francisco Chronicle* from 1877 to 1879; editorial writer for the *Springfield* (Mass.) *Republican* from 1879 to 1881 and the Philadelphia *Press* from 1881 to 1912; and the first director of the School of Journalism at Columbia University from 1912 until his retirement in 1919. He twice collected anthropological material in Morocco for the Smithsonian Institution and the University Museum. He wrote *Turkey, A World Problem of Today* (Garden City, N.Y., 1921). Died January 24, 1928, in New York

City. *References*: Papers, Historical Society of Pennsylvania; *DAB*; Elizabeth Dunbar, *Talcott Williams, Gentleman of the Fourth Estate* (Brooklyn, 1936); *NCAB* 15:306; and *WWWA*.

WILLIAMS, WILLIAM FREDERIC (1919–1871). Missionary, born January 11, 1818, in Utica, New York. Williams graduated from Yale College, was engaged in engineering until 1844, graduated from Auburn Theological Seminary, and was ordained in 1848. He became a missionary under the American Board of Commissioners for Foreign Missions (ABCFM)* in 1846. In 1849 he joined the Syria Mission,* went to Mosul in 1851, and remained there until 1859, when he moved to Mardin. He acquired Assyrian antiquities from the archaeological excavations at Nineveh. Died February 14, 1871, at Mardin, Turkey. *References*: *EM*; *AuburnTS*.

WILLIS, BAILEY (1857–1949). Geologist, born May 31, 1857, in Idlewild-on-Hudson, New York. Willis graduated from the Columbia School of Mines. He became a geologist for the Northern Pacific Railway in 1880 and explored Washington Territory. He was with the U.S. Geological Survey from 1882 to 1915, conducted geological explorations in China, helped the Argentine government establish a geological survey, and examined the geological features of Turkey in 1905. He was professor of geology at Stanford University from 1915 to 1922 and became a consulting geological engineer in 1922. He was seismologist of the Carnegie Institute of Washington expedition to Palestine and Cyprus in 1927, studied the Rift Valley and earthquakes in Palestine, and wrote articles on the Dead Sea, the Jordan Valley, and earthquakes in Palestine. In 1929 he was in Egypt, explored the East African Rift, and wrote *Living Africa: A Geologist's Wanderings Through the Rift Valleys* (New York, 1930), which is mostly autobiographical. Died February 19, 1949, in Palo Alto, California. *References*: *BGSA* 73 (1962): 55–72; *BMNAS* 35 (1961): 333–350; *DAB S4*; *DSB*; *NCAB* 37:53; and *WWWA*.

WILLOUGHBY, JAMES W(ALLACE) (1898–1986). Missionary, born October 6, 1898, in Albany, Alabama. Willoughby graduated from Wabash College and Western Theological Seminary. He was a missionary under the Presbyterian Church in the USA Board of Foreign Missions* in Iran from 1922 to 1924, when he was transferred to the United Mission in Mesopotamia and served in Mosul until 1946. He was a pastor in Ottawa, Ohio, from 1947 to 1949; was reassigned to the Syria-Lebanon Mission in 1949; was stationed at Deir-ez-Zor on the Euphrates River from 1949 to 1952; became the executive secretary of the Syria-Lebanon Mission, 1952 to 1954, and again from 1956 to 1959; and was a pastor in Nabatiya, Lebanon. He retired in 1964. Died May 7, 1986.

WILSON, EDWARD LIVINGSTON (1838–1903). Photographer. Wilson became the editor and owner of *Wilson's Photographic Magazine* in 1864. He conducted several large photographic expeditions and photographed the Middle East in 1882. He was the first American to photograph Petra, and he wrote his impressions in the September 1886 issue of *Century Magazine*. In 1883 he published the "Eastern Series" of 650 stereo cards of Palestine, Syria, and Anatolia, and *In Scripture Lands: New Views of Sacred Places; with One Hundred and Fifty Illustrations from Original Photographs* (New York, 1890). He was later the permanent secretary of the National Photographic Association. *References*: *NYT*, June 25, 1903; *WWWA*; and *WWWE*.

WILSON, EDWIN CARLTON (1893–1972). Diplomat, born February 7, 1893, in Palatka, Florida. Wilson graduated from Harvard University and served in World War I in the ambulance corps first with the French Army and later with the U.S. Army. He entered the foreign service in 1920; served in Santiago and Tegucigalpa; was first secretary in Paris; chief of the Division of Latin American Affairs from 1931 to 1935; counselor in Paris from 1935 to 1939; minister to Uruguay from 1939 to 1941; ambassador to Panama from 1941 to 1943; representative to the French Committee of Liberation with the rank of ambassador; and the president's diplomatic representative in Algiers in 1943. He was ambassador to Turkey from 1945 until his retirement in 1948, and chief of mission to supervise aid agreement with the Turkish government. He was later co-president of the American Turkish Association. Died September 10, 1972, in Washington, D.C. *References*: *MENA*; *NYT*, September 11, 1972; and *WWWA*.

WILSON, EDWIN P(AUL) (1928–   ). Intelligence agent and arms dealer, born May 28, 1928, near Nampa, Idaho. Wilson graduated from the University of Portland and served in the marines. He was an employee of the Central Intelligence Agency's Office of Security from 1951 until 1971, and a member of Task Force 157 of the Office of Naval Intelligence from 1970 until he was fired in 1971. Between 1976 and 1979 he was involved in illegal arms deals and terrorist training in Libya and lived near Tripoli, Libya, until he was arrested in the United States in 1983 and convicted of illegally shipping explosives and arms to Libya. *References*: Joseph C. Goulden with Alexander W. Raffio, *The Death Merchant: The Rise and Fall of Edwin P. Wilson* (New York, 1984); P. Edward Haley, *Qaddafi and the United States Since 1969* (New York, 1984), ch. 8; and Peter Maas, *Manhunt* (New York, 1986).

WILSON, EVAN M(ORRIS) (1910–1984). Diplomat, born January 20, 1910, in Rosemont, Pennsylvania. Wilson graduated from Haverford College, Oxford University, and the Geneva School of International Studies. He entered the foreign service in 1937 and served in Guadalajara, Mexico, Cairo, and Mexico City. He was secretary to the American delegation to the Anglo-American Commission of Inquiry on Palestine in 1945–1946; second secretary and vice consul and first secretary and consul in Teheran from 1947 to 1949; consul general in Calcutta from 1950 to 1953; first secretary in London from 1953 to 1957; counselor in Beirut from 1961 to 1964; and consul general in Jerusalem with the personal rank of minister from 1964 until his retirement in 1967. *Jerusalem, Key to Peace* (New York, 1975) describes the consulate's operations during the 1967 war. He was later a consultant for the Middle East Institute. Died March 13, 1984, in Washington, D.C. *References*: *CA*; *NYT*, March 15, 1984; and *WWWA*.

WILSON, J. CHRISTY (1891–1973). Missionary, born July 22, 1891, in Columbus, Nebraska. Wilson graduated from the University of Kansas and Princeton Theological Seminary, and was ordained in 1918. He was a missionary under the Presbyterian Church in the U.S.A. Board of Foreign Missions* and was stationed in Tabriz from 1919 to 1940. He was chairman of the Near East Relief Committee for Persia from 1921 to 1923 and chairman of the Near East Christian Counsil from 1937 to 1940. He was an interpreter and epigraphist for the expeditions of the Iranian Institute of New York. In 1941 Wilson became the director of fieldwork and associate professor of ecumenics at Princeton Theological Seminary, and he was a pastor in Princeton from 1962 to 1965, and in Monrovia, California, from 1965 to 1970. He wrote *An Introduction to Colloquial Kabul Persian* (Presidio of Monterey, California, 1955) and a biography of Samuel M. Zwemer. Died April 8, 1973, in Duarte, California. *Reference*: *WWWA*.

WILSON, JOHN ALBERT (1899–1976). Egyptologist, born September 12, 1899, in Pawling, New York. Wilson graduated from Princeton University and the University of Chicago. He was a teacher at the American University of Beirut* from 1920 to 1923, and an epigrapher to the Oriental Institute expedition to Luxor from 1926 to 1931. He was a professor at the University of Chicago from 1936 until his retirement in 1968, and director of the Oriental Institute from 1936 to 1945 and again in 1960–1961. He served with the Office of Strategic Services in Washington in 1942–1943, and with the State Department in 1943–1944. In 1958–1959 he directed the work of the epigraphic expedition in Luxor. Wilson served on the UNESCO consultative committee for the preservation of the ancient Nubian monuments. He wrote *Signs and Wonders upon Pharoah: A History of American Egyptology* (Chicago, 1964), as well as his memoirs, *Thousands of Years: An Archaeologist's Search for Ancient Egypt* (New York, 1972). Died August 30, 1976, in Hightstown, New Jersey. *References*: *DAS*; *NCAB* 59:256; *NYT*, August 31, 1976; and *WWWA*.

WILSON, MARY FLORENCE (1884–1977). Librarian, born January 29, 1884, in Lancaster, Pennsylvania. Wilson graduated from Drexel Institute and Columbia University. She was a librarian at Columbia University and became the librarian and a researcher for the Inquiry and the American Commission to Negotiate Peace in 1918–1919. She was assistant librarian and later librarian of the League of Nations Library in Geneva, and organized that library. In 1926 she traveled in the Near East for the Carnegie Endowment for International Peace, and wrote *Near East Educational Survey* (London, 1928). She later lectured at the Ecole de Bibliothécaires in Paris and did volunteer work in Europe. Died January 4, 1977, in La Tour de Peilz, Switzerland. *References*: *BDI*; Doris C. Dale, "An American in Geneva: Florence Wilson and the League of Nations Library," *Journal of Library History* 7 (1972): 366–371; and *NCAB* C:420.

WILSON, SAMUEL GRAHAM (1858–1916). Missionary and author, born February 11, 1858, in Indiana, Pennsylvania. Wilson graduated from Princeton University and Western and Princeton theological seminaries, and was ordained in 1880. He became a missionary under the Presbyterian Church in the U.S.A. Board of Foreign Missions* in Persia in 1880 and was stationed in Tabriz, becoming principal of the boys' school there in 1882. In 1892 he became head of a training and theological school and the treasurer of the mission. He wrote *Persian Life and Customs: With Scenes and Incidents of Residence and Travel in the Land of the Lion and the Sun* (New York, 1895), *Persia: Western Mission* (Philadelphia, 1896), and *Mariam, a Romance of Persia* (New York, 1906). He lived in the United States from 1912 to 1915 and returned to Persia again in 1915 as chairman of the Persian Commission of the American Committee for Armenian and Syrian Relief. Died July 2, 1916, in Tabriz, Persia. *References*: *DAB*; *WWWA*.

WINLOCK, HERBERT EUSTICE (1884–1950). Egyptologist, born February 1, 1884, in Washington, D.C. Winlock graduated from Harvard University. He joined the staff of the Metropolitan Museum of Art, was assistant curator of Egyptian art from 1909 to 1922, associate curator from 1929 to 1929, and curator from 1929 to 1939. He was engaged in excavations in Egypt 1906 to 1931, excavating at Lisht, the Oasis of Kharga, and Luxor for the Metropolitan Museum of Art, and was director of the Egyptian expedition from 1928 to 1932, excavating primarily at Deir el Bahri. He wrote *The Tomb of Queen Meryet-Amun at Thebes* (New York, 1932), *The Treasure of El Luhun* (New York, 1934), *Excavations at Deir el Bahri 1911–1931* (New York, 1942), and *The Treasure of Three Egyptian Princesses* (New York, 1948). He also published *El Dakhleh Oasis; Journal of a Camel Trip Made in 1908* (New York, 1936). Winlock was the director of the Metropolitan Museum of Art from 1932 until his retirement in 1939. Died January 26, 1950, in Venice, Florida. *References*; *DAB S4*; *NCAB* 37:217; *NYT*, January 27, 1950; and *WWWA*.

WINSLOW, WILLIAM COPLEY (1840–1925). Clergyman and archaeologist, born January 13, 1840, in Boston. Winslow graduated from Hamilton College and General Theological Seminary, and was ordained in 1867. He was a pastor in Lee, Massachusetts, from 1867 to 1870, and was then involved in literary work. In 1880 he went to Egypt to study its monuments and sites, and later founded the American branch of the Egypt Exploration Fund. Died February 2, 1925, in Boston. *References*: *ACAB*; *DAB*; *NCAB* 4:83; and *WWWA*.

WISHARD, JOHN G. (1863–1940). Medical missionary, born September 9, 1863, in Danville, Indiana. Wishard graduated from Central Normal (now Canterbury) College and Indiana Medical College. He served as a missionary under the Presbyterian Church in the U.S.A. Board of Foreign Missions* in Teheran from 1889 to 1899 and from 1903 to 1910. He managed to get a hospital built and to train a group of Persians in modern medical methods. He wrote *Twenty Years in Persia: A Narrative of Life Under the Last Three Shahs* (New York, 1908), and *Reminiscences of a Doctor: A Personal Narrative* (Wooster, Ohio, 1935). In 1910 he began to practice medicine in Wooster, Ohio. Died July 15, 1940, in Wooster. *References*: *IAB*; *OAB*; and *WWWA*.

WISTAR, EDWARD MORRIS (1852–1941). Banker, born January 3, 1852, in Abington, Pennsylvania. Winstar graduated from Haverford College. He was involved in banking, life insurance, real estate, and the cotton yarn business. He served as a special field agent for the American Red Cross* and was in charge of an American Red Cross expedition for Armenian relief in Anatolia in 1896. His report is included in Clara Barton, *The Red Cross: A History of This Remarkable Movement in the Interest of Humanity* (Washington, D.C., 1898). Died January 21, 1941, in Germantown, Philadelphia. *References*: Papers, Haverford College Library, Haverford, Pennsylvania; *NYT*, January 23, 1941.

WOLCOTT, SAMUEL (1813–1886). Missionary, born July 2, 1813, in South Windsor, Connecticut. Wolcott graduated from Yale College and Andover Theological Seminary in 1837, and was ordained in 1839. He went to Syria as a missionary under the American Board of Commissioners for Foreign Missions (ABCFM)* and was stationed in Beirut from 1839 to 1843. He was then sent to work in Dair al-Qamar, among the Druzes of Mount Lebanon, and opened a school there. He made discoveries in Syria and Palestine which he recorded in *Bibliotheca Sacra* and *Biblical Repository*. He visited Masada and provided the first modern description of the place. He was later pastor in Longmeadow and Belchertown, Massachusetts, Providence, Rhode Island, Chicago, and Cleveland. Died February 21, 1886, in Longmeadow, Massachusetts. *References*: *NCAB* 8:72; Yigael Yadin, *Masada: Herod's Fortress and the Zealots' Last Stand* (New York, 1966).

WOLF, SIMON (1836–1923). Lawyer, born October 28, 1836, in Hinzweiler, Bavaria. Wolf attended the University of Strassburg and Ohio Law College (Cleveland), came to the United States in 1848, and settled in Ulrichville, Ohio. He was admitted to the bar in 1861, began to practice in Washington, D.C., in

1862, was recorder of deeds for the District of Columbia from 1869 to 1878, and judge of the municipal court from 1878 to 1881. He was diplomatic agent and consul general in Egypt in 1881–1882. He resumed the practice of law and was lobbyist for the Jewish community. He wrote *Some Reminiscences at Home and Abroad* (Washington, D.C., 1914) and an autobiography, *The Presidents I Have Known from 1860 to 1918* (Washington, D.C., 1918). Died June 4, 1923, in Washington, D.C. *References*: Papers, American Jewish Historical Society; *ACAB*; *DAB*; *EJ*; *OAB*; David H. and Esther L. Panitz, "Simon Wolf as United States Consul to Egypt," *AJHSP* 47 (1957): 76–100; and *WWWA*.

WOODBERRY, GEORGE EDWARD (1855–1930). Author, born May 12, 1855, in Beverly, Massachusetts. Woodberry graduated from Harvard University. He was professor of English at the University of Nebraska in 1877–1878 and from 1880 to 1882, and professor of comparative literature at Columbia University from 1891 to 1904. He contributed to the *Atlantic Monthly* and the *Nation*, and wrote many books. He spent the years after 1904 traveling, lecturing and wandering in the Mediterranean. He traveled in North Africa and wrote *North Africa and the Desert: Scenes and Moods* (New York, 1914). Died January 2, 1930, in Beverly, Massachusetts. *References*: *ACAB*; *DAB*; *NCAB* 23:186; *NYT*, January 3, 1930; and *WWWA*.

WOODSMALL, RUTH FRANCES (1883–1963). Leader in welfare work for women, born September 20, 1883, in Atlanta, Georgia. Woodsmall graduated from the University of Nebraska, Wellesley College, and Columbia and Heildelberg universities. She was a teacher and a principal in Ouray, Colorado, Reno, Nevada, and Pueblo and Colorado Springs, Colorado. She was a director of the Young Woman's Christian Association (YWCA)* from 1917 to 1920; made a social survey of Constantinople for the YWCA; was an executive secretary in Turkey and Syria and secretary of the Eastern Mediterranean Federation; studied the changing status of Muslim women in the Middle East and India from 1928 to 1930; and wrote *Moslem Women Enter a New World* (New York, 1936). She was a member of Laymen's Foreign Missions inquiry in India from 1930 to 1932, served on the national staff of the YWCA in New York City from 1932 to 1935, and was general secretary of the World's YWCA council in Geneva from 1935 to 1947. She reassessed the role of women in the Middle East in 1954–1955, wrote *Study of the Role of Women, Their Activities and Organizations, in Lebanon, Egypt, Iraq, Jordan, and Syria* (New York, 1956), made a similar study in Turkey, Iran, and Afghanistan in 1956–1957, and wrote *Women and the New East* (Washington, D.C., 1960). Died May 25, 1963, in New York City. *References*: *CB* 1949; *NAW*; *NYT*, May 27, 1963; and *WWWA*.

WOODWARD, JOHN DOUGLAS (1846–1924). Illustrator, born July 12, 1846, in Middlesex County, Virginia, and grew up in Kentucky. Woodward studied art in Cincinnati, Richmond, and at Cooper Union in New York City.

He illustrated several pictorial works for D. Appleton and Company, and in 1878–1879 traveled in the Middle East, where he drew many of the original drawings that were included in the profusely illustrated *Picturesque Palestine, Sinai and Egypt* (New York, 1881–1884). In the 1890s he was curator for the Philadelphia Academy of Fine Arts, and after 1894 he devoted his full time to painting. Died June 5, 1924, in New Rochelle, New York. *References*: "An Artist Abroad in the Seventies: Letters by John Douglas Woodward," Ms., Virginia State Library, Richmond; *NCAB* 20:346; and L. Moody Simms, Jr., "John Douglas Woodward: Landscape Painter and Illustrator," *The Richmond Literature and History Quarterly* 2 (Spring 1980): 41–43.

WORKMAN, FANNY (BULLOCK) (1859–1925). Traveler, mountain climber, and explorer, born January 8, 1859, in Worcester, Massachusetts. Workman spent most of her life traveling. She was in North Africa, Egypt, and Palestine in the mid–1890s, traveled by bicycle through Algeria, and wrote *Algerian Memories: A Bicycle Tour Over the Atlas to the Sahara* (New York, 1895). She later traveled in South and Southeast Asia and explored the Himalaya Mountains. Died January 22, 1925, in Cannes, France. *References*: *DAB*; *NAW*; and *WWWA*.

WORLD'S GOSPEL UNION. *See* Gospel Missionary Union.

WRIGHT, AUSTIN HAZEN (1811–1865). Medical missionary, born November 11, 1811, in Hartford, Vermont. Wright graduated from Dartmouth College, Union Theological Seminary (Va.), and the University of Virginia Medical Department. He became a missionary under the American Board of Commissioners for Foreign Missions (ABCFM)* in Persia in 1840, replacing Asahel Grant* in Urmia, Persia. He sent antiquities to Dartmouth College. In 1863 he began the revision of the New Testament in Syriac. Died January 4, 1865, in Urmia. *References*: Wright family papers, Dartmouth College Library; *EM*; Oliver P. Hubbard, "An Account of How Dartmouth College Obtained Its Collection of Nineveh Slabs," Ms., Dartmouth College Library; and *UnionTS*.

WRIGHT, EDWIN MILTON (1897–   ). Missionary, born January 12, 1897, in Tabriz, Iran, to American parents. Wright graduated from the College of Wooster and Columbia University. He was involved with refugee resettlement in Iraq from 1921 to 1924, and was principal of an American high school in Tabriz from 1924 to 1937, lecturer in history at Columbia University from 1938 to 1941, research analyst for the Office of Strategic Services and for the Army Military Intelligence in Iran during World War II, country specialist at the State Department in 1946, and special assistant director in the Office of Near Eastern, South Asian, and African Affairs until 1953. He wrote *Azerbaijan: A Case History of Soviet Infiltration* (Washington, D.C., 1946) and *The Great Zionist*

Cover-up: A Study and Interpretation (Cleveland, 1975). *References*: "A Personal Narrative—A Retrospective View," Ms. in private hands; and *MENA*.

WRIGHT, ELIZABETH WASHBURN (1874–1952). Author, born November 19, 1874, in Minneapolis. Wright graduated from Radcliffe College. She assisted her husband Hamilton Kemp Wright (1867–1917), a medical researcher, in studying the narcotics problem. She was an assessor of the Opium Advisory Committee of the League of Nations from 1921 to 1925, and a delegate to the Geneva Opium Conference of 1924–1925. In 1923 she studied the production of opium in Turkey and Iran, and in 1927 she visited Turkey again to investigate the possibility of introducing substitute crops. In 1930–1931 she was an investigator of the opium problem in the Philippines for the U.S. Bureau of Narcotics. She wrote travel observations and articles about the opium trade. Died February 11, 1952, in Washington, D.C. *References*: *BDI*; *NYT*, February 14, 1952; and *WWWA*.

WRIGHT, G(EORGE) ERNEST (1909–1974). Archaeologist and biblical scholar, born September 5, 1909, in Zanesville, Ohio. Wright graduated from Wooster College, McCormick Theological Seminary, and Johns Hopkins University, and was ordained in 1934. He was instructor, assistant professor, and associate professor of Old Testament at McCormick Theological Seminary from 1939 to 1945, professor of Old Testament history and theology at Harvard University from 1945 to 1958, professor of divinity from 1958 until his death, and curator of the Harvard Semitic Museum. He was a member of the Bethel expedition in Palestine in 1934, archaeological director of the Drew-McCormick-American Schools of Oriental Research (ASOR)* expedition to Balata from 1956 to 1964, director of the Hebrew Union College excavation at Gezer in 1964–1965, and the American Expedition to Idalion, Cyprus, from 1971 to 1974. He was co-author of *Ain Shems Excavations* (Haverford, Pa., 1938–1939), wrote *Shechem, Biography of a Biblical City* (New York, 1965), and co-edited *American Expedition to Idalion, Cyprus: First Preliminary Report* (Cambridge, Mass., 1974). Died August 29, 1974, in Jaffrey, New Hampshire. *References*: *Magnalia Dei, the Mighty Acts of God: Essays on the Bible and Archaeology in Memory of G. Ernest Wright*, ed. Frank M. Cross et al. (Garden City, N.Y., 1976); *Archaeology* 28 (January 1975): 59; *BA* 37 (1974): 83–84; *DAS*; *CA*; William G. Dever, "Biblical Theology and Biblical Archaeology: An Appreciation of G. Ernest Wright," *Harvard Theological Review* 73 (1980): 1–15; Carney E.S. Gavin, "G. E. Wright at the Harvard Semitic Museum," *BA* 50 (March 1987): 10–21; *NYT*, August 31, 1974; *OAB*; and *WWWA*.

WRIGHT, HERBERT E(DGAR), JR. (1917–   ). Geologist, born September 13, 1917, in Malden, Massachusetts. Wright graduated from Harvard University and served in the army air force in World War II. In 1947 he became assistant professor and was later associate professor and professor of geology, ecology, and botany at the University of Minnesota, and became director of the Limnological Research Center in 1963. He was a geologist for the Minnesota Geological Survey from 1948 to 1963. He was field geologist of the Boston College-Fordham archaeological excavations at the Kasr Akil cave, Lebanon, in 1947, and member of the Oriental Institute's Jarco project in the Middle East in 1951, 1954–1955, 1960, 1963, 1964, and 1970. He pioneered the use of pollen to study the Middle East and first took pollen cores in the Zagros Mountains of Iran in the 1960s. *References*: *AMWS*; *WWA*

WRIGHT, WALTER LIVINGSTON, JR. (1900–1949). Historian, born May 15, 1900, at Lincoln University, Pennsylvania. Wright graduated from Princeton University and the American University of Beirut.* He was an instructor in history at the American University of Beirut from 1921 to 1925, resident researcher in Turkish language and history from 1928 to 1930, and assistant professor at Princeton University from 1930 to 1935. He was the secretary and an expert on Turkish history and affairs for the Hines-Kemmerer economic mission to Turkey in 1934, and president of Robert College* and the American College for Girls* from 1935 to 1944. He was chief of the Near East Section of the U.S. Office of the Coordinator of Information in Washington in 1941–1942, chief historian in the War Department General Staff in 1943, and professor of Turkish language and history at Princeton University. Died May 16, 1949, in Princeton, New Jersey. *References*: *NYT*, May 17, 1949; *WWWA*.

WYSNER, GLORA MAY (1898–   ). Missionary, born July 4, 1898, in Anderson, Indiana. Wysner graduated from Ohio and Western Reserve universities, and Hartford Seminary Foundation, and was ordained in 1932. She was a teacher in Ohio public schools from 1917 to 1921, and social worker in Cleveland from 1923 to 1926. She was a missionary under the Methodist Church in Algeria from 1926 to 1939, and in 1928 organized the first Woman's Home Missionary Society in North Africa. She was later the secretary of the Near East Committee and the Committee on Missionary Personnel and secretary of the International Missionary Council. She wrote *The Kabyle People* (New York, 1945), *Near East Panorama* (New York, 1950), and *Caught in the Middle* (New York, 1958). *References*: *IAB*; *OAB*; and *WWAW*.

Y

YALE, WILLIAM (1887–1975). Intelligence agent and political scientist, born August 6, 1887, in Dobbs Ferry, New York. Yale graduated from Yale University. He was a laborer on the Panama Canal, a private tutor, and a roustabout in the oil fields. In 1913 he went to Constantinople and was employed by the foreign service of the Standard Oil Company of New York (later Socony Vacuum Oil Company). He was in Jerusalem from 1915 to 1917, explored for oil deposits in Palestine, and traveled disguised through Turkey, Syria, Palestine, and Egypt. In 1917–1918 he was a special agent for the State Department in Cairo. He returned to Jerusalem in 1918 as a liaison to General Edmund Allenby's forces in Palestine and Syria. He served as a technical adviser to the King-Crane Commission* and adviser on Arab affairs to the American delegation at the Paris Peace Conference in 1919. He ran a shipping and tourism business in Cairo from 1919 to 1922, and was later assistant professor of history at the University of New Hampshire. In World War II he served briefly in the State Department. Died February 26, 1975, in Derry, New Hampshire. *References*: "Autobiography," Ms. and papers, Mugar Memorial Library, Boston University. Papers, Sterling Library, Yale University; *CA*; *NYT*, February 27, 1975; and Aileen Vincent-Barwood, "The Many Hats of William Yale," *AWM* 36 (September-October 1984): 38–40.

YEWELL, GEORGE HENRY (1830–1923). Painter, born January 20, 1830, in Havre de Grace, Maryland, and grew up in Iowa City, Iowa. Yewell studied in New York City, went to Paris in 1856, and lived in Rome from 1869 to 1875. In 1875 he visited Egypt where he painted street scenes in Cairo, works which he later exhibited in Iowa City. He returned to the United States in 1878 and maintained a studio in New York City. Died September 26, 1923, in Lake George, New York. *References*: *ACAB*; Zenobia B. Ness and Louise Orwig, *Iowa Artists of the First Hundred Years* (Des Moines, 1939); *NYHSD*; *NYT*, September 27, 1923; Mildred W. Pelzer, "George H. Yewell," *Palimpset* 11 (1930): 483–498; and *WWWA*.

YOUNG, ARTHUR NICHOLS (1890–1984). Economist, born November 21, 1890, in Los Angeles. Young graduated from Occidental College, Princeton and George Washington universities. He was employed in China as an economist from 1929 to 1946, was an adviser to the Central Bank of China, helped establish the Central Reserve Bank of China, was director of China National Aviation Company, and chairman of the Chinese National Commission on Relief and Rehabilitation during World War II. He was financial adviser to Saudi Arabia in 1951–1952 and head of the American economic mission, and helped set up the Saudi Arabian Monetary Agency. He wrote *Saudi Arabia: The Making of a Financial Giant* (New York, 1983), a personal account and an economic history. He was later an adviser to Mexico, Argentina, and Honduras. Died July 19, 1984, in Claremont, California. *References*: *CA*; *NCAB* C:84; *NYT*, August 24, 1984; and *WWWA*.

YOUNG, G(EORGE) DOUGLAS (1910–1980). Evangelist, born September 2, 1910, in Ham Heung, Korea, to American parents. Young graduated from Acadia University, Westminster and Faith theological seminaries, and Dropsie College. He was principal of an academy in Kingston, Nova Scotia, from 1942 to 1944; registrar and instructor in Hebrew at Faith Theological Seminary from 1944 to 1948; dean of the National Bible Institute (New York City) from 1948 to 1953; dean of Northwestern College and Seminary (Minneapolis) from 1953 to 1957; and dean and professor of Semitic studies at Trinity Evangelical Divinity School (Deerfield, Ill.) from 1957 to 1962. He went to Israel in 1956, founded the American Institute of Holy Land Studies in Jerusalem in 1957, and was its president and professor of Semitic studies until 1978. He published a newsletter, *A Dispatch from Jerusalem*. He moved to Israel in 1963 and was a member of the Jerusalem Street and Suburb Naming Commission and the Town Planning Commission. Died May 21, 1980, in Jerusalem. *References*: *Christianity Today* 24 (June 27, 1980): 51–52; Calvin B. Hanson, *A Gentile . . . With the Heart of a Jew* (Nyack, N.J., 1979); and *WWA*.

YOUNG, JAMES M., JR. (1924–   ). Medical missionary, born November 13, 1924, in Choudrant, Louisiana, and grew up in Ruston, Louisiana. Young graduated from Louisiana Polytechnic Institute (Ruston) and Louisiana State University School of Medicine, and served as a navy pilot. He was the superintendent of the Baptist Hospital in Gaza from 1955 to 1964, opened a clinic in Taiz, Yemen, in 1964, and was administrator and chief of physicians at the Baptist Hospital in Jibla, Yemen, from 1964 to 1983. *Reference*: James C. Hefley, *The Cross and the Scalpel* (Waco, Tex., 1971), pp. 42–49.

YOUNG, RODNEY STUART (1907–1974). Archaeologist, born August 1, 1907, in Bernardsville, New Jersey. Young graduated from Princeton and Columbia universities and studied at the American School of Classical Studies at Athens. He was associate curator at the University Museum in 1949–1950, and in 1950 he became curator and professor of classical archaeology at the University of Pennsylvania. He was ambulance driver in Greece after the German occupation, head of the Greek desk in the Office of Strategic Services from 1942 to 1944, and special assistant to the chief of the Greek mission of United Nations Relief and Rehabilitation Administration (UNRRA) from 1944 to 1946. He excavated in Greece before and after World War II. Young directed the excavations in Gordion, Phrygia, Turkey, from 1950 to 1964, and in 1953 excavated in Balkh, Persia. He wrote *Gordion, a Guide to the Excavations and Museum* (Ankara, 1968), and *Three Great Early Tumuli* (Philadelphia, 1981). Died October 25, 1974, in an automobile accident in Philadelphia. *References: From Athens to Gordion: The Papers of a Memorial Symposium for Rodney S. Young*, ed. Keith DeVries (Philadelphia, 1980); *AJA* 79 (1975): 112; *Archaeology* 28 (1975): 129; *DAS*; *NYT*, October 27, 1974; and *WWWA*.

YOUNG MEN'S CHRISTIAN ASSOCIATION OF THE UNITED STATES OF AMERICA (YMCA).

Nonsectarian Christian lay organization, founded in London in 1844 and in the United States in 1851. The International Committee was formed in 1879 and established overseas operations in foreign countries. Its first salaried representative in the Middle East was appointed in 1910, and it established operations in Turkey in 1910, in Egypt in 1913, and in Palestine in 1919. *References*: Archives, YMCA Historical Library, St. Paul, Minnesota; Kenneth S. Latourette, *World Service: A History of the Foreign Work and World Service of the Young Men's Christian Association of the United States and Canada* (New York, 1957).

YOUNG WOMEN'S CHRISTIAN ASSOCIATION OF THE U.S.A. (YWCA).

Nonsectarian lay Christian organization, founded in London in 1855 and in the United States in 1858. The International Board established operations in Turkey, and operated in Syria from 1920 to 1928. *References*: Nancy Boyd, *Emissaries: The Overseas Work of the American YWCA, 1895–1970* (New York, 1987); Anna V. Rice, *A History of the World's Young Women's Christian Association* (New York, 1947).

Z

ZIMPEL, CHARLES F. (1801– ?). Engineer, born in Germany. Zimpel lived in Jena and Thuringia, and later in America and was naturalized. He took part in the construction of railroads in the United States. In 1852 he visited Palestine, wrote a pamphlet on the Jews in Jerusalem, prepared a topographical map of Jerusalem, and drew up proposals for the colonization of Palestine. In 1864 he visited Palestine again, presented plans for a breakwater at Jaffa and for a railroad linking Jaffa with Jerusalem and Damascus, and published *Railway Between the Mediterranean, the Dead Sea and Damascus by Way of Jerusalem* (London, 1865). *Reference*: N. M. Gelber, "A Pre-Zionist Plan for Colonizing Palestine: The Proposal of a Non-Jewish German-American in 1852," *Historia Judaica* 1 (1939): 81–90.

ZORACH, MARGUERITE THOMPSON (1887–1968). Painter, born September 25, 1887, in Santa Rosa, California, and grew up in Fresno, California. Zorach graduated from Stanford University, went to Paris in 1903, and studied art. In 1911–1912 she traveled in Egypt and Palestine, painted there, and published her impressions in the *Fresno Morning Republican* in 1912. She later lived and painted in New York City. Died June 27, 1968, in Brooklyn, New York. *References*: *NYT*, June 29, 1968; Roberta Tarbell, *Marguerite Zorach: The Early Years, 1908–1930* (Washington, D.C., 1973); and *WWAW*.

ZWEMER, PETER JOHN (1868–1898). Missionary, brother of Samuel Marinus Zwemer,* born September 2, 1868, in South Holland, Illinois. Zwemer graduated from Hope College and the New Brunswick Theological Seminary, and was ordained in 1892. He served in the Arabian Mission* from 1892 until his death. He visited Muscat in 1893 and established a mission station in the town of Muscat. He printed on a hand printing press the first Christian tract ever printed in Arabia. Died October 18, 1898, in New York City. *References*: *HDRCA*.

ZWEMER, SAMUEL MARINUS (1867–1952). Missionary, born April 12, 1867, in Vriesland, Michigan. Zwemer graduated from the New Brunswick Theological Seminary and was ordained in 1890. One of the founders of the Arabian Mission,* he served as a missionary in various stations in Arabia from 1891 to 1912. He traveled widely, making three important journeys into the northern parts of Oman in 1900–1901, and wrote *Arabia: The Cradle of Islam: Studies in the Geography, People and Politics of the Peninsula, With an Account of Islam and Mission Work* (New York, 1900). He also visited Sanaa in Yemen in 1892 and 1904 and Hofhoff in Hassa. Another travel book was *Zigzag Journey in the Camel Country* (New York, 1911). He wrote extensively on Islam and missionary work among Muslims, was chairman and organizer of the Moham-medan Missionary Conference in Cairo in 1906, and became known as "the modern apostle to the Muslim world." In 1914 he was assigned to Cairo, returned to the United States in 1929, was professor of the history of religion and Christian missions at Princeton Theological Seminary, and editor of the *Moslem World*. He and James Cantine* wrote their reminiscences, *The Golden Milestones: Reminiscences of Pioneer Days Fifty Years Ago in Arabia* (New York, 1938). Died April 2, 1952, in Port Chester, New York. *References*: *HDRCA*; *MW* 42 (1952): 157–159; *NYT*, April 3, 1952; Lyle L. Vander Werff, *Christian Mission to Muslim: The Record* (South Pasadena, Calif., 1977), ch. IV; J. Christy Wilson, *Apostle to Islam: A Biography of Samuel M. Zwemer* (Cedar Rapids, Mich., 1952); *Flaming Prophet: The Story of Samuel Zwemer* (New York, 1970); and *WWWA*.

Chiefs of American Diplomatic Missions in the Middle East, 1831–1986

*Akins, James Elmer (1926–   ), AE/P Saudi Arabia 1973–1975
*Allen, George Venable (1903–1970), AE/P Iran 1946–1948
Alling, Paul Humiston (1896–1949), DiplAgt/CG Morocco 1945–1947
Anderson, G. Norman (1932–   ), AE/P Sudan 1986–
Anderson, John Alexander (1834–1892), Agt/CG Egypt 1891–1892
Anderson, Robert (1922–   ), AE/P Morocco, 1976–1978
Angell, James Burrill (1829–1916), EE/MP Turkey 1897–1898
Arnold, Olney (1861–1916), Agt/CG Egypt 1913–1916
*Atherton, Alfred Leroy, Jr. (1921–   ), AE/P Egypt 1979–1983
*Badeau, John Stothoff (1903–   ), AE/P United Arab Republic 1961–1964
*Barbour, Walworth (1908–1982), AE/P Israel 1961–1973
Barnes, Robert Gaylord (1914–1977), AE/P Jordan 1964–1966
Bartholomew, Reginald (1936–   ), AE/P Lebanon 1983–1986
Battle, Lucius Durham (1918–   ), AE/P United Arab Republic 1964–1967
Beach, Arthur Eugene (1907–1973), Chd'Aff Sudan 1956
*Beale, Truxton (1856–1936), MR/CG Persia 1891–1892
Beardsley, Richard (1838–1876), Agt/CG Egypt 1872–1876
Belcher, Taylor Garrison (1920–   ), AE/P Cyprus 1964–1969
*Benjamin, Samuel Greene Wheeler (1837–1914), MR/CG Persia 1883–1885
Bergus, Donald Clayton (1920–   ), AE/P Sudan 1977–1980
*Berry, Burton Yost (1901–1985), AE/P Iraq 1952–1954
*Blake, Maxwell (1877–1959), Agt/CG Morocco 1917–1922; DiplAgt/CG 1925–1940
Boehm, Richard Wood (1926–   ), AE/P Cyprus 1984–
Bocker, Paul Harold (1938–   ), AE/P Jordan 1984–
*Boker, George Henry (1923–1890), MR Turkey 1871–1875
Bonsal, Philip Wilson (1903–   ), AE/P Morocco 1961–1962
Bosworth, Stephen Warren (1939–   ), AE/P Tunisia 1979–1981
*Bowen, Herbert Wolcott (1856–1927), MR/CG Persia 1899–1901
Brewer, William Dodd (1922–   ), AE/P Sudan 1973–1977

* See entry in dictionary.
† See list of abbreviations at the end of this section.

Brown, Lewis Dean (1920–   ), AE/P Jordan 1970–1973
Buffum, William Burnside (1921–   ), AE/P Lebanon 1970–1974
Burns, Findley, Jr. (1917–   ), AE/P Jordan 1966–1967
Butler, George H. (?   –   ?   ), Agt/CG Egypt 1870–1872
Byroade, Henry Alfred (1913–   ), AE/P Egypt 1955–1956; AE/P Afghanistan 1959–
      1962
*Caffery, Jefferson (1886–1974), AE/P Egypt 1949–1955
Caldwell, John Lawrence (1875–1922), EE/MP Persia 1914–1921
Calhoun, John Archibald (1918–   ), AE/P Tunisia 1969–1972
Cannon, Cavendish Wells (1895–1962), EE/MP Syria 1950–1952; AE/P Morocco 1956–
      1958
Cardwell, John (?   –?   ), Agt/CG Egypt 1885–1889
Carpenter, Fred Warner (1873–1957), EE/MP Morocco 1910–1912
Carr, Dabney Smith (1802–1854), MR Turkey 1843–1844
Chapin, Selden (1899–1963), AE/P Iran 1955–1958
*Childs, James Rives (1893–   ), EE/MP Saudi Arabia 1946–1949; Yemen 1946–1950;
      AE/P Saudi Arabia 1949–1950
Cluverius, Wat Taylor, IV (1934–   ), AE/P Bahrain 1976–1978
Cottam, Howard Rex (1910–1984), AE/P Kuwait 1963–1969
Countryman, John R. (1933–   ), AE/P Oman 1981–1985
*Cox, Samuel Sullivan (1824–1889), EE/MP Turkey 1885–1886
Crawford, William Rex, Jr. (1928–   ), AE/P Yemen Arab Republic 1972–1974; AE/
      P Cyprus 1974–1978
Crocker, Edward Savage, 2nd (1895–1968), AE/P Iraq 1948–1952
Cutler, Walter Leon (1931–   ), AE/P Tunisia 1981–1984; AE/P Saudi Arabia 1984–
Davies, Rodger Paul (1921–1974), AE/P Cyprus 1974
Davis, Monnett Bain (1893–1953), AE/P Israel 1951–1953
Dean, John Gunther (1926–   ), AE/P Lebanon 1978–1981
*DeLeon, Edwin (1818–1891), Agt/CG Egypt 1853–1861
Denning, Joseph M. (1866–1927), Agt/CG Morocco 1922–1924
Dickman, Francois Moussiegt (1924–   ), AE/P United Arab Emirates 1976–1979; AE/
      P Kuwait 1979–1984
Dillon, Robert Sherwood (1929–   ), AE/P Lebanon 1981–1983
Dodge, Henry Percival (1870–1936), EE/MP Morocco 1909–1910
Drew, Gerald Augustin (1903–1970), EE/MP Jordan 1950–1952
Dreyfus, Louis Goethe, Jr. (1889–1973), EE/MP Iran 1939–1943; EE/MP Afghanistan
      1940–1942; AE/P Afghanistan 1949–1951
Dubs, Adolph (1920–1979), AE/P Afghanistan 1978–1979
Duke, Angier Biddle (1915–   ), AE/P Morocco 1979–1981
Dunbar, Charles Franklin, Jr. (1937–   ), AE/P Qatar 1983–1985
Eagleton, William Lester, Jr. (1926–   ), AE/P Syria 1984–
*Eddy, William Alfred (1896–1962), EE/MP Saudi Arabia 1944–1946
*Eilts, Hermann Frederick (1922–   ), AE/P Saudi Arabia 1965–70; AE/P Egypt 1974–
      1979
Eliot, Thedore Lyman, Jr. (1928–   ), AE/P Afghanistan 1973–1978
*Elkus, Abram Isaac (1867–1947), AE/P Turkey 1916–1917
*Engert, Cornelius Van Hemert (1887–1985), EE/MP Afghanistan 1942–1945
Ewing Raymond C. (1936–   ), AE/P Cyprus 1981–1984

Farland, Joseph Simpson (1914–   ), AE/P Iran 1972–1973
Farman, Elbert Eli (1831–1911), Agt/CG Egypt 1876–1881
Ferguson, John Haven (1915–1970), AE/P Morocco 1962–1964
*Fish, Bert (1875–1943), EE/MP Egypt 1933–1941; EE/MP Saudi Arabia 1939–1941
*Gallman, Waldemar John (1899–1980), AE/P Iraq 1954–1958
*Gary, Hampson (1873–1952), Agt/CG Egypt 1917–1919
Ghougassian, Joseph (1944–   ), AE/P Qatar 1985–
Godley, George McMurtie, 2nd (1917–   ), AE/P Lebanon 1974–1976
Grady, Henry Francis (1882–1957), AE/P Iran 1950–1951
Green, Joseph Coy (1887–1978), EE/MP Jordan 1952–1953; AE/P 1952–1953
*Grew, Joseph Clark (1880–1965), AE/P Turkey 1927–1932
*Griffis, Stanton (1887–1974), AE/P Egypt 1948–1949
*Griscom, Lloyd Carpenter (1872–1959), EE/MP Persia 1901–1902
*Gummeré, Samuel René (1849–1920), EE/MP Morocco 1905–1909
Gunther, Franklin Mott (1885–1941), EE/MP Egypt 1928–1930
*Hale, Charles (1831–1882), Agt/CG Egypt 1864–1870
Handley, William Jules (1918–1979), AE/P Turkey 1969–1973
Hardy, Arthur Sherburne (1847–1930), MR/CG Persia 1897–1899
*Hare, Raymond Arthur (1901–   ), AE/P Saudi Arabia & EE/MP Yemen 1950–1953;
        AE/P Lebanon 1953–1954; AE/P Egypt 1956–1959; AE/P United Arab Republic
        1958–1959; EE/MP Yemen 1959; AE/P Turkey 1961–1965
*Harrison, Thomas Skelton (1837–1919), Agt/CG Egypt 1897–1899
*Hart, Charles Calmer (1878–1956), EE/MP Persia 1929–1933
*Hart, Parker Thompson (1910–   ), AE/P Saudi Arabia 1961–1965; EE/MP Yemen
        1961–1962; AE/P Kuwait 1961–1963; AE/P Turkey 1965–1968
Haynes, Ulric St. Clair, Jr. (1931–   ), AE/P Algeria 1977–1980
Heath, Donald Read (1894–1981), AE/P Lebanon 1955–1958; AE/P Saudi Arabia 1957–
        1961
*Helms, Richard McGarrah (1913–   ), AE/P Iran 1973–1977
*Henderson, Loy Wesley (1892–1986), EE/MP Iraq 1943–1945; AE/P Iran 1951–1954
Hirsch, Solomon (1839–1902), EE/MP Turkey 1889–1892
Holmes, Julius Cecil (1899–1968), DiplAgt/CG Morocco 1955–1956; AE/P Iran 1961–
        1965
Horan, Hume Alexander (1934–   ), AE/P Sudan 1983–1986
Hornibrook, William Harrison (1884–1946), EE/MP Persia 1933–1936; EE/MP Afghan-
        istan 1935–1936
*Howell, Joseph Morton (1863–1937), Agt/CG Egypt 1921–1922; EE/MP 1922–1927
Hughes, Morris Nelson (1901–   ), Chd'Aff Tunisia 1956
Iddings, Lewis Morris (1850–1921), Agt/CG Egypt 1905–1910
*Jackson, John Brinckerhoff (1862–1920), EE/MP Persia 1907–1909
*Jardine, William Marion (1874–1955), EE/MP Egypt 1930–1933
Jay, Peter Augustus (1877–1933), Agt/CG Egypt 1909–1913
Jernegan, John Durnford (1911–1981), AE/P Iraq 1958–1962; AE/P Algeria 1965–1967
Johnstone, Larry Craig (1942–   ), AE/P Algeria 1985–
Jones, George Lewis, Jr. (1907–1971), AE/P Tunisia 1956–1959
Jones, John Wesley (1907–   ), AE/P Libya 1958–1962
Jones, Richard B. (? – ?), Agt/CG Egypt 1852–1853
Keating, Kenneth Barnard (1900–1975), A/P Israel 1973–1975

Keeley, James Hugh, Jr. (1895–1985), EE/MP Syria 1947–1950
Kelly, John (1939–   ), AE/P Lebanon 1986–
Killgore, Andrew Ivy (1919–   ), AE/P Qatar, 1977–1980
Kirk, Alexander Comstock (1888–1979), EE/MP Egypt 1941–1944; EE/MP Saudi Arabia
      1941–1943
*Knabenshue, Paul (1883–1942), MR/CG Iraq 1932–1942
Knight, Ridgway Brewster (1911–   ), AE/P Syria 1961–1965
Komer, Robert William (1922–   ), AE/P Turkey 1968–1969
Kontos, Constantine William (1922–   ), AE/P Sudan 1980–1983
Kornfeld, Joseph Saul (1876–1943), EE/MP Persia 1921–1924
Lane, George M. (1928–   ), AE/P Yemen Arab Republic 1978–1981
Lawson, Edward Burnett (1895–1962), AE/P Israel 1954–1959
Leidel, Donald Charles (1927–   ), AE/P Bahrain 1983–
*Leishman, John G. A. (1857–1924), EE/MP Turkey 1900–1906; AE/P 1906–1909
*Lewis, Samuel Winfield (1930–   ), AE/P Israel 1977–1985
Lightner, Edwin Allan, Jr. (1907–   ), AE/P Libya 1963–1965
Little, Edward Campbell (1858–1924), Agt/CG Egypt 1892–1893
Long, John G. (1846–1903), Agt/CG Egypt 1899–1903
Longstreet, James (1821–1904), MR Turkey 1880–1881
Lumsden, George Quincey, Jr. (1930–   ), AE/P United Arab Emirates 1982–1986
MacArthur, Douglas, II (1909–   ), AE/P Iran 1969–1972
Mack, David Lyle (1940–   ), AE/P United Arab Emirates 1986–
*MacMurray, John Van Antwerp (1881–1960), AE/P Turkey 1936–1941
Macomber, William Butts, Jr. (1921–   ), AE/P Jordan 1961–1963; AE/P Turkey 1973–
      1977
MacVeagh, Isaac Wayne (1833–1917), MR Turkey 1870–1871
Maestrone, Frank Eusebio (1922–   ), AE/P Kuwait 1976–1979
Mak, Dayton Seymour (1917–   ), Chd'Aff Kuwait 1961–1962
Mallory, Lester DeWitt (1904–   ), AE/P Jordan 1953–1958
*Marsh, George Perkins (1801–1882), MR Turkey 1849–1853
Marthinsen, Charles E. (1931–   ), AE/P Qatar 1980–1983
Maynard, Horace (1814–1882), MR Turkey 1875–1880
*McCauley, Daniel Smith (?   –1852), Agt/CG Egypt 1848–1852
*McClintock, Robert Mills (1909–1976), AE/P Lebanon 1957–1961
McCloskey, Robert James (1922–   ), AE/P Cyprus 1973–1974
McDonald, Alexander (1827?–1897), MR/CG Persia 1893–1897
*McDonald, James Grover (1886–1964), AE/P Israel 1949–1950
*McGhee, George Crews (1912–   ), AE/P Turkey 1951–1953
Meloy, Francis Edward, Jr. (1917–1976), AE/P Lebanon 1976
Merrell, George Robert, Jr. (1898–1962), AE/P Afghanistan 1951–1952
Meyer, Armin Henry (1914–   ), AE/P Lebanon 1961–1965; AE/P Iran 1965–1969
Mills, Sheldon Tibbetts (1904–   ), AE/P Afghanistan 1956–1959; AE/P Jordan 1959–
      1961
Minor, Harold Bronk (1902–1984), EE/MP Lebanon 1952; AE/P 1952–1953
Montgomery, George Cranwell (1944–   ), AE/P Oman 1984–
*Moose, James Sayle, Jr. (1903–   ), MR/C Saudi Arabia 1943–1944; EE/MP Syria
      1952; AE/P 1952–1957; AE/P Sudan 1958–1962
*Morgenthau, henry (1856–1946), AE/P Turkey 1913–1916

*Morris, Edward Joy (1815–1881), MR Turkey 1861–1870
*Morris, Leland Burnette (1886–1950), AE/P Iran 1944–1945
Mulcahy, Edward William (1921–   ), AE/P Tunisia 1976–1979
Murphy, Richard William (1929–   ), AE/P Syria 1974–1978; AE/P Saudi Arabia
    1981–1984
Murray, Wallace Smith (1887–1965), AE/P Iran 1945–1946
Nassif, Thomas Anthony (1941–   ), AE/P Morocco 1985–
*Neumann, Robert Gerard (1916–   ) AE/P Afghanistan 1966–1973; AE/P Morocco
    1973–1976; AE/P Saudi Arabia 1981
Newlin, Michael H. (1926–   ), AE/P Algeria 1984–
*Newsom, David Dunlap (1918–   ), AE/P Libya 1965–1969
Newton, David George (1935–   ), AE/P Iraq 1985–
*Noel, Cleo Allen, Jr. (1918–1973), AE/P Sudan 1972–1973
Paganelli, Robert Peter (1931–   ), AE/P Qatar 1974–1977; AE/P Syria 1981–
*Palmer, Ely Eliot (1887–1977), EE/MP Afghanistan 1945–1948; AE/P 1948
Palmer, Joseph, 2nd (1914–   ), AE/P Libya 1969–1972
*Parker, Richard Bordeaux (1923–   ), AE/P Algeria 1974–1977; AE/P Lebanon 1977–
    1978; AE/P Morocco 1978–1979
Pearson, Richmond (1852–1923), EE/MP Persia 1902–1907
Pelletreau, Robert Halsey, Jr. (1935–   ), AE/P Bahrain 1979–1980
*Penfield, Frederic Courtland (1855–1922), Agt/CG Egypt 1893–1897
*Philip, Herman Hoffman (1872–1951), EE/MP Persia 1925–1928
Pickering, Thomas Reeve (1931–   ), AE/P Jordan 1974–1978; AE/P Israel 1985–
Pinkerton, Lowell Call (1894–1959), EE/MP Lebanon 1947–1951; AE/P Sudan 1956–
    1957
Plitt, Edwin August (1891–1977), DiplAgt/CG Morocco 1947–1951
Pomeroy, George Potwin (1837–1887), Agt/CC Egypt 1882–1884
Popper, David Henry (1912–   ), AE/P Cyprus 1969–1973
*Porter, David (1780–1843), Chd'Aff Turkey 1831–1839; MR 1839–1843
Porter, Dwight Johnson (1916–   ), AE/P Lebanon 1965–1970
Porter, William James (1914–   ), AE/P Algeria 1962–1965; AE/P Saudi Arabia 1975–
    1977
Pratt, E. Spencer (? – ?), MR/CG Persia 1886–1891
Quainton, Anthony Cecil Eden (1934–   ), AE/P Kuwait 1984–
Reed, Joseph Verner, Jr. (1937–   ), AE/P Morocco 1981–1985
Reid, Odgen Rogers (1925–   ), AE/P Israel 1959–1961
Reinhardt, George Frederick (1911–1971), AE/P United Arab Republic & EE/MP Yemen
    1960–1961
Riddle, John Wallace (1864–1941), Agt/CG Egypt 1903–1905
*Rockhill, William Woodville (1854–1914), AE/P Turkey 1911–1913
Rockwell, Stuart Wesson (1917–   ), AE/P Morocco 1970–1973
*Rountree, William Manning (1917–   ), AE/P Sudan 1962–1965
Rugh, William Arthur (1936–   ), AE/P Yemen Arab Republic 1984–
*Russell, Charles Wells (1856–1927), EE/MP Persia 1909–1914
Russell, Franis Henry (1904–   ), AE/P Tunisia 1962–1969
Satterthwaite, Joseph Charles (1900–   ), DipAgt/CG Morocco 1953–1955
*Schuyler, Eugene (1840–1890), Agt/CG Egypt 1889–1890
Scotes, Thomas James (1932–   ), AE/P Yemen Arab Republic 1974–1978

Sebastian, Peter (1926–   ), AE/P Tunisia 1984–
Seelye, Talcott Williams (1922–   ), AE/P Tunisia 1972–1976; AE/P Syria 1978–1981
*Sherrill, Charles Hitchcock, Jr. (1867–1936), AE/P Turkey 1932–1933
Skinner, Robert Peet (1866–1960), AE/P Turkey 1933–1936
Sloan, Alexander Kilgore (1882–1944), Chd'Aff Iraq 1931–1932
Smythe, Hugh Heyne (1913–   ), AE/P Syria 1965–1967
*Spence, Carroll (1818–1896), MR Turkey 1853–1857
Sperry, Watson Robertson (1842–1926), MR/CG Persia 1892–1893
Spiers, Ronald Ian (1925–   ), AE/P Turkey 1977–1980
Sprigg, Carroll (1880– ?), Agt/CG Egypt 1920–1921
Steeves, John Milton (1905–   ), AE/P Afghanistan 1962–1966
*Steinhardt, Laurence Adolph (1892–1950), AE/P Turkey 1942–1945
Sterner, Michael Edmund (1928–   ), AE/P United Arab Emirates 1974–1976
Stoltzfus, William Alfred, Jr. (1924–   ), AE/P Kuwait 1971–1976; AE/P Bahrain
        1972–1974; Qatar 1971–1976; AE/P Oman & United Arab Emirates 1972–1974
Stone, Galen Luther (1921–   ), AE/P Cyprus 1978–1981
*Straus, Oscar Solomon (1850–1926), EE/MP Turkey 1887–1889, 1898–1899; AE/P
        1909–1910
Strausz-Hupé, Robert (1903–   ), AE/P Turkey 1981–
Strong, Robert Campbell (1915–   ), AE/P Iraq 1963–1967
*Sullivan, William Healy (1922–   ), AE/P Iran 1977–1979
Sutherland, Peter Adams (1933–   ), AE/P Bahrain 1980–1986
Symmes, Harrison Matthews (1921–   ), AE/P Jordan 1967–1970
Tappin, John Lindsley (1906–1964), AE/P Libya 1954–1958
Tasca, Henry Joseph (1912–1979), AE/P Morocco 1965–1969
Terrell, Alexander Watkins (1827–1921), EE/MP Turkey 1893–1897
Thacher, Nicholas Gilman (1919–   ), AE/P Saudi Arabia 1970–1973
*Thayer, William Sydney (1830–1864), CG Egypt 1861–1864
Thompson, Davis Preston (1834–1901), EE/MP Turkey 1892–1893
Toon, Malcolm (1916–   ), AE/P Israel 1975–1976
*Tuck, Somerville Pinkney, Jr. (1891–1967), EE/MP Egypt 1944–1946; AE/P 1946–
        1948
Twinam, Joseph Wright (1934–   ), AE/P Bahrain 1974–1976
*Veliotes, Nicholas Alexander (1928–   ), AE/P Jordan 1978–1981; AE/P Egypt 1983–
        1986
Viets, Richard Noyes (1930–   ), AE/P Jordan 1981–1984
*Villard, Henry Serrano (1900–   ), EE/MP Libya 1952–1954
Vincent, John Carter (1900–1972), DiplAgt/C Morocco 1951–1953
*Wadsworth, George, 2nd (1893–1958), DiplAgt/CG Lebanon & Syria 1942–1944; EE/
        MP 1944–1947; AE/P Iraq 1947–1948; AE/P Turkey 1948–1952; AE/P Saudi
        Arabia and EE/MP Yemen 1953–1958
Wailes, Edward Thompson (1903–1969), AE/P Iran 1958–1961
*Wallace, Lewis (1827–1905), MR Turkey 1881–1885; EE/MP 1882–1885
Walmsley, Walter Newbold, Jr. (1904–1973), AE/P Tunisia 1959–1962
Walsh, John Patrick (1918–   ), AE/P Kuwait 1969–1971
Ward, Angus Ivan (1893–1969), AE/P Afghanistan 1952–1956
Warren, Avra Milvin (1893–1957), AE/P Turkey 1953–1956
Warren, William Fletcher (1896–   ), AE/P Turkey 1956–1960

Weathersby, William Henry (1914–   ), AE/P Sudan 1965–1967
West, John Carl (1922–   ), AE/P Saudi Arabia 1977–1981
White, John Campbell (1884–1967), DiplAgt/CG Morocco 1940–1941
Wiley, John Cooper (1893–1967), AE/P Iran 1948–1950
Wiley, Marshall Wayne (1925–   ), AE/P Oman 1978–1981
Wilkins, Fraser (1908–   ), AE/P Cyprus 1960–1964
*Williams, James (1796–1869), MR Turkey 1858–1861
Wilson, Edwin Carleton (1893–1972), AE/P Turkey 1945–1948
Wilson, Thomas Murray (1881–1967), MR/CG Iraq 1942–1943
Winston, Frederick Hampden (1830–1904), MR/CG Persia 1885–1886
Wisner, Frank George, 2nd (1938–   ), AE/P Egypt 1986–
*Wolf, Simon (1836–1923), Agt/CG Egypt 1881–1882
Wolle, William Down (1928–   ), AE/P Oman 1974–1978; AE/P United Arab Emirates
        1979–1981
Yost, Charles Woodruff (1907–1981), AE/P Syria 1957–1958; AE/P Morocco 1958–
        1961
Zakheim, Sam H. (1935–   ), AE/P Bahrain 1986–
Zweifel, David Eugene (1934–   ), AE/P Yemen Arab Republic 1981–1984

ABBREVATIONS

AE/P	Ambassador Extraordinary and Plenipotentiary
Agt/CG	Agent and Consul General
Chd'Aff	Chargé d'Affaires
CG	Consul General
DiplAgt/CG	Diplomatic Agent and Consul General
EE/MP	Envoy Extraordinary and Minister Plenipotentiary
MR	Minister Resident
MR/CG	Minister Resident and Consul General

List of Individuals by Profession and Occupation

ADVENTURERS
English, George Bethune
Harland, Josiah
Khalil Agha
Smith, Edwin

AGRICULTURISTS
Campbell, Thomas Donald
Clark, Stanley Penrhyn
Davis, John Herbert
Forbes, Robert Humphrey
Freeman, George Fouche
Harland, Jack Rodney
Harris, Franklin Stewart
Hayden, Lyle Johnson
Ryerson, Knowles Augustus
Sacks, Mendes
Whitehouse, William Edwin

ANTHROPOLOGISTS
Adams, Robert McCormick
Antoun, Richard Taft
Barclay, Harold Barton
Coon, Carleton Stevens
Dupree, Louis Benjamin
Fairservis, Walter Ashlin, Jr.
Fernea, Elizabeth Warnock
Fernea, Robert Alan
Field, Henry
Gulick, John
Hart, David Montgomery
Hole, Frank
McCown, Theodore Doney

Reed, Charles Allen
Sweet, Louise E. Elizabeth

ARCHAEOLOGISTS. *See also*
PREHISTORIANS.
Adams, Robert McCormick
Adams, William Yewdale
Albright, William Foxwell
Bade, William Frederic
Banks, Edgar James
Bass, George Fletcher
Bates, Oric
Blegen, Carl William
Bliss, Frederic Jones
Bowen, Richard Le Baron, Jr.
Braidwood, Linda Schreiber
Breasted, James Henry
Buckler, William Hepburn
Bull, Robert Jehu
Butler, Howard Crosby
Callaway, Joseph Atlee
Cameron, George Glenn
Campbell, Edward Fay, Jr.
Carter, Theresa Howard
Cesnola, Luigi Palma Di
Chiera, Edward
Cleland, Ray Leroy
Colt, Harris Dunscomb
Dales, George Franklin
Daniel, John Franklin
Delougaz, Pinhas Pierre
Detweiler, Albert Henry
Dever, William Gwinn

Downey, Glanville
Duell, Prentice
Dyson, Robert Harris, Jr.
Eisen, Gustavus Augustus
Elderkin, George Wicker
Erim, Kenan Tavfik
Fisher, Clarence Stanley
Free, Joseph Paul
Freedman, David Noel
Garrett, Robert
Glueck, Nelson
Goetze, Albrecht Ernst Rudolf
Goldman, Hetty
Goodyear, William Henry
Grabar, Oleg
Haines, Richard Carlton
Hall, Lindsley Foote
Hammond, Philip
Hanfmann, George Maxim Anossov
Hauser, Walter
Haynes, John Henry
Hopkins, Clark
Howe, Bruce
Kelsey, Francis Willey
Kelso, James Anderson
Kraeling, Carl Herman
Kyle, Melvin Grove
Lamberg-Karlovsky, Clifford Charles
Lance, Hubert Darrell
Lapp, Paul Wilbert
Loud, Gordon
Love, Iris Cornelia
McCown, Chester Charlton
McCown, Donald Eugene
McEwan, Calvin Wells
Mellink, Machted Johanna
Merrill, Selah
Meyers, Eric Mark
North, Robert Grady
Norton, Richard
O'Callaghan, Roger Timothy
Paine, John Alsop
Peters, John Punnett
Peterson, Enoch Ernest
Pfeiffer, Robert Henry
Pier, Garrett Chatfield
Pritchard, James Bennett
Reed, William Laforest

Reisner, George Andrew
Robinson, Goerge Livingstone
Rostovtzev, Mikhail Ivanovich
Rowe, Louis Earle
Saller, Sylvester John
Sanborn, Cyrus Ashton Rollins
Schmidt, Erich Friedrich
Schumacher, Gottlieb S.
Seger, Joe Dick
Sellers, Ovid Rogers
Simpson, William Kelly
Smith, Myron Bement
Smith, Ray Winfield
Smith, Robert Houston
Solecki, Ralph Stefan
Stager, Lawrence E.
Titus, Robb de Peyster
Van Beek, Gus Willard
Ward, Lauriston
Waterman, Leroy
White, Donald
Whitehouse, Frederic Cope
Whittemore, Thomas
Wright, George Ernest
Young, Rodney Stuart

ARCHITECTS
Bacon, Francis Henry
Gallier, James, Sr.
Harmon, Arthur Loomis
Hunt, Richard Morris

ARMY OFFICERS
Campbell, William P. A.
Chaille-Long, Charles
Colston, Raleigh Edward
Connolly, Donald Hilary
Dennison, James Alfred
Dye, William McEntyre
Fechet, Eugene Oscar
Field, Charles William
Greely, John Nesmith
Harbord, James Guthrie
Haskell, William Nafew
Hutchison, Elmo Harrison
Lockett, Samuel Henry
Loring, William Wing
Marcus, David

Maxwell, Russell Lamonte
McClure, Robert Alexis
Mott, Thaddeus Phelps
Purdy, Erastus Sparrow
Reed, Horatio Blake
Reynolds, Alexander Welch
Rhett, Thomas Grimke
Ridley, Clarence Self
Riley, William Edward
Roosevelt, Kermit (1889–1943)
Shingler, Don Gilmore
Sibley, Henry Hopkins
Somerwell, Brehon Burke
Steever, Edgar Zell
Stone, Charles Pomeroy
Tevis, Charles Carrol
Wayne, Henry Constantine
Wheeler, Raymond Albert

ART HISTORIANS
Pope, Arthur Upham
Weitzmann, Kurt

ASSOCIATION EXECUTIVES
Allen, Harold Boughton
Barton, James Levi
Blatchford, Edward Williams
Clary, Cora A. Phoebe
Davis, Darius Alton
Finley, John Huston
Gage, Frances Cousens
Hall, Harvey Porter
Harte, Archibald Clinton
Hayden, Lyle Johnson
Jennings, Asa Kent
Judson, Harry Pratt
Kerr, Stanley Elphinstone
Miller, Alvah Leslie
Mott, John Raleigh
Neumann, Emanuel
St. Aubin, Wilfrid de
Smith, Wilbert B.
Williams, George St. John
Wistar, Edward Morris
Woodsmall, Ruth Frances

ASSYRIOLOGISTS
Chiera, Edward
Dougherty, Raymond Philip

Gelb, Igance Jay
Goetze, Albrecht Ernst Rudolf
Harper, Robert Francis
Hilprecht, Hermann Volrath
Jacobsen, Thorkild
Langdon, Stephen Herbert
Luckenbill, Daniel David

AUTHORS
Andrews, Fannie Fern Phillips
Appleton, Thomas Gold
Benjamin, Samuel Greene Wheeler
Blashfield, Evangeline Wilbour
Borden, Mary Spears
Bowles, Jane Sydney
Bowles, Paul Frederic
Brown, Demetra Vaka
Browne, John Ross
Colton, Walter
Cooper, Clayton Sedgwick
Cooper, Elizabeth Goodnow
Crabites, Pierre
Crawford, Francis Marion
De Forest, John William
Dos Passos, John Roderigo
Dunning, Harry Westbrook
Dupree, Nancy March Wolfe
Dwight, Harrison Griswold
Eddy, Daniel Clarke
Ellis, Harry Bearse
Ethridge, Willie Snow
Field, Henry Martyn
Gibbons, Helen Davenport Brown
Gibbons, Herbert Adams
Groseclose, Elgin Earl
Grosvenor, Edwin Augustus
Hale, Susan
Hamersley, John William
Harland, Marion
Johnson, Sarah Barclay
Jones, George
Keith, Agnew Newton
Lane, Rose Wilder
Leland, Charles Godfrey
Mayo, William Starbuck
McQueen, Elizabeth Lippincott
Melville, Herman
Michener, James Albert

Morris, Robert
Noyes, James Oscar
Rihani, Ameen Fares
Sampter, Jessie Ethel
Savage, Richard Henry
Seabrook, William Buehler
Stoddard, Charles Warren
Terhune, Albert Payson
Todd, Mabel Loomis
Twain, Mark
Van Dyke, Henry
Wallace, Susan Arnold Elston
Warner, Charles Dudley
Wharton, Edith
Woodberry, George Edward
Wright, Elizabeth Washburn

AVIATION EXECUTIVES
Robertson, William Bryan

AVIATORS
Hall, Melvin Adams
Kerr, Richard Caldwell
Kerwood, Charles W.
Sweeny, Charles

BACTERIOLOGISTS
Kligler, Israel Jacob

BANKERS
Blowers, George Albert
MacCormack, Daniel William
Pearson, Thomas

BIBLICAL SCHOLARS
Adams, James McKee
Burrows, Millar
Clark, Kenneth Willis
Cross, Frank Moore, Jr.
Lake, Kirsopp
Montgomery, James Alan
Robinson, Edward
Trever, John Cecil
Vincent, John Heyl

BUSINESSMEN
Clergue, Francis Hector
Crane, Charles Richard

CARTOONISTS
Davenport, Homer Calvin

CHEMISTS
Beam, William
Smith, John Lawrence
Tweddle, Herbert W. C.

CLERGYMEN
Anderson, Rufus
Ascham, John Bayne
Bartlett, Samuel Colcord
Barton, William Eleazer
Bausman, Benjamin
Bayley, James Roosevelt
Bellows, Henry Whitney
Bowen, Marcellus
Bridgeman, Charles Thorley
Burt, Nathaniel Clark
Crosby, Howard
Curtiss, Samuel Ives
Dorr, Benjamin
Durbin, John Price
Fosdick, Harry Emerson
Fulton, John
Gage, William Leonard
Gray, Albert Zabrisie
Holmes, John Haynes
Leary, Lewis Gaston
Lee, James Wideman
McGarvey, John William
McMahon, Thomas John
Millard, David
Mitchell, Hinckley Gilbert Thomas
Moulton, Warren
Newman, John Philip
Nies, James Buchanan
Odenheimer, William Henry
Olin, Stephen
Paxton, John D.
Potter, Henry Codman
Powell, Adam Clayton, Sr.
Rice, William A.
Ridgaway, Henry Bascom
Robinson, Paschal
Schaff, Philip
Smith, Eustace John
Spencer, Jesse Ames

Sweeney, Zachary Taylor
Talmage, Thomas De Witt
Thompson, Joseph Harrison
Thompson, Leander
Trumbull, Henry Clay
Wainwright, Jonathan Mayhew
Walker, Charles Thomas
Wallace, Edwin Sherman
Young, George Douglas

COLLECTORS
Cohen, Mendes Israel
Garrett, Robert
Smith, Edwin

COLONIZERS
Berman, Simeon
Leighton-Floyd, Mary Clark
Leighton-Floyd, Albert W.
Minor, Clorinda S.
Rosenberg, Adam
Spafford, Horatio Gates
Spafford, Anna Tubena Lawson
Vester, Bertha Hedges Spafford
Whiting, John D.

CONSULS. *See* **DIPLOMATS.**

CORRESPONDENTS. *See*
JOURNALISTS.

CRIMINOLOGISTS
Huffman, Arthur Vincent

DIPLOMATS
Akins, James Elmer
Allen, George Venable
Atherton, Alfred LeRoy, Jr.
Badeau, John Stothoff
Ballantine, Henry
Barbour, Walworth
Barclay, Thomas
Barlow, Joel
Beale, Truxton
Benjamin, Samuel Greene Wheeler
Berry, Burton Yost
Blake, Maxwell
Boker, George Henry

Bowen, Herbert Wolcott
Bradish, Luther
Bristol, Mark Lambert
Brown, John Porter
Bunche, Ralph Johnson
Caffery, Jefferson
Cathcart, James Leander
Childs, James Rives
Clark, Harlan Bendell
Clark, Lewis
De Hass, Franks S.
De Leon, Edwin
Dickinson, Charles Monroe
Donaldson, Joseph, Jr.
Doolittle, Hooker Austin
Doty, William Furman
Eddy, William Alfred
Eilts, Hermann Frederick
Einstein, Lewis David
Elkus, Abraham Isaac
Engert, Cornelius Van Hemert
Farman, Elbert Eli
Fish, Bert
Fox, William Carlton
Gallman, Waldemar John
Gary, Hampson
Gillespie, Julian Edgeworth
Gillman, Henry
Glazebrook, Otis Allen
Gorham, John Warren
Grew, Joseph Clark
Griffis, Stanton
Griscom, Lloyd Carpenter
Gummere, Samuel Rene
Habib, Philip Charles
Hale, Charles
Hare, Raymond Arthur
Harrison, Thomas Skelton
Hart, Charles Calmer
Hart, Parker Thompson William
Heap, Gwinn Harris
Heap, Samuel Davies
Henderson, Loy Wesley
Hollis, William Stanley
Horton, George
Howell, Joseph Morton
Imbrie, Robert Whitney
Jackson, Jesse Benjamin

Jackson, John Brinckerhoff
Jardine, William Marion
Johnson, Jeremiah Augustus
Knabenshue, Paul
Lamb, John
Lear, Tobias
Leishman, John G. A.
Lewis, Samuel Winfield
MacMurray, John Van Antwerp
Marsh, George Perkins
McCauley, Daniel Smith
McClintock, Robert Mills
McDonald, James Grover
McGhee, George Crews
Merrill, Selah
Moose, James Sale, Jr.
Morgenthau, Henry
Morris, Edward Joy
Morris, Leland Burnette
Moser, Charles Kroth
Murphy, Robert Daniel
Neumann, Robert Gerhard
Newsom, David Dunlap
Noah, Mordecai Manuel
Noel, Cleo Allen, Jr.
Nolte, Richard Henry
O'Brien, Richard
Offley, David
Ozmun, Edward Henry
Paddock, Gordon
Palmer, Ely Eliot
Parker, Richard Bordeaux
Payne, John Howard
Pendar, Kenneth W.
Penfield, Frederic Courtland
Perry, Amos
Philip, Herman Hoffman
Porter, David
Ravndal, Gabriel Bie
Rhind, Charles
Rhodes, Albert
Roberts, Edmund
Rockhill, William Woodville
Roosevelt, Archibald Bulloch
Rossow, Robert J.
Rountree, William Manning
Russell, Charles Wells
Sanger, Richard Harlankenden

Schuyler, Eugene
Shaler, William
Shaw, Gardiner Rowland
Sherrill, Charles Hitchock, Jr.
Southard, Addison E.
Spain, James William
Spence, Carroll
Steinhardt, Laurence Adolph
Straus, Oscar Solomon
Sullivan, William Healy
Tarler, George Cornell
Thayer, William Sidney
Veliotes, Nicholas Alexander
Vidal, Michel
Villard, Henry Serrano
Wadsworth, George
Wallace, Edwin Sherman
Wallace, Lewis
Wasson, Thomas Campbell
Williams, James
Wilson, Edwin Carlton
Wilson, Evan Morris
Wolf, Simon

ECONOMISTS
Atkins, Paul
Burns, Norman
Davis, John Herbert
Dunaway, John Allder
Groseclose, Elgin Earl
Gunter, John Wadsworth
Haskell, Earl Stanley
Kemmerer, Edwin Walter
Mears, Eliot Grinnell
Meyer, Albert Julius
Mikesell, Raymond French
Mohr, Emanual Nehemiah
Morgan, Ora Sherman
Polk, Judd Knox
Young, Arthur Nichols

EDITORS
Dana, Charles Anderson
Gilmore, Albert Field
Marden, Philip Sanford
Miller, Daniel Long
Rees, Thomas
Rowland, Joseph Medley

EDUCATORS. *See also* MISSIONARY EDUCATORS.

Adams, Kathryn Newell
Badeau, John Stothoff
Ballantine, Duncan Smith
Ballantine, William Gay
Barnard, Charles Inman
Baskerville, Howard C.
Berkson, Isaac Baer
Black, Floyd Henson
Black, Robert Pierpont
Brown, Julius Arthur
Brown, Philip Marshall
Burns, Norman
Cleland, William Wendell
Cobb, Stanwood
Davis, Moshe
Dewey, John
Dodge, Bayard
Dushkin, Alexander Mordecai
Fisher, Edgar Jacob
Gallagher, Charles Frederick
Galt, Russell
Gates, Caleb Frank
Grant, Elihu
Halkin, Shimon
Hall, William H.
Hamlin, Cyrus
Horton, Allan Williams
Huntington, George Herbert
Hutchison, Ralph Cooper
Jaquith, Harold Clarence
Jones, Arleigh Willard
Jones, Christina Hendry
Jordan, Samuel Martin
Kerr, Malcolm Hooper
Kirkwood, Samuel Brown
Knight, Edgar Wallace
Leavitt, Leslie Westbrook
Leonard, John Paul
Magnes, Judah Leon
Matthews, Roderic Donald
McLain, Raymond Francis
Miller, Burnette
Monroe, Paul
Parker, Beryl
Patrick, Mary Mills
Paton, Louis Bayles

Penrose, Stephen Beasly Linnard
Perry, Walter Scott
Polk, William Roe
Reed, Cass Arthur
Rice, William A.
Scipio, Lynn Adolphus
Shelton, William Arthur
Walsh, Edmund Aloysius
Washburn, George
Watson, Charles Roger
Wright, Walter Livingston, Jr.

EGYPTOLOGISTS

Breasted, James Henry
Bull, Ludlow Seguine
Caminos, Ricardo Augusto
Davis, Theodore Monroe
Dennis, James Teackle
Dunham, Dows
Edgerton, William Franklin
Gliddon, George Robins
Groff, William N.
Hayes, William Christopher
Lansing, Ambrose
Loring, Charles Greely
Lythgoe, Albert Horton
McCauley, Edward Yorke
Murch, Chauncy
Nelson, Harold Hayden
Parker, Richard Anthony
Reisner, George Andrew
Seele, Keith Cedric
Simpson, William Kelly
Smith, William Stevenson
Wilbour, Charles Edwin
Wilson, John Albert
Winlock, Herbert Eustice
Winslow, William Copley

ENGINEERS. *See also* MINING ENGINEERS.

Bunger, Mills Emerson
Butler, Millard Angle
Carroll, Charles Joseph
Clark, Wallace
Colt, James Wood
Cooper, Hugh Lincoln
Davies, Fred Alexander

Delano, Frederic Adrian
Derrick, Henry Clay
Gotshall, William Charles
Hays, James Buchanan
Huss, George Morehouse
Jewett, Albert C.
Johnston, Clarence Thomas
Lane, James Crandell
Lowdermilk, Walter Clay
Mead, Elwood
Poland, William Babcock
Prout, Henry Goslee
Schumacher, Gottlieb B.
Snograss, Cornelius Stribling
Thornburg, Max Weston
Zimpel, Charles F.

ENTOMOLOGISTS
Ballou, Henry Arthur

EPIDEMIOLOGISTS
Rosenau, Milton Joseph

EPIGRAPHERS
De Cou, Herbert Fletcher

EXPLORERS. *See* **TRAVELERS.**

FINANCIAL ADMINISTRATORS
McCaskey, Charles Irving
Millspaugh, Arthur Chester
Shuster, William Morgan

FLORISTS
Greene, Harvey Bartlett

GEOGRAPHERS
Huntington, Ellsworth
Robinson, Edward

GEOLOGISTS. *See also*
PETROLEUM GEOLOGISTS
Anderson, Robert Van Vleck
Barger, Thomas Charles
Brown, Glen Francis
Clapp, Frederick Gardner
Diller, Joseph Silas
Finch, John Wellington

Libbey, William
Paige, Sidney
Rhoades, Ralph Omer
Spurr, Josiah Edward
Washington, Henry Stephens
Willis, Bailey
Wright, Herbert Edgar, Jr.

GOVERNMENT OFFICIALS
Carrel, Morton Drew
Clapp, Gordon Rufus
Crane, Charles Richard
Culbertson, William Smith
Dorr, Goldthwaite Higginson
Ethridge, Mark Foster
Hines, Walker Downer
Hoskins, Harold Boies
Jackson, Charles Douglas
Johnston, Eric Allen
King, Henry Churchill
Kissinger, Henry Alfred
Landis, James McCauley
McFarlane, Robert Carl
Nielsen, Frederick Kenelm
Porter, Paul Aldermandt
Toulmin, John Edwin
Warne, William Elmo
Washington, George Thomas
Wilber, Donald Newton

HORTICULTURISTS
Fenzi, Emanuele Orazio
Mason, Silas Cheever
Nixon, Roy Wesley
Roeding, George Christian

HORSE BREEDERS
Richards, Alexander Keene

ICHTHYOLOGISTS
Clark, Eugenie

ILLUSTRATORS. *See also*
PAINTERS.
Bandiner, Alfred
Fenn, Harry
Hoppin, Augustus
Gibson, Charles Dana

Guerin, Jules
Mitchell, Bruce Handyside
Woodward, John Douglas

INVENTORS
Cochran, John Webster
Lay, John Louis

INTELLIGENCE AGENTS
Copeland, Miles
Eveland, Wilbur Crane
Roosevelt, Kermit (1916–   )
Wilson, Edwin Paul
Yale, William

JOURNALISTS
Agron (Agronsky), Gershon
Barnard, Charles Inman
Bell, Archibald
Bird, William
Brooks, Noah
Bryant, William Cullen
Bullard, Arthur
Carpenter, Frank George
Cooley, John Kent
Curtis, George William
Curtis, William Eleroy
Davis, Richard Harding
Ellis, Harry Bearse
Ellis, William Thomas
Harrison, Marguerite Elton Baker
Hepworth, George Hughes
Levy, Joseph M.
McCracken, William Dennison
Noah, Mordecai Manuel
Prime, William Cowper
Rue, Lars Larry
Sayre, Joel Grover
Schmidt, Dana Adams
Sheean, James Vincent
Southworth, Alvan S.
Williams, Talcott

JUDGES
Agranat, Shimon
Barringer, Victor Clay
Batcheller, George Sherman
Brinton, Jasper Yeates

Crabites, Pierre
Farman, Elbert Eli
Tuck, Somerville Pinkney

LAWYERS
Hamilton, Lloyd Nelson
Shields, Floyd Francis
Smith, Walter George
Stevens, Harley Crawford
Vester, Horatio

LEXICOGRAPHERS
Thomas, Joseph

LIBRARIANS
Wilson, Mary Florence

MACHINISTS
Hidden, Warren H.

MARINE CORPS OFFICERS
Cochrane, Henry Clay
Eaton, William
O'Bannon, Presley Neville

MEDICAL MISSIONARIES. *See also* PHYSICIANS AND SURGEONS.
Bennett, Arthur King
Bennett, Christine Iverson
Calverley, Eleanor Jane Taylor
Cochrane, Joseph Plumb
Dame, Louis Paul
De Forest, Henry Albert
Dodd, Edward Mills
Dodd, William Schauffler
Dodge, Asa
Eddy, Mary Pierson
Grant, Asahel
Haas, Cyril Herbert
Harrison, Paul Wilberforce
Henry, Vellora Meek
Holmes, George Washington
Hosmon, Sarah Longworth
Kimball, Grace Niebuhr
Lambie, Thomas Alexander
Lobdell, Henry
Marden, Jesse Krekore
Parmelee, Moses Christopher

Pratt, Andrew Tully
Raynolds, George Clark
Shepard, Frederick Douglas
Shepard, Lorrin Andrews
Smith, Azariah
Storm, William Harold
Thoms, John Sharon
Thoms, William Wells
Van Dyck, Cornelius Van Alen
West, Henry Sergeant
Wishard, John G.
Wright, Austin Hazen
Young, James M., Jr.

MEDICAL RESEARCHERS
Barlow, Claude Herman
Headlee, William Hugh

MERCHANTS
Offley, David
Osgood, John Felt
Rhind, Charles
Ropes, Joseph
Stewart, William
Stith, Griffin
Wilcocks, Benjamin Chrew
Wilcocks, James

MILITARY HISTORIANS
Marshall, Samuel Lyman Atwood

MINING ENGINEERS
Fox, Ernest Franklin
Gunther, Charles Godfrey
Hunt, Leigh Smith John
Lamson, Robert Shuyler
Mitchell, Lebbens H.
Twitchell, Karl Saben
Van Siclen, Matthew

MISSIONARIES. *See also* MEDICAL MISSIONARIES; MISSIONARY EDUCATORS.
Adams, Charles Clarence
Alexander, John Romich
Allen, Orson Parda
Andrus, Alpheus Newell
Antes, John

Baldwin, E. F.
Baldwin, Mary Briscoe
Barclay, James Turner
Barnett, James
Barnum, Henry Samuel
Barnum, Herman Norton
Barrows, John Otis
Barton, James Levi
Bassett, James
Benjamin, Nathan
Bilkert, Henry Arjen
Bird, Isaac
Bird, William
Bliss, Edwin Elisha
Bliss, Edwin Munsell
Bliss, Isaac Grout
Brewer, Josiah
Calhoun, Simeon Howard
Calverley, Edwin Elliott
Cantine, James
Carleton, Alford
Cary, Maude
Coan, Frederick Gaylord
Coan, George Whitefield
Cochran, Joseph Gallup
Dales, Sarah B.
Dennis, James Shepard
Dickson, Walter
Dodd, Edward Mills
Donaldson, Bess Allen
Dunmore, George Washington
Dwight, Harrison Gray Otis
Dwight, Henry Otis
Dykstra, Dirk
Eddy, William Woodbridge
Esselstyn, Lewis Fillmore
Farnsworth, Wilson Amos
Fisk, Pliny
Ford, George Alfred
Ford, Joshua Edwards
Fossum, Ludvig Olsen
Fowle, Luther Richardson
Frease, Edwin Field
Gates, Caleb Frank
Giffen, John Kelly
Goodell, William
Graffam, Mary Louise
Greene, Joseph Kingsbury

Gridley, Elnathan
Hawkes, James Woods
Herrick, George Frederick
Hollister, Mary Guillaume
Holmes, Mary Caroline
Homes, Henry Augustus
Hoskins, Franklin Evans
Jessup, Henry Harris
Jessup, Samuel
Jones, Eli
Jones, Sybil
Jones, William Mead
Jordan, Samuel Martin
Kelly, Caleb Guyer
King, Jonas
Knapp, George Cushing
Knapp, George P.
Knapp, Grace Higely
Krum, John Henry
Labaree, Benjamin
Labaree, Benjamin Woods
Ladd, Daniel
Lansing, Gulian
Laurie, Thomas
Lindsey, Robert Lisle
Lowther, William Ernest
March, Frederick William
Marden, Henry
Marsh, Dwight Whitney
McCague, Thomas
McGreery, Elbert L.
McDowell, Edmund Wilson
McKown, Martha J.
Merrick, James Lyman
Miller, William McElwee
Montgomery, Giles Foster
Murch, Chauncy
Nathan, Albert J.
Nelson, William Shedd
Nicol, James Houden
Oster, John Frederick
Oyler, David Smith
Parsons, Justin Wright
Parsons, Levi
Partridge, Ernest Crocker
Pease, Lorenzo Warriner
Peet, William Wheelock
Perkins, Justin

Porter, Harvey
Post, George Clinton
Powers, Philander Oliver
Reed, George Clinton
Rhea, Samuel Audley
Riggs, Charles Trowbridge
Riggs, Edward
Riggs, Elias
Riggs, Ernest Wilson
Riggs, Henry Harrison
Righter, Chester Newell
Ryan, Arthur Clayton
Saunders, Charles
Saunders, Martha Brudick
Schauffler, William Gottlieb
Schneider, Benjamin
Shedd, John Haskell
Shedd, William Ambrose
Shields, Reid Frampton
Smith, Eli
Smith, Frederick George
Southgate, Horatio, Jr.
Stoddard, David Tappan
Temple, Daniel
Thomson, William McClure
Tidrick, Ralph W.
Trasher, Lillian Hunt
Trowbridge, Tillman Conklin
Van Ess, John
Van Lennep, Henry John
Washburn, George
Watson, Andrew
West, Maria Abigail
Wheeler, Crosby Howard
Whiting, George Backus
Williams, William Frederic
Willoughby, James Wallace
Wilson, J. Christy
Wilson, Samuel Graham
Wolcott, Samuel
Wright, Edwin Milton
Wysner, Glora May
Zwemer, Peter John
Zwemer, Samuel Marinus

MISSIONARY EDUCATORS. *See also*
EDUCATORS; MISSIONARIES.
Bartlett, Cornelia Storrs
Birge, John Kinglsey

Blakley, Ellen M.
Blatter, Dorothy Gerturde
Bliss, Daniel
Bliss, Howard Sweester
Boyce, Arthur Clifton
Christie, Thomas Davidson
Elder, Earl Edgar
Ely, Charlotte Elizabeth
Ely, Mary Ann Caroline
Fiske, Fidelia
Goodsell, Fred Field
Greene, Olive
Harlow, Samuel Ralph
McClenahan, Robert Seward
McDowell, Margaret Dean
Merrill, John Ernest
Proctor, Myra Allen
Rappleye, Julia A.
Shattuck, Corinna
Tracy, Charles Chapin
Van Ess, Dorothy Firman
White, George Edward
Willard, Charlotte Richards

MISSIONARY NURSES. *See also*
MEDICAL MISSIONARIES;
MISSIONARIES.
Cushman, Emma Darling
Dalenberg, Cornelia
Lambert, Rose
Storm, Ida Adams Paterson

MORMON LEADERS
Hyde, Orson
Smith, George Albert

MOTION PICTURE DIRECTORS
Cooper, Marian C.

MOTION PICTURE
PHOTOGRAPHERS
Schoedsack, Ernest Beaumont

MOTORISTS
Glidden, Charles Jasper

NATURALISTS
Pickering, Charles
Ward, William Hayes

NAVAL OFFICERS
Bainbridge, William
Barron, Samuel
Biddle, James
Bristol, Mark Lambert
Chauncy, Issac
Chester, Colby Mitchell
Crane, William Montgomery
Dale, Richard
Decatur, Stephen Jr.
DeKay, George Colman
Elliott, Jesse Duncan
English, Earl
Goodrich, Caspar Frederick
Gorringe, Henry Honeychurch
Graves, Charles Iverson
Hall, Wilburn Briggs
Hepburn, Arthur Japy
Hull, Isaac
Ingraham, Duncan Nathaniel
Jones, Jacob
Laing, Frederic Williams
Lynch, William Francis
Mason, Alexander McComb
Morris, Richard Valentine
Nicholson, James William Augustus
Porter, David
Porter, David Dixon
Preble, Edward
Rodgers, John
Shubrick, John Templer
Shufeldt, Robert Wilson
Smith, Joseph
Somers, Richard

NURSES
Kaplan, Rose

ORIENTAL RUG CONNOISSEURS
Jones, Quill

ORIENTALISTS
Adams, Charles Clarence
Barton, George Aaron
Brown, John Porter
Chiera, Edward
Clay, Albert Tobias
Frye, Richard Nelson

Hall, Isaac Hollister
Hodgson, William Brown
Jackson, Abraham Valentine Williams
Lyon, David Gordon
Muller, Wilhelm Max
Olmstead, Albert Teneyck
Schmidt, Nathaniel
Speiser, Ephraim Avigdor
Spoer, Hans Henry
Torrey, Charles Cutler
Ward, William Hayes

PAINTERS. *See also* ILLUSTRATORS.

Bacon, Henry
Banvard, John
Blashfield, Edwin Howland
Bridgman, Frederick Arthur
Church, Frederic Edwin
Clague, Richard
Colman, Samuel, Sr.
De Forest, Lockwood
Gay, Winckworth Allan
Gifford, Robert Swain
Gifford, Sanford Robinson
Gould, Walter
Hall, George Henry
Jones, Hugh Bolton
Kellogg, Miner Kilbourne
Longfellow, Ernest Wordsworth
Metcalf, Willard Leroy
Newman, Henry Roderick
Powell, Lucien Whiting
Rolshoven, Julius
Sargent, John Singer
Sartain, William
Smith, Francis Hopkinson
Smith, Joseph Lindon
Suydam, James Augustus
Tanner, Henry Osawa
Thompson, Alfred Wordsworth
Tiffany, Louis Comfort
Troye, Edward
Vedder, Elihu
Waller, Frank
Waterman, Marcus Mark A.
Weeks, Edwin Lord

Yewell, George Henry
Zorach, Marguerite Thompson

PETROLEUM EXECUTIVES

Barger, Thomas Charles
Davies, Fred Alexander
Hull, Burton Elias
Rhoades, Ralph Omer

PETROLEUM GEOLOGISTS

Bramkamp, Richard Allen
Davies, Fred Alexander
DeGolyer, Everette Lee
Fohs, Ferdinand Julius
Henry, Schuyler B.
Isenberger, Nathan Perry
Kirk, Howard M.
Mason, Shirley Lowell
Miller, Robert Perry
Notestein, Frank B.
Ohliger, Floyd William
Rea, Henry Carter
Steineke, Max
Walton, Paul Talmage

PHILANTHROPISTS

Crane, Charles Richard
David, Theodore Monroe
Straus, Lina Gutherz
Straus, Nathan
Warren, Edward Kirk

PHOTOGRAPHERS

Bain, Robert Edward Mather
Elmendorf, Dwight Lathrop
Greene, John Bulkley
Kilburn, Benjamin West
Rau, William Herman
Rubin, Gail
Underwood, Bert Elias
Underwood, Elmer Judson
Wilson, Edward Livingston

PHYSICIANS AND SURGEONS. *See also* MEDICAL MISSIONARIES.

Anderson, Henry James
Avery, Bennett Franklin
Cowdery, Jonathan

Elliott, Mabel Evelyn
Fort, Joseph Marstain
Friedenwald, Harry
Johnson, Thomas Dickson
Kirkwood, Samuel Brown
Lansing, Elmer Ellsworth
Lewis, Edwin Rufus
Mott, Valentine
Noyes, James Oscar
Parmelee, Ruth Azniv
Post, George Edward
Rubinow, Isaac Max
Ruschenberger, William Samuel Waitman
Smith, Jerome Vancrowninshield
Turner, William Mason
Ward, Edwin St. John
Warren, Edward

PLANT EXPLORERS
Fairchild, David Grandison
Kearney, Thomas Henry
Koelz, Walter Norman
Popenoe, Paul Bowman
Swingle, Walter Tennyson
Westover, Harvey Leroy

PLANTERS
David, James Bolton

POLICEMEN
Schwarzkopf, Herbert Norman

PREHISTORIANS
Braidwood, Robert John
Haynes, Henry Williamson
Hencken, Hugh O'Neill

PRINTERS
Breath, Edwin
Hallock, Homan

PSYCHOLOGISTS
Prothro, Edwin Terry

QUAKER LEADERS
Jackson, Elmore

RELIGIOUS ZEALOTS
Adams, George Washington
Cresson, Warder
Livermore, Harriet
Minor, Clorinda S.
Spafford, Horatio Gates

REPORTERS. *See* JOURNALISTS.

ROYAL PERSONAGES
Nur el Hussein

SAILORS
Ray, William
Saunders, Daniel Jr.

SCIENTISTS
Anderson, Henry James
Harris, James Edward

SCULPTORS
Partridge, William Ordway

SEA CAPTAINS
Page, Rufus
Page, William Rufus
Riley, James
Ropes, Joseph

SHIPBUILDERS
Bucknam, Ransford D.
Eckford, Henry
Rhodes, Foster

SOCIAL WORKERS
Hexter, Maurice Beck
Jennings, Asa Kent
Mohr, Sophie Berger
Seligsberg, Alice Lillie
Thurber, Christopher Carson

SOCIOLOGISTS
Dodd, Stuart Carter
Huffman, Arthur Vincent
Ross, Frank Alexander

SOLDIERS. *See* **ARMY OFFICERS.**

SUMEROLOGISTS
Crawford, Vaughn Emerson
Kramer, Samuel Noah

TEACHERS. *See* **EDUCATORS.**

TOURIST GUIDES
Clark, Herbert Edgar
Floyd, Rolla

TRAVELERS
Browne, John Ross
Brownell, Clarence Melville
Carpenter, Frank George
Chaille-Long, Charles
Cohen, Mendes Israel
DeKay, James Ellsworth
Dodge, Wendell Phillips
Dulles, John Welsh
Furlong, Charles Wellington
Howe, Fisher
Kirkland, Elizabeth Cabot
Knox, Thomas Wallace

Ledyard, John
Lowell, John
Norton, Roy
Osborn, Henry Stafford
Phillips, Wendell
Powell, Edward Alexander
Rawson, Albert Leighton
Shoemaker, Michael Myers
Smith, Joseph Allen
Southworth, Alvan S.
Stephens, John Lloyd
Swift, John Franklin
Taylor, Bayard James
Thomas, Lowell Jackson
Ward, Aaron

TURCOLOGISTS
Birge, John Kingsley

ZIONISTS
Lindheim, Irma Levy
Neumann, Emanuel
Rosenblatt, Bernard Abraham
Szold, Henrietta
Weisgal, Meyer

Bibliographical Essay

In his article, "American Relations with the Middle East: Some Unfinished Business," in *Issues and Conflicts: Studies in Twentieth Century American Diplomacy*, ed. George L. Anderson (Lawrence, Kan.: University of Kansas Press, 1959), pp. 63–98, John A. DeNovo reviewed the existing literature on U.S. relations with the Middle East. He reviewed the literature again in 1970, in "Researching American Relations with the Middle East: The State of the Art, 1970," in *The National Archives and Foreign Relations Research*, ed. Milton O. Gustafson (Athens, Ohio: Ohio University Press, 1974), pp. 243–264. Much of the literature on this subject published before 1970 is listed in these two articles. A recent survey is Roger R. Trask, "United States Relations with the Middle East in the Twentieth Century: A Developing Area in Historical Literature," in *American Foreign Relations: A Historiographical Review*, ed. Gerald K. Haines and J. Samuel Walker (Westport, Conn.: Greenwood Press, 1981), pp. 293–309.

Other bibliographies dealing with specific topics of U.S.-Middle East relations include Thomas A. Bryson, *United States/Middle East Diplomatic Relations 1784–1978: An Annotated Bibliography* (Metuchen, N.J.: Scarecrow Press, 1979); and Rivka Demsky and Ora Zimmer, "America and the Holy Land: A Select Bibliography of Publications in English," *The Jerusalem Cathedra* 3 (1983): 327–358. The *Guide to American Foreign Relations Since 1700*, ed. Richard D. Burns (Santa Barbara, Calif.: ABC-Clio, 1983), especially chs. 18 and 33, is more selective.

Doctoral dissertations are recorded in Anne M. Avakina, *Armenia and the Armenians in Academic Dissertations* (Berkeley, Calif.: Professional Press, 1974); Frank Joseph Shulman, *American and British Doctoral Dissertations on Israel and Palestine in Modern Times* (Ann Arbor, Mich.: Xerox University Microfilm, 1973); George A. Selim, *American Doctoral Dissertations on the Arab World, 1883–1974* (Washington, D.C.: Library of Congress, 1976); *Supplement 1975–1981* (Washington, D.C.: Library of Congress, 1983); and Bryson's *United States/Middle East Diplomatic Relations*, pp. 173–196.

In 1959 DeNovo stated that there was as yet no full-scale survey of American relations with the Middle East. The situation has not changed, and the only exception is Philip L. Groisser, *The United States and the Middle East* (Albany, N.Y.: State University of New York Press, 1982), a textbook. Several studies, however, cover large or small parts of this history, or of United States relations with specific countries, and one can piece together much of the story by combining several of these books. The more important books which deal with segments of the history include David H. Finnie, *Pioneers East: The Early American Experience in the Middle East* (Cambridge, Mass.: Harvard University Press, 1967); James A. Field, Jr., *America and the Mediterranean World, 1776–1882* (Princeton, N.J.: Princeton University Press, 1969); Robert L. Daniels, *American Philanthropy in the Near East, 1820–1960* (Athens, Ohio: Ohio University Press, 1970); Joseph L. Grabill, *Protestant Diplomacy and the Near East: Missionary Influence on American Policy, 1810–1927* (Minneapolis: University of Minnesota Press, 1971); and John A. DeNovo, *American Interests and Policies in the Middle East 1900–1939* (Minneapolis: University of Minnesota Press, 1963). Several of these books include extensive bibliographical essays. ''America and the Middle East,'' ed. Parker T. Hart, *The Annals of the American Academy of Political and Social Science*, (Vol. 401, May 1972); and the ''Bicentennial Issue'' of the *Middle East Journal* (Vol. 30, No. 3, Summer 1976), are devoted to articles on U.S. relations with Middle Eastern countries.

The majority of scholars have concentrated on the diplomatic story. For example, Thomas A. Bryson, *American Diplomatic Relations with the Middle East, 1784–1975: A Survey* (Metuchen, N.J.: Scarecrow Press, 1977), and *Seeds of Mideast Crisis: The United States Diplomatic Role in the Middle East During World War II* (Jefferson, N.C.: McFarland, 1981); Phillip J. Baram, *The Department of State in the Middle East 1919–1945* (Philadelphia: University of Pennsylvania Press, 1978); Bruce R. Kuniholm, *The Origins of the Cold War in the Middle East: Great Power Conflict and Diplomacy in Iran, Turkey, and Greece* (Princeton, N.J.: Princeton University Press, 1980); Barry Rubin, *The Great Powers in the Middle East 1941–1947: The Road to the Cold War* (London: Cass, 1980); Seth Tillman, *The United States in the Middle East: Interests and Obstacles* (Bloomington, Ind.: Indiana University Press, 1982); William Stivers, *America's Confrontation with Revolutionary Change in the Middle East, 1948–83* (New York: St. Martin's Press, 1968); Donald Neff, *Warriors of Suez: Eisenhower Takes America into the Middle East* (New York: Linden Press/Simon & Schuster, 1981); Alan Dowty, *Middle East Crisis: U.S. Decision-Making in 1958, 1970 and 1973* (Berkeley, Calif.: University of California Press, 1984); Ishaq I. Ghanayem and Alden H. Voth, *The Kissinger Legacy: American Middle East Policy* (New York: Praeger, 1984); and Haim Shaked and Hanan Rabinovich, eds., *The Middle East and the United States: Perceptions and Policies* (New Brunswick, N.J.: Transaction Books, 1980).

The story of the U.S. Navy in the Middle East is covered by William N. Still, Jr., *American Sea Power in the Old World: The United States Navy in European and Near Eastern Waters, 1865–1917* (Westport, Conn.: Greenwood Press, 1980); and Thomas A. Bryson, *Tars, Turks, and Tankers: The Role of the U.S. Navy in the Middle East, 1800–1980* (Metuchen, N. J.: Scarecrow Press, 1980). The story of the American soldiers who served in nineteenth century Egypt is told in Pierre Crabites, *Americans in the Egyptian Army* (London, G. Routledge & Sons, 1938); and William B. Hesseltine and Hazel C. Wolf, *The Blue and the Gray on the Nile* (Chicago: University of Chicago Press, 1961).

Several studies of United States relations with specific countries in the Middle East have been written: THE ARAB WORLD. John S. Badeau, *The American Approach to the Arab World* (New York: Harper & Row, 1969); Robert W. Stookey, *America and the Arab States: An Uneasy Encounter* (New York: Wiley, 1975); and Faiz S. Abu-Jaber, *American-Arab Relations from Wilson to Nixon* (Washington, D.C.: University Press of America, 1974).

TURKEY. Roger R. Trask, *The United States Response to Turkish Nationalism and Reform* (Minneapolis: University of Minnesota Press, 1971); Laurence Evans, *United*

States Policy and the Partition of Turkey, 1914–1924 (Baltimore: Johns Hopkins University Press, 1965); Harry N. Howard, *Turkey, the Straits and U.S. Policy* (Baltimore: Johns Hopkins Press, 1974); George Harris, *Troubled Alliance: Turkish American Problems in Historical Perspective, 1945–1971* (Washington, D.C.: American Enterprise Institute for Public Policy Research, 1972); and Theodore A. Couloumbis, *The United States, Greece and Turkey: The Troubled Triangle* (New York: Praeger, 1983).

PERSIA/IRAN. Abraham Yeselson, *United States-Persian Diplomatic Relations, 1883–1921* (New Brunswick, N.J.: Rutgers University Press, 1956); Yonah Alexander and Allan Names, eds., *The United States and Iran: A Documentary History* (Frederick, Md.: Aletheia Books/University Publications of America, 1980); Mehdi Heravi, *Iranian-American Diplomacy* (Brooklyn, N.Y.: Gaus' Sons, 1969); Michael K. Sheehan, *Iran: The Impact of United States Interests and Policies 1941–1954* (Brooklyn, N.Y.: Gaus' Sons, 1968); Mark H. Lytle, *The Origins of the Iranian American Alliance 1941–1953* (New York: Holmes & Meier, 1987); Barry Rubin, *Paved with Good Intentions: The American Experience and Iran* (New York: Oxford University Press, 1980); R. K. Ramazani, *The United States and Iran: The Patterns of Influence* (New York: Praeger, 1982); and Garry Sick, *All Fall Down; America's Tragic Encounter with Iran* (New York: Random House, 1985).

EGYPT. L. C. Wright, *United States Policy Toward Egypt 1830–1914* (New York: Exposition, 1969); Jasper Y. Brinton, *The American Effort in Egypt: A Chapter in Diplomatic History in the Nineteenth Century* (Alexandria, Egypt: [Impr. du Commerce], 1972); Gail E. Meyer, *Egypt and the United States: The Formative Years* (Rutherford, N.J.: Fairleigh Dickinson University Press, 1980); Marvin G. Weinbaum, *Egypt and the Politics of U.S. Economic Aid* (Boulder, Colo.: Westview Press, 1986); and William J. Burns, *Economic Aid and American Policy Toward Egypt 1955–1981* (Albany, N.Y.: State University of New York Press, 1985).

PALESTINE AND ISRAEL. Frank E. Manuel, *The Realities of American-Palestine Relations* (Washington, D.C.: Public Affairs Press, 1949); *With Eyes Toward Zion: Scholars Colloquium on America-Holy Land Studies*, ed. Moshe Davis (New York: Arno Press, 1977); *With Eyes Toward Zion: Volume 2: Themes and Sources in the Archives of the United States, Great Britain, Turkey, and Israel*, ed. Moshe Davis (New York: Praeger, 1986); Peter Grose, *Israel in the Mind of America* (New York: Knopf, 1983); Hertzel Fishman, *American Protestantism and a Jewish State* (Detroit: Wayne State University Press, 1973); Kenneth R. Bain, *The March to Zion: United States Policy and the Founding of Israel* (College Station, Tex.: Texas A&M University Press, 1979); Cheryl Rubenberg, *Israel and the American National Interest: A Critical Examination* (Urbana, Ill., University of Illinois Press, 1986); Steven L. Spiegel, *The Other Arab-Israeli Conflict: Making America's Middle East Policy, from Truman to Reagan* (Chicago: University of Chicago Press, 1985); Gabriel Sheffer, ed., *Dynamics of Dependence: U.S.-Israeli Relations* (Boulder, Colo.: Westview Press, 1987). Edward B. Glick, *The Triangular Connection: America, Israel, and American Jews* (London: George & Unwin, 1982); Bernard Reich, *The United States and Israel: Influence in the Special Relationship* (New York: Praeger, 1984); Stephen Green, *Taking Sides: America's Secret Relations with a Militant Israel* (New York: W. Morrow, 1984); Bruce R. Kuniholm and Michael Rubner, *The Palestinian Problem and U.S. Policy: A Guide to Issues and References* (Claremont, Calif.: Regina Books, 1986); Mohammed K. Shadid, *The United States and the Palestinians* (New York: St. Martin's Press, 1981); Dan Tschirgi, *The Politics of Indecision: Origins and Implications of American Involvement with the Palestine Problem* (New York: Praeger, 1983);

Bernard Reich, *Quest for Peace: United States-Israel Relations and the Arab-Israeli Conflict* (New Brunswick, N.J.: Transaction Books, 1977); and William B. Quandt, *Decade of Decisions: American Policy Toward the Arab-Israeli Conflict 1967–1976* (Berkeley, Calif.: University of California Press, 1977).

SAUDI ARABIA. David E. Long, *The United States and Saudi Arabia: Ambivalent Allies* (Boulder, Colo.: Westview Press, 1985).

PERSIAN GULF. James H. Noyes, *The Clouded Lens: Persian Gulf Security and U.S. Policy*, 2nd ed. (Stanford, Calif.: Hoover Institution Press, 1982); Emile A. Nakhleh, *The Persian Gulf and American Policy* (New York: Praeger, 1982); and Hussein Sirriyeh, *U.S. Policy in the Gulf, 1968–1977: Aftermath of British Withdrawal* (London: Ithaca Press, 1984).

MOROCCO: Luella J. Hall, *The United States and Morocco, 1776–1956* (Metuchen, N.J.: Scarecrow Press, 1971); and Leon B. Blair, *Western Window in the Arab World* (Austin, Tex.: University of Texas Press, 1970).

LIBYA. P. Edward Haley, *Qaddafi and the United States Since 1969* (New York: Praeger, 1984).

The part played by missionary societies and missions in described by Kenneth S. Latourette, *History of the Expansion of Christianity* (New York: Harper & Brothers, 1937–1945), Vols. 6–7; Julius Richter, *A History of Protestant Missions in the Near East* (New York: Revell, 1910); A. L. Tibawi, *American Interests in Syria, 1800–1901: A Study of Educational, Literary and Religious Work* (Oxford: Clarendon Press, 1966); Adnan Abu-Ghazaleh, *American Missions in Syria: A Study of American Missionary Contribution to Arab Nationalism in 19th Century Syria* (Brattleboro, Vt.: Center for Arab and Islamic Studies, 1983); Frank A. Stone, *Academies for Anatolia* (Lanham, Md.: University Press of America, 1984); and the histories of the various missionary societies and missions listed in the respective articles.

There is a growing literature about American archaeology in the Middle East. It includes W. B. Dinsmoor, "Early American Studies of Mediterranean Archaeology," *Proceedings of the American Philosophical Society* 87 (1943): 70–104; John A. Wilson, *Signs and Wonders upon Pharaoh: A History of American Egyptology* (Chicago: University of Chicago Press, 1964); C. Wade Meade, *Road to Babylon: Development of U.S. Assyriology* (Leiden: Brill, 1974); Andrew Oliver, Jr., *Beyond the Shores of Tripoli: American Archaeology in the Eastern Mediterranean, 1789–1879* (Washington, D.C.: Washington Society of the Archaeological Institute of America, 1979); and Philip J. King, *American Archaeology in the Mideast: A History of the American Schools of Oriental Research* (Philadelphia: American Schools of Oriental Research, 1983).

Mira Wilkins, *The Emergence of Multinational Enterprises: American Business Abroad from the Colonial Era to 1914* (Cambridge, Mass.: Harvard University Press, 1970); and *The Maturing of Multinational Enterprise: American Business Abroad from 1914 to 1970* (Cambridge, Mass.: Harvard University Press, 1974) provide a general survey, including historical information on American firms operating in the Middle East. The histories of several companies also provide information about their activities in the Middle East. For example, Robert B. Davies, *Peacefully Working to Conquer the World: Singer Sewing Machines in Foreign Markets, 1854–1920* (New York: Arno Press, 1976); and Mira Wilkins and Frank E. Hill, *American Business Abroad: Ford on Six Continents* (Detroit: Wayne State University Press, 1964), as well as the histories of petroleum companies such as the Standard Oil Company of New Jersey. Many of the books dealing with Middle East petroleum devote space to U.S. policies and activities, including Edward W. Chester,

United States Oil Policy and Diplomacy: A Twentieth-Century Overview (Westport, Conn.: Greenwood Press, 1983); Benjamin Shwadran, *The Middle East, Oil and the Great Powers* (Boulder, Colo.: Westview Press, 1985), and *Middle East Crises Since 1973* (Boulder, Colo.: Westview Press, 1986); William Stiver, *Supremacy and Oil: Iraq, Turkey, and the Anglo-American World Order, 1918–1930* (Ithaca, N.Y.: Cornell University Press, 1982); Irvine H. Anderson, *Aramco, the United States, and Saudi Arabia: A Study in the Dynamics of Foreign Oil Policy, 1930–1950* (Princeton, N.J.: Princeton University Press, 1981); Aaron D. Miller, *Search for Security: Saudi Arabian Oil and American Foreign Policy, 1939–1949* (Chapel Hill, N.C.: University of North Carolina Press, 1980); and David S. Painter, *Oil and the American Century: The Political Economy of U.S. Foreign Oil Policy 1941–1954* (Baltimore: Johns Hopkins University Press, 1986).

Index

About the Author

DAVID SHAVIT is Associate Professor of Library Science at Northern Illinois University. His publications include *Federal Aid and State Library Agencies: The Implementation of Federal Policy* and *The Politics of Public Librarianship* (Greenwood Press, 1986). He was also contributing editor of *Personalities in Eretz-Israel 1799–1948: A Biographical Dictionary.*